T0331021

PERSPECTIVES ON CORPORATE GOVERNANCE

The events at Enron, WorldCom, Tyco, Adelphia, and elsewhere taught us a key lesson: corporate governance matters. The financial crisis of 2008 taught us that corporate governance can matter a great deal. But while it is now widely acknowledged that good corporate governance is a linchpin of good corporate performance, a significant debate remains over exactly how to improve corporate governance and its impact on corporate and overall economic performance. *Perspectives on Corporate Governance* offers a uniquely diverse and forward-looking set of approaches from leading experts, covering the major areas of corporate governance reform and analyzing the full range of issues and concerns, to offer a host of innovative and original suggestions for how corporate governance can continue to improve. Written to be both theoretically rigorous and grounded in the real world, the book is well suited for practicing lawyers, managers, lawmakers, and analysts, as well as academics conducting research or teaching in a range of courses in law schools, business schools, and in economics departments, at either the undergraduate or graduate level.

This volume is one of several collaborations between F. Scott Kieff and Troy A. Paredes through the Hoover Project on Commercializing Innovation, which studies the law, economics, and politics of innovation, including entrepreneurship, corporate governance, finance, economic development, intellectual property, antitrust, and bankruptcy, and is available on the Web at www.innovation. hoover.org.

F. Scott Kieff is a professor at the George Washington University Law School in Washington, DC, and also Ray and Louise Knowles Senior Fellow at Stanford University's Hoover Institution in Stanford, CA. He previously was Professor at the Washington University School of Law in Saint Louis, MO, and has also been a visiting professor in the law schools at Northwestern, Chicago, and Stanford. Having trained in law at the University of Pennsylvania and in science and economics at the Massachusetts Institute of Technology, he practiced law for several years for firms in New York and Chicago. He regularly serves as a testifying and consulting expert, mediator, and arbitrator to law firms, businesses, government agencies, and courts, and on a range of government panels relating to the business and technology sectors.

Troy A. Paredes is a professor at the Washington University School of Law in Saint Louis, MO, with a courtesy appointment at Washington University's Olin Business School, and has been a visiting professor in the law schools at the University of California in Los Angeles and Georgetown University. Having trained in law at Yale University and in economics at the University of California at Berkeley, he practiced law for several years for firms in Los Angeles and San Francisco. He is a co-author (beginning with the fourth edition) of a multi-volume securities regulation treatise with Louis Loss and Joel Seligman entitled "Securities Regulation," and is presently on leave from his academic appointments, having been appointed by President George W. Bush to the U.S. Securities and Exchange Commission, where he was sworn in on August 1, 2008.

Perspectives on Corporate Governance

Edited by

F. SCOTT KIEFF

George Washington University Law School
Stanford University Hoover Institution

TROY A. PAREDES

Washington University in St. Louis, School of Law

CAMBRIDGE
UNIVERSITY PRESS

University Printing House, Cambridge CB2 8BS, United Kingdom

One Liberty Plaza, 20th Floor, New York, NY 10006, USA

477 Williamstown Road, Port Melbourne, VIC 3207, Australia

314-321, 3rd Floor, Plot 3, Splendor Forum, Jasola District Centre, New Delhi - 110025, India

79 Anson Road, #06-04/06, Singapore 079906

Cambridge University Press is part of the University of Cambridge.

It furthers the University's mission by disseminating knowledge in the pursuit of
education, learning and research at the highest international levels of excellence.

www.cambridge.org
Information on this title: www.cambridge.org/9780521458771

© F. Scott Kieff and Troy A. Paredes 2010

First published 2010

A catalogue record for this publication is available from the British Library

Library of Congress Cataloging in Publication data
Perspectives on corporate governance / edited by F. Scott Kieff, Troy A. Paredes.
     p.   cm.
Includes bibliographical references and index.
ISBN 978-0-521-45877-1
1. Corporate governance – Law and legislation – United States.   I. Kieff, F. Scott.
II. Paredes, Troy.   III. Title.
KF1422.P47   2010
346.73´0664–dc22   2010000990

ISBN 978-0-521-45877-1 Hardback

Contents

Contributors

Stephen M. Bainbridge, William D. Warren Professor of Law, UCLA School of Law

Lucian A. Bebchuk, William J. Friedman and Alicia Townsend Friedman Professor of Law, Economics, and Finance and Director of the Program on Corporate Governance, Harvard Law School; Research Associate, National Bureau of Economic Research

William W. Bratton, Peter P. Weidenbruch, Jr., Professor of Business Law, Georgetown University Law Center

Kathleen F. Brickey, James Carr Professor of Criminal Jurisprudence, Washington University in St. Louis, School of Law

James D. Cox, Brainerd Currie Professor of Law, Duke University School of Law

Lawrence A. Cunningham, Professor of Law, The George Washington University Law School

Christine Di Guglielmo, Weil, Gotshal & Manges, LLP

Merritt B. Fox, Michael E. Patterson Professor of Law, Columbia Law School

Jesse M. Fried, Professor of Law, Harvard Law School

Jeffrey N. Gordon, Alfred W. Bressler Professor of Law and Albert E. Cinelli Enterprise Professorship, Columbia Law School

Hideki Kanda, Professor of Law, University of Tokyo

F. Scott Kieff, Professor of Law, The George Washington University Law School, and Ray and Louise Knowles Senior Fellow, Stanford University Hoover Institution on War, Revolution, and Peace

Rainer Kulms, Senior Research Fellow, Max Planck Institute for Comparative and Private International Law, and Lecturer-at-Law, University of Hamburg, Germany

Lawrence E. Mitchell, Theodore Rinehart Professor of Business Law, The George Washington University Law School

Troy A. Paredes, Professor of Law, Washington University in St. Louis, School of Law*

Shawn Pompian, Attorney Adviser, Office of the Legal Adviser at the U.S. Department of State

Joel Seligman, President, University of Rochester

E. Norman Veasey, Chief Justice, Delaware Supreme Court (Retired); Senior Partner, Weil, Gotshal & Manges, LLP

---

* Paredes is presently on leave for government service as a Commissioner at the Securities and Exchange Commission ("SEC"). Paredes worked on this book while working as a Professor of Law at Washington University School of Law before being sworn in and taking office as a Commissioner of the SEC. The views expressed in this book are those of the authors of the various chapters and do not necessarily reflect those of the co-editors. Nor are the views expressed in this book properly attributable to the SEC.

Acknowledgments and Dedication

The chapters in this book were presented at a conference on "The 'New' Corporate Governance" held at the Washington University School of Law in St. Louis. The conference was sponsored and hosted by the Center for Interdisciplinary Studies, along with support from the Whitney R. Harris Institute for Global Legal Studies, both of which are housed at the Washington University School of Law. The conference was held in honor of Joel Seligman – to whom this book is dedicated – and the contributions he has made to the study of securities regulation and corporate governance during his distinguished career. Before becoming the President of the University of Rochester in 2005, Joel Seligman served as the Dean and Ethan A. H. Shepley University Professor at the Washington University School of Law.

This book is part of broader work through the Project on Commercializing Innovation at Stanford University's Hoover Institution, which studies the law, economics, and politics of the range of legal and business relationships that can be used to bring ideas to market. We thank James E. Daily, who is a Postdoctoral Fellow and Administrative Director of the Project, for his excellent help editing the manuscript. More about the Project is available on the Web at www.innovation.hoover.org.

Let us thank Professor John Drobak, who directs the Washington University School of Law's Center for Interdisciplinary Studies. Without John's support, this book would not have been possible. We also recognize Linda McClain for her energetic efforts coordinating the conference behind this book; Tom Ferguson, Lucas Gredell, Rebecca Keyworth, Sarah Lampe, Erin Nave, and Timothy O'Connell for their editorial and research assistance; Sherrie Malone for her help preparing the manuscript; and John Berger, our Cambridge University Press editor, for his efforts and patience. We are particularly grateful to the individuals whose work makes up this book.

We also must point out that while Paredes is presently on leave for government service as a Commissioner at the Securities and Exchange Commission
("SEC"), he worked on this book while working as a Professor of Law at Washington University School of Law before being sworn in and taking office as
a Commissioner of the SEC. The views expressed in this book are those of
the authors of the various chapters and do not necessarily reflect those of the
co-editors. Nor are the views expressed in this book properly attributable to the
SEC.

F. Scott Kieff and Troy A. Paredes

PERSPECTIVES ON CORPORATE GOVERNANCE

Introduction

F. Scott Kieff and Troy A. Paredes

Although a number of factors contributed to the stock market decline that started in 2000 – including the bursting of the "dot-com" bubble, a softer economy than many expected, September 11 and the ongoing terrorist threat, and the wars in Afghanistan and Iraq – one factor that weighed on stocks stands out for present purposes: corporate scandal. Beginning with Enron in the fall of 2001, a wave of corporate scandal crashed on the U.S. economy. In addition to Enron, the scandals involved companies such as WorldCom, Tyco, HealthSouth, Adelphia, and Global Crossing. They also ensnared mutual funds and leading financial institutions up and down Wall Street, along with major accounting firms, such as the collapsed Arthur Andersen. As if the *bona fide* scandals that made the headlines were not enough to drag the markets down, a record number of earnings restatements – increasing steadily from 116 restatements in 1997, to 158 in 1998, 234 in 1999, 258 in 2000, and 305 in 2001 when the scandals began to break[1] – fueled doubt about companies' governance, finances, and business plans. These doubts became particularly sharp as the overall market tumbled through 2008.

Broad and deep securities markets, where ownership and control are widely separated, depend on a healthy dose of investor confidence to convince

---

[1] JOEL SELIGMAN, THE TRANSFORMATION OF WALL STREET: A HISTORY OF THE SECURITIES AND EXCHANGE COMMISSION AND MODERN FINANCE 624 (3d ed. 2003).

Kieff is Professor of Law, The George Washington University Law School, and Ray and Louise Knowles Senior Fellow, Stanford University Hoover Institution on War, Revolution, and Peace. Paredes is Professor of Law, Washington University in St. Louis, School of Law, presently on-leave for government service as a Commissioner at the Securities and Exchange Commission ("SEC"). Paredes worked on this chapter while working as a Professor of Law at Washington University School of Law before being sworn in and taking office as a Commissioner of the SEC; and the views expressed in this chapter are those of himself and Kieff and are not properly attributable to the SEC. This chapter is part of their work on the Hoover Project on Commercializing Innovation, which is available on the Web at www.innovation.hoover.org.

investors to hand over trillions of dollars to directors and officers over whom they exercise relatively little influence.[2] Although the nature of business is that some enterprises will succeed and others will fail, shareholders need to trust that the management team holding the company's reins will run the business honestly, in good faith, competently, and loyally – in short, that the company will be run in the best interests of the shareholders as opposed to in the best interests of the directors and officers. The abuses at what amounted to a handful of companies, given that there are thousands of public companies in the United States, rocked investor confidence, resulting in a major sell-off of equities and deep concerns market-wide. Investors understandably became skittish and, unable to distinguish the "good" companies from the "bad" ones, dashed to the sidelines with cash in hand as events at Enron, WorldCom, and elsewhere unfolded. Although the scandals affected relatively few companies overall, the seeming perfect storm of corporate governance failures disillusioned many about the U.S. corporate governance system and the integrity of U.S. securities markets.

If the debacle at Enron had been an isolated incident that could have been written off as the work of a few rotten apples at the company, perhaps Congress and the President would have sat tight. But once WorldCom broke in mid-June of 2002, it seemed apparent that the U.S. corporate governance system was suffering from deep flaws that needed fixing. As political pressures mounted, and as stock prices continued to plummet, something was bound to be done. In late July, within weeks of the news of WorldCom's massive fraud, Congress almost unanimously approved the Sarbanes-Oxley Act of 2002.

The Sarbanes-Oxley Act has proven to be the most important federal corporate governance and securities legislation since Congress adopted the original federal securities acts as part of President Franklin Roosevelt's New Deal. Once President George W. Bush signed the legislation into law on July 30, 2002, the markets were given additional assurance that fraud and corporate abuses would not be tolerated.[3] In addition to the legislative efforts of Congress and the President, a number of cops on the beat stepped up their efforts to detect and root out corporate wrongdoing: new listing standards were proposed for companies trading on the New York Stock Exchange or Nasdaq;

---

[2] For the classic treatment of the separation of ownership and control, see ADOLF A. BERLE, JR. & GARDINER C. MEANS, THE MODERN CORPORATION AND PRIVATE PROPERTY (1932).

[3] For overviews of events leading to the adoption of the Sarbanes-Oxley Act, see LOUIS LOSS, JOEL SELIGMAN, & TROY PAREDES, 2 SECURITIES REGULATION 510–659 (4th ed. 2007); William W. Bratton, *Enron and the Dark Side of Shareholder Value*, 76 TUL. L. REV. 1275 (2002); Roberta Romano, *The Sarbanes-Oxley Act and the Making of Quack Corporate Governance*, 114 YALE L.J. 1521 (2005); Joel Seligman, *No One Can Serve Two Masters: Corporate and Securities Law After Enron*, 80 WASH. U. L.Q. 449 (2002).

the U.S. Securities and Exchange Commission (SEC) engaged in wide-scale rulemaking and intensified its enforcement efforts; the Department of Justice began to focus its attention on corporate fraud; and New York Attorney General Eliot Spitzer assumed an unprecedented role in going after corporate corruption.

There is no doubt that new legal mandates and credible threats of massive civil fines and prison time reshaped the corporate landscape. But in addition to all of this, shareholders, led by institutional investors and increasingly by hedge funds, have become much more active, recognizing that they have a role in protecting their own interests instead of simply relying on the government to protect them. Consider, for example, the outrage over executive pay; the spike in the number of shareholder proposals; and the growing push for majority voting for boards of directors. Such shareholder activism is assisted by a discerning financial and business media that has shined a bright light on corporate wrongdoing and mismanagement.

As a result of all of this, it is fair to say that we have entered a new and especially controversial era in debates about corporate governance. The hallmark feature of this era is greater scrutiny of corporate actors by Congress, the SEC, state attorneys general, federal prosecutors, other corporate actors, judges, the public, and the media. Louis Brandeis said, "Sunlight is said to be the best of disinfectants; electric light the most efficient policeman."[4] Without question, closer tabs are being kept on corporate America now than ever before. But recognizing that more is not always better, this book's purpose is to consider what such close scrutiny has meant for corporate behavior so far and what it will mean for corporate behavior in the future.

This book begins in Part I with chapters by Lawrence Mitchell, Lawrence Cunningham, Scott Kieff, and Troy Paredes that study a fundamental relationship in the firm – that is, the relationship between the board of directors and the chief executive officer. Part II turns to executive pay, one of the most controversial issues in corporate governance. Chapters by Lucian Bebchuk and Jesse Fried, William Bratton, and Jeffrey Gordon address the structure of executive pay, the incentives executive pay creates for managers running the business, and opportunities for reform. The chapters in Part III cover various mechanisms for holding accountable managers and directors who loot the business, shirk, or "cook the books." Stephen Bainbridge considers shareholder activism. Merritt Fox considers the role of securities regulation. And Kathleen Brickey looks into the media's role. Part IV focuses on the source of regulation. In other words, should Congress or the states regulate corporate

[4] Louis D. Brandeis, Other People's Money and How the Bankers Use It 92 (1914).

conduct? James Cox's chapter takes Delaware to task for its handling of corporate governance in the post-Enron era. Norman Veasey, a former Delaware Supreme Court Justice, along with co-authors Shawn Pompian and Christine Di Guglielmo, defend federalism and the role of the states in corporate governance regulation. Part V looks outward, considering corporate governance in foreign countries. Hideki Kanda's chapter looks at the differences between bank and capital market regulation with a special emphasis on Japan, while Rainer Kulms discusses ongoing developments in European corporate governance. While these chapters cover different countries, they both engage the broader debate of whether corporate governance around the globe is converging to the U.S. model. This book concludes with an epilogue by Joel Seligman. Seligman's contribution identifies three trends in corporate governance that have impacted corporate conduct so far and that are bound to impact corporate governance in the future.

Part I starts with Lawrence Mitchell's "The Trouble with Boards." Mitchell studies the history of the board of directors. Mitchell starts by recounting the board's evolution from its early beginning to the present-day monitoring model of the board. Mitchell argues that the board, as it functions today, was designed principally to protect its members from legal liability and to leave corporate power with management. Consider, for example, the deferential business judgment rule and the fact that directors can be exonerated from monetary liability for breaching the duty of care. Against the historical backdrop he paints, Mitchell asks a fundamental question: "Is the board of directors of the modern American public corporation a useful institution?" Put differently, Mitchell asks if we should even bother having boards. Shareholders are told that the board is the corporation's keeper and exists to represent the shareholders' interests. Yet, according to Mitchell, the board does not do this. Thus, the board's existence fosters a false sense of security for shareholders, as well as other corporate constituencies. Mitchell is down on the board, but he does note some possible remedies for what ails it. One option is simply to do away with the board entirely. A very different choice is for the board to step up and exercise real power. Another option is to have several boards at a company, each with a different function. For example, one board could be responsible for legal compliance, while a separate board takes charge of shaping corporate strategy. A particularly thought-provoking suggestion stems from Mitchell's claim that real power rests not with the board, but with the CEO. If real power resides with the CEO, then perhaps shareholders, and not the board, should get to elect the CEO, according to Mitchell. Such direct-shareholder election of the CEO would be a fundamental shift in corporate internal affairs. Mitchell stresses that the starting point for any meaningful reform is to reconceptualize the board's purpose, since in his view the predominant monitoring model has let us down.

The second chapter in Part I is "Rediscovering Board Expertise: Legal Implications of the Empirical Literature" by Lawrence Cunningham. Cunningham examines the balance between expertise and independence in the boardroom. Historically, independence has been favored over expertise, but Cunningham argues that theory, empirical evidence, and new legal pressures support placing a greater value on expertise. Accounting expertise, in particular, is called for among the members of board audit committees. Cunningham goes on to discuss the questions that arise naturally: what should be required of experts and in whose interest should they act? To the first question, he argues that accounting experts should take a broad role, monitoring both accounting earnings management and real earnings management. To the second, he proposes that the audit committee accounting experts themselves should determine the balance of their constituency among equity investors, debt investors, bonus-compensated employees, and society.

Cunningham also considers whether independence and expertise are necessarily mutually exclusive. Although expertise derived from inside knowledge of the corporation is often opposed to independence, expertise derived from substantive knowledge in a discipline (e.g., accounting) is not. Cunningham argues that it is in fact this latter variety of expertise that is especially valuable when combined with independence. Promoting this combination requires realigning legal doctrine with the empirical evidence favoring expertise.

"The CEO and the Board: On CEO Overconfidence and Institutionalizing Dissent in Firms" by Scott Kieff and Troy Paredes concludes Part I. A great deal of attention has been aimed at going after corporate malfeasance in the post-Enron era. Fraud and looting are problems. But in trying to craft a corporate governance regime that remedies such agency costs, a different problem often is overlooked. That is, a great deal of firm value is destroyed when companies are run poorly. Even when directors and officers are acting loyally and are properly incentivized to maximize profits, the company can struggle, and possibly go under, if corporate strategy is not properly tended to and if particular business opportunities are not properly evaluated. Bad business decisions, or even good business decisions that are then implemented poorly, are a very real concern. Kieff and Paredes encourage more attention to be paid to improving the strategic decision making of corporate actors who are well-intentioned and hard-working and who are acting in good faith. They stress that it is important for management and its advisers to have good information and to deliberate earnestly to ensure there is a full airing of issues. The hallmark of good decision making is a balanced assessment of risks and rewards. Kieff and Paredes worry that boards and subordinate officers are too deferential to the CEO in how the enterprise is run, such that one view, the CEO's, too frequently dominates corporate decision making. So they explore a particular fix – namely, institutionalizing dissent in firms by appointing a formal devil's advocate on the board. The express job of the devil's advocate would be to challenge assumptions, identify risks, offer competing options, and press counterarguments.

"Pay Without Performance: Overview of the Issues" by Lucian Bebchuk and Jesse Fried starts off Part II of this book. What accounts for the structure of executive pay? Why are CEOs paid as much as they are? What does it mean for CEO pay to be "excessive"? To what extent do CEOs set their own pay? Bebchuk and Fried have developed one of the most influential theories of executive compensation – the so-called "managerial power" theory. Bebchuk and Fried contend that too often there is no meaningful arm's-length negotiation between managers and boards when boards fix managerial pay, and their chapter details the various ways in which managers influence their pay, even as boards have become more independent. Hence, it should come as no great surprise that executive compensation has skyrocketed. The managerial power theory highlights a cognate feature of executive compensation arrangements – that is, the need to avoid public outrage over outsized pay packages. Bebchuk and Fried claim that managers often structure their pay to "camouflage" their compensation to avoid public outrage. Instead of taking an especially large salary, senior executives may obscure their pay through pension plans, deferred compensation arrangements, and retirement perks. Managers and directors may also try to legitimize executive compensation with the stamp of approval from a supposedly independent outside compensation consultant. Having problematized executive compensation, Bebchuk and Fried offer a number of reforms. Among other things, they argue for improving transparency by having companies reduce all forms of compensation to a single dollar value. They also suggest having companies disclose the extent to which an executive's pay is attributable to general market and industry developments and not the executive's own efforts. The SEC has recently followed a similar reform agenda in revamping the agency's executive compensation disclosure requirements for public companies. Bebchuk and Fried do not stop with urging better disclosure, however. They also recommend several separate substantive provisions for compensation arrangements. These terms are designed to link pay to performance. Their most provocative suggestion strikes at the heart of the firm. Bebchuk and Fried argue that shareholders should be given more direct authority over the enterprise and greater freedom to remove directors and to put forth their own nominees.

The next chapter is William Bratton's "Supersize Pay, Incentive Compatibility, and the Volatile Shareholder Interest." Commentators and policy makers generally agree that executive compensation should be structured not only to compensate senior managers for their efforts, but to incentivize them to run the business in the shareholders' best interests. Put differently, the CEO and other top executives should be financially motivated to enhance shareholder value. But as Bratton highlights, this overlooks a key concern. It typically is assumed that all shareholders are the same, in which case they all have the same interests – say, a higher stock price today. Bratton explains that this view of shareholders is too simplistic. Shareholders are not monolithic. Bratton catalogues the different types of shareholders as follows: long-term investors, speculators, noise traders, fundamental value investors, long-term holders, "dumb money," and "smart money." Once the shareholder class is unpacked this way, what maximizing shareholder value means in practice is unclear, as Bratton illustrates. For example, a manager may make an imprudent investment in some fashionable new venture, such as an on-line business strategy, if that is what the market will reward in the short term. This may get today's stock price up, which is good for a speculator, but it may mean a lower stock price in the future, at the expense of long-term investors. Similarly, a manager who makes capital budgeting decisions with an eye toward hitting this quarter's earnings target may sacrifice future firm value by delaying or foregoing important investments. Further, executives may feel pressured to manage earnings or, worse yet, engage in actual fraud to meet earnings targets. Bratton says that compensation arrangements often align managers' interests with those of short-term speculators and that managers instead should be motivated to maximize the long-term fundamental value of the firm. How can this be done? One strategy that Bratton stresses is to turn managers into long-term investors by restraining the alienability of their equity grants.

The third chapter in Part II is "'Say on Pay': Cautionary Notes on the U.K. Experience and the Case for Muddling Through" by Jeffrey Gordon. Gordon describes two strands in the executive compensation debate: pay for performance and social responsibility. Although both have focused on giving the board and possibly shareholders more power to evaluate and constrain executive compensation, Gordon argues that pay for performance is likely to dominate the decision making of boards and shareholders, leaving social responsibility concerns to the political process.

Unfortunately, pay for performance does not produce an easy answer in all situations, and Gordon suggests that it is best understood as a goal rather than a simple, measurable output variable. With that in mind, Gordon turns to current reform efforts, particularly shareholder involvement in compensation setting. After describing a theoretical framework for understanding various approaches to the issue, Gordon analyzes the U.K. approach to "say on pay" and finds it lacking. Instead of a one-size-fits-all solution from the legislature, he suggests "muddling through" with a refined version of the existing US combination of firm-by-firm consideration of "say on pay" and shareholder threats to remove compensation committee members. Although such an approach may lead to socially unacceptably high levels of compensation, Gordon argues that such considerations are best addressed through tax policy rather than corporate governance reform.

Stephen Bainbridge opens Part III with his chapter, "Shareholder Activism in the Obama Era." Investors have long subscribed to the "Wall Street Rule" – if the company you invest in is underperforming, sell. Today, shareholders are much more active than in the past. Most notably, institutional investors have been exercising their voice in an effort to influence management and the board. Shareholder proposals are on the rise, for example, and shareholders have resorted to "just vote no" campaigns, withholding their votes for disfavored board nominees. As Bainbridge explains, there has been support for giving shareholders even more influence by facilitating the exercise of their franchise. Among other developments, the SEC proposed new rules that would have given shareholders access to the corporate ballot to nominate directors to compete with the company's slate. So-called "majority voting" for director elections has also gained steam. Bainbridge defends the separation of ownership and control and argues against shareholder activism in general and against extending the shareholder franchise in particular.

In key respects, Bainbridge's argument centers on his claim that the most active investors are union and public pension plans, which are often motivated by political considerations or the interests of non-shareholder constituencies, such as union or government employees. He makes three primary arguments. First, Bainbridge reasons that activist shareholders often pursue objectives that are not shared by passive investors and that often cut against the interests of passive investors. Second, he explains that shareholder activism undercuts board authority over the enterprise. Third, Bainbridge argues that greater investor activism simply relocates agency problems. For example, as institutional investors become more active, we have a new worry about whether pension fund managers are acting in the best interests of fund beneficiaries, in addition to traditional concerns over whether directors and officers are managing the business in the shareholders' best interests. In sum, Bainbridge argues against empowering shareholders to hold directors and managers more accountable.

Merritt Fox's "After *Dura*: Causation in Fraud-on-the-Market Actions" is next. At the core of the federal securities laws is a mandatory disclosure regime. The federal regime is designed to remedy the informational asymmetries that exist between companies and investors. The logic is that by arming investors with information, mandatory disclosure promotes informed investor decision making, capital market integrity, and capital market efficiency. Once they are empowered with information, investors can protect themselves against corporate abuses and mismanagement, and there is no need for the government to engage in more substantive securities regulation. All of this presumes that the information disclosed is complete and accurate. In reality, disclosures are not always truthful. Fox's chapter addresses the legal regime that empowers private litigants to enforce the federal securities laws to ensure the accuracy of corporate disclosures. Fox's chapter examines the civil liability system under the federal securities laws. Fox focuses his attention on an important Supreme Court decision handed down in 2005, *Dura Pharmaceuticals, Inc. v. Broudo*. *Dura* defines the loss causation element under the general federal antifraud provisions, section 10(b) of the Securities Exchange Act of 1934 and Rule 10b-5 promulgated thereunder. In finding that plaintiff-shareholders cannot show loss causation by pleading that an alleged misstatement led to an inflated stock price, the case has made it more difficult for shareholders to bring actions alleging fraud. Fox gives a detailed account of *Dura*, loss causation, and fraud-on-the-market actions generally. More pointedly, he argues that the loss causation requirement is nonsensical in fraud-on-the-market cases. Fox concludes that the Supreme Court has left several key issues unanswered, and he offers a number of important suggestions for lower courts to follow as they flesh out *Dura* in the years ahead. Depending on how the lower courts apply *Dura*, private litigation for fraud will be more or less impactful in holding parties to account under the federal securities laws and thus shaping corporate behavior.

In Part III's third chapter, "From Boardroom to Courtroom to Newsroom: The Media and the Corporate Governance Scandals," Kathleen Brickey studies the media. To the extent that sunlight is a disinfectant – and the mandatory disclosure regime of the federal securities laws is premised on the view that it is – the media play an important role shaping corporate conduct by shining light on wrongdoing and mismanagement. The media also influences lawmakers by stirring up opposition to certain corporate practices. Reports in the *New York Times* and the *Wall Street Journal* and on television often prod public outrage and capture the attention of lawmakers, thus influencing the agenda of legislators and regulators. Further, investors can use the media to wage a public campaign against particular senior officers and board members, and lawmakers can exhort particular reforms by taking to the airwaves and the op-ed pages. That said, as Brickey describes, the media sometimes gets it wrong and can be used as a tool to thwart corporate accountability. Through the lens of high-profile cases involving individuals such as Martha Stewart, Dennis Kozlowski, and Richard Scrushy, Brickey tackles a number of fundamental concerns. Has the media's rush to provide instantaneous coverage compromised journalistic integrity? Has reporting by the press risked causing mistrials? Is the media manipulated by corporate actors or their opponents? Is the media being used to influence juries? The media plays a more complex role in securities markets than simply disseminating information to investors and other stakeholders.

Part IV begins with "How Delaware Law Can Support Better Corporate Governance" by James Cox. Delaware is the most important source of corporate law in the United States. Cox takes Delaware to task for falling short in regulating corporate behavior. He censures Delaware for not more actively cultivating best practices for corporate actors and for too readily deferring to management and the board. Cox goes so far as to describe the law of fiduciary duty in Delaware as "vacuous" and says that "there is no there there." Cox spares almost no important corporate law doctrine, criticizing Delaware's duty of care, its lack of a meaningful duty of good faith, the demand requirement in derivative litigation, the law governing the usurpation of a corporate opportunity, and Delaware's takeover law. In so doing, Cox analyzes numerous leading Delaware cases, including *Disney, Aronson, Van Gorkom, Caremark, Broz, Unocal, Moran,* and *Blasius.* Cox concludes that the Delaware courts must see themselves as being in the "norms business" and must announce judicial expectations for directors and officers more sharply and sternly. He also argues that the Delaware courts should defer less to management and the board and should not be beholden to the standard claim that the Delaware courts must tread lightly to avoid discouraging risk taking. Cox thus calls into question longstanding judicial practice under the business judgment rule. Why have the Delaware courts gone easy on directors and officers, if indeed they have as Cox suggests? Cox notes one explanation – namely, that in order to ensure that Delaware remains the jurisdiction of choice for incorporation, the Delaware courts have decided to be friendly to management and boards.

Norman Veasey is much more sanguine about Delaware's success crafting corporate law. He is a unique authority on the topic, having served as the Chief Justice of the Delaware Supreme Court. In his chapter in Part IV, "Federalism versus Federalization: Preserving the Division of Responsibility in

Corporation Law," Veasey, along with Shawn Pompian and Christine Di Guglielmo, takes up the federalization of corporate law. Corporate law, which can best be understood as regulating corporate internal affairs and fixing the allocation of authority among directors, officers, and shareholders, has been the domain of the states, with the federal government focusing on securities regulation. Congress is seen to have upset this federal-state balance when it adopted the Sarbanes-Oxley Act in response to the frauds at Enron and World-Com. According to Veasey and his co-authors, Congress unwisely intruded upon the traditional sphere of the states. The authors begin by describing the longstanding federal-state regulatory balance and how the balance has changed in recent years with federal regulation of non-audit services, board committee composition, executive compensation, executive loans, lawyer conduct, and director elections. Veasey, Pompian, and Di Guglielmo argue against the further federalization of corporate law. First, they reason that federal intervention hurts investors because it imposes a top-down regime that deprives investors of the benefits of the regulatory competition that results when states compete for corporate charters. In other words, Veasey and his co-authors believe that competition among the states has resulted in a "race to the top," with Delaware "winning" because it has offered a corporate law regime superior to the rest of the country. Second, Veasey et al. argue that states have a comparative advantage over the federal government in regulating corporate internal affairs. Because fiduciary relationships are highly particularized, they do not lend themselves to the types of detailed bright-line rules that characterize federal regulation. The states, particularly through courts like the Delaware Chancery Court that are expert in business matters, are better equipped to apply open-ended fiduciary standards in a granular, fact-specific way case-by-case. No two companies are the same, and so no single regulatory regime should be imposed.

Part V opens with Hideki Kanda's chapter, "Regulatory Differences in Bank and Capital Market Regulation." The United States financial system is based on capital markets, whereas in much of the rest of the world, such as in Asia, financial systems center on banks. Kanda starts his analysis by providing a very useful overview comparing the structure and regulation of bank-based financial systems and capital market-based financial systems. These different systems of finance present different challenges and opportunities and thus call for different regulatory schemes. A logical extension of Kanda's analysis is that financial regulation around the globe will not (and should not) converge to a single model. In fact, the regulatory pattern is likely to be one of divergence, not convergence. Even more provocatively, Kanda explains which type of financial system should exist in a country. He theorizes that the cost of regulation and enforcement determines the type of financial system that is and should be found. For example, Kanda says that in a bank system, regulation is targeted to providing deposit insurance and preventing bank failures. By contrast, he summarizes as follows the three types of regulations a capital market system requires: (1) strong investor protections, such as mandatory disclosure, stringent antifraud protections, and uniform accounting standards; (2) an active government enforcement agency, such as the SEC, complemented by private enforcement; and (3) strong regulation of financial intermediaries, such as broker-dealers, underwriters, and pension funds. Kanda concludes that the regulatory regime needed to buttress a capital market system of finance is more complex and costly and that not every country is up to the task of crafting and enforcing such a regime. Kanda ultimately concludes that a bank system is better when a country's economy is small and that a capital market system is better when a country's economy is large. Kanda points to Japan as one country that has slowly graduated from a bank-based financial system to a capital market-based financial system as its economy has grown and become better equipped to shoulder the regulatory burden needed to sustain capital markets.

The other chapter in Part V, "European Corporate Governance After Five Years with Sarbanes-Oxley" by Rainer Kulms, takes the reader from Asia to Europe. Company law in Europe is undergoing major change. A persistent question continues to be whether company law should be harmonized throughout Europe. The debate over company law harmonization in Europe recalls the decades-long debate in the United States over whether competition for corporate charters among the states has led to a "race to the top" or a "race to the bottom" and the more recent debate, captured in Part IV of this book, over the Sarbanes-Oxley Act and the federalization of corporate law. Kulms' analysis, which includes an effective overview of European regulation, centers on recent proposals by the European Commission for harmonizing European corporate law and securities regulation. Kulms offers a thoroughgoing assessment of the choice between harmonization as compared to regulatory competition among European Union member states. For example, harmonization (or centralization), particularly when reflected in mandates, may help address externalities. On the other hand, one size of company law may not fit the needs of each of the diverse member states and mandates crowd out private ordering. Interestingly, as the debate continues over the pros and cons of centralizing regulatory decision making in Europe, the United States has recently experienced more centralized decision making as Congress undertook a more active role regulating corporate governance when it adopted the Sarbanes-Oxley Act.

This book concludes with an Epilogue comprising an essay by Joel Seligman entitled, "Three Secular Trends of Corporate Law." Seligman identifies and explicates the following three trends, which he believes will continue to influence corporate governance. First, state corporate law, according to Seligman, has become increasingly irrelevant. Seligman claims that the states, including Delaware, have abdicated their responsibility for regulating corporate behavior. Second, federal securities regulation has become a more prominent feature of the U.S. corporate governance system. That said, Seligman predicts that federal securities regulation will continue to have a kind of "binge/purge" quality to it, with periods of regulatory inactivity interrupted by flurries of hyperactivity after crises. Enron and WorldCom, for example, ushered in historic reforms after years of understaffing and underfunding at the SEC. Third, the SEC itself has become more bureaucratized. The SEC is a larger agency with a more aggressive agenda than in the past. Its rules are extremely detailed and often affect change not just at the margins, but at the core. Consequently, SEC rulemaking often results in more complex and more costly regulatory regimes that increasingly spur backlash. Seligman claims that it may become more difficult for the agency to perform its job in the future as the leading securities regulator in the United States. Just as there are risks that the agency can be too aggressive, there also are risks that it can become too tentative in the face of criticism.

* * *

It is hoped that this book enriches our understanding of the impact that the new era of corporate governance, ushered in by Enron and WorldCom, has had on corporate conduct for better and for worse. We should continue to give securities markets and corporate governance a hard look, even when times are good and no scandals are hitting the headlines. We should similarly give a hard look to corporate and securities regulations, enacted and proposed, regardless of whether headlines cry out for regulation, de-regulation, or are silent on the topic. The regime regulating corporate behavior needs to be nimble and able to accommodate changing business and investor needs and concerns, which can arise when stock prices are climbing, as well as when they are crashing. If there is one fundamental lesson to take away, it is that our regulatory regime must remain "state of the art." We must learn from our past, including the natural experiments that history has run, and the ideas that have previously been offered in the debates of our history. We must also anticipate developments and not simply react to them.

When thinking about how to structure or improve a system of laws focused on more market based, financial activities, as compared with those laws focused on fairness and civil rights, etc., we should try hard to determine how future parties will engage similar situations in the face of various possible legal responses to present ones. That is, we should see things as dynamic not static. We also should fully expect that we won't be able to select the true, correct, outcome in a given case with certainty and so we should try to develop a set of comparative analyses of relative magnitudes and frequencies of the inevitable over inclusiveness and under inclusiveness that are associated with different legal regimes designed to address the problem. We should also develop an understanding of who is the lowest cost provider and evaluator of the information needed to make an appropriate decision and be vigilant about administrative costs in different decision-making processes. We should be vigilant about the transaction costs of those deals needed to help ensure resources regularly move to their highest and best use as well as those agency costs for those hierarchies we create within organizations. Throughout it all, we should be very skeptical of comparative exposure to public choice problems for each different available approach.

In the end, we must constantly endeavor to develop well reasoned approaches to corporate and securities regulation. The contributions to this book are designed to do just that.

PART ONE

THE BOARD OF DIRECTORS AND THE CEO

1 The Trouble with Boards

Lawrence E. Mitchell

On Tuesday afternoon, December 2, 1913, Thomas W. Lamont and Louis D. Brandeis met for a three-hour luncheon at the University Club in New York. The famous Pujo Committee hearings had reached their controversial end, convincing many Americans that the accusations of Brandeis and others as to the existence of a Money Trust were right. The Money Tust appeared as a small group of mostly New York bankers centered on the House of Morgan. It allegedly controlled corporate America and its access to capital by placing its members on the boards of many of the nation's largest corporations.[1]

Lamont was a relatively new partner of J. P. Morgan and Co.[2] Like his partners, he served as a director of a number of corporations in which interlocking bank directorates had been exposed by the Pujo investigations. Within just a few years, he would take effective leadership of the Morgan firm and become perhaps the most prominent financier of his generation.

---

[1] The Pujo Committee was a subcommittee of the House Committee on Banking and Currency appointed in April 1912 to investigate the existence of a so-called Money Trust on Wall Street. The Committee delivered its report the following year. REP. OF THE COMM. APPOINTED PURSUANT TO H. RES. 429 AND 504 TO INVESTIGATE THE CONCENTRATION OF CONTROL OF MONEY AND CREDIT (Comm. Print 1913). For a detailed discussion of the committee and its work, see LAWRENCE E. MITCHELL, THE SPECULATION ECONOMY: HOW FINANCE TRIUMPHED OVER INDUSTRY (2007).

[2] RON CHERNOW, THE HOUSE OF MORGAN: AN AMERICAN BANKING DYNASTY AND THE RISE OF MODERN FINANCE (1990).

Lawrence E. Mitchell is Theodore Rinehart Professor of Business Law, George Washington University. I would like to thank Bill Bratton, Mel Eisenberg, Jim Fanto, Jeff Gordon, Theresa Gabaldon, Kent Greenfield, Tom Joo, and Dalia Tsuk Mitchell for their helpful advice and comments. Participants in conferences at Columbia Law School and Washington University School of Law also made helpful remarks. Finally, I would also like to thank Leslie Kramer for her research help. Portions of this chapter previously were published in *The Board as a Path Toward Corporate Social Responsibility*, in THE NEW CORPORATE ACCOUNTABILITY: CORPORATE SOCIAL RESPONSIBILITY AND THE LAW 279–306 (Doreen McBarnet et al. eds., 2008).

The conversation was polite, as befitted both the setting and the character of
the two men. Needless to say, they disagreed about much. The most interesting
turn in the conversation came during Brandeis's remarks about the potential
conflicts of interest created by the fact that many of the same men sat on the
boards of competing corporations. Passing the point in complete disagreement
with Lamont's response, Brandeis took a different tack, questioning Lamont
as to the sheer physical ability of Morgan's men to do their work as directors:

> LDB: Take your own house alone. Here are all you gentlemen, from all
> accounts, worked half to death. How, in the nature of things, can you pos-
> sibly attend intelligently to the affairs of railroad management? It is simply
> impossible. . . .

> TWL: But, Mr. Brandeis, we don't attempt to manage railroads. The public has
> an idea that we do, but that is just what we don't do. Nobody realizes better
> than we do that that is not our function. We give the best counsel that we
> can in the selection of good men, making mistakes sometimes of course . . . ,
> but on the whole we do fairly well and we give our very best advice on the
> financial policy, looking both backward and forward over a series of years, for
> the purpose of building up and entrenching the company's credit.[3]

For much of the succeeding ninety-four years, lawyers and businesspeople
have engaged in debates about the role of the board that are little more than
variations on Brandeis and Lamont's exchange. It was not until the mid-1970s
that we came to accept Lamont's description as the appropriate legal model.

Lamont was describing a version of what we have come to know as the
monitoring board. Since the 1980s, the monitoring board, composed largely
of outside directors, has been the received and dominant model of the board
of the large U.S. public corporation.[4] But the monitoring board, or at least its
implementation, has come under fire from academics and reformers in recent
years. Critics see the monitoring board as outmoded and ineffectual and have
suggested a variety of reforms.[5]

---

[3] The entire conversation is reported in Paul P. Abrahams, *Brandeis and Lamont on Finance
Capitalism*, 47 BUS. HIST. REV. 72, 82–83 (1973).

[4] Robert Hamilton, *Corporate Governance in America, 1950–2000: Major Changes but Uncertain
Benefits*, 25 J. CORP. L. 349, 363 (2000); THE BUSINESS ROUNDTABLE, STATEMENT ON CORPO-
RATE GOVERNANCE (Sept. 1997) [hereinafter 1997 BUSINESS ROUNDTABLE STATEMENT]. The
concept of the monitoring board as the dominant legal model was recently reinforced. *In re*
Walt Disney Co. Derivative Lit., 906 A.2d 27 (Del. 2006), *aff'g* 907 A.2d 693 (Del. Ch. 2005).

[5] See, e.g., Lynne L. Dallas, *The Multiple Roles of Boards of Directors*, 40 SAN DIEGO L. REV.
781 (2003); Jill E. Fisch, *Taking Boards Seriously*, 19 CARDOZO L. REV. 265 (1997); Donald
C. Langevoort, *The Human Nature of Corporate Boards: Law, Norms, and the Unintended
Consequences of Independence and Accountability*, 89 GEO. L.J. 797 (2001).

The reform literature ignores history. It typically assumes the monitoring board as a given.[6] Reform literature that begins with the assumption of the monitoring board typically ends with suggestions for improving or modifying the monitoring board. Once we understand the history of the development of the monitoring board, we should not be surprised to see that reformers fail to make it work. It was not designed to work.[7]

The exception to scholarly ahistoricism is a recent piece by Jeff Gordon. Gordon traces the history of the independent board from the 1950s and observes a roughly parallel development of the shareholder-value norm.[8] From this, he concludes that the monitoring board consisting of independent directors grew as a way of fulfilling the shareholder-value norm and has had a positive impact on corporate governance by better aligning managerial and shareholder interests.[9]

My reading of the history is different. First, as I argue elsewhere, the concept of shareholder valuism, if not the term, has been a constant since the creation of the giant modern U.S. corporation at the turn of the twentieth century.[10] Almost from the beginning, the interests of shareholders were protected, during what is commonly known as the managerialist era, which ran through the 1970s, by close corporate control combinations consisting of managers with substantial equity stakes in their corporations, performance-based compensation, and controlling stockholders. It was only a series of economic and political events in the 1970s, which I will later describe, that broke this structure in a way that led to the need for a new control model.

---

[6] Indeed, it assumes the board of directors as a given.

[7] As I will later explain, Mel Eisenberg, who developed the monitoring model, did intend it to be a real reform effort and worked as reporter for the American Law Institute's Corporate Governance Project to impose real standards on the board. The story of how that process was hijacked by the corporate bar is well known, and I will retell only a brief synopsis of it here. For a good example of the corporate bar's response to the reporter's efforts to impose standards on the monitoring board, see Bay Manning's scolding classic *The Business Judgment Rule and the Director's Duty of Attention: Time for Reality*, 39 BUS. LAW. 1477 (1984). My point, however, is that, even if that process hadn't been hijacked, the very concept of the monitoring board itself is flawed. The problem, as Eisenberg well saw, is that there does not appear to be much of an alternative.

[8] The shareholder-value norm captures the idea that the corporation is to be run solely for the purpose of maximizing shareholder value. Its desirability as a governing principle is hotly contested in contemporary scholarship but has largely been accepted as a business matter. LAWRENCE E. MITCHELL, CORPORATE IRRESPONSIBILITY: AMERICA'S NEWEST EXPORT (2001).

[9] Jeffrey N. Gordon, *The Rise of Independent Directors in the United States, 1950–2005: Of Shareholder Value and Stock Market Prices*, 59 STAN. L. REV. 1465 (2007).

[10] For an extended history of the development of the shareholder-value norm through the creation of the modern giant corporation, the modern stock market, and their relationship to one another, see MITCHELL, *supra* note 1.

Second, and the subject of this chapter, is my argument that Gordon's optimistic reading of the historical development of the independent monitoring board misses a darker story, a story grounded not in economics but in politics, a story not of enhanced board accountability but of the loss of board accountability.[11] Simply put, the corporate board as we know it today was developed primarily for the purpose of protecting directors from liability.[12] Although it first came into being as an innovative and good-faith reform exercise, it rapidly was refined to shield management directors from liability while providing virtually no exposure for outsiders. The model's use of nominating, compensation, and audit committees gave rise to the practice of periodic intervention by experts as a means of allowing outside directors to fulfill the light duties contemplated by the monitoring board.[13] Once the monitoring model was fully embraced by the Delaware courts in the 1980s, it played a substantial role in the diminished standards of fiduciary obligation, and particularly the duty of care, that exist today.[14]

[11] Gordon's reading is optimistic only if one accepts his favorable appraisal of the shareholder-value norm.

[12] This is the case despite some substantial business opposition to the monitoring board. James W. Walker Jr., *Comments on the ALI Corporate Governance Project*, 9 DEL. J. CORP. L. 580 (1984); STATEMENT OF THE BUSINESS ROUNDTABLE ON THE AMERICAN LAW INSTITUTE'S PROPOSED "PRINCIPLES OF CORPORATE GOVERNMENT AND STRUCTURE: RESTATEMENT AND RECOMMENDATIONS" (1983) [hereinafter 1983 BUSINESS ROUNDTABLE STATEMENT]. I believe that much of this opposition was intricately related to perceived increased liability standards, especially with respect to the duty of care, that accompanied the first formal introduction of the monitoring board in Tentative Draft No. 1 of the American Law Institute's Principals of Corporate Governance. While that project (or at least that draft) showed real potential for reform of corporate governance, the monitoring board had by that time come to be accepted, for the most part, in legal doctrine, in a manner that diluted rather than enhanced director liability, as I will explain herein. Daniel Fischel at the time suggested another ulterior motive – that the use of an independent board (which he does not necessarily assume to be a monitoring board) would compel managers to behave in more socially responsible ways. Daniel R. Fischel, *The Corporate Governance Movement*, 35 VAND. L. REV. 1259, 1284 (1982). I would suggest, without arguing the point, that history has demonstrated either the incorrectness of this insight or the failure of the project at the same time that it has demonstrated a strong protection of directors from legal liability. Roberta Karmel, almost in passing, appears to have seen the liability-protective possibilities of the monitoring board rather early. Roberta S. Karmel, *The Independent Corporate Board: A Means to What End?* 52 GEO. WASH. L. REV. 534, 553 (1984).

[13] I will discuss the growth of the director search firm and compensation consultant herein.

[14] One can, of course, dispute the propriety of the current level of the duty of care. That is not my issue. My point is that, whatever one might think of the duty of care, it is a considerably lower standard than it might have been and that the institution of the monitoring board as the dominant model bears substantial responsibility for that result.

Before I proceed, let me be clear about what I am not discussing as much as about what I am discussing. I am not especially concerned with the institution of the outside director per se. Outside directors are a logical (if perhaps unnecessary) corollary to the monitoring board. Eisenberg himself appears to have considered independent directors a necessary component

This chapter proceeds as follows. Section I provides a brief overview of the history of the board prior to the 1970s. The overview is necessarily brief because the board generally was not a serious subject of legal study during that time. Section II discusses the business and political failures during the

of the monitoring board, although others do not. Melvin A. Eisenberg, *The Modernization of Corporate Law: An Essay for Bill Cary*, 37 U. MIAMI L. REV. 187, 205 (1983). *But see* Lawrence E. Mitchell, *Structural Holes, CEOs, and Informational Monopolies: The Missing Link in Corporate Governance*, 70 BROOK. L. REV. 1313 (2005) (arguing that inside directors have an ability lacking among outside directors to perform important informational and monitoring functions).

   While much of the reform literature of the late 1970s and 1980s discusses the utility of outside directors, my concern is with the monitoring board as an institution of corporate governance, regardless of its composition. Brudney is almost alone among scholars of the era in making the careful distinction between the use of outside directors and the reconceptualization of the board as a monitoring board as qualitatively different phenomena. Victor Brudney, *The Independent Director: Heavenly City or Potemkin Village?* 95 HARV. L. REV. 597, 632 (1982). The distinction was also observed in a note published in the *Vanderbilt Law Review* in 1987. Note, *The Corporate Governance Debate and the ALI Proposals: Reform or Restatement?* 40 VAND. L. REV. 693, 706 (1987). *See also* James S. Mofsky & Robert D. Rubin, *Introduction: A Symposium on the ALI Corporate Governance Project*, 37 U. MIAMI L. REV. 169, 179 (1983) (implicitly acknowledging the conceptual distinction between a monitoring board and a board of independent directors); Kenneth E. Scott, *Corporation Law and the American Law Institute Corporate Governance Project*, 35 STAN. L. REV. 927, 934 (1983) (same). The history of the former and its co-optation by the corporate establishment is a story that has been told. The historical development of the latter and its consequences for reform has not. The latter is the purpose of this chapter.

   Moreover, it is not my purpose to accuse anybody of intentionally creating a dysfunctional board. Determining motive is beyond my ability simply from reading the available historical evidence. What I do argue is that the legal system rapidly came to see the way in which the monitoring board could provide a greater liability shield than other models of board governance at the same time that it left corporate power where it had always been, in the hands of management. Boards and their lawyers lost little time in implementing the monitoring model, notwithstanding a puzzling diversion during the early debates over the American Law Institute's Principles of Corporate Governance.

   I should also be clear about terminology. In its basic form, the monitoring board is a model of board governance that relies upon directors principally to hire, compensate, and terminate the CEO and perhaps other senior officers; provide a check on the corporation's auditing processes; vote on conflict of interest transactions; and act on the most important (and therefore episodic) corporate decisions. This contrasts with other board models, such as a board that actually manages the corporation or a board that engages in strategic decision making. These models and others do suggest that the board could provide a meaningful governance function. My argument is that it does not and will not as long as we accept the monitoring model as our starting point for reform. The Business Roundtable, in its 1983 response to the ALI Principles, identified five types of boards – "legitimating, advisory, participating (monitoring or overseeing), judicial, and dominating." 1983 BUSINESS ROUNDTABLE STATEMENT, at 25. The statement was drawn from Kenneth R. Andrews, *Rigid Rules Will Not Make Good Boards*, HARV. BUS. REV. Nov–Dec. 1982 (citing Jeanne Lynch, *Activating the Board of Directors*, unpublished doctoral thesis, Harvard Business School, 1979). While there has been a great deal written about the board since then, the participating board is clearly accepted as dominant in the literature on public corporations.

1970s that led to the first serious calls for board reform. The emergence of
the monitoring board as the favored model is grounded in an understanding
of this history. Section III, the heart of this chapter, describes and analyzes
the gradual acceptance of the monitoring board as the favored model, from
its early embrace by the American Bar Association (ABA), the Conference
Board, and the Business Roundtable, to its abandonment by these organizations in the heated political fights over the development of the American Law
Institute's (ALI) *Principles of Corporate Governance*, and the eventual acceptance of the model by all relevant professional groups by the early 1990s as
they came to see its director-protective qualities. Section IV shows the gradual
acceptance of the monitoring board by the Delaware courts throughout the
1980s and its most recent strong support of the model in the *Disney* case, even
as they rearticulated the legal standards for directors' conduct as formulaic,
procedural, and minimal. Section V concludes with some reflections on the
appropriate role of the board of directors in the modern public corporation.

I. EARLY UNDERSTANDINGS OF THE ROLE OF THE BOARD

Boards of directors, or institutions like them, have been around for centuries,
long before the development of the modern public business corporation.[15]
But, at least in the United States, we had no major reason to be concerned
with the proper role of boards of directors until the development of the large
modern public corporation in the last few years of the nineteenth century.
Until that time, we had very few large public corporations besides the railroads, and these were often tightly controlled by a single shareholder or small
group of shareholders.[16] When concern about boards was expressed during
that era, it was a different sort of concern from the concern developed later
in the century. Talk about the board was not so much about corporate governance and shareholder matters as it was a proxy for larger public issues, such as
antitrust, railroad regulation, and the control of securities speculation. Questions of board behavior principally involved questions of corporate finance
that related to these issues.[17]

---

[15] Franklin A. Gevurtz, *The Historical and Political Origins of the Corporate Board of Directors*,
33 HOFSTRA L. REV. 89 (2004).

[16] ALFRED D. CHANDLER, THE VISIBLE HAND: THE MANAGERIAL REVOLUTION IN AMERICAN
BUSINESS (1977) dates the development of the large modern corporation to the 1880s. Although
there were some large extraction and marketing corporations, almost all of the corporations
Chandler talks about are railroads. There were very few manufacturing corporations approach-
ing modern size until the late 1890s. LAWRENCE E. MITCHELL, THE SPECULATION ECONOMY:
HOW FINANCE TRIUMPHED OVER INDUSTRY (2007); WILLIAM ROY, SOCIALIZING CAPITAL
(1997).

[17] MITCHELL, *supra* note 1.

The famous Pujo Committee hearings of 1911 and 1912 gave Congress the chance to investigate the existence of an alleged Money Trust that controlled corporate America by virtue of its position on corporate boards.[18] Although interlocking directorships that were said to result in concentrated board control by the Money Trust banks were a focus of the hearings, the main problem caused by this control was restrained competition and access to capital. Evidence ranged from such relatively arcane matters as clearinghouse membership and stock certificate printing to stock underwriting; margin financing; and finally, business and credit control.[19] The function of the board in terms of the corporation's business was not a significant issue.

The disinterest in the board per se, or rather the interest in other aspects of board control, is evident from the consequence of the hearings, the passage of the Federal Reserve Act, the Federal Trade Commission Act, and the Clayton Antitrust Act early in the first Wilson administration. There was some early concern for the welfare of minority shareholders. At this point, the principal public concern was over issues of corporate capitalization and finance, which, at the end of the day, were proxies for concern about monopoly and consumer protection. It was only with the widespread ownership of common stock by the American public that developed in the 1920s that a focus on what the board of directors was doing and should do with respect to the corporation and its stockholders began to matter.[20]

---

[18] MONEY TRUST INVESTIGATION, INVESTIGATION OF FINANCIAL AND MONETARY CONDITIONS IN THE U.S. UNDER H. RES. NOS. 429 AND 504, BEFORE A SUBCOMM. OF THE COMM. ON BANKING AND CURRENCY (Comm. Print 1913).

The money-trust investigation was a delayed response to the panic of 1907, which combined a bank panic and a stock market collapse that for the first time hurt the new and larger numbers of American investors. The phrase "Money Trust" appears to have been coined by Congressman Charles A. Lindbergh of Minnesota. While the investigation was a bit of a show trial, it did lead to serious hearings on securities markets and some legislative action (although there were no results). Lindbergh's stability remains in question. In 1917, he introduced a resolution in the House proffering articles of impeachment against the five members of the Federal Reserve Board, including the draftsman of the predecessor to the Federal Reserve Act, the investment banker Paul Warburg, of the important railroad house Kuhn, Loeb, alleging that the act itself and the Federal Reserve was created by its members as part of a vast international banking conspiracy to bilk America of its wealth. The committee report declaring a lack of sufficient evidence to proceed with the impeachment was a terse single sentence. H.R. 450, 64th Cong. (1917); 54 CONG. REC. 3126–30 (1917); 54 CONG. REC. 4953 (1917).

[19] Market manipulation was another important concern and led to the introduction of the first investor-centered securities regulation bill in Congress in 1914. MITCHELL, *supra* note 16.

[20] Concern with this last issue certainly existed from the 1890s and was bound up with these other issues, but my point is that it did not become the principal issue until the role of big corporations in American life had largely been resolved as a political matter. MITCHELL, *supra* note 16. It had nonetheless been so well established by this point that, apart from financing decisions, if that, many boards did little or nothing. The literature was more concerned with directorial abuse of power than defining the role of the board itself, which appears to have been

Corporate governance reform in the modern sense traditionally is traced from the publication in 1932 of what is widely considered its *ur*-text, Berle and Means's *The Modern Corporation and Private Property*.[21] Despite their justifiable fame in opening broad debate about the legitimacy of corporate dominance based both on their statistical demonstration of the separation of ownership and control and on the enormous amount of economic and social power held by management, Berle and Means actually had very little to say about the appropriate role of the board. A large proportion of the book is devoted to an examination of the ways in which the statutory rules of corporate finance, which are directed to the board, can harm various classes of share-holders, though they do discuss the legal rules (care and loyalty) governing directors' conduct.[22] Beyond that, a few pages are devoted to the way that proxy voting disempowers shareholders (and, by implication, empowers managers) and the elimination of shareholders' rights to remove directors at will.

The book really makes no contribution to the debate over the role of the board in terms of corporate governance. The authors' principal concern was the economic, social, and political power the separation of ownership from control gave corporate directors.[23] The separation between ownership and management led to a focus on shareholder democracy and the fiduciary duties of directors, with the latter issue also reflected in the famous Berle-Dodd debates.[24]

Nothing in Berle and Means's argument necessarily required a focus on the board from a corporate governance standpoint. They treated management as a class, including not only directors but executives, too (except in the corporate

perceived as rather minimal. *See generally* Frederick Dwight, *Liability of Corporate Directors*, 17 YALE L.J. 34 (1907); H. A. Cushing, *The Inactive Corporate Director*, 8 COLUM. L. REV. 21 (1908); M. C. Lynch, *Diligence of Directors in the Management of Corporations*, 3 CAL. L. REV. 21 (1914).

[21] ADOLF A. BERLE JR. & GARDINER C. MEANS, THE MODERN CORPORATION AND PRIVATE PROPERTY (1932).

[22] It is worth noting that Berle and Means discuss these duties as duties of management more broadly than those of directors. *Id.*

[23] Dalia Tsuk, *From Pluralism to Individualism: Berle and Means and 20th Century American Legal Thought*, 30 LAW & SOC. INQUIRY 179 (2005).

[24] A.A. Berle Jr., *Corporate Powers as Powers in Trust*, 44 HARV. L. REV. 1049 (1931); A.A. Berle Jr., *For Whom Are Corporate Managers Trustees? A Note*, 45 HARV. L. REV. 1365 (1932); E. Merrick Dodd, *For Whom Are Corporate Managers Trustees?* 45 HARV. L. REV. 1145 (1932). It is important to understand that neither *The Modern Corporation and Private Property* nor the Berle-Dodd debates were about corporate governance in any modern understanding of the term, because it is customary in the literature to genuflect to these works as the starting point of our corporate governance debate. While they were important works in debates over corporate power and responsibility, they are not about corporate governance but rather about corporate purpose.

finance discussion, in which the board was the necessary subject because of its statutory role). And, indeed, there was some (although not a lot) of scholarship after Berle and Means in the literature of business and sociology devoted to the role and power of executives and managers as distinct from the board of directors itself.[25] But managers and employees generally played a very little role in the legal structure of corporate law.[26]

The first important discussion of the appropriate function of the board appears to be William O. Douglas's 1934 article "Directors Who Do Not Direct."[27] Douglas observes that the responsibility of directors to direct had become "a popular theme in recent years," citing to House hearings on the 1933 federal securities legislation. The various ideas and criticism he surveys all go to the question of board size and composition. The reform that Douglas advocates is an independent board composed of nonmanagement shareholders, serving as trustees of the shareholders, in control of the proxy machinery, and truly independent of managers (in a direct nod to Berle and Means), governed by a code of conduct laying out the directors' responsibilities.[28]

The board envisioned by Douglas is at least in part an early version of the monitoring board, and the article appears to be the first significant (if implicit) description of this board function. As Berle and Means had described concentrated board power and proxy capture by management, and others had noted the problems of figurehead directors, Douglas focused mainly on board capture by management, with the well-known consequence of highly conflicted and self-referential management structures resulting in lack of corporate vision, excessive compensation, and the use of corporate funds by

[25] *See, e.g.*, CHESTER I. BARNARD, THE FUNCTIONS OF THE EXECUTIVE (1938).

[26] Kent Greenfield, *The Place of Workers in Corporate Law*, 39 B.C. L. REV. 293 (1998). Brandeis's view of the managing board was apparently still quite current. In his 1931 treatise on directors, Howard Hilton Spellman examines in detail the entire range of board powers, claiming power for the board to make ordinary business decisions and even to purchase necessary supplies, showing the full sweep of what we would consider managerial powers as well as all of the financial powers identified by Berle and Means. HOWARD HILTON SPELLMAN, A TREATISE ON THE PRINCIPLES OF LAW GOVERNING CORPORATE DIRECTORS, *esp.* §§ 134, 137, 143, 149, & 151 (1931). Ballantine and Lattin's 1939 casebook on corporations does not even address the function of the board of directors. HENRY WINTHROP BALLANTINE & NORMAN DUNHAM LATTIN, CASES AND MATERIALS ON THE LAW OF CORPORATIONS (1939); *see also* HENRY WINTHROP BALLANTINE, BALLANTINE ON CORPORATIONS (1946); ALEXANDER HAMILTON FREY, CASES AND MATERIALS ON CORPORATIONS AND PARTNERSHIPS (1951); LUDWIG TELLER, CORPORATIONS (1949).

[27] William O. Douglas, *Directors Who Do Not Direct*, 47 HARV. L. REV. 1305 (1934).

[28] There is no strong indication that Berle was overly dubious about the actual function of the board. For example, in a 1932 review of Howard Hilton Spellman, A Treatise on the Principles of the Law Governing Corporate Directors, 80 U. PA. L. REV. 145 (1931–32), he mentions nothing about the role of the board at all.

managers for their own benefit. Managerialism, replacing the early century control by Morgan and his allies, was the result of board capture, with the potentially pernicious consequence of unmonitored conflicting interests in management.

While Douglas seems to anticipate the monitoring board (without using the term), he remains equally tied to the statutory idea that directors supervise management and formulate "financial and commercial policies."[29] Thus, at the same time that he hints at a more modern version of the board, he remains grounded in the early century view reflected by Brandeis that directors have a strong managerial role in addition to the monitoring role he contemplates. Douglas's article had little influence on corporate scholarship and practice as far as board function goes. Nor did it have any particular influence in stimulating a debate over the role of boards. To the extent it had any importance, it was in perpetuating Berle and Means's concerns about insular boards protected by the fortress of the proxy machinery.

The general understanding that boards no more made the corporation's "financial and commercial policies" than they managed the corporation came relatively late. Eisenberg places this recognition as revelatory in 1945.[30] Thus, perhaps we can mark 1945 as the beginning of the debate on modern board functions, although there is very little legal literature on the subject following that work until the 1970s. The discussion of board function took place more among economists, management scholars, and sociologists than among legal academics, and even the literature reflecting this discussion was relatively sparse.[31] Indeed, in 1960, the *University of Chicago Law Review* published an article from a lawyer's point of view suggesting that the board itself was an "anachronism."[32]

---

[29] Douglas, *supra* note 27, at 1322.

[30] MELVIN A. EISENBERG, THE STRUCTURE OF THE CORPORATION: A LEGAL ANALYSIS 140 (1976). Eisenberg marks the publication of Robert Aaron Gordon's *Business Leadership in the Large Corporation* as the "early" point at which it was revealed that "the boards of large companies initiated decisions on either specific matters or broad policies." Gordon clearly describes both a modern-sounding monitoring function for the board and the fact that the board was considerably more passive than even the light description of its monitoring function would indicate. ROBERT AARON GORDON, BUSINESS LEADERSHIP IN THE LARGE CORPORATION 116–125 (1945).

[31] George Hornstein noted in 1948 that critiques of boards were principally the province of judges and sociologists. George D. Hornstein, *The Board of Directors and Business Management, by Melvin T. Copeland & Andrew R. Towl*, 48 COLUM. L. REV. 164 (1948) (book review). A leading example is JAMES BURNHAM, THE MANAGERIAL REVOLUTION: WHAT IS HAPPENING IN THE WORLD (1941).

[32] Robert A. Kessler, *The Statutory Requirement of a Board of Directors: A Corporate Anachronism*, 27 U. CHI. L. REV. 696 (1960). Kessler was not in favor of an outright abolition of the board but rather that shareholders have the option to abolish it and elect officers directly.

Most of the legal literature concerned with boards, from Berle and Means through the 1960s, was focused on board control of the proxy machinery[33] and the fiduciary duties of directors.[34] (There was also heavy attention to the role of the board in close corporations.[35]) The assumption continued to be that boards had at least a policy-making function if not a management function, the latter of which they simply were not performing,[36] even as it remained clear that the real corporate power was held by management.[37] As late as 1976, Eisenberg could announce as news that "most of the powers supposedly vested in the board are actually vested in the executives."[38] Yet the board remained as the last, best hope against the increasing displacement of all other interests by rampant managerialism.[39]

II. REFORMING THE BOARD

Matters had changed dramatically by the 1970s. It is fair to say that the early 1970s were a time when directors and their counsel were looking with deep

[33] See, e.g., Mortimer M. Caplin, Proxies, Annual Meetings, and Corporate Democracy: The Lawyer's Role, 37 VA. L. REV. 653 (1951); Mortimer M. Caplin, Shareholder Nominations of Directors: A Program for Fair Corporate Suffrage, 39 VA. L. REV. 141 (1953); Note, Corporations – Payment of Proxy Solicitation Expenses – An Aspect of Corporate Democracy, 31 N.Y.U. L. REV. 504 (1956). Another area of board concern was restrictions on board functions by shareholder agreement, of interest principally in the close corporation area and a subject that also assumed some degree of managerial power in the board. See, e.g., Comment, Shareholders' Agreements and the Statutory Norm, 43 CORNELL L.Q. 68 (1957).

[34] "The very heart and soul of the development of corporate law in the last two decades has been the immense flood of cases and statutes concerned with the director's duty of loyalty." Samuel M. Fahr, What Every Corporation Director Should Know, by Percival E. Jackson, 35 IOWA L. REV. 150 (1949) (book review).

[35] See, e.g., George D. Hornstein, Stockholders' Agreements in the Closely Held Corporation, 59 YALE L.J. 1040 (1950); Charles W. Steadman, Maintaining Control of Close Corporations, 14 BUS. LAW. 1077 (1959).

[36] Fahr, supra note 34; Hornstein, supra note 35 (noting that "corporations . . . function through their directors"); Arthur A. Ballantine, Directors and Their Functions, by John C. Baker, 59 HARV. L. REV. 151 (1945) (book review).

[37] Sigmund Timberg, Corporate Fictions: Logical, Social and International Implications, 46 COLUM. L. REV. 533, 564–66 (1948). Timberg sees corporate power as pluralistic, much like the state's political pluralism.

[38] EISENBERG, supra note 30, at 141. This actually was not news to Eisenberg or any other careful observer, but the fact that it was worth noting suggests the tenacity of old ideas about board management. JOHN C. BAKER, DIRECTORS AND THEIR FUNCTIONS (1945); PETER DRUCKER, THE PRACTICE OF MANAGEMENT 178 (1954); HAROLD KOONTZ, THE BOARD OF DIRECTORS AND EFFECTIVE MANAGEMENT 21 (1967); MYLES MACE, DIRECTORS: MYTH AND REALITY 73, 76–77, 80 (1971).

[39] Perhaps the apex of managerialism is illustrated by the wonderful description of IT&T's management meeting in RALPH NADER ET AL., TAMING THE GIANT CORPORATION (1975).

concern at a series of legal and social developments, developments that threatened them with significant liability.[40] As one commentator put it in 1979:
"Corporate governance has, within approximately the last five years, again
become a subject of intense national debate in Congress, the federal regulatory agencies, the academic community, the organized bar, public interest
groups, and the business community itself."[41] It was these developments that
motivated this activity and that chased directors and their counsel to run to
safety. It was in the monitoring board that they found shelter.

The reasons for board concern are fairly clear. The middle of the twentieth
century was a time when U.S. industry unquestionably ruled the world. By the
early 1970s, the conglomeration movement was rapidly bringing that development to a crisis point, and the stock market was faltering.[42] The new conglomerates themselves presented problems for directors, including conflicts
of interest among various conglomerate boards and an overwhelming complexity of worldwide business.[43] The Watergate investigation's revelation of
illegal corporate campaign contributions followed by the SEC's questionable
payments investigations, with its discovery of corporate domestic and foreign
bribery, often unknown to directors, also diminished confidence in corporate
America and brought forth calls for reform.[44] The impregnable Pennsylvania
Railroad, once the nation's largest corporation, had gone bankrupt without
ever missing a dividend, and with that came an SEC investigation into its
causes, numerous suits against directors, and the development of the securities class action.[45] Numerous other bankruptcies and severe financial losses,

[40] Roberta S. Karmel, *The Independent Corporate Board: A Means to What End?* 52 Geo. Wash.
L. Rev. 534, 539 (1984); Bryan F. Smith, *Corporate Governance: A Director's View*, 37 U. Miami
L. Rev. 273, 276 (1983).
[41] Marshall L. Small, *The Evolving Role of the Director in Corporate Governance*, 30 Hastings
L.J. 1353 (1979); Melvin A. Eisenberg, *The Modernization of Corporate Law: An Essay for Bill
Cary*, 37 U. Miami L. Rev. 187, 209–10 (1983).
[42] Nader, Green, and Seligman describe 1975 as "a year of reckoning for a dozen major conglomerates." Nader et al., *supra* note 39, at 78.
[43] Richard J. Farrell & Robert W. Murphy, *Comments on the Theme: "Why Should Anyone Want
to Be a Director?"* 27 Bus. Law. 7 (1972).
[44] The story is well told in Joel Seligman, *A Sheep in Wolf's Clothing: The American Law Institute
Principles of Corporate Governance Project*, 55 Geo. Wash. L. Rev. 325, 333–36; SEC, Rep.
on Questionable and Illegal Corporate Payments and Practices (1976). Karmel gives
a less sympathetic account of the era. Roberta S. Karmel, *Realizing the Dream of William O.
Douglas: The Securities and Exchange Commission Takes Charge of Corporate Governance*, 30
Del. J. Corp. L. 79 (2005).
[45] *SEC Staff Study of the Financial Collapse of the Penn Central Co.: Summary* [1972–73 Transfer
Binder], Fed. Sec. L. Rep. (CCH) ¶ 78,931 (1972). Numerous lawsuits resulted from the
collapse of Penn Central. *See, e.g., In re* Penn Central Transp. Co., 484 F.2d 1300 (3d Cir.
1973); *In re* Penn Central Transp. Co., 452 F.2d 1107 (3d Cir. 1971); *SEC v.* Penn Central Co.,
Fed. Sec. L. Rep. (CCH) ¶ 94,527 (E.D. Pa. May 2, 1974). The securities class action first

brought on in part by recession, occurred, and with them the resignations or firings of some prominent CEOs. Chrysler was in need of its eventual federal bailout, and even New York City faced bankruptcy. An activist SEC, aided by the Second Circuit, had a string of successes starting with *BarChris*[46] and *Texas Gulf Sulphur*,[47] in attempting to make the securities laws into a body of federal corporate law with far more teeth than state law had presented.[48] Shareholder proposals by activist groups advocating a variety of social causes were being thrust on corporations and litigated in court.[49]

These events by themselves would have been enough to spur on reform. But they also suggested a particular type of reform, one for which the raw ingredients were readily available. Outside directors had, by the early 1970s, come to constitute the majority of directors on most corporate boards. Outside directors first became prominent as a way of helping to insulate boards from liability for conflict-of-interest transactions, but now they were beginning to be seen as a way of ensuring responsibility to – if not appeasing – different corporate constituencies.[50] The role of managerial directors was well understood – they worked for the corporation and were answerable to the CEO. But questions arose as to what exactly the role of outsiders was to be.[51] Moreover, Congress itself was investigating the structure of corporate law, with particular attention to the social purpose of the corporation and the role of the shareholder, which of course implicated the board as well.[52] And, in 1971, Myles Mace published his famous study demonstrating the almost complete passivity of corporate

became a practical remedy for shareholders after 1966. J. Vernon Patrick Jr., *The Securities Class Action for Damages Comes of Age (1966–1974)*, 29 Bus. Law. 159 (1974).

[46] Escott v. BarChris Constr. Corp., 283 F. Supp. 643 (S.D.N.Y. 1968); *see also* Gould v. American-Hawaiian 5.5. Co., 535 F. 2d 761 (3d Cir. 1976).

[47] SEC v. Tex. Gulf Sulphur Co., 446 F. 2d 1301 (2d Cir. 1971), *cert. denied*, 404 U.S. 1005 (1972).

[48] Roberta Karmel relates the history of the SEC's attempts to federalize corporate law. Karmel, *supra* note 44.

[49] *See, e.g.*, Med. Comm. for Human Rights v. SEC, 432 F. 2d 659 (D.C. Cir. 1970).

[50] Victor Brudney, *Panel Discussion*, 37 U. Miami L. Rev. 319, 321 (1983).

[51] Noyes E. Leech & Robert H. Mundheim, *The Outside Director of the Publicly Held Corporation*, 31 Bus. Law. 1799 (1976); Cyril Moscow, *The Independent Director*, 28 Bus. Law. 9 (1972). It was this increase (or recognition of the increase) in the number of outside directors that led the Committee on Corporate Laws to amend section 35 of the Model Business Corporation Act in 1974 to move to a monitoring model of the board. Model Bus. Corp. Act § 143 (1974) [hereinafter MBCA]. By 1973, according to data published by the Conference Board and the American Society of Corporate Secretaries, 77 percent of 855 corporations surveyed had a majority of outside directors considering former or retired employees as such, and 62 percent considering them as management directors. By 1977, the data were 84 percent and 66 percent. *Corporate Director's Guidebook*, 33 Bus. Law. 1595 (1978), app. C.

[52] *Hearings on Corporate Rights and Responsibilities Before the Senate Comm. on Commerce*, 94th Cong. (1976); *The Role of the Shareholder in the Corporate World: Hearings Before the Subcomm. on Citizens and Shareholder Rights and Remedies of the Senate Comm. on the Judiciary*, 95th Cong. (1977).

boards.[53] All of these developments put increasing pressure on boards to figure out how to avoid liability. The first question that had to be answered was, What was the board to do?

Board reform became an important subject of discussion for the first time in the 1970s.[54] But, as Eisenberg points out, most reform proposals began with "the received legal model of the board," that is, the board as manager.[55] And the variety of proposals demonstrates that this idea of board as manager retained a strong hold on the legal imagination, as Eisenberg classifies them into "those calling for professional directors; those calling for full-time directors; and those calling for fully-staffed boards."[56]

On one level, the move to board reform was an attempt to break managerial control of U.S. corporations for the purpose of greater political and social accountability. Perhaps the high point of the attack on entrenched managerialism for social reform is Nader, Green, and Seligman's *Taming the Giant Corporation*, published the same year as Eisenberg's *Structure of Corporate Law*.[57] *Taming the Giant Corporation* captured the deep fear of insulated corporate power characterizing the social moment, and perhaps nowhere better than in a description of an IT&T management meeting.[58] The story reads like a Cold War era description of a secret conclave of the Evil Empire's politburo and, except for the absence of nuclear weapons, is almost as frightening. Nader, Green, and Seligman also targeted their reform suggestions by looking to an older model of board management as the means to break managerialism, but their choice was a board composed of representatives from all corporate constituencies and working in the overall public interest.[59]

Breaking corporate power over the powerless was their goal. In fact, Nader, Green, and Seligman, perhaps more than any other legal authors to that time, picked up on Berle and Means's central concern, unrestrained managerial power run amok in society.[60] Management uncontrolled was management running the country.[61] But the problem with managerialism was not

---

[53] MACE, *supra* note 38.

[54] Indeed, Brudney, who observed in 1982 that "[l]awyers, both academic and practicing, have long been concerned with the function of the board," cites literature almost exclusively from the 1970s to support his claim. Brudney, *supra* note 14, at 603 nn.15–16.

[55] EISENBERG, *supra* note 30, at 139.   [56] *Id.* at 149.

[57] Christopher Stone, *Where the Law Ends* (1975), though not as focused on governance, is another important contribution to the reform literature of the era.

[58] NADER ET AL., *supra* note 39, at 76–77 (quoting Anthony Sampson).

[59] *Id.* at 125. For a more moderate exploration of the social responsibilities of business and a description of a board model to accompany it, see THE AMERICAN ASSEMBLY, CORPORATE GOVERNANCE IN AMERICA (1978).

[60] In this respect, one can see *Taming the Giant Corporation* a worthy successor to *The Modern Corporation and Private Property*.

[61] NADER ET AL., *supra* note 39, at 76.

management. After all, management still runs corporate America, just as it did then. The problem with managerialism was board capture, or, as Nader, Green, and Seligman saw it, board composition and the complacency of plutocratic directors.

This may sound like a precious distinction, but on a moment's thought it will appear that it is not. Board capture as a result of management's control of the proxy machinery was a major focus of corporate scholarship from the New Deal until the late 1960s. But what was the goal of the arguments to reform the proxy machinery and put it back into the hands of – whom? The shareholders? While scholarship calls for shareholder, and sometimes stakeholder, control, there was no practical expectation that shareholders would stir from their historical lethargy and take control of their capital. Nor did the investment logic of diversification, always a typical American practice but further strengthened by the development in the 1960s of mutual funds, suggest any reason to believe that this would be the case. So who would regain control of the proxy machinery from management? The board. To do what? Until the monitoring model of the board developed, to manage, which, by common consensus, they did not and could not do. So even if complete proxy reform had been achieved, the result would have been the substitution of one set of managers by another.

An extended analysis of managerialism is beyond the scope of this chapter, but the relevant point is that, until we could develop an appropriate function for the board, proposals for proxy reform would have allowed us to rearrange deck chairs on the *Titanic*. Once the proxy-reform theories had played out, it was naturally time to figure out what it was we wanted the board to do. Eisenberg helped to provide the answer to this question. But the dominant shape of reform was not, in the end, political, in the way contemplated by Nader, Green, and Seligman, although political agitation surely contributed to the atmosphere of fear in which the monitoring model was developed. Reform was, instead, legal, and shaped to protect the board from liability.

III. THE DEVELOPMENT OF THE MONITORING BOARD

It was only in 1976, with the publication of Mel Eisenberg's *The Structure of the Corporation*, that the idea of the monitoring board was clearly formulated and put forth as the appropriate description of the board's function.[62]

---

[62] Eisenberg based the book on an earlier set of law review articles, including *Legal Models of Management Structure in the Modern Corporation: Officers, Directors, and Accountants*, 63 CALIF. L. REV. 375 (1975). Harvey Goldschmid had also described the monitoring board in a speech given in 1973. Harvey J. Goldschmid, *The Greening of the Board Room: Reflections on Corporate Responsibility*, 10 COLUM. J. L. & SOC. PROBS. 15, 24–25 (1973).

Eisenberg provides what is probably the first coherent statement of the monitoring model.[63] (It is interesting to note that almost all of the material cited by Eisenberg in compiling and supporting this model is drawn from the late 1960s and early 1970s, further reinforcing my conclusion that there had been no significant earlier interest in board function.[64]) Eisenberg reviews the traditionally accepted function of the managing board and the reform efforts to enhance it and concludes, correctly in my view, that the board in fact can perform none of these functions.[65] The deductive process takes us from the received legal model of a board that actually manages to the working model in which power is mostly vested in executives. He then examines and takes apart reform proposals, from professional directors to full-time directors and fully staffed boards, before turning to the various functions attributed to the board. These include giving advice and counsel to the CEO; authorizing (rather than initiating) major corporate transactions; providing a mechanism by which major shareholders and creditors might influence control over corporate action; and finally, the monitoring function, including the selection and firing of the CEO. Eisenberg concludes:

[63] EISENBERG, *supra* note 30, at 162–68. Others have also credited Eisenberg with the development of the monitoring model. George W. Dent Jr., *The Revolution in Corporate Governance, The Monitoring Board, and the Director's Duty of Care*, 61 B.U. L. REV. 623 (1981); Karmel, *supra* note 40, at 543; *see also* Note, *The Corporate Governance Debate and the ALI Proposals: Reform or Restatement?* 40 VAND. L. REV. 693, 705 (1987). A more nuanced understanding of the practical functioning of the board, despite the received legal managerial model, can be found earlier in the business literature. *See, e.g.*, MELVIN T. COPELAND & ANDREW R. TOWL, THE BOARD OF DIRECTORS AND BUSINESS MANAGEMENT 4 (1947).

[64] Eisenberg's footnotes on the board, both in the book and in the article, are almost exclusively drawn from the late 1960s and early 1970s. The few older citations are to books by business scholars in the late 1940s and 1950s that principally discuss the power centers of U.S. business as the senior executives and the role of the board as minimal. Indeed, the legal literature on board reform almost exclusively began in the 1970s. *See* Brudney, *supra* note 14, at 597–98 nn.1–2 (cataloging the reform literature). Alfred Conard, in his well-regarded *Corporations in Perspective*, published in the same year as Eisenberg's book, gives very little attention to the role of the board except to recognize the managerial latitude given the board by law and the very limited supervisory function the board actually provides. *See* ALFRED CONRAD, CORPORATIONS IN PERSPECTIVE §§ 197, 210 (1976).

[65] A different and more elaborate reform proposal for a series of divisional boards corresponding to divisions of corporate responsibility and following the logic of a corporation's internal organization was proposed by Jack Coffee a year later. John C. Coffee Jr., *Beyond the Shut-Eyed Sentry: Toward a Theoretical View of Corporate Misconduct and an Effective Legal Response*, 63 VA. L. REV. 1099 (1977). Given its complexity and substantive content, it would have been considerably harder for business to co-opt Coffee's model than the monitoring model. But it is precisely the complexity of Coffee's model, as well as the significantly greater obligation that it would have put on directors, that would have almost certainly prevented its adoption.

The major effect of according central importance to the policymaking function . . . has been to divert legal and corporate institutions from implementing
a cluster of functions which the board can perform and which cannot easily
be performed by any corporate organ except the board: selecting, monitoring,
and removing the members of the chief executive's office.[66]

As Eisenberg realized, the only functions left were hiring and firing the chief
executive and monitoring his or her performance. These are the functions he
targeted for reform by describing oversight boards with adequate information
to perform their tasks. In other words, having correctly eliminated all other
possible functions of the board, Eisenberg was left with the monitoring model.

Eisenberg was making an empirical claim about what boards actually did
and a commonsense normative claim about the limits of what boards were
capable of doing. He notes that the board is the only corporate organ that can
perform the monitoring function (with a similar observation made roughly
contemporaneously in financial economics by Michael Jensen and William
Meckling.[67]) He also saw a decided virtue in the monitoring board as a means
of controlling managerial power. Thus, there is a strong normative component
to the monitoring model as well. Monitoring might be all the board could
do, but if it was a necessary corporate function and the board was uniquely
equipped to perform it, then the board ought to do it.

For the monitoring board to work as the reform that Eisenberg planned, the
board needed the kind of true independence that would provide for serious
monitoring. Thus Eisenberg concludes with a normative recommendation.
Legal rules must "to the extent possible: (1) make the board independent of
the executives whose performance is being monitored; and (2) assure a flow
of, or at least a capability for acquiring, adequate and objective information
on the executives' performance."[68] Had Eisenberg's suggestions been fully
adopted, with a substantially independent and adequately informed board,
the monitoring board might have developed with a meaningful function.[69]
Instead, businesses and their lawyers hijacked the model, embracing its structure without its substance. They turned it into a shell of what Eisenberg had
imagined – and a very protective shell at that. Through no fault of his own,
Eisenberg's reform effort was sandbagged by America's corporate bar when

---

[66] EISENBERG, *supra* note 30, at 170.

[67] Michael C. Jensen & William H. Meckling, *Theory of the Firm: Managerial Behavior, Agency
Costs, and Ownership Structure*, 3 J. FIN. ECON. 305 (1976); *see also* Eugene Fama, *Agency
Problems and the Theory of the Firm*, 88 J. POL. ECON. 288 (1980).

[68] Eisenberg, *supra* note 30, at 170.

[69] ALI, PRINCIPLES OF CORPORATE GOVERNANCE: ANALYSIS AND RECOMMENDATIONS (1994).

the model received its only real chance for implementation, in the American Law Institute's (ALI) *Principles of Corporate Governance.*

The following pages detail the story of the rise, fall, and resurrection of the monitoring model as the accepted description of board function. It is a story of how business came to embrace the monitoring model, only to reject it in the 1980s even as it had become a more or less accomplished fact. The debate over the monitoring board that took place in the 1970s was modest, and not so much over the idea of the monitoring board itself than the treatment of the model largely as a structural concept. Critics called for a more substantive description of the board's duties.[70] Commentators attempted to supply that substance, as did Eisenberg himself, serving as reporter for the third part of the *Principles of Corporate Governance.* But, as I soon demonstrate, acceptance of the monitoring model in the 1970s was left to the American Bar Association and business groups that rapidly seized upon it for their own reasons.

The monitoring model was controversial when it appeared but hardly as controversial as it would become in 1982. Most of the early controversy was among legal scholars and remained on the level of scholarly discourse.[71] When the ALI published its *Tentative Draft No. 1* in 1982, the earlier skirmish among academics became a full-blown battle among businesspeople and practicing lawyers, on one side (including a healthy cadre of corporate academics), and much of corporate legal academia on the other. But initially, as I show, the business community generally welcomed the idea of the monitoring board. Victor Brudney, puzzling in 1983 over the controversy surrounding the adoption of the monitoring model by the ALI *Principles,* noted that the very monitoring model about which the opponents were incensed was precisely the model corporate America and the corporate bar had claimed they wanted in the 1970s.[72]

A. *The Monitoring Board as Liability Shield*

Three highly influential groups embraced the monitoring model in different ways and with different emphases in the late 1970s. But, despite their differences, the American Bar Association, the Conference Board, and the Business

---

[70] Dent, *supra* note 63; Small, *supra* note 41. Eisenberg's substantial aspect of the model was to require independent directors. Again, there was significant debate over whether this would be enough to make the monitoring model work.

[71] Karmel, *supra* note 12, at 550.

[72] Victor Brudney, *The Role of the Board of Directors: The ALI and Its Critics,* 37 U. Miami L. Rev. 223 (1983).

Roundtable all understood how the structure of the monitoring model could be used to protect directors from serious threats of legal liability.

1. The ABA's Contribution – The Corporate Director's Guidebook, 1978–2004

Political agitation for board reform in the 1970s was symptomatic of the problems that had led to such broad legal and political concern with the public corporation. As the problems of business were revealed, so, too, were social issues and dislocations that had been masked at the height of the successful conglomeration movement. These issues were important in helping to create the atmosphere of reform, and the debate over directors' roles during the 1970s developed in the atmosphere of fear and uncertainty they created. All of this concern led to the ABA's publication of the first *Corporate Director's Guidebook* in 1976,[73] with the revised edition published in 1978.[74] The *Guidebook* placed the ABA's imprimatur on the monitoring board as the best board model.

The *Guidebook* is important. It was drafted by the Committee on Corporate Laws of the American Bar Association. This was the same ABA committee responsible for drafting and maintaining the Model Business Corporation Act (Model Act). The 1978 edition was endorsed, after comment on the 1976 draft, by the American Society of Corporate Secretaries (ASCS).[75] As the preface to the *Guidebook* notes, the Model Act embodies "the collective judgment of experienced corporate lawyers and academicians from diverse locations in the United States," which contributed to entitling that act to "persuasive weight."[76] Not surprisingly, the *Guidebook* is based upon the Model Act. Certainly the endorsement of the powerful corporate bar and the ASCS, along with the relationship between the *Guidebook* and the Model Act, made it reasonably likely that compliance with the *Guidebook* would protect directors from liability.

The 1978 edition makes it clear that the *Guidebook* was in large part a response to directorial fears of liability. The introduction notes: "As a general observation, it is believed that directors who act within the framework of conduct outlined in this *Guidebook* will not only be performing their directorial functions competently, but will also be reducing the risk of being charged with

[73] *Corporate Director's Guidebook*, 32 BUS. LAW. 5 (1976).
[74] *Corporate Director's Guidebook*, 33 BUS. LAW. 1595 (1978).
[75] *Corporate Director's Guidebook: Comments Submitted by the American Society of Corporate Secretaries*, 33 BUS. LAW. 321 (1977).
[76] *Corporate Director's Guidebook, supra* note 74.

deficient individual performance as a director."[77] Not only does this situate the
development of the *Guidebook* in an atmosphere in which corporate directors
feared liability, but the statement itself is an attempt to put the quasi-official
legal imprimatur of the ABA on the monitoring board and its relatively light
directorial responsibilities.

Among its many functions, the *Guidebook* took upon itself the task of presenting a "proposed model for the governance of a publicly-owned business
corporation." While the model was admittedly not prescribed by statute, the
Guidebook presented it as a starting point for the development of best practices,
taking account of "current concerns in areas of public policy and emerging
trends of corporate governance."[78]

The *Guidebook* importantly describes its board model as a "structural
model," intended to "produce an appropriate environment for the governance
of publicly-owned corporations."[79] The choice of a structural model in contrast
to a model embracing substantive board duties is revealing. As an innocent
and entirely practical matter, it implicitly acknowledges significant variations
among the business practices and corporate structures of publicly held corporations. These led to differences in effective board functioning, so it might be
impractical to prescribe substantive directors' roles.

Structure has other advantages over substance. Structure is relatively easy to
adjust, especially when talking about something like a balance between inside
and outside directors. So the structural approach has an additional practical
dimension as well.

But the ABA's decision to adopt a structural model has somewhat darker
significance. A structural model cleverly avoids the need to establish standards
of substantive behavior. The role of directors is not to be specified beyond the
broad legal duties of care and loyalty already judicially imposed. Those duties,

---

[77] *Id.* at 1597.

[78] There was not, nor is there, any model of the board prescribed by statute. To the extent that
the law prescribes a model of the board, it can be inferred from the duty of care. Brudney,
in 1982, notes that "courts have not yet formally addressed the distinction between a duty to
manage and a duty to monitor in assessing whether the common law duty of care has been
met." Brudney, *supra* note 14, at 632 n.90. One could argue that the Delaware Supreme Court's
opinion in *Graham v. Allis-Chalmers Manufacturing Co.*, 188 A.2d 125 (Del. 1963), though it
long antedated the concept of the monitoring board, did just that. Certainly, it has been argued
that Chancellor Allen's opinion *In re Caremark International Inc. Derivative Litigation*, 698
A.2d 959 (Del. Ch. 1996), has the potential to establish a duty to monitor, at least in terms of
requiring effective information systems in a corporation operating within a regulated industry.
This requirement appears in almost all of the descriptions of the monitoring board.

[79] *Corporate Director's Guidebook*, *supra* note 74, at 1619. The *Guidebook* took as its starting point
the proposition adopted in section 35 of the recently revised Model Business Corporation Act
that the board is not expected to manage the corporation on a day-to-day basis. MBCA (1974).

especially the duty of care, are dependent upon the director's role to define their scope. A structural model simply allows for adjustment in the overall relationship of directors to the corporation that provides a distancing that necessarily limits the director's role and thus the scope of substantive duties. Substantive models of directorial behavior would have been far more difficult to implement and therefore far more constraining, and would have worked contrary to the effect of the *Guidebook* by exposing directors to even greater liability.[80]

As events played out, the structural model set out in the *Guidebook* paved the way for future judicial developments of the application of the duties of care and loyalty in a manner that allowed them to be filled almost exclusively by process.[81] This is certainly true as a matter of Delaware law and also led to the growth of compensation consulting firms and a boom in business for executive search firms in recruiting board members as protective adjuncts to the compensation committee and nominating committee.[82] It would have been difficult, if not impossible, for a substantive model to have been adapted so readily to procedural duties. And process is considerably easier to comply with than substance. Thus judicial developments helped to seal the protective nature of the monitoring model.[83]

The main thrust of the structural model was to focus on the distinction between management and nonmanagement directors and suggest that the good board should contain a significant quota of the latter. This is consistent with the increase of outside directors that had begun in the 1950s and accelerated through the early 1970s, both as a response to corporate scandals arising because of the unchecked insularity of managerialism and as a way for corporations to demonstrate their attempts to behave responsibly in an age of turmoil.[84] It was also consistent with Eisenberg's view of the necessary predicate to a successful monitoring board. Indeed, it was the remedy of outside

---

[80] Brudney, *supra* note 14.

[81] For the process-based nature of modern fiduciary adjudication, see Lawrence E. Mitchell, *Fairness and Trust in Corporate Law*, 43 DUKE L.J. 425 (1993).

[82] It is worth noting that in the recent *Disney* opinion, Chancellor Chandler was far more critical of compensation consultant Graef Crystal than he was of the Disney board's compensation committee. *In re* Walt Disney Co. Derivative Litig., 907 A.2d 693, 770 (Del. Ch. 2005). The process of employing a compensation consultant and the committee's (and thus the board's) right to rely on his report shows the relationship between structure and process and the protective nature of compliance with the latter.

[83] I have made the argument at length in earlier works. *See, e.g.*, Lawrence E. Mitchell, *Fairness and Trust, supra* note 81; Lawrence E. Mitchell, *Trust, Contract, Process, in* PROGRESSIVE CORPORATE LAW (Lawrence E. Mitchell ed., 1995).

[84] The principal function of outside directors up to this point had been to sanitize conflict of interest transactions. Brudney, *supra* note 50, at 322.

directors, rather than the more refined conceptual solution of the monitoring board itself, that dominated corporate legal scholarship in the years following Eisenberg's statement of the model.[85]

The rest of the *Guidebook* describes the monitoring board in little detail, but it is beyond question that the monitoring model is the model the *Guidebook* endorsed.[86] Directors are to review and confirm basic corporate objectives, as well as select and monitor the CEO and senior management. They also have to perform their few statutorily prescribed duties, such as approving mergers and calling special meetings as set out in the Model Business Corporation Act.[87] The monitoring model described by the *Guidebook* had a single focus. Unlike Eisenberg's structural model, that focus cabined possible director liability at the same time that it completely rejected the possibility of corporate reform along the political lines that reformers like Nader were arguing for:

> It is important to emphasize that the role of the director is to monitor, in an environment of loyal but independent oversight, the conduct of the business and affairs of the corporation in behalf of those who invest in the corporation. The director should not be perceived as, or perceive himself as, a representative of any other constituency, either private or public. Were the role of any director – whether management or non-management – to be otherwise, profound changes would be required in defining the director's rights and obligations in a variety of contexts.[88]

And there it all is. The model is a monitoring model. The monitoring model is a structural model. Independent directors are to be the key. And the social role of the corporation was clear. Shareholders, and shareholders only, are to be the objects of directors' concern.[89]

Obviously, there is much that is unclear in this description of the monitoring model, and the subsequent burgeoning literature on corporate governance is, in many respects, an attempt to fill in the blanks. But it is striking to note that the first quasi-official statement of what the board should do appeared as

---

[85] *See, e.g.*, Statement of the Business Roundtable, *The Role and Composition of the Board of Directors of the Large Publicly Owned Corporation*, 33 Bus. Law. 2083 (1978); Brudney, *supra* note 14; Leech & Mundheim, *supra* note 51; Lewis D. Solomon, *Restructuring the Corporate Board of Directors: Fond Hope – Faint Promise?* 76 Mich. L. Rev. 581 (1978).

[86] David Ruder, *Panel Discussion*, 37 U. Miami L. Rev. 319, 337 (1983) ("I was on the committee that drafted the *Corporate Director's Guidebook*, and I agree with you that the monitoring model was part of the *Corporate Director's Guidebook*.")

[87] *Corporate Director's Guidebook, supra* note 74, at 1607.

[88] *Id.* at 1621.

[89] While the phrase "those who invest in the corporation" as the sole constituent is ambiguous, it clearly contemplates shareholders. It is possible that the language could include creditors, but that interpretation is improbable given the modern position of creditors in corporate law.

late as 1978. It is even more striking to see the minimal nature of the duties prescribed for directors to fulfill the duty of care, duties that easily could be discharged even by relatively detached outside directors. And in light of the later controversy over the ALI's description of the monitoring model, it is at least interesting to note that one corporate director wrote, in 1983 at the height of that debate, that the arguments over the role of the board during the 1970s produced a consensus model of the board, and that model was the monitoring model. Moreover, he noted, "most corporations have voluntarily implemented so many elements of this theory."[90]

2. *Guidebook* II

A lot happened in the corporate world between 1978 and the next edition of the *Guidebook* in 1994. One of the most significant legal developments was the Delaware Supreme Court's decision in *Smith v. Van Gorkom*.[91] It was generally accepted at the time that *Van Gorkom* challenged the minimalist monitoring model. But one could easily read *Van Gorkom* as setting out a procedural road map for the duties of the monitoring board in perhaps its most significant context, that of a takeover, and others have so read it.[92] The way to avoid liability after *Van Gorkom* simply was to follow the road map. But there was no need to fear even the potential mischief of *Van Gorkom* for long. The Delaware legislature quickly restored the safety of minimal monitoring by enacting section 102(b)(7) of the Delaware General Corporation Law.

The 1994 edition of the *Guidebook* acknowledges that "a lot has happened and continues to happen, in the corporate governance world since 1978," justifying a revision of the *Guidebook*.[93] But while the takeover decade had passed, the ALI had adopted its *Principles of Corporate Governance*, institutional investors were beginning to arise from their slumber, and the savings and loan crisis and insider-trading scandals of the 1980s were history, the ABA found itself in a position to declare victory in the revised edition. No longer was it modest about its adoption of the monitoring board.

We deleted the "proposed model" of the board of a publicly held corporation for two reasons: first, much of this material is now found in the discussion of

---

[90] Bryan F. Smith, *Corporate Governance: A Director's View*, 37 U. Miami L. Rev. 273, 277–79 (1983); *see also* Andrews, *supra* note 14, at 36 ("And who can quarrel with the monitoring model?").

[91] Smith v. Van Gorkom, 488 A.2d 858 (Del. 1985).

[92] In the post-*Disney* era, it is almost impossible to claim that *Van Gorkom* had serious consequences.

[93] American Bar Association Committee on Corporate Laws, *Corporate Director's Guidebook: 1994 Edition*, 49 Bus. Law. 1243, 1247 (1994).

the structure of the board and its committees; and second, developments in applicable law have removed much of the need for the tentativeness reflected in the concept of a model.[94]

The monitoring board was an accomplished fact.

That reality did not prevent the *Guidebook* from specifying again the functions of the new monitoring board. Although slightly more detailed, the same responsibility for approving corporate objectives and monitoring management form the core of the directors' role as they had sixteen years earlier. Added to this are the obligations to adopt plans for senior executive succession, adopt policies of corporate conduct, review procedures for financial information flows, and "evaluate the overall effectiveness of the board." In substance, this added little and seems merely to be specification of the early duties tailored to the events intervening between the two versions of the *Guidebook*.

3. *Guidebook* III

Skipping a 2001 revision of the *Guidebook*, the final interesting ABA document is the *Guidebook* revision of 2004.[95] The reason for revision is obvious:

> Since the publication of the third edition, the stunning failures of several prominent U.S. corporations, and the disclosure of abuses of office by some of their senior executives, have led to widespread public concerns about the role and responsibilities of corporate directors.... The public belief that good corporate governance could have prevented these corporate failures has resulted in a new reality in which corporations perceived not to have good corporate governance will be penalized in the marketplace.[96]

Left unsaid was that, in the new era, penalization in the marketplace also meant penalization in the boardroom and the executive suite. The director-protective monitoring board needed some reconsideration.

What was that reconsideration? Not much. One aspect was a clearer definition of the director's role, a definition that, as I show, had been adopted by the Business Roundtable thirty years earlier. "As a general matter, a business corporation's core objective in conducting its business activities is to create and increase shareholder value."[97] But monitoring was still the mode of behavior. "Although recent changes in corporate governance standards effected by the Sarbanes-Oxley Act... increase the compliance and disclosure requirements

---

[94] *Id.* at 1248.
[95] *Corporate Director's Handbook (Fourth Edition)*, 59 Bus. Law. 1057 (2004).
[96] *Id.* at 1060.   [97] *Id.* at 1063.

that the board and management of public companies must address, they do not change the fundamental principles governing director action."[98]

What were those principles? The *Guidebook* provides a longer list this time, but the only new features were that the board should adopt ethical policies and compliance programs, understand "the risk profile of the corporation," and pay greater attention to board and committee composition, all clearly responsive to the problems that helped to bring down Enron. But taken individually, and the list as a whole, they reinforce the simple monitoring model proposed in 1978, albeit with greater specificity. True, directors might have to spend a little more time on the corporation's affairs. But to satisfy their duties, they really had to do little more than was expected of them thirty years earlier.[99] The only new advice, essentially, was to let the shareholders see you sweat a bit.

Thus, the monitoring model proposed and refined by the ABA, begun in a climate of fear and most recently revised in a similar climate, specifies relatively minimal duties for directors that, if minimally performed, will allow them to avoid liability. And in the years between the adoption of the 1978 model up to and including the present, with the singular exception of *Van Gorkom* and a few cases involving takeovers, the monitoring board has performed its protective function admirably well.

4. Business Protects Its Own – The Conference Board and the Business Roundtable

The history and development of the *Guidebook* are revealing. But there were other significant discussions surrounding the new monitoring model, and both the Conference Board and the Business Roundtable endorsed it in the late 1970s for the same reason – fear. Again, their reasons for favoring the monitoring board seem clearly aimed at liability protection.

The Conference Board had long paid attention to boards, but its modern contribution began in 1967, with the publication of its report *Corporate Directorship Practices* (the Report).[100] The Conference Board reported that by 1953 a majority of manufacturing companies had a majority of outside directors, growing to 63 percent by the time of the Report. Nonetheless, the function of these directors as, indeed, the function of all directors, remained a question. It was clear on one level that the function of outside directors was to sanitize

---

[98] *Id.* at 1064.

[99] Chancellor Chandler confirms this observation in *Disney*. *In re* Walt Disney Co. Derivative Litig., 907 A.2d 693 (Del. Ch. 2005).

[100] NAT'L INDUS. CONFERENCE BD. AND AM. SOC'Y OF CORP. SEC'YS, CORPORATE DIRECTORSHIP PRACTICES: STUDIES IN BUSINESS POLICY NO. 125 (1967) [hereinafter CORPORATE DIRECTORSHIP PRACTICES].

conflict of interest transactions. But beyond that, they had no particular purpose other than to ratify management's decisions. What else they might do, if
anything, was uncertain.[101]

The Report directly confronts the issue, noting that "it is difficult, if not
impossible, to delineate with precision the boundaries between the functions
of the board of directors and those of corporate management," a problem that
was particularly difficult in corporations that had boards principally composed
of inside directors.[102] The ambiguity of state law led to a wide variety in board
practices, with some of the best boards specifically enumerating their own
functions. In counseling directors as to their legal liability, however, the Report
was careful to state that "the fundamental legal responsibility of the board of
directors is to manage the company in the interests of the stockholders."[103]
While recognizing the directors' right to delegate, the Report cautions that
this does not relieve a director from liability but is simply a way of fulfilling
the director's duties. As a general matter, and on this background, the Report
describes the board's appropriate role as a cross between an advisory board and
a monitoring board.[104]

By 1975, the Conference Board had revisited and modified its views. It begins
its 1975 report, *Corporate Directorship Practices* (the 1975 Report), by noting,
"This Report is appearing at a time when, perhaps more than ever before, the
corporate board of directors is being seriously reexamined."[105] Interestingly,
the 1975 Report's authors begin their study with the question not of what the
board should do but to whom it is accountable. This question, they write,
is a necessary precondition to determining the board's role, and it is one we
have seen the ABA answer in the *Guidebook*, though rather more indirectly.
The 1975 Report describes some sort of a monitoring board, though not quite
as pure a one as Eisenberg's model, as its description leaves some significant
managerial powers in the board itself. For example, strategic planning remains

---

[101] The reality of outsider-dominated boards by the 1970s suggests that the outpouring of conversation about outside directors was more about their purpose than their need, although it is fair
to say that there was considerable debate about their appropriate identity and the definition of
outside directors.

[102] CORPORATE DIRECTORSHIP PRACTICES, *supra* note 100, at 96.

[103] *Id.* at 109.   [104] *Id.* at 93.

[105] JEREMY BACON & JAMES K. BROWN, CORPORATE DIRECTORSHIP PRACTICES: ROLE, SELECTION,
AND LEGAL STATUS OF THE BOARD 1 (1975). For further evidence of the recent focus on board
function, see NOYES E. LEECH & ROBERT H. MUNDHEIM, THE OUTSIDE DIRECTOR OF THE
PUBLIC CORPORATION 3 (Korn-Ferry International 1976). ("At this time of reexamination for
many institutions of American life, the board of directors of the publicly held corporation is
drawing substantial attention"). Leech & Mundheim, *supra* note 51. And, of course, Myles
Mace's 1971 classic, *Directors: Myth and Reality*, had already demonstrated that boards did
not actually manage the corporations they served. Instead, his model was close to that of a
monitoring and advisory or planning role contemplated by the Conference Board.

a significant function of the board, a function that still rings of the board's managerial role that was in the process of being phased out. Nonetheless, the 1975 Report can be seen as a serious attempt at giving greater specificity to the role of the board at a time when directors felt as if they were coming under increasing legal attack.

While the Conference Board Report attributed the new focus on board function to more aggressive enforcement both of securities and corporate laws, the ABA saw the increase in outside directors as the motivating force in shifting from a managing board to some form of monitoring board.[106] And a 1976 report by Robert Mundheim and Noyes Leech for Korn-Ferry International, while agreeing both with the Conference Board and the ABA, accepted as its model Eisenberg's monitoring board, but with a twist. The focus of the Korn-Ferry report was on the increasingly prominent outside director, because inside directors act "primarily as managers . . . they cannot perform objectively in any capacity other than as managers and . . . , at the worst, they merely duplicate the thinking of the chief executive officer."[107]

All of this can be seen as a general movement not only to specify the functions of directors but also to specify them away from any substantive engagement in management that might have been practiced under older board models or at least contemplated by older ideas about the proper role of the board. Monitoring restricted what it was reasonable to expect the board to do. Increasing the number of outside directors limited what it was reasonable for the board to know.[108] And increasing the number of outside directors also provided a protective shield for the inside directors, as the Delaware courts were quick to recognize.[109]

---

[106] "Before the advent of the so-called 'outside' director, it was not unreasonable to expect the board to be actively involved in the corporation's business; however, with the development of board participation by individuals not otherwise actively involved with the corporation, any such expectation can no longer be viewed as feasible." MBCA add. B at 143 (1974). The Korn-Ferry report, mentioned subsequently, tended to agree with the Conference Board that increased directorial litigation, including the landmark *BarChris* case, had a major role in intensifying attention to boards.

[107] LEECH & MUNDHEIM, *supra* note 105, at 7.

[108] The then-recent *Francis v. United Jersey Bank*, 432 A.2d 814 (N.J. 1981), much cited at the time both for its clear acceptance of the monitoring model and for its imposition of liability on a director, is probably best seen in context as suggested by Elliott Weiss. "*Francis* . . . , much cited by the ALI Project, is remarkable not because a director was actually held liable, but as an illustration of the difficulty courts find in imposing due care liability on directors." Elliott Weiss, *Economic Analysis, Corporate Governance Law, and the ALI Corporate Governance Project*, 70 CORNELL L. REV. 1, 14 n.61 (1984).

[109] In a series of mostly takeover cases in the early 1980s (along with some derivative suit cases), the Delaware Supreme Court made it rather clear that a corporate board composed of a majority of outside directors had substantial insulation from liability. LAWRENCE E. MITCHELL ET AL., CORPORATE FINANCE AND GOVERNANCE 825 n.2 (2d ed., 1996).

A final important endorsement of the monitoring board appeared in *The Business Lawyer* as a companion piece to the ABA's 1978 *Guidebook*. The Business Roundtable, like the other organizations, began its own *Statement on the Role and Composition of the Board of Directors of the Large Publicly Owned Corporation* (the Statement) in fear.[110] It concludes its brief introduction by noting, "Some unfortunate developments of the last few years have caused the U.S. business community to reexamine intensively board operations and procedures as well as board composition."[111] The same liability environment that had prompted the ABA and the Conference Board to act also motivated the Business Roundtable.

It was motivated by fear but adopted a tone of defiance. The Statement begins with a defense of the role of U.S. business in our democracy. In the note "Corporate Legitimacy and Corporate Power" it states: "We think it incontestable that the U.S. system has led to greater political freedom, to better economic performance, and to more personal autonomy, than any other actual – as distinct from idealized – system with which it might be compared."[112] Defending its members further, it briefly summarizes the regulatory and competitive environments in which American corporations operated, noting the restraints they imposed on excessive or antisocial behavior. While the Business Roundtable understood the legitimating effect these restraints created, it was not without remorse. "We enumerate all these legal, regulatory and political constraints on U.S. business organizations with some mixed emotions because a number of them impose excessive and unnecessary costs – costs borne ultimately by the consuming public."[113] Having asserted its own primacy and exculpation and having tied its own victimization to that of the American public, it was ready for a substantive discussion of board reform.

That discussion was both more philosophical and considerably more defensive than the statements of the ABA and the Conference Board. Its general thrust was less one of board reform than of corporate legitimacy, defending the corporate enterprise against the legal and social onslaught that characterized the decade. It defined the board's role in terms of whom it was to serve instead of defining the board's role in terms of what the directors were to do, although it did the latter as well. And the answer to that question was the same as the ABA's and the Conference Board's – the shareholders. The Business Roundtable's approach to protecting directors from increasing liability was to

[110] *The Role and Composition of the Board of Directors of the Large Publicly Owned Corporation: Statement of the Business Roundtable*, 33 BUS. LAW. 2083 (1978).
[111] *Id.* at 2087.   [112] *Id.* at 2089.
[113] *Id.* at 2091.

accept the inevitability of the monitoring board and to make sure that the focus of that board was crystal clear, thus also accomplishing the purpose of limiting the scope of director behavior and liability.

The Statement does go into some detail as to the nature of the board. Implicitly objecting to the rise of independent directors, the Statement recognized the impossibility of "a board composed partly of 'outsiders' to conduct" day-to-day business, giving pride of place to "the indispensable role played by operating management in the conduct of day-to-day corporate affairs."[114] It went on to sing the praises of hierarchy and centralized authority as serving the needs of efficiency and rapid decision making. But, bowing to political reality, it also acknowledged that "operating management derives its authority and legitimacy from the board of directors."[115]

Here was a somewhat different take on the contemporary debate on board reform. The role of the board was clear – it provided the legitimacy necessary to allow the experts – the management – to operate. What the board actually did to fulfill that role was less important, as long as it did not interfere with management any more than was absolutely necessary to provide that legitimation.

The Business Roundtable did make an effort to define the role of the board. That role included monitoring top management and compliance with law. But it also included a significant role for strategic planning, what the Statement referred to as "resource allocation." Finally, the Statement described the board's role in maintaining the corporation's social responsibility, the board function perhaps most in keeping with its view of the board as legitimating corporate management. But that responsibility was heavily circumscribed. Long-term profit maximization that might indirectly benefit other constituents was legitimate, but the interests of the stockholders (and, interestingly, the employees) were first and foremost. While this long-term approach could well be good for business, the Statement cautioned, "[O]ther groups affected by corporate activities cannot be placed on a plane with owners," shareholder proposals under Rule 14a-8 should be limited to business, and "many of the social causes pursued by activist groups represent minority views rather than a prevailing consensus."[116]

The Business Roundtable bowed to the inevitability of outside directors, noting both the importance of experienced businesspeople on boards and the significant diversification of board membership it had perceived to have already taken place. At the same time, it resoundingly rejected the idea of

---

[114] *Id.* at 2094. [115] *Id.*
[116] *Id.* at 2100.

constituency directors or codetermination, perhaps with the recent publication of *Taming the Giant Corporation* in mind.[117] As to the overall board, the Statement recommended that a corporation have enough outsiders "at least sufficient to have a substantial impact on the board decision process. . . . " It recommended that in most cases this should be a majority of the directors. At the same time, it was also reformist enough to suggest that the audit, compensation, and nominating committees – the three committees most important to the legitimating role of the board – be composed entirely of outside directors.[118] The outside directors, with their minimal monitoring duties, could serve not only a legitimating function but also as a shield to protect insiders from liability.

Thus the 1970s ended with substantial convergence by academics, lawyers, and businesspeople on the monitoring model as the dominant vision of board function. That happy state of agreement was about to be blown apart in the 1980s. The political and social atmosphere had rapidly changed and the chance for meaningful corporate reform evaporated. The Supreme Court decision in *Santa Fe Industries Inc. v. Green* in 1977 and the election of Ronald Reagan in 1980 significantly diminished the immediate range of political possibilities.[119] It was in this new environment that the American Law Institute was to introduce its version of the monitoring board. The *American Law Institute Principles of Corporate Governance* (the *Principles* or the Project) did as much as anything to cement the monitoring board as the dominant model of board governance. But it did not do so until the controversy surrounding the *Principles* almost destroyed the monitoring board. The ABA, the Conference Board, and the Business Roundtable collectively did a volte-face from their position in the 1970s to attack the very model they had unanimously promoted. From the publication of its *Tentative Draft No. 1* in 1982 until the ALI's final adoption of the *Principles* in 1992, the almost hysterical controversy surrounding the Project could well have led to very different models of corporate governance.

---

[117] *Id.* at 2105–06.
[118] *Id.* at 2108. As the debate in the 1980s would show, the definition of outsiders contemplated by the Business Roundtable was quite different from that contemplated by Eisenberg and the ALI.
[119] By the time of publication of Elliott Weiss's *Social Regulation of Business Activity: Reforming the Corporate Governance System to Resolve an Institutional Impasse*, 28 UCLA L. REV. 343 (1981), the chances for political reform had more or less passed. Ronald Reagan had been elected president, and the next decade for corporate law was to be centered on the work of lawyers employing the tools of neoclassical economics to make the case for a corporation more strongly grounded in the sanctity of private property. Jensen and Meckling's work had begun to have its influence: the new scripture for this movement was FRANK EASTERBROOK & DANIEL FISCHEL, THE ECONOMIC STRUCTURE OF CORPORATE LAW (1991).

Virtually every aspect of those *Principles* came under aggressive attack by the corporate bar and corporate America. I will now explain both the controversy surrounding the monitoring board and the reasons for it.

5. The ALI – Fear and Loathing in Corporate America

It must have been a foregone conclusion that the *Principles* would adopt the model of the monitoring board. Mel Eisenberg was reporter for the first three sections, the last of which deals with (and indeed is titled) "The Structure of the Corporation." And the first item cited in the reporter's note following section 3.02, which delineated the function of the board, is *The Structure of Corporate Law*, a reference that remained throughout every revision from that first tentative draft to the final draft adopted in 1994.

The ALI had enough influence to make the corporate bar take the Project seriously. The bar was so concerned about the possible results that it created a lobbying group known as CORPRO to mold the *Principles* to their clients' interests.[120] The members of CORPRO were representatives from the Section's Committees on Corporate Laws, Corporate Law Departments, Corporate Counsel, and Federal Regulation of Securities. The principal concern of CORPRO was that the reporters were enshrining aspiration as law in the *Principles*, including "expand[ing] the directors' duty of care to include concern for the effectiveness of monitoring programs. . . ."[121] But there was more.

The monitoring model described in the first tentative draft was, in substance, exactly the same monitoring model that in the 1970s had been embraced by the *Guidebook*, the Conference Board, and the Business Roundtable.[122]

---

[120] For the story of CORPRO's efforts as well as its successes, see Alex Elson & Michael L. Shakman, *The ALI Principles of Corporate Governance: A Tainted Process and a Flawed Product*, 49 BUS. LAW. 1761 (1994); Elliot Goldstein, *CORPRO: A Committee That Became an Institution*, 48 BUS. LAW. 1333 (1993) (Goldstein was president of CORPRO from its formation until 1986); Richard B. Smith, *An Underview of the Principles of Corporate Governance*, 48 BUS. LAW. 1297 (1993) (Smith was also a member of CORPRO).

[121] Goldstein, *supra* note 120, at 1334.

[122] The *Guidebook* is, of course, not law, and the Committee on Corporate Laws might well have been concerned that greater specificity of the role of directors in a form that appeared to be statutory (although it was not) would have undue influence on courts in increasing directors' duties. The Business Roundtable notes the voluntary nature of the *Guidebook* approvingly and its pronounced evolutionary purpose, 1997 BUSINESS ROUNDTABLE STATEMENT, *supra* note 4, at 30–31, although as I noted earlier the *Guidebook* itself has remained unchanged in its fundamental principles over thirty years. Nonetheless, the 1974 comment on section 35 of the Model Business Corporation Act not only describes a broad monitoring model almost identical to that suggested by Eisenberg in his academic work. The comment further states: "The purpose of the modification of the first sentence of section 35 is to eliminate any ambiguity as to the director's role in formulating major management policy as opposed to direct involvement

Section 3.02 of the *Principles* was somewhat more specific in describing what that model meant, but even a casual look at the earlier literature, not to mention the cases, supports Victor Brudney's conclusion that the reporters put forth a "quite faithful interpretation of current law on the duty of care" and their adoption of "the structural principles of the monitoring board and the role of independent directors."[123] But the reporters in Part IV – this time under the authorship of Harvey Goldschmid – dared to attempt to draft a detailed statement of the business judgment rule (BJR). While not my present concern, one could have read the BJR provisions to have upped the ante a bit by increasing the rigor of the duty of care and that, as the preceding quote indicates, suggests a major reason for the corporate bar's forceful opposition to the *Principles*.[124] But in attacking the BJR provisions, CORPRO and its allies failed to distinguish between the standard of care and the concept of the monitoring board that its members had already embraced (and was well on its way toward becoming mainstream Delaware law). As a result, the board model described by the ALI came in for the same kind of rough treatment as the business judgment rule, despite the fact that, upon sober reflection, the utility of that model as a liability shield should have been as obvious as it was less than a decade earlier and a decade later.

The Business Roundtable, perhaps the most virulent opponent of the ALI Project, published a lengthy statement in opposition to the *Principles* after the release of *Tentative Draft No. 1*.[125] That organization was agitated by the entire Project, which it saw as creating new law and imposing new and greater responsibilities on boards and corporations. The Business Roundtable was particularly troubled by the form of the *Principles*, which was written as a classic Restatement, implying that the *Principles* were indeed law even though the *Principles* themselves clearly stated their aspirational character.[126]

The Roundtable's Statement, based in part on a study it commissioned by Paul McAvoy, practically predicts the destruction of corporate America if

---

in day-to-day management." Of course, it is precisely this role contemplated by section 3.02 of the *Principles*, with additional but obvious specifications as to the board's role in hiring and compensating senior management. One last possibility for agitation by the ABA is its acknowledgment in 1974 of its desire to retain flexibility in the hope that courts would adopt liability rules "in this dynamic corporate area" that "more accurately recognize the proper role of the corporate director." MBCA, *supra* note 51, at 147.

[123] ALI, PRINCIPLES OF CORPORATE GOVERNANCE AND STRUCTURE: RESTATEMENT AND RECOMMENDATIONS, TENTATIVE DRAFT NO. 1 (1982); Brudney, *supra* note 72, at 225.

[124] *See also* Elliott Goldstein, *The Relationship Between the Model Business Corporation Act and the Principles of Corporate Governance: Analysis and Recommendation*, 52 GEO. WASH. L. REV. 501 (1984).

[125] 1983 BUSINESS ROUNDTABLE STATEMENT, *supra* note 12.

[126] As I suggested *supra* note 122, this same issue of format may well have troubled the ABA.

the *Principles* were to be adopted.[127] Among the targets was the monitoring
board itself, although at least in the Delaware courts the monitoring board
had already become an established fact and indeed had demonstrated its
effectiveness in shielding directors from liability. The Business Roundtable
had been comfortable with the monitoring board in the late 1970s. Indeed, it
was quite happy with the monitoring board again, in 1997, when it published
a new statement fully embracing the monitoring model in terms that are
substantially identical to those proposed in *Tentative Draft No. 1*.[128] But matters
were different in 1983.

One objection made by the Business Roundtable was that the *Principles*
selected the monitoring model as the best-practices model for corporate boards.
The Business Roundtable argued that business research had identified at least
five kinds of boards, of which the monitoring board was one, and that it would
be foolhardy to adopt a single model in a dynamic field like business.[129] But
it was also clear that the Business Roundtable read the monitoring model
as implying far more active board involvement in the business than appears
justified by the text of section 3.02(a) and the reporter's comment. It objected to
the model on the grounds of technical, financial, and international complexity
in business. Reading all of the materials from the perspective of 2007 leads me
to conclude that the Business Roundtable saw the monitoring model to require
significantly more directorial work and allowed considerably less flexibility
in determining its function than it actually did. (Indeed, section 3.02(a) is
rather explicit about flexibility.) The development of the legal treatment of
the monitoring board since 1983 clearly supports this conclusion.

I have already suggested that a major cause for concern was the general
conflation of the monitoring model with the carefully articulated business
judgment rule. It is clear that this was the Business Roundtable's perspective. The Statement muddles together the monitoring board and the business
judgment rule. In describing the monitoring board, the Statement includes
as inextricably related to that model the ALI's requirement of a majority of
independent directors on boards and the establishment of an audit committee
of independent directors, with its perception that the duty of care would be
significantly expanded, the protection currently afforded to directors under

[127] *See* 1983 BUSINESS ROUNDTABLE STATEMENT, *supra* note 12, at 6–7, setting forth in executive summary form a parade of horribles, including corporate inflexibility, increased costs,
decreased productivity, diminished risk taking, and short-term business focus.
[128] 1997 BUSINESS ROUNDTABLE STATEMENT, *supra* note 4, at 4–5.
[129] 1983 BUSINESS ROUNDTABLE STATEMENT, *supra* note 12, at 25. *See also* Bryan F. Smith, *Corporate Governance: A Director's View*, 37 U. MIAMI L. REV. 273 (1983).

the business judgment rule would be narrowed, and derivative suits would be easier to sustain.

The Statement addresses the monitoring model directly only in its observation that "a series of enumerated oversight responsibilities would be imposed on the board and specific committees." And in its specification of its objection to this last point, the Statement is clear about some of its fears. Directors themselves could be subject to much greater liability because of the imposition of increased responsibility. The Statement notes in particular section 3.02(a)'s requirement that directors be responsible for "assuring the existence of compliance programs" and betrays its anxiety that directors would become liable for antitrust violations and conflict of interest transactions.[130] In fact, section 3.02(a)'s description of board responsibilities is nothing more than a broad statement of the minimal requisites for compliance with the duty of care as articulated in contemporaneous cases.[131]

The fight over the *Principles* was also a turf war. The ABA's Section on Business Law has responsibility for drafting and revising the Model Business Corporation Act. It was evident from the inception of the Project that the *Principles* would cover much the same ground as the Model Act. A charitable description of the ABA's concern, expressed by CORPRO member Richard Smith, was its fear of conflicting principles of law governing the same subject area.[132] A somewhat less charitable view would describe the conflict between the ABA and the ALI as a dogfight over territory.[133]

The turf war was multilateral. The ALI was taking on nothing less than a prescription for good corporate practice (and a good deal more). It was not just about whose law governed but also about who decided how business should be run. "Business school professors regard themselves as at least the equal of law professors in dealing with organizational structures of business entities."[134] While the ALI did include some business academics and practitioners in the debate, their interests were represented mainly by their counsel, largely in the form of CORPRO. And if business academics were miffed by their relative exclusion, businesspeople were furious at the idea that law professors might tell them how to run their corporations. The chair of the Business Roundtable, referring to the ALI drafters, said: "We don't require four law professors to tell us how to run our business. . . . I find it appalling arrogance that they think they can vote on how America is managed."[135] And so a turf war among lawyers,

---

[130] 1983 BUSINESS ROUNDTABLE STATEMENT, *supra* note 12, at 16.
[131] *See* Francis v. United Jersey Bank, 432 A.2d 814 (N.J. 1981) decided that same year.
[132] Smith, *supra* note 120, at 1301.   [133] *See also* Goldstein, *supra* note 124.
[134] Smith, *supra* note 120, at 1303.   [135] Andrews, *supra* note 14, at 35.

businesspeople, and academics was also part of the story. All of this created a furor over *Tentative Draft No. 1*.[136]

A final fear that led to controversy was the statement in *Tentative Draft No. 1* that boards should be composed of a majority of independent directors and that the audit, nominating, and compensation committees be exclusively composed of outside directors.[137] In light of what I have said of the liability-shielding features of the monitoring model, cool thinking should have made it apparent that outside directors serving in these capacities would have been the ultimate shield for insiders. So something more has to explain the furor. The background of the agitations of the 1970s suggests a reason. Business groups and their legal allies were afraid that outsider-controlled boards would be established for the purpose of changing the responsibilities of business, and indeed the ALI was accused of pursuing this goal.[138] Rather than serving as a shield, then, the business perception was that the ALI's monitoring model was a backhanded way to impose upon business the social responsibilities it had escaped with the change in the political climate in 1980. The fear was that outside directors would be drawn from the multiple constituencies identified by Nader, Green, and Seligman. This fear – one of the most pronounced fears of the 1970s – blinded the business groups to the obvious truth that they would control the composition of the outside board and that it would protect them.

The development of the monitoring board as liability shield is what happened and what logic should have predicted would happen. After all, the sources of most board candidates and their backgrounds, the well-known psychological processes of director's assimilation onto boards,[139] and the obvious ability of management to dominate a board of part-timers should have made it clear to insiders and managers that the outside directors on the new monitoring boards would continue to be just like them. But with fresh memories of the 1970s, and the takeover decade poised to begin, this was not the way the opposition saw matters.

These fears were a major factor in business opposition to the Project. Also significant was the fact that the neoclassical, free-market model of the

---

[136] Among the objections of the Business Roundtable was the ALI's failure to consult business experts. 1983 BUSINESS ROUNDTABLE STATEMENT, *supra* note 12, at 20.

[137] For my purposes it is not important here to follow the ALI's distinction among different types of outside directors. As Karmel points out, the New York Stock Exchange had required independent audit committees since 1977. Karmel, *supra* note 44, at 18.

[138] *See* Karmel, *supra* note 12.

[139] James D. Cox & Harry L. Munsinger, *Bias in the Boardroom: Psychological Foundations and Legal Implications of Corporate Cohesion*, 48 LAW & CONTEMP. PROBS. 83 (1985).

corporation had been developing and was now reaching maturity.[140] A vision
of the corporation, restrained in its behavior principally by market mechanisms and able to operate with a freedom that would not be possible when
constrained by law, had to be very attractive to businesspeople. The evidence
suggests that they did have a keen awareness of this relatively new scholarship.[141]
Any specification of director's functions or duties would have restricted this
freedom.

Seligman offers a final explanation. The reforms of the 1970s evolved on
the background of a great deal of agitation, including SEC and congressional
investigations, for changes in the way and, perhaps, the purposes for which
corporate America was run. A monitoring board must have seemed to business
groups and their lawyers to be a more attractive alternative during the mid-
1970s than allowing public pressure to result in legislation. The atmosphere
following Reagan's election in 1980 was different: "The ALI project was the
only significant corporate governance initiative with any reform component
remaining."[142] As Seligman sees it, with real pressure for reform out of the
way, all criticism was focused on the one remaining reform project, however
pallid.

This explanation is plausible and surely is at least partly correct. But it
cannot explain the complete reversal of business attitudes.[143] The monitoring
board was quite a modest reform (if indeed a reform at all), it was accepted
in Delaware law, and it was ideally suited to director protection. Enlightened
self-interest should have led to continued business support for the monitoring
board. Besides, while the ALI is influential, it does not make law, and one
could reasonably expect that the Delaware courts in particular would have
charted their own course. Thus, an attitude of graceless victory might well have
stimulated the opposition, but the other factors I've mentioned are necessary
for a complete explanation.

The ALI won the war, as Delaware's perfection of the monitoring model
and the Business Roundtable's embrace of it in 1997 demonstrate. But it was a
Pyrrhic victory, one not for reform but, ultimately, for a recasting of the status
quo. This is demonstrated not only by the director-protective nature of the

---

[140] EASTERBROOK & FISCHEL, *supra* note 119; Fama, *supra* note 67; Jensen & Meckling, *supra* note 67.
[141] 1983 BUSINESS ROUNDTABLE STATEMENT, *supra* note 12, at 24, 29; Goldstein, *supra* note 124, at 502; Seligman, *supra* note 44, at 346–49.
[142] Seligman, *supra* note 44, at 359.
[143] Seligman does discuss the law and economics movement as a "new mode" of criticism in addition to this explanation. I see it as something more than that, although the difference is subtle – as a justification for nonregulation and at the same time a vision of a deregulated corporate society that provided affirmative ammunition.

contemporary legal model of the monitoring board[144] but also by a comment to section 3.02 that first appears in *Tentative Draft No. 11*, published in 1991 and embodying the first significant changes to section 3.02 (which changes survive in the adopted the *Principles*):

> Section 3.02 is intended as a statement of the rules that a court would adopt, giving full weight to all of the considerations (including the judicial precedents) that the courts deem it appropriate to weigh. Section 3.02 is not intended ... to enlarge the scope of a director's legal obligations and liability, the performance expected from directors to comply with the duty of care, or the role and accountability of directors concerning the corporation's compliance with law.[145]

Section 3.02 was intended to clarify, not expand. It was not about reform at all. There was no need for anybody to be upset.

It is clear from the literature that section 3.02 was not to create radical reform. Roswell Perkins, president of the ALI, writing in the 1986 *Business Lawyer* seems somewhat (and, in my view, understandably) perplexed as to what all the fuss was about. He notes as to the monitoring board: "The statement of the required functions of the board of directors ... is essentially a simple one, placing emphasis on the election, evaluation, and dismissal, where appropriate, of the principal senior executives. ... The board can be as active as it wants to be, but the drafts impose very few functions as being essential." He goes on to observe the concerns raised by those who saw this model as increasing liability, arguing to the contrary that "the statement of the board's functions in section 3.02(a) is essentially a limiting one ... ," and that oversight is intended to be indirect and general, not direct and active.[146] That, indeed, is how it reads to a disinterested observer in 2007. But the factors I have identified, as well as the 1985 *Van Gorkom* decision,[147] blinded observers to the modesty of the function and the utility of the model to corporate directors. In addition, by the mid-1980s, we were thick in the boom of hostile takeovers, insider-trading scandals, the proliferation of junk bonds, and renewed congressional attention to corporate America in an atmosphere that bore some of the characteristics of the earlier decade of business fear.

---

[144] *In re* Walt Disney Co. Derivative Litig., 907 A.2d 693 (Del. Ch. 2005).

[145] ALI, Principles of Corporate Governance and Structure: Analysis and Recommendations, Tentative Draft No. 11, 110–11 (1991).

[146] Roswell B. Perkins, *The ALI Corporate Governance Project in Midstream*, 41 Bus. Law. 1195, 1201–02 (1986).

[147] Smith v. Van Gorkom, 488 A.2d 858 (Del. 1985).

IV. DELAWARE SEALS THE DEAL

The creation of the monitoring board, with its emphasis on limited and attenuated directorial responsibility, could not have come soon enough for business
development. Just as the conglomeration movement marked the high point of
managerialism in the 1960s and early 1970s, the end of the latter decade and
the beginning of the next brought the deconglomeration movement, what we
have come to know as the great takeover decade of the 1980s with its bust-up
leveraged takeover. There is little point here in replaying the business history
of that decade. It is too well-known to require extended comment. Equally
well known but highly relevant to this discussion is Delaware's response. For
as the Delaware courts grappled with the application of traditional doctrines
to a new transactional form that presented ineradicable conflicts of interest,
the development of the monitoring board gave the courts just the matrix they
needed on which to shape a director-protective doctrine.

It would be tedious and somewhat pointless to analyze the cases. What is
important, however, is the leitmotif of those cases. All directors were faced
with conflicting interests in hostile takeovers. But inside directors faced far
more serious conflicts than did outsiders. After all, the insiders derived their
livelihoods from their positions with the target corporations, positions almost
sure to be eliminated (at least for them) if the hostile offer were to succeed.
Outsiders presumably valued their jobs, as well. But if the corporation were
sold, they still had generally lucrative positions with their own corporations to
keep them occupied. And the 1980s were still before that time when directors'
compensation became truly significant. So while outsiders had some prestige
to lose, and perhaps an enjoyable avocation, they were hardly in the position
of insiders.

The *Unocal* proportionality test was artfully created by the Delaware court to
steer a course between the board's entrenched conflict without doing violence
either to the business judgment rule (and its underlying precept that directors
manage the corporation) or the fairness test, designed to ensure directorial
fealty that invariably put the board on the defensive.[148] Taken on its own, the
test was a substantial advance in corporate doctrine and well suited to the
problem it addressed. But the Delaware Supreme Court's decision to forgo
the fairness test presented a substantial danger in the case of insider-dominated
boards. True, the first part of the *Unocal* test provided some metric of objectivity
for a board's decision to resist a hostile takeover, and the second part, the
proportionality test, similarly provided some objective balance to evaluate the

---

[148] Unocal Corp. v. Mesa Petroleum Co., 493 A.2d 946 (Del. 1985).

methods used to ensure their consistency with the board's objectively perceived threats to the corporation. But the application of that test to a managing board of insiders would have presented its own difficult issues. While the Delaware courts have been consistent in their refusal to inquire into directors' subjective motivations, an insider board would have made the *Unocal* test look more like a procedural whitewash than a hard look at board behavior.

Fortunately, by the 1980s, a majority of major American corporations had outside boards and the monitoring model was well established. The outsiders, at least, were meant to cast a baleful eye on the conflicting transactions of insiders. Both this role, and the status of outside directors, made takeover doctrine that provided board deference far more plausible than would have been the case with inside boards.

The Delaware courts were keenly aware of this. In case after case – in *Moran*,[149] *Revlon*,[150] *Newmont Mining*,[151] *Mills*,[152] and *Paramount*;[153] in merger cases like *Weinberger*;[154] and in derivative lawsuits like *Zapata*[155] and *Grobow*[156] – the court repeatedly made clear the almost sanitizing effect that a majority-independent board, which at this point necessarily meant a monitoring board, would have on judicial evaluation of corporate behavior in conflict of interest transactions. And, as has frequently been noted, this cleansing effect – this protective effect – of the new board allowed the courts to look not at the substance of the actions but the procedures pursuant to which they had been taken. Good process – decision making by reasonably informed, rational, independent boards – allowed the courts to bypass entirely the substance of the decision making and even the substance of the process of the decision making. Chancellor Allen went so far as to proclaim the incomprehensibility of a rational process producing an irrational result.[157] The monitoring board had achieved its purpose. Directors serving on properly composed monitoring boards, behaving in accordance with the model, were almost exempt from liability.

The problem was that the monitoring board could serve as an effective liability shield only for as long as directors were willing to abide by the script. The very nature of a monitoring board, as a minimalist board, presented

---

[149] Moran v. Household Int'l, Inc., 500 A.2d 1346 (Del. 1985).
[150] Revlon, Inc. v. MacAndrews & Forbes Holding, Inc., 506 A.2d 173 (Del. 1985).
[151] Ivanhoe Partners v. Newmont Mining Corp., 535 A.2d 1334 (Del. 1987).
[152] Mills Acquisition Co. v. MacMillan, Inc., 559 A.2d 1261 (Del. 1988).
[153] Paramount Commc'ns v. Time, Inc., 571 A.2d 1140 (Del. 1989).
[154] Weinberger v. UOP, Inc., 457 A.2d 701 (Del. 1983).
[155] Zapata Corp. v. Maldonado, 430 A.2d 779 (Del. 1981).
[156] Grobow v. Perot, 539 A.2d 180 (Del. 1988).
[157] *In re* Caremark Intl'l Derivative Litig., 698 A.2d at 967 (Del. Ch. 1996).

still-unresolved issues of inadequate board time and information, the almost-intractable problem of structural bias, the continuing issues of proxy capture, and real power vested where it always had been – the CEO and top management. These lingering issues could and, in the late 1990s, did lead to problems. Monitoring can be a serious and active engagement. But the unresolved issues of board limitation combined with little corporate incentive to resolve them almost ensured that boards would become lax in discharging their responsibilities. And, as Brudney observed, if monitoring directors did their jobs properly, their discovery of corporate problems would be "to expose the independent directors to responsibility for failures or shortfalls over which they have little control."[158]

Take, for example, even the simplest and clearest of board responsibilities, removing an underperforming CEO. That almost never happened. So rare an occurrence was it that Robert Stempel's termination as CEO of General Motors in 1992 was widely viewed as a cataclysmic event.[159] The fact that CEO removal is such a rare occurrence is completely understandable. Leaving aside all of the issues that we know help reinforce CEO power and board complacency, the circumstances in which corporate underperformance can be traced to the CEO are few, and the magnitude of the corporate problem that has to exist to motivate a board to oust the CEO is large. For a variety of reasons like stability, long-term vision, and corporate consistency that are beyond the scope of this chapter, it is probably a good thing that CEOs are not so easily removed. But the reluctance of monitoring boards to cross their CEOs is legendary.[160] This deference even extends to former CEOs, as was demonstrated recently by Sandy Weill's negotiations over his departure package from Citigroup.

As everyone knows, the pace of CEO removal has quickened following the corporate scandals of 2002.[161] Those scandals occurred under the eyes of properly constructed monitoring boards, most of which, by all accounts, engaged in precisely the processes that the monitoring model expected of them. While some of the CEO removals have nothing to do directly with the scandals, it is in a similar atmosphere of well-publicized scandal, increased legal activity, new regulation, shareholder agitation (at least on the part of institutional

---

[158] Brudney, *supra* note 14, at 633.

[159] *See* Doron P. Levin, *Shakeup at GM; Stempel Quits Job as Top G.M. Officer in Rift with Board*, N.Y. TIMES, Oct. 27, 1992, at A1; Mark J. Roe, *Clearing Boardrooms Like G.M.'s*, WALL ST. J., Oct. 27, 1992, at A16.

[160] *See* Eliezer M. Fich & Lawrence J. White, *CEO Compensation and Turnover: The Effects of Mutually Interlocked Boards*, 38 WAKE FOREST L. REV. 935, 936 (2003).

[161] Chuck Lucier et al., *CEO Succession 2005: The Crest of the Wave*, STRATEGY + Business, Summer 2006, *available at* http://www.strategy-business.com/press/article/06210?pg=0.

shareholders), and serious questions about corporate responsibility that existed in the 1970s that these removals have occurred.

The model of the outsider-dominated monitoring board may be the principal legal variable that differentiates the early 2000s from the 1970s. It is the fact that this model has worked so well that has protected so many boards from liability. But in an age of anxiety, there is always a response. The only defensive response available to the monitoring board is to exaggerate its behavior within the context of its responsibilities. Because CEO selection and removal is first and foremost among these responsibilities, it is no surprise that we see more CEO removals. When the atmosphere of crisis abates, as has already begun, we can expect a return to the procedurally oriented, relatively passive monitoring board.

On August 9, 2005, Chancellor Chandler of the Delaware Court of Chancery handed down his long-awaited opinion in *In re Walt Disney Company Derivative Litigation.*[162] It was no surprise in his long, thoughtful, measured opinion that he absolved the Disney board from breach of its duty of care and obligation to act in good faith. But there is one aspect of the opinion in particular that is highly relevant to my argument, and that is the chancellor's introductory remarks, well worth quoting at length. "As I will explain in painful detail hereafter, there are many aspects of defendants' conduct that fell significantly short of the best practices of ideal corporate governance." Noting that the Disney board's actions (and inactions) had occurred a decade earlier than the decision, a decade that had seen the failures of Enron and World-Com, he went on to write "that applying 21st century notions of best practices in analyzing whether those decisions were actionable would be misplaced." He added:

> Unlike ideals of corporate governance, a fiduciary's duties do not change over time. How we understand those duties may evolve and become refined, but the duties themselves have not changed, except to the extent that fulfilling a fiduciary duty requires obedience to other positive law. This Court strongly encourages directors and officers to employ best practices, as those practices are understood at the time a corporate decision is taken. But Delaware does not – indeed, the common law cannot – hold fiduciaries liable for a failure to comply with the aspirational ideal of best practices. . . . [163]

---

[162] *In re* Walt Disney Co. Derivative Litig., 907 A.2d 693 (Del. Ch. 2005). The ruling was affirmed on June 8, 2006, by the Delaware Supreme Court in an opinion written by Justice Jacobs. 906 A.2d 27 (Del. 2006).

[163] *Disney*, 907 A.2d at 697–98. Justice Jacobs noted this language approvingly in the Delaware Supreme Court's opinion. *Disney*, 906 A.2d at 72.

The monitoring board began as a model both of best practice and of appropriate law reform. And the monitoring board – like so many other best practices such as interested director statutes, stakeholder legislation, directors' indemnification, and antitakeover devices – became adopted as the law. We saw the monitoring board develop as a response both to corporate crisis and confusion about the proper role of the board. We saw how it was taken up by board-friendly reform groups as a way of shielding directors from liability. We saw how the Delaware courts accepted the monitoring board through its decisions in the 1980s and 1990s. And now, with the *Disney* decision, we see not only a court approving the minimal actions at least of outside members of a monitoring board but also acceptance of that very low level of board conduct as the metric of fiduciary obligation. Whatever talk there is of reinvigorated or newly activist boards, Chancellor Chandler's undoubtedly correct and disarmingly frank assessment of the relationship between law and best practice makes it clear that the monitoring board has become a striking success in its function of protecting directors from liability. All a director need do is to comply with that minimal standard of monitoring, and he should be free. Whatever aspirations corporate reformers may have, those who work in boardrooms, and those who protect them, have absolutely no incentive to change the contemporary model of board governance.

V. CONCLUSION

The historical lesson is important both in understanding the trouble with boards and in providing some insight into meaningful board reform. An institution born in fear and designed for defense is unlikely to be useful when aggressive action is necessary.

Our history began in a miasma of confusion over what precisely it was that boards did or were supposed to do, a confusion that presented relatively few serious problems in times of unquestioned general prosperity and corporate stability and in an era when hierarchy was expected and respected. The question of the role of the board began to arise only as corporate America destabilized during the age of conglomeration and began to come apart at the seams in the 1970s. With no clearly defined role for the board and no practical managerial role, the way was open to recast the board in the only role it reasonably could perform, the minimal role of board as monitor. And in a time of fear, it was particularly easy to shape that board in a way that provided maximum protection for the directors. I do not claim that protection was the principal reform motivation. I only claim that, with increasing attention to the board and calls for reform in a climate of aggressive regulation and enforcement, an atmosphere of fear and uncertainty, it was a natural response to mold reform to be protective.

The problem for contemporary board reform is to understand the climate in which our dominant board model was created and the forces that shaped it as it is. The contemporary board is a defensive institution. As such, it is little surprise that it is the first line of attack for corporate critics, the first line of litigation for plaintiffs' lawyers, and the first line of complaint for activist shareholders. To recast the Business Roundtable's understanding of the board as a legitimating device, we can see that the board has been molded to serve as a scapegoat. But this scapegoat institution protects its members with a legal superstructure that permits the wolves to bray at the gates but rarely to enter. Such a board is not and, I argue, was not, designed to serve the goal of ensuring the responsible and efficient management of the large public corporation. Building reform on this model is almost certain to fail. Reformers who truly believe in boards must reconceptualize the very purpose of a board before engaging in meaningful reform. In this case, building on the past simply won't do.

The story of the development of the modern monitoring board raises an important question: is the board of directors of the modern American public corporation a useful institution? In light of the *Disney* opinion, which came on the heels of a series of major corporate scandals that took place under the eyes of properly constituted and apparently functioning monitoring boards, one is entitled to ask why we bother to have boards at all. The economic and social consequences of maintaining the institution of the board are significant in light of the time, talent, expense, and litigation and compliance costs that go into propping up the board as the facade of corporate governance. Its existence requires justification and an explanation of its benefits, not simple assumptions.

An in-depth examination of these issues requires empirical study and is therefore beyond the scope of this chapter, which is designed to explain how the modern board came to be what it is. But consistent with that history and, perhaps, most dangerous of all of the board's failings, the dominance of the monitoring board, if not the existence of the board itself, has engendered a false sense of security for all of those dependent upon the corporation. This is not simply a matter of disappointed expectations when boards find themselves embroiled in corporate scandals or even simply criticized for poor corporate performance. Rather, and more mundanely, an institution that is so structurally handicapped in performing serious and meaningful functions and that at the same time is held out as the oversight mechanism of

U.S. corporate capitalism leads even sophisticated investors and stakeholders as well as the government and general public to believe that serious, meaningful, and thoughtful oversight exists over the business and conduct of U.S. corporations. Sometimes it does, though not always at the board level.[164] Quite often it does not.[165] The board's very existence creates a kind of false consciousness in U.S. business and financial life.

All of these problems may be resolvable if we can infuse some substantive content into board functions. Suggestions for this kind of reform have been made.[166] But while we fiddle with the board, perhaps more important problems go unaddressed. Before the development of the monitoring board, serious people knew that the top corporate officers were the center of corporate power.[167] Our widespread acceptance of the monitoring board has masked that continuing reality and diverted scholarly attention from this power.[168] If all goes well, the consequence is simply the enormous expense in money, time, and talent that I have already mentioned. When something goes wrong, we are left essentially helpless and uninformed in constructing appropriate remedies.[169] Nowhere is this more evident than in the Sarbanes-Oxley Act of 2002, passed in response to the corporate scandals of the turn of the century, which in its corporate aspects does little more than reinforce our unrelenting focus on the board. In so doing, it, too, merely undergirds our reliance upon an institution that time and again has disappointed us.

With whom or what would we replace the board? Perhaps no one and nothing. Perhaps we will conclude that, flawed or not, the board should remain largely as it is, and we will continue to muddle our way through to a meaningful and effective role for the board. Perhaps we need multiple boards

---

[164] As Lyman Johnson and David Millon have pointed out, corporate scholarship generally ignores the central role of corporate officers. Lyman P.Q. Johnson & David Millon, *Recalling Why Corporate Officers Are Fiduciaries*, 46 WM. & MARY L. REV. 1597 (2005); Lyman P.Q. Johnson, *Corporate Officers and the Business Judgment Rule*, 60 BUS. LAW. 439 (2005).

[165] James P. Holdcroft & Jonathan R. Macey, *Corporate Governance: Flexibility in Determining the Role of the Board of Directors in the Age of Information*, 19 CARDOZO L. REV. 291, 294–95 (1997) (corporate complexity may make boards' task impossible).

[166] *See, e.g.*, George W. Dent, *The Revolution in Corporate Governance, the Monitoring Board, and the Director's Duty of Care*, 61 B.U. L. REV. 623, 661–80 (1981).

[167] JOHN CALHOUN BAKER, DIRECTORS AND THEIR FUNCTIONS: A PRELIMINARY STUDY 12 (1945); PETER DRUCKER, THE PRACTICE OF MANAGEMENT 178 (1954).

[168] This is true despite somewhat increased institutional investor activism. While institutions may pressure CEOs, they do so largely through the board. There has been recent legal scholarly attention paid to the CEO and top executives, though principally limited to the problems of executive compensation. LUCIAN ARYE BEBCHUK & JESSE M. FRIED, PAY WITHOUT PERFORMANCE: THE UNFULFILLED PROMISE OF EXECUTIVE COMPENSATION (2004).

[169] Even the board is left bewildered, as the Enron and WorldCom scandals demonstrate.

with very distinct functions;[170] or a return to boards with real managerial powers; or some other substantive modification of the role of the board and, with it, its composition. Perhaps we need direct shareholder elections of CEOs. Whatever the solution, it is with an understanding of how our board came to be, and why it does not work, that we can arm ourselves properly to answer these questions.

[170] John C. Coffee Jr., *Beyond the Shut-Eyed Sentry: Toward a Theoretical View of Corporate Misconduct and an Effective Legal Response*, 63 VA. L. REV. 1099 (1977); Lynne L. Dallas, *The Multiple Roles of Boards of Directors*, 40 SAN DIEGO L. REV. 781 (2003).

2   Rediscovering Board Expertise

Legal Implications of the Empirical Literature

Lawrence A. Cunningham

People are rediscovering the value of expertise on corporate boards of directors. The rediscovery occurs after several decades of celebrating independent directors under the guise of the monitoring model of boards. While independence remains fashionable, and the Sarbanes-Oxley Act of 2002 (SOX) continues its long-standing promotion, SOX also requires companies to disclose whether their boards have expertise on the board audit committee and, if not, why not.[1] This hastens an inchoate ten-year trend favoring expertise. The value of expertise is supported by theory and empirical research. Accidents of political history appear to explain its subordination, until recently, to independence.

As a matter of theory, board expertise harmonizes with basic division of labor principles, yet little attention is paid to the specific expertise that directors offer. The most prominent model of director expertise, developed during the rise of the monitoring board, envisioned an expertise in "decision control."[2] But this views boards as monoliths and hides the significance of individuals in group decision making.[3] Accompanying the rise of the monitoring board and its privileged place for independence was the rise of the board committee, especially the audit committee. Although committees have designated functions, until recently, the focus has been on member independence rather than expertise benefiting from division of labor.

---

[1] Sarbanes-Oxley Act of 2002 § 301, 15 U.S.C. § 78j-1(m)(2) (2007).

[2] Eugene F. Fama & Michael C. Jensen, *Separation of Ownership and Control*, 26 J.L. & Econ. 301, 315 (1983).

[3] *See* Darian M. Ibrahim, *Individual or Collective Liability for Corporate Directors?*, 93 Iowa L. Rev. 929 (2008).

Lawrence A. Cunningham is Professor of Law, The George Washington University Law School. Thanks to Richard Baker, Donald Clarke, Renee Jones, Troy Paredes, and Robert Prentice. Another version of this chapter appeared in the *Cincinnati Law Review*.

As an empirical matter, the value of expertise is supported by a large body of research. Most strikingly, research shows that accounting expertise is valuable in promoting audit committee effectiveness, while general financial and other expertise contribute less value. The rise of independence and its displacement of expertise were due largely to periodic needs to quell political disputes or respond to crises. The appeal to independence helped generate consensus. The rediscovery of the value of expertise appears after an abundance of empirical research showing that independence on boards of directors is of uncertain value at best.

Despite this rediscovery of the value of expertise, no statement of purpose accompanies the new imperatives for expertise. Legal doctrines developed over several decades, based on the independence construct, should be reviewed to adapt to increased value resulting from reintroduction of expertise into the boardroom. Restoring expertise requires revisiting basic conceptions of corporate governance, including some encrusted principles of state corporation law and some recently developed gestures in securities regulation.

After a brief summary of the rise of board independence, showing its political roots and uncertain economic value, the analysis below considers the origins and current state of interest in director expertise. This includes a review of the considerable body of recent empirical evidence showing high value of accounting expertise among directors on audit committees. Analysis suggests that desired expertise for board audit committees centers on accounting expertise rather than other types of expertise. SOX rightly contemplated that kind of expertise but, under pressure, the SEC instead adopted an expansive conception of expertise that dilutes its value.

Discussion then explores more complex challenges that arise from rediscovering the value of expertise. First, the purpose of accounting expertise on audit committees is not self-evident. One issue concerns what scope of burden those experts bear: whether their enlistment to control accounting earnings management (artificial bookkeeping manipulations) extends to a mandate to control real earnings management (substantive business decisions taken to generate desired bookkeeping consequences). Another is to whom audit committee accounting experts should be beholden, a twenty-first century twist on last century's debate concerning for whom managers are trustees. The current issue hinges on the meaning and beneficiaries of conservatism in accounting, considering competing demands for relative conservatism from varying corporate constituencies.

Second, it is customary to see independence and expertise as trade-offs. This view seems correct when expertise arises from insider status but incorrect when the expertise is substantive knowledge in a discipline. It should be possible for a director to be both an expert and independent. Indeed, empirical evidence shows that the combination of independence and expertise is uniquely valuable and should be encouraged. Yet while law has long promoted independence, it discourages expertise. This appears to reflect unintended doctrinal consequences of the decades-long independence bias. Accordingly, the rediscovered value of expertise demands doctrinal adjustments so that courts can bring law into line with what is known to work in corporate governance.

I. THE POLITICS AND ECONOMICS OF INDEPENDENCE

Two schools of thought have influenced conceptions of the corporation: a private law account based in trust and contract law, with shareholders as beneficiaries, and a public law account based on state concessions of charter grants with multiple constituencies. During the twentieth century, the dominant view came to center on private shareholder interests to be advanced by boards – although standard formulations of directorial duty retain vestiges of the dueling schools when invariably announcing that directors must act in the interests of "the corporation and its shareholders."[4]

A. *Politics*

The assumptions of private ordering were first tested amid the economic upheavals of the 1930s and the ensuing regulatory frenzy and academic debates. A series of exchanges from 1931 to 1935 between Professors Adolph Berle and Merrick Dodd reflect the familiar positions.[5] Professor Berle saw the corporation as involving a relinquishment of control by shareholders to corporate managers and believed that the resulting separation of ownership from control required imposing trustlike duties on managers to act for shareholder benefit. Professor Dodd, accepting that separation existed, proposed to fill it not with managerial duties to shareholders but with managerial duties to various corporate constituencies that included employees and communities.[6]

---

[4] *See* William T. Allen, *Our Schizophrenic Conception of the Business Corporation*, 14 CARDOZO L. REV. 261 (1992).

[5] Adolph A. Berle, *Corporate Powers as Powers in Trust*, 44 HARV. L. REV. 1049 (1931); Adolph A. Berle, *For Whom Corporate Managers Are Trustees: A Note*, 45 HARV. L. REV 1365 (1932); E. Merrick Dodd Jr., *For Whom Are Corporate Managers Trustees?*, 45 HARV. L. REV. 1145 (1932); E. Merrick Dodd Jr., *Is Effective Enforcement of the Fiduciary Duties of Corporate Managers Practicable?*, 2 U. CHI. L. REV. 194 (1935).

[6] This is obviously an overgeneralized summary of these stances, which are far more complex and must be understood in their historical context. For those purposes, see William W. Bratton &

With a nod to Dodd, contemporaneous legislative reforms occurred at the federal level. But they mostly embraced Berle's stance, with the role for independent directors to promote investor interests, not broader public ones. The political role of independent directors thus appears at this early stage, reflecting how the new federal securities laws were "a pragmatic compromise between proponents of direct federal control over corporations through chartering [and] those who sought to leave all regulation of corporations to the states."[7]

This model was tested again during the turmoil from the mid-1960s to the late 1970s. Investigations into the Watergate scandal revealed that U.S. corporations made extensive and illicit bribes to foreign officials – without accurately accounting for them.[8] Flurries of SEC consent orders mandated corporate governance reforms, with an emphasis on installing independent directors.[9] This began a custom, which continues today, of responding to corporate crises by looking to independent directors. Then, Congress banned such bribes and mandated systems of internal control and the maintenance of books and records to promote faithful financial reporting.[10]

The period's lack of directorial oversight is understandable, however, for Delaware courts had told directors a decade earlier (in 1963) that they had no duty to maintain internal control or to discover misreporting within corporations whose boards they occupied.[11] Joining Congress in the wake of the bribery scandals, Delaware courts began a decades-long process of rewarding the use of independent directors. In opinions arising out of related derivative litigation, they accorded special deference to decisions of independent directors serving on special litigation committees and made this role pivotal to the law of demand futility in derivative litigation.[12]

Michael L. Wachter, *Shareholder Primacy's Corporatist Origins: Adolf Berle and "The Modern Corporation"* (Univ. of Penn. Inst. for Law & Econ., Research Paper No. 07-24, 2007), *available at* http://ssrn.com/abstract=1021273.

[7] *See* Roberta S. Karmel, *The Independent Corporate Board: A Means to What End?*, 52 GEO. WASH. L. REV. 534 (1984).

[8] *See, e.g.*, SEC v. ITT Corp., [1979 Transfer Binder] Fed. Sec. L. Rep. (CCH) ¶ 96,948 (D.D.C. Aug. 8, 1979); SEC v. Lockheed, [1975–76 Transfer Binder] Fed. Sec. L. Rep. (CCH) ¶ 95,509 (D.D.C. Apr. 13, 1976).

[9] *See* Arthur F. Mathews, *Recent Trends in SEC Requested Ancillary Relief in SEC Level Injunctive Actions*, 31 BUS. LAW. 1323 (1976); Lewis D. Solomon, *Restructuring the Corporate Board of Directors: Fond Hope, Faint Promise?*, 76 MICH. L. REV. 581 (1978).

[10] Foreign Corrupt Practices Act, 15 U.S.C. § 78m(b)(2); *see* SEC v. World-Wide Coin Invs., Ltd., 567 F. Supp. 724 (N.D. Ga. 1983).

[11] Graham v. Allis-Chalmers Mfg. Co., 188 A.2d 125 (Del. 1963).

[12] Zapata v. Maldanado, 430 A.2d 779 (Del. 1981); *see also* Auerbach v. Bennett, 393 N.E.2d 994 (N.Y. 1979).

Amid a campaign for corporate social responsibility led by Ralph Nader and Joel Seligman,[13] Melvin Eisenberg[14] focused inquiry on variation between state law, which indicated that boards were to manage the corporation, and practice, which showed that they did no such thing.[15] A brilliant political compromise resulted in the demise of the advisory board model – seen as non-functional – and its replacement with the monitoring board and a heightened emphasis on independence and subordination of expertise. Yet no consensus existed concerning exactly what independent directors were to do[16] – or how independence was to be defined.[17]

The 1980s takeover boom gave independent directors a specific role. Delaware courts, continuing a pattern dating at least to the bribery scandal litigation, strengthened the appeal of independent directors by increasingly deferring to their decisions.[18] Using independent directors insulated from judicial review a variety of recurring classes of cases, including: self-interested transactions,[19] cash-out mergers,[20] adoption of poison pills,[21] resisting hostile takeover threats[22] and simply "saying no" to hostile takeover bids.[23] Delaware law eschewed the question of director expertise, although the New Jersey Supreme Court famously announced that the duty of care requires directors to examine and understand a corporation's financial statements.[24]

By the 1990s, director independence was heralded to solve virtually all corporate governance challenges.[25] The construct became a routine policy tool,

[13] See RALPH NADER ET AL., TAMING THE GIANT CORPORATION 123–28 (1976).
[14] MELVIN A. EISENBERG, THE STRUCTURE OF THE CORPORATION: A LEGAL ANALYSIS (1976).
[15] See MYLES MACE, DIRECTORS: MYTH AND REALITY (1971); William O. Douglas, *Directors Who Do Not Direct*, 47 HARV. L. REV. 1305 (1934); Myles L. Mace, *Directors: Myth and Reality – Ten Years Later*, 32 RUTGERS L. REV. 293 (1979).
[16] The monitoring model and its independent directors arrived with critics, including well-chronicled debates within the American Law Institute (ALI) and between the ALI and the Business Roundtable and the American Bar Association. For a thorough analytical review of this history, see Jeffrey N. Gordon, *The Rise of Independent Directors in the United States, 1950–2005: Of Shareholder Value and Stock Market Prices*, 59 STAN. L. REV. 1465 (2007).
[17] See Donald C. Clarke, *Three Models of the Independent Director*, 32 DEL. J. CORP. L. 73 (2007).
[18] On the previous pattern, see Lawrence E. Mitchell, "The Trouble with Boards," included in this volume (the principal role of independent directors before the 1970s, and to a lesser extent since, was sanitizing interested director transactions and providing insulation from liability).
[19] Marciano v. Nakash, 535 A.2d 400 (Del. 1987); see also Fliegler v. Lawrence, 361 A.2d 218 (Del. 1976).
[20] Weinberger v. UOP, Inc., 457 A.2d 701 (Del. 1983).
[21] Moran v. Household Int'l, Inc., 500 A.2d 1346 (Del. 1985).
[22] Unocal Corp. v. Mesa Petroleum, Inc., 493 A.2d 946 (Del. 1985).
[23] Paramount Commc'ns, Inc. v. Time, Inc., 571 A.2d 1140 (Del. 1990).
[24] Francis v. United Jersey Bank, 432 A.2d 814 (N.J. 1981).
[25] See Richard A. Epstein, *In Defense of the Corporation*, 2004 NZ L. REV. 707, 719 (2004).

used in numerous contexts.[26] Independence was to promote optimal compensation and recruiting despite directors lacking expertise in the relevant subjects. Some promoted "perspective and diversity" on boards,[27] which may be seen as a kind of expertise, such as sensitivity to the interests of other constituencies, although it remained true that no expertise was sought on behalf of traditional shareholder constituencies. State courts made using independent directors irresistible to corporations, giving deference to decisions that were widely condemned and hard to defend so long as made by independent directors.[28]

These ambitions continued in response to the parade of accounting scandals that erupted in the early 2000s at numerous companies – epitomized by revelation at Enron Corp., nominally the seventh-largest U.S. corporation – that were elaborate frauds. In their immediate aftermath, politically astute corporate leaders sought to avert regulation by advocating reforms that concentrated on increasingly using independent directors.[29] While this effort failed, when Congress intervened by passing SOX, it continued the habit of celebrating director independence. Despite continuing resort to independent directors for political purposes or in response to crisis, there has never been much evidence of related benefits.[30]

B. Economics

At Enron and firms that committed other frauds of the early 2000s, boards were endowed with abundant independence, yet they failed miserably. This is unsurprising considering a comprehensive 1999 survey of empirical studies that found little correlation between independence and corporate performance.[31] In fact, as two recent updated reviews of this literature attest, the considerable

---

[26] These included concerning (1) compensation disclosure (1992), (2) tax deductibility of certain compensation expenses (1994), and (3) application of short-swing profit rules (1996).

[27] *See* Martin Lipton & Jay W. Lorsch, *A Modest Proposal for Improved Corporate Governance,* 48 Bus. Law. 59, 67–68 (1992).

[28] *See, e.g.,* Brehm v. Eisner, 746 A.2d 244 (Del. 2000); *In re* The Walt Disney Co. Derivative Litig., 907 A.2d 693 (Del. Ch. 2005).

[29] *See* Stephen M. Bainbridge, *A Critique of the NYSE's Director Independence Listing Standards,* 30 Sec. Reg. L.J. 370 (2002).

[30] See Laura Lin, *The Effectiveness of Outside Directors as a Corporate Governance Mechanism: Theories and Evidence,* 90 Nw. U. L. Rev. 898 (1996).

[31] Sanjai Bhagat & Bernard Black, *The Non-Correlation Between Board Independence and Long-Term Firm Performance,* 27 J. Corp. L. 231 (2002); Sanjai Bhagat & Bernard Black, *The Uncertain Relationship Between Board Composition and Firm Performance,* 54 Bus. Law. 921 (1999).

evidence shows at best weak correlation between board independence and corporate performance.[32]

Evidence is slightly stronger of correlations between director independence and specific tasks. Some evidence suggests that independence associates with prudent cash management and facilitating or resisting changes in corporate control. Independent directors may be better at firing subpar managers, although evidence is slight and scattered.

There is little or no evidence that independent directors achieve greater gains for takeover targets or adopt different defensive profiles from those of other directors. Evidence conflicts on whether firms with independent boards are less likely to make value reducing takeover bids; any effect that appears is small. Research does not show any particular effects of independence on CEO compensation. Evidence does show a relation between board and audit committee independence – and expertise – and various measures of financial reporting quality (but that gets ahead of the story and will be discussed in the next section of this chapter).

While scholars generally construe the empirical evidence as not supporting claims that independent directors improve firm performance, that conclusion is not inevitable. Professor Jeffrey Gordon reinterprets the empirical relations by explaining the data on other grounds.[33] This reinterpretation emphasizes diminishing returns to independence, because the data all look at changes in independence levels during periods after the construct had achieved normative status. The more important effects may be systemic, not unique to individual enterprises, and include more accurate stock prices and fuller financial disclosure that benefit all enterprises, according to Professor Gordon.

Another basis for reinterpreting the studies that examine corporate performance is how independent directors may contribute other skills, such as promoting compliance or advancing social interests. This view seems plausible given how some original proponents of the monitoring board sought to promote compliance amid the bribery scandals and how some current champions continue to seek compliance, especially with financial reporting requirements.[34] These purposes may not translate into measurable

---

[32] The comprehensive reviews are Gordon, *supra* note 16, and Robert A. Prentice & David B. Spence, *Sarbanes-Oxley as Quack Corporate Governance: How Wise Is the Received Wisdom?*, 95 Geo. L.J. 1843 (2006). Readers are referred to these works for citations to the research summarized in the following paragraphs.

[33] Gordon, *supra* note 16.

[34] *See* Prentice & Spence, *supra* note 32, at 1868.

improvements in corporate performance (indeed, Professor Daniel Fischel warned of, and some proponents advocated, the opposite).[35]

On the other hand, this reinterpretation fits uneasily alongside studies showing weak correlations between independence and specific tasks, suggesting yet other possibilities: that nominal independence was subverted by managerial control over the appointments process[36] or that nominal independence transforms into structural bias once an outsider joins a board.[37] In any event, the independent director remains a powerful norm, despite initial and continuing disagreement about its purposes or effects. However, there is an emerging appeal for expertise that promises to alter conventional attitudes toward boards in corporate governance.[38]

II. THE EMERGING APPEAL FOR EXPERTISE

The fascination for independent directors that arose in the 1970s brought increased attention to board committees, especially audit, compensation, and nominating committees.[39] This attention implicitly recognized the value of division of labor on a board of directors. Yet there was little discussion of the qualifications that would be put to use by these committees. Instead, the motivation was to put certain kinds of decisions in the hands of independent directors, whether they had expertise or not.

A changing of the guard is afoot, with expertise becoming at least as important as independence in corporate governance. That change was led by stock exchanges in the late 1990s and reinforced with SOX's encouragement of expertise on audit committees in 2002. In the years since SOX, the percentage of accountants on board audit committees increased significantly.[40]

---

[35] *See* Daniel J. Fischel, *The Corporate Governance Movement*, 35 VAND. L. REV. 1259 (1982).

[36] *See* William W. Bratton & Joseph A. McCahery, *Regulatory Competition, Regulatory Capture, and Corporate Self-Regulation*, 73 N.C. L. REV. 1861, 1867–68 (1995).

[37] *See* James D. Cox & Donald E. Schwartz, *The Business Judgment Rule in the Context of Termination of Derivative Suits by Independent Committees*, 61 N.C. L. REV. 541, 542–43 (1983).

[38] Previous efforts to overcome the independence obsession have called for accountability, although that is not the same as the call for expertise. *E.g.*, Ronald J. Gilson & Reinier Kraakman, *Reinventing the Outside Director: An Agenda for Institutional Investors*, 43 STAN. L. REV. 863, 865 (1991).

[39] *See* ABA Comm. on Corporate Laws, *Corporate Director's Guidebook*, 33 BUS. LAW. 1591, 1619–20 (1978); Business Roundtable, Statement, *The Role and Composition of the Board of Directors of the Large Publicly Owned Corporation*, 33 BUS. LAW. 2083, 2108–10 (1978).

[40] *See* Stephen Taub, *Audit Committees Embracing Accountants*, CFO MAG., Sept. 20, 2007 (referring to a report from Huron Consulting Group), *available at* http://www.cfo.com/article.cfm/9853512?f=search.

A. Audit Committees

It has long been recognized that the audit committee is the most important board committee.[41] Proposals for mandatory audit committees date to the late 1930s and early 1940s.[42] Interest resumed in the late 1960s and gathered momentum through the 1970s.[43] In the 1970s, the SEC encouraged the use of independent directors on audit committees;[44] adopted rules requiring companies to disclose whether or not they had an audit committee;[45] and published guidelines addressing audit committee attributes.[46] As a result, audit committee use expanded dramatically from the mid-1960s, when they were relatively rare, to the mid-1970s, when they became commonplace.[47]

In 1977, the New York Stock Exchange adopted a listing requirement mandating independent directors on audit committees.[48] The provision offered a capacious conception of independence. It allowed persons to have "customary" commercial and professional relationships with the company, so long as this did not otherwise pose a threat to independent judgment. This formulation may strike contemporary students as nearly empty given current sensibilities about independence. But at the time, the provision was a significant change, and the "customary relationships" exception was not seen to nullify

---

[41] See PRICEWATERHOUSECOOPERS, WHAT DIRECTORS THINK ANNUAL SURVEY (2005).

[42] See In re McKesson & Robbins, Inc., Exchange Act Release No. 2707, [1940 Transfer Binder] Fed. Sec. L. Rep. (CCH) ¶ 72,020 (Dec. 5, 1940); Edward F. Greene & Bernard B. Falk, *The Audit Committee: A Measured Contribution to Corporate Governance [and] A Realistic Appraisal of Its Objectives and Functions*, 34 BUS. LAW. 1229, 1233 n.16 (1979) (noting 1939 NYSE proposal).

[43] See Greene & Falk, *supra* note 42, at 1233 & 1234 n.16 (noting 1967 proposal made by the AICPA); Subcomm. on Oversight & Investigations of the H. Comm. on Interstate and Foreign Commerce, 94th Cong., Report on Federal Regulation and Regulatory Reform 29–42 (Subcomm. Print 1976).

[44] See SEC, *Standing Audit Committees Composed of Outside Directors*, [1971–1972 Transfer Binder] Fed. Sec. L. Rep. (CCH) ¶ 78,670, at 81,424 (No. 9548, Mar. 23, 1972).

[45] Item 8(e), Schedule 14A, 17 C.F.R. § 240.14a-101 (1978).

[46] SEC, Notice of Amendments to Require Increased Disclosure of Relationships Between Registrants and Their Independent Public Accountants, 40 Fed. Reg. 1010 (1974), reprinted in [Accounting Series Release Transfer Binder] Fed. Sec. L. Rep. (CCH) ¶ 72,187, at 62,394 (No. 11147, Dec. 20, 1974); Proposed Rules Relating to Shareholder Communications, Shareholder Participation in the Corporate Electoral Process and Corporate Governance Generally, Exchange Act Release No. 14,970, 15 SEC Docket (CCH) 291 (July 18, 1978).

[47] See Gordon, *supra* note 16, at n.211 (citing evidence that in 1967 from one-third to one-fifth of companies boasted audit committees, whereas by 1977 nearly all did).

[48] Proposed Rule Change by Self-Regulatory Organizations, 42 Fed. Reg. 8737 (Feb. 11, 1977); Securities Exchange Act Release No. 13,346 (Mar. 9, 1977), 11 SEC Docket (CCH) 1945, 1946 (1977); Order Approving Proposed Rule Change, 42 Fed. Reg. 14,793 (Mar. 16, 1977).

the innovation.[49] The other exchanges followed the NYSE's lead during the 1980s.[50]

A series of audit failures in the early 1980s sparked interest in accounting aspects of corporate governance. In 1987, the American Institute of Certified Public Accountants (AICPA) and others sponsored the National Commission on Fraudulent Financial Practices. In addition to founding the Committee of Sponsoring Organizations of the Treadway Commission (COSO) – which became the chief architect of corporate internal controls[51] – it produced the Report of the National Commission on Fraudulent Financial Reporting.[52] This Commission, named for Chairman James Treadway, recommended that boards be required to have independent audit committees and suggested the high value of accounting expertise for audit committee members. No official action was taken on the recommendations as the late 1980s turned into the roaring 1990s.

In 1994, the Public Oversight Board of the SEC Practice Section of the AICPA formed an advisory panel to give auditing a central role in corporate governance and return auditing to an important place in society.[53] It urged that audit committees be informed as to the appropriateness of a company's accounting principles and the degree of conservatism in their application.[54] This demand for information is a precursor to ensuing calls for actual knowledge – expertise – on audit committees.

Those calls began in the late 1990s, when SEC Chairman Arthur Levitt launched a campaign to improve corporate governance by emphasizing expertise, not mere independence.[55] He urged companies to recruit more audit committee members with financial experience. A group he impaneled echoed the point, urging that audit committees have at least three financially literate members and one with financial management experience.[56] The NYSE and Nasdaq adopted these recommendations under rules, still in effect, requiring

[49] *See* Karmel, *supra* note 7, at 536 (citing Securities Exchange Act Release No. 13,346 (Mar. 9, 1977), 11 SEC Docket (CCH) 1945, 1946 (1977)).

[50] *See* Karmel, *supra* note 7, text at nn.69–70.   [51] *See* http://www.coso.org.

[52] REPORT OF THE NATIONAL COMMISSION ON FRAUDULENT FINANCIAL REPORTING (1987), *available at* http://www.coso.org/Publications/NCFFR.pdf.

[53] *See* http://www.publicoversightboard.org/about.htm.

[54] *See* Public Oversight Board of the SEC Practice Section of the AICPA Rep. (1994).

[55] *See* Arthur Levitt, Chairman, SEC, Remarks at the New York University Center for Law and Business (Sept. 28, 1998), *available at* www.sec.gov/news/speeches/spch220.txt.

[56] *See* Ira M. Millstein, *Introduction to the Report and Recommendations of the Blue Ribbon Committee on Improving the Effectiveness of Corporate Audit Committees*, 54 BUS. LAW. 1057 (1999). The group also followed the tradition of boosting independence, including by recommending eliminating the allowance of the "customary relationships" loophole appearing in previous definitions.

all audit committee members to be financially literate and show financial sophistication, demonstrated by oversight responsibilities, past experience, or professional certification.[57]

Sarbanes-Oxley reformed structural features as well as highlighted abstract independence and substantive expertise. Previously, power over the audit function was lodged with outside auditors and internal management, with limited audit committee oversight.[58] Managers hired, fired, and paid auditors, so auditors were beholden to them – not to the committee. An independent and expert committee under those circumstances might be worth little. However, SOX puts the committee in charge and vests it with important powers.[59] This alters the monitoring model, equipping independent – and now expert – directors with power they never had before.[60]

Moreover, SOX injects expertise into the audit committee indirectly. It requires companies to disclose whether the audit committee boasts expertise or not (and if not, why not). Even so, this gesture toward expertise is a dramatic change from the traditional habit of simply adding formal independence (although SOX indulges that habit too, as noted).[61] SOX conceives of the required audit committee expertise in explicit, focused terms, measuring expertise by formal training and experience in accounting.[62] But SOX also directed and deferred to the SEC to define the requisite expertise in implementing the statute.

In its first proposed definition, the SEC followed SOX's language to draw expertise narrowly, emphasizing knowledge of accounting through extensive

[57] NYSE, Inc., Listed Company Manual §§ 303.01(B)(2)(a) and 303.01(B)(2)(b)-(c) (2007); NASD By-Laws, art. 9, § 5; NASD Marketplace Rules, § 4350(d)(1)-(2). NYSE listing rules also currently require compensation and nominating committees, both with independent directors, but are silent as to desired expertise. NYSE, Inc., Listed Company Manual § 303A.04-.05 (2007).
[58] On the problems embedded in the old relationship, see Melvin A. Eisenberg, *Legal Models of Management Structure in the Modern Corporation: Officers, Directors and Accountants*, 63 CAL. L. REV. 375 (1975).
[59] Sarbanes-Oxley Act of 2002 § 301, 15 U.S.C. § 78j-1(m)(2) (2007); *see* Strengthening the Commission's Requirements Regarding Auditor Independence, Exchange Act Release No. 47,265, 79 SEC Docket (CCH) 1284 (Jan. 28, 2003).
[60] William W. Bratton, *Enron, Sarbanes-Oxley and Accounting: Rules versus Principles versus Rents*, 48 VILL. L. REV. 1023, 1034–36 (2003).
[61] Sarbanes-Oxley Act of 2002 § 301, 15 U.S.C. § 78j-1(m)(2) (2007) ("to be considered to be independent for purposes of this paragraph, a member of an audit committee of an issuer may not, other than in his or her capacity as a member of the audit committee, the board of directors, or any other board committee (i) accept any consulting, advisory, or other compensatory fee from the issuer; or (ii) be an affiliated person of the issuer or any subsidiary thereof").
[62] Sarbanes-Oxley Act of 2002 § 407, codified at 15 U.S.C. § 7265 (2007).

experience in the field.[63] This conception is now described in the literature as an accounting financial expert – only professional accountants qualified. Critics objected to the narrow definition. Some claimed that, under it, financial heavyweights like Warren Buffett and Alan Greenspan would not qualify as experts; others said it would be hard to attract people who met the narrow definition and that the narrow skills would absorb limited resources needed to recruit other persons with other desirable skill sets.[64]

In response to objections, the SEC broadened the definition beyond accounting experience to include experience in finance, financial statement analysis or evaluation, and even supervision of accounting and financial executives or personnel.[65] The revised definition resembles the definitions of expertise adopted a decade earlier by the NYSE and Nasdaq. No longer limited to professional accountants, nearly anyone in business qualifies – managers of other companies, investment bankers, commercial bankers, and venture capitalists. Reflecting this broad definition, three categories of audit committee experts are now described in the literature: accounting experts, nonaccounting financial experts, and nonfinancial experts.

B. Evidence

Empirical evidence on the correlation between director independence and corporate performance reveals weak links, as discussed above.[66] The exception is a well-developed body of evidence demonstrating a strong, positive

---

[63] Disclosure Required by Sections 404, 406, and 407 of the Sarbanes-Oxley Act of 2002, Exchange Act Release No. 34-46701, 78 SEC Docket (CCH) 1907 (Oct. 22, 2002). The SEC's proposed definition of financial expert mimicked SOX's language, saying that SOX requires the SEC, in defining financial expert:

> [T]o consider whether a person has, through education and experience as a public accountant or auditor or a principal financial officer, or controller, or principal accounting officer of an issuer, or from a position involving the performance of similar functions: (1) an understanding of [GAAP] and financial statements; (2) experience in (a) the preparation or auditing of financial statements of generally comparable issuers and (b) the application of such principles in connection with the accounting for estimates, accruals and reserves; (3) experience with internal accounting controls; and (4) an understanding of the audit committee functions.

Id.

[64] *See* C. Bryan-Low, *Defining Moment for SEC: Who's a Financial Expert?*, WALL ST. J., Dec. 9, 2002, at C1.

[65] Disclosure Required by Sections 406 and 407 of the Sarbanes-Oxley Act of 2002, Exchange Act Release No. 47,235, 79 SEC Docket (CCH) 1077 (Jan. 23, 2003) (coining the designation "audit committee financial expert").

[66] *See supra* text accompanying notes 31–38.

correlation between director independence and financial reporting quality (measured in various ways, as discussed below).[67] Researchers and theorists struggled to interpret this exception and soon ascertained that it operates through audit committees.[68] Increasingly, evidence shows that this correlation strengthens significantly when accounting experts serve on audit committees (and strengthens incrementally when audit committee members have other expertise encompassed in the SEC's expansive, criticism-induced definition).

Research has long examined the correlation between board-level independence and various proxies for financial reporting quality. Evidence shows a strong, negative correlation between relative board independence and accounting fraud.[69] A similar pattern appears in relation to the probability of financial misreporting, with pending SEC enforcement actions and shareholder lawsuits serving as a proxy.[70] These results are corroborated in tests that use other proxies of financial statement reliability, including the presence of abnormal accruals and other signs of earnings management.[71] Similar results were obtained when the independence of audit committees was examined

---

[67] *See* Prentice & Spence, *supra* note 32, at 1869 (explaining that "the vast bulk of existing empirical studies indicates that more board independence does translate into more accurate financial reporting"); *id.* at 1869 ("[M]ost evidence supports the... conclusion that more independence means less financial monkey business.").

[68] *See* Gordon, *supra* note 16, at 1504 (explaining that the "best-developed evidence" is a "positive association between board independence and financial reporting accuracy" [and why it occurs is not certain], but "some studies suggest it could be through the independent audit committee").

[69] Mark S. Beasley, *An Empirical Analysis of the Relation Between the Board of Director Composition and Financial Statement Fraud*, 71 ACCT. REV. 443, 455 (1996) (negative association between accounting fraud and relative board independence); *see also* Mark S. Beasley et al., *Fraudulent Financial Reporting: Consideration of Industry Traits and Corporate Governance Mechanisms*, 14 ACCT. HORIZONS 441, 452 (2000) (negative association between independence and fraud in several industries); Hatice Uzun et al., *Board Composition and Corporate Fraud*, FIN. ANALYSTS J., May-June 2004, at 33 (similar relationship using broader proxy for fraud).

[70] Patricia M. Dechow et al., *Causes and Consequences of Earnings Manipulation: An Analysis of Firms Subject to Enforcement Actions by the SEC*, 13 CONTEMP. ACCT. RES. 1, 21 (1996) (comparing firms with high likelihood of accounting fraud, as signaled by SEC enforcement action, with a control group of firms); David W. Wright, *Evidence on the Relation Between Corporate Governance Characteristics and the Quality of Financial Reporting* (Stephen M. Ross Sch. of Business at the Univ. of Mich., Working Paper, 1996), *available at* www.ssrn.com/abstract=10138 (firms facing SEC enforcement actions sport less audit committee independence compared to sample of industry or size cohort); Eric Helland & Michael E. Sykuta, *Who's Monitoring the Monitor? Do Outside Directors Protect Shareholders' Interests?*, 40 FIN. REV. 155, 171 (2005) (association between independence and fewer shareholder lawsuits).

[71] April Klein, *Audit Committee, Board of Director Characteristics, and Earnings Management*, 33 J. ACCT. & ECON. 375, 387 (2002) (negative association between board independence and abnormal accruals); Sarah E. McVay et al., *Trading Incentives to Meet the Analyst Forecast*, 11 REV. ACCT. STUD. 575, 575 (2006) (earnings management "is weaker in the presence of an independent board").

discretely, finding that independence is associated with lower levels of earnings manipulation or accounting fraud.[72]

The idea that audit committee expertise might contribute to more accurate financial reporting is intuitive.[73] This intuition was the basis for early interest in promoting expertise, including the Treadway Commission's recommendations.[74] Experimental studies show the relativity of expertise, ranging from the command of rudimentary knowledge ("literacy") to experiential knowledge derived from extensive applications in practice ("actual expertise").[75] Also intuitively, neither independence nor expertise contributes to results unless those commanding such traits have power to implement recommendations (a result that SOX's structural audit committee reforms make promising).[76]

Empirical evidence supports these intuitions. Extensive research investigates the correlation between various conceptions of audit committee expertise and related proxies for financial reporting quality (sometimes thought of as audit committee effectiveness). Studies show an inverse relationship between

---

[72] Jeffrey Cohen et al., *The Corporate Governance Mosaic and Financial Reporting Quality*, 23 J. ACCT. LIT. 87, 99–102 (2004) (surveying studies of relationship between governance characteristics, especially of audit committee independence, and earnings manipulation or fraud); *compare* Klein, *supra* note 71 (association between abnormal accruals and independent directors but "no meaningful relation between abnormal accruals and having an audit committee comprised solely of independent directors").

[73] *E.g.*, Todd DeZoort, *An Investigation of Audit Committees' Oversight Responsibilities*, 33 ABACUS 208 (1997); Dorothy A. McMullen & Kannan Raghunandan, *Enhancing Audit Committee Effectiveness*, J. ACCOUNTANCY 182 (1996) (companies with deficient financial reporting less likely to have CPAs on audit committee); Kannan Raghunandan et al., *Audit Committee Composition, "Gray Directors," and Interaction with Internal Auditing*, 15 ACCT. HORIZONS 105 (2001); F. Kannan Raghunandan & William J. Read, *The State of Audit Committees*, 191 J. ACCOUNTANCY 57 (2001); Stephen A. Scarpati, *CPAs as Audit Committee Members*, 196 J. ACCOUNTANCY 32 (2003).

[74] *See* I. Bull & Florence C. Sharp, *Advising Clients on Treadway Audit Committee Recommendations*, 167 J. ACCOUNTANCY 46 (1989).

[75] *See* Linda S. McDaniel et al., *Evaluating Financial Reporting Quality: The Effects of Financial Expertise vs. Financial Literacy*, 77 ACCT. REV. 139 (Supp. 2002) (experimental research using audit managers as "experts" and executive MBA graduates as "literates" and finding that experts are better than literates at evaluating financial reporting quality).

[76] *See* Lawrence P. Kalbers & Timothy J. Fogarty, *Audit Committee Effectiveness: An Empirical Investigation of the Contribution of Power*, 12 AUDITING: J. PRAC. & THEORY 24 (1993) (examining relation between audit committee power and effectiveness, finding that "expert power" is highly associated with financial reporting effectiveness). The internal control apparatus within an enterprise also has a bearing on the effectiveness of both corporate governance and financial reporting. *See* Robert A. Prentice, *Sarbanes-Oxley: The Evidence Regarding Section 404*, 29 CARDOZO L. REV. (2007), *available at* www.ssrn.com/abstract=991295 (reviewing empirical studies concentrating on the association between internal control aspects of Sarbanes-Oxley and various proxies for corporate governance and reporting effectiveness).

expertise and likelihood of financial reporting irregularities,[77] artificial earnings management,[78] fraud,[79] and restatements.[80] Various degrees of expertise also are associated with higher financial statement quality,[81] more conservative accounting,[82] and a propensity to provide or update managerial forecasts containing adverse rather than favorable news.[83] Studies show that greater expertise is associated with less-frequent suspicious auditor switching[84] and a lower likelihood of material weaknesses in internal controls.[85]

Recent research examines more closely various conceptions of audit committee expertise. This is motivated by debates concerning how to define expertise, especially by comparing the SEC's initial and revised definitions of expertise for audit committees.[86] Evidence is strong that there is a correlation between accounting expertise and high-quality financial statements and audit committee effectiveness.[87] There is also some (but limited) evidence of

[77] See Dorothy A. McMullen & Kannan Raghunandan, *Enhancing Audit Committee Effectiveness*, 182 J. ACCOUNTANCY 79 (1996).

[78] See Biao Xie et al., *Earnings Management and Corporate Governance: The Role of the Board and the Audit Committee*, 9 J. CORP. FIN. 295 (2003).

[79] See Anup Agrawal & Sahiba Chadha, *Corporate Governance and Accounting Scandals*, 48 J. L. & ECON. 371 (2005).

[80] See Lawrence J. Abbott et al., *Audit Committee Characteristics and Restatements*, 23 AUDITING: J. PRAC. THEORY 69 (2004).

[81] See Andrew J. Felo et al., *Audit Committee Characteristics and the Perceived Quality of Financial Reporting: An Empirical Analysis* (Working Paper, 2003), *available at* http://papers.ssrn.com/sol3/papers.cfm?abstract_id=401240.

[82] See Gopal V. Krishnan & Gnanakumar Visvanathan, *Does the SOX Definition of an Accounting Expert Matter? The Association Between Audit Committee Director's Expertise and Conservatism* (Working Paper, 2007), *available at* http://www.ssrn.com/abstract=866884.

[83] See L. Karamanou & Nicos Vafeas, *The Association Between Corporate Boards, Audit Committees, and Management Earnings Forecasts: An Empirical Analysis*, 43 J. ACCT. RES. 453 (2005) (propensity to update forecasts for bad news more likely when audit committee boasts expertise).

[84] See Deborah Archambeault & F. Todd DeZoort, *Auditor Opinion Shopping and the Audit Committee: An Analysis of Suspicious Auditor Switches*, 5 INT'L J. ACCT. 33 (2001).

[85] See Yan Zhang et al., *Audit Committee Quality, Auditor Independence and Internal Control Weaknesses*, J. ACCT. & PUBLIC POLICY (2006) (SOX internal control weakness more likely for firms with audit committees boasting less accounting financial expertise).

[86] As discussed above, SOX and the SEC first floated a narrow definition of expertise limited to accounting expertise, but the SEC, under pressure, expanded it to include other kinds of financial expertise (nonaccounting financial expertise) as well as expertise in supervising accountants and other financial experts (nonfinancial expertise).

[87] See, e.g., Dan Dhaliwal et al., *The Association Between Audit Committee Accounting Expertise, Corporate Governance and Accruals Quality: An Empirical Analysis* (Working Paper, 2006), *available at* http://papers.ssrn.com/sol3/papers.cfm?abstract_id=906690; Joseph V. Carcello et al., *Audit Committee Financial Expertise, Competing Corporate Governance Mechanisms, and Earnings Management* (Working Paper, 2006), *available at* http://papers.ssrn.com/sol3/papers.cfm?abstract_id=887512.

a correlation between nonaccounting financial expertise and those virtues.[88] Evidence is strong that there is no particular correlation between nonfinancial expertise and various measures of financial statement reliability or general audit committee effectiveness.[89]

Some of this research emphasizes normative implications. Several studies expressly support the SEC's original narrow definition of expertise as opposed to the broader definition it later adopted under pressure. Classifying audit committee members as boasting accounting, nonaccounting financial, and other nonfinancial expertise, one study finds a significant, positive correlation between accounting expertise and accruals quality but no such correlation with the other two kinds of expertise.[90] The prescription is to favor SOX's and the SEC's first narrow definition – recognizing that other committee features can influence effectiveness, too.[91] Using similar definitions, another study likewise finds a correlation between accounting expertise and accounting conservatism but no correlation between other expertise and that quality – also expressly supporting SOX's and the SEC's original narrow definition.[92]

Another study stating normative implications finds the strongest correlation is with accounting expertise, following similar definitional classifications.[93] Accounting expertise and some nonaccounting financial expertise are

---

[88] *See, e.g.,* Jean Bedard et al., *The Effect of Audit Committee Expertise, Independence and Activity on Aggressive Earnings Management,* 23 AUDITING: J. PRAC. & THEORY 13 (2004); Lawrence J. Abbott et al., *Audit Committee Characteristics and Financial Misstatement: A Study of the Efficacy of Certain Blue Ribbon Committee Recommendations* (Working Paper, 2002), *available at* http://ssrn.com/abstract=319125.

[89] *See, e.g.,* Joseph V. Carcello & Terry L. Neal, *Audit Committee Characteristics and Auditor Dismissals Following "New" Going Concern Reports,* 78 ACCT. REV. 95 (2003); Robert C. Anderson et al., *Board Characteristics, Accounting Report Integrity and the Cost of Debt,* 37 J. ACCT. & ECON. 315 (2004).

[90] Dhaliwal et al., *supra* note 87. Following an emerging standardization of these classifications in the empirical literature, the study delimits them as follows: accounting expertise is current or past experience as CPA, CFO, comptroller, VP finance, or "any other major accounting positions"; finance expertise is current or past experience as investment banker, financial analyst, or "any other financial management roles"; and supervisory expertise is current or past experience as CEO or company president or the like. Dhaliwal et al., *supra* note 87.

[91] Notably, the Dhaliwal, Naiker, and Navissi study also finds significant positive interaction between audit committee accounting expertise and attributes that signal strong audit committee governance (namely independence, a relatively larger size, and more frequent meetings). Dhaliwal et al., *supra* note 87.

[92] Gopal V. Krishnan & Gnanakumar Visvanathan, *Does the SOX Definition of an Accounting Expert Matter? The Association Between Audit Committee Director's Expertise and Conservatism* (Working Paper, 2007), *available at* http://www.ssrn.com/abstract=866884.

[93] Joseph V. Carcello et al., *Audit Committee Financial Expertise, Competing Corporate Governance Mechanisms, and Earnings Management* (Working Paper, 2006), *available at* http://papers.ssrn.com/sol3/papers.cfm?abstract_id=887512.

associated with lesser earnings management for firms with weak alternate
corporate governance mechanisms. But independent audit committee members with financial expertise are most successful in mitigating earnings
management. The researchers emphasize that "alternative corporate governance mechanisms are an effective substitute for audit committee financial
expertise."[94] The normative implication: firms should have flexibility to choose
the governance mechanisms that fit their unique situations, recognizing the
likely value of accounting expertise on audit committees.

Research also considers market reaction to adding various kinds of expertise
to audit committees. A widely cited study found favorable market reactions
to companies naming new audit committee members who boasted accounting expertise, especially when other good governance attributes exist, but no
reaction to nonaccounting expertise.[95] These researchers emphasize that the
findings are consistent with accounting expertise on audit committees improving corporate governance, but only when the expert and the corporation's other
governance attributes empower experts to make a difference.[96] This market-
based study thus is consistent with the other empirical research as well as with
long-standing intuition that accountants will contribute accounting expertise
when empowered to do so.

Given the normative prescriptions of such studies, it is worth noting that
some studies find a correlation between broader conceptions of expertise and
desirable financial reporting traits. For example, one study found a correlation between financial and governance expertise and lower levels of earnings
management and even some correlation between other kinds of firm-specific
expertise and that quality.[97] This study's findings are also generally consistent with the view that independent directors contribute to quality financial
reporting.

In summary, there are many ways to promote financial reporting quality and
audit committee effectiveness, including through independence, accounting
expertise, and possibly other kinds of expertise. This may suggest that legal mandates are neither wise nor necessary.[98] Indeed, despite the empirical evidence

[94] *Id.*
[95] Mark DeFond et al., *Does the Market Value Financial Expertise on Audit Committees of Boards of Directors?*, 43 J. ACCT. RES. 153 (2005).
[96] *Id.*
[97] *See* Jean Bedard et al., *The Effect of Audit Committee Expertise, Independence and Activity on Aggressive Earnings Management*, 23 AUDITING: J. PRAC. & THEORY 13 (2004).
[98] *See* Roberta Romano, *The Sarbanes-Oxley Act and the Making of Quack Corporate Governance*, 114 YALE L. J. 1521 (2005) (making this point in light of the lack of evidence supporting association between independence and firm performance and the mixed evidence on the association between audit committee independence and financial reporting quality although

suggesting that audit committee accounting experts contribute to financial statement quality, there are contrasting scenarios. At Enron, for example, both independent directors and experts on its audit committee failed to catch manifest irregularities.[99] Even so, the evidence suggests that some combinations are stronger and others weaker, with the optimal combining independence and accounting expertise. Yet numerous policy and legal issues arise from the intuition and evidence, to which the next section turns.

III. THE FUTURE ROLE OF EXPERTISE

A normative implication of the empirical evidence on expertise is to encourage – if not mandate – the appointment of accounting experts to audit committees. After all, CEOs – and many other business experts – rarely have knowledge of generally accepted accounting principles (GAAP), generally accepted auditing standards (GAAS), or rules and regulations of the SEC and applicable securities laws.[100]

Objections to a mandatory or even hortatory commitment to board expertise, including on audit committees, concern the considerable burden of expectations that would befall those members. The burden is significant as a practical matter, given lack of specification of what those expectations should be. It is exacerbated by uncertainty as to what legal consequences follow from the fact that a director has expertise. The following sections consider each of these problems in turn.

A. *Specifications*

Rediscovering the value of expertise underscores a significant shift at the basic level of specifying the expertise that boards of directors should wield. Before the SOX era spawned interest in substantive expertise, theorizing about expected expertise was limited. Professor Eugene Fama offered the general theory that independent directors contributed expertise in "decision control."[101] It is possible that decision control is the expertise that all independent directors offer,[102]

not exploring the evidence concerning audit committee expertise and financial reporting quality).

[99] *See* William W. Bratton Jr., *Enron and the Dark Side of Shareholder Value*, 76 Tul. L. Rev. 1275, 1333–38 (2002); Paul M. Healy & Krishna G. Palepu, *Governance and Intermediation Problems in Capital Markets: Evidence from the Fall of Enron* (Harvard NOM Working Paper No. 02–27, 2002), *available at* http://ssrn.com/abstract=325440.

[100] *See* Dennis Beresford, *Take a Seat in the Boardroom*, 200 J. Accountancy 104 (2005).

[101] Fama & Jensen, *supra* note 2.

[102] For criticism, see Lucian Arye Bebchuk et al., *Managerial Power and Rent Extraction in the Design of Executive Compensation*, 69 U. Chi. L. Rev. 751, 771 (2002).

yet that imagines boards as monoliths without attention to particular skills that, under the division of labor, contribute individualized value.

While focusing on expertise associated with quality financial reporting, SOX recognizes that directors, independent and otherwise, each can contribute different expertise. In the future, one should expect increased attention to other kinds of expertise that exploit the division of labor, too, such as in recruiting business leadership through nominating committees that boast not merely independence but also knowledge of relevant labor markets and through designing compensation systems using directors who are not merely independent but also knowledgeable on the subject. Sparked by SOX, the following focuses solely on specifying the expertise that it seems to contemplate in order to highlight both the importance and difficulty of doing so.

First, SOX appears to demand expertise to promote financial reporting quality. True, SOX covers much ground by tinkering with many aspects of corporate governance. But there is no doubt that SOX was inspired by problems with accounting and control systems and sought to respond with tools to improve both.[103] Thus, it emphasizes internal control, adding its most elaborate provisions, sections 103 and 404 concerning maintaining, certifying, and auditing internal control.[104] Many consider the rearrangement of the audit supervision function to be among SOX's most important changes.[105] In short, SOX is about accounting, and so the expertise on audit committees should be accounting expertise – not necessarily the broader conceptions reflected in the SEC's final definition.

The historical catalyst for independent directors and developments in intervening decades also supports this view. During the 1970s, and since SOX, the expertise expected from independent directors appears more in the nature of expertise in internal control systems designed to promote financial reporting quality and compliance with law.[106] The 1970s bribery scandals that led to laws requiring internal control systems and independent directors were logical servants of compliance. In the late 1990s, even a Delaware court, in

---

[103] *See* Sarbanes-Oxley Act of 2002, preamble.
[104] *See* Lawrence A. Cunningham, *Facilitating Auditing's New Early Warning System: Control Disclosure, Auditor Liability and Safe Harbors*, 55 HASTINGS L.J. 1449 (2004).
[105] JOHN C. COFFEE JR., GATEKEEPERS: THE ROLE OF THE PROFESSIONS IN CORPORATE GOVERNANCE 367 (2006); Erica Beecher-Monas, *Corporate Governance in the Wake of Enron: An Examination of the Audit Committee Solution to Corporate Fraud*, 55 ADMIN. L. REV. 357 (2003); Bratton, *supra* note 60, at 1034–36.
[106] *See* Michael P. Dooley, *Two Models of Corporate Governance*, 47 BUS. LAW. 461 (1992); Melvin A. Eisenberg, *The Board of Directors and Internal Control*, 19 CARDOZO L. REV. 237 (1997).

Caremark,[107] questioned the continuing validity of the 1963 *Graham* decision that minimized director responsibilities over internal control.[108]

The demand for accounting expertise is reflected in audit committee charters widely adopted in SOX's wake. A survey of selected charters is revealing. First, there is substantial standardization of these documents across a variety of enterprises.[109] Second, they tend to concentrate on fundamentals of accounting, along with internal controls. A reasonable inference from the objectives stated in these charters is that the implicit expectations can be met only by those with accounting expertise.[110] Meeting the objectives in these charters likely calls for directors who understand not only accounting principles and inherent need for estimates but also (1) the various maneuvers available to massage reported accounting results and (2) the scope of relative conservatism and the consequences of achieving any given level of conservatism.

Despite this plausible claim that SOX and current audit committee members seek to use accounting expertise and internal control to promote financial reporting quality, such statements are broad and conceal trade-offs. Expertise may enable an enterprise to promote quality financial reporting in conformity with GAAP, GAAS, and SEC regulations – including internal control requirements – but these subjects allow for considerable leeway in application. The following explores two examples of the challenges that result: (1) earnings management raises the issue of how involved audit committee accounting experts must be in substantive decisions that managers make in pursuing desired accounting results, and (2) conservatism raises the issue of whose interests audit committee accounting experts should seek to promote.

1. Earnings Management

Managers can deliberately influence reported financial results through manipulation of discretionary accounting estimates and allocations (called accounting earnings management) or though manipulation of discretionary

---

[107] *In re* Caremark Int'l Inc. Derivative Litig., 698 A.2d 959 (Del. Ch. 1996).

[108] *Caremark's* language and subsequent Delaware court applications of it suggest that it poses no real liability threat to directors. *See Stone ex rel. AmSouth Bancorp. v. Ritter*, 911 A.2d 362 (Del. 2006). Delaware law rarely does, yet its admonitions can play a norm-shaping function. *See* Melvin A. Eisenberg, *Corporate Law and Social Norms*, 99 COLUM. L. REV. 1253 (1999); Edward B. Rock, *Saints and Sinners: How Does Delaware Corporate Law Work?*, 44 UCLA L. REV. 1009 (1997); David A. Skeel Jr., *Shaming in Corporate Law*, 149 U. PA. L. REV. 1811 (2001).

[109] *See also* LAWRENCE A. CUNNINGHAM, LAW & ACCOUNTING: CASES AND MATERIALS 612–15 (2005) (presenting illustrative audit committee charter).

[110] *See also* Krishnan & Visvanathan, *supra* note 82, at 13–14 (noting that audit committee charters are standardized, giving examples from Ruby Tuesday and eBay).

expenditures (referred to as real earnings management).[111] Survey evidence indicates that managers engage in real earnings management when necessary to meet targeted or expected accounting results, such as earnings per share.[112] Empirical evidence is strong that accounting expertise on audit committees reduces accounting earnings management.[113] Empirical evidence concerning whether audit committee accounting expertise influences real earnings management is both limited[114] and conflicting, with studies showing both the absence[115] and the presence[116] of a negative correlation.

Whether audit committee experts influence real earnings management may depend, in part, on whether they believe that doing so is their responsibility, because no authority specifies what their purpose is. The SEC, SOX, and the exchanges only suggest or require expert presence without saying anything about its purpose. Authoritative silence on the purpose of expertise leads to two competing views in the literature.

One view sees audit committees as monitors and enforcers, whose presence is solely to assure compliance with what law, accounting, and regulations

---

[111] *See* Sugata Roychowdhury, *Management of Earnings Through the Manipulation of Real Activities That Affect Cash Flow from Operations* (Working Paper, 2005), *available at* http://papers. ssrn.com/sol3/papers.cfm?abstract_id=477941 (providing a model to measure real earnings management; relating levels of actual operating cash flows, discretionary expenditures such as research and development and selling, general and administrative expenses, and production costs to normal levels estimated by industry and company experience; and finding evidence of real earnings management for sample of enterprises from 1987 to 2001). Real earnings management can be achieved through any means that enables the acceleration or delay of recognizing events, thus including decisions concerning investment, inventory, training, and so on.

[112] *See* John R. Graham et al., *The Economic Implications of Corporate Financial Reporting*, 40 J. ACCT. & ECON. 3 (2005); John R. Graham et al., *Value Destruction and Financial Reporting Decisions* (Working Paper 2006) (fall 2003 survey reveals that CFOs think earnings per share are important and are willing to use real earnings management to meet expectations or to smooth, with 80 percent saying they would decrease discretionary spending on research and development, advertising, and maintenance to meet earnings expectations and 55 percent saying they would delay a positive net-present-value investment project to meet earnings expectations), *available at* http://papers.ssrn.com/sol3/papers.cfm?abstract_id=871215.

[113] *See supra* text accompanying notes 77–89.

[114] *See* Krishnan & Visvanathan, *supra* note 82, at 34 ("there is limited evidence on whether audit committees are able to constrain real earnings management").

[115] *See* Carcello et al., *supra* note 93 (finding no negative association between audit committee expertise and real earnings management). This study actually finds a positive association between audit committee expertise and the component of real earnings management involving the level of discretionary expenditures. *Id.* at 5.

[116] *See* Krishnan & Visvanathan, *supra* note 82, at 7 (finding negative association between audit committee accounting expertise and real earnings management); *id.* at 34 (greater audit committee accounting expertise "mitigates tendencies to manipulate earnings through real activities").

require.[117] If so, then accounting earnings management is their bailiwick, but real earnings management is not. Under the other view, audit committee experts are present for the purposes of directing and monitoring the management of the enterprise, including decisions concerning internal resource allocation.[118] That role includes understanding whether resource allocation decisions are driven by substantive business judgments concerning long-term value enhancement or by short-term aspirations or pressures to achieve designated accounting results, such as meeting earnings-per-share expectations.

The latter view seems compelling as a matter of law, logic, and policy. As a matter of law, committee experts are directors, too, and directors are not excused from understanding, reviewing, or even controlling internal firm resource allocations – whatever their specific purpose. As a matter of logic, the distinction between accounting earnings management and real earnings management is ultimately superficial – both are artificial exercises. Most important, as a matter of policy, evidence is strong that the post-SOX reduction in accounting earnings management has increased managerial appetite and resolve to pursue real earnings management.[119] Determining that audit committee accounting experts should police accounting earnings management but not real earnings management would produce a policy backfire.

The backfire would be at least as serious as the problem that accounting earnings management presents, although the problems differ slightly. The problem with accounting earnings management is that investors are misled into suboptimal capital allocation decisions that could result in investment losses. The problem with real earnings management is that managers deliberately commit to suboptimal capital allocation decisions that almost certainly,

---

[117] *See* Carcello et al., *supra* note 93 ("Since real earnings management is within the bounds of GAAP, we argue that it is not in the purview of the audit committee."); *id.* ("Real earnings management . . . is not illegal[,] not a violation of financial reporting rules, and even if discovered would not result in charges of financial fraud or create cause for an earnings restatement. Thus, we argue that it is beyond the scope of the audit committee's responsibility to filter out real earnings management."); *id.* at 29 (real earnings management "is generally not fraudulent and would be well within the accepted province of management's discretion"); *see also* Hillary A. Sale, *Independent Directors as Securities Monitors*, 61 Bus. Law. 1375 (2006).

[118] *See* Krishnan & Visvanathan, *supra* note 82, at 35 (also opining that audit committee member incentives to constrain real earnings management are the same as those for accounting earnings management: knowledge base, job expectations stated in charter, plus litigation and reputation risk).

[119] *See* Carcello et al., *supra* note 93, at 31 (findings suggest that accounting experts "can mitigate earnings management via discretionary accruals" but that managers "react by increasing real earnings management"); Daniel A. Cohen et al., *Trends in Earnings Management in the Pre- and Post-Sarbanes Oxley Periods* (Working Paper, 2005) (finding that post-SOX accounting earnings management has declined but that real earnings management has increased), *available at* http://papers.ssrn.com/sol3/papers.cfm?abstract_id=658782.

although stealthily and indirectly, inflict investment losses on investors.[120] Accordingly, the expectations and duties of audit committee experts should include controlling real earnings management precisely as much as accounting earnings management.[121] At least, specification of expectations is in order.

2. Conservatism

A general definition of conservatism in accounting is a prudential preference, in the face of uncertainty, to understate economic reality rather than overstate it.[122] In practice, this entails the understatement of net assets by more timely recognition of losses compared to gains.[123] These concepts can be unpacked by specifying the circumstances in which such asymmetric recognition can occur.[124]

Strong conservatism would describe a pervasive preference so that no or few circumstances depart from that norm, epitomized in such traditional dicta as the lower of cost or market principle. Weak conservatism would describe a limited preference so that numerous contexts allow departures from that kind of dictum, such as where fair value accounting allows using actual or estimated current fair-market values for designated asset classes (like marketable securities or property, plant, and equipment). Neutral conservatism would designate a median position between the extremes.

Different corporate constituencies have different appetites and demand for relative conservatism.[125] Consider four classes of potential constituents:

---

[120] *See* Carcello et al., *supra* note 93 ("Real earnings management may diminish firm and shareholder value. . . . "); Graham et al., *supra* note 112.

[121] *See* Graham et al., *supra* note 112 (suggesting that boards and audit committees should exercise oversight to prevent managerial decisions that promote real earnings management while destroying corporate and shareholder value).

[122] FIN. ACCT. STNDS. BD., STATEMENT OF FINANCIAL ACCOUNTING CONCEPTS No. 2 ¶¶ 91–95 (1980).

[123] *See* Sudipta Basu, *The Conservatism Principle and the Asymmetric Timeliness of Earnings*, 24 J. ACCT. & ECON. 3 (1997). A variety of definitions of conservatism appear in the literature, including proxying it by the level of verification required to support recognition or measurement of an accounting item. The variety of definitions and the range of emphasis placed on the principle reflect the breadth of discretion in application.

[124] The concept of conservatism also can be tested using a wide variety of proxies. *See* Krishnan & Visvanathan, *supra* note 82, at 16. In addition to asymmetric loss recognition, examples include book-to-market ratio, correlation between cash flows and contemporaneous accruals, and correlation between changes in current earnings and lagged changes in earnings. *See* Anne Beatty et al., *Conservatism and Debt* (Working Paper, 2006).

[125] *See* Donald C. Langevoort, *The Social Construction of Sarbanes-Oxley*, 105 MICH. L. REV 1817, 1839 (2007) ("conservative financial reporting is comforting to creditors, shareholders, and others who see it as a disciplinary or monitoring tool [but with a] corresponding loss in accuracy. . . . [C]onservative GAAP reporting on average understates the true economic value of the firm. . . . How much, if at all, conservative reporting deprives investors of useful

equity investors; debt investors; employees compensated using accounting-based bonus systems; and society, governmental taxation being the proxy. All other things being equal, debt demands strong conservatism to protect downside risks,[126] employees demand weak conservatism to exploit bonus payments,[127] and equity demands weak or neutral conservatism depending on time horizons and prevailing market conditions.[128] While government may prefer weak conservatism to maximize immediate tax revenue (setting aside supply-side effects), to minimize tax obligations, enterprises prefer strong conservatism (to the extent that financial and tax accounting regimes are coextensive). In whose interests should audit committee accounting experts draw the conservatism line amid resulting trade-offs?

Two constraints ameliorate the magnitude of these trade-offs, but they are incomplete, leaving the question and significant challenges open. First, accounting standards established through formal standard setting limit the discretionary range. But they do not eliminate it. GAAP historically embedded a conservatism principle, generally favoring asymmetric recognition of losses compared to gains. But it allowed a range within which conservatism could be relatively stronger or weaker in designated contexts, such as estimating warranty reserves and loss contingencies.[129] Moreover, GAAP is becoming less conservative through expanded use of fair value accounting and by moving away from traditional dictums such as the lower of cost or market principle.[130]

---

information is controversial" (*citing* Anil Arya et al., *Are Unmanaged Earnings Always Better for Shareholders?*, 17 Acct. Horizons 111 (Supp. 2003)).

[126] *See* William W. Bratton, *Shareholder Value and Auditor Independence*, 53 Duke L.J. 439, 477 (2003) (debt investors prefer conservative accounting because they do not enjoy capital appreciation and so concentrate on negative analysis of default risk and rely on hard assets for ultimate recovery). Other advantages of conservatism for debt investors include how resulting accounting would sooner signal adversity and trigger applicable remedial rights such as acceleration. *See* Raymond J. Ball et al., *Is Accounting Conservatism Due to Debt or Equity Markets? An International Test of "Contracting" and "Value Relevance" Theories of Accounting* (Working Paper, 2005), *available at* http://www.csom.umn.edu/Assets/51165.pdf.

[127] Other employees likely exhibit risk aversion akin to debt investors. *See* Bratton, *supra* note 126, at 477.

[128] *See* Bratton, *supra* note 126, at 455–63 (providing a taxonomy of equity investors arrayed according to their diverse types: speculators, investors, short-term holders, long-term holders, noise traders, fundamental value investors, dumb money, and smart money); *id.* at 465–72 (illustrating range of shareholder demand functions using examples of relatively benign cookie-jar reserves to more aggressive earnings management through the timing of revenue recognition and finding that even in the more extreme contexts, the shareholder interest, subject to changing environments over time, "does not unite against management and aggressive accounting").

[129] *See* Cunningham, *supra* note 109, at 39–40 (excerpting selections from relevant standards).

[130] *See* Stanley Siegel, *The Coming Revolution in Accounting: The Emergence of Fair Value as the Fundamental Principle of GAAP*, 42 Wayne L. Rev. 1839 (1996); Fin. Acct. Stnds. Bd., Statement of Financial Accounting Concepts No. 7, Using Cash Flow Information

Accordingly, managers – and audit committee accounting experts – face choices along the conservatism continuum within existing standards and will have more discretion under broadening fair value standards.

Second, debt contract covenants can be used to supply conservatism that lenders demand, without regard to relative conservatism of official standards or decisions enterprises make when producing published financial statements.[131] While there is some modest empirical evidence that lenders use covenants to do this,[132] the weight of the evidence indicates that contractual modifications only partly satisfy lender demand for accounting conservatism.[133] For example, studies show a positive correlation between contractual tailoring toward conservatism and conservative financial reporting apart from that tailoring.[134] The costs of contracting are too great to meet lender demand for conservatism entirely by contract.[135] The empirical results support conjectures and historical evidence that the conservatism principle in GAAP arose from lender demand for standardization of conservatism to reduce costs of contracting.[136]

Two other factors amplify the magnitude of the trade-offs, increasing their significance and accentuating the question of audit committee beneficiaries. First, managers are commonly those employees who are compensated

---

AND PRESENT VALUE IN ACCOUNTING MEASUREMENTS (Feb. 2000); FIN. ACCT. STNDS. BD., STATEMENT OF FINANCIAL ACCOUNTING STANDARDS NO. 133, ACCOUNTING FOR DERIVATIVE INSTRUMENTS AND HEDGING ACTIVITIES, STATEMENT OF FINANCIAL ACCOUNTING STANDARDS NO. 133 (1998); FIN. ACCT. STNDS. BD., STATEMENT OF FINANCIAL ACCOUNTING STANDARDS NO. 142 GOODWILL AND OTHER INTANGIBLE ASSETS (2001).

[131] Debt contract terms invariably reflect conservatism, as where covenants count losses fully and credit gains only partly. *See* Beatty et al., *supra* note 124.

[132] *See* Wayne R. Guay & Robert E. Verrecchia, *Discussion of Bushman and Piotroski and Theory of Conservative Accounting* (Working Paper, 2006), *available at* http://papers.ssrn.com/sol3/papers.cfm?abstract_id=884302.

[133] Roy L. Watts, *Conservatism in Accounting* Part I: Explanations and Implications, 17 ACCT. HORIZONS 207 (2003) [hereinafter Watts, *Conservatism* Part I]; Roy L. Watts, *Conservatism in Accounting Part II: Evidence and Research Opportunities*, 17 ACCT. HORIZONS 287 (2003) [hereinafter Watts, *Conservatism Part II*]; *see also* Ball et al., *supra* note 126 (international data showing economies with larger debt markets than equity markets produce more conservative reports, implying that lender demand influences financial reporting outcomes).

[134] Beatty et al., *supra* note 124.

[135] *Id.* ("findings suggest that lenders may find it too costly to meet their demand for conservatism through contract modifications [so that] [a]s GAAP becomes less conservative, borrowers may be forced to make more conservative accounting choices within GAAP to avoid the costly modifications to contract GAAP").

[136] Roy L. Watts, *A Proposal for Research on Conservatism* (Working Paper, 1993), *available at* http://papers.ssrn.com/sol3/papers.cfm?abstract_id=6044; *see also* FIN. ACCT. STNDS. BD., STATEMENT OF FINANCIAL ACCOUNTING CONCEPTS NO. 2, QUALITATIVE CHARACTERISTICS OF ACCOUNTING INFORMATION, 94 (1980) (noting a preference of lenders for conservative accounting).

according to accounting-based measurements. They have strong incentives against conservatism and essentially set its level. Again, this reality partly explains why U.S. accounting standards historically embed the conservatism principle.[137] Audit committee accounting experts have an important monitoring and control function to play in negotiating the competing demands for relative conservatism, particularly when managers have incentives to demand weak conservatism, at best.[138]

Second, equity investors exhibit demand for neutral to weak conservatism according to respective time horizons and market conditions.[139] Short-term equity investors demand weaker conservatism, while long-term investors demand stronger conservatism. In periods of economic expansion and rising stock prices, equity investors tend to demand weaker conservatism, and in economic downturns and bear markets, preferences tend to return to stronger conservatism.[140] This variation adds competing demand functions that audit committee accounting experts should be expected to balance.

Finally, the tax function cuts both ways.[141] Supply-side theory aside, government may seek weaker conservatism in corporate financial reporting, but other constituents – equity, debt, and employees – prefer comparatively stronger conservatism. At least this is true to the extent that GAAP and tax accounting impose uniform requirements, which is not always the case in the United States. But there are important contexts in which the two requirements are coextensive, as with inventory accounting to take an example for merchandising enterprises. And empirical evidence demonstrates that tax-paying enterprises use more conservative accounting than tax-exempt entities.[142] The result is an additional factor that influences the degree of conservatism that financial reports supply – and additional challenges for audit committee financial experts.

[137] *See* Watts, *Conservatism Part I* (conservatism facilitates monitoring of managers and contracts by constraining overpayments to managers); Watts, *Conservatism Part II* (same).

[138] If audit committee financial experts were compensated in any part using accounting-based measures, these functions would become more difficult to perform. The role of incentive compensation also points to the importance of related expertise – not so much independence – on the board compensation committee. It also suggests developing critical relationships between experts on the audit committee and compensation committee to coordinate tasks to achieve optimal enterprise policies.

[139] Beatty et al., *supra* note 124 (noting how lenders demand conservative accounting given asymmetric nature of claims, in contrast to equity, which prefer symmetric or neutral accounting).

[140] Bratton, *supra* note 126, at 455–63.

[141] *See* Watts, *Conservatism Part I.*

[142] Watts, *Conservatism Part II* (empirical evidence showing that tax-paying enterprises use more conservative accounting than tax-exempt entities).

This is not to suggest that the trade-offs are cannot be resolved. They frequently are resolved, among standard setters and preparers alike.[143] The critical point is that the demand for conservatism is relative and varies across corporate constituencies. GAAP grants extensive discretion, even under its conservatism principle, and contracts do not satisfy all lender demand for conservatism. Conflicting interests are acute for managers enjoying accounting-based bonuses. Resolving these trade-offs suggests an important role for audit committee accounting experts, even though authoritative guidance is lacking.[144]

To the extent that such experts are expected to perform new functions in the post-SOX environment, clarifying these trade-offs would be desirable. In theory, the prescription may simply be that, as directors, the audit committee should act in the interests of shareholders.[145] But shareholder demand for conservatism varies across shareholder types and with market conditions. And the greater the bias for weak conservatism, the greater is the managerial discretion.[146] The new expertise on audit committees is intended to address managerial abuse of accounting discretion. This opens an alternative prescription: audit committee accounting experts have duties akin to those of auditors, meaning duties owed equally to shareholders and debt investors.[147]

These plausible alternatives suggest that the need is acute to clarify to whom audit committee accounting experts should be beholden. This inquiry is not to say that all audit committees should work to supply any particular level of conservatism or that law should supply the incentives to achieve such an objective. The exact demand and supply of conservatism varies among enterprises and across time according to varying capital structures and constituency demographics (including use of accounting-based bonus compensation and tax status).

[143] See Watts, *Conservatism Part I* (lender demand drives conservatism in law, standards, contracts, and practice; Financial Accounting Standards Board and reporting enterprises all balance competing demands of equity and debt when setting and applying standards); Watts, *Conservatism Part II* (same).

[144] See Krishnan & Visvanathan, *supra* note 82 (despite importance of conservatism principle, there is "limited empirical evidence of the relation between audit committee characteristics and conservatism").

[145] Cf. Homer Kripke, *The SEC, the Accountants, Some Myths and Some Realities*, 45 N.Y.U. L. Rev. 1151, 1188–91 (1970); Lynn A. Stout, *The Investor Confidence Game*, 68 Brook. L. Rev. 407, 433–34 n.71 (2002).

[146] See Melvin A. Eisenberg, *Legal Models of Management Structure in the Modern Corporation: Officers, Directors, and Accountants*, 63 Cal. L. Rev. 375, 417–19, 424–30 (1975); Faith Stevelman Kahn, *Transparency and Accountability: Rethinking Corporate Fiduciary Law's Relevance to Corporate Disclosure*, 34 Ga. L. Rev. 505, 507–18 (2000).

[147] See United States v. Arthur Young & Co., 465 U.S. 805 (1984) ("The independent public accountant performing this special [public] function owes ultimate allegiance to the corporation's creditors and stockholders, as well as to the investing public.").

Moreover, there is no way for accounting standards or external auditors to define the optimal supply and demand intercept in general or for a particular enterprise. But someone must exercise the resulting discretion among competing trade-offs. Managers do so in the first instance, but isn't it reasonable to ask experts within the enterprise to promote the optimal supply in response to varying demand? If so, the logical persons to do so are audit committee accounting experts. This does not, *ipso facto*, warrant judicial or regulatory intrusion into those decisions. On the contrary, if directors command expertise, judges and regulators – lacking it – should grant them as much latitude as independent directors have enjoyed for four decades.

The next section pursues this line of inquiry further, but before proceeding, the observation concerning fair value accounting mentioned above bears elaboration. Conservative accounting traditions, such as the lower of cost or market principle, emphasize reliability over relevance when these traits are at odds. Fair value accounting is not conservative, being symmetrical to gains and losses and having no preference for lower or higher asset amounts. It purports to emphasize relevance over reliability. But, as noted, relevance may differ across constituents. Fair value accounting may be more "relevant" to equity investors and less relevant to debt investors.[148]

Yet even this proposition is doubtful, because fair value accounting simply uses prevailing valuations over other measures. Those values may not be relevant either to equity investors or to debt investors (or to any other constituents). Prevailing valuations are drawn from market transactions, if available, and from managerial estimates, if they are not. That expands managerial discretion and points to an important particular function for audit committee experts: to police fair value assumptions. The move toward fair value accounting thus will underscore the challenge for audit committee experts in determining their purpose and how best to meet it.

B. Adjustments

Audit committee accounting experts add value to corporate governance, yet receive no special benefits from contributing it compared to other directors and can face disincentives and threatened penalties. Both points require review. The following first explores disincentives that arise from the curious but common habits of celebrating independence, rewarding it over expertise, and holding that independence and expertise are mutually exclusive. Discussion

---

[148] *See* Bratton, *supra* note 126, at 478–79.

then explores how law, especially Delaware corporate law, reinforces those biases by rewarding independence and penalizing expertise.

1. Compatibility

It is customary to observe a trade-off between director independence and director expertise. This relationship may hold for expertise that arises from corporate knowledge commanded only by senior executives. That kind of expertise, which may be called status expertise, is mutually exclusive with attributes of detachment associated with most definitions of independence. Both sorts of directors contribute different kinds of value. The status expert may have greater ability than the outsider to identify excesses or duplicities of a CEO. The outsider may have greater freedom or capacity to act on that ability to interdict CEO shenanigans. Not only are the roles mutually exclusive in this sense; they are also mutually complementary. The challenge is to find the optimal combination of these different kinds of expertise.[149]

The customary trade-off analysis has less force when expertise is considered as substantive command of a specialized field of knowledge, such as accounting. A director having no other affiliation with a corporation and providing accounting expertise presents none of the trade-offs between independence and that particular kind of expertise. Rather, the independent expert director adds mutually complementary value by bringing detachment, along with useful knowledge. Considering the weight of empirical evidence, the value that independence alone adds is tenuous compared to the strong contributions to quality financial reporting that independence plus accounting expertise makes.[150]

Seen in this light, existing federal law and exchange rules are unobjectionable. They leave corporations with substantial flexibility to achieve optimal board design. Independence is rewarded in certain circumstances, such as concerning executive compensation and taxation matters at the board level.[151] The goal of independence is addressed by SOX's rules speaking to audit committee obligations.[152] But companies are free to have as many or as few independent

---

[149] See Epstein, *supra* note 25, at 719 (stating that the optimal combination may be determined by thinking of the relationship between the marginal cost and the marginal benefit of an additional independent director compared to inside directors).

[150] This remains so even if independence alone contributes advantages to corporate governance that elude capture in statistical models testing its association with corporate performance, *supra* text accompanying notes 31–37, and despite how independence alone sometimes associates with financial reporting quality, *supra* text accompanying notes 67–72.

[151] See *supra* text accompanying notes 26–28.   [152] See *supra* text accompanying notes 61–62.

directors as they wish.[153] They are also free to have any number and type of persons wielding any variety of expertise. Although SOX's have-or-disclose provision encourages having experts on audit committees and exchange rules require some expertise, neither definition of expertise is rigorous. Further, federal law provides that designation of an audit committee member as such an expert imposes no greater or different duty or liability risk on that director compared to other directors.[154]

Despite the empirical reality and federal law flexibility, it may be tempting to believe that the customary trade-off between independence and status expertise carries over to the context of substantive expertise. In some federal securities law contexts and in exchange rules, the definition of independence concentrates on the amount of money and benefits a person receives in various capacities from the corporation. Too much is said to impair independence. For example, exchange rules provide that one loses independence if income from advisory, consulting, or related activities exceeds designated dollar amounts ($60,000 under Nasdaq rules and $100,000 for NYSE companies).[155]

However, SOX goes further, saying that independence and expertise are mutually exclusive as a functional matter, denying that anyone can be independent if performing expert services, outside a directorial capacity, for a given corporation. One corporate governance scholar testified before Congress that if a person is to provide consulting services, he or she should be retained as a consultant, and if the person is to provide directorial services, he or she is to be nominated and elected as a director; in binary fashion, the witness testified that "[y]ou cannot blend the two."[156] While this view is congruent with the customary trade-off applicable to outsiders compared to those with status expertise (insiders), it is harder to square with the injection of substantive expertise where that trade-off dissolves.

---

[153] *See, e.g.*, Bhagat & Black, *The Uncertain Relationship, supra* note 31, at 941–42 (summarizing studies suggesting difficulty in establishing optimal size); Dan R. Dalton, *Number of Directors and Financial Performance: A Meta-Analysis,* 42 ACAD. MGMT. J. 674, 676 (1999) (surveying studies); Charu G. Raheja, *Determinants of Board Size and Composition: A Theory of Corporate Boards,* 40 J. FIN. & QUANT. ANALY. 283 (2005).

[154] *See* Disclosure Required by Sections 406 and 407 of the Sarbanes-Oxley Act of 2002, Exchange Act Release No. 47,235, 79 SEC Docket (CCH) 1077 (Jan. 23, 2003) (text accompanying notes 34–38 explaining inclusion of safe harbor against exposing audit committee financial expert to any different legal liability than other directors and expressing the opinion that this should obtain under both federal securities laws and state corporation laws).

[155] Nasdaq Rule 4200(a)(15); NYSE Listed Company Manual, Rule 303A.02(b)(ii).

[156] *See* Douglas M. Branson, *Too Many Bells? Too Many Whistles? Corporate Governance in the Post-Enron, Post-WorldCom Era,* 58 S.C. L. REV. 65, 82–90 (2006) (quoting testimony of Professor Charles Elson, University of Delaware).

An expert in accounting remains an expert in accounting when serving either as a director or as a consultant. Treating the activities as mutually exclusive gives content to the makeweight arguments opposing the SEC's original definition of the relevant expertise: fewer qualified people will be available, and attracting them will absorb resources from other recruiting efforts.[157] Corporations that recognize the value of expertise among directors will pay expert directors more – and classify payments as director compensation, not as outside compensation.[158] This reveals the constraints as formalistic (evidenced further by how exchange rules use fixed dollar figures for all directors rather than specify compensation in meaningful terms such as a percentage of a person's adjusted gross income or net worth).

In such an environment, experts may prefer consulting to serving as members of a board of directors. Consultancy became an increasingly appealing line of work throughout the period of the monitoring board's ascendancy, which may be explained by the decline of interest in board expertise as the advisory model ceded to the monitoring model.[159] The appeal of consulting was reinforced by how consultants can serve in capacities that are equivalent to other gatekeepers – including independent directors, auditors, and lawyers – but without associated burdens or liability risks.[160] Under the mutually exclusive approach, rules drive more experts off boards and into consulting. Yet if expertise is desired on boards – as intuition, evidence, and brewing change suggests – this framework requires adjustment. This is not to say that pristine definitions of independence must be forsaken but that to appreciate that zealous commitment to such purity carries a higher price than seems to be appreciated.

2. Incentives

More acute talent pool contraction arises from the strange reality that, in Delaware at least, independent directors enjoy extraordinary deference and

---

[157] See *supra* text accompanying notes 64–65.

[158] See Clarke, *supra* note 17, at 80 & 84.

[159] See Gordon, *supra* note 16, at 1513–14 & n.185 (the "advisory board...included... knowledgeable parties [who] could serve as a useful sounding board for the CEO, a kitchen cabinet, and could provide expertise.... In an important sense, boards were an extension of management.... Thus another way to understand the movement from the advisory to the monitoring board is in terms of the rise of consultants, who can better provide cross-industry expertise and strategic counseling than board members recruited by the CEO.").

[160] See CHRISTOPHER D. McKENNA, THE WORLD'S NEWEST PROFESSION: MANAGEMENT CONSULTING IN THE TWENTIETH CENTURY (2006). True, also, is that expert consulting firms can face liability risks for breach of contract or perhaps negligence when advice they give or projects they contribute backfire in ways that breach contracts or constitute torts. But that kind of liability exposure differs considerably from that imposed on recognized gatekeepers. *Id.*

face essentially no risk of judicial rebuke, whereas expert directors are held to a higher standard of performance. These strange consequences follow from the awkward structure of director duties, which traditionally are classified as the duties of loyalty and care.[161] Allegations of loyalty breaches are defended by showing independence and that showing enables invoking the business judgment rule under which discharge of the duty of care is presumed. So directors able to establish their independence are rewarded with complete deference under state law. The theory of this deference is that judges are not competent to make business decisions (or at least are less competent than independent directors).

In contrast, a director who is an expert suffers a burden rather than enjoying a benefit. A director expert in financial matters, for example, is expected to exercise that expertise. If one does not, that weakens the defense against allegations of breaching any fiduciary duty.[162] The doctrine purports to enable judicial inferences from unexercised expertise that a person has acted with volition – with scienter using securities law parlance or in breach of the duty of loyalty in corporate law terms. Thus, directors are penalized for commanding expertise but rewarded for independence.

Rewarding ignorance over knowledge is ironic. Moreover, to hold an expert director liable for failing to exercise expertise, a judge must have first decided, as a substantive matter, that a transaction was unfair, as when a merger price is too low. Irony thickens: directors who are independent but nonexpert win deference from judges who say they lack business acumen while directors who are expert (without regard to independence) are second-guessed by those same (self-confessed) incompetent judges.

Incrementally punishing expertise while privileging independence may not matter much, of course, when few directors of any kind ever face personal liability for any decisions they make. But to capitalize on the recognized value of this expertise, policy should be alert to signals being sent. After all, signaling norms is one of the few important functions that Delaware courts perform.

More important is how this stance conflicts with the concept of the division of labor. Incentives for independence may be desirable to promote the optimal mixture of independence and status expertise on a board and even to maintain

---

[161] More recently, a splinter duty that Delaware courts call good faith has appeared, although it is in fact a long-standing component of the other duties. *See* Melvin A. Eisenberg, *The Duty of Good Faith in Corporate Law*, 31 DEL. J. CORP. L. 1 (2005); *see also Stone ex rel. AmSouth Bancorp. v. Ritter*, 911 A.2d 362 (Del. 2006) (acknowledging that any duty of good faith is a component of the duty of loyalty).

[162] *See In re* Emerging Commc'ns, Inc., Civil Action No. A-16415, 2004 WL 1305745, at 40 (Del. Ch. May 3, 2004, rev'd June 4, 2004) (expert director liable for failing to use financial expertise in testing financial fairness of cash out merger benefiting controlling shareholder).

some independence while adding substantive expertise. But as a matter of intuition, extensively supported by empirical evidence, incentives should be offered for substantive expertise, too.

Benefits of the division of labor are advanced by substantive expertise in multiple disciplines not by increasing the outsider status of directors for the sake of achieving outsider status. Encouraging substantive expertise should be at least as important – or more so – than encouraging independence. Delaware courts have to wrestle with this problem. The solution could include following federal law, which provides that expert directors face no different or greater legal duty or liability risk than other directors.[163] Attracting valuable expertise to boards of directors may depend on it.

V. CONCLUSION

Board independence has been the product of political compromise in most corporate governance debates during the past several generations. It has been possible for independence to be heralded so that all sides seem to get something from it – a reduction in agency costs for investors (both equity and debt) and protection of the interests of other corporate constituencies and perhaps society. One consequence of the political dimension is absence of consensus as to exactly what role independent directors are to play. While definitions of independence are regularly rewritten, no one knows exactly what independent directors are supposed to do and most evidence suggests that they do not do anything particularly well.

Gestures in SOX signal a sharp, yet still inchoate, conception of expertise on audit committees to promote superior financial reporting. Empirical evidence suggests that this works – directors with accounting expertise on audit committees are associated with more faithful financial reporting. However, it remains to specify the functions and expectations for these experts, including the role experts are to play in policing real earnings management and the degree of conservatism to supply. Real earnings management raises questions about how involved such directors should be in nominally substantive business decisions that amount to subterfuges to achieve accounting results; conservatism compels asking for whom audit committee expert directors are

---

[163] Notably, in its release adopting final rules on audit committee financial experts, the SEC opined that neither the Sarbanes-Oxley Act nor the SEC regulations should affect liability, under federal or state law, of directors designated as audit committee financial experts. *See* Disclosure Required by Sections 406 and 407 of the Sarbanes-Oxley Act of 2002, Exchange Act Release No. 47,235, 79 SEC Docket (CCH) 1077 (Jan. 23, 2003) (text accompanying notes 34–38).

trustees, particularly whether their conduct should be guided according to the interests of equity or debt investors.

Taking the empirical evidence on expertise together with the history of redefining independence, one can predict that, in the wake of future financial scandals, reforms will redefine expertise, too. Reforms will most likely consider using the SEC's initial proposal and may even fiddle with the possibility of mandating expertise. Debate probably will have to address exactly what directors are supposed to do with their expertise. It seems prudent to begin these discussions before the next scandals erupt – which might even delay their timing, reduce their magnitude, or tame their character.

3   The CEO and the Board

On CEO Overconfidence and Institutionalizing Dissent in Firms

F. Scott Kieff and Troy A. Paredes

I. INTRODUCTION

In describing the "effective executive," Peter Drucker said:

> Unless one has considered alternatives, one has a closed mind.
>
> This, above all, explains why effective decision makers deliberately disregard the second major command of the textbooks on decision making and create dissension and disagreement, rather than consensus.
>
> Decisions of the kind the executive has to make are not made well by acclamation. They are made well only if based on the clash of conflicting views, the dialogue between different points of view, the choice between different judgments. The first rule in decision-making is that one does not make a decision unless there is disagreement.[1]

He continued:

> The effective decision-maker . . . organizes disagreement. This protects him against being taken in by the plausible but false or incomplete. It gives him the alternatives so that he can choose and make a decision, but also so that

[1] PETER F. DRUCKER, THE EFFECTIVE EXECUTIVE 148 (1985).

F. Scott Kieff is Professor of Law, The George Washington University Law School, and Ray and Louise Knowles Senior Fellow, Stanford University Hoover Institution on War, Revolution, and Peace. Troy A. Paredes is Professor of Law, Washington University in St. Louis, School of Law, presently on leave for government service as a commissioner at the Securities and Exchange Commission. Paredes worked on this chapter while working as a professor of law at Washington University School of Law before being sworn in and taking office as a commissioner of the SEC; the views expressed in this chapter are those of himself and Kieff and are not properly attributable to the SEC. This chapter is part of the authors' work on the Hoover Project on Commercializing Innovation, which is available on the Web at www.innovation.hoover.org. Special thanks to Chris Bracey, Bill Bratton, Kathleen Brickey, and Mike Meurer for their comments and insights. This chapter is adapted from Troy A. Paredes, *Too Much Pay, Too Much Deference: Behavioral Corporate Finance, CEOs, and Corporate Governance*, 32 FLA. ST. U. L. REV. 673 (2005).

he is not lost in the fog when his decision proves deficient or wrong in execution. And it forces the imagination – his own and that of his associates. Disagreement converts the plausible into the right and the right into the good decision.[2]

Managing a company as CEO is about making decisions. Making decisions is not the hard part.[3] The hard part, as Drucker suggests, is making good decisions and then implementing them successfully.

Without question, chief executives make astute, effective decisions routinely but not always.[4] Lots of possibilities explain why bad decisions get made and why even good decisions get implemented poorly. A CEO, for example, may lack important information or suffer from a "blind spot," failing, say, to identify a competitor's countermoves in response to the CEO's initiative.[5] A CEO simply may not be up to the task of being CEO; he may not be well equipped to run the company. Even a highly capable individual with very good information may not manage the business successfully if she does not spend enough time and effort thinking through issues in all of their complexity. A CEO may make a bad decision from the company's perspective and the viewpoint of its stakeholders if the chief executive acts disloyally, such as by "empire building" that manifests itself in imprudent acquisitions.[6] And at least from the perspective of the company's shareholders, the CEO may make a bad decision in aggressively fending off a bid for the company to entrench himself as CEO.[7] A chief executive who believes that she will be ousted unless there is a major success (i.e., who believes that she is in a final period) may reasonably conclude that there is little to lose personally by taking a big risk, even if it jeopardizes the enterprise's future. On the other hand, a CEO may be risk

---

[2] *Id.* at 153. *See also id.* at 148–55 (more by Drucker on the role of disagreement in decision making).

[3] To be more precise, being seen as making decisions is not hard. But being seen as making a decision is different from making one. When a leader or decision maker acts in the case of a broad consensus that has welled up before him or her, the seeming act of leadership or decision making is nothing more than an act of following.

[4] For present purposes, I consider a decision that maximizes the value of the enterprise on an expected basis to be effective or good.

[5] *See, e.g.,* Edward J. Zajac & Max H. Bazerman, *Blind Spots in Industry and Competitor Analysis: Implications of Interfirm (Mis)Perceptions for Strategic Decisions,* 16 ACAD. MGMT. REV. 37 (1991); *see also* Colin Camerer & Dan Lovallo, *Overconfidence and Excess Entry: An Experimental Approach,* 89 AM. ECON. REV. 306 (1999).

[6] *See, e.g.,* Bernard S. Black, *Bidder Overpayment in Takeovers,* 41 STAN. L. REV. 597, 626–28 (1999); John C. Coffee Jr., *Regulating the Market for Corporate Control: A Critical Assessment of the Tender Offer's Role in Corporate Governance,* 84 COLUM. L. REV. 1145, 1167–69, 1224–29, 1269–80 (1984).

[7] *Cf.* Unocal Corp. v. Mesa Petroleum Co., 493 A.2d 946 (Del. 1985).

averse and thus too cautious. A CEO, for example, may manage the business conservatively to protect his firm-specific human capital – in other words, his job.

This catalog of well-studied types of ineffective CEO decision making essentially breaks down into two categories. First, managers may make poor decisions because of imperfect information; and second, managers may make poor decisions because of traditional agency (or conflict-of-interest) problems.[8] But there is a third category that has more recently been receiving growing attention: poor business decisions that result from various psychological biases that impact managerial decision making. The study of such psychological influences on managers is a focus of the field called behavioral corporate finance.[9]

The behavioral model of corporate decision making does not adhere to the standard assumption that people are rational, and instead it openly takes account of human psychology by focusing on how a range of cognitive biases affect how executives decide things.[10] When matters of managerial psychology are addressed, the discussion tends to stress CEO overconfidence. The essential concern when it comes to CEO overconfidence is that a CEO may make a bad decision by overvaluing projects or strategic initiatives, which leads the CEO to make too much investment in them, thereby failing to maximize

[8] On agency problems, see generally Eugene F. Fama, *Agency Problems and the Theory of the Firm*, 88 J. POL. ECON. 288 (1980); Eugene F. Fama & Michael C. Jensen, *Separation of Ownership and Control*, 26 J.L. & ECON. 301 (1983); Michael C. Jensen & William H. Meckling, *Theory of the Firm: Managerial Behavior, Agency Costs and Ownership Structure*, 3 J. FIN. ECON. 305 (1976).

[9] For a concise discussion, see Malcolm P. Baker et al., *Behavioral Corporate Finance: A Survey* (2005), *available at* http://ssrn.com/abstract=602902. For another excellent overview, see MAX H. BAZERMAN, JUDGMENT IN MANAGERIAL DECISION MAKING (2002).

[10] For a sampling from the growing field of behavioral law and economics that focuses on corporate governance and securities regulation, see Stephen M. Bainbridge, *Why a Board? Group Decisionmaking in Corporate Governance*, 55 VAND. L. REV. 1 (2002); Lawrence A. Cunningham, *Behavioral Finance and Investor Governance*, 59 WASH. & LEE L. REV. 767 (2002); Lynne L. Dallas, *A Preliminary Inquiry into the Responsibility of Corporations and Their Officers and Directors for Corporate Climate: The Psychology of Enron's Demise*, 35 RUTGERS L.J. 1 (2003); James A. Fanto, *Quasi-Rationality in Action: A Study of Psychological Factors in Merger Decision-Making*, 62 OHIO ST. L.J. 1333 (2001); Kimberly D. Krawiec, *Accounting for Greed: Unraveling the Rogue Trader Mystery*, 79 OR. L. REV. 301 (2000); Donald C. Langevoort, *Organized Illusions: A Behavioral Theory of Why Corporations Mislead Stock Market Investors (and Cause Other Social Harms)*, 146 U. PA. L. REV. 101 (1997) [hereinafter Langevoort, *Organized Illusions*]; Donald C. Langevoort, *Taming the Animal Spirits of the Stock Markets: A Behavioral Approach to Securities Regulation*, 97 NW. U. L. REV. 135 (2002); Donald C. Langevoort, *The Organizational Psychology of Hyper-Competition: Corporate Irresponsibility and the Lessons of Enron*, 70 GEO. WASH. L. REV. 968 (2002); Robert Prentice, *Whither Securities Regulation? Some Behavioral Observations Regarding Proposals for Its Future*, 51 DUKE L.J. 1397 (2002). See also the symposium published by the *Lewis & Clark Law Review* (2006), "Behavioral Analysis of Corporate Law: Instruction or Distraction?"

firm value or perhaps even destroying firm value. Put differently, the legitimate worry is that a business decision is prone to turn out badly when, as a result of overconfidence, a manager overestimates a project's benefits while underestimating its costs and risks.[11]

This chapter's goal is to offer some suggestions to consider for improving corporate decision making, with particular focus on the risk of overconfidence. Corporate decision making may improve if senior management and the board better appreciate the reasons poor decisions sometimes get made. To this end, section II of this chapter amplifies the above introduction to CEO overconfidence. The discussion briefly fleshes out how overconfidence can lead even a well-intentioned CEO who is working diligently to maximize firm value to make poor decisions. Simply recognizing the risk of overconfidence can lead to better decision making as CEOs and the board take steps to guard against it. Section III offers a particular suggestion for improving corporate decision making, picking up on the thrust of Drucker's statements quoted above. Namely, section III discusses the prospect of institutionalizing dissent in firms by appointing a member or members of the board of directors to serve as a formal devil's advocate. Formalizing the devil's advocate function not only might help debias and manage CEO overconfidence but also might improve the flow of information and help identify and thus remedy conflicts of interest. Section IV concludes.

II. SOME OBSERVATIONS ON CEO OVERCONFIDENCE

An extensive literature shows that people tend to be overconfident.[12] The long and short of overconfidence is that individuals tend to be overly optimistic

---

[11] Lovallo and Kahneman refer to managers who see business opportunities through "rose-colored glasses," in effect "setting themselves up for failure." Dan Lovallo & Daniel Kahneman, *Delusions of Success: How Optimism Undermines Executives' Decisions*, HARV. BUS. REV., July 2003, at 56, 57–58. Consider also the literature on the "hubris hypothesis" of takeovers and the "winner's curse." *See* RICHARD H. THALER, THE WINNER'S CURSE: PARADOXES AND ANOMALIES OF ECONOMIC LIFE (1992) [hereinafter THALER, WINNER'S CURSE]; Richard Roll, *The Hubris Hypothesis of Corporate Takeovers*, 59 J. BUS. 197 (1986); Richard H. Thaler, *Anomalies: The Winner's Curse*, J. ECON. PERSP., Winter 1998, at 191 (1988); *see also* G. ANANDALINGAM & HENRY C. LUCAS JR., BEWARE THE WINNER'S CURSE: VICTORIES THAT CAN SINK YOU AND YOUR COMPANY (2004).

[12] As De Bondt and Thaler have noted, "[p]erhaps the most robust finding in the psychology of judgment is that people are overconfident." Werner F. M. De Bondt & Richard H. Thaler, *Financial Decision-Making in Markets and Firms: A Behavioral Perspective, in* 9 HANDBOOKS IN OPERATIONS RESEARCH AND MANAGEMENT SCIENCE: FINANCE 385–410 (R.A. Jarrow et al. eds., 1995).

The following discussion draws from a wide-ranging literature on overconfidence, overoptimism, and self-attribution biases. For a small sampling, see Stephen J. Choi & A. C. Pritchard,

about the future they have in some way selected as they place too much
faith in themselves and their ability to generate good results. Two ingredients
seem to mix to create overconfidence. Not only do people overestimate their
abilities, but they also tend to suffer from a so-called illusion of control – that
is, people tend to believe that they control outcomes more than they actually
do.[13] Correspondingly, people tend to take too much credit for their success
and to blame other factors when they underperform. As a result, studies suggest
that prior success leads a person to become increasingly confident.[14]

For business, the risk is that an overconfident CEO will make bad business decisions, at least in terms of expected payoffs. An overconfident CEO's
assessment of business opportunities is not objective, but rather it accentu-
ates the benefits of some course of action while downplaying the costs and
uncertainties. In terms of any net-present-value calculation, this translates into
benefits that are perceived as too high and costs that are too low, causing the
risk of overinvestment as the CEO initiates and undertakes projects that in
reality have lower or even negative net present value. March and Shapira put

Behavioral Economics and the SEC, 56 STAN. L. REV. 1, 28–30 (2003); Christine Jolls, *Behav-
ioral Economics Analysis of Redistributive Legal Rules*, 51 VAND. L. REV. 1653, 1659–61 (1998);
Asher Koriat et al., *Reasons for Confidence*, 6 J. EXPERIMENTAL PSYCHOL.: HUM. LEARNING
& MEMORY 107 (1980); Russell B. Korobkin & Thomas S. Ulen, *Law and Behavioral Science:
Removing the Rationality Assumption from Law and Economics*, 88 CAL. L. REV. 1051, 1091–
95 (2000); Sarah Lichtenstein & Baruch Fischhoff, *Do Those Who Know More Also Know
More About How Much They Know?*, 20 ORGANIZATIONAL BEHAV. & HUM. PERFORMANCE
159 (1977); Paul J. Healy & Don A. Moore, *The Trouble with Overconfidence* (2007), *available
at* http://ssrn.com/abstract=1001821; Paul J. Healy & Don A. Moore, *Bayesian Overconfidence*
(2007), *available at* http://ssrn.com/abstract=1001820; Jeffrey J. Rachlinski, *Misunderstanding
Ability, Misallocating Responsibility*, 68 BROOK. L. REV. 1055, 1080–82 (2003). For work that
focuses on corporate decision making from which the discussion in this section II draws, see
infra note 16.
[13] *See, e.g.*, Daniel Kahneman & Dan Lovallo, *Timid Choices and Bold Forecasts: A Cognitive
Perspective on Risk Taking*, 39 MGMT. SCI. 17, 27 (1993); Lovallo & Kahneman, *supra* note 10,
at 58–59; James G. March & Zur Shapira, *Managerial Perspectives on Risk and Risk Taking*,
33 MGMT. SCI. 1404, 1410–11 (1987).
[14] For additional consideration of this point and citations to the literature, see Troy A. Paredes,
*Too Much Pay, Too Much Deference: Behavioral Corporate Finance, CEOs, and Corporate
Governance*, 32 FLA. ST. U. L. REV. 673, 713–20 (2005).
   Relatedly, managers may have "blind spots" leading them to underestimate the competition.
See, e.g., Zajac & Bazerman, *supra* note 4.
   Further, commitment and confirmation biases can exacerbate the impact of overconfidence.
Individuals are prone to commit increasingly to a course of action once a decision has been
made and tend to search for and welcome evidence that confirms their choice while failing to
search for disconfirming evidence and discounting it when it is discovered. *See, e.g.*, Choi &
Pritchard, *supra* note 11, at 30–33; Pamela R. Haunschild et al., *Managerial Overcommitment
in Corporation Acquisition Processes*, 5 ORG. SCI. 528 (1994); Langevoort, *Organized Illusions*,
at 142–43; Barry M. Staw & Jerry Ross, *Knowing When to Pull the Plug*, HARV. BUS. REV.,
Mar.–Apr. 1987, at 68.

it this way: "managers accept risks, in part, because they do not expect that they will have to bear them."[15] Camerer and Lovallo similarly characterize the impact of overconfidence: "Overconfidence predicts that agents will be relatively insensitive to risk; indeed, when risk is high their overconfidence might lead them to *prefer* riskier contracts because they think they can beat the odds."[16] Overly aggressive business expansions, overpayment in acquisitions, and rejections of premium bids for the company represent some of the potential concrete consequences flowing from CEO overconfidence.[17]

We do not want to overstate the concern. Although studies support the claim that CEOs are overconfident, it is hard to measure the extent of overconfidence, and it is even more difficult to ascertain its impact on actual business decisions. In fact, results that are consistent with overconfidence might be attributable to imperfect information or conflicts of interest. More

---

[15] March & Shapira, *supra* note 12, at 1411 (discussing managerial belief in the ability to control risks, thereby distinguishing taking "good" risks from "gambling").

[16] Camerer & Lovallo, *supra* note 4, at 315. *See also* Lovallo & Kahneman, *supra* note 10, at 59 (explaining that managers' "self-confidence can lead them to assume that they'll be able to avoid or easily overcome potential problems in executing a project").

[17] An extensive literature, both theoretical and empirical, has considered managerial overconfidence and its impact on corporate decision making. *See, e.g.*, THALER, WINNER'S CURSE; Ball et al., *infra* note 18; Roland Benabou & Jean Tirole, *Self-Confidence and Personal Motivation*, 117 Q.J. ECON. 871 (2002); Antonio Bernardo & Ivo Welch, *On the Evolution of Overconfidence and Entrepreneurs*, 10 J. ECON. & MGMT. STRATEGY 301 (2001); Marianne Bertrand & Antoinette Schoar, *Managing with Style: The Effect of Managers on Firm Policies*, 118 Q.J. ECON. 1169 (2003); Camerer & Lovallo, *supra* note 4; John A. Doukas & Dimitris Petmezas, *Acquisitions, Overconfident Managers and Self-Attribution Bias* (working paper on file with Troy Paredes); Simon Gervais & Itay Goldstein, *Overconfidence and Team Coordination* (Rodney L. White Ctr. for Fin. Res., Working Paper No. 08–04, 2004), *available at* http://finance.wharton. upenn.edu/~rlwctr/papers/0408.pdf; Simon Gervais et al., *infra* note 27; Goel & Thakor, *infra* note 27; Haunschild et al., *supra* note 13; Mathew L. A. Hayward & Donald C. Hambrick, *Explaining the Premiums Paid for Large Acquisitions: Evidence of CEO Hubris*, 42 ADMIN. SCI. Q. 103 (1997); J. B. Heaton, *Managerial Optimism and Corporate Finance*, 31 FIN. MGMT. 33 (2002); Pekka Hietala et al., *What Is the Price of Hubris? Using Takeover Battles to Infer Overpayments and Synergies*, 32 FIN. MGMT. 5 (2003); Kahneman & Lovallo, *supra* note 12, at 24–29 (distinguishing between an "inside view" of a problem and an "outside view" in explaining various causes and consequences of optimistic biases in organizations); Roderick M. Kramer, *The Harder They Fall*, HARV. BUS. REV., Oct. 2003, at 58 (discussing how overconfidence and ego can lead to a CEO's fall); Lovallo & Kahneman, *supra* note 10, at 58 (explaining how a more objective "outside view" can act as a "reality check" that counteracts managerial overconfidence); Dan Lovallo et al., *Deals Without Delusions*, HARV. BUS. REV., Dec. 2007, at 92; Ulrike Malmendier & Geoffrey Tate, *Does Overconfidence Affect Corporate Investment? CEO Overconfidence Measures Revisited*, 11 EUR. FIN. MGMT. 649 (2005); David M. Messick & Max H. Bazerman, *Ethical Leadership and the Psychology of Decision Making*, SLOAN MGMT. REV., Winter 1996, at 9; David de Meza & Clive Southey, *The Borrower's Curse: Optimism, Finance and Entrepreneurship*, 106 ECON. J. 375 (1996); Roll, *supra* note 10; Zajac & Bazerman, *supra* note 4.

to the point, there is no bright line indicating when a CEO has become overconfident. More importantly, while there is reason to be concerned about CEO overconfidence, overconfidence may be self-correcting, at least for some executives and at least to some degree. Studies indicate that feedback can help debias overconfidence. In other words, CEOs can learn from their mistakes and from the mistakes of others. For example, a CEO may infer the risk of overconfidence by having himself overpaid in some earlier acquisition or observing transactions involving other companies that were overly optimistic and turned out poorly.

The central cause of trouble is that CEOs often do not receive the kind of pointed feedback needed to remedy or avoid overconfidence. Rather, feedback is often noisy and delayed. As Zajac and Bazerman have explained, the kind of "accurate and timely" feedback required to improve managerial judgment

> is rarely available [to managers] because (1) outcomes are commonly delayed and not easily attributable to a particular action, (2) variability in the environment degrades the reliability of feedback, (3) there is often no information about what the outcome would have been if another decision had been made, and (4) many important decisions are unique and therefore provide little opportunity for learning.[18]

While each of these reasons explains why the CEO may not know of more, there are additional, incentive-based reasons why the CEO and others might not want this information. For example, potential dissenters may not want to take on the risk of challenging the CEO or others. The CEO also may not want to be challenged.[19]

Even when a CEO makes a bad decision, plenty of other factors that the CEO does not determine can plausibly be blamed for a bad outcome –

[18] Zajac & Bazerman, *supra* note 4, at 42 (citing Amos Tversky & Daniel Kahneman, *Rational Choice and the Framing of Decisions*, 59 J. Bus. S251, S274–75 (1986)). *See also* Sheryl B. Ball et al., *An Evaluation of Learning in the Bilateral Winner's Curse*, 48 ORGANIZATIONAL BEHAV. & HUM. DECISION PROCESSES 1 (1991); Kahneman & Lovallo, *supra* note 12, at 18 (explaining that learning can occur "when closely similar problems are frequently encountered, especially if the outcomes of decisions are quickly known and provide unequivocal feedback"). J. Edward Russo & Paul J.H. Schoemaker, *Managing Overconfidence*, SLOAN MGMT. REV., Winter 1992, at 10 ("Overconfidence persists in spite of experience because we often fail to learn from experience.").

For more on feedback, see, for example, Garland, *infra* note 29; Therese A. Louie, *Decision Makers' Hindsight Bias After Receiving Favorable and Unfavorable Feedback*, 84 J. APPLIED PSYCHOL. 29 (1999); Rachlinski, *infra* note 29, at 1212; Stone & Opel, *infra* note 29; Zakay, *infra* note 29.

[19] For more on the relationships among these cognition and incentive effects, see Troy A. Paredes, *Too Much Pay, Too Much Deference: Behavioral Corporate Finance, CEOs, and Corporate Governance*, 32 FLA. ST. U. L. REV. 673, 702-736 (2005).

climbing interest rates, an economic slowdown, bad lawyers, bad bankers, an unforeseen regulatory change or judicial opinion, and so on. Further, it can be years before a bad decision is identified as a failure – again, with lots of intervening events along the way to take the blame. In addition, a manager can always reasonably claim that she made a good decision, even when the outcome is bad, given that business is inherently risky. Put differently, an executive can deflect responsibility by pointing out that business failures are an unavoidable cost of taking action and doing business and that a CEO who never fails is not taking enough risks.[20]

Whether or not learning debiases managerial overconfidence, markets may keep it in check.[21] In this view, product market competition, capital market pressures, the market for corporate control, and the market for management, or some combination thereof, discipline executives to run their companies profitably. The implication is that ineffective managers – such as those prone to make bad decisions as a result of overconfidence (or otherwise) – either will be chased from the market or will improve their decision making. In short, the argument is that overconfident CEOs (and the companies they run) cannot survive.

This market discipline argument has currency, but it also has limits. First, although CEO turnover has appeared to increase in more recent years – especially since the collapse of Enron and WorldCom, as boards have become more demanding of management – a company still has to struggle considerably for some period of time before the CEO is removed.[22] A great deal of firm value can be destroyed during the period of underperformance leading to a CEO's displacement. When the chief executive finally is replaced, there are no guarantees that the new CEO will successfully turn things around. The damage already done may be irreparable. Even if things can be turned around, it takes time to craft and implement a new strategy.

Second, capital market discipline does not bite particularly hard for a company that does not have to tap capital markets to any meaningful extent to meet its business needs.

---

[20] *Cf.* Lovallo & Kahneman, *supra* note 10, at 58: "According to standard economic theory, the high failure rates are simple to explain: The frequency of poor outcomes is an unavoidable result of companies taking rational risks in uncertain situations. Entrepreneurs and managers know and accept the odds because the rewards of success are sufficiently enticing. In the long run, the gains from a few successes will outweigh the losses from many failures."

[21] For discussions of the disciplining effect of markets, see, for example, Black, *supra* note 5, at 630–32; Langevoort, *supra* note 9, at 148.

[22] *See, e.g., Making Companies Work,* ECONOMIST, Oct. 25, 2003, at 14–15; Eric Dash, *Boards More Likely to Oust Underperforming Chief Executives, a Study Finds,* N.Y. TIMES, May 22, 2007, at C6; Patrick McGeehan, *Study Finds Number of Chiefs Forced to Leave Jobs Is Up,* N.Y. TIMES, May 12, 2003, at C5.

Third, boards of directors can adopt defensive tactics that fend off unsolicited bids, thus undercutting the disciplining effect of hostile takeovers.

Fourth, market discipline is thought to remedy conventional agency problems by incentivizing managers to maximize shareholder value. However, debiasing CEOs who are overconfident is not primarily about encouraging CEOs to focus on running the business profitably instead of helping themselves. In addition, CEO overconfidence is not about conflicts of interest between the CEO and shareholders; it is about unconscious psychological biases that can impact well-intentioned, hardworking CEOs. Put differently, there is somewhat of a mismatch between the solution of market discipline and the problem of cognitive bias. In fact, studies have shown that greater accountability can actually worsen the CEO overconfidence problem.[23]

[23] See Philip E. Tetlock, *The Impact of Accountability on Judgment and Choice: Toward a Social Contingency Model,* in 25 ADVANCES IN EXPERIMENTAL SOCIAL PSYCHOLOGY 331, 344–59 (Mark P. Zanna ed., 1992) (explaining that "defensive bolstering" – that is, "efforts to generate as many justifications as possible" – can lead to greater confidence and commitment); Hal R. Arkes, *Costs and Benefits of Judgment Errors: Implications for Debiasing,* 110 PSYCHOL. BULL. 486, 493 (1991) ("Incentives are not effective in debiasing association-based errors because motivated subjects will merely perform the sub-optimal behavior with more enthusiasm. An even more assiduous search for confirmatory evidence will not lower one's over-confidence to an appropriate confidence level."); Christina L. Brown, *"Do the Right Thing:" Diverging Effects of Accountability in a Managerial Context,* 18 MARKETING SCI. 230, 231 (1999) ("[S]ince accountability can encourage defensive thinking or 'bolstering,' it may create overconfidence in one's predictions and encourage decision makers to stick with a losing course of action. This leads to the discouraging implication that accountability can distort decisionmaking exactly when it makes its adherents feel more certain they are 'doing the right thing.'" (citations omitted)); *id.* at 244 ("This effect is exacerbated if accountability also creates overconfidence in one's predictions, either because providing reasons for one's predictions makes one more confident (whether or not the reasons are good ones), or because concern over being evaluated encourages one to express one's ideas more confidently (whether or not one is genuinely confident)."); Jennifer S. Lerner & Philip E. Tetlock, *Accounting for the Effects of Accountability,* 125 PSYCHOL. BULL. 255, 257 (1999) ("Defensive bolstering should also lead people to generate as many reasons as they can why they are right and potential critics are wrong. This generation of thoughts consistent with one's views then leads people to hold even more extreme opinions." (citations omitted)); *id.* at 258 ("Research on attitude change reveals that people who sense that an audience wants to control their beliefs will often respond to the threat to their autonomy by asserting their own views all the more vigorously."); Philip E. Tetlock & Richard Boettger, *Accountability: A Social Magnifier of the Dilution Effect,* 57 J. PERSONALITY & SOCIAL PSYCHOL. 388 (1989); Philip E. Tetlock & Jae Il Kim, *Accountability and Judgment Processes in a Personality Prediction Task,* 52 J. PERSONALITY & SOCIAL PSYCHOL. 700 (1987). *See also* Mark Seidenfeld, *Cognitive Loafing, Social Conformity, and Judicial Review of Agency Rulemaking,* 87 CORNELL L. REV. 486, 508–26 (2002) (summarizing accountability literature).

For others suggesting a similar mismatch, see, e.g., Koriat et al., *supra* note 11, at 117 ("Working harder will have little effect unless combined with a task restructuring that facilitates more optimal cognitive functioning."); Amos Tversky & Daniel Kahneman, *Rational Choice and the Framing of Decisions,* 59 J. BUS. S251, S274–75 (1986) (explaining that there is little experimental support for the view that "proper incentives" remedy cognitive bias).

Beyond all of this, it is important to acknowledge that CEO overconfidence is not necessarily bad and something that needs to be rooted out. An overconfident CEO ultimately may advance the best interests of the corporation, at least compared to the prospect of a halting chief executive. The clarity of purpose, commitment, and charisma that mark effective CEOs may best be realized when a CEO is overconfident.

First, to be effective, a CEO needs to be decisive and willing and able to act quickly when necessary.[24] More to the point, incrementalism is not always feasible in business; boldness often is called for. And once a decision is made, a CEO has to be confident and determined enough to push through adversity, as there will always be challenges and doubts. Put bluntly, overconfidence can give managers the guts to take the risks and make the business changes necessary for a company to remain competitive, even if it sometimes means they take too much risk.[25]

Second, an overconfident CEO can be an inspiring leader. A charismatic, self-confident chief executive can boost morale and motivate others in the organization to work hard.[26]

Third, by projecting confidence, a top executive can signal to competitors a plan, willingness, and ability to compete aggressively that may give the CEO and her company an advantage in future business dealings.[27]

Fourth, overconfidence may offset a CEO's incentive to be cautious to avoid jeopardizing his job.[28] A CEO who is risk averse, managing to the downside,

---

[24] See Langevoort, *Organized Illusions*, at 153 (explaining that the benefit of a determined focus is that it can "avoid the informational paralysis that often comes from seeing and thus dwelling on too many risks or opportunities" and that "[h]igh levels of self-esteem and self-efficacy are associated with aggressiveness, perseverance, and optimal risk-taking").

[25] Cf. Clayton M. Christensen, The Innovator's Dilemma: When New Technologies Cause Great Firms to Fail (1997); Clayton M. Christensen & Michael E. Raynor, The Innovator's Solution: Creating and Sustaining Successful Growth (2003). These works reflect the view that companies have to continue to innovate to succeed over the long run.

[26] Maccoby expressed a similar sentiment as follows: "Why do we go along for the ride with narcissistic leaders? Because the upside is enormous.... When narcissists win, they win big. Narcissists create a vision to change the world; they are bold risk takers who think and act independently, pursuing their vision with great passion and perseverance. This is exactly the kind of leader we expect to take us to places we've never been before, to build empires out of nothing." Michael Maccoby, The Productive Narcissist: The Promise and Peril of Visionary Leadership xiv (2003). See also Rakesh Khurana, Searching for a Corporate Savior: The Irrational Quest for Charismatic CEOs (2002).

[27] See generally Andrew D. Brown, *Narcissism, Identity, and Legitimacy*, 22 Acad. Mgmt. Rev. 643 (1997) (summarizing literature regarding reputation and signaling).

[28] On the prospect of overconfidence counterbalancing CEO risk aversion, see, for example, Simon Gervais et al., *Overconfidence, Investment Policy, and Executive Stock Options* (Rodney L. White Ctr. for Fin. Res., Working Paper No. 15–02, 2003), *available at*

usually does not maximize the firm's value, although it is recognized that when everything in the market is going down, this strategy may actually turn out best for the firm.

Where does this leave things when it comes to CEO overconfidence? There are pros and cons of overconfidence; not every CEO is overconfident to the same degree; and a given CEO may be overconfident to different degrees – including not at all – under different circumstances. In other words, there is a great deal of uncertainty when trying to assess CEO overconfidence generally, let alone with respect to a particular chief executive.

That said, it is important for all constituents to recognize the risk of overconfidence to position themselves to guard against it. Metacognition concerns thinking about and understanding how one thinks. Alerting a chief executive to her cognitive tendencies can mitigate flawed decision making.[29] Put simply, recognizing overconfidence can itself go a long way toward remedying it to the extent it is a problem. A CEO who recognizes and accepts that she may be overconfident can institute decision-making techniques, such as seeking out disagreement (as Drucker urges) and explicitly interrogating her own assumptions and analysis. A loyal manager looking to maximize firm value has an incentive to try and make better decisions once she realizes her own cognitive shortcomings and biased judgment.

It is important to underscore that the goal is not to avoid taking risks. Businesses have to take risks to survive. Rather, the goal is for CEOs and the companies they run to avoid taking excessive risks unknowingly. Overconfidence can lead to the inadvertent taking of unrecognized risks.

http://ssrn.com/abstract=361200 (showing that CEO overconfidence and optimism can ameliorate conflicts of interest between risk-averse managers and shareholders); Anand Mohan Goel & Anjan V. Thakor, *Rationality, Overconfidence and Leadership* 29 (Univ. of Mich. Bus. Sch., Working Paper No. 00–022, 2000), *available at* http://ssrn.com/abstract=244999 ("CEO overconfidence turns out to be a virtue for risk-neutral shareholders ... because it helps overcome to some extent the risk aversion of managers and thus closes the 'preference gap' between shareholders and managers.").

[29] *See* METACOGNITION, COGNITION, AND HUMAN PERFORMANCE (D.L. Forrest-Pressley et al. eds., 1985); Mahzarin R. Banaji et al., *How (Un)ethical Are You?*, HARV. BUS. REV., Dec. 2003, at 56–58 (explaining that to remedy bias, "managers must bring a new type of vigilance to bear. To begin, this requires letting go of the notion that our conscious attitudes always represent what we think they do. It also demands that we abandon our faith in our own objectivity and our ability to be fair."); Lovallo & Kahneman, *supra* note 10, at 61 ("Simply understanding the sources of overoptimism can help planners challenge assumptions, bring in alternative perspectives, and in general take a balanced view of the future."); Russo & Schoemaker, *supra* note 17, at 8–11, 13–15 (discussing the debiasing effects of metaknowledge – that is, knowing what you do not know – and explaining that "awareness alone may be all that is needed" to remedy overconfidence); Staw & Ross, *supra* note 13, at 71 (explaining that, to counteract overcommitment, "[t]he most important thing for managers to realize is that they may be biased toward escalation").

III. DEVIL'S ADVOCATE

Generally, better business decisions result when a firm's corporate governance structure is designed to promote a full airing of issues. In other words, some degree of disagreement is important. An engaging deliberative process not only ensures that information is uncovered and shared but also can help ensure that conflicts of interest manifest themselves. Furthermore, studies show that dissent can mitigate overconfidence.[30] By considering arguments

---

[30] The discussion of dissent in this section III draws from an extensive literature. *See, e.g.,* BAZER-MAN, *supra* note 8, at 155–59; CASS R. SUNSTEIN, WHY SOCIETIES NEED DISSENT (2003); USING CONFLICT IN ORGANIZATIONS (Carsten De Dreu & Evert Van De Vliert eds., 1997); Hal R. Arkes, *Costs and Benefits of Judgment Errors: Implications for Debiasing*, 110 PSYCHOL. BULL. 486, 494 (1991); Hal R. Arkes et al., *Two Methods of Reducing Overconfidence*, 39 ORGANIZA-TIONAL BEHAVIOR & HUMAN DECISION PROCESSES 133, 141–42 (1987); William K. Balzer et al., *Effects of Cognitive Feedback on Performance*, 106 PSYCHOL. BULL. 410 (1989); Carsten K.W. De Dreu & Michael A. West, *Minority Dissent and Team Innovation: The Importance of Partic-ipation in Decision Making*, 86 J. APPLIED PSYCHOL. 1191 (2001); Baruch Fischhoff, *Debiasing*, in JUDGMENT UNDER UNCERTAINTY: HEURISTICS AND BIASES (Daniel Kahneman et al. eds., 1982), at 422; Howard Garland et al., *De-Escalation of Commitment in Oil Exploration: When Sunk Costs and Negative Feedback Coincide*, 75 J. APPLIED PSYCHOL. 721 (1990); Heather K. Gerken, *Dissenting by Deciding*, 57 STAN. L. REV. 1745 (2005); Theodore T. Herbert & Ralph W. Estes, *Improving Executive Decisions by Formalizing Dissent: The Corporate Devil's Advocate*, 2 ACAD. MGMT. REV. 662 (1977); Stephen J. Hoch, *Counterfactual Reasoning and Accuracy in Predicting Personal Events*, 11 J. EXPERIMENTAL PSYCHOL.: LEARNING MEMORY & COGNITION 719 (1985); Koriat et al., *supra* note 11; Kramer, *supra* note 16, at 64–66; Laura J. Kray & Adam D. Galinsky, *The Debiasing Effect of Counterfactual Mind-Sets: Increasing the Search for Disconfirmatory Information in Group Decisions*, 91 ORGANIZATIONAL BEHAV. & HUM. DECISION PROCESSES 69 (2003); Martin Landau & Donald Chisholm, *The Arrogance of Optimism: Notes on Failure-Avoidance Management*, 3 J. CONTINGENCIES & CRISIS MGMT. 67 (1995); Charles G. Lord et al., *Considering the Opposite: A Corrective Strategy for Social Judgment*, 47 J. PERSONALITY & SOCIAL PSYCHOL. 1231 (1984); Messick & Bazerman, *supra* note 16, at 20; Charlan Jeanne Nemeth, *Dissent as Driving Cognition, Attitudes, and Judg-ments*, 13 SOCIAL COGNITION 273 (1995); Charlan Jeanne Nemeth, *Differential Contributions of Majority and Minority Influence*, 93 PSYCHOL. REV. 23 (1986); Charlan Nemeth & Cyn-thia Chiles, *Modelling Courage: The Role of Dissent in Fostering Independence*, 18 EUR. J. SOCIAL PSYCHOL. 275 (1988); Charlan Nemeth et al., *Devil's Advocate Versus Authentic Dis-sent: Stimulating Quantity and Quality*, 31 EUR. J. SOCIAL PSYCHOL. 707 (2001); Randall S. Peterson & Charlan J. Nemeth, *Focus Versus Flexibility: Majority and Minority Influence Can Both Improve Performance*, 22 PERSONALITY & SOCIAL PSYCHOL. BULL. 14 (1996); Ran-dall S. Peterson et al., *Group Dynamics in Top Management Teams: Groupthink, Vigilance, and Alternative Models of Organizational Failure and Success*, 73 ORGANIZATIONAL BEHAV. & HUM. DECISION PROCESSES 272 (1998); S. Plous, *A Comparison of Strategies for Reducing Interval Overconfidence in Group Judgments*, 80 J. APPLIED PSYCHOL. 443 (1995); Jeffrey J. Rachlinski, *The Uncertain Psychological Case for Paternalism*, 97 NW. U. L. REV. 1165, 1214 (2003); William Remus et al., *Does Feedback Improve the Accuracy of Recurrent Judgmental Forecasts?*, 66 ORGANIZATIONAL BEHAV. & HUM. DECISION PROCESSES 22 (1996); Russo & Schoemaker, *supra* note 18, at 10–13; Stefan Schulz-Hardt et al., *Productive Conflict in Group*

against some course of action – such as by asking probing questions and follow-ups, challenging key assumptions, focusing on counterfactuals, or developing other options – risks become more salient to a decision maker and she may realize that she exerts less control over outcomes than she thought. Relatedly, research shows that conflict in decision making can spawn creativity and open-mindedness and more expansive thinking.

At bottom, dissent in a firm can help ensure that a more informed and balanced assessment of some course of conduct prevails and that more business options are considered. In addition, the careful exploration of contrasting views often leads to a fulsome ventilation of ideas, thereby revealing the reasons for particular decisions; and the elucidation of those reasons *ex ante* can help managers better manage whatever problems eventually arise from those decisions, *ex post.*

Presumably, more dissent exists today in boardrooms and executive suites in Sarbanes-Oxley's wake than did in the past.[31] Nonetheless, companies still

Decision Making: Genuine and Contrived Dissent as Strategies to Counteract Biased Information Seeking, 88 Organizational Behav. & Hum. Decision Processes 563 (2002); David M. Schweiger et al., *Group Approaches for Improving Strategic Decision Making: A Comparative Analysis of Dialectical Inquiry, Devil's Advocacy, and Consensus,* 29 Acad. Mgmt. J. 51 (1986); David M. Schweiger et al., *Experiential Effects of Dialectical Inquiry, Devil's Advocacy, and Consensus Approaches to Strategic Decision Making,* 32 Acad. Mgmt. J. 745 (1989); Charles R. Schwenk, *Devil's Advocacy in Managerial Decision-Making,* 21 J. Mgmt. Stud. 153 (1984); Charles Schwenk, *A Meta-Analysis on the Comparative Effectiveness of Devil's Advocacy and Dialectical Inquiry,* 10 Strategic Mgmt. J. 303 (1989); Charles R. Schwenk, *Effects of Devil's Advocacy and Dialectical Inquiry on Decision Making: A Meta-Analysis,* 47 Organizational Behav. & Hum. Decision Processes 161 (1990); Charles R. Schwenk & Richard A. Cosier, *Effects of the Expert, Devil's Advocate, and Dialectical Inquiry Methods on Prediction Performance,* 26 Organizational Behav. & Hum. Performance 409 (1980); Charles Schwenk & Joseph S. Valacich, *Effects of Devil's Advocacy and Dialectical Inquiry on Individuals Versus Groups,* 59 Organizational Behav. & Hum. Decision Processes 210 (1994); Eric R. Stone & Ryan B. Opel, *Training to Improve Calibration and Discrimination: The Effects of Performance and Environmental Feedback,* 83 Organizational Behav. & Hum. Decision Processes 282 (2000); Dan N. Stone et al., *Formalized Dissent and Cognitive Complexity in Group Processes and Performance,* 25 Decision Sci. 243 (1994); Cass R. Sunstein, *Group Judgments: Statistical Means, Deliberation, and Information Markets,* 80 N.Y.U. L. Rev. 962 (2005); David Trafimow & Janet A. Sniezek, *Perceived Expertise and Its Effect on Confidence,* 57 Organizational Behav. & Hum. Decision Processes 290 (1994); Vincent A. Warther, *Board Effectiveness and Board Dissent: A Model of the Board's Relationship to Management and Shareholders,* 4 J. Corp. Fin. 53 (1998); Dan Zakay, *The Influence of Computerized Feedback on Overconfidence in Knowledge,* 11 Behav. & Info. Tech. 329 (1992).

[31] *See generally* Alan Murray, Revolt in the Boardroom: The New Rules of Power in Corporate America (2007); Arthur Levitt Jr., *The Imperial CEO Is No More,* Wall St. J., Mar. 17, 2005, at A16; Joann S. Lublin & Erin White, *Deferential No More, Directors Are Speaking Out More Often: When Is Dissent Dysfunctional?,* Wall St. J., Oct. 2, 2006, at B1; Alan Murray, *Calling Ebbers and Other CEOs to Account,* Wall St. J., Feb. 23, 2005, at A2.

might consider whether more should be done in this regard to improve corporate decision making, at least when it comes to especially material matters. One possibility is to formally appoint a devil's advocate from the board of directors to participate in corporate decision making, an idea that has received some attention recently.[32]

---

[32] *See* COLIN B. CARTER & JAY W. LORSCH, BACK TO THE DRAWING BOARD: DESIGNING CORPORATE BOARDS FOR A COMPLEX WORLD 174–75 (2004) (proposing that boards appoint a "designated critic" as a means of "legitimizing dissent" to better ensure that management is challenged but without creating "resentment and conflict"); Randall Morck, *Behavioral Finance in Corporate Governance – Independent Directors and Non-Executive Chairs* (Nat'l Bureau of Econ. Res., Working Paper No. 10644, 2004) (recommending that nonexecutive chairmen of the board and independent directors counter the psychological tendency of individuals to obey authority), *available at* http://www.nber.org/papers/w10644; BARRY NALEBUFF & IAN AYRES, WHY NOT? HOW TO USE EVERYDAY INGENUITY TO SOLVE PROBLEMS BIG AND SMALL 6–9 (2003) (arguing that boards should identify a devil's advocate to make counterarguments and in effect to ask "Why not?" pursue some alternative course of action when presented with a proposal); Marleen A. O'Connor, *The Enron Board: The Perils of Groupthink*, 71 U. CIN. L. REV. 1233, 1304–06 (2003) (advocating a devil's advocate on the board to counter groupthink); Harold J. Ruvoldt Jr., *A Way to Get to "What if . . . ?,"* DIRECTORS & BOARDS, Fall 2003, at 31, 33 (stressing the importance of directors asking, "What if?" and suggesting the development of "black papers" to articulate the worst-case scenario); *cf.* David Gray, *Wanted: Chief Ignorance Officer*, HARV. BUS. REV., Nov. 2003, at 22 (explaining that ignorance is a "precious resource," in part because it can spawn new ideas); Diane L. Coutu, *Putting Leaders on the Couch: A Conversation with Manfred F.R. Kets de Vries*, HARV. BUS. REV., Jan. 2004, at 70 (quoting Manfred F.R. Kets de Vries as saying that leaders, including CEOs, need a "fool" or, more generally, "people with a healthy disrespect for the boss – people who feel free to express emotions and opinions openly, who can engage in active give-and-take"); Lynne L. Dallas, *The Multiple Roles of Corporate Boards of Directors*, 40 SAN DIEGO L. REV. 781, 784–86, 817–18 (2003) (recommending "business review boards" that would be charged with evaluating business decisions); James A. Fanto, *Whistleblowing and the Public Director: Countering Corporate Inner Circles*, 83 OR. L. REV. 435, 490–524 (2004) (advocating the election of so-called public directors who would bring an "oppositional" attitude to boards to counter groupthink). *See also* JAY LORSCH, PAWNS OR POTENTATES: THE REALITY OF AMERICA'S CORPORATE BOARDS 91–93, 182–83 (1989); MYLES L. MACE, DIRECTORS: MYTH AND REALITY 52–65, 180, 186–88 (1986) (discussing the role of the board when it comes to "asking discerning questions"). For a relevant assessment focusing on the CEO, see BOB FIFER & GORDON QUICK, THE ENLIGHTENED CEO: HOW TO SUCCEED AT THE TOUGHEST JOB IN BUSINESS (2007).

Kahneman and Lovallo have suggested a complementary approach, emphasizing that managers should take an outside view when evaluating a project. In particular, to introduce more objectivity into forecasting, the outside view would have managers: (1) select a reference class for the proposed project, (2) assess the distribution of outcomes, (3) make an intuitive prediction of the project's position in the distribution, (4) assess the reliability of one's prediction, and (5) correct the intuitive estimate. Lovallo & Kahneman, *supra* note 10, at 62; *see also* Kahneman & Lovallo, *supra* note 12.

For another discussion of the importance of dissent in corporations, see Jeffrey A. Sonnenfeld, *What Makes Great Boards Great*, HARV. BUS. REV., Sept. 2002, at 106. Sonnenfeld explains:

> If you're the CEO, don't punish mavericks or dissenters, even if they're sometimes pains in the neck. Dissent is not the same thing as disloyalty. Use your own resistance as an

A key benefit of actually appointing a formal devil's advocate as part of corporate decision making is that it institutionalizes dissent in the firm. This may be most important when it comes to ensuring that the CEO does not dominate decision making. With a devil's advocate appointed, tough, persistent questioning does not depend on directors or subordinate officers deciding to step forward to press the CEO, which can be difficult. Rather, it becomes the specific job of an identified director or small group of directors to develop counterarguments, ask pointed questions, challenge assumptions, and otherwise ensure an open and frank discussion of issues. Even if a CEO says that he welcomes disagreement, individuals may be reluctant to take him at his word and may thus temper their probing or simply go along. Furthermore, once a devil's advocate speaks up, others on the board and in the senior management ranks may be more comfortable speaking out and contributing their independent views.

The devil's advocate function could be implemented in many different ways. That said, some features of the approach come to mind as particularly important.

First, directors serving in the devil's advocate role need access to good information. Good information will equip the devil's advocate to ask hard questions that are worth asking, to sniff out misleading or evasive answers, and to offer helpful alternatives. Second, the director must not be concerned about the potential costs of expressing an opposing view to the CEO. In other words, the director must be independent – that is, not beholden to or otherwise unduly under the control or other influence of the CEO. To aid in this regard,

opportunity to learn. Probe silent board members for their opinions, and ask them to justify their positions. If you're asked to join a board, say no if you detect pressure to conform to the majority. Leave a board if the CEO expects obedience. Otherwise, you put your wealth and reputation – as well as the assets and reputation of the company – at risk.

Id. at 110. *See also* Kenneth R. Andrews, *Corporate Strategy as a Vital Function of the Board,* HARV. BUS. REV., Nov.–Dec. 1981, at 174; Kathleen M. Eisenhardt et al., *How Management Teams Can Have a Good Fight,* HARV. BUS. REV., July–Aug. 1997, at 77; Lovallo et al., *supra* note 16; *see generally* J. EDWARD RUSSO & PAUL J.H. SCHOEMAKER, WINNING DECISIONS (2002).

For an influential treatment, see IRVING L. JANIS, GROUPTHINK: PSYCHOLOGICAL STUDIES OF POLICY DECISIONS AND FIASCOES (2d ed. 1982).

The idea of appointing one or more directors to serve as a devil's advocate suggests that there is room for the board to serve a more active managerial role. For excellent discussions of the different models of boards of directors, see the chapters by Lawrence Mitchell and Lawrence Cunningham. *See also* MELVIN A. EISENBERG, THE STRUCTURE OF THE CORPORATION: A LEGAL ANALYSIS (1976); LORSCH, *supra*; MACE, *supra*.

A company's decision to institute a devil's advocate should be voluntary. One could imagine that enhanced dissent could in effect be mandated through evolving fiduciary duties. For an assessment of such an eventuality, see Paredes, *supra* note 13, at 747–57.

it might be prudent to rotate the devil's advocate role among directors or even to randomly choose which director will serve this function when a particular issue meriting serious consideration arises. Third, individuals serving as a devil's advocate should have sufficient stature so that they and their views are respected and taken seriously. Fourth, the devil's advocate needs to take her responsibility seriously, spending enough time and effort to do the job earnestly and effectively. Simply going through the motions, having adopted a check-the-box approach to dissent, could do more harm than good. If the devil's advocate does not approach her task diligently, she risks being ignored and may simply provide cover for a bad decision. Fifth, it may be important to ensure that an individual serving as devil's advocate does not have any, or at least not too much, ambition of becoming CEO herself.[33] Otherwise, she may exploit her role as devil's advocate to undercut and ultimately edge out the incumbent CEO. It is one thing for the devil's advocate to dissent in the spirit of trying to ensure a good decision is reached. It is another thing for the devil's advocate to compete for power.

This fifth point suggests a troubling risk inherent in appointing a devil's advocate or otherwise institutionalizing dissent in an organization. It is important that the devil's advocate does not take himself too seriously and actively try to block a course of action the CEO prefers after appropriate reflection. The devil's advocate is not a co-CEO and is not there to usurp the CEO's role. Rather, the devil's advocate exists to ensure that information is disclosed, arguments are heard, risks are recognized, assumptions are studied, and flawed logic is exposed. In other words, the devil's advocate function exists to improve the CEO's decision making, as well as that of the board; the purpose is not to wrest power from the CEO or even to unduly influence the rest of the board. A word of caution for the rest of the board, then, is in order. The other directors should seriously engage and consider the devil's advocate's views and probing but should not readily defer to the devil's advocate. There is no reason to presume that the devil's advocate is right. The board also should avoid rushing to question whether the CEO is right for the company if the CEO changes his or her mind in response to the devil's advocate. The board should not rush

---

[33] *Cf.* Robert F. Felton & Simon C.Y. Wong, *How to Separate the Roles of Chairman and CEO*, McKinsey Q., No. 4, 2004, at 59, stating about nonexecutive chairs:

> For chairmen, the most important characteristic – over and above the usual ones, such as integrity and leadership ability – is a lack of ambition to be CEO: only someone content to serve in a secondary, behind-the-scenes role can have a productive and trusting relationship with the chief executive. The lack of rivalry fosters cooperation, eases the flow of information, and helps chairmen to serve as effective mentors to CEOs and to revel in their success.

Id. at 65.

to see the CEO as too tentative or, worse yet, as lacking the judgment and knowledge required to succeed as the business's top executive.

The added challenge in instituting a devil's advocate is to get the benefit of dissent without too much disruption or ill will being fostered or causing things to grind to a halt. At a minimum, a CEO who has to tend to a devil's advocate may be distracted from other serious matters and may become frustrated and even demoralized when faced with repeated questioning. More to the point, when disagreement focuses attention on risk, a CEO might be dissuaded from taking even prudent risks and might become too tentative. In other words, dissent may push a CEO off good business decisions and turn even an overconfident CEO into a weak one. Even if the CEO remains committed to some course of action, the earlier dissent may undercut the conviction with which others implement the CEO's decision. Support for the CEO and his initiatives may wane so that good decisions do not get the organizational support needed to succeed. At the same time, well-recognized team-building strategies can go a long way toward mitigating these risks.

Given these general guideposts, before implementing the devil's advocate role, a company should consider its own particular needs and circumstances, including the rest of its corporate governance structure. No single approach is optimal for each firm or each circumstance. Indeed, an active lead director or nonexecutive chairman of the board may already ensure adequate dissent within a firm,[34] as might a chief risk officer. And some chief executives bring a trusted senior adviser on board to provide the chief executive counsel, which presumably includes asking tough questions and delivering bad news, as one would expect from a devil's advocate.[35]

IV. CONCLUSION

A fundamental goal of corporate governance is to ensure that corporate executives and directors make good business decisions. Given the complexity of business, making good decisions is not easy. Even well-intentioned individuals who are working earnestly and in good faith to run a business successfully will make mistakes, sometimes disastrous ones. Accordingly, it is important that we constantly strive to find ways to improve corporate decision making.

This chapter explores the problem of CEO overconfidence and the possible solution of a devil's advocate on the board. The chapter connects and extends

[34] Cf. John Roberts et al., *Beyond Agency Conceptions of the Work of the Non-Executive Director: Creating Accountability in the Boardroom*, 16 BRITISH J. MGMT. S5 (2005).
[35] Cf. David A. Nadler, *Confessions of a Trusted Counselor*, HARV. BUS. REV., Sept. 2005, at 68.

a wealth of diverse literatures from different areas of study – management, economics, psychology, law, political science, and so on – to explore some of the ways this solution can help solve this problem. The chapter's authors themselves are sufficiently aware of the overconfidence problem that we recognize the proposals we explore here also are fraught with their own serious limitations and so should not be received with too much confidence. For example, the strategies offered here for mitigating problems of overconfidence bring with them other risks, including having the devil's advocate try too hard to compete for the CEO's job, having the devil's advocate be seen as a mere straw man whose ideas never have any value, and having the team as a whole not act as a sufficiently coherent team after decisions have been made. While well-known techniques for maintaining team spirit can mitigate these risks, the net benefit or cost of any set of strategies will vary across different settings. In addition, while procedures may succeed in mitigating overconfidence in some ways, they may still lead to their own form of overconfidence in other ways. For example, a decision-making process that includes rich ventilation of concerns about issues of one type may yield a decision that is not sufficiently robust to issues of a second type, leaving the CEO potentially overconfident about problems relating to that second type.

At bottom, the overall effort toward better management can be advanced when corporate governance takes into account managerial psychology, in addition to managerial incentives. That said, it is critical that we do not assume that we know more than we actually do about how corporate actors make decisions and exercise judgment. While it is prudent to consider psychology, we must appreciate that important gaps remain in our understanding of how people make choices and why. Because we still have a great deal to learn about decision making, we need to be cautious and deliberate in making recommendations for reforming corporate governance based on our present understanding of managerial psychology.

PART TWO

THE WHY, WHEN, HOW, AND HOW MUCH OF EXECUTIVE PAY

4 Pay Without Performance

Overview of the Issues

Lucian A. Bebchuk and Jesse M. Fried

I. INTRODUCTION

In our recent book *Pay without Performance*,[1] and in several accompanying and subsequent papers,[2] we seek to provide a full account of how managerial power and influence have shaped executive compensation in publicly traded U.S. companies. Financial economists studying executive compensation have typically assumed that pay arrangements are produced by arm's-length contracting, contracting between executives attempting to get the best possible

[1] LUCIAN A. BEBCHUK & JESSE M. FRIED, PAY WITHOUT PERFORMANCE: THE UNFULFILLED PROMISE OF EXECUTIVE COMPENSATION (2004). Earlier articles by us on which the book draws include Lucian A. Bebchuk & Jesse M. Fried, *Executive Compensation as an Agency Problem*, 17 J. ECON. PERSP. 71 (2003); Lucian A. Bebchuk, Jesse M. Fried, & David I. Walker, *Managerial Power and Rent Extraction in the Design of Executive Compensation*, 69 U. CHI. L. REV. 751 (2002).

[2] These studies include Lucian A. Bebchuk & Jesse M. Fried, *Executive Compensation at Fannie Mae: A Case Study of Perverse Incentives, Nonperformance Pay, and Camouflage*, 30 J. CORP. L. 807 (2005); Lucian A. Bebchuk & Robert Jackson Jr., *Executive Pensions*, 30 J. CORP. L. 823 (2005); Lucian A. Bebchuk & Yaniv Grinstein, *The Growth of Executive Pay*, 21 OXFORD REV. ECON. POL'Y 282 (Summer 2005); Lucian A. Bebchuk & Jesse M. Fried, *Stealth Compensation via Retirement Benefits*, 2 BERKELEY BUS. L.J. 291 (2004); Lucian A. Bebchuk & Yaniv Grinstein, *Firm Expansion and CEO Pay* (2005) (unpublished manuscript, on file with Lucian A. Bebchuk).

Lucian A. Bebchuk is William J. Friedman and Alicia Townsend Friedman Professor of Law, Economics, and Finance and Director of the Program on Corporate Governance, Harvard Law School, and Research Associate, National Bureau of Economic Research. Jesse M. Fried is Professor of Law, Harvard Law School. For financial support, the authors would like to thank the John M. Olin Center for Law, Economics, and Business; the Guggenheim Foundation; the Lens Foundation for Corporate Excellence; and the Nathan Cummins Foundations (Bebchuk); and the Boalt Hall Fund and the University of California, Berkeley, Committee on Research (Fried). This piece was originally published in the *Journal of Corporation Law* and subsequently reprinted with minor adjustments in the *Journal of Applied Corporate Finance* and *Academy of Management Perspectives*. This version reflects some additional revisions.

deal for themselves, and boards trying to get the best possible deal for shareholders. This assumption has also been the basis for the corporate law rules
governing the subject. We aim to show, however, that the pay-setting process
in U.S. public companies has strayed far from the arm's-length model.

Our analysis indicates that managerial power has played a key role in shaping executive pay. The pervasive role of managerial power can explain much of
the contemporary landscape of executive compensation, including practices
and patterns that have long puzzled financial economists. We also show that
managerial influence over the design of pay arrangements has produced considerable distortions in these arrangements, resulting in costs to investors and
the economy. This influence has led to compensation schemes that weaken
managers' incentives to increase firm value and even create incentives to take
actions that reduce long-term firm value.

The dramatic rise in CEO pay during the past two decades has been the
subject of much public criticism, which intensified following the corporate
governance scandals that began erupting in late 2001. The wave of corporate
scandals shook confidence in the performance of public company boards and
drew attention to possible flaws in their executive compensation practices. As
a result, there is now widespread recognition that many boards have employed
compensation arrangements that do not serve shareholders' interests. But there
is still substantial disagreement about the scope and source of such problems
and, not surprisingly, about how to address them.

Many take the view that concerns about executive compensation have been
exaggerated. Some maintain that flawed compensation arrangements have
been limited to a relatively small number of firms and that most boards have
carried out effectively their role of setting executive pay. Others concede that
flaws in compensation arrangements have been widespread but maintain that
those flaws have resulted from honest mistakes and misperceptions on the
part of boards seeking to serve shareholders. According to this view, now that
the problems have been recognized, corporate boards can be expected to fix
them on their own. Still others argue that even though regulatory intervention
was necessary, recent reforms that strengthen director independence will fully
address past problems; once the reforms are implemented, boards can be
expected to adopt shareholder-serving pay policies.

Our work seeks to persuade readers that such complacency is unwarranted.
To begin with, flawed compensation arrangements have not been limited to
a small number of bad apples; they have been widespread, persistent, and
systemic. Furthermore, the problems have not resulted from temporary mistakes or lapses of judgment that boards can be expected to correct on their
own. Rather, they have stemmed from structural defects in the underlying

governance structure that enable executives to exert considerable influence over their boards. The absence of effective arm's-length dealing under today's system of corporate governance has been the primary source of problematic compensation arrangements. Finally, while recent reforms that seek to increase board independence will likely improve matters, they will not be sufficient to make boards adequately accountable. Much more needs to be done.

Another broader aim of our work has been to contribute to a better understanding of some basic problems with the U.S. corporate governance system. The study of executive compensation opens a window through which we can examine our current reliance on boards to act as guardians of shareholders' interests. Our corporate governance system gives boards substantial power and counts on them to monitor and supervise company managers. As long as corporate directors are believed to carry out their tasks for the benefit of shareholders, current governance arrangements, which insulate boards from intervention by shareholders, appear acceptable. Our analysis of the executive pay landscape casts doubt on the validity of this belief and on the wisdom of insulating boards from shareholders.

A full understanding of the flaws in current compensation arrangements, and in the governance processes that have produced them, is necessary to address these problems. After providing a full account of the existing problems, our work also puts forward a set of proposals that could be considered for improving both executive pay and corporate governance. We provide detailed suggestions for how both the amount of pay and its performance sensitivity could be made more transparent. Such transparency will provide a better check on managers' power to influence their own pay. It will also eliminate existing incentives to choose compensation arrangements that are less efficient but more effective in camouflaging either the amount of pay or its insensitivity to managers' own performance.

Furthermore, our analysis of the many ways in which pay schemes weaken or distort managerial incentives provides a basis for examining how corporate boards could strengthen the link between pay and performance and thereby improve incentives. Finally, we put forward a number of reforms that would make directors not only more independent of insiders but also more dependent on shareholders, thus improving board accountability to shareholders. Such reforms could well offer the most promising route for improving executive compensation and corporate governance more generally.

In this chapter, we outline some of the main elements of our critique of contemporary executive compensation and corporate governance arrangements, as well as some suggested reforms. We start by describing the limitations of the official arm's-length model of executive compensation. We then turn to the managerial power perspective. We show that managerial influence can explain many features of the compensation landscape, and we explain how this influence has led to opaque and distorted pay arrangements. We conclude with a discussion of suggestions for making pay more transparent, improving the design of pay arrangements, and increasing board accountability.

Before proceeding, we want to emphasize that our critique of existing pay arrangements and pay-setting processes does not imply that most directors and executives have acted less ethically than others would have in their place. Our problem is not with the moral caliber of directors and executives but with the system of arrangements and incentives within which directors and executives operate. As currently structured, the U.S. corporate governance system unavoidably creates incentives and psychological and social forces that distort pay choices. Such incentives and forces can be expected to lead most people serving as directors to go along with arrangements that favor their firms' executives, as long as these arrangements are consistent with prevailing practices and conventions and thus not difficult to justify to themselves and to others. If we were to maintain the basic structure of the system and merely replace current directors and executives with a different set of individuals, the new directors and executives would be exposed to the very same incentives and forces as their predecessors, and by and large, we would not expect them to act any differently. To address the flaws in the pay-setting process, we need to change the governance arrangements that produce such distortions.

II. THE STAKES

What is at stake in the debate over executive pay? Some might question whether executive compensation has a significant economic impact on shareholders and the economy. The problems with executive compensation, it might be argued, do not much affect shareholders' bottom line and instead are mainly symbolic. However, the questions of whether and to what extent pay arrangements are flawed are important for shareholders and policy makers because defects in these arrangements can impose substantial costs on shareholders.

Let's start with the excess pay that managers receive as a result of their power – that is, the difference between what managers' influence enables them to obtain and what they would get under arm's-length contracting. As a recent study by Yaniv Grinstein and one of us documents in detail,[3] the amounts involved are hardly pocket change for shareholders. Among other

---

[3] Bebchuk & Grinstein, *The Growth of Executive Pay, supra* note 2.

TABLE 4.1. *Aggregate top-five compensation, 1993–2003 (in $ billions)*

Period	All ExecuComp firms	Non-ExecuComp firms	All firms
1993–2003	212	139	351
1993–1997	68	55	123
1999–2003	122	70	192

Source: Lucian A. Bebchuk, *The Case for Increasing Shareholder Power*, 118 HARV. L. REV. 833 (2005).

things, this study provides figures for aggregate compensation of the top five executives of publicly traded U.S. firms. According to the study's estimates, which are shown in Table 4.1, these companies paid their top five executives a total of $351 billion during the eleven-year period from 1993 to 2003, with about $192 billion of this amount paid during the five-year period from 1999 to 2003. Note that the aggregate compensation figures reported by the study reflect only those amounts reported in each firm's annual summary compensation table. As will be discussed later, standard executive compensation data sets (like the ExecuComp data set used in the study) omit many significant forms of compensation, such as the substantial amounts of retirement benefits received by executives. Thus, the aggregate compensation figures may significantly understate the actual compensation received by firms' top executives during this period.

Table 4.1 shows aggregate compensation paid by a large set of public firms to their top five executives. The set of firms includes all ExecuComp firms and Compustat firms with a market capitalization larger than $50 million, except for firms for which there is no net income information in Compustat as well as real estate investment trusts, mutual funds, and other investment funds (SIC codes 67XX). All figures are in 2002 dollars. The compensation paid to executives of non-ExecuComp firms is estimated using the coefficients from annual regressions of compensation on firm characteristics in ExecuComp firms.

Table 4.2 displays the ratio of the aggregate top-five compensation paid by publicly traded U.S. firms to their aggregate corporate earnings. Such aggregate compensation accounted for 6.6 percent of the aggregate earnings (net income) of publicly traded U.S. firms during the period from 1993 to 2003. Moreover, during the most recent three-year period examined by the study (2001–2003), aggregate top-five compensation jumped to 9.8 percent of aggregate earnings, up from 5 percent during the period from 1993 to 1995. Income information is obtained from Compustat, and the estimates

TABLE 4.2. *Compensation and corporate earnings*

	Period	Aggregate top-five compensation to aggregate earnings (%)
Three-year periods	1993–1995	5.0
	1994–1996	4.9
	1995–1997	5.2
	1996–1998	5.5
	1997–1999	6.0
	1998–2000	6.5
	1999–2001	8.6
	2000–2002	12.8
	2001–2003	9.8
Five-year periods	1993–1997	5.2
	1999–2003	8.1
Full period	1993–2003	6.6

Source: Lucian A. Bebchuk, *The Case for Increasing Shareholder Power*, 118 HARV. L. REV. 833 (2005).

of aggregate top-five compensation are calculated in the same way as in Table 4.1.

These figures indicate that if compensation levels could be cut without weakening managerial incentives, the gain to investors would not be merely symbolic. It would have a discernible effect on corporate earnings. But excess pay is unlikely to be the only or even the main cost of current compensation practices. Managers' influence over their compensation arrangements can result in the weakening and distortion of managerial incentives. In our view, the dilution and distortion of incentives could well impose a larger cost on shareholders than excessive compensation per se.

Existing pay arrangements have been producing two types of incentive problems. First, compensation arrangements have provided weaker incentives to increase shareholder value than would have been provided under arm's-length contracting. Both the nonequity and equity components of managerial compensation have been more severely decoupled from managers' contributions to company performance than appearances might suggest. Making pay more sensitive to performance could therefore have substantial benefits for shareholders.

Second, prevailing practices not only fail to provide cost-effective incentives to increase value but also create perverse incentives. For example, managers' broad freedom to unload company options and stock can lead them to act in ways that reduce shareholder value. Executives who expect to unload shares have incentives to report misleading results, suppress bad news, and choose projects and strategies that are less transparent to the market. The efficiency costs of such distortions may well exceed – possibly by a large margin – whatever liquidity or risk-bearing benefits executives obtain from being able to unload their options and shares at will. Similarly, because existing pay practices often reward managers for increasing firm size, they provide executives with incentives to pursue expansion through acquisitions or other means, even when that strategy is value reducing.

III. THE ARM'S-LENGTH CONTRACTING VIEW

According to the official view of executive compensation, in setting pay arrangements, corporate boards are guided solely by shareholder interests and operate at arm's length from the executives whose pay they set. The premise that boards contract at arm's length with executives has long been and remains a central tenet in the corporate world and in most research on executive compensation by financial economists. In the corporate world, the official view serves as the practical basis for legal rules and public policy. It is used to justify directors' compensation decisions to shareholders, policy makers, and courts. These decisions are portrayed as being made largely with shareholders' interests at heart and therefore deserving of deference.

The premise of arm's-length contracting has also been shared by most of the research on executive compensation. Managers' influence over directors has been recognized by those writing on the subject from legal, organizational, and sociological perspectives, as well as by media commentary on executive pay. But the vast majority of research on executive pay has been done by financial economists, and most of their work assumes that corporate boards adopt pay arrangements that serve shareholders by providing managers with cost-effective incentives to maximize value. Because boards and executives operating at arm's length have incentives to avoid inefficient provisions, the arm's-length contracting view has led researchers to assume that executive compensation arrangements will tend to increase value.[4] Some financial economists, whose studies we discuss at length in our book, have reported findings that they viewed as inconsistent with the arm's-length model.[5] However, most work in

---

[4] *See* Bebchuk, Fried, & Walker, *supra* note 1; Bebchuk & Fried, *Executive Compensation as an Agency Problem, supra* note 1 (noting that the link between arm's-length contracting and efficient arrangements has led us to label arm's-length contracting as "efficient contracting" or "optimal contracting" in some of our earlier work).

[5] *See, e.g.*, Marianne Bertrand & Sendhil Mullainathan, *Are CEOs Rewarded for Luck? The Ones Without Principals Are*, 116 Q.J. ECON. 901 (2001); Olivier Jean Blanchard et al., *What*

the field has started from the premise of arm's-length contracting between boards and executives.

Financial economists, both theorists and empiricists, have largely worked within the arm's-length model in attempting to explain common compensation arrangements and differences in compensation practices among companies.[6] In fact, upon discovering practices that appear inconsistent with the cost-effective provision of incentives, financial economists have labored to come up with clever explanations for how such practices might be consistent with arm's-length contracting after all. Practices for which no explanation has been found have been described as anomalies or puzzles that will ultimately either be explained within the paradigm or disappear.

In our book, we identified many compensation practices that are difficult to understand under the arm's-length contracting view but that can readily be explained by managerial influence over the pay-setting process. In response, critics suggested reasons some of these practices could still have an explanation within an arm's-length contracting framework and argued that we therefore have not succeeded in completely ruling out the possibility of arm's-length dealing. For example, in response to our account of the significant extent to which pay is decoupled from performance, Core, Guay, and Thomas argued that there are circumstances in which large amounts of nonperformance pay might be desirable.[7] Similarly, in response to our criticism of the widespread failure of firms to adopt option plans that filter out windfalls, both Gordon and Holmstrom argue that our analysis has not completely ruled out the possibility of explaining such failure within the arm's-length contracting model.[8]

These arguments reflect an implicit presumption in favor of arm's-length contracting: pay arrangements are assumed to be the product of arm's-length contracting unless one can prove otherwise. The presumption of arm's-length contracting, however, does not seem warranted. As we discuss below, an

---

Do Firms Do with Cash Windfalls?, 36 J. Fin. Econ. 337 (1994); David Yermack, *Good Timing: CEO Stock Option Awards and Company News Announcements*, 52 J. Fin. 449 (1997).

[6] For surveys from this perspective in the finance and economics literature, see, e.g., John M. Abowd & David S. Kaplan, *Executive Compensation: Six Questions That Need Answering*, J. Econ. Persp., Fall 1999, at 145; John E. Core et al., *Executive Equity Compensation and Incentives: A Survey*, 9 Econ. Pol'y Rev. 27 (2003).

[7] See, e.g., John E. Core et al., *Is U.S. CEO Compensation Inefficient Pay Without Performance?*, 103 Mich. L. Rev. 1142 (2005).

[8] See Jeffrey Gordon, *Executive Compensation: If There's a Problem, What's the Remedy? The Case for "Compensation Disclosure and Analysis,"* 30 J. Corp. L. 675 (2005); Bengt Holmstrom, *Pay Without Performance and the Managerial Power Hypothesis: A Comment*, 30 J. Corp. L. 703 (2005).

examination of the pay-setting process suggests that managerial influence is likely to play a key role. Thus, given the *a priori* likelihood of managerial influence, the burden of proof should be on those who argue that the executive pay arrangements are not significantly shaped by such influence. In any event, the fact that financial economists continue to implicitly or explicitly use arm's-length contracting as their baseline presumption indicates the dominance and power of this long-held view.

IV. LIMITS OF THE ARM'S-LENGTH VIEW

The official arm's-length story is neat, tractable, and reassuring. But it fails to account for the realities of executive compensation. The arm's-length contracting view recognizes that managers are subject to an agency problem and do not automatically seek to maximize shareholder value. The potential divergence between managers' and shareholders' interests makes it important to provide managers with adequate incentives. Under the arm's-length contracting view, the board attempts to provide such incentives cost-effectively through managers' compensation packages. But just as there is no reason to assume that managers automatically seek to maximize shareholder value, there is no reason to expect that directors will, either. Indeed, an analysis of directors' incentives and circumstances suggests that director behavior is also subject to an agency problem.

Directors have had and continue to have various economic incentives to support, or at least to go along with, arrangements that favor the company's top executives. A variety of social and psychological factors – collegiality, team spirit, a natural desire to avoid conflict in the board, friendship and loyalty, and cognitive dissonance – exert additional pull in that direction. Although many directors own some stock in their companies, their ownership positions are too small to give them a financial incentive to take the personally costly, or at the very least unpleasant, route of resisting compensation arrangements sought by executives. In addition, limitations on time and resources have made it difficult for even well-intentioned directors to do their pay-setting job properly. Finally, the market constraints within which directors operate are far from tight and do not prevent deviations from arm's-length contracting outcomes in favor of executives. Below we briefly discuss each of these factors.

A. *Incentives to Be Reelected*

Besides an attractive salary, a directorship is also likely to provide prestige and valuable business and social connections. The financial and nonfinancial benefits of holding a board seat naturally give directors an interest in keeping their positions.

In a world where shareholders select individual directors, board members might have an incentive to develop reputations as shareholder serving. Typically, however, the director slate proposed by management is the only one offered. The key to retaining a board position is thus being placed on the company's slate. And because the CEO has had significant influence over the nomination process, displeasing the CEO has been likely to hurt one's chances of being put on the company slate. Directors thus have an incentive to go along with the CEO's pay arrangement, a matter dear to the CEO's heart, at least as long as the compensation package remains within the range of what can plausibly be defended and justified. In addition, developing a reputation as a director who blocks compensation arrangements sought by executives can only hurt a director's chances of being invited to join other boards.

The new stock exchange listing requirements, which attempt to give independent directors a greater role in director nominations, weaken but do not eliminate executives' influence over director nominations. The CEO's wishes can be expected to continue to influence the decisions of the nominating committee; after all, the directors appointed to the board are expected to work closely with the CEO. As a practical matter, director candidates who are opposed by the CEO are not expected to be offered board nomination and would likely decline nomination if it were offered.[9] Even if the CEO had no influence over nominations, members of the nominating committee would be unlikely to look favorably on an individual who has taken a tough position on the CEO's pay. They might wish to avoid the friction and unpleasantness accompanying disputes over the CEO's pay or might simply side with the CEO because of the other factors discussed below.

B. CEO Power to Benefit Directors

There are a variety of ways in which CEOs can benefit individual directors or board members as a group. For one thing, CEOs have influence over director compensation. As the company leader, usually as a board member, and often as board chairman, the CEO can choose to either discourage or encourage director pay increases. Independent directors who are generous toward the CEO might reasonably expect the CEO to use his or her bully

---

[9] Daniel Nasaw, *Opening the Board: The Fight Is on to Determine Who Will Guide the Selection of Directors in the Future*, WALL ST. J., Oct. 27, 2003, at R8.

pulpit to support higher director compensation. At a minimum, generous treatment of the CEO contributes to an atmosphere that is conducive to generous treatment of directors. And, in fact, a study finds that companies with higher CEO compensation have higher director compensation as well – and that such high pay levels appear to reflect insider "cooperation" rather than superior corporate performance.[10]

In addition, CEOs have often used their power over corporate resources to reward individual directors who were particularly cooperative. The new stock exchange listing standards place some limits on the ability of CEOs to reward independent directors, but they do leave CEOs with substantial power in this area. For example, the requirements allow the company to pay $100,000 in additional compensation to an independent director. And there is no limit to how much the firm can pay an independent director's immediate family members, as long as they are nonexecutive employees.

Similarly, the requirements limit but do not prohibit business dealings between a company and an independent director's firm, and they place absolutely no limit on the company's dealings with the director's firm before or after the director qualifies for independent director status. The standards also permit unlimited contributions to charitable organizations that independent directors run, are affiliated with, or simply favor. In sum, executives' control over corporate resources continues to enable them to provide many directors with rewards. These rewards generally outweigh the small, direct personal cost to most directors of approving pay arrangements that fail to serve shareholder interests.

C. Friendship and Loyalty

Many independent directors have some prior social connection to the company's CEO or other senior executives. Even directors who did not know the CEO before their appointment may well have begun their service with a sense of obligation and loyalty to the CEO. The CEO often will have been involved in recruiting the director to the board. As a result, directors often start serving with a reservoir of goodwill toward the CEO, which will contribute to a tendency to favor the CEO on compensation matters. This kind of reciprocity is expected and observed in many social and professional contexts. Not surprisingly, studies find that compensation committees whose chairs have

---

[10] Ivan E. Brick et al., *CEO Compensation, Director Compensation, and Firm Performance: Evidence of Cronyism*, 12 J. Corp. Fin. 403 (2006).

been appointed after the CEO takes office have tended to award higher CEO compensation.[11]

D. Collegiality and Authority

In addition to friendship and loyalty considerations, there are other social and psychological forces that make it difficult for directors to resist executive-serving compensation arrangements. The CEO is the directors' colleague, and directors are generally expected to treat their fellow directors collegially. The CEO is also the company's leader, the person whose decisions and visions have the most influence on the firm's future direction. In most circumstances, directors treat the CEO with respect and substantial deference. Switching hats to contract at arm's length with one's colleague and leader is naturally difficult.

E. Cognitive Dissonance and Solidarity

Many members of compensation committees are current and former executives of other companies. Because individuals have a tendency to develop views that are consistent with their self-interest, executives and former executives are likely to have formed beliefs that support the type of pay arrangements from which they themselves have benefited. An executive who has benefited from a conventional option plan, for example, is more likely to resist the view that such plans provide executives with excessive windfalls.

Further reinforcing such cognitive dissonance, an executive who serves as a director in another firm might identify and feel some solidarity or sympathy with that firm's executives. She naturally would be inclined to treat these executives the same way she would like to be treated. Not surprisingly, there is evidence that CEO pay is correlated with the pay levels of the outside directors serving on the compensation committee.[12]

F. The Small Cost of Favoring Executives

Directors typically own only a small fraction of the firm's shares. As a result, the direct personal cost to board members of approving compensation arrangements that are too favorable to executives – the reduction in the value of their shareholdings – is small. This cost is therefore unlikely to outweigh the

[11] Brian G. Main et al., *The CEO, the Board of Directors, and Executive Compensation: Economic and Psychological Perspectives*, 4 INDUS. CORP. CHANGE 293 (1995).
[12] *Id.*

economic incentives and social and psychological factors that induce directors to go along with pay schemes that favor executives.

G. Ratcheting

It is now widely recognized that the rise in executive compensation has in part been driven by many boards seeking to pay their CEOs more than the industry average. This widespread practice has led to an ever-increasing average and a continuous escalation of executive pay.[13] A review of reports of compensation committees in large companies indicates that a large majority of them used peer groups in determining pay and set compensation at or above the 50th percentile of the peer group.[14] Such ratcheting is consistent with a picture of boards that do not seek to get the best deal for their shareholders but are happy to go along with whatever can be justified as consistent with prevailing practices.

H. Limits of Market Forces

Some writers have argued that, even if directors are under the considerable influence of corporate executives, market forces will cause boards and executives to adopt the compensation arrangements that arm's-length contracting would produce. Our analysis, however, finds that market forces are neither sufficiently fine-tuned nor sufficiently powerful to compel such outcomes. The markets for capital, corporate control, and managerial labor impose some constraints on executive compensation. But these constraints are by no means stringent, and they permit substantial deviations from arm's-length contracting.

Consider, for example, the market for corporate control – the threat of a takeover. Most companies have substantial defenses against takeovers. For example, a majority of companies have a staggered board, which prevents a hostile acquirer from gaining control before two annual elections are held and often enables incumbent managers to block hostile bids that are attractive to shareholders. To overcome incumbent opposition, a hostile bidder must be prepared to pay a substantial premium.[15] The disciplinary force of the market for corporate control is further weakened by the prevalence of golden

[13] Kevin J. Murphy, *Executive Compensation, in* HANDBOOK OF LABOR ECONOMICS 2485, 2517–18 (Orley Ashenfelter & David Card eds., 1999).

[14] John M. Bizjak et al., *Has the Use of Peer Groups Contributed to Higher Levels of Executive Compensation?* (2000) (unpublished manuscript, on file with Jesse M. Fried).

[15] Lucian Bebchuk et al., *The Powerful Antitakeover Force of Staggered Boards: Theory, Evidence, and Policy,* 54 STAN. L. REV. 887 (2002).

parachute provisions, as well as by payoffs made by acquirers to target managers to facilitate the acquisition. The market for corporate control thus exerts little disciplining force on managers and boards, leaving them with considerable slack and the ability to negotiate manager-favoring pay arrangements.

I. New CEOs

Some critics of our work have assumed that our analysis of managerial influence does not apply when boards negotiate pay with a CEO candidate from outside the firm.[16] However, while such negotiations might be closer to the arm's-length model than negotiations with an incumbent CEO, they still fall quite short of this benchmark.

Among other things, directors negotiating with an outside CEO candidate know that after the candidate becomes CEO, he or she will have influence over their renomination to the board and over their compensation and perks. The directors will also wish to have good personal and working relationships with the individual who is expected to become the firm's leader and a fellow board member. And while agreeing to a pay package that favors the outside CEO imposes little financial cost on directors, a breakdown in the negotiations, which might embarrass the directors and force them to reopen the CEO selection process, would be personally costly to them. Finally, directors' limited time forces them to rely on information shaped and presented by the company's human resources staff and compensation consultants, all of whom have incentives to please the incoming CEO.

J. Firing of Executives

Some have suggested that the increased willingness of directors to fire CEOs over the past decade, especially in recent years, provides evidence that boards do in fact deal with CEOs at arm's length.[17] However, firings are still limited to unusual situations in which the CEO is accused of legal or ethical violations or is viewed by revolting shareholders as having a record of terrible performance. Without strong outside pressure to fire the CEO, mere mediocrity is far from enough to get a CEO pushed out. Furthermore, in the rare cases in which boards fire executives, boards often provide the departing executives with benefits beyond those required by the contract to sweeten the CEO's departure

---

[16] Kevin J. Murphy, *Explaining Executive Compensation: Managerial Power vs. the Perceived Cost of Stock Options*, 69 U. CHI. L. REV. 847 (2002).

[17] *See, e.g.*, Holman W. Jenkins, *Outrageous CEO Pay Revisited*, WALL ST. J., Oct. 2, 2002, at A17.

and alleviate the directors' guilt and discomfort. All in all, boards' record of dealing with failed executives does not support the view that boards treat CEOs at arm's length.

In sum, a realistic picture of the incentives and circumstances of board members reveals many incentives and tendencies that lead directors to behave very differently than boards contracting at arm's length with their executives over pay. Recent reforms, such as the new stock exchange listing requirements, may weaken some of these factors but will not eliminate them. Without additional reforms, the pay-setting process will continue to deviate substantially from arm's-length contracting.

VI. POWER AND PAY

The same factors that limit the usefulness of the arm's-length model in explaining executive compensation suggest that executives have had substantial influence over their own pay. Compensation arrangements have often deviated from arm's-length contracting, because directors have been influenced by management, insufficiently motivated to insist on shareholder-serving compensation, or simply ineffectual. Executives' influence over directors has enabled them to obtain rents, or benefits greater than those obtainable under true arm's-length contracting.

In our work, we find that the role of managerial power can explain many aspects of the executive compensation landscape. It is worth emphasizing that our conclusion is not based on the amount of compensation received by executives. In our view, high absolute levels of pay do not by themselves imply that compensation arrangements deviate from arm's-length contracting. Our finding that such deviations have been common is based primarily on an analysis of the process by which pay is set and an examination of the inefficient, distorted, and nontransparent structure of pay arrangements that emerge from this process. For us, the smoking gun of managerial influence over pay is not high levels of pay but such things as the correlation between power and pay, the systematic use of compensation practices that obscure the amount and performance insensitivity of pay, and the showering of gratuitous benefits on departing executives.

A. *Power-Pay Relationships*

Although top executives generally have some degree of influence over their boards, the extent of their influence depends on various features of the company's governance structure. The managerial power approach predicts that executives who have more power should receive higher pay – or pay that is less sensitive to performance – than their less powerful counterparts. A substantial body of evidence does indicate that pay is higher, and less sensitive to performance, when executives have more power.

First, there is evidence that executive compensation is higher when the board is relatively weak or ineffectual vis-à-vis the CEO. In particular, CEO compensation is higher: (1) when the board is large, which makes it more difficult for directors to organize in opposition to the CEO; (2) when more of the outside directors have been appointed by the CEO, which could cause them to feel gratitude or obligation to the CEO; and (3) when outside directors serve on three or more boards, and thus are more likely to be distracted.[18] Also, CEO pay is between 20 percent and 40 percent higher if the CEO is the chairman of the board, and it is negatively correlated with the stock ownership of compensation committee members.[19]

Second, studies find a negative correlation between the presence of a large outside shareholder and pay arrangements that favor executives. A large outside shareholder might engage in closer monitoring and thereby reduce managers' influence over their compensation. One study finds a negative correlation between the equity ownership of the largest shareholder and the amount of CEO compensation. More specifically, doubling the percentage ownership of a large outside shareholder is associated with a 12–14 percent reduction in a CEO's nonsalary compensation.[20] Another study finds that CEOs in companies without a 5 percent (or larger) outside shareholder tend to receive more "luck-based" pay – that is, pay associated with profit increases that are generated entirely by external factors (such as changes in oil prices and exchange rates) rather than by managers' own efforts.[21] This study also finds that, in companies lacking large, outside shareholders, boards make smaller reductions in cash compensation when they increase CEOs' option-based compensation.

Third, there is evidence linking executive pay to the concentration of institutional shareholders, which are more likely to monitor the CEO and the board. One study finds that more concentrated institutional ownership leads to lower and more performance-sensitive compensation.[22] Another study finds that the

---

[18] John E. Core et al., *Corporate Governance, Chief Executive Compensation, and Firm Performance*, 51 J. Fin. Econ. 371 (1999).

[19] *Id.*; Richard M. Cyert et al., *Corporate Governance, Takeovers, and Top-Management Compensation: Theory and Evidence*, 48 Mgmt. Sci. 453 (2002).

[20] Cyert et al., *supra* note 19.

[21] Marianne Bertrand & Sendhil Mullainathan, *Agents With and Without Principals*, Am. Econ. Rev., May 2000, at 203.

[22] Jay C. Hartzell & Laura T. Starks, *Institutional Investors and Executive Compensation*, 58 J. Fin. 2351 (2003).

effect of institutional shareholders on CEO pay depends on the nature of their relationships with the firm.[23] This study reports that CEO pay is negatively correlated with the presence of pressure-resistant institutions, institutions that have no other business relationship with the firm and presumably are concerned only with the firm's share value. But CEO pay is positively correlated with the presence of pressure-sensitive institutions – institutions that have business relationships with the firm (such as managing its pension funds) and are thus more vulnerable to management pressure.

Fourth, studies find a connection between pay and antitakeover provisions, arrangements that make CEOs and their boards less vulnerable to a hostile takeover. One study finds that CEOs of companies adopting antitakeover provisions enjoy above-market compensation before adoption of the provisions and that adoption is followed by further significant increases in pay.[24] This pattern is not readily explainable by arm's-length contracting. Indeed, if risk-averse managers' jobs are more secure, shareholders should be able to pay the managers less. Another study finds that CEOs of companies that became protected by state antitakeover legislation enacted during the period from 1984 to 1991 reduced their holdings of shares, which became less important for the purpose of maintaining control, by an average of 15 percent.[25] Arm's-length contracting, by contrast, might predict that CEOs protected by antitakeover legislation would be required by their boards to increase their shareholdings to restore their incentive to generate shareholder value.

Finally, there is evidence that managerial power affects the likelihood that firms opportunistically time executives' option grants via backdating or otherwise. A study by Yaniv Grinstein, Urs Peyer, and one of us finds that grants to a CEO were more likely to be lucky – to have a reported grant date resulting in an exercise price equal to the lowest price of the month – when the board lacked a majority of independent directors.[26] The study also found that such grants were more likely to be lucky when the CEO had served in the role for a long time – and therefore could be expected to have greater influence over internal pay-setting processes. [27]

---

[23] David Parthiban et al., *The Effect of Institutional Investors on the Level and Mix of CEO Compensation*, 41 ACAD. MGMT. J. 200 (1998).

[24] Kenneth A. Borokhovich et al., *CEO Contracting and Anti-Takeover Amendments*, 52 J. FIN. 1495 (1997).

[25] Shijun Cheng et al., *Identifying Control Motives in Managerial Ownership: Evidence from Antitakeover Legislation*, 8 REV. FIN. STUD. 637 (2005).

[26] Lucian Bebchuk et al., *Lucky CEOs* (Nat'l Bureau of Econ. Res., Discussion Paper No. 12771, 2006), *available at* www.nber.org/papers/w12771.

[27] *Id.* For a discussion of the literature finding a link between backdating and managerial power, see Jesse M. Fried, *Option Backdating and Its Implications* (working paper, on file with Jesse M. Fried, 2007).

B. Limits of Managerial Influence

There are, of course, limits to the arrangements that directors will approve and executives will seek. Although market forces are not sufficiently powerful to prevent significant deviations from arm's-length outcomes, they do impose some constraints on executive compensation. If a board were to approve a pay arrangement viewed as egregious, for example, shareholders would be less willing to support incumbents in a hostile takeover or a proxy fight.

In addition, directors and executives adopting such an arrangement might bear social costs. Directors approving a clearly inflated and distorted pay package might be subject to ridicule or scorn in the media or in their social and business circles. Most directors would wish to avoid such treatment, even if their board positions were not at risk, and these potential social costs reinforce the constraints imposed by market forces. Like market forces, the potential costs cannot preclude significant deviations from shareholder-serving arrangements, but they may discourage the adoption of arrangements that are patently abusive and indefensible.

One important building block of the managerial power approach is, therefore, outrage costs. When a board approves a compensation arrangement favorable to managers, the extent to which directors and executives bear economic costs (such as heightened risk of takeover) and social costs (such as embarrassment) will depend on how the arrangement is perceived by outsiders whose views matter to the directors and executives. The more outrage a compensation arrangement is expected to generate, the larger the potential economic and social costs will be, and thus the more reluctant directors will be to approve it and the more hesitant managers will be to propose it in the first place.

There is evidence that the design of compensation arrangements is indeed influenced by how outsiders perceive them. One study finds that, during the 1990s, CEOs who were the target of shareholder resolutions criticizing executive pay had their annual (industry-adjusted) compensation reduced over the subsequent two years.[28]

C. Camouflage and Stealth Compensation

The critical role of outsiders' perception of executives' compensation and the significance of outrage costs explain the importance of yet another

---

[28] Randall S. Thomas & Kenneth J. Martin, *The Effect of Shareholder Proposals on Executive Compensation*, 67 U. CIN. L. REV. 1021 (1999).

component of the managerial power approach: camouflage. The desire to minimize outrage gives designers of compensation arrangements a strong incentive to try to legitimize; justify; obscure; or more generally, camouflage the amount and performance insensitivity of executive compensation.

The desire to camouflage has an important effect on pay structures. We show that compensation designers' attempts to obscure the amount and performance insensitivity of compensation have led to arrangements that undermine and distort managerial incentives, thereby weakening firm performance. Overall, the camouflage motive turns out to be quite useful in explaining many otherwise-puzzling features of the executive compensation landscape.

Among the arrangements that have been used in the past to disguise or downplay the amount and performance insensitivity of compensation are executive pension plans and deferred compensation arrangements. Most executive pensions and deferred compensation arrangements do not enjoy the large tax subsidy granted to the standard retirement arrangements provided to other employees. In the case of executives, such arrangements merely shift tax liability from the executive to the firm. The efficiency grounds for providing compensation through in-kind retirement perks are also far from clear.

All of these arrangements, however, have made executives' compensation less visible to investors, regulators, and the general public. Among other things, until recently, disclosure rules did not require companies to place a dollar value on, or include in their publicly filed summary compensation tables, the amounts provided to executives after they retire. Although the existence and terms of executives' retirement arrangements had to be disclosed in various places throughout the firm's public filings, this disclosure was less visible because outsiders, including compensation researchers and the media, focus on the dollar amounts reported in the compensation tables.

In a recent empirical study, Robert Jackson and one of us used information provided in proxy statements to estimate the value of the executive pension plans of S&P 500 CEOs.[29] About two-thirds of CEOs have such plans, and the study estimates the value of these plans for all CEOs who had recently left their firms or were close to retirement age. For the median CEO in the study's sample, the actuarial value of the CEO's pension was $15 million, which made up about one-third of the total compensation (both equity and nonequity based) they had received during their service as CEOs.

Furthermore, the study indicates that when pension value is included in calculating executive pay, compensation is much less linked to performance than is commonly perceived. After pension value is included, the percentage

---

[29] *See* Bebchuk & Jackson, *supra* note 2.

of a CEO's total compensation that is salary like (that is, the portion that consists of fixed annual payments, such as basic salary during the CEO's service and pension payments afterward), increases from 16 percent to 39 percent. The study documents that the omission of retirement benefits from standard compensation data sets has distorted investors' picture of pay arrangements. In particular, this omission has led to (1) significant underestimations of the total amount of pay, (2) considerable distortions in comparisons among executive pay packages, and (3) substantial overestimations of the extent to which executive pay is linked to performance.

In our book and subsequent work, we advocated that companies be required to disclose the monetary value of the benefits awarded to executives via executive pensions and deferred compensation.[30] The SEC subsequently adopted enhanced disclosure requirements for these types of compensation.[31] While the SEC's new disclosure rules will make it more difficult for firms to use executive pensions and deferred compensation plans to hide the amount and performance insensitivity of executive pay, the motive to camouflage pay persists. After all, it took SEC intervention to get companies to disclose the monetary value of executive pensions and deferred compensation arrangements. Thus, we can expect many firms to seek other types of arrangements that can camouflage pay.

D. Gratuitous Good-Bye Payments

In many cases, boards give departing CEOs payments and benefits that are not required under the terms of a CEO's compensation contract. Such gratuitous good-bye payments are common even when CEOs perform so poorly that their boards feel compelled to replace them. For example, when Mattel's CEO Jill Barad resigned under fire, the board forgave a $4.2 million loan, gave her an additional $3.3 million in cash to cover the taxes for forgiveness of another loan, and allowed her unvested options to vest prematurely. These gratuitous benefits were offered in addition to the considerable benefits that she received

---

[30] See LUCIAN A. BEBCHUK & JESSE M. FRIED, PAY WITHOUT PERFORMANCE: THE UNFULFILLED PROMISE OF EXECUTIVE COMPENSATION (2004); Bebchuk & Jackson, *supra* note 2; Bebchuk & Fried, *Stealth Compensation via Retirement Benefits*, *supra* note 2.

[31] See Executive Compensation and Related Person Disclosure, Sec. Act Release No. 8732A, 88 SEC Docket (CCH) 2353 (Aug. 29, 2006); Executive Compensation Disclosure, Sec. Act Release No. 8765, 89 SEC Docket (CCH) 1921 (Dec. 22, 2006). For comments filed by us and Robert Jackson in support of the new disclosure requirements, see Letter from Lucian A Bebchuk, Jesse M. Fried, & Robert Jackson to Nancy M. Morris, SEC Secretary (Apr. 14, 2006), *available at* http://www.law.harvard.edu/faculty/bebchuk/Policy/Bebchuk-Fried-Jackson%20Comment.pdf.

under her employment agreement, which included a termination payment of $26.4 million and a stream of retirement benefits exceeding $700,000 per year.

It is not easy to reconcile such gratuitous payments with the arm's-length contracting model. The board has the authority to fire the CEO and pay no more than the CEO's contractual severance benefits. There should be no need to "bribe" a poorly performing CEO to step down. In addition, the signal sent by the gratuitous good-bye payment will, if anything, only weaken the incentive of the next CEO to perform.

The making of such gratuitous payments, however, is quite consistent with the existence of managerial influence over the board. Because of their relationship with the CEO, some directors might be unwilling to replace the existing CEO unless the CEO is very generously treated. Other directors might be willing to replace the CEO even without a gratuitous good-bye payment but prefer to give it either to reduce their personal discomfort in forcing out the CEO or to make the separation process less personally unpleasant. In all of these cases, directors' willingness to make such payments stems from their relationships with the CEO.

Of course, taking managerial power as given, providing gratuitous payments to fired CEOs could be beneficial to shareholders in some instances. If many directors are loyal to the CEO, such payments might be necessary to assemble a board majority in favor of replacing the executive. In this case, the practice helps shareholders when the CEO's departure yields a benefit larger than the cost of the good-bye payment. For our purposes, however, what is important is that the gratuitous payments, whether or not they are beneficial to shareholders (given managers' power), reflect the existence and significance of managerial influence.

VII. THE DECOUPLING OF PAY FROM PERFORMANCE

In the early 1990s, prominent financial economists such as Michael Jensen and Kevin Murphy urged shareholders to be more accepting of large pay packages that would provide high-powered incentives.[32] Shareholders, it was argued, should care much more about providing managers with sufficiently strong incentives than about the amounts spent on executive pay. Defenders of current pay arrangements view the rise in pay over the past fifteen years

---

[32] *See, e.g.*, Michael C. Jensen & Kevin J. Murphy, *CEO Incentives – It's Not How Much You Pay, But How*, Harv. Bus. Rev., May-June 1990, at 138; Michael C. Jensen & Kevin J. Murphy, *Performance Pay and Top-Management Incentives*, 98 J. Pol. Econ. 225 (1990).

as the necessary price – and one worth paying – for improving executives' incentives.

The problem, however, is that executives' large compensation packages have been much less sensitive to their own performance than has been commonly recognized. Shareholders have not received the most bang for their buck. Companies could have generated the same increase in incentives at a much lower cost to their shareholders, or they could have used the amount spent to obtain more powerful incentives.

A. Nonequity Compensation

Although the equity-based fraction of managers' compensation has increased considerably during the past decade and has therefore received more attention, nonequity compensation continues to be substantial. In 2003, nonequity compensation represented, on average, about half of the total compensation of both the CEO and the top five executives of S&P 1500 companies not classified as new-economy firms.[33]

Although significant nonequity compensation comes in the form of base salary and sign-up, or golden hello, payments that do not purport to be performance related, much nonequity compensation comes in the form of bonus compensation that does purport to be performance based. Nonetheless, empirical studies have failed to find any significant correlation between nonequity compensation and managers' own performance during the 1990s.[34]

A close examination of compensation practices suggests why nonequity compensation is not tightly connected to managers' own performance. First of all, many companies use subjective criteria for at least some of their bonus payments. Such criteria could play a useful role in the hands of boards guided solely by shareholder interests. However, boards favoring their top executives can use the discretion provided by these plans to ensure that executives are well paid even when their performance is substandard.

Furthermore, when companies do use objective criteria, these criteria and their implementation are usually not designed to reward managers for their own contribution to the firm's performance. Bonuses are typically based not on how the firm's operating performance or earnings increased relative to its peers but on other metrics. And when companies fail to meet the established targets, the board can reset the target (as happened at Coca-Cola in 2001 and

[33] See Bebchuk & Grinstein, The Growth of Executive Pay, supra note 2.
[34] See Murphy, supra note 13.

at AT&T Wireless in 2002) or compensate the executives by setting even lower figures going forward.

Finally, many boards award bonuses to managers simply for buying other companies. In about 40 percent of large acquisitions during the period from 1993 to 1999, the acquiring-firm CEO received a multimillion-dollar bonus for completing the deal.[35] But making acquisitions hardly appears to be something for which managers should receive a special reward – that is, a payment above and beyond whatever benefit they get from the effect of the acquisition on the value of the managers' options, shares, and earnings-based bonuses. Executives do not lack incentives to make value-increasing acquisitions. If anything, investors' concern is that executives may engage in empire building and make too many acquisitions. Thus, although the making of a large acquisition might provide a convenient excuse for a large bonus, acquisition bonuses are not called for by incentive considerations.

B. Windfalls in Equity-Based Compensation

In light of the historically weak link between nonequity compensation and managerial performance, shareholders and regulators wishing to make pay more sensitive to performance have increasingly encouraged the use of equity-based compensation, often in the form of stock options. We strongly support equity-based compensation, which in principle can provide managers with desirable incentives. In practice, however, the design of executives' stock options has enabled executives to reap substantial rewards even when their own performance was merely passable or even poor.

1. Rewards for Marketwide and Industrywide Movements

Conventional stock options enable executives to gain from any increase in the nominal stock price beyond the grant-date market value. This, in turn, means that executives can profit even when their companies' performance significantly lags behind that of their peers, as long as marketwide and industrywide movements provide sufficient lift for the stock price. A substantial fraction of stock price increases is due to such movements rather than to firm-specific factors that might reflect the manager's own performance.

Although there are a variety of ways in which market- and industry-driven windfalls could be filtered out, very few companies have adopted equity-based plans that even attempt to filter out such windfalls. Unfortunately, most of

---

[35] Yaniv Grinstein & Paul Hribar, *CEO Compensation and Incentives: Evidence from M&A Bonuses*, 73 J. FIN. ECON. 119 (2004).

the boards now changing their equity-based compensation plans in response to outside pressure still choose to avoid plans that would effectively eliminate such windfalls. Instead, they are moving to plans based on restricted stock that fail to eliminate, and sometimes even increase, these windfalls.

2. Rewards for Short-Term Spikes

Option plans have been designed, and largely continue to be designed, in ways that enable executives to make considerable gains from temporary spikes in the company's stock price, even when long-term stock performance is poor. Companies have given executives broad freedom to unwind equity incentives, a practice that has been beneficial to executives but costly to shareholders. In addition to being granted the freedom to exercise their options as soon as they vest and sell the underlying stock, executives often have considerable control over the timing of sales, thus enabling them to benefit from their inside information. Compounding the problem, many firms have adopted reload plans that make it easier for executives to lock in profits from short-term spikes. The features of option plans that reward managers for short-term spikes not only decouple pay from managers' own performance but also provide incentives to manipulate earnings. There is, in fact, significant evidence linking executives' freedom to unload options with earnings manipulation and financial misreporting.[36]

C. Compensation at and after Departure

As we have already noted, the dollar value of a substantial portion of executive compensation has not been reported in firms' publicly filed summary compensation tables and has therefore not been included in standard compensation data sets. This stealth compensation has included executive pensions, deferred compensation arrangements, and postretirement consulting contracts and perks. These less visible forms of compensation have tended to be insensitive to managerial performance, thus further contributing to a decoupling of pay from performance.

Take, for example, Franklin Raines, who was forced to retire as Fannie Mae's CEO in late 2004. On Raines's departure, Fannie owed him (and his surviving spouse after his death) an annual pension of approximately $1.4 million, an amount specified without any connection to the firm's stock performance

---

[36] See, e.g., Daniel Bergstresser & Thomas Philippon, CEO Incentives and Earnings Management: Evidence from the 1990s, 80 J. FIN. ECON. 511 (2006); Scott L. Summers & John T. Sweeney, Fraudulently Misstated Financial Statements and Insider Trading: An Empirical Analysis, 73 ACCT. REV. 131 (1998).

under Raines. In a case study of his compensation, we estimated the value of this nonperformance element of pay at about $25 million.[37]

Further decoupling pay from performance are severance payments given to departing executives. Executives pushed out by their boards are typically paid a severance amounting to two or three years' worth of annual compensation. The payments are not reduced even when the executive's performance has been clearly and objectively dismal. Furthermore, standard severance provisions do not reduce the severance payment even if the executive quickly finds other employment.

It is doubtful that severance arrangements reflect efficient and arm's-length contracting. Nonexecutive employees are generally both more likely to be terminated than executives and less financially capable of bearing this risk. But they are not protected from having to bear a substantial monetary loss in the event of termination. If executive severance provisions were driven by risk-bearing considerations, one would expect nonexecutive employees to have such provisions as well.

More important, if executives' high pay is justified by the importance of providing them with incentives, one would expect their compensation arrangements to be more sensitive to performance than nonexecutive pay and to provide less protection in the event of dismal failure. Current corporate severance practices not only fail to strengthen the link between pay and performance but also undermine it by diminishing the difference between payoffs for good and bad performance.

VIII. IMPROVING TRANSPARENCY

We now consider ways of improving pay arrangements and the governance processes that produce those arrangements. We start with a proposition that could be viewed as a no-brainer, one for which there seems to be no reasonable basis for opposition. Specifically, the SEC should vigilantly ensure that public companies make the amount and structure of their executive pay packages transparent.

Financial economists have paid little attention to transparency. They tend to focus on stock price behavior and assume that any publicly available information – even if understood by only a small number of professionals – becomes incorporated into stock prices. Thus, economists are commonly interested in whether certain information is publicly available, not in how it is disclosed.

---

[37] Bebchuk & Fried, *Executive Compensation at Fannie Mae: A Case Study of Perverse Incentives, Nonperformance Pay, and Camouflage, supra* note 2.

As we have discussed, SEC regulations already require detailed disclosure of the compensation of a company's CEO and of the four other most highly paid executives. Thus, from economists' stock-pricing perspective, there is already a significant amount of information available about executive compensation.

In our view, however, is it important to recognize the importance of making such disclosures transparent. The purpose of executive compensation disclosure is not merely to enable accurate pricing of corporate securities. Its purpose is also to provide some check on arrangements that are too favorable to executives. This goal is not well served by disseminating information in a way that makes the information understandable to a small number of market professionals but opaque to others.

Transparency provides shareholders with a more accurate picture of total pay and its relationship to performance, thereby providing some check on departures from arrangements that serve shareholder interests. Furthermore, transparency can eliminate the distortions that arise when pay designers choose particular forms of compensation for their camouflage value rather than for their efficiency. Finally, transparency imposes little cost on companies, because it would simply require them to clearly disclose information they have or can obtain at negligible cost.

In our work, we have proposed various ways in which disclosure and transparency could be improved.[38] The SEC subsequently adopted new disclosure rules that implement some of our proposals.[39] Among other things, firms must now report each year the increase in actuarial value of executives' defined benefit pension plans. In addition, firms must disclose the balances under executives' deferred compensation arrangements.

Nonetheless, these reforms and current practices fall short of complete transparency. Investors still lack a clear picture of many aspects of executives' compensation arrangements. For example, shareholders will still find it hard to figure out the extent to which the arrangements shift tax costs from the executives to the firm and the degree to which the compensation reflects market and industry windfalls rather than firm-specific performance. We believe that additional steps – such as the ones we describe here – would be desirable.

---

[38] See, e.g., LUCIAN A. BEBCHUK & JESSE M. FRIED, PAY WITHOUT PERFORMANCE: THE UNFUL-FILLED PROMISE OF EXECUTIVE COMPENSATION (2004); Bebchuk & Jackson, *supra* note 2; Bebchuk & Fried, *Stealth Compensation via Retirement Benefits, supra* note 2.

[39] See Executive Compensation and Related Person Disclosure, Sec. Act Release No. 8732A, 88 SEC Docket (CCH) 2353 (Aug. 29, 2006); Executive Compensation Disclosure, Sec. Act Release No. 8765,89 SEC Docket (CCH) 1921 (Dec. 22, 2006).

First, firms could be required to disclose all nondeductible compensation. The tax code permits companies to deduct certain payments to executives but not others. Companies routinely include in their disclosure boilerplate language notifying shareholders that some of the arrangements may result in the firm being unable to deduct a portion of an executive's compensation, but they do not provide details about what particular amounts end up not being deductible. Companies could be required to provide full details about the components of pay that are not deductible, place a monetary value on the costs of this nondeductibility to the firm, and disclose this dollar cost to investors.

Second, companies could be required to report to their shareholders how much of their executives' profits from equity and nonequity compensation is attributable to general market and industry movements. This could be done by requiring firms to calculate and report the gains made by managers from the exercise of options (or the vesting of restricted shares, in the case of restricted share grants) and to report what fraction, if any, reflects the company's success in outperforming its industry peers. Such disclosure would help clarify the extent to which the company's equity-based plans reward the managers for good relative performance.

Third, companies could be required to make transparent to shareholders on a regular basis the extent to which their top five executives have unloaded any equity instruments received as part of their compensation. Although a diligent and dedicated researcher can obtain this information by sifting through stacks of executive trading reports filed with the SEC, requiring the firm to compile and report such information would highlight for all investors the extent to which managers have used their freedom to unwind incentives.

Of course, even before improved mandatory disclosure requirements are put in place, companies could voluntarily make pay more transparent. Companies need not follow a lawyerly approach of disclosing only what is legally required. Given executives' and directors' strong interest in camouflaging CEO pay, we do not expect many firms to disclose more than what is absolutely required. However, there may well be some boards that are willing to provide more investor-friendly compensation disclosure.

While we have suggested above some ways in which current pay practices can be made more transparent, we must emphasize that the task of keeping disclosure requirements sufficient and adequate is an ongoing one. As long as pay designers are motivated to camouflage CEO pay, firms will seek new ways of delivering stealth compensation to executives. Thus, it is important that public officials, governance reformers, and investors scrutinize developments in compensation practices to ensure that disclosure requirements remain up to date.

IX. IMPROVING PAY ARRANGEMENTS

Well-designed executive compensation can provide executives with cost-effective incentives to generate shareholder value. We have argued, however, that the promise of such arrangements has not yet been realized. Below we note various changes that companies could consider in order to strengthen the link between pay and performance and thereby improve executives' incentives.

A. *Proposal 1: Reduce Windfalls in Equity-Based Compensation*

Firms would do well to consider adopting equity compensation plans that filter out at least some of the gains in the stock price that are due to general market or industry movements. With such filtering, the same amount of incentives can be provided at a lower cost, or stronger incentives can be provided at the same cost. This can be done not only by indexing the exercise price of stock options but in other ways as well. For example, by linking the exercise price of options to changes in the stock price of the worst-performing firms in the industry, marketwide movement can be filtered out without imposing excessive risk on executives.

It is also important to note that moving to restricted stock is not a good way to address the windfall problem. In fact, restricted stock grants provide even larger windfalls than conventional options.

B. *Proposal 2: Reduce Windfalls in Bonus Plans*

For similar reasons, companies should consider designing bonus plans that filter out improvements in financial performance due to economy- or industrywide movements. Even assuming that it is desirable to focus on accounting rather than stock price performance, as most bonus plans seek to do, rewarding executives for improvements in accounting measures enjoyed by all companies in the industry is not a cost-effective way to provide incentives. Thus, bonus plans should be based not on absolute increases in earnings, sales, revenues, and so forth, but rather on such increases relative to peer companies.

C. *Proposal 3: Limit the Unwinding of Equity Incentives*

Pay arrangements could be improved by curtailing executives' broad freedom to unwind the equity-based incentives provided by their compensation plans. It may well be desirable to separate the vesting of options and managers' ability to unwind them. By requiring that executives hold vested options (or the shares resulting from the exercise of such options) for a given period after vesting, boards would ensure that options already belonging to executives will remain in their hands for some time, continuing to provide incentives to increase shareholder value. Furthermore, such restrictions would eliminate the significant distortions that can result from rewarding executives for short-term spikes in the stock price that do not subsequently hold. To prevent circumvention, such restrictions could be backed by contractual prohibitions on executives' hedging or using any other scheme that effectively eliminates some of their exposure to declines in the firm's stock price.

It would also be desirable to make it more difficult for executives to profit by selling ahead of bad news. Letting executives sell their shares when their inside information indicates that the stock price is about to decline can dilute and distort their incentives. Firms could reduce executives' ability to profit from insider selling by requiring them to predisclose their trades. Under such an approach, executives would disclose in advance their intention to sell shares, providing detailed information about the intended trade and including the number of shares to be sold.[40] If the sale were large or otherwise unusual, the announcement would trigger enhanced scrutiny of the firm. If investors believe the company is hiding bad news, the stock price would decline before managers sell, reducing their insider-trading profits. Alternatively, firms could create a hands-off option plan that takes unwinding decisions out of the hands of executives. Under such a plan, options would be cashed out according to a prearranged, predisclosed schedule. Executives thus could not use inside information to inflate their option profits.[41]

D. Proposal 4: Tie Bonuses to Long-Term Performance

Even assuming it were desirable to reward managers for improvements in accounting results, it might be desirable to give such rewards not for short-term results but only for improvements that are sustained over a considerable period of time. Rewarding executives for short-term improvements is not an effective way to provide beneficial incentives and indeed might create incentives to manipulate short-term accounting results.

It also might be desirable for compensation contracts to include general clawback provisions that require managers to return payments based on

---

[40] For a detailed proposal, see Jesse M. Fried, *Reducing the Profitability of Corporate Insider Trading Through Pretrading Disclosure*, 71 S. CAL. L. REV. 303 (1998).

[41] For a more detailed description of hands-off option plans, see Jesse M. Fried, *Hands-Off Options*, 61 VAND. L. REV. 453 (2008).

accounting numbers that are subsequently restated. Such return of payments is warranted, regardless of whether the executive was in any way responsible for the misreporting. When the board believes it is desirable to tie executive payoffs to a formula involving a metric whose value turns out to have been inflated, correctly applying the formula requires reversing payments that were based on erroneous values. The governing principle should be this: what wasn't earned must be returned.

E. *Proposal 5: Be Wary of Paying for Expansion*

Because running a larger company increases managers' power, prestige, and perquisites, executives might have an incentive to expand the company at the expense of shareholder value. Executive compensation arrangements should seek to counter rather than reinforce this incentive. A recent study by Yaniv Grinstein and one of us finds that executives' decisions to expand company size – by issuing new equity to finance acquisitions or investments or by avoiding distributions – are associated with increases in subsequent executive pay.[42] Controlling for past performance, the compensation of continuing CEOs is positively and substantially correlated with firm expansion during their service. While a larger firm size might lead the board to raise executive pay, boards should keep in mind that the expectation that expansion results in higher pay can provide executives with incentives to expand even when doing so would not be value maximizing.

F. *Proposal 6: Restore Dividend Neutrality*

Under current option plans, terms are not updated to reflect the payment of dividends and, as a result, executives' payoffs are reduced when they decide to pay a dividend. There is evidence that companies run by executives whose pay has a large option component tend to pay lower dividends and instead distribute cash through share repurchases,[43] which have a less adverse effect on the value of managers' options but may not be the most efficient form of payout.[44] To reduce distortions in managers' payout decisions, it might be desirable to design all equity-based compensation in such a way that it neither

---

[42] Bebchuk & Grinstein, *Firm Expansion and CEO Pay, supra* note 2.

[43] Christine Jolls, *Stock Repurchases and Incentive Compensation* (Nat'l Bureau of Econ. Res., Working Paper No. 6467, 1998), *available at* http://www.nber.org/papers/w6467; George Fenn & Nellie Liang, *Corporate Payout Policy and Managerial Stock Incentives*, 60 J. Fin. Econ. 45 (2001) (confirming Jolls's findings).

[44] *See* Jesse M. Fried, *Informed Trading and False Signaling with Open Market Repurchases*, 93 Cal. L. Rev. 1326 (2005).

encourages nor discourages the payment of dividends. In particular, in the case of option plans, the exercise price of options could be adjusted downward to reflect a dividend payment.

G. Proposal 7: Rethink Executive Pensions

There are reasons to doubt the efficiency of the widespread practice of using supplemental executive retirement plans (SERPs) to provide executives with a major component of their career compensation. Unlike pension plans used for nonexecutive employees, SERPs do not enjoy a tax subsidy. And given that companies have been moving away from defined benefit plans to defined contribution plans for nonexecutive employees, it is far from clear that providing executives with defined benefit plans is required by risk-bearing considerations. Unlike defined contribution plans, which force the employee to bear the risk of poor investment performance, defined benefit plans shift the risk of investment performance to the firm. However, executives do not seem less able to bear such risk than other employees. Although the efficiency benefits of SERPs are far from clear, SERPs impose incentive costs. They provide executives with pay that is largely independent of performance, thereby weakening the overall link between total pay and performance. Boards would thus do well to reconsider their heavy use of SERPs.

H. Proposal 8: Avoid Soft-Landing Arrangements

Soft-landing arrangements, which provide managers with a generous exit package when they are pushed out due to failure, dilute executives' incentives. While companies spend large amounts on producing a payoff gap between good and poor performance, the money spent on soft-landing arrangements works in the opposite direction, narrowing the payoff gap between good and poor performance.

At present, executives are commonly promised generous severance arrangements in the event of termination, unless the termination is triggered by an extremely narrow set of circumstances (such as criminal indictment or malfeasance). Boards should consider provisions that make the termination payoff depend on the reasons for the executive's termination and the terminated executive's record. Even if companies stick to the existing, broad definition of termination without cause, the payoff in such a termination should depend in part on the firm's performance relative to its peers during the executive's service. An executive who is terminated against a background of extremely poor stock performance should get less than an executive who is terminated when the company's performance is reasonable.

X. IMPROVING BOARD ACCOUNTABILITY

Past and current flaws in executive pay arrangements have resulted from under-lying problems in the corporate governance system: specifically, directors' lack of sufficient incentives to focus solely on shareholder interests when setting pay. If directors could be relied on to focus on shareholder interests, the pay-setting process, and board oversight of executives more generally, would be greatly improved. The most promising route to improving pay arrangements is thus to make boards more accountable to shareholders and more focused on shareholder interests. Such increased accountability would transform the arm's-length contracting model into a reality. It would improve both pay arrangements and board performance more generally.

Recent reforms require most companies listed on the major stock exchanges (the New York Stock Exchange, Nasdaq, and the American Stock Exchange) to have a majority of independent directors, which are directors who are not otherwise employed by the firm or in a business relationship with it. These companies must also staff compensation and nominating committees entirely with independent directors. Although such reforms are likely to reduce managers' power over the board and improve directors' incentives somewhat, they fall far short of what is necessary.

Our analysis shows that the new listing requirements weaken executives' influence over directors but do not eliminate it. More important, there are limits to what independence can do by itself. Independence does not ensure that directors have incentives to focus on shareholder interests or that the best directors will be chosen. In addition to becoming more independent of insiders, directors also must become more dependent on shareholders. To this end, it might be desirable to eliminate the arrangements that currently entrench directors and insulate them from shareholders.

To begin, it might be desirable to turn shareholders' power to replace directors from myth into reality. Even in the wake of poor performance and shareholder dissatisfaction, directors now face very little risk of being ousted. Shareholders' ability to replace directors is extremely limited. A recent study by one of us provides evidence that outside the hostile takeover context the incidence of electoral challenges to directors has been practically negligible in the past decade.[45] It might well be desirable to change this state of affairs.

To improve the performance of corporate boards, it might be desirable to reduce impediments to director removal.[46] As a first step, shareholders could

[45] Lucian Arye Bebchuk, The Case for Shareholder Access to the Ballot, 59 Bus. Law. 43 (2003).
[46] For a fuller analysis of the ways in which shareholder power to remove directors could be made viable, see Lucian A. Bebchuk, The Myth of the Shareholder Franchise, 93 Va. L. Rev. 675 (2007).

be given the power to place director candidates on the corporate ballot. In addition, proxy contest challengers that attract sufficient support could have their expenses reimbursed by the company. Furthermore, it might be desirable to limit the use of staggered boards, a feature of most public companies, to impede director removal. Staggered boards provide powerful protection from removal in either a proxy fight or a hostile takeover. Also, a recent study by Alma Cohen and one of us finds that staggered boards are associated with economically significant reductions in firm value. It might be desirable to enable shareholders to replace all the directors each year or at least every other year.[47]

In addition to making shareholder power to remove directors viable, it might be undesirable for boards to have veto power, which current corporate law grants them, over proposed changes to governance arrangements in the company's charter. Shareholders could be given the power, which they now lack, to initiate and adopt changes in the corporate charter. Under current rules, shareholders can pass only nonbinding resolutions. And, as documented in a recent empirical study by one of us, boards often choose not to follow resolutions that receive majority support from shareholders, even after the resolutions have passed two or three times.[48] This state of affairs might well be undesirable.

Allowing shareholders to amend the corporate charter would eventually improve the entire range of corporate governance arrangements without outside regulatory intervention. If there is concern that shareholders are influenced by short-term considerations, shareholder-initiated changes could require approval by majority vote in two successive annual shareholder meetings. But denying shareholders the power to change the corporate charter, no matter how widespread and long lasting shareholder support for such a change may be, is unlikely to be desirable. Allowing shareholders to set governance arrangements would help make boards more accountable to shareholders.

To fully address the existing problems in executive compensation and corporate governance, structural reforms in the allocation of power between boards and shareholders may be necessary. Given political realities, such reforms would not be easy to pass. But the corporate governance flaws that we have discussed – and have shown to be pervasive, systemic, and costly – make considering such reforms worthwhile.

---

[47] Lucian A. Bebchuk & Alma Cohen, *The Costs of Entrenched Boards*, 78 J. Fin. Econ. 409 (2005).

[48] Lucian A. Bebchuk, *The Case for Increasing Shareholder Power*, 118 Harv. L. Rev. 833 (2005).

5 Supersize Pay, Incentive Compatibility, and the Volatile Shareholder Interest

William W. Bratton

The compensation of chief executive officers (CEOs) increased by a factor of six over the past two decades,[1] with the overwhelming share of the increase coming not as salary but as "incentive pay," mostly in the form of stock options and cash bonuses triggered by performance metrics.[2] Observers from outside the corporate governance arena perceive a social problem and question the magnitude of this raise. They worry about the fact that executives in the United States are by far the world's best paid.[3] On the domestic level, observers also worry about a growing inequality of income: the average CEO of an S&P 500 company made 30 times more than the average American production worker in 1970, but 210 times more in 1996.[4] By 2005, the multiplier was 262.[5]

[1] See Bengt Holmström & Steven N. Kaplan, *The State of U.S. Corporate Governance: What's Right and What's Wrong?* 10 (ECGI Finance Working Paper No. 23/2003, 2003), *available at* http://ssrn.com/abstract=441100.

[2] Average total remuneration of executives of S&P 500 companies (adjusted for inflation) went from $850,000 in 1970 to $14 million in 2000, falling with the stock market to $9.4 million in 2002. At the same time, average base salaries merely doubled, going from $850,000 to $2.2 million. Michael C. Jensen & Kevin J. Murphy, *Remuneration: Where We've Been, How We Got to Here, What Are the Problems, and How to Fix Them* 24–25 (Harv. NOM Working Paper No. 04–28, 2004), *available at* http://ssrn.com/abstract=561305. Amounts have risen since then. The CEO of an S&P 500 company made on average $14.78 million in total compensation in 2006, according to a preliminary analysis by the Corporate Library. *See* AFL-CIO Executive Pay Watch, AFL-CIO, *available at* http://www.aflcio.org/corporatewatch/paywatch/.

[3] *See* Randall S. Thomas, *Explaining the International CEO Pay Gap: Board Capture or Market Driven?*, 57 VAND. L. REV. 1171 (2004) (suggesting reasons to justify the transnational pay gap).

[4] Kevin J. Murphy, *Executive Compensation* 51 (University of Southern California Working Paper, 1998), *available at* http://ssrn.com/abstract=163914.

[5] Jeanne Sahadi, *CEO Paycheck*, CNN Money, June 21, 2006, available at http://money.cnn.com/2006/06/21/news/companies/ceo_pay_epi/index.htm (based on all firms earning more than $1 billion annually).

William W. Bratton is Peter P. Weidenbruch Jr. Professor of Business Law, Georgetown University Law Center. This chapter was previously published by the *Virginia Law & Business Review*, at 1 VA. L. & BUS. REV. 55 (2006).

Inside the world of corporate governance, the question is different, because the level of compensation is not by itself seen as a problem.[6] Tournament economics provides a widely accepted justification for supersize amounts. The tournament sweeps in the entire set of aspiring executives, who then compete for a small number of top-tier jobs. High-powered competition ensues among executives, which is thought to result in better management.[7] The corporate governance question is whether compensation mechanisms within the winner's circle should be subject to exacting standards of incentive compatibility. Critics of prevailing practices argue that large payoffs to managers should be strictly conditioned on the creation of shareholder value.[8] According to critics, prevailing arrangements fail to impose such conditions because the bargaining framework is skewed in management's favor.[9] Defenders of the prevailing practice answer that the governance framework is effective, if not perfect. To support this view, they point to rational risk-return trade-offs embodied in the contracts.[10]

This chapter intervenes in the debate to assert that an evaluation of compensation practices should concern more than the attributes of the bargaining space. The discussants all posit the maximization of shareholder value as the firm's objective and agree that value can be enhanced by aligning management's interests with those of the shareholders. A follow-up question rarely arises: how should the shareholder-beneficiary be modeled for the purpose of designing incentives? This chapter unpacks the notion of the shareholder, introducing a more particularized account in which the unitary model of the shareholder disintegrates into a differentiated cast of characters made up of investors, speculators, noise traders, fundamental value investors, short-term holders, long-term holders, dumb money, and smart money. The model is not only fragmented but also volatile, for different shareholder types predominate in different firms and in different stock markets. A normative question emerges concerning the design of equity incentive compensation: what kind of a shareholder do we wish the incentivized manager to be?

---

[6] Lucian Bebchuk & Jesse Fried, Pay Without Performance: The Unfulfilled Promise of Executive Compensation 5, 70–74 (2004).

[7] *See, e.g.,* Sherwin Rosen, *The Economics of Superstars*, 71 Am. Econ. Rev. 845, 846, 857 (1981); *see also* Edward P. Lazear, *Output-Based Pay: Incentives, Retention or Sorting?* (IZA Discussion Paper No. 761, 2003), *available at* http://ssrn.com/abstract=403900.

[8] Professors Lucian Bebchuk and Jesse Fried are the leading critics. *See generally* Bebchuk & Fried, *supra* note 6.

[9] *Id.* at 6, 9.

[10] For a theoretical showing along these lines, see Benjamin E. Hermalin, *Trends in Corporate Governance* 13–20 (University of California, Berkeley Working Paper, Sept. 3, 2003), *available at* http://ssrn.com/abstract=441360.

Most will agree that compensation should be designed to encourage managers to take the view of a long-term, fundamental value investor rather than a short-term speculator sensitive to market moods. Yet prevailing compensation practices align management interests with those of speculative, short-term shareholders. Three possible perverse effects result, all well known in the compensation literature.[11] First, speculatively inclined managers can rationalize investments in projects that decrease the long-term value of the firm. Second, speculative incentives encourage aggressive accounting and distorted corporate reporting. Third, speculative incentives skew payout policy away from dividends and toward open-market repurchases of firm stock, with possible adverse consequences. Long-term restraints on the alienation of equity awards, whether purchased through the exercise of stock options or granted outright, would ameliorate all three problems. These are not seen in practice because they diminish the value of equity grants by impairing liquidity and inhibiting the reduction of risk by means of diversification.

Strict incentive compatibility, then, decreases the compensation value of equity grants. A question accordingly arises concerning the appropriate mediation of this conflict between compensation value and incentive effects. Economic theory holds out no calculative solution; there is no general theory of optimal incentive contracting with respect to corporate managers.[12] Pending such a theory's appearance, three alternative approaches can be suggested. First, the imposition of alienation restraints can be offset by an increase in the number of shares awarded, leaving the present value of compensation unaffected. Here a question arises respecting the amount paid, for at some point the value of the concession becomes unreasonably large. Second, a decrease in value for the sake of incentive compatibility could be deemed noncompensable as a normative proposition: why should shareholders have to pay more for correctly aligned incentives? In this case, the problem lies in the tournament payoff, because at some point a pay cut hurts the firm by dulling incentives. The third approach, which recognizes the problems just noted, deems the matter ill suited to rule-based resolution and leaves it to case-by-case negotiation. Here, the problem lies in the flawed bargaining context.

Although there is no theoretical template that correctly determines tradeoffs between compensation and incentive compatibility, economic theory does

---

[11] *See, e.g.,* Randall Thomas & Thomas Martin, *The Determinants of Shareholder Voting on Stock Option Plans,* 35 Wake Forest L. Rev. 31, 40–46 (2000).

[12] If we had such a theory, there would be nothing to dispute except the level of pay. *See* Patrick Bolton et al., *Pay for Short-Term Performance: Executive Compensation in Speculative Markets* 33 (ECGI Finance Working Paper No. 79/2005, 2005), *available at* http://ssrn.com/abstract=691142.

TABLE 5.1. *Shareholder types*

Speculation	Investment
Noise trading	Fundamental value investment
Short term	Long term
Dumb money (smart money)	Smart money (dumb money)

hold out normative guidance. Equity grants make no sense when viewed as pure compensation. If a supersize pay package were the sole objective in view, the shareholders would get more bang for their buck by paying cash. Equity grants accordingly can be justified only to the extent that they hold out positive incentive effects, effects that can be maximized only by imposing retention constraints that detract from compensation value. An ordering of priorities is implied. Incentive compatibility should come first, with the level of compensation being set only in an incentive-compatible framework. So long as corporate boards treat incentive alignment and compensation as coequal objectives, trade-offs will follow, and equity compensation schemes will continue to hold out perverse incentives.

This chapter's first part describes behavioral variations in the shareholder population. The second part looks at stock option and bonus plans to see what kind of shareholder they usher into corporate headquarters. Speculators emerge in significant numbers. The third part shows that this chapter's analysis holds negative implications for both sides of the debate over executive pay.

I. MODELING THE SHAREHOLDER

To value a share is to project returns and then find a factor with which to discount them. The appraiser studies facts presently ascertainable about the company, the industry, and the economy, and then takes out a crystal ball. Valuations are just guesses, albeit some are better calculated than others. That being the case, it comes as no surprise that financial economics has never managed to come up with a robust asset-pricing model. Absent such a model, which would provide a means to verify present prices, there is much room for behavioral variation, diversity of approach, and opinion among shareholders on matters of valuation. And nearly all matters of concern to shareholders ultimately come down to matters of value. Behaviorally speaking, then, there is no unitary, empirical shareholder. One only can describe a series of binary alternatives, which are shown in Table 5.1.

It follows that when the shareholder interest is called on to provide a normative benchmark (whether better to align the incentives of executives or for some other purpose), the shareholder must be modeled. Modeling means choosing among the different shareholder types above. The choice proceeds under constraint: one can mix and match characteristics from the various rows and from either column of Table 5.1, but if one includes too many characteristics from both columns at once, a model providing a coherent normative instruction will not emerge.

The shareholder is indeed modeled routinely in boardrooms and in corporate and securities law. But the more particular attributes of such shareholder constructs tend to be implicit and often vary with the context or over time. Securities law provides an example. Historically, it has regulated from the perspective of the investment column, but it has been increasingly solicitous of the speculative side during the past two decades. Corporate law presents a contrasting case. It often models its shareholder beneficiary so vaguely as to elide the problem of making menu choices. This is not necessarily a failing; the governance problems on corporate law's table often do not require further inquiry into the shareholders' financial and behavioral profiles. For example, when the question is whether managers should be able to line their pockets with an unfair self-dealing transaction, the law may fairly assume a unitary shareholder interest in a fiduciary duty of loyalty. Sometimes, however, corporate law does model the shareholder interest more particularly. For example, it draws selectively from the investment column in articulating the law of takeover defense,[13] aligning the long-term shareholder with the manager against short-term speculators, so as to justify management takeover defenses.[14] There follows a more particular look at the columns and the categories.

A. *Speculation versus Investment*

The typology's headings come from the classic conservative treatise on finance and valuation, Graham and Dodd's *Security Analysis*.[15] Graham and Dodd divided stockholders into two types. On one side, they placed those who play the market looking for quick gains. Against this category of speculators, Graham and Dodd contrasted a second category of investors, which itself comprises two subsets. The more conservative subset of investors looks for

---

[13] *Compare* Martin Lipton, *Pills, Polls, and Professors Redux*, 69 U. CHI. L. REV. 1037 (2002), with Lucian Bebchuk, *The Case Against the Board Veto in Corporate Takeovers*, 69 U. CHI. L. REV. 973 (2002).

[14] *See, e.g.*, Paramount Commc'ns, Inc. v. Time, Inc., 571 A.2d 1140, 1155 (Del. 1989) (approving defensive tender offer on the ground of protection of long-term investment plan).

[15] BENJAMIN GRAHAM & DAVID L. DODD, SECURITY ANALYSIS: PRINCIPLES AND TECHNIQUE 33–36 (3d ed. 1951).

safe income streams, analyzing past performance and avoiding any forward-looking projection. The less conservative subset looks for capital appreciation rather than income and invests based on projections of future growth. They thereby resemble speculators, with the difference lying in the approach taken. Investment in growth requires something "more tangible than the psychology of the purchaser," specifically the safety of the principal and a satisfactory return, and these goals are best achieved by thorough analysis.[16] Such analysis has to address the quality of the company, but it cannot stop there. Quantity, in the sense of the relation of the stock price to the company's fundamental value, matters just as much. In Graham and Dodd's picture, the market price is not necessarily the best-available evidence of the value on offer. Given a market full of speculators, it certainly will not be: the best firm in the world is the issuer of just another speculative stock if speculators have bid its price to the stratosphere.[17]

Investment, said Graham and Dodd, is "good for everybody and at all times."[18] But speculation is not always bad, depending on who does the speculating and the prevailing conditions. Unfortunately, speculation often turns out badly. The failure properly to distinguish between the two activities, they said, brought about the disaster of 1929.

B. Noise Trading versus Fundamental Value Investment

The essence of Graham and Dodd's distinction between speculation and investment shows up in the contemporary noise-trading theory of stock market pricing.[19] The noise theorists, looking to behavioral psychology, divide the market into two types of shareholders: noise traders and fundamental value investors.[20] The fundamental value investors resemble the less conservative subset of Graham and Dodd's investors. These actors know that value lies in hard cash flows and invest in those flows even as they look for growth. Their time lines tend to be longer, and their information sets include only facts respecting the investee and the economy (so-called fundamental value

---

[16] *Id.* at 37.

[17] Contemporary observers term their approach *value investing*. Warren Buffett, a student of Graham and Dodd, is a famously successful exemplar. *See* ROGER LOWENSTEIN, BUFFETT: THE MAKING OF AN AMERICAN CAPITALIST 36–59 (1995) (describing Buffett's relationship with Graham).

[18] GRAHAM & DODD, *supra* note 15, at 34.

[19] *See, e.g.,* Andrei Shleifer & Lawrence Summers, *The Noise Trader Approach to Finance,* 4 J. ECON. PERSP. 19, 19–22, 23–26 (Spring 1990).

[20] For a leading model, see Joseph Lakonishok et al., *Contrarian Investment, Extrapolation, and Risk,* 49 J. FIN. 1541, 1542–44, 1575–76 (1994).

information) rather than the latest word from Wall Street. Market trends and daily noise do not impress them.

The noise traders resemble Graham and Dodd's speculators, although this model adds an overlay of psychology to reinforce the description of the speculative mindset. Noise traders chase trends: when they see somebody make a killing on a rising stock, they assume that actor to be smart rather than lucky, and they imitate the strategy.[21] Noise traders also display behavioral biases. They are overconfident in their own investment abilities.[22] When the stock price is trending upward, they react too favorably to good news. Once a downward trend becomes manifest, they react too unfavorably to bad news. In both cases, they suffer from availability bias and place too great a weight on recent events and easily available information.[23] An availability bias also leads noise traders to make poorly considered risk-return projections, in which they underweight the importance of risks of low probability and high magnitude. Finally, at the moment when the trend turns, noise traders can be slow to read the handwriting on the wall. Their irrational inaction[24] results from a hindsight bias, in which traders overweight past events that actually occurred rather than those that might have occurred.[25] It also follows from confirmation bias, which is the tendency to confirm earlier decisions regardless of their intrinsic soundness.[26] Noise traders get embedded notions about their strategies and shut out information.

Trends dominate the resulting picture of market pricing.[27] When the market trends upward, too much is made of good news, and bad news is filtered out. Indeed, market information may influence the price as much as (or even more than) fundamental value information. Market information most clearly dominates in a bubble, where a feedback loop takes over as one stock price

---

[21] *See* Shleifer & Summers, *supra* note 19, at 28–30.

[22] Robert Prentice, *Whither Securities Regulation? Some Behavioral Observations Regarding Proposals for Its Future*, 51 DUKE L. J. 1397, 1459–60 (2001).

[23] *See* Amos Tversky & Daniel Kahneman, *Judgment Under Uncertainty: Heuristics and Biases*, 185 SCIENCE 1124, 1127–28 (1974).

[24] *See* Donald C. Langevoort, *Selling Hope, Selling Risk: Some Lessons for Law from Behavioral Economics About Stockbrokers and Sophisticated Customers*, 84 CAL. L. REV. 627, 659–60 (1996).

[25] *See* Baruch Fischhoff, *Hindsight Is Not Equal to Foresight: The Effect of Outcome Knowledge on Judgment Under Uncertainty*, 104 J. EXPERIMENTAL PSYCH.: HUM. PERCEPTION & PERFORMANCE 288, 297 (1975).

[26] *See* Charles G. Lord et al., *Biased Assimilation and Attitude Polarization: The Effects of Prior Theories on Subsequently Considered Evidence*, 37 J. PERSONALITY & SOC. PSYCH. 2098, 2099 (1979).

[27] For models, see Nicholas C. Barberis et al., *A Model of Investor Sentiment*, 49 J. FIN. ECON. 307 (1998); Kent Daniel et al., *Investor Psychology and Security Market Under- and Overreactions*, 53 J. FIN. 1839 (1998).

increase feeds the next increase.[28] The trend turns only sometime after information about fundamental value has ceased to justify the price.[29] Eventually, the accumulation of bad news causes investors to substitute a new, negative model. Then the trend turns downward, with investors thereafter tending to underweight good news.[30]

Restating the above in less formal terms, speculative investors experience mood swings. Uncertainty is the ultimate cause: no shareholder, whether a speculator or an investor, can ascertain fundamental value with surety, even while staking significant sums in a highly competitive marketplace. Cool rationality can turn out to be the behavioral exception rather than the rule.

C. Short Term versus Long Term

The speculative interest tends to have a short-term time horizon, with the investment interest more likely to look long. This follows from speculators' differing behavioral characteristics. The market information that drives the speculators bears primarily on the near term. The fundamental value that drives the investment side tends to have meaning only over the intermediate or long term.

The appellations *short term* and *long term* have come to stand in for Graham and Dodd's terms *speculation* and *investment*. The change in usage has normative implications, as reference to a short-term time horizon avoids the pejorative implication of the "speculation" label[31] when coupled with strong assumptions about the accuracy of market pricing. Under this approach, widely prevalent in the 1990s, different time horizons hold out no complications for the model of the shareholder, and the phrase "shareholder value maximization," when keyed to today's stock price, carries a positive normative connotation. Present-value theory brings all time horizons together into today's market price and, under the efficient market hypothesis (EMH), today's price reflects fundamental value. It follows that maximizing today's stock price maximizes fundamental value and that directing management to maximize present value holds out no risk of perverse effects. The converse also obtains under this market-favorable view: maximizing fundamental value maximizes today's

---

[28] ROBERT J. SHILLER, IRRATIONAL EXUBERANCE 44–68 (2000).

[29] *See* Barberis et al., *supra* note 27, at 307–08 (describing price underreaction to news).

[30] ANDREI SHLEIFER, INEFFICIENT MARKETS: AN INTRODUCTION TO BEHAVIORAL FINANCE 113–14 (2000).

[31] Graham and Dodd pointed out that there is no clear line separating the short and long terms and that one can "invest" in the short term and "speculate" in the long term. GRAHAM & DODD, *supra* note 15, at 35.

stock price, so that management confidently can invest for the long term, without having to worry about being punished by the speculative interest in the stock market.

Problems come up if the EMH drops out of the picture and market underpricing and overpricing become possible. If the market price does not automatically self-correct, then it can be driven in incorrect directions by short-term, noise-trading shareholders. If pursuing a shareholder value strategy causes management to align the business plan with these shareholders' preferences, the result could be underinvestment in productive projects and overinvestment in suboptimal projects.

D. Dumb Money versus Smart Money

The final binary – dumb money versus smart money – complicates the typology's division of the world into speculators and investors, as indicated by the parentheticals in the chart. The noise traders make up the core of the dumb-money shareholders. But the category can also sweep in an uninformed fundamental value investor – someone, for example, who collects stocks with high price-to-earnings ratios in an underdiversified portfolio for the long term. The core smart-money investor is a well-informed fundamental value investor. But the category includes speculative actors as well. Some smart money will combine fundamental and market value information, watching the noise traders and the market trend. When the noise traders push the market upward, bidding up stocks in a feedback loop where an uptick is good news that triggers another uptick, smart money certainly can ride along. After all, there is money to be made as prices rise; thus did momentum funds make an appearance in the institutional investment community during the 1990s. But the smart money knows when fundamentals do not support the market price and, being (relatively) free of behavioral biases, will be ready to be the first to bail out when the trend turns. The same insights invite the smart money to profit by bucking the trend. If fundamental value does not support the market price, then the price inevitably falls. Accordingly, money can be made by shorting the stock (or the whole market). More generally, given a lot of noise, some smart money will be contrarian.

In its contrarian posture, the smart money plays a key role in the scenario cited in support of the EMH. The EMH asserts that the market price is the best reflection of fundamental value and that new fundamental value information gets into the stock price almost immediately, even as it accepts the existence of dumb money and noise trading. It can do both at once because it asserts that smart money trumps dumb money. Dumb money goes off in every direction, canceling itself out in the random-error term. Smart money goes consistently in the direction of fundamental value, keeping stock prices correctly aligned with fundamentals.

Under the EMH it follows that supply and demand do not determine stock prices. What is on offer in the stock market is money in the future, and demand for money is consistently high. The valuation questions go only to the amount of money, the time of payment, and the quantum of risk – questions answered by fundamental value information. Since demand is a constant, the only thing that can cause a price to change is new fundamental value information. Noise traders, meanwhile, always get wiped out in the long run.

Although the EMH continues to have defenders,[32] the contrasting noise-trading description of the market has been ascendant for more than a decade. Erratic stock market behavior encouraged the shift. Under the present consensus view, the stock market is a place where noisy supply and demand intermix with fundamental value because there is not enough smart money to trump the dumb money in the short term.[33] Contrarian investment is just too risky. Overpricing and underpricing are constant possibilities. But in the long run, fundamental value always prevails.

E. Summary: Shareholders and Fundamental Value

The division of shareholders into variegated speculators and investors does not preclude the employment of a unitary model, depending on the question presented. For example, all shareholders want managers to create long-term fundamental value (or at least to be seen as so doing). To see why this is the case, try to imagine a stock market bubble occurring in the absence of a plausible fundamental value story. Absent the story, investors will have no cause to get excited in the first place. Even the dot-com bubble of the late 1990s began within a fundamental value scenario. The Internet was new, and more and more people were becoming acquainted with it, giving rise to the reasonable projection that it would become an important center of commerce. According to the story, that meant there were going to be fantastic profits for a handful of winners who got in early with attractive Web sites, gained market share, and established a brand. Unfortunately, the story, although rational, also was highly probabilistic. Worse, it became exaggerated in the telling, in the interpretation, and in the wake of actual stock price increases. When the market puts present money on the table, the connection between that market

---

[32] For a contemporary defense, see Eugene Fama, *Market Efficiency, Long-Term Returns, and Behavioral Finance*, 49 J. FIN. ECON. 283, 284–85 (1998).

[33] *See, e.g.*, Andrei Shleifer & Robert Vishny, *The Limits of Arbitrage*, 52 J. FIN. 35, 39–54 (1997).

value and the supporting fundamental value story can become attenuated. But the story has to be in place before the market takes off; even at the crest of tulip mania, there was an operative fundamental value story.[34]

All of this implies that for a stockholder, whether a noise trader or a fundamental value investor, news about fundamental value always matters. Beyond that base point, however, a unitary shareholder perspective on value cannot be assumed. As the next part of this chapter demonstrates, shareholder preferences respecting investment policy, financial reporting, and payout policy vary with behavioral characteristics, time horizons, and the state of the market.

II. THE VOLATILE SHAREHOLDER INTEREST AND INCENTIVE COMPENSATION

We now draw on the variant shareholder perspectives just described to evaluate prevailing compensation practices and ask two questions. First, what sort of manager-shareholder is likely to be produced by prevailing incentive compensation practices? Second, does shareholder interest provide a coherent normative yardstick with which to evaluate prevailing practices? Section A outlines the terms of standard stock option plans, along with the main points made by their critics. Section B asks how the plans affect incentives to invest for the long term. Section C looks into the plans' impact on financial reporting. Section D shows how stock option compensation affects payout policy. Section E looks into the incentive compatibility of two additional components of standard pay packages: cash bonuses and exit payments. Section F summarizes.

A. *Stock Option Plans: Prevailing Practice and Critique*

Under prevailing practices, stock option plans have ten-year durations, with options granted under the plans vesting gradually over the period.[35] When an option vests, the manager is free to exercise it and sell the stock. The exercise price is the stock's market price at the time the option is granted. The price remains fixed for the life of the option.[36] Critics question both the pricing and the vesting practices. [37]

---

[34] Peter Garber, *Tulipmania*, 97 J. POL. ECON. 535, 555–57 (1989) (arguing that rare bulbs had high fundamental value due to sales of offshoots).

[35] YALE D. TAUBER & DONALD R. LEVY, EXECUTIVE COMPENSATION 663 (2002). Vesting usually occurs ratably over time but could be based on performance incentives. *Id.*

[36] Thomas & Martin, *supra* note 11, at 39.

[37] Bebchuk and Fried also question the numbers granted. They think that fewer would be better. According to the empirical evidence they cite, the positive incentive effect declines as the

As to exercise prices, the critics make a simple behavioral point: higher hurdles require greater effort and therefore hold out a bigger payoff for shareholders. If exercise prices were set higher than the market price, the manager would have to create some value in order to put the option into the money. Yet despite the apparent sacrifice of incentive effect, only a small subset of companies price options out of the money, that is, above the market price of the stock at grant. The practice of leaving the price fixed for the life of the option also arguably softens the incentive effect. A fixed price rewards the executive for marketwide and sectorwide upward price movement, in addition to upward movement due to the company's own performance (which is said to account for only 30 percent of stock growth on average).[38] So long as the market rises over time, a payoff is virtually guaranteed. Indexing solves the problem. Under this, the exercise price is reset upward and downward over time to filter out changes attributable to the market or sector. Alternatively, vesting could be conditioned on meeting a fixed performance target. Neither palliative was seen much in practice before 2003. Since then, mounting criticism has caused a minority of boards to attach performance targets.[39]

The critics also question the vesting rules. Once the option vests, the executive is free to exercise it and sell the underlying stock. And executives do sell 90 percent of the stock purchased on exercise.[40] This, of course, defeats the purpose of aligning their interests with that of the shareholders. No nefarious intentions need be read in, however. The managers sell in order to diversify their portfolios, acting no different from other rational investors. At the same time, nefarious deeds do occur. Executives use inside information to time their sales,[41] and firms use inside information to time option grants. A notorious subset even backdated grants.[42]

Other common features of option plans come under fire, most notably reloading and replacement. A reloading feature automatically grants the beneficiary a new option for every option exercised, with the exercise price

---

number granted increases, so that the benefits of the last option granted may be less than the cost. BEBCHUK & FRIED, *supra* note 6, at 138.

[38] *Id.* at 139.

[39] *See* Joann S. Lublin, *Boards Tie CEO Pay More Tightly to Performance*, WALL ST. J., Feb. 21, 2006, at A1 (noting that "30 of 100 major U.S. corporations" base a "portion" of equity grants on performance targets, up from seventeen in 2003, but that the targets tend to remain undisclosed).

[40] *Id.* at 176–77. Stock sales are not the only problem. Executives also can employ derivative contracts to put themselves in the economic position of diversified stockholders, even as they continue to own the stock purchased under the plan. *See* Steven A. Bank, *Devaluing Reform: The Derivatives Market and Executive Compensation*, 7 DEPAUL BUS. L.J. 301, 323–24 (1995) (describing risk shifting in the derivatives market).

[41] BEBCHUK & FRIED, *supra* note 6, at 179–83, 191.

[42] *See* Ryan v. Gifford, 918 A.2d 341 (Del. Ch. 2007).

set at the stock's price at the time of reloading. According to the critics, the new option can serve as a form of protection against subsequent price volatility respecting the shares purchased. So long as the stock price manages to spike above the exercise price of the replacement option at some point during its life, the executive gets a chance to profit on the stock purchased even if the overall price trend is downward. Stock price volatility thereby becomes a potential source of personal profit.[43] Replacement occurs when options expire out of the money. The firm creates new options to replace them, with the exercise price pegged at the lower market price at the time of the replacement grant.[44] The critics assert that this insures against performance failure and works at cross-purposes with the original option, which was granted to discourage the stock price decline that triggers the new option grant.[45]

As a theoretical matter, many of the criticisms are as contestable as the prevailing practice. As already noted, we have no ironclad theory of optimal incentive contracting. If we did, the theory would tell us how to design the contracts, and there would be nothing to dispute except the level of pay.[46] Absent a theory, there is room for debate about means to induce the productive incentives. As to exercise prices, it can be noted that the stock price at the time of the option grant reflects the market's present expectation about all future value scenarios, expectations shaped in light of the incentive compensation scheme. Strictly speaking, as the option goes into the money, value has been created with the executive's participation. As to the absence of indexing, it has been argued that there may be reason to reward executives for general market increases: the value of good managers may go up during good times, creating a retention incentive. Even reloading could be the means to the end of an optimal long-term incentive arrangement. Perhaps the additional options also have a positive effect; it all depends on the overall mix of incentives, and nobody has a guiding template. Finally, replacement options may not look plausible *ex ante*, but *ex post*, at the time of expiration, new options import continued incentives to succeed.[47]

None of these back-and-forth arguments can be settled here. But a complex model of the shareholder sharpens understanding of the stakes. The following sections take up three matters particularly likely to trigger conflicting interests in the group of shareholders, namely investment policy, reporting practice, and payout policy. In all of these cases, the particular shareholder incentive

[43] BEBCHUK & FRIED, *supra* note 6, at 169–70.

[44] Formerly, the result also was accomplished by amending the plan to lower the price, a practice that ceased when the Financial Accounting Standards Board changed the accounting treatment in 1998. *Id.* at 165–67.

[45] *See* Thomas & Martin, *supra* note 11, at 43.   [46] *See* Bolton et al., *supra* note 12, at 33.

[47] *Id.* at 34–37.

profile fostered by an equity compensation scheme can skew the firm's choices in unproductive directions.

B. Investment Policy

Hypothesize a choice of investments. The firm can invest in a line of business much favored in the stock market – say, a broadband network or Internet-access business in the late 1990s. Alternatively, it can invest in a less glamorous extension of its core business. The firm does not have the capacity to make both investments. Its managers know three things: (1) the market will reward the glamorous investment in the near term, (2) the glamorous investment is highly risky, and (3) the firm's capital-budgeting analysis yields a slightly higher present value for the less glamorous investment in the core business.

In theory, the firm should make the less glamorous investment due to its higher net present value. Only an irrationally risk-prone actor would opt for glamour. A properly designed equity compensation scheme should not cause the firm's managers to stray from this rational choice.

Stock option compensation is defended on the theory that it encourages the very risk-neutral investment policy favored in financial economic theory. It does so by counterbalancing the perverse effects of straight salary. Managers on straight salary are thought to tend toward risk aversion. They have an undiversifiable human capital investment in the firm and a consequent interest in institutional stability. This contrasts with the interest of the shareholders, who tend to hold well-diversified portfolios and approach risk neutrality in their evaluation of new investments. The conflict of interest ripens when the managers choose a low-risk, low-return investment instead of the high-risk, high-return investment preferred by the shareholders. Stock options counterbalance the managers' risk-averse tendencies by holding out the possibility of future stock ownership. But they do not thereby automatically make managers risk neutral. Prior to an option's expiration or exercise, its holder is benefited by an increase in the underlying asset's volatility; high volatility enhances the probability of exercise in the money. This creates a potential problem. High-risk choices made from an option holder's perspective may be too risky, decreasing the firm's long-term fundamental value even as they make the option more valuable. This is just the possibility held out by the glamour investment in the hypothetical. Defenders of standard stock option plans acknowledge the problem, counseling that the solution lies in setting the right mix between options granted and the flow of straight salary tied to the managers' low-risk human capital investment.[48]

---

[48] Thomas & Martin, *supra* note 11, at 40.

Although the theory may well be sound, realizing the theoretically correct mix of incentives presents a serious practical problem. To see why, let us examine the hypothetical from the various shareholders' points of view.

We begin on the investment side. A long-term shareholder will want management to expand the core competency, despite the short-term opportunity cost to the stock price. On a long-term basis, the core investment causes the stock price to increase. A fundamental value investor, viewed without regard to the time horizon, will make the same choice, because dispassionate risk appraisal shows the investment to be more valuable. But a caveat must be entered: a smart fundamental value investor with a short time horizon might see things differently, opting for a near-term bump in the stock price.

The noise trader and the short-term holder also will see things differently. The market's near-term reaction matters greatly to both of them, so both favor the glamour investment. Dumb money, impressed by a stock price uptick, also will favor glamour; indeed, additional dumb money might be induced to invest in the wake of the glamour investment's announcement, thus further driving up the stock price.

If the firm makes the glamour investment, some smart-money observers will conclude that the market overvalues it and short the stock. If the smart money thereby corrects the overvaluation, there is little risk that stock option compensation will encourage suboptimal investing by the firm. But how much smart money will be out there to perform the price correction function? The investment decisions of publicly traded firms tend to be opaque. Their periodic reports do not lay out precise decision parameters such as those assumed in the hypothetical. Accordingly, to perform its job of correcting prices, the smart money needs to be more conversant with the fundamentals of the firm's business than any reference to publicly available information permits. Quite apart from the costs and risks of short positions, smart money will not necessarily be available to correct the stock price.

We now turn to the managers, assuming that they are the beneficiaries of a generous, conventional stock option plan in the middle of its term. They hold vested, exercisable options; unvested options that can be exercised in the near term; and unvested options that can be exercised only in the intermediate term. They also hold stock purchased through the past exercise of options. How these holdings affect the investment decision depends on the numbers projected and the managers' personal preferences. From a long-term, fundamental value point of view, the glamour investment is suboptimal. But it also will cause the stock price to be significantly higher in the short term. If the executives are ready to sell the stock they now own or will soon acquire through option exercise during the period in which the firm's stock is overpriced due to the glamour investment, they have an incentive to choose it. If, on the other hand, the glamour investment is so risky that it holds out a possibility of future distress, they may reject it because their job-term projections extend into the intermediate or long terms.

Three points emerge from this exercise. First, shareholder interest does not necessarily send a clear signal on the choice of investment. Second, conventional stock option compensation does not necessarily incent managers to create long-term fundamental value. Third, managers make stock-price-based calculations from a smart-money position. Even if they realize that the glamour investment presents significant negative long-term possibilities, they may opt for it anyway, knowing that they can adjust their stockholdings during the projected period of overvaluation. They can even act before astute market players. There arises a high risk of opportunism.

Two adjustments advocated by the critics of stock option plans address these problems. First, vesting practices could be changed so that the managers are locked into long-term positions in the stock. Plans have typically required executives to retain a minimum amount of stock, but the minimums set have been too low to be meaningful.[49] Stricter retention policies have been mooted,[50] but it is too early to tell whether these will significantly constrain an executive's tendency to dispose of stock in the wake of option exercise. Second, executives could be forced to disclose their stock sales in advance (rather than after the fact), so as to minimize their smart-money advantage and increase the stock of information moving market prices in correct directions.[51]

Some advocate a different approach, suggesting that stock options be abandoned and replaced by restricted stock plans. Such plans award the stock outright and thus ameliorate perverse effects respecting investment policy. As has been noted, options gain value as the firm's stock becomes more volatile, perversely tying executive wealth to stock volatility. To the extent that the executives' risk-averse attachment to their jobs does not counteract this incentive, a problem is presented. Restricted stock addresses the problem by importing more stable incentives. Where options allow for value only in the event that the stock price exceeds the exercise price after vesting and before expiration, long positions in stock have value on both the upside and the downside.[52]

---

[49] *See* JAMES F. REDA ET AL., COMPENSATION COMMITTEE HANDBOOK 259 (2d ed. 2005).

[50] *Id.* To be effective, these would have to bar risk shifting through derivative contracting. *See* Bank, *supra* note 40, at 323–24.

[51] BEBCHUK & FRIED, *supra* note 6, at 179–81, 191; Jensen & Murphy, *supra* note 2, at 68.

[52] Brian J. Hall & Kevin J. Murphy, *The Trouble with Stock Options* 19 (Harv. NOM Working Paper No. 03–33, 2003), *available at* http://ssrn.com/abstract=415040. The corporate world's failure to take advantage of these asserted benefits can be explained in part by reference to

The restricted stock argument is correct so far as it goes, subject to the important caveat that the substitution of long holdings for options does not by itself achieve incentive compatibility. Note that the managers in the hypothetical have long holdings of the stock from past option exercises in addition to options under the present plan. So long as the executives hold significant numbers of shares that may freely be sold in the overpriced market, the suboptimal glamour investment may make them better off. Absent retention constraints on those long holdings, the incentive problem remains unsolved. The same goes for restricted stock plans.

Restricted stock has an additional shortcoming. Compared to stock options, it holds out an opportunity cost respecting incentives to create value.[53] Restricted stock amounts to an option with an exercise price of zero, and there is no reason to believe zero is an optimal exercise price.[54] To see the point, compare the award of an option to buy one hundred shares at $100 and an outright grant of one hundred shares, both awarded with the stock trading at $100. Assume that the stock price declines to $80 on the day after the grant and stays at $80 forever because the firm is badly managed. The holder of the option is wiped out; the holder of the stock emerges with 80 cents on the dollar despite poor performance.

These value implications help explain the trend toward restricted stock after 2001.[55] From one point of view, it looks like a healthy reaction to option-related excesses of the 1990s. But at a time when stock market averages showed little forward motion, it also neatly dovetailed with managers' self-interest. In a retrenching market, restricted stock increases net management compensation, not only compared to the alternative of indexed options but even compared to conventional, fixed-price options. The restricted stock alternative accordingly makes economic sense only if the grants are conditioned on the firm's meeting strict performance targets, or, in the alternative, the firms take care to make the grant in the form of a trade-off, with the executive taking the stock in lieu of cash salary or bonus payments otherwise to be received.[56]

In summary, given variegated shareholders and the possibility of market mispricing, equity compensation holds out negative possibilities respecting investment policy. The incentive problem is time sensitive: mispricing occurs in the short and intermediate term, but in the long term, fundamental value

accounting and tax regimes, which have pushed preferences in the direction of options. *Id.* at 24.

[53] *See* REDA ET AL., *supra* note 49, at 244.

[54] BEBCHUK & FRIED, *supra* note 6, at 170–71; Jensen & Murphy, *supra* note 2, at 58.

[55] *See* REDA ET AL., *supra* note 49, at 244.   [56] *See* Jensen & Murphy, *supra* note 2, at 59.

controls. It follows that time holds out the cure. Equity incentive schemes, whether in option or in long form, should restrict alienation so as to align the incentives of managers with the long-term stock price and thus the long-term shareholder interest.

The analysis changes for a firm with underpriced stock. Here, two scenarios present themselves. The first is benign. The firm's managers, as smart money, have a strong incentive to hold until the stock price reaches fundamental value, whatever the terms of the plan. The second scenario is more troubling. Here, a lack of upward movement in the stock price induces impatience and ill-advised investment in overpriced assets. Retention constraints are irrelevant in the first case but beneficial in the second. Across-the-board restrictions on alienation accordingly appear to be in order.

Just how long such retention constraints should endure is another question, with the answer presumably varying from firm to firm, depending on the nature of the business and the state of the market. A one-size-fits-all standard still can be suggested: the executive should be required to retain an amount of stock that is material in light of the executive's overall net worth until a year after the termination of employment at the firm.

A final caveat should be entered. For most purposes, long-term stock price enhancement and long-term fundamental value creation amount to different terms for the same objective. However, they may send different signals when an unwanted merger bid appears. The long-term fundamental value objective has been used to justify management resistance to a premium bid on the ground that the firm's long-term value under present management exceeds the price offered by the bidder. The justification rings hollow in the eyes of many because long-term fundamental value investors still tend to favor the premium bid. In the hostile-offer case, the conflict between long-term and short-term interests occurs not among the outside shareholders but between inside managers and the outside shareholders as a group. Prevailing stock option practices help to realign managers' interests with those of the outside shareholders. Significant, vested, and alienable equity stakes make managers less likely to oppose the takeover. Thus did stock option compensation apparently counteract the tendency to resist, facilitating unprecedented numbers of friendly mergers during the 1990s. Strict, enduring restraints on alienation would change this. Managers with an equity interest that remains unvested in the wake of a takeover paid for in bidder stock will have every reason to resist, preferring to leave the pursuit of long-term value in their own hands rather than those of a hostile stranger. A united shareholder interest, then, would want revised vesting restrictions made contingent on events in the control market.

C. The Quality of Financial Reports

Now consider the impact of equity-based compensation on management's incentives respecting financial reporting. We take a simple, relatively benign example of 1990s earnings management: the cookie-jar reserve. The firm takes an extraordinary loss in a given quarter respecting an unsuccessful line of business. The stock price effect of the bad news is muted because the loss is a one-time-only affair. Given, say, a $15 billion company, the market will not be overly concerned as between a write-off of $1.5 billion or $1.75 billion. So, management, which expects actual write-offs over time to total $1.5 billion, tops up the present deduction from earnings to $1.75 billion. The extra $250 million goes to the cookie jar. In a subsequent quarter when the earnings come in a tad less than expected, management conveniently revisits the loss reserve and reduces it. The released sum supports earnings in the subsequent quarter.[57] A cookie-jar stash also can derive from any overestimated cost, such as unrealistically high estimates of any of sales returns, loan losses, or warranty costs.

Managers in the 1990s held out the shareholder interest in justifying the manipulation. It was said that investors prefer a time series of smoothly increasing income figures.[58] The drawdowns from the cookie jar let management construct that steadily rising line of earnings, avoiding volatile income results that mean a higher discount rate and a lower stock price. Such income smoothing does not necessarily corrupt the trend, even as it beneficially reduces volatility. And since the trend determines the long-term run value, any misrepresentation is not material.

Managers cited the noise traders in the alternative. In the overheated 1990s market, the noise interest hyped every piece of news about fundamental value to such a degree as to make it plausible to argue that earnings management serves a higher shareholder interest.[59] If, to take a much-used example, the firm misses its expected quarterly earnings number by $0.01 and the

---

[57] The use of the big-bath write-off to increase cookie-jar reserves is constrained for business exits commenced after December 31, 2002; liabilities incurred in respect of closures must now be recognized on incurrence and not in advance. FIN. ACCT. STANDS. BD., ACCOUNTING FOR COSTS ASSOCIATED WITH EXIT OR DISPOSAL ACTIVITIES, STATEMENT OF FIN. ACCOUNTING STANDARDS NO. 146 (2002).

[58] Mary E. Barth et al., *Market Rewards Associated with Patterns of Increasing Earnings*, 37 J. ACCT. RES. 387, 398, 412 (1999) (showing that firms with patterns of greater earnings have higher price-per-earnings ratios, after controlling for other factors).

[59] For a detailed description of quarter-to-quarter earnings pressures in the late 1990s, see Joseph Fuller & Michael C. Jensen, *Just Say No to Wall Street*, 14 J. APPLIED CORP. FIN. 41 (Winter 2002), *available at* http://ssrn.com/abstract=297156.

overheated market as a result punishes the stock by bidding it down 10 percent, then a reserve that holds out the missing penny benefits the shareholders. It allows management to anticipate and counteract the shareholders' behavioral shortcomings, protecting the stock price from short-term market mood swings.

Shareholder responses to these justifications depend on the state of the market and the makeup of the particular shareholder. We begin on the investment side. The fundamental value investor will not favor the manipulation of earnings figures through loss reserves. Because these investors only care about cash flows in the future, they want an unvarnished present report. Management advocacy that results in smoother numbers makes it harder to work through to the most accurate valuation. Since greater volatility means a higher discount factor, the appraiser needs accurate information about volatility so as to make the adjustment.

The profiles of long-term and smart-money investors will differ. The long-term investor, once situated in a stock, presumably will not be destabilized when management turns up a couple of cents short of expectations in the current quarter. At the same time, earnings management, pursued in moderation, will not inflict any significant injury on this investor. In the long run, the empirical cash flow absolutely controls, and the long-run question is whether the company produces competitively. Therefore, the long-term investor could profess indifference to earnings management keyed to the short-term interest. The profile alters as accounting manipulation becomes more aggressive and holds out a risk of *ex post* enforcement. An accounting scandal means deadweight costs of defense and accompanying institutional instability. All of these impair long-term value. Better to submit accurate reports in the first place.

The smart money is supposed to be able to see through the ruse to the periodic cash flows, at least so long as the published reports give it an adequate basis for so doing. It incurs the cost of the analysis, but, since it is smart, it will be doing the analysis in any event. For example, from a smart-money point of view, there arguably would have been nothing wrong with Enron's practice of pumping up its earnings numbers with results from sham transactions with special-purpose entities, so long as Enron fully disclosed the transactions in the footnotes to its financials.[60] Enforcement costs remain a negative, but the smart money, by definition, gets out first.

Now let us consider the speculators. Assume a shareholder buys a stock on a trend-chasing basis. The trend is that earnings are rising. The holding period is short or intermediate, without a definite termination date. Given

---

[60] For a description of the Enron fraud, see William W. Bratton, *Enron and the Dark Side of Shareholder Value*, 76 TUL. L. REV. 1275, 1314–22 (2002).

this profile, an earnings shortfall hyped as bad news could be destabilizing, causing the shareholder to sell and incur tax and transaction costs. It follows that a little finagling to avoid the firm being short on its earnings projections will not be objectionable. Just by arranging the numbers, management protects a shareholder from herself and from the manic nature of the market.

Unfortunately, earnings management also holds out problems for speculators, even as they are its nominal beneficiaries. It works well only so long as management massages the numbers to protect an upward trend that responds by staying on trajectory for at least the intermediate term. Let us suppose that the upward trend stalls, causing management to draw down from the cookie jar to protect the slope of the line. There will be some shareholders who are influenced to hold who might otherwise have sold because of the stall. As to these, the income smoothing may or may not be beneficial. It will certainly turn out to be detrimental if events make clear that the upward trend was history as of the time of the income smoothing. Once the trend turns down, the manipulation undertaken protectively turns out to be injurious. Indeed, all speculative investors' interests then presumptively lie in getting out in the first wave. Where the unvarnished truth prompts that sale, income smoothing injures the holder. The injury is even worse for the holder buying in reliance on the manipulated numbers at or after the turning point in the trend. With earnings management, then, the speculative investor to which management caters could turn out to be an injured party.

Standard stock option plans do nothing to skew management's incentives to a long-term, fundamental value view of financial reporting. Managers who massage numbers protect a trend into which they can sell stock purchased through option exercise, pocketing a premium over fundamental value. They do so as the smartest of smart money, for they control the reports. Bolton, Scheinkman, and Xiong show this in a formal model in which, given large differences of opinion about the value of the stock, even a contract that optimally trades off risk sharing and management incentives will induce a short-term orientation and encourage actions that feed speculation.[61]

Presumably, smart-money shareholders of managers thus incentivized, whether noise traders or value investors, will be closely watching the managers' selling activity so as to benefit along with them. These holders can protect themselves. A sharper conflict of interest opens up between managers employing aggressive accounting and noise-trading, dumb-money shareholders who rely on the trend and hold on to the stock.[62]

---

[61] Bolton et al., *supra* note 12, at 6.

[62] Note also an additional conflict between management and the dumb-money interest. Prior to the change of the accounting rules in 2005, stock option compensation did not entail

Speculative shareholders acted out this volatile behavior pattern in the real world over the past decade. In the standard account of the recent corporate reporting crisis, managers in the late 1990s, incentivized by stock options, used consulting rents to induce auditors to accord a free hand to manage bottom-line numbers. Auditors defended the practice by reference to the shareholder interest: if the threat to independence did not upset the shareholders, then regulators should not intervene to impose their more conservative views about accounting choices.[63] At the time, the supply-and-demand dynamic respecting audit services operated to make auditors sensitive to the speculative shareholder interest. Unfortunately for the auditors, stock market reverses later caused the speculators to take a fundamental value view of financial reporting, condemning accounting formerly viewed with favor or indifference. The experience of Enron, WorldCom, and other scandals ameliorated the incentive problem respecting financial reports by prompting a shift in the way investors view the numbers.

The recent shift in shareholder demand respecting reporting does not solve the incentive problem, however. The same shift in demand occurred after 1929, with conservatism prevailing long thereafter. But speculative demands for aggression eventually returned during the bull markets of the 1960s and early 1970s. A similar, cyclical return to the speculative perspective on financial reporting thus can be predicted to occur at some point in the future. When the time comes, unrestricted management stockholdings will hasten the transition.

There again arises a powerful case for retention constraints. A long-term restraint on alienation ties management's interest to long-term cash flows rather than constructed numbers in present reports. Here again, the need for constraint is reduced in undervalued firms, whose managers only want to get the markets to see the truth. But a clear distinction cannot be made in practice between overvalued and undervalued firms – no one ever knows for certain which firm is which. Indeed, if the manager of an overvalued firm believes the firm to be undervalued, an incentive to overstate results could follow. Strict retention rules again are signaled across the board.

---

a charge to periodic earnings. *See* FIN. ACCT. STANDS. BD., ACCOUNTING FOR STOCK-BASED COMP., STATEMENT OF FIN. ACCOUNTING STANDARDS NO. 123 (1995). Thus could management compensate itself without reporting the arrangement's economic cost to existing shareholders. Of course, smart-money shareholders, whether speculators or investors, were not fooled. Dumb money presumably would have taken the earnings reports at face value.

[63] Rick Antle et al., *An Economic Analysis of Auditor Independence for a Multi-Client, Multi-Service Public Accounting Firm* (Report for AICPA, 1997), *available at* http://ftp.aicpa.org/public/download/members/div/secps/isb/0117194.doc. The industry's advocates also pointed to informational advantages and the adequacy of legal liability constraints.

D. Payout Policy

Hypothesize a firm with free cash flow. Management has a choice as to how to disgorge the money. It can raise the regular dividend (or declare a special dividend), or it can cause the firm to repurchase its shares in the open market. If the EMH were true and the choice had no tax consequences, the shareholders would be indifferent.[64] In the real world, however, the choice has tax implications. In addition, the real world holds out the complicating possibility that stock may be overpriced or underpriced at the time of the repurchase.

Different shareholders will have a different view of the choice. Long-term taxpaying holders who view the stock as correctly priced or underpriced will favor repurchase. Even under the regime of rate parity between ordinary income and capital gains introduced by the Jobs and Growth Tax Relief Reconciliation Act of 2003,[65] repurchase holds out the benefit of a tax deferral for long-term holders.[66] Short-term and noise-trading holders need not disagree. Repurchase announcements are taken as good news and tend to trigger a 3 percent announcement-period gain. They thus can figure into the stock's momentum. Disagreement breaks out only if the stock is overpriced at the time of repurchase. Here, repurchase programs disadvantage long-term, fundamental value investors, particularly if they are not smart enough to see the temporary overvaluation. A noise trader who overcredits the signal might be similarly disadvantaged.

Meanwhile, standard stock options skew management's choice away from dividends and toward repurchases in all states of the world. Consider the choice between a dividend and a repurchase from an option holder's point of view. Dividends are paid to shareholders but not to option holders. One dollar paid out as a dividend does an option holder no good unless the option is dividend-protected, that is, unless the option contract provides for a diminution of the exercise price to make up for the dividend. But only 1 percent of executives have dividend-protected stock options.[67] It follows that stock option value is negatively related to the firm's expected dividend payout. Assume a manager with a ten-year option. Further assume that the firm's stock price has a volatility

---

[64] This follows from the irrelevance hypothesis of Modigliani and Miller. *See* Franco Modigliani & Merton Miller, *The Cost of Capital, Corporation Finance, and the Theory of Investment*, 48 AM. ECON. REV. 261 (1958).

[65] Jobs and Growth Tax Relief Reconciliation Act of 2003, Pub. L. No. 108–27, 117 Stat. 752 (codified as amended in scattered sections of 26 U.S.C., 42 U.S.C., and 46 U.S.C.).

[66] William W. Bratton, *The New Dividend Puzzle*, 93 GEO. L. J. 845, 852–55 (2005).

[67] Kevin J. Murphy, *Executive Compensation*, *in* 3B HANDBOOK OF LABOR ECONOMICS 2485, 2509–10 (Orley Ashenfelter & David Card eds., 1999).

of 30 percent and that the risk-free rate of return is 5 percent. Under the Black-Scholes option-pricing model, a cut in the dividend yield from 2 percent to 1 percent increases the option's value by 18 percent. Cutting the dividend entirely raises option value by 39 percent.[68]

Stock options, then, raise the financial stakes of the choice between dividends and repurchases, giving managers a strong incentive to prefer repurchases. Unsurprisingly, empirical studies show a strong correlation between stock options and payout choices. The probability of stock repurchase is positively related to the presence of stock options.[69] Firms with large stock option plans are more likely to announce share repurchase plans.[70] Dividends are strongly negatively correlated with options.[71] A study of the largest S&P 500 firms from 1994 to 1997 shows that even as the repurchase payout rose from 17 percent to 41 percent as a percentage of income, the dividend yield dropped steadily from 2.76 percent to 1.41 percent.[72]

In addition, the number of shares repurchased in open-market repurchase programs relates positively to the total number of options exercisable.[73] Some studies report that firms repurchase gradually over the lives of options to reduce the options' dilutive effect.[74] But there also is evidence that firms time repurchase announcements around the times stock options are being exercised.[75] Whatever the timing, the numbers are large. One survey finds that firms repurchase roughly 38 percent of the shares underlying their option grants prior to exercise.[76] The more stock options that are outstanding, the more stock the firms repurchase. Managers admit this. Three-fifths of the

[68] Scott J. Weisbenner, *Corporate Share Repurchases in the 1990s: What Role Do Stock Options Play?* 9 (Fed. Reserve Bd. Working Paper No. 2000–29, 2000), *available at* http://www.federalreserve.gov/pubs/feds/2000/200029/200029pap.pdf.

[69] Christine Jolls, *Stock Repurchases and Incentive Compensation* 15–17 (Nat'l Bureau of Econ. Res., Working Paper No. 6467, 1998), *available at* http://www.nber.org/papers/w6467.

[70] Mary E. Barth & Ron Kasznik, *Share Repurchases and Intangible Assets*, 28 J. ACCT. & ECON. 211, 238 (1999).

[71] *See* George W. Fenn & Nellie Liang, *Corporate Payout Policy and Managerial Stock Incentives*, 60 J. FIN. ECON. 45, 47–48 (2001) (using the Lambert model to show that a 1 percent standard-deviation change in the stock option variable reduces dividends by thirty-eight basis points).

[72] Nellie Liang & Steven A. Sharpe, *Share Repurchases and Employee Stock Options and Their Implications for S&P 500 Share Retirements and Expected Returns* 17 (Fed. Reserve Bd. Working Paper No. 1999–59, 1999), *available at* http://www.federalreserve.gov/pubs/feds/1999/199959/199959pap.pdf.

[73] Kathleen M. Kahle, *When a Buyback Isn't a Buyback: Open Market Repurchases and Employee Options*, 63 J. FIN. ECON. 235, 238 (2002).

[74] Weisbenner, *supra* note 68, at 3.

[75] Konan Chan et al., *Do Firms Knowingly Repurchase Stock for Good Reason?* 2 n.4 (2001), *available at* http://www.ruf.rice.edu/~jgspaper/W_Ikenberry_insiderv6.pdf.

[76] Weisbenner, *supra* note 68, at 23.

executives reporting in one survey acknowledged that they instituted an open-market repurchase program to prepare for stock option exercise.[77]

The situation can be corrected in part. Interpolating dividend protection in option plans removes the incentive skew toward repurchases. Of course, given a dividend-paying firm, dividend protection increases the value of the options; the giveback would be a decrease in the number granted or an increase in the exercise price. But even given dividend protection, management may retain the urge to warehouse in advance of exercise, particularly in light of the new rules requiring that the option's cost must be deducted from periodic earnings. Now that options cause earnings to be lower, there appears to be more reason than ever to reduce the number of shares outstanding so that the earnings-per-share figure, so critical in the eye of the noise traders, stays as high as possible.

E. Bonuses and Exit Payments

Stock option plans, whatever the shortcomings in their design, have one great merit: they condition rewards on the stock price, which in turn is determined by free-market actors. Firms also dispense large cash bonuses. These could be tied to the stock price but tend not to be. This section looks first into periodic performance bonuses and then into bonuses paid on exit.

1. Performance Bonuses
Many cash bonus plans employ periodic earnings targets. This practice returns us to incentives respecting financial reports. Accounting standards give management room to manipulate numbers to magnify current results. Conditioning bonuses on earnings encourages this, with possible benefits for short-term holders and noise traders, at least where the earnings reports cause the stock to be overvalued. However, to the extent that smart-money investors determine the market price and the stock is valued correctly, earnings ruses do not hold out stock price benefits. But the perverse incentive remains: the cash bonus scheme still rewards management for putting numbers on a page, without spillover benefits to shareholders of any type.

Other periodic cash bonus awards are tied to particular performance targets. To the extent the targets are tied to the improvement of bottom-line performance, these bonuses may be unobjectionable. Indeed, in the case of a firm with undervalued stock, they may be an effective means to provide periodic rewards to effective managers pending the stock's recovery. In addition, these

---

[77] *Id.* at 8 (citing a 1999 survey of 1,600 CFOs).

bonuses can be tailored to the performance of particular tasks. Unfortunately, however, the practice often falls short. Some performance targets lack a strong connection to the improvement of bottom-line performance. Consider one common target – spending all the funds in an annual budget.[78] This has the benefit of being cash-flow-based and thus less subject to manipulation than an earnings target. On the other hand, it holds out a bonus for the act of investment rather than for the longer process of investing successfully and realizing projected returns.[79] Compare a bonus paid for closing an acquisition.[80] As with the budget bonus, the target's accomplishment lies within the discretion of the executive payee, and the bonus is paid for the act of investing rather than the result of investing successfully.[81] Recent results have been particularly dismaying. Despite stock option compensation, the period 1998–2001 was the worst in history with respect to acquirer losses from bad mergers.[82] In these cases, a unified model of the shareholder suffices to condemn the practice; no shareholder interest is advanced.

The criticisms trigger a question. If accounting numbers fall short as a performance metric and the stock price suffices only on a long-term basis, is there any reliable bonus metric available from quarter to quarter? Critics of prevailing practice point to cash flow as an alternative metric. Private equity firms use cash flows to reward the managers of leveraged-buyout firms, triggering bonuses on the generation of cash flows sufficient to service debt.[83] Other firms reward managers when cash flows exceed the cost of capital.[84]

Consider, as a possible variation on this theme, the dividend. Oliver Hart shows that in an ideal (and taxless) world, first-best results easily can be achieved with an all-common-stock capital structure and a simple incentive compensation system. Hart describes a simple two-period situation where the firm is founded at $t = 0$ and liquidated at $t = 2$, with an intermediate decision respecting liquidation or continuance to be made at $t = 1$, along with a dividend payment. Hart would make the compensation of the manager depend entirely on the dividend d. That is, incentive compensation I should equal

---

[78] *See* JAMES F. REDA, COMPENSATION COMMITTEE HANDBOOK 115–16 (2002).

[79] Unfortunately, these budget-based bonus plans tend to open doors for manipulation. By setting thresholds and caps, they encourage smoothing and manipulation of the capital budgeting process. *See* Jensen & Murphy, *supra* note 2, at 69–75, which recommends a linear approach that is not keyed to any particular year's capital budget.

[80] In addition, when performance targets are not met, they often are lowered *ex post*. BEBCHUK & FRIED, *supra* note 6, at 124–27.

[81] *Id.*

[82] *See* Sara B. Moeller et al., *Wealth Destruction on a Massive Scale? A Study of Acquiring Firm Returns in the Recent Merger Wave*, 60 J. FIN. 757, 758, 770 (2005).

[83] *See* Jensen & Murphy, *supra* note 2, at 76.   [84] *Id.* at 76–77.

B $(d_1 + d_2)$, where B is a proportion of the firm's total returns. If the payment also covers liquidation proceeds, where $I = B\,[d_1 + (d_2, L)]$, the manager can be expected to make an optimal decision respecting liquidation at $t = 1$. If the expected value of L at $t = 1$ is greater than the total returns expected at $t = 2$, the firm is liquidated at $t = 1$, and no costly contracting designed to align the manager's incentives with those of outside investors is necessary.[85] The problem, in Hart's conception, is that the bribe B required to align management incentives with those of outside security holders is unfeasibly large.[86] Accordingly, a complex capital structure must be devised to align incentives in the direction of optimal investment and to ensure that the actor with the appropriate incentives controls the assets.

In theory, then, the dividend cannot feasibly serve as the exclusive basis for measuring executive pay. But might it serve a limited purpose as a metric for periodic cash bonuses? Unlike accounting numbers such as periodic earnings, the dividend follows from actual operations and cash flows. Unlike the stock price, it is not the product of valuation under uncertainty. A dividend-based bonus scheme would encourage firms to pay dividends, thereby alleviating problems of overinvestment and excess reliance on open market stock repurchases. The question is whether a dividend-contingent bonus would cause the opposite problem, underinvestment. Dividends, like bonuses contingent on acquisition closings, follow from actions within the zone of management discretion. Managers seeking larger bonuses could divert cash flows needed to finance good projects into dividend flows. But there could be countervailing incentives. Managers holding stock options subject to retention constraints would retain an incentive to make good long-term investments. Given such a long-term incentive alignment, a dividend-based bonus might have the limited effect of causing the managers to raise by one notch the hurdle rate applied in evaluating investments, which need not be a bad thing. The matter would come down to the amount of the dividend-based bonus: it should import an

---

[85] OLIVER HART, FIRMS, CONTRACTS, AND FINANCIAL STRUCTURE 146–48 (1995); *see also* Anat R. Admati & Paul Pfleiderer, *Robust Financial Contracting and the Role of Venture Capitalists*, 49 J. FIN. 371 (1994) (articulating a fixed-fraction model of venture capitalist participation in the decision of whether to continue). In the model, there is no *ex ante* prospect of firm continuance in the event of poor results; in the real world, managers derive private benefits from asset management and might opt to continue.

[86] The large B is conceded in venture-capital financings and private-equity restructurings. But the context is different from that of the pay debate. Venture capital and private equity both involve arm's-length negotiations with outside equity capital that exercises control, and transaction structures share a limited duration. The pay debate concerns mature publicly traded firms, with their separation of ownership and control, and an implicit, unlimited time horizon.

incentive toward objective evaluation of new investments, without skewing hurdle rates to destructive, uneconomically high levels.

That said, a dividend-based bonus suits only mature firms with steady cash flows. For a contrast, hypothesize a firm at an early growth stage of its life cycle with an investment set that holds out excellent returns for the indefinite future. Further hypothesize that the firm seriously pursues an incentive-compatible, long-term equity compensation scheme. Stock purchases through option exercises are locked down so that executives at all times have a material portion of their wealth tied to the long-term performance of the firm's stock. Regular salaries are capped at $1 million per year in light of Internal Revenue Code section 162(m).[87] Finally, cash bonuses are paid only in tandem with dividend announcements, with the payment mechanism designed so that no perverse incentives arise respecting investment policy. The scenario implies a problem: as of $t = 0$, the top team has to wait for the long term to come about before receiving big payoffs. The long wait fails to synchronize with tournament economics. As of $t = 0$, any potential manager with bargaining power will reject the terms of the compensation plan. At $t = 1$, an impatient manager might look for a job elsewhere. This firm, then, will be thrown back to more problematic bonus calculations.

2. Exit Payments

Firms also pay bonuses on entry and exit. Bonuses for signing are unsurprising, assuming a competitive market for the best managers. Bonuses for leaving, whether by firing, retirement, or acquisition, are more disturbing, competitive market or not. The average severance package equals three or more years of compensation, with only 2 percent of firms reducing it in the event that the CEO finds new work. The critics argue that firing should not be a cash bonanza.[88]

Exit payments still can be defended in theory. Long-term value creation follows from long-term investment under uncertainty. A payment that cushions failure arguably encourages risk taking, for whatever the reputational consequences of forced exit, the executive does not have to worry about personal cash flow. This argument resonates especially well with respect to undervalued firms whose executives might be unjustly blamed for a languishing stock price. It also comes to bear in defense of golden parachutes triggered by

---

[87] Internal Revenue Code § 162(m) (2006), enacted in 1994, limits the deductibility of straight salaries to $1 million; compensation beyond $1 million is not deductible unless conditioned on a link to performance.

[88] BEBCHUK & FRIED, *supra* note 6, at 88–89, 132–35.

acquisitions, as the bonus encourages a neutral posture with respect to sale of the company.[89]

Questions still arise, however. The golden parachute makes sense because exit coincides with a premium payment to the other shareholders more easily secured with the executive's cooperation. Other terminations, whether for retirement or for incompetence, do not coincide with such upside events. If these exiting executives already are the beneficiaries of supersize pay packages, cash flow should not be a near-term problem. In addition, the exit payment, by ensuring against failure even as the executive is richly compensated at present, could diminish incentives to succeed. The tournament incentive obtains only for those trying to reach the top team. For the winners, continued high-powered incentives depend on the posttournament compensation package. Of course, reputational incentives motivate executives whatever their pay arrangements. But recent decades' experience counsels against reliance on reputation. If reputation mattered greatly, firms presumably would revert to the practice of three decades ago and remit the lion's share of compensation in the form of straight salary, saving the shareholders the dilution costs of supersize equity compensation. The system abandoned reliance on reputation a decade and a half ago when it shifted its focus to high-powered incentives. Whatever the system's present shortcomings, turning back is not a plausible option.

F. Summary

This section began with two questions. First, what kind of manager-shareholders are prevailing incentive compensation practices likely to produce? Second, does the shareholder interest provide a coherent normative yardstick with which to evaluate prevailing practices?

The answer to the first question depends on the case. With an undervalued firm, managers are likely to resemble long-term, fundamental value shareholders. With an overvalued firm, present practice aligns their interest with short-term noise traders, making it rational for managers to make suboptimal investments, distort financial reports, and follow suboptimal payout practices. The informational advantage that comes with the managers' inside positions exacerbates the problem.

The answer to the second question is yes and no. Sometimes, as with some bonus payments, the shareholder interest answers normative questions with a unitary voice. But responses often depend on the shareholders' type, the state of the market, and the undervaluation or overvaluation of the particular

---

[89] *See* REDA ET AL., *supra* note 49, at 231–32.

firm's stock. The noisier the stock market and the more overvalued the firm's stock, the less coherent is the signal from the shareholder interest. The shareholder interest will more likely be united, and management's incentives will more likely be well aligned with it when the firm's stock is undervalued. Undervalued firms attract the fundamental value interest; noise traders stay away.

But suppose that managers of all firms are prone to believe that the market undervalues their stock. One often enough hears managers complaining that the market underappreciates their firms' stock. If widespread belief in undervaluation is the case, it helps explain the laxity in prevailing practice, for conventional plans make more economic sense assuming undervalued stock. But the incentive problem is simultaneously aggravated. Some managers may believe their stock to be underappreciated when the stock in fact is overvalued. Managers of other overvalued firms may accurately appraise the situation. Either way, incentive pay schemes invite suboptimal investment, inaccurate financial reports, and skewed payout policy.

III. THE VOLATILE SHAREHOLDER INTEREST AND THE DEBATE OVER SUPERSIZE PAY

The debate over executive compensation focuses on the quality of the bargaining space in which corporate boards and top team members effect trade-offs between incentives and compensation.

The leading critics, Lucian Bebchuk and Jesse Fried, charge that compensation practices fail to satisfy the validation standard of an arm's-length contract. Managers, they say, possess and effectively wield power, assuring that compensation prevails over incentives and that performance rewards come on easy terms. Bebchuk and Fried make a short, direct prescription, reasoning as follows: given that (1) the victims of the imbalanced arrangement are the shareholders and (2) the injury is the result of management empowerment, it follows that (3) the only plausible cure lies in empowering the shareholders.[90]

Those who view the governance system more favorably offer three defenses of pay practices. First, the same phenomena that the critics ascribe to executive empowerment can be better explained in terms of the economic relationship between risk and return, as higher risks attending equity-based pay must be compensated with higher upside payouts. Second, to the extent the practice falls short of the arm's-length ideal, informational shortcomings are responsible. Boards incorrectly believe that stock options are a bargain mode of compensation and tend to overvalue them in comparison to cash payments.

[90] BEBCHUK & FRIED, *supra* note 6, at 4–5, 10–12, 61–117, 189–216.

Third, whatever the shortcomings of the practice, the system is fundamentally sound. Managers have on the whole done well for the shareholders since shifting to performance pay in the early 1990s. Loud attacks only enhance the political credibility of the outsider social critics, whose calls for social justice will only crimp the incentive system.

This section reviews this debate against the background of volatile shareholder behavior. It shows that less ground separates the various positions than first appears. Both sides agree that incentive compatibility must be traded off against present compensation. They thus together hold open a door for the perverse effects of speculative shareholding.

A. Power and Rents

Bebchuk and Fried's normative base point is a model of arm's-length bargaining. Under the model, executive pay packages should reward an executive with a sum in excess of his or her reservation price, should contain terms that encourage the executive to increase the value of the firm, and should avoid terms that reduce the value of the firm. More particularly, "arm's length" means modifying existing arrangements to add more upside pull. Stock options should be priced out of the money at grant and the price should be indexed so as to filter out marketwide advances. Reloading and backdoor repricing should be prohibited. Retention constraints should be imposed. Bonus triggers should be performance sensitive, and exit payments should be curtailed.[91]

1. The Arm's-Length Bargain

Compensation packages, say Bebchuk and Fried, do not conform to the arm's-length model because managers influence independent directors. Restating the point, managers use power to extract rents, defined as benefits better than those available under an arm's-length bargain. A prediction follows: the more power a manager possesses, the greater the rents in the pay package.[92] Power, of course, cannot be observed and quantified directly, forcing Bebchuk and Fried to back their positive assertion with inferences drawn from institutional arrangements. They point out that corporate institutions are ill suited to foster arm's-length bargaining between top managers and their corporate employers, drawing on a list of shortcomings well known to students of corporate governance.

Bebchuk and Fried's assertions about power, rents, and the boardroom bargaining context all follow from a basic assumption concerning the appropriate

---

[91] *Id.* at 18–19, 121–46, 159–62, 164–70, 174–85.   [92] *Id.* at 63.

trade-off between incentives and compensation: an arm's-length deal, they assert, would tightly tie pay to performance. At first this seems surprising; one somehow expects a firmer foundation than an intuitive association of hurdle height and value creation. But on reflection, Bebchuk and Fried have no basis for proceeding other than by raw assertion. After all, we have no robust positive theory of optimal incentive compensation. The absence of a theory also explains why process infirmities figure so prominently in Bebchuk and Fried's substantive case, for if managers possess a bargaining advantage and intrinsically prefer more compensation and less incentive compatibility, then the resulting contract will reflect their preference. Given Bebchuk and Fried's assumption respecting the appropriate trade-off, the contract is *ipso facto* substantively infirm.

Bebchuk and Fried bump up against the problem of trading off incentives and compensation at two critical points in their analysis. The issue arises when they propose stricter terms for option plans, like out-of-the-money pricing and indexing. Both of these increase the option price and thus decrease the value of each option granted. They propose a reciprocal adjustment: the number of options granted can be increased to adjust for the price increase so that the present value of the grant (and thus the compensation) remains unchanged.[93] Here, in effect, incentives and compensation synchronize perfectly so that the firm's value can be increased as a result of intensified management effort without management having to give up even a single dollar of compensation value. Although the managers may end up working harder in exchange for the same overall compensation value, the harder work is rewarded with a bigger upside payoff.

The trade-off problem also arises with respect to retention constraints. All other things being equal, a tighter restraint on alienation decreases the pay plan's compensation value by blocking the executive's access to liquidity and portfolio diversification. But here, Bebchuk and Fried propose no Pareto-optimal swap. Instead, they see a pie to be sliced. An "efficient" contract, they say, slices carefully, striking a balance between the competing interests with staged holding periods that would vary from case to case.[94] A question arises: why not gross up again in this case, compensating the executive with a larger number of inalienable shares so as to make up for the loss in value to the alienation restraint? Bebchuk and Fried appear to intuit a limit to usefulness of tit-for-tat trades of compensation for incentives.

The differential treatment is puzzling, given the strong commonalities in the two cases. In both, present value would be increased in exchange for incentive compatibility. The difference is that in the first case, the gross-up pays for forward motion in the stock price, while in the second case, it guards against perverse effects. Perhaps the benefits of forward motion justify increased compensation because the firm is projected to be more valuable net of the trade, where downside-avoided costs of misalignment with the speculative shareholder interest are more difficult to confront and gauge. Note that such a judgment is more likely to follow if the shareholder is modeled in a unitary and benign mold.

Other factors also may be at work. Perhaps the problem identified by Hart creeps into the option compensation scenario at some point: full incentive compatibility may just cost too much in terms of the percentage interest in the firm conceded. But trade-offs made in practice probably follow from a very different intuition. Corporate actors may perceive a small-scale trade-off or no trade-off at all because they perceive the management interest at stake in the case of retention constraints to be more legitimate than that implicated in a negotiation over price. In this view, diversification and liquidity are to shareholding what freedom of movement is to citizenship, and only a limited concession can reasonably be expected at the bargaining table. So limited is the concession demanded that the question of countervailing compensation never arises. Significantly, this approach also tends to imply a unitary and benign model of the shareholder.

A contrasting approach to the trade-off should be put on the table for consideration. Under this, the firm just says no to short-term liquidity and diversification because proper incentive alignment should not be negotiable. To remit the matter of a long-term time horizon to the black box of arm's-length contracting leaves open the possibility of perverse effects. Even assuming an arm's-length bargaining context, the more bargaining power brought to the table by the executive, the more the incentives are skewed toward the speculative shareholder model. Executive pay plans have two purposes: to compensate and to incentivize. If, in the context of a package that mixes straight salary, cash bonuses, and equity awards, it is the incentive purpose that justifies the equity-based component, then it is unclear why retention constraints automatically must be countered by significant concessions to the compensation objective.

2. Shareholder Empowerment

The skew toward the speculative interest persists when Bebchuk and Fried set out a menu of governance improvements. Some of the items on the list would tweak the present system so as to make it more likely that the shareholder voice registers inside boardrooms. For example, transparency could be enhanced.

All compensation could be reported with a dollar value attached, and executive stock sales could be directly reported by the company.[95] In addition, the shareholder vote could be made more meaningful, with separate votes on different segments of compensation plans giving shareholders the opportunity to pinpoint objectionable provisions. Other proposals on the menu are more radical and would empower the shareholders, fundamentally changing the system. For example, binding shareholder initiatives on compensation could be permitted. More than that, the board could lose its legally vested control of the agenda over important corporate legislation so that shareholders could remove entrenching provisions. Finally, shareholders could have access to the ballot on terms broader than those recently proposed by the Securities and Exchange Commission.[96]

As the proposals become more radical, volatile shareholder behavior becomes more of a problem, or at least holds out no circumstantial guarantee of a solution. To see why, consider the counterfactual possibility of a decade in all respects like the 1990s, except that Bebchuk and Fried's shareholder access reforms are in place. The question is whether the shareholder voice rises up to insist on reforms assuring that compensation packages hold out no perverse effects respecting investments, financial reports, and payout policy. The scenario is highly unlikely. Shareholders at the time, including the institutional investors on which access schemes rely, were happy to ride market momentum. It took a bear market and scandals to trigger shareholder demands about bad mergers and the quality of financial reports. At the same time, on some compensation issues, shareholders probably have unified and unproblematic interests. Out-of-the-money pricing and indexing stand out as possibilities. As to these matters, which go purely to the issue of bang for the buck, shareholder access might have a consistently beneficial effect. Meanwhile, the access cure holds out minuses as well as pluses.

B. Defensive Tactics

Defenders of the practice respond to the critics at three levels. The first level presents a full-dress defense of prevailing practice. The second level steps back to admit process infirmities but to reject the unequal bargaining power

---

[95] *Id.* at 192–94. The SEC, apparently influenced by all the criticism, has adopted new rules requiring more extensive disclosures of executive compensation arrangements. *See* Executive Compensation and Related Person Disclosure, Securities Act Release No. 33-8732A, 88 SEC Docket (CCH) 2353 (Aug. 29, 2006).

[96] BEBCHUK & FRIED, *supra* note 6, at 197–98, 210–12.

description. The third level steps farther back still to admit management empowerment but to argue that the system is robust nonetheless.

1. The Fair Deal

The full-dress defense, put forward by Professor Murphy and others, draws on the economic relationship between risk and return to describe prevailing compensation practice as a fair trade.[97] This analysis turns on comparison of outside and insider option valuation. From the firm's point of view, the cost of an executive stock option is the cash consideration the firm would receive from a third-party investor for the same contingent interest in the stock. But third-party investors and firm employees differ in a critical respect as option buyers. Third-party investors are fully diversified and positioned to hedge the risk attending the option position.[98] They accordingly are risk neutral, where employees are underdiversified and risk averse. It follows that the option's value to the employee is less than its value to the third party.[99] It further follows that an option makes no sense when considered as pure compensation in comparison to cash: in order to constitute $1 of pay in the eyes of the employee, option compensation must be increased to make up for the employee's valuation discount. The option thereby costs the firm more than the $1 in value the employee receives. An option nevertheless might make sense as incentive compensation. But the overall terms of an arm's-length option package should be expected to reflect the employee's risk aversion. This explains terms that otherwise could be seen as giveaways, such as exercise prices set at the money rather than at a discount, the failure to index the exercise price, and the allowance of both early exercise and stock sales after exercise.[100]

This fair deal emerges only on a critical assumption – that the employee's compensation objective and the firm's incentive objective may be traded off without any further scrutiny of the resulting contract's incentive properties. This contrasts sharply with Bebchuk and Fried's assumption that an arm's-length deal tightly ties pay to performance and avoids harm to the firm. It also leads to a strange result when viewed through the lens of this chapter's typology of shareholding. In the fair deal story, the executive bargains to attain the status of a fully diversified outside shareholder with full exit rights. The bargained-for status invites the executive to take the speculative mind-set, much like an

---

[97] *See* Brian J. Hall & Kevin J. Murphy, *Stock Options for Undiversified Executives* (Harv. NOM Research Paper No. 00–05, 2001), *available at* http://ssrn.com/abstract=252805.

[98] Kevin J. Murphy, *Explaining Executive Compensation: Managerial Power Versus the Perceived Cost of Stock Options*, 69 U. CHI. L. REV. 847, 859–60 (2002).

[99] Jensen & Murphy, *supra* note 2, at 38.   [100] Hall & Murphy, *supra* note 97, at 3, 13.

aggressive mutual fund. The question asked above comes up again: why should a bargaining zone holding out that result be deemed normatively acceptable?

Substantive scrutiny of incentive effects cannot be avoided under the fair-deal story's own basic assumptions. The trade-offs that make the deal fair follow from the assumption that stock options, viewed solely as compensation, amount to an intrinsically inefficient form of compensation. It follows that option compensation can be justified based on the incentives it creates.

A justificatory standard can be set loosely or strictly. The relaxed standard takes a Kaldor-Hicks approach; that is, the value of the incentives created must exceed the options' opportunity cost as compensation and the costs of perverse effects. This allows incentive incompatibility to be traded for compensation so long as the overall result makes the firm more valuable. Real-world trade-offs could be evaluated only by intuition, of course; here, as with any other exercise in valuation, present verification is not a possibility. The strict standard takes the just-say-no approach mooted above and aspires to a Pareto-optimal result, in which the value of the incentives created must exceed the options' opportunity cost, and the scheme may allow no foreseeable perverse effects. This standard's benefit lies in the imposition of retention constraints on a *per se* basis. Bargaining and unverifiable cost-benefit trade-offs proceed in respect of the other elements of the deal. Assuming an arm's-length context, the executive with bargaining power gets a gross-up in the number of shares granted; the executive with fewer chips at the table comes away with reduced compensation value.

2. The Free-Lunch Fallacy

Now we turn to a process defense mooted to counter the charge of executive empowerment. This begins with the same assertion as the fair-deal defense: stock options, viewed as compensation, fail to pass the cost-benefit test. The follow-up assertion is that board members fail to appreciate the costs. They incorrectly believe stock options to be a bargain mode of compensation and overvalue options in comparison to cash payments by underestimating the options' economic cost to the shareholders whose stakes they dilute.[101]

Jensen and Murphy use this point to account for a number of practices. For example, during the 1990s, firms continued to grant the same number of stock options year after year, even as their stock prices doubled, causing the value of incentive grants to balloon. Had pay plans been tightly focused on performance sensitivity, the number of options would have been cut back as the market rose. In contrast, when the market fell after 2000, option value decreased in lockstep

---

[101] Jensen & Murphy, *supra* note 2, at 37–39.

with it. Had the value of the grants been the center of attention, rather than the absolute number of shares granted, further adjustments would have been required.[102] (Indeed, if management were all-powerful, the market decline by itself should have caused a gross-up in the numbers.) For Jensen and Murphy, this free-lunch fallacy does a better job of accounting for practices during the past decade and a half than executive empowerment. They also look to lack of sophistication to explain the absence of indexing: prior to 2005,[103] firms were required under generally accepted accounting principles (GAAP) to expense the value of indexed options from their earnings, but no deduction was required for fixed-price, unindexed options. It follows that boards gave up performance sensitivity not because they were dominated but because they were naively fixated on earnings per share (EPS), and the applicable GAAP was badly articulated.[104]

Murphy takes this a step farther, folding the free-lunch fallacy into the fair-deal story. The firm grants options not to incentivize but because it mistakenly believes them to be cheap compensation.[105] It follows that concessions keyed to the managers' risk aversion – the fixed price set at market and the absence of restraints on alienation – bother the firm little because it does not view them as costly. The manager would prefer an exercise price set below market; the firm would prefer an exercise price above market; and they split the difference when they set the price at the market.[106]

This analysis suffers from the same infirmity as the substantive defense in chief. The mistaken perception of low cost starts out as a positive observation that counters the power description, casting board decision making in the positive light of good faith. But the observation ends up as a statement of purpose, and the purpose is compensation taken alone. The transformation creates a normative problem. Given that stock options are intrinsically inefficient when viewed only as compensation, a board that proceeds on this basis and trades away incentive properties may be making a bad deal.

The lack of sophistication resonates better as pure description. Of course, one can go only so far in depicting board members as dumb money. But the characterization still carries due to the agency context: board members are not trading for their own accounts when approving compensation packages, and they operate in a cooperative environment. Given these qualifications, it is plausible to model businesspeople reacting differently to cash and scrip. At the

[102] See id. at 37.
[103] See Fin. Acct. Stands. Bd., Share-Based Payment, Statement of Fin. Accounting Standards No. 123 (2004).
[104] Murphy, *supra* note 4, at 21.
[105] Murphy, *supra* note 98, at 865–66.
[106] Id. at 863–64.

same time, EPS matters in the boardroom because it matters to noise traders in the markets. A boardroom seminar on basic financial economics accordingly would fall short as a cure. For whatever reason – and the fact that someone else's money is being spent provides a good reason – the economic costs of equity kickers are not perceived as equivalent to those of cash payments.

Admitting lack of sophistication into the picture detracts from the power explanation only if we define power narrowly as the authority to direct the actions of others, the power possessed by a sovereign or a military superior. If we relax the definition and describe power in terms of a position to exploit others economically, lack of sophistication fits neatly into the power description. The unequal bargaining power described in contract law is power in this lesser mode. It is also the mode of empowerment referenced by the critics.

3. Substantial Performance

The third defense makes still more concessions. Just as management power is hard to prove, so is its presence hard to deny. Many defenders accordingly concede it a place in the institutional description.[107] Some even concede that some managers take excessive rewards, that equity compensation is more liquid than shareholders would want, and that perverse incentives have cropped up in the form of accounting manipulation.[108] The dispute goes to the normative implications of the diagnosis of systemic imperfection. Here is the question: to what extent does the system succeed or fail in cost-effectively channeling the energy of empowered managers to productive ends that serve the shareholder interest? To answer the question is to make a judgment call. Defenders of the practice make a three-part case for relative success.

The first part of the defensive case takes a broad view and looks at the bright side. Shareholders, it is said, should be pleased with the way things have gone in the past decade and a half. Returns, measured net of the cost of executive compensation, have been generally higher since the switch to option-based compensation. And the shift did succeed in aligning management interests with those of the shareholders to a greater extent than in the past. Meanwhile, from 1992 to 2000, growth of gross domestic product in the United States was higher than in any of Italy, France, Britain, Germany, or Japan.[109]

Defenders also point to governance improvements initiated in the 1990s. Boards became smaller and more independent, shareholders became more

---

[107] *See* Hall & Murphy, *supra* note 52, at 27–28; Holmström & Kaplan, *supra* note 1, at 13; Jensen & Murphy, *supra* note 2, at 54; *see also* John E. Core et al., *Is U.S. CEO Compensation Inefficient Pay Without Performance?*, 103 MICH. L. REV. 1142, 1160–61 (2005).

[108] Holmström & Kaplan, *supra* note 1, at 3–4, 12–14.

[109] *Id.* at 3–4.

vigilant, compensation committees became the norm, and federal disclosure regulations required greater transparency than ever before.[110] Shareholders apparently welcomed the shift to option compensation as they enjoyed the bull market of the 1990s. In contrast, a much smaller net-pay increase to management during the 1980s triggered a populist backlash, due to the association of high salaries with layoffs, plant closings, and downsizing.[111]

Finally, the defenders argue that problems with executive compensation after the year 2000 mainly concern a few cases of abuse, and that any breakdowns due to the strain of the 1990s boom market have been addressed quickly.[112] Cases where high pay and poor performance coincide can be identified statistically and dealt with accordingly. The existence of bad apples does not compel the conclusion that the whole economy suffers from governance problems.[113]

No one on either side of the debate questions any of these points. The matter comes down to a dispute over the characterization accorded to a system that is admittedly dysfunctional. There is no objective resolution. Meanwhile, the whole discussion deflects attention from the important question: Assuming that equity incentive compensation can be better designed, should it be better designed? The answer clearly is yes.

IV. CONCLUSION

Supersize pay can have unpleasant side effects. To the extent that equity incentive compensation turns managers into speculative shareholders, perverse effects will follow. Redirecting incentives to the investment mode of shareholding cures those problems but creates new ones. A compensation plan designed to create manager-investors delays supersize cash payoffs in order to keep the focus on long-term fundamental value. The delay reduces the value of the compensation package. One must then ask whether the purpose of incentive compensation is actually to incentivize or merely to compensate. To the extent that the answer is both, perverse effects remain a constant possibility. It is time to raise the bar and emphasize incentives. Incentive compatibility should be the first priority, with the level of compensation being fixed in a framework that lacks foreseeable perverse effects.

[110] Hall & Murphy, *supra* note 52, at 27–28.   [111] Murphy, *supra* note 4, at 1.
[112] Jensen & Murphy, *supra* note 2, at 3–4.   [113] Core et al., *supra* note 107, at 1166.

6 "Say on Pay"

*Cautionary Notes on the U.K. Experience and the Case for Muddling Through**

Jeffrey N. Gordon

I. INTRODUCTION AND OVERVIEW

Executive compensation seems always on the public agenda. At a 2003 Columbia Law School conference that debated the newly published *Pay without Performance* by Lucian Bebchuk and Jesse Fried, an editor of *Fortune* magazine showed a series of magazine covers beginning with the early 1950s to illustrate the persistent fascination with the pay of the chief executive of large public companies. Excessive CEO pay led to tax law changes in the early 1990s. Large stock option payoffs and megagrants made for especially vivid magazine cover stories in the late 1990s. Golden parachute payouts to fired CEOs made for lurid headlines in the 2000s. The changing ratio in the compensation level of CEO versus line worker from 20 to 1 in the 1950s to 350 to 1 today has taken on traction in the political realm as well as the boardroom. Add to the uneasy contemporary mix the preening of hedge fund managers, whose billion-dollar annual paychecks dwarf the typical CEO package.

Thus, there are really two strands in the contemporary executive compensation debate. One is the pay-for-performance strand, which accepts that managers should be paid commensurate with performance but focuses on management's purported ability to extract compensation beyond an arm's-length bargaining outcome. The other is the social-responsibility strand, which focuses on the social demoralization and economic justice concerns that high

* Note: This work was previously published as *"Say on Pay": Cautionary Notes on the U.K. Experience and the Case for Shareholder Opt-in*, 46 HARV. J. ON LEGISL. 323 (2009).

Jeffrey N. Gordon is Alfred W. Bressler Professor of Law, Columbia Law School, and Fellow, European Corporate Governance Institute. I am grateful to Fabrizio Ferri for discussion and insightful comments on an earlier draft. In honor of Joel Seligman, whose scholarship on the Securities and Exchange Commission, securities regulation, and corporate governance has been mandatory reading even before he entered law teaching, and with the hope that he will find time to continue this valuable work in addition to his new duties.

levels of CEO compensation may raise. Pay without performance may be especially demoralizing on this view, but performance would be an insufficient basis for current levels of executive compensation, in part because the firm's performance is the result of a team's effort in an environment created by stakeholders. A major reform focus in both debates, however, has been corporate governance, namely the role of the board and possibly the shareholders in evaluating and constraining executive compensation.

The fundamental inconsistency in the two strands is reminiscent of the tensions behind the initial burst of corporate governance reform energy in the 1970s, which focused on the composition of the board, specifically the case for independent directors. The analogous strands were reflected by advocacy for a monitoring board, principally in service of shareholder interests, versus a stakeholder board, which would balance the interests of shareholders against other important stakeholders. The shareholder-value position triumphed because of critical changes in the 1980s: the rise of hostile takeover bids, which were necessarily geared to the shareholders, and the increasing equity ownership positions of institutional investors, who were, as a matter of fiduciary law, concerned to maximize the value of their investments. Thus, independent directors – the major corporate governance innovation of the period – came to see their principal role as serving shareholders, not other constituencies.[1]

In the current debate over executive compensation, the balance of forces within the corporation today is, if anything, more tilted in the shareholder direction than it was in the 1970s, when critical corporate objectives seemed up for grabs. Institutional shareholders own even more stock; shareholder activism has spread beyond transactions in control. The social responsibility strand in the debate is likely to have far more influence in the political and legislative realm than in corporate governance reform. For example, marginal tax rates have, historically, had a large effect on executive compensation.[2] This is not to rule out a feedback loop between the political traction of the executive compensation debate and subsequent public corporation practice, only that boards and shareholders are likely, in the end, to give much greater emphasis to pay-for-performance considerations.[3]

[1] See generally Jeffrey N. Gordon, The Rise of Independent Directors in the United States, 1950–2005: Of Shareholder Value and Stock Market Prices, 59 STAN. L. REV. 1465 (2007).
[2] See Carola Frydman & Raven Saks, Executive Compensation: A New View from a Long-Term Perspective, 1936–2005 (July 6, 2007), FEDS Working Paper No. 2007-35, available at http://ssrn.com/abstract=972399.
[3] Note that if high levels of CEO compensation lead to own-firm employee demoralization, that becomes a pay-for-performance issue because it directly affects the profitability of the firm. This is why CEO compensation in a firm facing financial distress becomes such a fraught problem.

A. *The Complexity of Pay for Performance: Why We Leave It to the Board*

But focusing on pay for performance as the lodestar of compensation practice hardly produces straightforward solutions in the real world or even provides an easy metric to determine which corporate boards have most faithfully adhered to that precept. Among other reasons, this is because executive compensation must serve four goals that are not in stable relationship with one another. The first goal is to provide a reward for successful prior service; the second is to provide incentives for future service; the third is to retain and attract managerial talent; the fourth is to align managerial and shareholder interests in light of embedded legal rules that favor managers.

Three examples illustrate the dilemma. The first example: the firm has not done well in the preceding period, but the board does not want to fire the CEO, either because it believes that the CEO has made *ex ante* correct strategic choices that worked out poorly because of unpredictable economic shocks or because, all things considered, the board believes the CEO is the leader most likely to lead the firm out of its present straits. The current environment of rapidly escalating oil prices and an abrupt turn in credit markets provide many examples of CEO decisions that might plausibly fit into this category. Assume that the CEO's stock options (or other long-term incentive arrangements) are now significantly underwater. To reprice the options (anathematized in the corporate governance literature) or to issue new options with a different strike price could be readily characterized as rewarding failure, inconsistent with the first goal. Yet to leave the situation unchanged may poorly incentivize the CEO for the next period, or even worse, leave the CEO with incentives to swing for the fences, as the upside-downside payoffs are so asymmetric.[4]

The second example: the firm has done extremely well; indeed, the CEO has been a star performer over a significant period, to the point that the CEO now owns a meaningful percentage of the firm's equity. What should be the shape of the CEO contract for the next period? From a rewards perspective, the compensation package should continue to include hefty stock-related compensation and bonus opportunities consistent with the value creation that the board hopes the CEO will continue to deliver. But from an incentives perspective, why should the board give the CEO more than a token? The

---

[4] This is one reason there is apparently little correlation between the value of stock option grants and performance. *See* Fabrizio Ferri & David Maber, *Say on Pay Vote and CEO Compensation: Evidence from the U.K.* (June 2008), *available at* http://ssrn.com/abstract=1169446, at 14 (citing sources).

largest part of the CEO's personal wealth is tied up in the firm's stock.[5] The CEO is already well incented to increase shareholder value. Would the CEO start shirking or otherwise make bad decisions with his or her personal wealth on the line just because the pay is less? Would he or she quit, putting the firm in the hands of someone whom the CEO probably believes will do a poorer job?[6] The polar case merely illustrates the more general claim: that rewards objectives and incentives objectives would not necessarily produce the same compensation contract and that the optimal CEO contract for a particular firm could well vary in CEO wealth accumulation.[7] This means that direct comparison of compensation packages across firms is much noisier and potentially misleading about board performance.

Awareness of rewards or incentives differences has already begun to percolate among professional executive compensation observers. For example, some have begun to complain that the Securities and Exchange Commission's newly revamped annual compensation disclosure, compensation discussion and analysis (CD&A), does not include sufficient disclosure of the CEO's accumulated ownership position, in particular, what is taken to be the critical variable (from an incentives perspective): the sensitivity of CEO wealth to changes in firm performance. Disclosure of the annual compensation package – what the firm is paying out on an annual basis to its CEO – incompletely informs investors about the CEO's performance incentives. But this is not simply a disclosure point, because the accumulation of ownership changes the optimal rewards-incentives mix. The board's role is not to benchmark compensation to some industry measure (though that may be relevant) but to tailor compensation to its actual CEO.

---

[5] This of course assumes that the CEO has not been able to unwind his or her equity exposure through stock dispositions or hedging transactions, itself a complicated matter for the board to monitor.

[6] The example implicitly includes some lock-in of the CEO's stock ownership position in the immediate postretirement period and some limit on the CEO's ability to find another firm that, to compete for the CEO's services, will simply replace the accumulated original firm equity with new firm equity.

[7] This intuition is behind some of the noticeable elements in executive compensation at private firms, particularly the inverse relationship of compensation to CEO ownership and to CEO age. *See* Rebel A. Cole & Hamid Mehran, *What Do We Know About Executive Compensation at Privately Held Firms?* (July 6, 2008), FRB of New York Staff Report No. 314, *available at* http://ssrn.com/abstract=1156089.

For a development of the idea of a CEO's "wealth leverage," see Stephen F. O'Byrne & S. David Young, *Top Management Incentives and Corporate Performance*, 17 J. App. Corp. Fin. 105 (Fall 2005); *id.*, *Why Executive Pay Is Failing*, 84 Harv. Bus. Rev. 28 (June 2006). For an evaluation of CEO wealth sensitivities in the United States, see John E. Core et al., *Is US CEO Compensation Broken?* 17 J. App. Corp. Fin. 97 (Fall 2005).

The third example: one area of great concern to many governance activists and critics has been the golden parachute, a special payment to the CEO triggered by a change in control or, commonly, termination without cause. Here a little history is in order. Golden parachutes arose in response to the hostile takeover movement of the 1980s. There are two ways to tell the story. On the bright side, golden parachutes compensated target managers, who typically faced displacement after such a takeover, for the loss of what an economist would call firm-specific human capital investments. But why should a laid-off CEO receive such compensation, and so generous, when a laid-off rank-and-file worker – also having made firm-specific human capital investments, often of equal or greater value relative to net worth – usually does not?

That brings us to the dark side. The courts, Delaware most important, gave managers what might be called a takeover-resistance endowment – that is, the right to fight a hostile takeover using corporate resources, including the power to "just say no."[8] One way to solve this dilemma is to structure compensation to align managerial and shareholder incentives in the face of a hostile bid – that's the polite way to describe the resulting golden parachute arrangement. So if the CEO receives approximately three times salary and bonus and the accelerated vesting of a large stock option grant to boot, the chance to become truly rich in a takeover solves the problem of managers fighting off hostile bidders. But the devil is in the details and the triggers for these chutes were crafted for broader situations than the core case of the takeover where the CEO loses his or her job. Most notably, the chutes broadened into a general severance arrangement that covered not only takeover situations but also virtually any case of termination without cause.[9] This had led to nightmare cases of $100-million-plus payouts, not pay for performance, not the CEO getting a share of

[8] *See* Paramount Commc'ns Inc. v. Time Inc., 571 A.2d 1140 (Del. 1989); Unitrin, Inc. v. Am. Gen. Corp., 651 A.2d 1361 (Del. 1995).

[9] Of course, firing a CEO is arguably just a lower-cost way to achieve the result of a significant fraction of hostile deals, which seek gains in the replacement of inefficient managers. The CEO's loss of human capital in such a case is equivalent to the actual takeover. The only difference is in the CEO's resistance right, which in the firing case comes from managerial control over the proxy machinery that has been a source of the CEO's ability to stack the board with allies. The corporate governance changes that have undercut the CEO's ability to dominate the board selection process are parallel to other changes in the corporate control markets that have reduced the antitakeover endowment.

Some would defend large severance payments as providing insurance to encourage CEO risk taking, particularly given the reality that even an *ex ante* correct decision that turns out badly may result in CEO turnover. The question is how large a payout is appropriate. The acceleration of unvested stock-related compensation seems hard to justify even a generous reading of that rationale. Moreover, many failed business decisions were *ex ante* wrong. Clawbacks are rarely invoked for failure short of fraud.

the upside when the firm is sold at a premium, but pay for failure so egregious that even a Chief Executive who has awarded the Medal of Freedom despite failure felt obliged to take notice.[10]

Conditional on the initial grant of the takeover-resistance endowment, the golden parachute may have been a locally efficient response. It is a familiar Coasean observation that the assignment of a legal entitlement does not necessarily interfere with attaining efficient outcomes (though wealth may be redistributed). The golden parachute payment can be seen as shareholder buyback of the resistance endowment so as to permit value-increasing transactions to occur. But changes in the corporate governance environment that have reduced CEO power over the board[11] and that have otherwise empowered shareholder activists[12] have reduced the value of the takeover-resistance endowment. We should expect to see significant changes in golden parachute arrangements, which will separate out compensatory features from hold-up features. But a simple pay-for-performance metric may not tell us how well a board is accomplishing this transition, given the loss-avoidance and endowment effects that make downward renegotiation difficult.

These three examples just illustrate the more general point that pay for performance is an objective rather than an easily measureable output variable and that the effort to attempt to reduce it to a simple output may lead boards (and the evaluators of boards) astray. Much additional complexity arises from the substitutability and the complementarity of the many different instruments in executive compensation. Restricted stock, for example, which can be seen as a combination of cash plus an option, substitutes for each separate element,

---

[10] Speaking before an audience of financial leaders in New York City on January 31, 2007, President Bush said:

> Government should not decide the compensation for America's corporate executives, but the salaries and bonuses of CEOs should be based on their success at improving their companies and bringing value to their shareholders. America's corporate boardrooms must step up to their responsibilities. You need to pay attention to the executive compensation packages that you approve. You need to show the world that American businesses are a model of transparency and good corporate governance.

"State of the Economy" address, Jan. 31, 2007, *available at* http://georgewbush-whitehouse. archives.gov/news/releases/2007/01/20070131-1.html. Among the recipients of the Medal of Freedom from President Bush have been Paul Bremer, head of reconstruction and humanitarian assistance and the Coalition Provisional Authority in postinvasion Iraq, 2003–04; Tommy R. Franks, leader of U.S. military forces in the invasion of Iraq and the postinvasion aftermath; and George Tenet, director of the Central Intelligence Agency from 1997 to 2004.

[11] Gordon, *supra* note 1, at 1468, 1470, 1520–23, 1531–33, 1539–40.

[12] An example is the use of equity swaps to accumulate significant economic ownership and "virtual" voting positions that do not trigger a poison pill. *See, e.g.,* CSX Corp. v. Children's Inv. Fund Mgmt. (U.K.) LLP, 2008 U.S. Dist. LEXIS 46039 (S.D.N.Y. June 11, 2008), *appeal pending.*

but the blending of such elements is complementary. A different combination of elements from even a standardized menu may produce quite different effects. The ultimate CEO performance incentive is threat of termination or nonrenewal, which means that managers may value identical compensation packages differently across firms depending on comparative performance delivery patience.

Moreover, when we say "pay for performance," what performance are we trying to reward and incentivize? Presumably stock price gains are of the greatest interest to shareholders, but measuring profits also has its appeal, because bottom-line results may be less susceptible to stock market fashion (though more vulnerable to accounting conventions). Profits also seem associated with a hard measure, like more cash in the bank or funds available for dividends. Yet current profits reflect past investments; how to reward and incent the firm's development of valuable real options?[13] Stock price measures may imperfectly measure the value of such investments, particularly given that the firm may resist disclosure to hold on to competitive rents. As the firm becomes more granular in its performance objectives, success and compensation become harder to measure and monitor.

Of course, even after performance has been defined and measured, there remains this question: how much pay for how much performance? We gave up on the idea of a just price a long time ago, relying instead on markets to set prices. But the market price for a CEO is hardly self-defining, as the market for senior managerial services has no posted prices (hence the hunt for comparators). Executive compensation at any particular firm seems inevitably the result of a bargaining process between the CEO and someone empowered to act for the firm. Thus, recent reform efforts have been principally process focused and have been particularly geared toward process reform for the large public firm without a controlling shareholder.

B. Boards and Shareholders

The consensus view in the United States is that the board of directors needs to serve as the shareholders' agent in negotiating CEO compensation. As

---

[13] "Real options" refer to business opportunities that become more or less valuable depending upon future states of the world. For example, a pilot plant in an area of technological uncertainty creates a real option for a major commercial rollout, whose exercise (or abandonment) is conditional on the arrival of new information about the technology's feasibility. So the return on the investment in the pilot plant includes not only expected profits on its output but also the value of the embedded real option associated with the investment. For accounts of how real options theory should figure in business decision making, see, for example, RICHARD A. BREALEY ET AL., PRINCIPLES OF CORPORATE FINANCE 597–615 (8th ed. 2006); AVINASH K. DIXIT & ROBERT S. PINDYCK, INVESTMENT UNDER UNCERTAINTY (1994); Timothy A. Luehrman, *Strategy as a Portfolio of Real Options*, 76 HARV. BUS. REV. 89 (1998).

with many other reforms in corporate governance, the standard move is to strengthen board independence, both generally and with respect to this particular function. This has meant tightening standards of director independence and attempting through a series of process reforms to imbue boards with a self-conception of independence.[14] On the functional dimension, stock exchange listing rules now mandate a special board committee, a compensation committee composed exclusively of independent directors, to focus specifically on the CEO compensation question.[15] This committee is empowered to hire outside experts. As part of the SEC's 2006 CD&A regulation, the compensation committee is required to prepare a compensation committee report over the name of each member that discloses whether the compensation committee "reviewed and discussed the [CD&A] with management . . . and recommended . . . that the [CD&A] be included in the . . . annual report,"[16] in effect, an ownership statement.

One of the major current issues is the extent to which this ostensibly independent committee has been captured by its advisers, the compensation consultants either generally or specifically. That is, does the fact that compensation consultants are often part of diversified human relations service providers hired by managements instill a CEO-favoring tilt to compensation consultant work? This raises the question of inherent bias in the compensation consultant industry as presently structured. Or is same-firm work by the compensation consultant (meaning, human relations work for the firm in addition to compensation work for the board) a specific (and limited) source of independence-undermining bias, as commonly hypothesized with accounting firms? Or do compensation consultants have a style, that is, a reputation for pay packages of a particular mix of compensation elements and level, so that boards pick consultants after a basic decision on the compensation approach? As part of its 2006 CD&A regulations, the SEC required public firms to disclose the role of compensation consultants in the executive compensation-setting process, and quite interesting data are beginning to emerge on these questions.[17]

---

[14] For a fuller account, see Gordon, *supra* note 1, at 1490–99.

[15] *Id.*, at 1490–93.

[16] Regulation S-K, item 407(e)(5), 17 C.F.R. § 229.407(e)(5).

[17] Alexandra Higgins, *The Effect of Compensation Consultants* (Corporate Library, Oct. 2007); U.S. H.R. Comm. on Oversight and Govt. Reform (Majority Staff), *Executive Pay: Conflicts of Interest Among Compensation Consultants* (Dec. 2007); Kevin Murphy & Tatiana Sandino, *Executive Pay and "Independent" Compensation Consultants* (WP June 2008), *available at* http://ssrn.com/abstract=114899; Christopher S. Armstrong et al., *Economic Characteristics, Corporate Governance, and the Influence of Compensation Consultants on Executive Pay Levels* (WP June 2008), *available at* http://ssrn.com/abstract=1145548; Brian Cadman et al., *The Role and Effect of Compensation Consultants on CEO Pay* (WP March 2008), *available at*

Another current issue, even more salient, is the extent to which shareholders should be involved in the pay-setting process. For most proponents of a shareholder role, the objective is not to substitute the shareholders' business judgment for the board's but to heighten the board's independence in fact given subsequent shareholder response. Alternatively, we can frame the shareholder role in compensation setting (and corporate governance more generally) in terms of accountability.[18] First, strengthen the board's independence; then strengthen the board's internal process; and finally, strengthen the board's accountability to shareholders. Of course, the annual election of directors provides a recurrent shareholder check on board action, an annual accountability moment. Additional disclosure of compensation information per the 2006 CD&A regulations now provides shareholders even more information to assess board performance on this critical element of corporate governance. Proponents of shareholder influence in compensation setting argue, however, that replacing directors or even targeting compensation committee members through a just-vote-no campaign is costly and cumbersome and therefore not a credible constraint on the board. They support a more specific shareholder role, one that unbundles executive compensation from other elements of board decision making, more granular accountability.

One way to categorize the shareholder role in compensation setting is with respect to a $2 \times 2 \times 2 \times 2$ matrix that sets up shareholder consultation choices between (1) before versus after, (2) binding versus advisory, (3) general versus specific compensation plans, and (4) mandatory versus firm optional. So, for example, the present U.S. system requires (via stock exchange listing rule) shareholder approval of stock option plans, meaning that consultation must occur before implementation, the consultation is binding, and consultation is mandatory. Yet U.S. shareholders have no role in the specific implementation

---

http://ssrn.com/abstract=1103682; Martin J. Conyon, *Compensation Consultants and Executive Pay: Evidence from the United States and the United Kingdom* (WP May 2008), *available at* http://ssrn.com/abstract=1106729.

In using the empirical studies, it's important to appreciate their methodological limitations. The House Report, the boldest in its suggestion of firm-specific conflict, relies on basic quantitative descriptions of the differences between firms that do and do not use compensation consultants, without assessing the statistical significance of those differences and without taking into account standard control variables. More sophisticated papers by financial economists necessarily rely on one year's disclosure data and thus the effects they observe are all cross-sectional. Policy makers customarily are interested in the dynamic effects of disclosure generally and for specific firms. Policy decisions are often taken without the benefit of authoritative empirical studies, but apart from seeking more disclosure, it might be wise to see how the compensation consultant industry practice unfolds, particularly given the complementary effects of shareholder voice.

[18] Fabrizio Ferri suggested this way of formulating the issue.

of stock option plans, that is, the decision to make specific grants to particular
officers, so this consultation right is general. Presumably, the basis for the
distinction is the sense that shareholders should have approval rights over
establishment of a compensation plan that may dilute shareholder interests
but that approval of specific grants (as with other compensation elements)
would interfere with the board's role in setting (and tailoring) compensation.
Current proponents of a larger shareholder role call for a shareholder advisory
vote on both general and specific compensation plans, so-called say on pay. In
terms of the matrix, this means an after consultation that is advisory with respect
to general and specific plans (bundled into a single vote). Some proponents
think say on pay should be mandatory, meaning shareholders at all firms should
have the right; others that the principle should be adopted on a firm-by-firm
basis, meaning optional.

This chapter addresses the say-on-pay question, in particular recent federal
legislative proposals modeled on U.K. legislation adopted in 2002 that makes
shareholder consultation mandatory. The advantage to mandatory legislation
is that the shock of greater shareholder consultation rights across the full
range of firms could well destabilize an equilibrium of accretions to executive
compensation that otherwise would be hard to prune and reset. The disadvantage is the likely evolution of a best-compensation-practices regime that
would ill suit many firms. The cookbook and normatively opinionated nature
of compensation best practices that are emerging in the United Kingdom
seems a cautionary tale. In the U.S. setting, the consequences might be even
more concerning, as the energized shareholder actors have even less basis for
independent business judgment than their U.K. counterparts and thus may
delegate these judgments to a small number of specialized advisers.

If pay for performance is the ultimate objective of compensation activism, it
could be that the jury-rigged version of shareholder consultation that is evolving in the United States, firm-by-firm consideration of say-on-pay proposals
and firm-specific threats to target compensation committee board members
through withhold-vote campaigns, is the best way to muddle forward. From the
public and social responsibility perspective, this form of muddling through[19]
may be insufficient because it will probably result in compensation that is
still "too much."[20] Resetting the basic equilibrium may be highly valued, and
a systemwide rule may offer a greater chance for that outcome. But if the
master problem is on the social responsibility dimension, how likely is it that

[19] *See* Charles A. Lindblom, *The Science of Muddling Through,* 19 PUB. ADMIN. REV. 79 (1959).
[20] *See* Jeffrey N. Gordon, *Executive Compensation: If There Is a Problem, What's the Remedy?
The Case for "Compensation Discussion and Analysis,"* 30 J. CORP. LAW 675 (2005) (reaction
to pay-for-performance compensation for Harvard endowment managers).

a corporate-governance-based solution will lead to a better outcome than a general tax policy change?

II. SHAREHOLDER CONSULTATION AND SAY ON PAY

A major goal of the SEC's 2006 adoption of a CD&A requirement was to stimulate shareholder reaction to the firm's executive compensation practices through the existing means of public and private response. These include media reactions, private shareholder interventions with managements and directors, precatory resolutions, and withhold-vote campaigns against compensation committee directors. Some have argued that these mechanisms are insufficient to check potential compensation excess,[21] most notably because of general shareholder debility in corporate governance, and have pushed for an explicit shareholder role in the compensation-setting process. This push is partly fueled by what has been revealed through CD&A disclosure, particularly pension and deferred-compensation benefits whose bottom-line dimensions may have startled even experienced directors. Some have been especially concerned by compensation inequities, including the large disparities between CEO compensation and even other C-level managers, not to say other members of the management team and line employees.[22] The sense of out-of-control compensation has been heightened both by enormous payouts to unsuccessful CEOs at a time of economic unease[23] and by the option backdating scandal,[24] which suggested widespread overreaching by already-well-paid senior managers.

---

[21] *See, e.g.*, John E. Core et al., *The Power of the Pen and Executive Compensation*, 88 J. Fin. Econ. 1 (2008) (finding that press coverage focuses on firms with higher excess compensation ("sophistication") and greater executive stock option exercise ("sensationalism") but also finding "little evidence that firms respond to negative press coverage by decreasing excess CEO compensation or increasing CEO turnover").

[22] Lucian Bebchuk et al., *CEO Centrality*, Harv. Law & Econ. Discussion Paper No. 601 (May 2008), *available at* http://ssrn.com/abstract=1030107.

[23] Dismissed CEOs of Pfizer and Home Depot, for example, received severance packages in the $200 million range. *See* Ylan Q. Mui, *Seeing Red over a Golden Parachute Home Depot's CEO Resigns, and His Hefty Payout Raises Ire*, Wash. Post, Jan. 4, 2007, at D1; Ellen Simon, *Pfizer's McKinnell to Get $180M Package*, Wash. Post., Dec. 21, 2006, *available at* http://www.washingtonpost.com/wp-dyn/content/article/2006/12/21/AR2006122101167.html.

[24] Erik Lie, *On the Timing of CEO Stock Option Awards*, 51 Mgmt. Sci. 802 (2005); Randall A. Heron & Erik Lie, *Does Backdating Explain the Stock Price Pattern Around Executive Stock Option Grants?*, 83 J. Fin. Econ. 271 (2007); Mark Maremont, *Authorities Probe Improper Backdating of Options: Practice Allows Executives to Bolster Their Stock Gains; A Highly Beneficial Pattern*, Wall St. J., Nov. 11, 2005, at A1. The backdating persisted even after the adoption of the Sarbanes-Oxley legislation, which imposed internal controls standards that should have ended it. *See* Jesse Fried, *Options Backdating and Its Implications*, 65 Wash. & Lee L. Rev. (2008).

In the search for remedies, governance activists, already inspired by the U.K. model of greater shareholder governance rights, looked to the United Kingdom's 2002 adoption of a mandatory shareholder vote on a firm's annual directors' remuneration report, in effect an advisory vote on the firm's executive compensation practices, as rejection of the report did not invalidate a compensation agreement.[25] After the Democratic takeover of the Congress in the November 2006 midterm elections, Congressman Barney Frank, the chair of the House Committee on Financial Services, and then Senator Barack Obama sponsored a similar bills calling for a mandatory annual shareholder advisory vote on executive compensation.[26] The House passed the legislation on April 20, 2007, but it was not taken up by the Senate. In the course of his presidential campaign, Senator John McCain has embraced the say-on-pay cause.[27] After the 2008 elections, it seems likely that the legislative push will be renewed.

A. *Self-Help Say on Pay in the United States*

In the meantime, governance activists have employed the shareholder proposal route to put precatory say-on-pay resolutions before shareholders. The issue apparently caught fire at a meeting of governance activists and professionals in December 2006.[28] For the 2007 proxy season, activists led by the American Federation of State, Country, and Municipal Workers (AFSCME) and Walden Asset Management, the social investor, put forward approximately sixty proposals.[29] The proposals generated average support of 42 percent and

---

[25] The U.K. legislation did two things. First, it expanded disclosure of executive compensation beyond the requirements of London Stock Exchange Listing Rule 12.43A(c), requiring a directors' remuneration report. *See* Schedule 7A of the Companies Act of 1985, effective Aug. 1, 2002. Second, it required an advisory shareholder vote on the report. *Id.* § 241A. The report must provide particularized disclosure for senior executives of the various sources of compensation as well as an explanatory statement by the company's compensation policy (including the company's comparative performance). The report must be signed by remuneration committee members, and its quantitative elements must be audited. Although a shareholder vote is mandatory for every public company, "No entitlement of a person to remuneration is made conditional on the resolution [required by this section] being passed . . . ." *Id.* § 241A.(8). *See* Directors' Remuneration Report Reg. 2002/1986 Explanatory Para. 1 [U.K. Stat. Inst. 2002/1986]; Palmer's Company Law from Sweet & Maxwell ¶ 8.207.3.

[26] H.R. 1257 (110th Cong, 1st Sess.); Sen. 1181 (110th Cong, 1st Sess.).

[27] *McCain Seeks Shareholders' Say on Pay*, Newsweek, June 10, 2008, *available at* http://www.businessweek.com/bwdaily/dnflash/content/jun2008/db20080610_480485.htm.

[28] Kristin Gribben, *Divisions Grow Within Say-on-Pay Movement*, Agenda, July 7, *available at* http://www.shareholderforum.com/sop/Library/20080707_Agenda.htm.

[29] Erin White & Aaron O. Patrick, *Shareholders Push for Vote on Executive Pay*, Wall St. J., Feb. 26, 2007, at B1.

passed at seven firms, including Verizon, Blockbuster, Motorola, and Ingersoll Rand.[30] Two of the firms, Verizon and Blockbuster, adopted annual say-on-pay bylaw provisions.

Anticipation grew that sentiment for these proposals would snowball.[31] Aflac voluntarily adopted say on pay; so did RiskMetrics, the keeper of corporate governance scorecards, and H&R Block, trying to make amends after an unfortunate foray into mortgage lending led to a successful shareholder insurgency. But 2008 was not the banner year that proponents had expected. Although tallies are not yet complete for the 2008 proxy season, the number of proposals grew only moderately, to seventy, and the level of support has remained at the same level, approximately 43 percent.[32] Majority support was attained at six firms, including Alaska Air, Pacific Gas and Electric, Lexmark, Motorola (again), and Apple (presumably because of its stock option backdating involvement). Interestingly, support for say on pay slipped at financial firms from near 40 percent to around 30 percent.[33] Proponents had thought that massive losses would occasion shareholder outrage, especially in light of large payouts to departing CEOs at Merrill Lynch and Citigroup. Apparently, investors were nervous about disrupting governance at a time of stress and concerned about retention of highly compensated employees in an industry with great job mobility. Indeed, the hesitation to press for say on pay in the financial services industry may show the complexity of trying to figure out what counts as good performance and how to devise an appropriate pay-for-performance scheme.

It appears that more traditional investors and even some governance professionals are rethinking the matter of an annual say on pay.[34] Some think that an annual vote will be divisive and will disrupt shareholder-board communications. Others think such a vote will provide cover for the board and the compensation committee, pointing to the U.K. experience of invariable shareholder approval, and is not a stern enough rebuke compared to the alternative of voting against retention of compensation committee members.[35] Others are

---

[30] RISKMETRICS GROUP, 2007 POSTSEASON REPORT 8 (Oct. 2007).

[31] George Anders, *Say on Pay Gets a Push, But Will Boards Listen?*, Wall St. J., Feb. 27, 2008 at A2.

[32] L. Reed Walton, *U.S. Midseason Review*, May 23, 2008, *available at* http://blog.riskmetrics.com/gov/2008/05/us-midseason-reviewsubmitted-by-l-reed-walton-publications.html.

[33] Tom McGinty, *Say-on-Pay Doesn't Play on Wall Street: Fewer Investors Back Plans to Weight in Executive Compensation*, WALL ST. J., May 22, 2008, at C1.

[34] Kristin Gribben, *supra* note 28.

[35] Claudi H. Deutsch, *Say on Pay: A Whisper or a Shout for Shareholders?*, N.Y. TIMES, Apr. 6, 2008, at BU9. *See* RISKMETRICS GROUP, *supra* note 30, at 10–12 (detailing significant withhold votes at seventeen firms over compensation issues).

wary of what they foresee as dependence on proxy advisory firms for voting guidance.

Because of the slow slog – the adoption of say-on-pay provisions by only eight firms over two years – proponents have put their hopes on mandatory adoption by federal legislation.

B. *Legislated Say on Pay in the United Kingdom*

So what of the U.K. experience? The relevant questions include the following: How successful has the United Kingdom been in reining in excessive compensation? Are there other effects that might be positive or negative? How would that experience translate to the U.S. setting? In particular, how does a U.K.-like rule compare with firm opt-in through shareholder-proposed bylaw amendments?

The stylized facts of the U.K. experience appear to be as follows: shareholders invariably approve the directors' remuneration report, with perhaps eight turndowns across thousands of votes over a six-year experience. This level of shareholder approval reflects (at least in part) board behavior that flows from direct and indirect shareholder influence. Such influence comes principally from best-practice compensation guidelines issued by the two largest shareholder groups, the Association of British Insurers (ABI) and the National Association of Pension Funds (NAPF), and further elaborated in the United Kingdom's Combined Code of Corporate Governance. Shareholder influence also comes, less commonly, from occasional firm-level shareholder consultation. In terms of direct effects on pay, U.K. executive compensation has continued to increase significantly in both the fixed and variable components. It may be that some performance-pay elements are more tightly geared to actual performance. There is also some empirical evidence that the pay-for-performance sensitivity of U.K. compensation increased after adoption of the advisory vote, particularly for firms that paid excess compensation or otherwise had controversial pay practices in the preadoption period.

The U.K. adoption of a shareholder advisory vote on executive compensation had its roots in a particularly U.K. experience of compensation "outrage."[36]

---

[36] This follows Jonathan Rickford, *Do Good Governance Recommendations Change the Rules for the Board of Directors?, in* Capital Markets and Company Law (Klaus J. Hopt & Eddy Wyrmeersch eds., 2003); Jonathan Rickford, *Fundamentals, Developments and Trends in British Company Law – Some Wider Reflections (Second Part),* 2 Eur. Corp. & Fin. L. Rev. 63 (2005) (Rickford was the former project director of the U.K. Company Law Review of the Department of Trade and Industry and a member of European Commission's High Level Group on Company Law); Guido Ferrarini & Niamh Moloney, *Executive Remuneration and*

One of the hallmarks of the Thatcher government in the 1980s was the privatization of many utilities, including the gas, water, electricity, and telecommunications monopolies. The salaries of the senior officers skyrocketed for doing allegedly the same job, and, in the case of all but British Telecom, not doing that very well. The public reaction to such "fat cats" (so labeled in the press) threatened to undermine privatization itself. In 1995, the Study Group on Directors' Remuneration produced the Greenbury Code,[37] which called on boards to establish a remuneration committee of independent directors to set executive compensation and for disclosure of an audited remuneration report. Subsequent corporate governance reform consolidation by the Hempel Committee in 1998 produced the Combined Code on Corporate Governance. The Combined Code was attached to the London Stock Exchange Listing Rules, which obliged firms to "comply or explain [noncompliance]" with Code provisions. In addition to remuneration report disclosure, boards were obliged to annually consider and minute their consideration of whether to seek shareholder approval of the firm's remuneration polices, especially in the case of significant changes or controversial elements.

The New Labor government that took power in 1997 began a review of various elements of the U.K. corporate governance system in light of a growing international consensus that good governance added a competitive economic edge. Escalating U.K. CEO pay, post-tech-bubble payouts to dismissed CEOs, and survey data that fewer than 5 percent of firms had brought compensation policy questions to shareholder vote[38] led to amendment of the U.K. Companies Act to require both a somewhat-more-detailed disclosure regime than under the Listing Rules and to require a shareholder advisory vote on a newly fashioned directors' remuneration report (DRR). The DRR was to supply not only audited compensation information but also a novel (for the United Kingdom) stock price performance graph and the board's compensation rationale.

What has been the effect on U.K. compensation of the shareholder advisory vote? It seems fair to say that the new regime brought about much greater shareholder engagement with the pay-setting process. In the initial year, there was a flurry of high visibility activity, most famously in the case of Glaxo-SmithKline, in which a large golden parachute (estimated by shareholders at $35 million) for the CEO triggered a shareholder revolt that led to rejection

Corporate Governance in the EU: Convergence, Divergence, and Reform Perspectives, 1 EUR. CORP. & FIN. L. REV. 251 (2004).

[37] Named after its chair Sir Richard Greenbury (then chairman of Marks and Spencer, the retailer).

[38] *See* PRICEWATERHOUSECOOPERS, MONITORING CORPORATE ASPECTS OF DIRECTORS' REMUNERATION (1999).

of the remuneration committee's report.[39] During that year, there were press accounts of shareholder interventions into the remuneration policy of perhaps a dozen large firms.[40]

In subsequent years, observers have noted four visible effects of the regime shift.[41] First, consultation has increased between firms and large shareholders, or at least with the leading institutional investor groups[42] and with the proxy services firms RREV and IVIS.[43] The communications range from the perfunctory to the serious. Second, rejections of remuneration reports have been rare, only eight over the six-year history of the new regime – all but GlaxoSmithKline have involved small firms. Deloitte has reported that, over the period, only 10 percent of a large sample of firms received a negative vote of 20 percent or more. Nevertheless, in recent years, the proxy services firms have recommended negative votes in 10–15 percent of cases, principally involving smaller firms. Presumably, most firms shape their compensation policies to avoid negative shareholder votes. There is also some evidence that firms receiving a significant negative vote in one year receive a much higher positive vote in the subsequent year, which suggests that most firms accommodate shareholder views.[44] Third, the leading associations of institutional investors, the ABI and the NAPF, have extended their compensation influence through the fashioning of compensation guidelines that provide a set of yellow and red lines.[45] These guidelines build on the best practices for executive pay

[39] Gautum Naik, *Glaxo Holders Reject CEO's Compensation Package*, WALL. ST. J., May 20, 2003, at D8; Heather Timmons, *Glaxo Shareholders Revolt Against Pay Plan for Chief*, N.Y. TIMES, May 20, 2003, at W1. The vote was narrow, 50.72 percent to 49.28 percent. Two large institutional investors voting against the report were Isis Asset Management, a U.K. money manager with nearly $100 billion in assets, and CalPERS, a U.S. public pension fund with more than $150 billion in assets that is a notable proponent of corporate governance reform worldwide.

[40] See Rickford, *supra* note 36; Ferrarini & Moloney, *supra* note 36, at 295–97.

[41] This draws generally from Stephen Davis, *Does "Say on Pay" Work? Lessons on Making CEO Compensation Accountable*, Policy Briefing No. 1 [Draft] (2007), which cites relevant sources.

[42] Joanna L. Ossinger, *Regarding CEO Pay, Why Are the British So Different?*, WALL ST. J., Apr. 10, 2006, at R6 (two hundred firms annually consult with ABI).

[43] RREV is owned by ISS in affiliation with the National Association of Pension Funds. IVIS is owned by the Association of British Insurers.

[44] See Kym Sheehan, *Is the Outrage Constraint an Effective Constraint on Executive Remuneration? Evidence from the U.K. and Preliminary Results from Australia* (March 18, 2007), *available at* http://ssrn.com/abstract=974965 (analyzing results for 2003–2005 votes); Ferri & Maber, *supra* note 4 (finding increase in performance sensitivity of CEO compensation in firms receiving more negative votes).

[45] See ABI & National Association of Pension Funds, *Best Practice on Executive Contracts and Severance – A Joint Statement*, initially issued in December 2002 and then reissued annually as part of ABI, *Principles and Guidelines on Remuneration*. The most recent version of the ABI's *Principles and Guidelines* (2007) is available on the IVIS Web site, http://www.ivis.co.uk/ExecutiveRemuneration.aspx.

built into the Combined Code.[46] The consultations often arise with respect to changes in a firm's approved compensation practices (because it passed muster the prior year) or practices that trench on the guidelines. Indeed, compliance or not with the guidelines often becomes the basis for the shareholder vote. Fourth, long-term CEO employment agreements, which in the U.K. setting gave rise to highly salient episodes of pay for failure, seem to have ratcheted down. GlaxoSmithKline was such a case. Indeed, the most dramatic changes have occurred in this area. Almost no large U.K. firms now enter into senior manager contracts of more than one year or provide for accelerated options on a change in control, thus putting to an end the U.K. version of the golden parachute.[47] This change, however, could have partly resulted from the government's initiation of a consultative process that raised the threat of legislation on termination payments, a threat made credible by legislation of the DRR regime.[48]

When it comes to looking at the effect of the new regime on actual pay, the results are much murkier. In the United Kingdom, CEO salaries and bonus payouts have increased at a double-digit rate in recent years.[49] The value of long-term incentive plans is harder to measure, but the growth rate is similar, indeed, higher than in the United States,[50] though U.K. observers have noted a tightening of performance triggers to vesting of particular benefits. The most thorough empirical analysis, albeit through 2005 only, is by Ferri and Maber (2008),[51] which analyzes U.K. compensation trends before and after adoption of the DRR regime. Using standard controls for documented influences on CEO compensation (such as firm size), they report a number of important findings. First, the overall growth rate of CEO pay is unchanged; there is no onetime

[46] *See* Fin. Reporting Council, Combined Code on Corporate Governance, Part B (rev'd June 2008) (prior versions issued in 1998, 2003, and 2006).

[47] *See* Deloitte, Report on the Impact of the Directors' Remuneration Report Regulations 6, 19–20 (Nov. 2004).

[48] *See* Department of Trade & Industry, Rewards for Failure: Directors' Remuneration – Contracts, Performance and Severance (Consultation, June 2003). Moreover, the ratcheting-back of pay for failure began with the Greenbury best-practice guidelines in this area, which had reduced the typical three-year managerial term to one year by 2002. *See* Steve Thompson, *The Impact of Corporate Governance Reforms on the Remuneration of Executives in the U.K.*, 13 Corp. Gov. 19, 22, 23 (2005) (suggesting that investors pushed to limit contract terms to one year, which generally produced relatively small savings, because shorter terms "facilitate[d] the ousting of under-performing executives").

[49] *See, e.g.*, RREV Executive Remuneration: Trends in Executive Remuneration 2006 (2007); Ferri & Maber, *supra* note 4, at 49, table 1, panel A.

[50] *Id.*, table 1 (and author's own calculations). This is merely a continuation of the narrowing of the compensation gap between U.S. and U.K. CEOs. *See* Martin J. Conyon et al., *How High Is US CEO Pay? A Comparison with U.K. CEO Pay* (WP June 2006), *available at* http://ssrn.com/abstract=907469.

[51] Ferri & Maber, *supra* note 4.

downward revision or a moderation in the trend. Second, they nonetheless find greater pay-performance sensitivity in certain categories of firms: firms with a controversial compensation history, namely those with high levels of shareholder dissent in the first year of the shareholder advisory vote and those with excess pay in the pre-DRR period (firms in the top 20 percent of CEO pay after controlling for standard pay determinants). These, by hypothesis, are the firms in which compensation is least tied to performance and in which a regime that brings shareholder focus to bear may have its strongest effect.

To counter the suggestion that contemporaneous U.K. governance changes, but not the DRR regime, drove the greater pay-performance sensitivity, they ran tests with firms listed on the Alternative Investment Market (AIM). They find AIM firms did not experience a comparable increase in pay-performance sensitivity. Similarly, to test the possibility that worldwide governance or competitive factors were the driver, they ran comparable tests on a sample of U.S. firms, which showed no comparable change in pay-performance sensitivity over the period.

Although Ferri and Maber's results are suggestive, only a body of literature, not any single empirical paper, can securely ground a conclusion about the positive effects of the DRR regime. Among the elements in their work that counsel against overenthusiasm on its finding of firms' greater responsiveness to pay-for-performance demands are factors that suggest the possibility of efficiency losses. For example, the demonstrated increased pay-performance sensitivity is generally with respect to losses, not gains (although they test both). In other words, after the DRR regime, pay is more likely to go down if performance declines, but there is no evidence of the reverse. This, of course, is consistent with avoiding pay for failure, certainly a major theme, if not the preoccupation, of the reform impulse behind the DRR. Similarly, the performance indicator that is associated with greater sensitivity is return on assets (ROA), an accounting measure, rather than stock price performance. Putting aside the matter of shareholder preference, stock prices measure expectations of future earnings, which relate to new investment. A possible message of the new regime is, "Don't overcompensate the 'failed' CEO; focus on today's safely measurable earnings, not tomorrow's." If that is the result of a shareholder advisory vote, it seems an odd way to build a system that relies on entrepreneurial energy and the risk of failure.[52]

[52] A more positive interpretation might be that because the U.K. compensation scheme is generally tilted toward cash payouts rather than stock-related compensation, 65 percent to 35 percent, pay-to-return-on-assets performance is the right, or at least more important, sensitivity measure. Then the concern becomes the guidelines that lock in a normatively controversial tilt against stock-related compensation. It is still a consequence of the regime as a whole.

An additional point is a possible size effect in Ferri and Maber's results, meaning that independent of performance, the DRR regime may have had a negative effect on CEO compensation at the largest firms. Since pay generally increases in size, this suggests that the DRR may have produced a decrease in the rate of compensation growth where pay was on average the highest and where high pay was most visible. This may serve perfectly fine social objectives, but it does not fit the pay-for-performance objectives of the DRR.[53]

A more technical factor that may confound the Ferri and Maber result is that the DRR regime consisted of two elements: extensive mandatory disclosure of executive compensation particulars, including the board's reasoning process in the award of compensation, and the shareholder advisory vote. As the authors observe, many compensation elements were already mandatorily disclosed via the London Stock Exchange's Listing Rule 12.43(c), though the report requires significantly more detail, particularly on long-term incentive plans and severance. Contemporary market participants, though they appreciated the improved disclosure, seemed to think that the new advisory vote was a more significant change than the improved disclosure. A 2004 Deloitte survey of leading institutional investors on the impact of the new DRR regime, commissioned by the Department of Trade and Industry, reported that 70 percent of respondents regarded the shareholder vote as having "very significant impact," whereas only 26 percent regarded the detailed disclosure of compensation particulars as having comparable significance, even though nearly 90 percent regarded the remuneration report as providing better understanding of compensation.[54] Thus, Ferri and Maber seem safe in attributing most of the effect to the shareholder empowerment elements of the scheme.

C. Lessons from the United Kingdom for the United States in Say on Pay

1. Side Effects of the U.K. System

The efficiency effects of the U.K. system are potentially a matter of concern. As noted previously, the only available empirical evidence shows pay-performance responsiveness tied to a current earnings measure, not a stock-based measure. Beyond that, the workings of the system seem ill suited for a dynamic environment. For example, immediately upon adoption of the DRR regime, the ABI and the NAPF adopted best practices of compensation guidance. Because of the dominance of those two actors, whose institutional

---

[53] The size effect looks to be separate from the excess-compensation effect.

[54] DELOITTE, REPORT ON THE IMPACT OF THE DIRECTORS' REMUNERATION REPORT REGULATIONS 34, 27 (2000). The Report used an intensity scale of 1–5. On a broader definition of significance that adds 4 and 5, the gap is less pronounced: 92 percent versus 74 percent.

investor members own 30 percent of the shares of large U.K. public firms, the annual shareholder vote is often a test of comply or explain with those guidelines. Indeed, an alternative approach, in which shareholders would annually evaluate firm compensation practices in light of the firm's performance and prospects as a whole, would be very costly.[55] The tendency for firms to herd in their compensation practices is very strong: follow the guidelines, stay in the middle of the pack, and avoid change from a prior year when the firm receives a favorable vote. Yet what is the normative basis for giving authoritative weight to the guidelines, whose conventional wisdom has not itself been tested for performance-inducing effect?

For example, the current ABI guidelines contain elaborate prescriptions for the issuance of stock options and other sorts of stock-related compensation, including a requirement of "performance based vesting" based on "challenging and stretching financial performance" (not just a high exercise price) that applies not only to shares from an initial grant but also to shares from a bonus grant, meaning that an option (or share) grant will not necessarily ever be in the money.[56] To a nonprofessional eye, this reads simply like a prejudice against stock-based compensation, and the expression of a preference for a U.K.-style of compensation that traditionally has been tilted toward cash salary and bonus. Indeed, this is consistent with the Ferri and Maber evidence that shows pay-performance responsiveness to earnings-based measures that commonly are used in bonus awards, not stock-based measures geared toward stock-related compensation. The guidelines may be correct in their outcome in particular instances of compensation form, but it is hard to believe that they will persistently produce a result similar to arm's-length bargaining, if that is the ultimate comparator. More concerning is that the implementation of the guidelines may transmit a particular form of compensation practice across an entire economy.

Deviations from the guidelines require, as a practical matter, a consultation with the proxy adviser of one of the institutional groups, either RREV or IVIS. To do otherwise may be to risk a negative recommendation on the advisory vote. There are no studies on the bureaucratic capabilities or expertise of either proxy adviser. The system as a whole seems to tilt toward stasis rather than innovation in compensation practices. Perhaps this is wise. In light of the generally greater shareholder power in the United Kingdom, it does, however,

---

[55] *See* Kristin Gribben, *U.K. Investors Warn U.S. About Say on Pay*, AGENDA (Nov. 12, 2007) (citing experience of U.K. fund managers, who nevertheless want to retain the advisory vote), *available at* http://www.shareholderforum.com/op/Publications/20071112_Agenda.htm.

[56] ABI, EXECUTIVE REMUNERATION – ABI GUIDELINES ON POLICIES AND PRACTICES §§ 4.1., 4.6, 4.12, 5.7 (2006).

seem ironic that the implementation practicalities of say on pay may reduce the freedom in fact of the shareholders' bargaining agent.

2. Translation of the U.K. Experience to the United States

Possible side effects do not necessarily negative the value of the shareholder advisory vote in the United Kingdom. But it could be that many of its benefits are bundled with an overall corporate governance system that gives shareholders considerably more power than in the United States, so that a transplant of say on pay alone would trade differently in the United States. Corporate governance in this sense is a function of ownership and legal rules. The U.K. ownership is characterized by what might be called concentrated institutional ownership, meaning that although U.K. firms are Berle-Means firms without controlling owners, the shares are held, first, by institutions rather than retail investors, and second, that these institutions are "concentrated" rather than "dispersed."[57] As noted previously, the dominant U.K. institutional investors have been insurers and private industry pension funds. They share a common address, the City of London, and common objectives, long-term holdings producing steady dividends and gains. Over a forty-year period, they have gained considerable experience in collaborative efforts to engage their investee firms on business and governance matters.

Part of the reason they are paid attention to is a legal regime that empowers shareholders to a much greater extent than in the United States. For example, shareholders can remove directors or amend the articles. Five percent of the shareholders can call a special meeting. The board may not interfere with shareholder choice in a takeover bid. Through the exercise of preemptive rights, shareholders can constrain the firm's access to equity capital markets. Yet it is the coordination possibilities of the U.K. form of concentrated institutional ownership that has transformed these statutory rights into governance power. Thus, the benefits of shareholder advisory voting in the United Kingdom need to be assessed against that backdrop. The dialogue about compensation may be genuinely informative in a two-sided sense and may inject leeway that is not immediately apparent. In the course of the compensation talk, the conversation may turn to performance more generally, including the performance of the CEO or perhaps consultation about business plans.

The U.S. statutory system empowers shareholders less, granting the board greater autonomy but taking greater pains to bolster its independence. The

---

[57] This and much of the succeeding discussion draws from John Armour & Jeffrey N. Gordon, *The Berle-Means Firm of the 21st Century* (working paper, Feb. 2008, on file with Jeffrey N. Gordon).

fraction of independent directors in the United States is considerably higher; the requirements of independence are stricter; the compensation committee is entirely independent. By comparison, the U.K. Combined Code currently permits the Chairman (if formerly an independent) to sit on the remuneration committee. But an equally important difference is ownership structure. Even as recently as 1980, most U.S. firms had a dispersed retail ownership base. Dramatic increases in institutionalization began in the 1980s, but the form of ownership was dispersed institutional ownership, meaning that the institutions were very different in investment objectives, anticipated holding periods, and geographic location. That diversity has, if anything, increased. Moreover, U.S. securities regulation has placed various barriers to coordination among institutional investors that increase its cost and legal risk.

So how would a say-on-pay regime work in the United States? There are many more firms in the United States (think S&P 1500 versus FTSE 350) and many more institutional investors, but a very limited practice of institutional consultation and much less coordinated consultation. The most active institutional investors have been public pension funds and union pension funds, and they certainly act from shareholder value economic motives but may have other motives as well. Hedge funds have recently joined the ranks of shareholder activism, but they are looked at warily, not just by boards but also by other institutions, whose managers cannot benefit from two and twenty compensation schemes.

Only a relative handful of the large public pension funds have independent corporate governance expertise to guide their share voting, and even the largest and most experienced of these, CalPERS and TIAA-CREF, depend on guidelines that they fashion with only limited company-specific accommodation. Most of the rest simply delegate most of the substantive decision making in the governance area to a proxy services firm, in particular Institutional Shareholder Services (ISS), now part of RiskMetrics.[58]

Like ABI and NAPF, ISS will establish guidelines on compensation; indeed, such guidelines already exist. As in the United Kingdom, firms that do not want to stir trouble will herd. Or firms with alternative ideas will engage ISS in negotiation – but the numbers of firms and the time for serious engagement could easily make the situation untenable. The propensity of many U.S. institutional investors to delegate such decisions could well give power to a handful of proxy service firms to make substantively very important decisions with

---

[58] See Stephen J. Choi & Jill E. Fisch, *On Beyond CalPERS: Survey Evidence on the Developing Role of Public Pension Funds in Corporate Governance*, 61 VAND. L. REV. 315 (2008).

potentially economywide ramifications. Indeed, the economywide embrace of stock options in the 1990s resulted in part from institutional investor pressure on firms to adopt this best-practice way to enhance managerial incentives.[59] The favored accounting treatment established plain-vanilla options as the best-practice implementation. In other words, much of what we now regret was the result of prior standardized practice that guidelines epitomize.[60] It is clear that legislated say on pay in the United States is one way to catch and stop the bad-behaving outliers. But there are costs and risks that cannot be ignored.

The major advantage of mandatory say-on-pay legislation is the powerful shock it might deliver to the executive compensation structure, which would destabilize the present equilibrium. This is some of what happened in the United Kingdom. Adoption of the DRR regime suddenly roused the U.K. institutions into a very significant role in reviewing and challenging compensation practices, a kind of big bang of compensation engagement. Some dubious practices like long-term contracts and lavish golden parachutes simply disappeared in the new equilibrium. The trend to more U.S.-style stock-based incentive compensation appears to have reversed. Yet even in the United Kingdom, the new equilibrium is not a dramatic change. As Ferri and Maber show, the trend line of compensation increases was not affected.

Moreover, there would be no big bang in the United States. As discussed above, U.S. shareholder activists have focused on executive compensation for some time, through both the shareholder proposal machinery and withhold-vote campaigns for offending compensation committee directors.[61] Rules on majority voting for directors that have been adopted by a majority of U.S. public firms only add to the potency of such withhold-vote campaigns. Ironically, such activity in the United States over the same period as the DRR regime may have produced a onetime downward revision lacking in the United Kingdom, according to Ferri and Maber's data.[62]

---

[59] Gordon, *Independent Directors*, at 1529 n.257.

[60] It is only now, with adoption of FAS 123R, that firms may feel free to experiment with alternative stock option forms, such as performance triggers for grant or vesting, possibly using industry indices to measure performance. Yet the concerns about valuation of tailored instruments for accounting purposes may have its own uniformity pressure.

[61] The one area in which U.S. law favors shareholders relative to that of the United Kingdom is with respect to the making of shareholder proposals. Rule 14a-8 under the U.S. 1934 Securities and Exchange Act, 17 C.F.R. § 240.14a-8(b) provides access to the issuer proxy to a small shareholder (owning the lesser of $2,000 in market value or 1 percent). By contrast, section 376 of the U.K. 1985 Companies Act 1985 imposes a 5 percent share-ownership threshold.

[62] Ferri & Maber, *supra* note 4, at 56, table 7, panel A. This finding may have resulted from exchange-rate fluctuations (see table 7, panel B), and so must be taken cautiously.

3. Executive Compensation as a Hard Problem

Putting aside agency cost consideration, devising an effective executive compensation scheme is hard. Private equity firms have a solution – very high levels of stock-related compensation that pays off only on a successful exit from the going-private transaction. Success results in very large payoff, but a fired private equity CEO typically loses unvested options and restricted stock (rather than obtaining acceleration through a U.S.-style golden parachute). Severance is typically limited to the equivalent of one or two years' salary, but of course the salary base is much smaller because of the concentration on incentive-based pay.[63] For such high-powered incentives to work well, a high-powered governance structure is also required.

So why isn't the private equity model an exemplar for public company practices? One possible answer is that it may be too demanding, both on the executives who bear enormous firm-specific risk and on the governance structure, which requires directors who are knowledgeable about the business and deeply engaged. For example, a recent paper by Leslie and Oyer observes that compensation patterns in reverse leverage buyouts begin to revert to the public company norm within one year of the going public transaction.[64] "Executive ownership drops quickly and substantially right after the IPO . . . to levels similar to public firms."[65] Salary levels take a little longer to reach the comparable public firm norm – three or four years. Private equity owners presumably have every incentive to maximize the value of their shares in the exit IPO and bear the cost of compensation structures, so it is hard to believe that they would knowingly install a suboptimal regime.

III. CONCLUSION: ON MUDDLING THROUGH

So we need public firms, and we need compensation mechanisms that reward, provide incentives, and are political sustainable – in short, that serve a number of social ends. My tentative view is that the current U.S. compensation reform project is headed in the right direction. Firm-specific say-on-pay campaigns can be targeted against compensation miscreants and can have useful demonstration effects for many other firms. Targeted just-vote-no campaigns against compensation committee members can have similar, perhaps even

---

[63] *See* David Carney, *Deliver and You Get Paid*, DEAL, June 1, 2007.
[64] Philip Leslie & Paul Oyer, *Managerial Incentives and Strategic Change: Evidence from Private Equity* (draft, Mar. 2008, manuscript on file with Jeffrey N. Gordon).
[65] *Id.* at 16–17.

more powerful, effects.[66] These efforts could be augmented by concerted efforts by institutional investors, other governance groups, and the securities analyst community to develop a set of compensation good practices, akin to the Greenbury Code, that could provide a focal point for engagement. In a 2005 article, I said that the regime launched by the SEC's CD&A regulation deserved a five-year trial before we undertook significant change.[67] Having looked more closely at the United Kingdom's say-on-pay regime, I am prepared to reaffirm my prior view. We need more information about the consequences of the U.K. system. And we need more experience about the possible success of present compensation-reform efforts by shareholder activists at particular firms. If this is not a satisfactory result from a social responsibility perspective, then the tax code would be a better place to look than adjustment with corporate governance.

Previously published as Say on Pay": Cautionary Notes on the U.K. Experience and the Case for Shareholder Opt-in, 46 Harv. J. on Legisl. 323 (2009).

---

[66] *See* Diane Del Guercio et al., *Do Boards Pay Attention When Institutional Investor Activists "Just Vote No"?* 90 J. Fin Econ. 84 (2008), *available at* http://ssrn.com/abstract=575242 (positive effects from just-vote-no campaigns"); Jie Cai et al., *Electing Directors* (WP March 2008), *available at* http://ssrn.com/abstract=1101924) (the fewer votes for directors are correlated with subsequent reductions in excess compensation). *See also* Yonca Ertimu et al., *Board of Directors' Responsiveness to Shareholders: Evidence from Shareholder Proposals* (WP April 2008), *available at* http://ssrn.com/abstract=816264 (greater board responsiveness to recent majority-vote shareholder proposals than prior proposals).

[67] *See* Gordon, *supra* note 20, at 701.

PART THREE

CONSTRAINING MANAGERS AND DIRECTORS

Investors, Securities Regulation, and the Media

7   Shareholder Activism in the Obama Era

Stephen M. Bainbridge

The first decade of the new millennium has seen repeated efforts by corporate governance activists to extend the shareholder franchise and otherwise empower shareholders to take an active governance role. The major stock exchanges, for example, implemented new listing standards expanding the number of corporate compensation plans that must be approved by shareholders.[1] The Delaware General Corporation Law (DGCL) and the Model Business Corporation Act (MBCA) were amended to allow corporations to require a majority vote – rather than the traditional plurality – to elect directors.[2]

The financial crisis of 2008, the election of Barack Obama as president of the United States, the expansion of Democratic majorities in both houses of Congress, and the installation of a Democratic majority at the Securities and Exchange Commission gave these efforts renewed impetus. Echoing such constituencies as unions and state and local government pension plans, Washington Democrats blamed the financial crisis in large part on corporate governance failures.[3] Accordingly, much of their response took the form of new shareholder entitlements. The Department of Treasury's implementation rules for the Troubled Assets Relief Program (TARP), for example, contained a so-called say-on-pay provision requiring TARP-recipient institutions to hold

---

[1] See, e.g., NEW YORK STOCK EXCHANGE, LISTED COMPANY MANUAL § 3.12.
[2] DEL. CODE ANN., tit. 8, § 141(b), 216; Mod. Bus. Corp. Act. § 10.22.
[3] See Transcript, *The Federalist Society – Corporations Practice Group: Panel on the SEC and the Financial Services Crisis of 2008*, 28 REV. BANKING & FIN. L. 237, 238 (2008) (remarks of Stephen M. Bainbridge) ("We have heard many calls for financial services reform, a so-called 'new New Deal'").

Stephen M. Bainbridge is William D. Warren Professor of Law, University of California, Los Angeles. Portions of this chapter were adapted from *The Case of Limited Shareholder Voting Rights*, 53 UCLA L. REV. 601 (2006).

an annual nonbinding shareholder vote on executive compensation.[4] Senator Charles Schumer's (D-NY) proposed Shareholder Bill of Rights Act "would add a new Section 14A to the Securities Exchange Act of 1934 requiring each proxy statement covered by it to provide for a non-binding shareholder vote on executive compensation as disclosed in the proxy statement," as well as requiring shareholder approval of golden parachutes in certain acquisition transactions.[5] Then Senator Barack Obama had sponsored similar say-on-pay legislation in the preceding Congress.[6] A pending SEC rule-making proposal would allow a shareholder to nominate 25 percent of the company's board of directors or one nominee, whichever is greater.[7]

In contrast to these incessant reforms, state corporate law has traditionally limited shareholder voting rights. Under the Delaware code, for example, shareholder voting rights are essentially limited to the election of directors and approval of charter or bylaw amendments, mergers, sales of substantially all of the corporation's assets, and voluntary dissolution.[8] As a formal matter, only the election of directors and amending the bylaws do not require board approval before shareholder action is possible.[9] In practice, of course, even the election of directors (absent a proxy contest) is predetermined by the existing board nominating the next year's board.[10]

These direct restrictions on shareholder power long have been supplemented by a host of other rules that indirectly prevent shareholders from exercising significant influence over corporate decision making. Three sets of statutes are especially noteworthy: (1) disclosure requirements pertaining to large holders,[11] (2) shareholder voting and communication

---

[4] DAVIS, POLK & WARDWELL, *"Say on Pay" Now a Reality for TARP Participants* (Feb. 25, 2009), *available at* http://www.davispolk.com/1485409/clientmemos/2009/02.25.09.say.on.pay.pdf.

[5] Joseph E. Bachelder III, *TARP, "Say on Pay" and Other Legislative Developments*, Harv. Law School Forum on Corporate Governance and Fin. Reg. (July 4, 2009), *available at* http://blogs.law.harvard.edu/corpgov/2009/07/04/.

[6] Stephen M. Bainbridge, *Is "Say on Pay" Justified*, REGULATION, Spring 2009, at 42.

[7] Stephen M. Bainbridge, *Rising Threat of Dysfunctional Boards*, AGENDA, May 25, 2009, at 3.

[8] *See* MICHAEL P. DOOLEY, FUNDAMENTALS OF CORPORATION LAW 174–77 (1995) (summarizing state corporate law on shareholder voting entitlements).

[9] DEL. CODE ANN., tit. 8, §§ 109, 211 (2000).

[10] *See generally* Bayless Manning, Book Review, 67 YALE L.J. 1477, 1485–89 (1958) (describing incumbent control of the proxy voting machinery).

[11] Securities Exchange Act § 13(d) and the SEC rules thereunder require extensive disclosures from any person or group acting together which acquires beneficial ownership of more than 5 percent of the outstanding shares of any class of equity stock in a given issuer. 15 U.S.C. § 78m (2001). The disclosures required by section 13(d) impinge substantially on investor privacy and may discourage some investors from holding blocks greater than 4.9 percent of a company's stock. U.S. institutional investors frequently cite section 13(d)'s application to groups and the consequent risk of liability for failing to provide adequate disclosures as an explanation for

rules,[12] and (3) insider-trading and short-swing profits rules.[13] These laws affect shareholders in two respects. First, they discourage the formation of large stock blocks.[14] Second, they discourage communication and coordination among shareholders.

This chapter contends that state corporate law gets it right. The director-primacy-based system of U.S. corporate governance has served investors and society well.[15] This record of success occurred not in spite of the separation of ownership and control but because of that separation. The shareholder empowerment proposals being driven by President Obama and the Democratic majorities in Congress and at the SEC thus threaten the very foundation of corporate governance.

I. IN DEFENSE OF THE SEPARATION OF OWNERSHIP AND CONTROL

The laws just described long solidified the phenomenon famously associated with Adolf Berle and Gardiner Means's 1932 book *The Modern Corporation*

the general lack of shareholder activism on their part. Bernard S. Black, *Shareholder Activism and Corporate Governance in the United States*, in THE NEW PALGRAVE DICTIONARY OF ECONOMICS AND THE LAW 459, 461 (1998).

[12] To the extent shareholders exercise any control over the corporation, they do so only through control of the board of directors. As such, shareholders are able to affect the election of directors, which determines the degree of influence they will hold over the corporation. The proxy regulatory regime discourages large shareholders from seeking to replace incumbent directors with their own nominees. See Stephen M. Bainbridge, *Redirecting State Takeover Laws at Proxy Contests*, 1992 WIS. L. REV. 1071, 1075–84 (describing incentives against proxy contests). It also discourages shareholders from communicating with one another. See Stephen Choi, *Proxy Issue Proposals: Impact of the 1992 SEC Proxy Reforms*, 16 J.L. ECON. & ORG. 233 (2000) (explaining that liberalization of the proxy rules has not significantly affected shareholder communication practices).

[13] See Stephen M. Bainbridge, *The Politics of Corporate Governance*, 18 HARV. J.L. & PUB. POL'Y 671, 712–13 (1995) (noting insider-trading concerns raised by shareholder activism).

[14] Large block formation may also be discouraged by state corporate law rules governing minority shareholder protections. Under Delaware law, a controlling shareholder has fiduciary obligations to the minority. See, e.g., Zahn v. Transam. Corp., 162 F.2d 36 (3d Cir. 1947). A controlling shareholder who uses its power to force the corporation to enter into contracts with the shareholder or its affiliates on unfair terms can be held liable for the resulting injury to the minority. See, e.g., Sinclair Oil Corp. v. Levien, 280 A.2d 717 (Del. 1971). A controlling shareholder who uses its influence to effect a freeze-out merger in which the minority shareholders are bought out at an unfairly low price likewise faces liability. See, e.g., Weinberger v. UOP, Inc., 457 A.2d 701 (Del. 1983).

[15] See generally Stephen M. Bainbridge, *Director Primacy: The Means and Ends of Corporate Governance*, 97 NW. UNIV. L. REV. 547 (2003) (describing the director-primacy model of the corporation and outlining its benefits).

and Private Property;[16] namely, that public corporations are characterized by a separation of ownership and control – the firm's nominal owners, the shareholders, exercised virtually no control over either day-to-day operations or long-term policy. Instead, control was vested in the board of directors and the professional managers to whom the board delegated authority, neither of which group typically owned more than a small portion of the firm's shares.

Berle and Means believed that this separation of ownership and control was both a departure from historical norms and a serious economic problem.[17] They were wrong on both scores.

According to Berle and Means, dispersed shareholder ownership arose as a consequence of the development of large capital-intensive industrial corporations during the late nineteenth century. These firms demanded capital investments far greater than any single entrepreneur could provide; instead, the capital they required could be raised only by attracting funds from many investors. Because investors recognized the necessity of diversification, even very wealthy individuals limited the amount they put at risk in any given firm, which further fragmented share ownership.

Professor Walter Werner dismissed this account as the erosion doctrine. As he explained, in this version of history, there was a time when the corporation behaved as it was supposed to:

> The shareholders who owned the corporation controlled it. They elected a board of directors to whom they delegated management powers, but they retained residual control, uniting control and ownership. In the nation's early years the states created corporations sparingly and regulated them strictly. The first corporations, run by their proprietors and constrained by law, exercised state-granted privileges to further the public interest. The states then curtailed regulation . . . , and this Eden ended. The corporation expanded into a huge concentrate of resources. Its operation vitally affected society, but it was run by managers who were accountable only to themselves and could blink at obligations to shareholders and society.[18]

In contrast, Werner demonstrated that the separation of ownership and control in fact was a feature of American corporations from the earliest periods: "Banks, and the other public-issue corporations of the [pre–Civil War] period, contained the essential elements of big corporations today: a tripartite internal government structure, a share market that dispersed shareholdings and

[16] ADOLF A. BERLE & GARDINER C. MEANS, THE MODERN CORPORATION AND PRIVATE PROPERTY (1932).
[17] *Id.* at 6–7.
[18] Walter Werner, *Corporation Law in Search of its Future*, 81 COLUM. L. REV. 1611, 1612 (1981).

divided ownership and control, and tendencies to centralize management in full-time administrators and to diminish participation of outside directors in management."[19]

If this version of history is correct, there never was a time in which unity of control and ownership was a central feature of U.S. corporations. To the contrary, it appears that ownership and control separated at a very early date. In turn, this analysis suggests that the separation of ownership and control may be an essential economic characteristic of such corporations. What survival value does the separation of ownership and control confer? In short, it creates a central decision-making body vested with the power of fiat. To be sure, Armen Alchian and Harold Demsetz famously claimed that the firm "has no power of fiat, no authority, no disciplinary action any different in the slightest degree from ordinary market contracting between any two people."[20] Hence, Alchian and Demsetz argued, an employer's control over its employees differs not all from the power of a consumer over the grocer with whom the consumer does business.

If they were right, however, the firm would be nothing more than a quasi-market arena within which a set of contracts between various factors of production are constantly renegotiated. It is not. Power exists within firms, however, and it matters. The corporation has a nexus – and that nexus wields a power of fiat different from that of a consumer over a grocer. Indeed, fiat is the chief characteristic that distinguishes firms from markets. As economist Ronald Coase explained long ago, firms emerge when it is efficient to substitute entrepreneurial fiat for the price mechanisms of the market.[21] By creating a central decision maker – a nexus – with the power of fiat, the firm thus substitutes *ex post* governance for *ex ante* contract.

Granted, coordination can be achieved without fiat, as demonstrated by the democratic decision-making processes of many partnerships and other small firms. As the contrast between such firms and the public corporation illustrates, governance arrangements fall out on a spectrum between consensus and authority. Authority-based decision-making structures are characterized by the existence of a central office empowered to make decisions binding on the firm as a whole and tend to arise when the organization's constituencies have different interests and access to information.

The necessity of a center of power capable of exercising fiat within the corporation thus follows as a matter of course from the asymmetries of information

---

[19] *Id.* at 1637.
[20] Armen A. Alchian & Harold Demsetz, *Production, Information Costs, and Economic Organization*, 62 AM. ECON. REV. 777, 777 (1972).
[21] Ronald Coase, *The Nature of the Firm*, 4 ECONOMICA (n.s.) 386 (1937).

and interests among the corporation's various constituencies. Shareholders care about the value of the residual claim on the corporation. Customers care about the quality and quantity of the goods produced by the corporation. Workers care about salary and conditions of employment – and so on. Under such conditions, efficient decision making demands an authority-based governance structure.

This is true even though corporation law confers rights to participate in corporate governance only to shareholders. Overcoming the collective action problems presented when one is dealing with many thousands of shareholders would be difficult and costly, of course, if not impossible. Even if one could do so, moreover, shareholders lack both the information and the incentives necessary to make sound decisions on either operational or policy questions. Under these conditions, it is "cheaper and more efficient to transmit all the pieces of information to a central place" and to have the central office "make the collective choice and transmit it rather than retransmit all the information on which the decision is based."[22] Accordingly, shareholders prefer to irrevocably delegate decision-making authority to some smaller group, namely the board of directors.

To be sure, the separation of ownership and control creates a principal-agent problem, as Berle and Means explained: "The separation of ownership from control produces a condition where the interests of owner and of ultimate manager may, and often do, diverge."[23] Associated with the shareholders' purchase of the residual claim on the corporation's assets and profits is an obligation on the part of the board of directors and managers to maximize shareholder wealth.[24] Given human nature, it would be surprising indeed if the board of directors (or some members thereof) did not occasionally use its control of the corporation to increase its members' own wealth rather than that of the shareholders. Consequently, much of corporate law is best understood as a mechanism for constraining agency costs.

In my view, however, corporate law academics are far too preoccupied with agency costs. In the first instance, corporate managers operate within a pervasive Web of accountability mechanisms that substitute for monitoring by residual claimants. The capital and product markets, the internal and external employment markets, and the market for corporate control all constrain shirking by firm agents.

[22] KENNETH J. ARROW, THE LIMITS OF ORGANIZATION 68–69 (1974).
[23] Berle & Means, *supra* note 16, at 6.
[24] *See generally* STEPHEN M. BAINBRIDGE, CORPORATION LAW AND ECONOMICS 418–29 (2002) (explaining that the basic corporate law principle that directors have a fiduciary duty to maximize shareholder wealth arises not out of shareholder ownership of the corporation but out of the terms of the shareholders' contract with the corporation).

In the second, agency costs are the inescapable result of placing ultimate decision-making authority in the hands of someone other than the residual claimant. We could substantially reduce agency costs by eliminating discretion. That we do not do so implies that discretion has substantial virtues.

A complete theory of the firm thus requires one to balance the virtues of discretion against the need to require that discretion be used responsibly. Neither the power to wield discretionary authority nor the necessity to ensure that power is used responsibly can be ignored, because both promote values essential to the survival of business organizations.[25] Unfortunately, however, they also are antithetical.[26] Because the power to hold to account differs only in degree and not in kind from the power to decide, one cannot have more of one without also having less of the other. As Kenneth Arrow explained:

> [Accountability mechanisms] must be capable of correcting errors but should not be such as to destroy the genuine values of authority. Clearly, a sufficiently strict and continuous organ of [accountability] can easily amount to a denial of authority. If every decision of A is to be reviewed by B, then all we have really is a shift in the locus of authority from A to B and hence no solution to the original problem.[27]

Hence, directors cannot be held accountable without undermining their discretionary authority.

The principal argument against shareholder activism follows ineluctably from this line of analysis. The chief economic virtue of the public corporation is not that it permits the aggregation of large capital pools but rather that it provides a hierarchical decision-making structure well suited to the problem of operating a large business enterprise with numerous employees, managers, shareholders, creditors, and other inputs. In such a firm, someone must be in charge: "Under conditions of widely dispersed information and the need for speed in decisions, authoritative control at the tactical level is essential for success."[28] While some argue that shareholder activism "differs, at least in form, from completely *shifting* authority from managers to" investors,[29] it is in fact a difference in form only. Shareholder activism necessarily contemplates that institutions will review management decisions, step in when management performance falters, and exercise voting control to effect a change in policy or personnel. For the reasons identified previously, giving investors this power of review differs little from giving them the power to make management

---

[25] *Cf.* Michael P. Dooley, *Two Models of Corporate Governance*, 47 Bus. Law. 461, 471 (1992).
[26] *Id.*   [27] Arrow, *supra* note 22, at 78.
[28] *Id.* at 69.
[29] Mark J. Roe, Strong Managers, Weak Owners: The Political Roots of American Corporate Finance 184 (1994) (emphasis in original).

decisions in the first place. Even though investors probably would not micro-manage portfolio corporations, vesting them with the power to review board decisions inevitably shifts some portion of the board's authority to them. This remains true even if only major decisions of A are reviewed by B.

If the foregoing analysis has explanatory power, it might fairly be asked why we observe any restrictions on the powers of corporate takeovers or any prospect for them to be ousted in a takeover or proxy contest. Put another way, why do we observe any right for shareholders to vote?

In the purest form of an authority-based decision-making structure, all decisions in fact would be made by a single, central body – here, the board of directors. If authority were corporate law's sole value, shareholders thus likely would have no voice in corporate decision making. As we have seen, however, authority is not corporate law's only value, because we need some mechanism for ensuring director accountability with respect to the shareholders' contractual right requiring the directors to use shareholder wealth maximization as their principal decision-making norm.[30] Like many intracorporate contracts, the shareholder-wealth-maximization norm does not lend itself to judicial enforcement except in especially provocative situations.[31] Instead, it is enforced indirectly through a complex and varied set of extrajudicial accountability mechanisms, of which shareholder voting is just one.

Importantly, however, like all accountability mechanisms, shareholder voting must be constrained in order to preserve the value of authority. As Arrow observes:

> To maintain the value of authority, it would appear that [accountability] must be intermittent. This could be periodic; it could take the form of what is termed "management by exception," in which authority and its decisions are reviewed only when performance is sufficiently degraded from expectations. . . . [32]

Accordingly, shareholder voting is properly understood not as an integral aspect of the corporate decision-making structure but rather as an accountability device of last resort to be used sparingly, at best. Indeed, as Robert Clark observes, the proper way in which shareholder voting rights are used to hold corporate directors and officers accountable is not through the

[30] *See* Bainbridge, *supra* note 24, at 419–29 (explaining why shareholder wealth maximization would emerge from hypothetical bargaining between directors and shareholders even in the director-primacy model).

[31] *See id.* at 422 (noting that "the business judgment rule (appropriately) insulates director from liability" in this context).

[32] Arrow, *supra* note 22, at 78.

exercise of individual voting decisions but rather collectively in the context of a takeover.[33] Because shares are freely transferable, a bidder who believes the firm is being run poorly can profit by offering to buy a controlling block of stock at a premium óver market and subsequently displacing the incumbent managers, which presumably will result in an increase in firm value exceeding the premium the bidder paid for control. Hence, just as one might predict on the basis of Arrow's analysis, shareholder voting properly comes into play as an accountability only "when [management] performance is sufficiently degraded from expectations" to make a takeover fight worth waging.[34]

In sum, given the significant virtues of discretion, one ought not lightly interfere with management or the board's decision-making authority in the name of accountability. Indeed, the claim should be put even more strongly: preservation of managerial discretion should always be default presumption. Because the separation of ownership and control mandated by U.S. corporate law has precisely that effect, by constraining shareholders both from reviewing most board decisions and from substituting their judgment for that of the board, that separation has a strong efficiency justification.

II. THE RISE OF INSTITUTIONAL INVESTORS

Does the foregoing analysis change when we take into account the rise of institutional investors? Since the early 1990s, various commentators have argued that institutional investor corporate governance activism could become an important constraint on agency costs in the corporation.[35]

A. *The Theory*

Institutional investors, they argued, will approach corporate governance quite differently than individual investors. Because institutions typically own larger blocks than individuals and have an incentive to develop specialized expertise in making and monitoring investments, the former should play a far more active role in corporate governance than dispersed shareholders. Their greater access to firm information, coupled with their concentrated voting power,

---

[33] ROBERT C. CLARK, CORPORATION LAW 95 (1986).

[34] Space does not permit an evaluation here of whether shareholders therefore ought to have unfettered rights to accept any takeover offer or, to put it another way, whether the board of directors properly has a gatekeeping function even with respect to corporate takeovers. I argue in favor of such a board function in Bainbridge, *supra* note 24, at 805–17.

[35] *See, e.g.,* Roe, *supra* note 29; Bernard S. Black, *Shareholder Passivity Reexamined*, 89 MICH. L. REV. 520 (1990).

should enable them to more actively monitor the firm's performance and to make changes in the board's composition when performance lags. Corporations with large blocks of stock held by institutional investors thus might reunite ownership of the residual claim and ultimate control of the enterprise. As a result, concentrated ownership in the hands of institutional investors might lead to a reduction in shirking and, hence, a reduction in agency costs.

B. In Practice

In the early 1990s, it seemed plausible that the story might eventually play out. Institutional investors increasingly dominated U.S. equity securities markets. They also began to play a somewhat more active role in corporate governance than they had in earlier periods: taking their voting rights more seriously and using the proxy system to defend their interests.

They began voting against takeover defenses proposed by management and in favor of shareholder proposals recommending removal of existing defenses. Many institutions also no longer routinely voted to reelect incumbent directors. Less visibly, institutions influenced business policy and board composition through negotiations with management. But while there seemed little doubt that institutional investor activism could have effects at the margins, the question remained as to whether the impact would be more than merely marginal.

By the end of the 1990s, the answer seemed to be no. A comprehensive survey found relatively little evidence that shareholder activism mattered.[36] Even the most active institutional investors spent only trifling amounts on corporate governance activism. Institutions devoted little effort to monitoring management; to the contrary, they typically disclaimed the ability or desire to decide company-specific policy questions. They rarely conducted proxy solicitations or put forward shareholder proposals. They did not seek to elect representatives to boards of directors. They rarely coordinated their activities. Most important, empirical studies of U.S. institutional investor activism found "no strong evidence of a correlation between firm performance and percentage of shares owned by institutions."[37]

---

[36] Bernard S. Black, *Shareholder Activism and Corporate Governance in the United States*, *in* The New Palgrave Dictionary of Economics and the Law 459 (1998). Because of a resurgence of direct individual investment in the stock market, motivated at least in part by the day-trading phenomenon and technology stock bubble, the trend toward institutional domination stagnated. Large blocks held by a single investor remained rare. Few U.S. corporations had any institutional shareholders who owned more than 5 percent or 10 percent of their stock.

[37] *Id.* at 462.

Today, institutional investor activism remains rare. It is principally the province of union and state and local public employee pension funds.[38] But while these investors' activities generate considerable press attention, they can hardly be said to have reunited ownership and control.

C. Even Institutions are Rationally Apathetic

One should not be surprised that most institutions appear to be just as apathetic as individual shareholders. Because institutional investors generally are profit maximizers, they will not engage in an activity whose costs exceed its benefits. Even ardent proponents of institutional investor activism concede that institutions are unlikely to be involved in day-to-day corporate matters. Instead, they are likely to step in only where there are serious long-term problems. On the benefit side of the equation, corporate governance activism is unattractive because in many cases activism is unlikely to be availing. In some cases, intervention will come too late. In others, the problem may prove intractable, as where technological changes undercut the firm's competitive position.

Turning to the cost side of the equation, because it is impossible to predict *ex ante* which corporations are likely to experience such problems, activist institutions will be obliged to monitor all of their portfolio firms.[39] Moreover, because corporate disclosures rarely give one a full picture of the corporation's prospects, additional and more costly monitoring mechanisms must be established.

In any case, monitoring costs are just the price of entry for activist institutions. Once they identify a problem firm, steps must be taken to address the problem. In some cases, it may suffice for the activist institution to propose some change in the rules of the game, but less tractable problems will necessitate more extreme remedial measures, such as removal of the incumbent board of directors.

---

[38] The chief exception to that rule, as of this writing, is an apparent increase in the willingness of private hedge funds to exercise the limited control rights granted to shareholders.

[39] It is for this reason that Professor Black's economies of scale arguments fail. Black contends that activist investors will find that monitoring issues cut across a wide range of companies, which permits them to make use of economies of scale by developing standard responses to managerial derelictions; see Black, *supra* note 35, at 580–84, while nonactivist investors can obtain economies of scale by developing standardized voting procedures. *Id.* at 589–91. If institutional activism is more likely to take the form of crisis intervention, however, such economies of scale are unlikely to obtain because different crises will necessitate differing responses. At most, we might expect institutions to adopt standard voting practices on issues such as takeover defenses, which is a low-cost technique consistent with observed institutional behavior. It is also consistent with the thesis that only marginal effects should be expected from institutional activism.

In public corporations with dispersed ownership of the sort under debate here, such measures necessarily require the support of other shareholders, which makes a shareholder insurrection against inefficient but entrenched managers a costly and difficult undertaking. Putting together a winning coalition requires, among other things, ready mechanisms for communicating with other investors. Unfortunately, SEC rules on proxy solicitations, stock ownership disclosure, and controlling shareholder liabilities have long impeded communication and collective action. Even though the 1992 SEC rule amendments somewhat lowered the barriers to collective action, important impediments remain.[40]

Yet even if there were further erosion in the barriers to shareholder communication, coordinating shareholder activism may remain a game not worth playing, because the benefits are low. Because many companies must be monitored, and because careful monitoring of an individual firm is expensive, institutional activism is likely to focus on crisis management. In many crises, however, institutional activism is unlikely to be availing. In some cases, intervention will come too late. In others, the problem may prove intractable, as where technological changes undercut the firm's competitive position.

Putting together a winning coalition requires, among other things, ready mechanisms for communicating with other investors. Unfortunately, SEC rules on proxy solicitations, stock ownership disclosure, and controlling shareholder liabilities have long impeded communication and collective action. Even though the 1992 SEC rule amendments somewhat lowered the barriers to collective action, important impediments remain.[41]

Even where gains might arise from activism, only a portion of the gains would accrue to the activist institutions. Suppose that the troubled company has 110 outstanding shares, currently trading at $10 per share, of which the potential activist institution owns ten. The institution correctly believes that the firm's shares would rise in value to $20 if the firm's problems can be solved. If the institution is able to effect a change in corporate policy, its ten shares will produce a $100 paper gain when the stock price rises to reflect the company's new value. All the other shareholders, however, will also automatically receive a *pro rata* share of the gains.[42] As a result, the activist institution confers a gratuitous $1,000 benefit on the other shareholders.

---

[40] *See* Black, *supra* note 35, at 49–52.

[41] *See* Bernard S. Black, *Next Steps in Proxy Reform*, 18 J. CORP. L. 2, 49–52 (1992).

[42] One could plausibly expect institutions to surmount this problem by seeking private benefits, which makes investor activism even less appealing. See *infra* notes 46–54 and accompanying text. Instructively, one of the highest-profile successes of shareholder activism was the effort to get investors to withhold authority for their shares to be voted to elect directors at Disney's 2004 annual shareholder meeting. In that case, however, the campaign had a central organizing figure – Roy Disney – with a private motivation for doing so. Even then, a plurality of the

As a result, free riding is highly likely. In a very real sense, the gains resulting from institutional activism are a species of public goods. They are costly to produce, but because other shareholders cannot be excluded from taking a *pro rata* share, they are subject to a form of nonrivalrous consumption. As with any other public good, the temptation arises for shareholders to free ride on the efforts of those who produce the good.

Granted, if stock continues to concentrate in the hands of large institutional investors, there will be marginal increases in the gains to be had from activism and a marginal decrease in its costs.[43] A substantial increase in activism seems unlikely to result, however. Most institutional investors compete to attract either the savings of small investors or the patronage of large sponsors, such as corporate pension plans. In this competition, the winners generally are those with the best relative performance rates, which makes institutions highly cost conscious.[44] Given that activism will only rarely produce gains, and that when such gains occur they will be dispensed upon both the active and the passive, it makes little sense for cost-conscious money managers to incur the expense entailed in shareholder activism. Instead, they will remain passive in hopes of free riding on someone else's activism. As in other free-riding situations, because everyone is subject to and likely to yield to this temptation, the probability is that the good in question – here, shareholder activism – will be underproduced.

In addition, corporate managers are well positioned to buy off most institutional investors that attempt to act as monitors. Bank trust departments are an important class of institutional investors, but they are unlikely to emerge as activists because their parent banks often have or anticipate commercial lending relationships with the firms they will purportedly monitor. Similarly, insurers "as purveyors of insurance products, pension plans, and other

shares was voted to reelect the incumbent board. *Disney: Restoring Magic*, ECONOMIST, July 16, 2005, *available at* 2005 WLNR 11134752. It is also instructive that Disney management later persuaded Roy Disney to drop his various lawsuits against the board and sign a five-year standstill agreement pursuant to which he would not run an insurgent slate of directors in return for being named a director emeritus and consultant to the company, which nicely illustrates how a company can buy off the requisite central coordinator when that party has a private agenda. *Roy Disney, Gold Agree to Drop Suits*, CORP. GOV. REP. (BNA), Aug. 1, 2005, at 86.

In contrast, when CalPERS, the biggest institutional investor of them all, struck out on its own in 2004, withholding its shares from being voted to elect directors at no less than 2,700 companies, including Coca-Cola director and legendary investor Warren Buffet, the project went nowhere. *See* Dale Kasler, *Governor's Plan Could Erode CalPERS Clout*, SACRAMENTO BEE, Feb. 28, 2005, at A1.

[43] Edward Rock, *The Logic and Uncertain Significance of Institutional Investor Activism*, 79 GEO. L.J. 445, 460–63 (1991).
[44] *Id.* at 473–74.

financial services to corporations, have reason to mute their corporate governance activities and be bought off."[45] Mutual fund families whose business includes managing private pension funds for corporations are subject to the same concern.

This leaves us with union and state and local pension funds, which in fact have generally been the most active institutions with respect to corporate governance issues.[46] Unfortunately for the proponents of institutional investor activism, however, these are precisely the institutions most likely to use their position to self-deal (i.e., to take a non–*pro rata* share of the firms assets and earnings) or to otherwise reap private benefits not shared with other investors. With respect to union and public pension fund sponsorship of shareholder proposals under existing law, Roberta Romano observes:

> It is quite probable that private benefits accrue to some investors from sponsoring at least some shareholder proposals. The disparity in identity of sponsors – the predominance of public and union funds, which, in contrast to private sector funds, are not in competition for investor dollars – is strongly suggestive of their presence. Examples of potential benefits which would be disproportionately of interest to proposal sponsors are progress on labor rights desired by union fund managers and enhanced political reputations for public pension fund managers, as well as advancements in personal employment. . . . Because such career concerns – enhancement of political reputations or subsequent employment opportunities – do not provide a commensurate benefit to private fund managers, we do not find them engaging in investor activism.[47]

This is not just academic speculation. The pension fund of the union representing Safeway workers, for example, used its position as a Safeway shareholder in an attempt to oust directors who had stood up to the union in collective bargaining negotiations.[48] This is not an isolated example. Union pension funds tried to remove directors or top managers, or otherwise affect corporate policy, at more than two hundred corporations in 2004

---

[45] Roe, *supra* note 29, at 62.

[46] *See* Randall S. Thomas & Kenneth J. Martin, *Should Labor Be Allowed to Make Shareholder Proposals?*, 73 WASH. L. REV. 41, 51–52 (1998).

[47] Roberta Romano, *Less Is More: Making Shareholder Activism A Valued Mechanism of Corporate Governance*, 18 YALE J. REG. 174, 231–32 (2001). None of this is to deny, of course, that union and state and local pension funds also often have interests that converge with those of investors generally. *See* Stewart J. Schwab & Randall S. Thomas, *Realigning Corporate Governance: Shareholder Activism by Labor Unions*, 96 MICH. L. REV. 1020, 1079–80 (1998).

[48] Iman Anabtawi, *Some Skepticism About Increasing Shareholder Power* 4 (unpublished manuscript on file with author).

alone.[49] Union pension funds reportedly have also tried shareholder proposals to obtain employee benefits they couldn't get through bargaining.[50]

Public employee pension funds are even more vulnerable to being used as a vehicle for advancing political or social goals unrelated to shareholder interests generally. Recent activism by CalPERS, for example, reportedly is being "fueled partly by the political ambitions of Phil Angelides, California's state treasurer and a CalPERS board member, who is considering running for governor of California in 2006."[51] In other words, Angelides allegedly used the retirement savings of California's public employees to further his own political ends.

Using public pension fund investments to support so-called socially responsible investments long has been a particularly popular program of politicians and others on the left. Some have gone so far as to suggest that "the road to socialism, or some substantial socialization of the investment process, might lie through an expanded, publicly regulated system of pension finance."[52] Somewhat to the right of that position was President Clinton's call for the Rebuild America Fund, which would have leveraged federal funding by tapping "state, local, private sector, and pension fund contributions."[53] Although that proposal never came to fruition, the Clinton Department of Labor did encourage pension funds to make "economically targeted investments" in such areas as infrastructure, housing, and job creation.[54]

To be sure, like any other agency cost, the risk that management will be willing to pay private benefits to an institutional investor is a necessary consequence of vesting discretionary authority in the board and the officers. It does not compel the conclusion that we ought to limit the board's power. It does suggest, however, that we ought not to give investors even greater leverage to extract such benefits by further empowering them.

D. Rearranging the Deck Chairs

The analysis to this point suggests that the costs of institutional investor activism likely outweigh any benefits such activism may confer with respect to

---

[49] Stephen M. Bainbridge, *Flanigan on Union Pension Fund Activism, available at* http://www.professorbainbridge.com/2004/04/flanigan_on_uni.html.

[50] *Id.*

[51] Stephen M. Bainbridge, *Pension Funds Play Politics*, TECH CENTRAL STATION, Apr. 21, 2004, *available at* http://www.techcentralstation.com/042104G.html.

[52] William H. Simon, *The Prospects of Pension Fund Socialism, in* CORPORATE CONTROL & ACCOUNTABILITY 165, 166 (Joseph McCahery et al. eds., 1993).

[53] BILL CLINTON & AL GORE, PUTTING PEOPLE FIRST: HOW WE CAN ALL CHANGE AMERICA 144 (1992).

[54] Jim Saxton, *A Raid on America's Pension Funds*, WALL ST. J., Sept. 29, 1994, at A20.

redressing the principal-agent problem. Even if one assumes that the cost-benefit analysis comes out the other way around, however, it should be noted that institutional investor activism does not solve the principal-agent problem; rather, it merely relocates its locus.

The vast majority of large institutional investors manage the pooled savings of small individual investors. From a governance perspective, there is little to distinguish such institutions from corporations. The holders of investment company shares, for example, have no more control over the election of company trustees than they do over the election of corporate directors. Accordingly, fund shareholders exhibit the same rational apathy as corporate shareholders. Kathryn McGrath, a former SEC mutual fund regulator, observes: "A lot of shareholders take ye olde proxy and throw it in the trash."[55] The proxy system thus "costs shareholders money for rights they don't seem interested in exercising."[56] Indeed, "Ms. McGrath concedes that she herself often tosses a proxy for a personal investment onto a 'to-do pile' where 'I don't get around to reading it, or when I do, the deadline has passed.'"[57] Nor do the holders of such shares have any greater access to information about their holdings, or ability to monitor those who manage their holdings, than do corporate shareholders. Worse yet, although an individual investor can always abide by the Wall Street rule with respect to corporate stock, he cannot do so with respect to such investments as an involuntary, contributory pension plan.

For beneficiaries of union and state and local government employee pension funds, the problem is particularly pronounced. As we have seen, those who manage such funds may often put their personal or political agendas ahead of the interests of the fund's beneficiaries. Accordingly, it is not particularly surprising that pension funds subject to direct political control tend to have poor financial results.[58]

III. CONCLUSION

If the separation of ownership and control is a problem in search of a solution, encouraging institutional investors to take an active corporate governance role simply moves the problem back a step: it does not solve it. Yet it is not at all clear that the separation of ownership and control is a pathology requiring treatment. For many years, the ability of our system of corporate governance

[55] Karen Blumental, *Fidelity Sets Vote on Scope of Investments*, WALL ST. J., Dec. 8, 1994, at C1, C18.
[56] *Id.*   [57] *Id.*
[58] Roberta Romano, *Public Pension Fund Activism in Corporate Governance Reconsidered*, 93 COLUM. L. REV. 795, 825 (1993).

to function largely without shareholder input worked pretty well. As the *Wall Street Journal* explained:

> The economy and stock market have performed better in recent years than any other on earth. "How can we have done marvelously if the system is fundamentally flawed?" [economist Bengt] Holmstrom asks. If the bulk of American executives were stealing from shareholders and financial markets were rigged, they reason, then capital would flow to the wrong places and productivity wouldn't be surging.[59]

Economists Holmstrom and Kaplan likewise concluded that the following:

> Despite the alleged flaws in its governance system, the U.S. economy has performed very well, both on an absolute basis and particularly relative to other countries. U.S. productivity gains in the past decade have been exceptional, and the U.S. stock market has consistently outperformed other world indices over the last two decades, including the period since the scandals broke. In other words, the broad evidence is not consistent with a failed U.S. system. If anything, it suggests a system that is well above average.[60]

Does the financial crisis require us to rethink that model, as President Obama, the Washington Democrats, and the corporate governance activist community insist? No. First, to the extent corporate governance contributed to the financial crisis, it did so because shareholders are already too strong, not because they were too weak. Professor Lawrence Mitchell explains:

> Managers thrive by increasing their portfolios' value. That is a hard thing to do and it takes time. So for years fund managers have increased their pay by putting pressure on corporate managers to increase short-term stock prices at the expense of long-term business health. Doing business that way puts jobs and sustainable industry at risk, now and in the future.

> For example, managers responded to the pressure by using their retained earnings to engage in large stock buybacks. In the three years to September 2007, companies in the S&P 500 used more money to buy back stock than to invest in production. With retained earnings gone, all that was left to finance production was debt. When the credit markets collapsed, these corporations could not borrow, and thus could not produce. Are boards and managers to blame? Sure. But so are the big shareholders who have been pushing

[59] David Wessel, *"The American Way" is a Work in Progress*, WALL ST. J., Nov. 13, 2003, at A2.
[60] Bengt R. Holmstrom & Steven N. Kaplan, *The State of U.S. Corporate Governance: What's Right and What's Wrong?* 1 (Sept. 2003), *available at* http://papers.ssrn.com/sol3/papers.cfm?abstract_id=441100.

management for this kind of behavior for years. They are more the problem than the solution. Enhancing their voting rights will only make things worse.[61]

Mitchell continues:

> The proposals [to enhance those rights] are fighting the last war. Inattentive boards of non-financial companies may have been a big factor in the corporate scandals at the start of the century. But it is hyperbolic to suggest, as the Schumer bill does, that this had anything significant to do with the current recession. The Schumer bill and the SEC proposal only exacerbate the problem by chaining boards to the ball of stock prices – which helped to cause those scandals in the first place.[62]

Mitchell therefore asks:

> Do we really want speculators telling corporate boards how to manage their businesses? Those who say "yes" want to increase short-term management pressure and thus share prices, regardless of the corporate mutilation this induces. They do not seem to care that their profits come at the expense of future generations' economic well-being. But if our goal is to give expert managers the time necessary to create long-term, sustainable, and innovative businesses, the answer is a clear "no."[63]

In sum, the separation of ownership and control did not cause the financial crisis of 2008. Efforts to reduce the degree to which ownership and control are separated by empowering shareholders will not help prevent future crises. To the contrary, such efforts undermine the system of corporate governance that served us well for a very long time and that, if protected from the reformists' zeal, can continue to do so when the current crisis abates.

---

[61] Lawrence Mitchell, *Protect Industry from Predatory Speculators*, FIN. TIMES, July 8, 2009.
[62] *Id.*   [63] *Id.*

8   After *Dura*

Causation in Fraud-on-the-Market Actions

Merritt B. Fox

Legal causation is sometimes called "proximate cause" or in recent years "loss causation" in federal securities cases. We have already observed that the proliferation of terms to describe causation in the federal securities law is not helpful.... What other field of law alternatively refers to causation in terms of an "in connection with" element; cause in fact; causal nexus; transactional causation; loss causation; legal cause; proximate cause; but for causation; or simply causation? This etymological mishmash is a breeder of confusion concerning both the cause in fact and the legal causation elements.[*]

The Supreme Court decision in *Dura* was notable for... how limited its impact is likely to be on future securities class actions.... The question is not must the plaintiff plead and prove that the defendant was responsible for the plaintiff's loss, but rather, how does the plaintiff plead and prove such responsibility. Here *Dura* is strikingly limited in its significance.[**]

On April 19, 2005, the Supreme Court announced its unanimous opinion in *Dura Pharmaceuticals, Inc. v. Broudo*,[1] concerning what a plaintiff must show

[*] 9 LOUIS LOSS & JOEL SELIGMAN, SECURITIES REGULATION 4401 n.463 (3d ed. 2004).
[**] LOUIS LOSS, JOEL SELIGMAN, & TROY PAREDES, SECURITIES REGULATION 1096 (Supp. 2007).
[1] Dura Pharms., Inc. v. Broudo, 544 U.S. 336 (2005).

Merritt B. Fox is Michael E. Patterson Professor of Law, Columbia Law School. Thanks for helpful comments go to Professor Jill Fisch and to participants at workshop conferences at the University of Iowa Law School, Georgetown Law School, and Tilburg University in the Netherlands. The author wishes to thank Neil Weinberg, Rachel Jacobs, Mehdi Miremadi, and Jason Rogers for their valuable research assistance. Another version of this piece appears as an article, Merritt B. Fox, *After* Dura: *Causation in Fraud-on-the-Market Actions*, 31 J. CORP. L. 829 (2006). Substantial portions of this piece are based on two earlier articles concerning causation in fraud-on-the-market cases. Merritt B. Fox, *Demystifying Causation in Fraud-on-the-Market Actions*, 60 BUS. LAW. 507 (2005); and Merritt B. Fox, *Understanding* Dura, 60 BUS. LAW. 1547 (2005). This chapter, in addition to tying the ideas of the two earlier articles together, extends their analysis by critiquing several academic commentaries that have been published since the Supreme Court's *Dura* decision and considering a number of relevant lower-court cases, both before and after *Dura*.

to establish causation in a Rule 10b-5 fraud-on-the-market suit for damages. The opinion had been awaited with considerable anticipation, being described at the time of oral argument in the *Financial Times,* for example, as the "most important securities case in a decade."[2] After the opinion was handed down, a representative of the plaintiffs' bar lauded it as a "unanimous ruling protecting investors' ability to sue."[3] A representative of the defendant's bar equally enthusiastically hailed it as "a significant victory for public companies and others named as defendants in securities fraud cases."[4] This chapter seeks to ascertain the opinion's real significance and to provide a framework for resolving the issues that remain open to be decided by future courts. Joel Seligman, with his usual prescience, has anticipated my conclusions as indicated by the two quotes that start this chapter.

The Supreme Court's grant of certiorari in *Broudo v. Dura Pharmaceuticals, Inc.*[5] came against the backdrop of years of highly confusing lower-court decisions concerning what a plaintiff needs to show to establish causation in a fraud-on-the-market suit. This confusion had arisen, I will argue, because the lower courts had tried to analyze causation in fraud-on-the-market cases using the twin concepts of transaction causation and loss causation. These concepts had been originally developed in connection with causation determinations in cases based on traditional reliance. Traditional reliance-based cases, unlike fraud-on-the-market cases, involve the plaintiff establishing that defendant's misstatement induced the plaintiff to enter into what turns out to be a losing transaction. In such cases, transaction causation was satisfied by the very showing of traditional reliance (i.e., the plaintiff would not have purchased but for the misstatement).[6] Loss causation in these cases involved, in turn, an additional showing that the purchased security declined in value from what was paid (or sold at a loss) and that the decline or loss was in some way reasonably related to the falsity of the statement that induced the purchase.[7] The function of the loss-causation requirement, like the function of proximate cause in actions for negligence, was to prevent the wrongdoer

[2] Patti Waldmeir, *Supreme Court to Rule on "Most Important Securities Case in a Decade,"* FIN. TIMES, Jan. 10, 2005, at 5.

[3] Press Release, Lerach Stoia Geller Rudman & Robbins, LLP (Apr. 19, 2005).

[4] Pamela S. Palmer et al., *Supreme Court in* Dura Pharmaceuticals *Unanimously Endorses "Loss Causation" Requirement in Fraud-on-the-Market Cases,* SEC. LITIG. & PROF. LIABILITY PRAC. (Latham & Watkins LLP, 2d quarter 2005), at 2, *available at* http://www.lw.com/upload/pubContent/_pdf/pub1370_1.pdf.

[5] Broudo v. Dura Pharms., Inc., 339 F.3d 933 (9th Cir. 2003), *cert. granted,* 542 U.S. 936 (2004).

[6] *See, e.g.,* Emergent Capital Inv. Mgmt. v. Stonepath Group, Inc., 343 F.3d 189, 197 (2d Cir. 2003).

[7] *See infra* section I.

from being responsible for all of the consequences for which his action was a but-for cause (i.e., all of the losses, however unrelated to the misstatement, that the plaintiff might suffer over time as a result of purchasing this security).

Fraud-on-the-market actions such as *Dura* are very different from traditional reliance-based actions. The plaintiff in a traditional reliance-based action is typically a purchaser involved in either a face-to-face transaction in shares of a nonpublicly traded issuer or an IPO. These are the only situations where plaintiffs are likely to be able to show traditional reliance. These are situations where there is no reason to assume that the price is an efficient one. In contrast, plaintiffs in fraud-on-the-market actions such as *Dura* are purchasers in active public secondary markets, where prices can be assumed to be efficient. Fraud-on-the-market actions involve a fundamentally different kind of causal connection between the defendant's misstatement and the plaintiff's injury. The defendant's misstatement injures the plaintiff not because it caused her to make a purchase that later, *ex post*, turned out to be a losing transaction. Rather, it injures her because, *ex ante*, it caused her to pay a purchase price that is higher than it would have been but for the misstatement. The purchase is one that she might well have made even if the defendant had not made the misstatement. This causal connection between the misstatement and an injury in the form of its effect on price at the time the plaintiff enters into the transaction was recognized by the Supreme Court when it originally approved fraud-on-the-market actions in *Basic Inc. v. Levinson*[8] almost twenty years ago.

---

[8] Basic Inc. v. Levinson, 485 U.S. 224, 243 (1988), in which the Supreme Court stated that the fraud-on-the-market theory, based on the idea that a material misstatement will affect the plaintiff's purchase price, provides the plaintiff with an alternative way to demonstrate "the requisite causal connection between a defendant's misrepresentation and a plaintiff's injury." Specifically, the Court said, "There is, however, more than one way to demonstrate the causal connection." Characterizing the Third Circuit's opinion in *Peil v. Speiser*, 806 F.2d 1154 (3d Cir. 1986), as "succinctly putting" the question of reliance and the fraud-on-the market theory, the Court quoted *Speiser*:

> [T]he price of a company's common stock is determined by the available material information regarding the company and its business. . . . Misleading statements will therefore defraud purchasers of stock even if the purchasers do not directly rely on the misstatements. . . . The causal connection in such a case is no less significant than in a case of direct reliance on misrepresentations.

Basic, 485 U.S. at 243–44 (citation omitted).

The rule in *Basic* applies both to suits by secondary market purchasers in cases of falsely positive statements and to suits by secondary-market sellers in cases of falsely negative statements. This chapter assumes throughout a suit by a purchaser based on a falsely positive statement. Everything I say here about the causation requirement in positive misstatement cases would, with the appropriate reversals, apply equally to a suit by a seller based on a falsely negative statement.

The fraud-on-the-market theory's *ex ante* focus on the price at the time of purchase is, for transactions occurring in efficient markets, what is called for by the modern, efficiency-oriented economic thinking that has been the driving force behind the evolution of securities regulation over the past two decades. Efficiency-oriented thinking considers problems from an *ex ante* perspective because its concern is with the law's effect on the structure of incentives of the various actors involved at the time the plaintiff enters into the transaction. Thus, it is these actors' expectations at the time of the transaction that matters. Other than the inflation in price due to the misstatement, the efficient market hypothesis guarantees that the purchase price is a fair one because the other factors affecting price in the future are as likely to increase price as decrease it.[9] Thus, the injury is the inflation in price at the time of purchase.

The twin concepts of transaction causation and loss causation are reasonably serviceable in helping to determine when causation is or is not present in an action for fraud based on traditional reliance. These twin concepts simply do not make sense in an action for fraud based on the fraud-on-the-market theory, however, because of the difference between the two kinds of actions in terms of the causal connections between misstatement and injury. The transaction causation requirement makes no sense in a fraud-on-the-market action, as the plaintiff is not required to show that she would not have purchased but for the defendant's misstatement. Indeed, often she would have. The typical plaintiff is a member of a class predominantly consisting of portfolio investors who have made impersonal purchases of shares in the secondary market on the New York Stock Exchange (NYSE) or Nasdaq and may not have been aware of the misstatement. Alternatively, the plaintiff may be an index fund. Even if the plaintiff had been aware of the misstatement and was investing speculatively, the misstatement is unlikely to have been decisive in the decision to purchase, as a believable misstatement, while making the stock appear more attractive than it really was, would also have made it commensurately more expensive.

---

[9] Stated more precisely, the efficient markets hypothesis holds that future returns from holding a security will be priced in an unbiased way given all publicly available information. RICHARD A. BREALEY ET AL., PRINCIPLES OF CORPORATE FINANCE 333–41 (8th ed. 2006). Combined with the capital asset pricing model, *see id.* at 188–92, the efficient markets hypothesis provides that other factors are as likely to add to as to subtract from what would be the price predicted on the basis of the return on a completely safe asset, such as U.S. government bonds, plus a premium reflecting the expected return on an investment in the market as a whole and the systematic riskiness of the issuer's shares. Thus, while the efficient markets hypothesis does not stand for the proposition that there will be no long-term growth in share prices on average over time, it says that the ordinary investor cannot on average make profits by trying to pick particular, unusually attractive stocks based on publicly available information.

The loss causation requirement makes no sense either in the context of a fraud-on-the-market action because the injury – that the plaintiff paid too much – flows directly from the misstatement. Requiring the defendant to compensate for such an injury presents no danger of providing compensation for risks unrelated to the misrepresentation because injury is unrelated to anything that happens to price after the purchase date. Thus, there is no need for some intervening proximate cause requirement to prevent the defendant from compensating a loss for which its misconduct is a but-for cause but is unrelated in the sense that it did not increase the risk that the plaintiff would suffer the loss.

Abandoning the transaction-causation and loss-causation framework would have permitted the Supreme Court, I argue, to have avoided the confusion exhibited by the lower courts as they struggled to redefine the twin concepts to make them fit the fraud-on-the-market context. By casting this rhetorical baggage aside, the Court could have used the *Dura* case self-consciously to develop standards concerning what an *ex ante* analysis suggests are the two main concerns relating to causation in fraud-on-the-market actions. One main concern involves identifying those situations where a misstatement actually did inflate the plaintiff's purchase price and hence create an injury. Rules are needed concerning what the plaintiff must plead and prove, and the acceptable forms of evidence, concerning this question.[10] The other main concern involves how to prevent damages from being paid to the subset of investors who suffer injury by purchasing shares at a price inflated by the misstatement but who recoup this injury in part or in whole by reselling sufficiently quickly that the price at the time of sale is still inflated. Thus, rules are also needed concerning who, at the pleading stage and at trial, has the burden of proof on the question of when the market realized the true situation, thereby dissipating the inflation in price, and what are the acceptable forms of evidence of the occurrence of such realization.

The design of each of these sets of rules has an impact on the extent to which we achieve two important public policy aims. One aim relates to the desirability of enhancing share-price accuracy, in particular by deterring corporate misstatements. The other relates to the desirability of limiting the variety of transaction costs associated with civil litigation, including, but not limited to, the costs associated with strike suits. These two aims are in part conflicting. Good design involves minimizing these conflicts to the extent

---

[10] As will be discussed in more detail here in section IV, under some circumstances this concern breaks down into two subquestions: did the misstatement inflate share price at some point in time; and was it still inflated at the time that the plaintiff purchased?

possible and then choosing the appropriate place in the inevitable remaining degree of trade-off between the two aims.

Unfortunately, the Supreme Court in its opinion in *Dura* did not abandon the bifurcated transaction-causation and loss-causation framework for fraud-on-the-market actions, and so it was not able to address the two main concerns in a fully self-conscious way. Rather, as the lower courts had been doing in various different ways, the Court redefined the twin concepts to try to make them fit fraud-on-the-market actions. The Court allowed plaintiffs to satisfy the transaction-causation requirement by use of *Basic's* "presum[ption] that the price reflects a material misrepresentation"[11] – in other words, a presumption that the price is inflated by the misrepresentation. This is a very different standard from the "but for the misstatement, the plaintiff would not have purchased" transaction-causation standard used in traditional reliance-based cases. As for loss causation, the Court ruled that a mere showing that the price has been inflated by the misstatement is not sufficient.[12] The Court was not specific concerning what kind of additional showing would be sufficient, thus creating a void that future courts are left to fill. The argument of this chapter is that, in doing so, these future courts should be mindful that whatever the legal rhetoric, the rules that they develop are best evaluated in terms of the two main concerns discussed above: how well and at what cost they (1) identify those situations where plaintiffs have purchased shares at a price that has genuinely been inflated by a misrepresentation, and (2) avoid payment of damages to the subset of such plaintiffs who recoup their injury by reselling sufficiently quickly that the price is still equally inflated.

This chapter develops the foregoing points in more detail. Section I explores the origins of the concepts of transaction causation and loss causation in Rule 10b-5 fraud cases based on traditional reliance. Section II explores the pre-*Dura* attempts of the lower courts to apply these concepts to fraud-on-the-market theory cases and the opportunity that *Dura* presented to the Supreme Court to clear up the resulting confusion. Section III discusses the history of the *Dura* litigation and the holding in the Supreme Court opinion. Section IV addresses what issues have been definitively decided by the Court in *Dura* and what issues remain open to be decided in future cases. Section V considers to what extent the reasoning used by the Supreme Court in reaching its decision is useful in determining how these open issues should be resolved. Section VI considers how, from a policy point of view, these open issues should be resolved. Section VII concludes.

---

[11] *Basic*, 485 U.S. at 341–42.   [12] *Id.*

I. CAUSATION IN ACTIONS BASED ON TRADITIONAL RELIANCE

A. *The Origins of the Transaction-Causation and Loss-Causation Framework*

The twin requirements of transaction causation and loss causation were developed in the context of Rule 10b-5 fraud cases where plaintiffs were able to show traditional reliance. The seminal case defining traditional reliance is the Second Circuit's 1965 opinion in *List v. Fashion Park*.[13] The district court in *List* found that the plaintiff, with regard to one of his allegations, would have purchased even if he had known the true situation.[14] On the basis of this finding, the district court dismissed the claim relating to this allegation. The Second Circuit affirmed.[15] In reaching its decision, the Second Circuit started with a ruling that the requirement in common law misrepresentation cases that the plaintiff show that reliance "carried over into civil suits under Rule 10b-5."[16] Citing common law authorities, the court found that "the test of 'reliance' is whether 'the misrepresentation is a substantial factor in determining the *course of conduct* which results in (the recipient's) loss.'"[17] Given the district court's finding that the plaintiff would have purchased anyway, which the appeals court did not find clearly erroneous, the plaintiff clearly failed the test. The court stated that "the reason for this requirement is to certify that the conduct of the defendant actually caused the plaintiff's injury."[18]

List left an open question. Suppose the plaintiff had been able to show that he would not have purchased had he known the true situation. Would that by itself have been sufficient to establish causation? A positive answer would mean that any person who made a misleading statement in violation of Rule 10b-5 would be liable to anyone who could show that the statement was a but-for cause of the purchase of a security that subsequently declined in price for any reason. The plaintiff would essentially be complaining to the defendant: "You got me into this through your violation and because I got into it, I suffered a

---

[13] List v. Fashion Park, 340 F.2d 457 (2d Cir. 1965). *List* was a nondisclosure case in which the plaintiff claimed injury because an insider stayed silent when he allegedly had a duty to speak, not a case based on an affirmative misleading statement. The court's analysis, however, drew on affirmative misleading statement cases in the common law, and the court's definition of reliance has been regularly cited as controlling in subsequent Rule 10b-5 affirmative misleading statement cases.

[14] *Id.* at 464.   [15] *Id.*

[16] *Id.* at 462–63.

[17] *Id.* at 462 (citations omitted) (emphasis added).

[18] *Id.*

loss for which you should make me whole." This, however, was not the route chosen by the federal courts in working out the contours of the implied right of action under Rule 10b-5. Over time, a clear requirement developed that for liability to be imposed, a plaintiff basing a claim on a showing that the defendant's Rule 10b-5 violation impelled her to make a securities purchase must show something more.

The first signs that a showing of something more was required appeared in 1969 in another Second Circuit opinion, *Globus v. Law Research Service, Inc.*[19] In *Globus*, the jury found that defendants, who had made misleading statements in violation of Rule 10b-5 in a circular for a stock offering, were liable to plaintiffs, who had presented evidence that they had been attracted by the misleading statements to purchase some of the offered shares and subsequently sustained a loss. On appeal, defendants argued that the jury instructions on causation were improper and that there was insufficient evidence of causation.[20] The jury instructions were that "the plaintiff is required to prove . . . that he or she suffered damages as a proximate result of the alleged misleading statements and purchase of stock in reliance on them . . . in other words that the damage was either a direct result or a reasonably foreseeable result of the misleading statement." The court described these as "clear instructions on causation"[21] and found that they "were sufficient to bring home the basic concept that causation must be proved else defendants could be held liable to the world."[22] As for the evidence, the appeals court observed not only that the plaintiffs introduced evidence that the statements were a but-for cause of the purchases but also that the jury could infer that the stock price was bloated as a result of the statement. The court held that this "was sufficient to support a finding of a causal relationship between the misrepresentation and the losses appellees incurred when they sold."[23] Thus, while the court did not explicitly say that a showing of more than just traditional reliance was required, it did, in response to a defendant's argument that more needed to be shown, approvingly recite jury instructions that appeared to call for a showing of more and point to evidence suggesting the existence of more than just but-for causation.

Five years later, in *Schlick v. Penn-Dixie Cement Corp.*, the Second Circuit moved one step closer to a clear requirement that a plaintiff who bases a claim on a showing that the defendant's Rule 10b-5 violation impelled her into making a securities purchase must show something more.[24] Introducing

[19] Globus v. Law Research Serv., Inc., 418 F.2d 1276 (2d Cir. 1969).
[20] *Id.* at 1291.   [21] *Id.*
[22] *Id.* at 1292.   [23] *Id.* at 1291–92.
[24] Schlick v. Penn-Dixie Cement Corp., 507 F.2d 374 (2d Cir. 1974).

for the first time into the case law the terms *loss causation* and *transaction causation,* the court stated in dicta:

> This is not a case where the 10b-5 claim is based solely upon material omis-
> sions or misstatements in the proxy materials. Were it so, concededly there
> would have to be a showing of both *loss causation* – that the misrepresenta-
> tions or omissions caused the economic harm – and *transaction causation* –
> that the violations in question caused the appellant to engage in the trans-
> action in question.[25]

The court added, however, that the something more that needed to be shown, what it termed *loss causation,* was "rather easily shown by proof of some kind of economic damage."[26] Finally in 1981, the Fifth Circuit provided a clear appellate court ruling that a showing of something more was required. In *Huddleston v. Herman & MacLean,* the court, in finding that the trial court's failure to submit issues of reliance and causation to the jury required a new trial, stated:

> The plaintiff must prove not only that, had he known the truth, he would not
> have acted, but in addition that the untruth was in some reasonably direct, or
> proximate, way responsible for his loss. The causation requirement is satisfied
> in a Rule 10b-5 case only if the misrepresentation touches upon the reasons
> for the investment's decline in value.[27]

The *Huddleston* court links these two requirements to the transaction-causation and loss-causation language used by other courts.[28]

B. The Transaction-Causation and Loss-Causation Framework Fits Traditional Reliance-Based Actions Reasonably Well

The twin requirements of transaction causation and loss causation are now firmly established.[29] In the context of an action based on traditional reliance,

---

[25] *Id.* at 380. The crux of the complaint was based on a "corporate mismanagement theory" that there was a scheme to defraud in violation of Rule 10b-5 based on "market manipulation and a merger on preferential terms" in connection with the purchase or sale of a security. *Id.* at 381.

[26] *Id.* at 380.

[27] Huddleston v. Herman & MacLean, 640 F.2d 534, 549 (5th Cir. 1981).

[28] The court in *Huddleston* says that courts sometimes consider reliance to be a component of causation and that "the term 'transaction causation' is used to describe the requirement that the defendant's fraud must precipitate the investment decision" and is "necessarily closely related to" reliance. *Id.* at 549 n.24. "Loss causation," the court continues, "refers to a direct causal link between the misstatement and the claimant's economic loss." *Id.*

[29] *See* Suez Equity Investors v. Toronto-Dominion Bank, 250 F.3d 87, 95 (2d Cir. 2001) ("It is settled that causation under federal securities laws is two-pronged: . . . both transaction causa-tion . . . and loss causation."). For a survey of the cases requiring loss causation, see MICHAEL J. KAUFMAN, SECURITIES LITIGATION: DAMAGES § 11:1 (2001).

their meanings are fairly settled. Transaction causation involves a showing that the plaintiff would not have purchased but for the misstatement.[30] Loss causation in this context follows on this first showing. It involves the additional showing that the purchased security declined in value from what was paid (or was sold at a loss) and that the decline or loss was in some way reasonably related to the falsity of the statement that induced the purchase.[31] These twin requirements fit neatly within traditional reliance-based actions and in this context have a reasonably sensible rationale. The objection to imposing liability based on a showing of transaction causation alone is the same as it would be to imposing liability for every injury for which an act of negligence is a but-for cause. As every first-year law student learns, the chain of but-for results flowing from any act of negligence can go on forever and encompass an infinite number of injuries. For most or all of these injuries, it would be ridiculous to hold the actor responsible. Thus, a showing of something more than but-for causation is required. In tort, the something more is proximate cause. In Rule 10b-5, misleading statement cases based on traditional reliance, the something more is loss causation. In each case, the something more involves at a minimum a showing that the wrongful act somehow raised the probability that the plaintiff would suffer a loss of the kind that he or she did in fact suffer.

There is also a reasonable, though not quite as compelling, rationale for the requirement that the loss be in the form of a sale at a lower price than the plaintiff paid (or, if the plaintiff still holds the security at the time suit is brought, a decline in the market price from the price paid) rather than in the form of the amount extra that the plaintiff paid as a result of the misstatement. The rationale involves an *ex post* perspective rather than the *ex ante* perspective that is characteristic of modern, economics-based securities law analysis.[32] It relies on the observation that being induced by a misstatement into making a securities purchase does not by itself inherently mean that the purchaser will ultimately be worse off. The inducement simply puts the purchaser in a position to enjoy all kinds of possible gains and suffer all kinds of possible losses. If the purchaser ultimately does realize a loss and the loss is one that would have been predictable, given knowledge of the true state of affairs, then, the thinking goes, an injury has occurred for which the person who made the misstatement in violation of Rule 10b-5 should be liable.

The critical first step in developing the rationale for this requirement of a loss at sale or decline in price is to recognize that an action based on a showing

---

[30] *See, e.g.*, Emergent Capital Inv. Mgmt. v. Stonepath Group Inc., 343 F.3d 189, 197 (2d Cir. 2003).

[31] *Id.*   [32] *See infra* section III.B.

of traditional reliance typically grows out of a face-to-face purchase of shares of a nonpublicly traded issuer or a purchase at or about the time of an IPO. In these situations, the price that the plaintiff pays is not one established in an efficient secondary market. As a consequence, the value of the security is much more subjective and the relationship between the misleading statement and the price that the plaintiff paid is unclear.[33] Unlike what I will contend should be the proper approach with fraud-on-the-market actions, the focus in traditional reliance-based actions should not, the argument for the rationale goes, be on the difference created by the misstatement between the price paid and value of the security or on the effect of the misstatement on the price paid. This is because just how low a price, if any, would have spurred this particular plaintiff to have been willing to buy had she been aware of the truth – the measure of price inflation for this particular plaintiff – is inherently unknowable. The focus instead should be on two facts. First, whatever the value of the security at the time of purchase relative to the price paid, this particular plaintiff would not have purchased at the price offered if she had known the truth. Second, the risks that the truth would have revealed have in fact revealed themselves.

It may be easiest to conceptualize the requirement of a loss at sale or decline in price as related to a modified form of recissionary damages. This form of damages is called for because of the special situations that typically give rise to traditional reliance-based actions, where the price the plaintiff paid has not been set in an efficient secondary trading market.[34] Pure recissionary damages would be the difference between the price paid and the price at

---

[33] As one district court, quoted in *Basic*, put it, "In face-to-face transactions, the inquiry into an investor's reliance upon information is in the subjective pricing of that information by that investor." Basic Inc. v. Levinson, 485 U.S. 224, 244 (1987) (quoting *In re* LTV Sec. Litig. 88 F.R.D. 134, 143 (N.D. Tex. 1980)).

[34] *See* 9 Louis Loss & Joel Seligman, Securities Regulation 4407–28 (3d ed. 2004) (discussing problems with calculating damages in close corporation and thin-market situations and the use of recissionary damages); Robert B. Thompson, *The Measure of Recovery Under Rule 10b-5: A Restitution Alternative to Tort Damages*, 37 Vand. L. Rev. 349, 361–62 (1984) (discussing modifications to the out-of-pocket measure of damages needed when there is no ready market for stock or when market price of traded stock does not reflect its actual value at the time of the transaction). Some of the early Rule 10b-5 misstatement cases even suggest that full recissionary damages are appropriate in such situations. *See* Baumel v. Rosen, 283 F. Supp. 128, 146 (D. Md. 1968) (calling for equitable recission in the case, where defendant close corporation sold shares to plaintiffs who relied on the corporation's misstatements); Esplin v. Hirschi, 402 F. 2d 94, 104–05 (10th Cir. 1968) (plaintiff entitled to recover the difference between price paid and value at time of discovery of the fraud); Harris v. Am. Inv. Co., 523 F.2d 220, 226–27 (8th Cir. 1975). The modification that damages would be reduced or eliminated to the extent that there were other causes for the loss at sale or decline in price can be regarded as reflecting a concern that full recissionary damages could result in unjustified compensation.

which the securities were sold (or, if still held, the price at the time suit was brought). Modified recissionary damages would start with this measure but reduce or eliminate the damages to the extent that the loss or decline was due to factors other than ones related to the false statement. This modified recissionary measure of damages fits nicely with the idea that plaintiff was put by the defendant's wrongful misstatement in the position of potentially suffering losses and that, as a result, there should be compensation for any losses that in fact do occur, but not if the losses arose from reasons unrelated to the misstatement.

It should be emphasized that this rationale for requiring an *ex post* loss is driven by the face-to-face or thin-market situations that are associated with most traditional reliance-based cases and the special measure of damages that such situations may suggest. It is only logical that in an action for compensatory damages, the form of loss for which we make a causation determination should correspond to the measure of damages. Compensatory damages, after all, are supposed to measure loss. The standard measure of damages in Rule 10b-5 cases is "out of pocket" damages – the extra amount the plaintiff pays because of the misstatement.[35] The form of loss that corresponds to this measure of damages is the amount by which the misstatement inflates the price the plaintiff pays. Thus, the particular situations in which traditional reliance-based fraud actions arise are what call for the special semirecissionary measure of damages, which in turn call for looking for the causes of an *ex post* injury rather than the causes of an injury at the time of purchase, as should be the case with standard Rule 10b-5 cases including fraud-on-the-market cases.

II. CAUSATION IN FRAUD-ON-THE-MARKET CASES

A. *The Difference in Causal Link*

Fraud-on-the-market actions are distinctly different from actions based on traditional reliance. As discussed above, the plaintiff in a traditional reliance-based action needs to show that she would have acted differently but for the wrongful misstatement. At a minimum, this requires that the plaintiff was aware of the statement. The fraud-on-the-market theory, approved by the Supreme Court in 1988 in *Basic Inc. v. Levinson*,[36] provides the plaintiff an

---

[35] Randall v. Loftsgaarden, 478 U.S. 647, 662 (1986); Estate Counseling Serv., Inc. v. Merrill Lynch, Pierce, Fenner & Smith, Inc. 303 F.2d 527, 532 (10th Cir. 1962); LOSS & SELIGMAN, *supra* note 34 at 4409–14.

[36] Basic Inc. v. Levinson, 485 U.S. 224 (1988).

alternative way to demonstrate "the requisite causal connection between a defendant's misrepresentation and a plaintiff's injury."[37] This alternative is to show that the misstatement caused the price the plaintiff paid at the time of purchase to be too high, an effect that can be presumed in the case of a material misstatement by an official of an issuer whose shares trade in an efficient market.

The Court insisted in *Basic* that its ruling maintained the need for plaintiff to show reliance, just in the form of "reliance on the integrity of [the market] price"[38] instead of reliance on the misstatement itself. There is a big difference between these two forms of reliance, however. Unlike traditional reliance, the plaintiff no longer needs to show he or she would have acted differently (i.e., not purchased the security) if the defendant had not made the misstatement.

B. *The Transaction-Causation and Loss-Causation Framework Fits Fraud-on-the-Market Actions Poorly*

As a result of this difference in causal link, the twin requirements of transaction causation and loss causation fit very poorly with fraud-on-the-market actions. In these actions, the typical plaintiff is a member of a class predominantly consisting of portfolio investors and index funds that have made impersonal purchases of shares in the secondary market on the NYSE or Nasdaq. As noted, the plaintiff need not allege that she relied on the misstatement. Indeed, she may well not even have been aware of it.[39] Even if she were, the misstatement is unlikely to have been decisive in her decision to purchase, since the misstatement, while making the stock appear more attractive than it really is, would also have made it commensurately more expensive. Thus, whether she was aware of the statement or not, she likely would have made the purchase even if the misstatement had not been made, just at a lower price. Consequently, the misstatement is not likely to be a but-for cause for the purchase. The fact that, for most fraud-on-the-market plaintiffs, the defendant's misstatement is not a but-for cause for their purchase renders nonsensical both elements of the

---

[37] *Id.* at 243. *See* discussion *supra* note 8. [38] *Basic,* 485 U.S. at 247.

[39] In *Basic,* the Court recognizes the difference between the kind of situation that gives rise to the traditional reliance-based fraud action and the one that gives rise to a fraud-on-the-market action: "The modern securities markets, literally involving millions of shares changing hands daily, differ from the face-to-face transactions contemplated by early fraud cases, and our understanding of Rule 10b-5's reliance requirement must encompass these differences." *Id.* at 244.

transaction-causation and loss-causation framework as developed in traditional reliance-based cases.

1. Transaction Causation

Transaction causation, as we have seen, involves a showing that the plaintiff would not have purchased but for the misstatement. Thus, transaction causation is just another name for traditional reliance. If courts were seriously to impose a transaction causation requirement in fraud-on-the-market cases, they would be acting in direct contradiction to *Basic*. The whole purpose of *Basic* was to provide the purchaser in the secondary trading markets, for whom demonstrating traditional reliance would be an unrealistic evidentiary burden, an alternative way to demonstrate the causal connection between a defendant's misrepresentation and her injury.[40]

2. Loss Causation

Once it is recognized that requiring fraud-on-the-market plaintiffs to show transaction causation is inconsistent with *Basic*, it becomes clear that the loss-causation requirement makes no sense, either. Remember that the loss-causation requirement is a follow on to transaction causation. If, to impose liability on a defendant, all that an investor has to show is that she was induced into purchasing shares by the defendant's misstatement (i.e., transaction causation), the defendant would be insuring the plaintiff against every risk that could possibly depress the price below the price paid at time of purchase, including risks totally unrelated to the misstatement. Loss causation is the requirement of something more, akin to proximate cause in negligence, which prevents such wide-ranging liability.

A loss-causation requirement serves no comparable purpose in a fraud-on-the-market action, because imposing liability based solely on a showing of this special kind of reliance does not lead to similarly wide-open results. The "causal connection between a defendant's misrepresentation and a plaintiff's injury"[41] is simply different. The plaintiff, rather than saying to the defendant, "You got me into this and now I've suffered a loss," is saying, "I might have purchased anyway even without your misstatement, but your misstatement made me pay more that I otherwise would have." The claimed loss – that the plaintiff paid too much – flows directly from the misstatement. If proved true, the resulting damages paid to the plaintiff compensate the plaintiff for that loss and nothing more. No insurance for any kind of risk would be provided.

[40] *Id.* at 245.   [41] *Id.* at 243.

C. The Pre-Dura History of the Application of the Transaction-Causation and Loss-Causation Framework to Fraud-on-the-Market Cases

While the Supreme Court had never discussed the matter prior to *Dura*, the lower courts had consistently said over the preceding twenty years that plaintiffs must show both transaction causation and loss causation in all Rule 10b-5 damage actions, whether based on traditional reliance or on the fraud-on-the-market theory.[42] Having developed the twin-requirement framework for traditional reliance-based actions, the lower courts apparently felt bound to apply it to fraud-on-the-market actions as well after the new alternative theory of liability became accepted. These efforts by the lower courts to cram fraud-on-the-market cases into the ill-fitting transaction-causation and loss-causation framework has led to muddy legal reasoning and arbitrary results.

1. Transaction Causation

While the lower courts continue to reiterate the idea that transaction causation means that the defendant's misstatement induced the plaintiff's purchase,[43] the success of plaintiffs in pleading and proving transaction causation never seems to be an issue in fraud-on-the-market cases. This is odd, given that a substantial portion of the plaintiffs in a typical fraud-on-the-market class action almost certainly would have purchased even if the misstatement had not been made. The courts seem satisfied by the fact that the plaintiffs have shown some sort of "reliance."[44] This effort at resolution ignores the fact that while *traditional reliance* and *transaction causation* are just two names for the same but-for concept of causation, the *Basic* type of reliance on the integrity of the market price that characterizes fraud-on-the-market cases is not the same as transaction causation.[45] By glossing over this distinction, the courts make the

---

[42] See Suez Equity Investors v. Toronto-Dominion Bank, 250 F.3d 87, 95 (2d Cir. 2001) ("It is settled that causation under federal securities laws is two-pronged: ... both transaction causation ... and loss causation"). As discussed *supra* section I, the origins of the twin requirements go back to *Globus v. Law Research Serv., Inc.*, 418 F.2d 1276 (2d Cir. 1969), and *Schlick v. Penn-Dixie Cement Corp.*, 507 F.2d 374 (2d Cir. 1974). By 1981, there was in *Huddleston v. Herman & MacLean*, 640 F.2d 534 (5th Cir. 1981), a clear appellate-court ruling that a showing of both elements was required. For a survey of the cases requiring loss causation, see MICHAEL J. KAUFMAN, SECURITIES LITIGATION: DAMAGES § 11:1 (2001).

[43] See, e.g., Robbins v. Koger Props., Inc., 116 F.3d 1441, 1147 (11th Cir. 1997); Bryant v. Apple South, Inc., 25 F. Supp. 2d 1372, 1382 (M.D. Ga. 1998); In re Valujet, Inc., 984 F. Supp. 1472, 1480 (N.D. Ga. 1997).

[44] See, e.g., Semerenko v. Cendant Corp., 223 F.3d 165, 178–83 (3d Cir. 2000).

[45] Some courts in fraud-on-the-market cases include as part of the required showing of loss causation a component that sounds more like transaction causation – that is, plaintiffs must plead and prove that if they had known the truth, they would not have purchased. See

transaction-causation requirement, which logically should not be there at all in this kind of case, trivially easy to meet. This tactic is innocent enough by itself. After all, as we have seen, if they seriously tried to apply the requirement, they would essentially be reversing the Supreme Court's decision in *Basic*, since the whole point of the fraud-on-the-market action is to allow suits to be brought by plaintiffs who cannot show that the defendant's misstatement caused their purchases. The tactic has had an unfortunate side effect, however. Allowing courts to avoid the reality that no real transaction causation exists creates much confusion as to what the standard for loss causation should be.

2. Decisions Finding That Price Inflation Constitutes Loss Causation

Recall the meaning of loss causation, as it was originally developed in the case law: a showing by the plaintiff that the purchased security declined in value from what was paid or was sold at a loss and that the decline or loss is in some way reasonably related to the falsity of the statement that induced the purchase. Some courts prior to *Dura* concluded that a showing that the price at the time of purchase was inflated by the misstatement is sufficient to constitute loss causation. Typically, they simply asserted this to be the case and made no attempt to explain how their conclusion relates to the meaning of loss causation as it was originally developed in the case law.[46]

The approach of these courts that a showing of price inflation satisfies the requirement of loss causation had at least two defects in terms of legal reasoning. First, while the courts acquiesced to the idea developed in the prior case law that the plaintiff must make a certain showing (i.e., loss causation), they provided no reasoning as to how the new meaning assigned to the term related to the meaning developed in the prior case law that established the requirement. Nor did they try to establish how, in the different context of fraud-on-the-market suits, showing price inflation satisfies the purposes for which the original loss causation requirement was developed. Second, the

Bryant v. Avado Brands, Inc., 100 F. Supp. 2d 1368, 1382 (M.D. Ga. 2000); In re Valujet Sec. Litig., 984 F. Supp. 1472, 1480 (N.D. Ga. 1997). Based on pleadings to this effect, the courts in these cases denied motions to dismiss the complaints. Such a pleading fails to address whether the plaintiff would have purchased the shares but for the misstatement, however – nor is it very believable in most cases arising out of purchases in an efficient secondary market. If the plaintiffs, who were outside investors, had known the truth, so would the market. The shares might therefore have been an equally attractive purchase since the market price would have been commensurately lower, compensating for the less rosy but true situation.

[46] This is the approach of the two leading appellate opinions that hold that, in a fraud-on-the-market case, a showing of price inflation satisfies loss causation. See, e.g., Knapp v. Ernst & Whinney, 90 F.3d 1431, 1438 (9th Cir. 1996); Gebhart v. ConAgra Foods, Inc., 335 F.3d 824, 831 (8th Cir. 2003). This is also the approach that was used in the Ninth Circuit opinion in *Dura*. Broudo v. Dura Pharms., Inc., 339 F.3d 933, 937–38 (9th Cir. 2003).

approach redefines loss causation in such a way that the same evidence that the courts found satisfied the transaction-causation requirement – that the misstatement caused inflation in the price the plaintiff paid at the time of purchase – satisfies loss causation, as well. Thus, their new definition rendered loss causation, which is supposed to be an additional requirement beyond transaction causation, totally redundant.

Although these courts did not do so, one could argue that allowing a showing of price inflation to satisfy the loss causation requirement in fraud-on-the-market cases sensibly relates to the traditional loss-causation formulation because, if a false statement inflates price at the time of purchase, the market ultimately will reflect the true situation. After that point, the price will be lower than it would have been if the market had never realized the true situation. This argument has defects of its own, however. First, it in essence simply redefines in *ex post* terms the *ex ante* reality that the plaintiff paid more for the security than he or she would have but for the wrongful misstatement. The *ex post* fact that the price is lower than it would have been if the market had never realized the true situation hardly seems by itself like a compelling reason for compensation. The reason for compensation, if there is one, comes from the *ex ante* reality that the plaintiff was forced to pay too much. Second, when the market realizes the true situation, the price will not necessarily be lower than the price the plaintiff paid because, between the time of the purchase and the point of market realization, other factors unrelated to the misstatements may have pushed price up by more than the removal of the misstatements' price inflation pushed it down. Therefore, even if the misstatement inflated the price paid, the plaintiff may not have suffered a loss *ex post*, as required by the traditional loss-causation formulation. Third, if all that the plaintiff has to show to satisfy the loss causation requirement is that the misstatement inflated price at the time of purchase, she does not need to show, as the traditional loss-causation formulation requires, that she held until the point that the market realized the true situation. If she sold earlier than that point, she may have recouped at sale the amount of overpayment at purchase.

3. Pre-*Dura* Decisions Finding a Showing of Price Inflation Insufficient to Satisfy the Loss-Causation Requirement

Other courts concluded that a showing that the price at the time of purchase was inflated by the misstatement is insufficient to constitute loss causation and appeared to require the same showing in fraud-on-the-market cases as in traditional reliance cases. *Robbins v. Koger Properties, Inc.*[47] and *Semerenko v.*

---

[47] Robbins v. Koger Props., Inc., 116 F.3d 1441 (11th Cir. 1997).

Cendant Corp.[48] are the two leading recent appellate-court opinions taking this position. The reasoning in each also has serious problems.

In *Robbins*, the Eleventh Circuit rejected the price inflation theory by the following route: First, it stated that transaction causation is equivalent to reliance and is "akin to actual or 'but for' causation."[49] Second, it said that the Supreme Court, in articulating the fraud-on-the-market theory in *Basic*, found that a showing of price inflation "creates a presumption of reliance," which, the *Robbins* court said, is "more related to transaction causation" and "not a presumption of causation."[50] Therefore the court refused to use the fraud-on-the-market theory to alter the loss-causation requirement and stated that it would continue to "require proof of a causal connection between the misrepresentation and the investment's subsequent decline in price."[51]

As discussed above, the reasoning in the *Robbins* opinion ignores the fact that the kind of reliance established by the Supreme Court in *Basic* is not but-for causation – hence, a showing that satisfies the fraud-on-the-market kind of reliance is not a showing of transaction causation.[52] The reasoning ignores as well that in *Basic* the Supreme Court describes a showing of price inflation as providing the plaintiff an alternative way to demonstrate "the requisite causal connection between a defendant's misrepresentation and a plaintiff's injury,"[53] thereby suggesting that the Court did regard a showing of price inflation as creating a presumption of causation. The reasoning also ignores the fact that, because the fraud-on-the-market reliance standard is not but-for causation, there is no need for a showing of something more in the form of traditional loss causation in order to save defendants from insuring risks unrelated to the subject matter of the misrepresentation. Finally, the reasoning in *Robbins* ignores the special situations existing in the traditional reliance-based cases, in which the loss-causation requirement was developed, that justified the unusual focus on *ex post* rather than *ex ante* injury (i.e., that these cases typically arose out of face-to-face or thin- or initial-market situations where the purchase price paid by the plaintiff was not determined in, or guided by, a price in an established, efficient secondary trading market).

In *Semerenko*, the Third Circuit also rejected the inflation theory, stating that "an investor must also establish that the alleged misrepresentation prox-imately caused the decline in the security's value to satisfy the element of loss causation."[54] It did so with a more policy-oriented focus, however. The

---

[48] Semerenko v. Cendant Corp., 223 F.3d 165, 185 (3d Cir. 2000).
[49] *Robbins*, 116 F.3d at 1147.   [50] *Id.* at 1148.
[51] *Id.*   [52] *See supra* section III.B.1.
[53] *Basic*, 485 U.S. at 243.
[54] Semerenko v. Cendant Corp., 223 F.3d 165, 185 (3d Cir. 2000).

Semerenko court's concern was that "where the value of the security does not actually decline as a result of an alleged misrepresentation . . . the cost of the alleged misrepresentation is still incorporated into the value of the security and may be recovered at any time simply by reselling the security at the inflated price."[55] The court was certainly right that a plaintiff who sells before full market realization of the truth should have his or her damages reduced or eliminated by the extent to which the price continues to be inflated by the misstatement. But full elimination of this price inflation, and hence of the Third Circuit's worry, does not require that price at time of plaintiff's sale be below the price paid, as is required under the traditional loss-causation formulation. Again, other unrelated factors may have increased share price by more than the full deflation reduced it. Moreover, as more fully discussed below, the problem of sales prior to partial or full deflation could be considered in terms of the determination of individual damages rather than causation and thus is not necessarily fatal to the use of the inflation theory of loss causation.[56]

D. The Supreme Court's Missed Opportunity in Dura

Dura presented the Supreme Court with an opportunity to clear up this lower-court confusion completely. The Court had not developed the twin requirements of transaction causation and loss causation; indeed, it had never even commented on them prior to *Dura*. The Court was therefore in a particularly free position to end the confusion caused by the lower courts' misapplication of a framework of their own making and to throw out these ill-fitting requirements for fraud-on-the-market suits. In their place, the Court could have in clear language substituted the simple requirement, consistent with its reasoning in *Basic* and the fundamental logic of the fraud-on-the-market theory, that the plaintiff plead and prove that the defendant's misstatement inflated the price the plaintiff paid. Because of the defendant's wrongful misstatement, plaintiff paid an amount extra equal to this inflation for something with no greater fundamental value than if the misstatement had not been made. This overpayment is the injury suffered by the plaintiff and thus the injury on which the causation analysis should focus (although the plaintiff's

---

[55] *Id.* The court made this statement to suggest that earlier Third Circuit opinions that appeared to adopt the price-inflation theory of loss causation might be wrong. What the Third Circuit rule is at this point was not tested by this case, however, since the court found that the complaint alleged that the stock involved "was 'buoyed' by the defendants['] alleged misrepresentations, and that it dropped in response to disclosure of the alleged misrepresentations," *id.* at 186, and so the appellate court would have vacated the district court's granting of defendants' motion to dismiss under either approach.

[56] *See infra* section III.D.

recovery in damages would be limited to the extent that she receives at the time of sale a benefit arising from the same wrong because of any continuing inflation).[57]

Abandoning the rhetorical confusion of the transaction-causation and loss-causation framework and instead straightforwardly addressing the underlying reality in the way suggested here would have done more than just clear up confusion. It would have brought the analysis of causation in fraud-on-the-market cases in line with the modern economic thinking that has been the driving force behind the evolution of securities regulation over the past two decades. This thinking has an *ex ante* focus and is concerned with the law's effects on the structure of incentives of the various actors involved at the time the plaintiff enters into the transaction. The *ex ante* focus calls for use of the out-of-pocket measure of damages (i.e., the extra amount the plaintiff pays at time of purchase because of the misstatement, assuming full market realization of the true situation prior to the sale). As we have seen, unlike actions based on traditional reliance, there are no strong reasons in the case of fraud-on-the-market actions to depart from this measure.[58] The out-of-pocket measure has in fact been the standard measure of damages all along in Rule 10b-5 cases generally.[59]

In this regard, it is worth noting that straightforwardly addressing the underlying reality in the way suggested here corresponds to the well-known 1982 article by Daniel Fischel, in which he argues, using modern finance theory, that in cases involving actively traded securities, proof of materiality, causation, and measure of damages should all go to the same issue: the amount by which the misstatement inflated share price.[60] While the Supreme Court cited Fischel's article in *Basic*,[61] the lower courts have largely ignored its implications, as they have fashioned a post-*Basic* theory of causation for fraud-on-the-market cases. As discussed below, the Court in its *Dura* opinion failed to seize this opportunity to end the confusion created by the lower courts. It retained the transaction-causation and loss-causation framework and rhetorically treated the case of the plaintiff who sells prior to the market beginning to realize the true situation as one involving an absence of loss causation rather than an absence of damages. Despite its rhetorical shortcomings, however, the Court's opinion leaves open ample room for the development of rules with substantive

---

[57] The reasoning for limiting recovery in this fashion corresponds to Judge Sneed's concurring opinion in *Green v. Occidental*, 541 F.2d 1335, 1341–46 (9th Cir. 1976) (Sneed, J., concurring).

[58] See *supra* section II.B.   [59] See text accompanying *supra* note 35.

[60] See Daniel Fischel, *Use of Modern Finance Theory in Securities Fraud Cases Involving Actively Traded Securities*, 38 BUS. LAW. 1, 12–13 (1982).

[61] *Basic*, 485 U.S. at 246 n.24.

results that make good policy sense. It is simply important that courts keep the underlying reality in mind as a guide in future action.

III. THE HISTORY OF *DURA* AND THE SUPREME COURT'S HOLDING

Dura involved a class action by plaintiffs who were open-market purchasers of defendant Dura Pharmaceutical's shares. They alleged that they had been damaged as a result of Dura falsely claiming progress on an asthma-medication delivery device that the FDA ultimately found not approvable. The alleged misstatements were made in a series of press releases issued from April 1997 through January 1998. On February 24, 1998, Dura publicly announced that it expected less-than-forecast earnings, which it attributed to slow sales of one of its current products, Ceclor CD. Dura's share price dropped sharply and the plaintiffs so alleged. In November 1998, Dura publicly announced the FDA finding that the asthma-medication device was not approvable. The plaintiffs did not allege that the November announcement was followed by a price drop.[62] The class consisted of all purchasers of Dura Pharmaceutical shares between April 15, 1997, when the firm reported strong progress selling Ceclor CD as well as the completion of patient dosing (a step in the tests needed as part of the FDA approval process for the asthma-medication delivery device) and February 24, 1998, the date of the less-than-forecast earnings announcement.

The district court dismissed the complaint in *Dura* for failure to state a claim, deciding that, because the complaint did not allege any relationship between the negative FDA finding and the February price drop, the plaintiff failed to plead "loss causation."[63] The Ninth Circuit reversed, requiring only a "pleading that the price at the time of purchase was overstated and sufficient indication of the cause."[64] The Supreme Court granted certiorari on whether, contrary to the Ninth Circuit's position, a plaintiff in a fraud-on-the-market suit such as *Dura* must demonstrate loss causation by pleading and proving a causal connection between the misstatement and a subsequent decline in price.[65] Defendants, in support of their position that such a demonstration was

---

[62] The price in fact fell 21 percent, from $12^3/_8$ to $9^3/_4$. Brief for the United States as Amicus Curiae Supporting Petitioners at 2–3, Broudo v. Dura Pharms., Inc., 544 U.S. 336 (2005) (No. 03–932), 2004 WL 2069564.

[63] *In re* Dura Pharms., Inc. Sec. Litig., Civil No. 99CV0151-L (NLLS), 2000 U.S. Dist. LEXIS 15258 (S.D. Cal. July 11, 2000).

[64] Broudo v. Dura Pharms., Inc., 339 F.3d 933, 938 (9th Cir. 2003), *rev'd*, 544 U.S. 336 (2005).

[65] Dura Pharms., Inc. v. Broudo, 542 U.S. 936 (2004) (mem.).

required, cited opinions from other circuits.[66] They were joined in their certiorari petition by an amicus brief from the solicitor general and the Securities and Exchange Commission.

The Supreme Court reversed the Ninth Circuit's judgment. The Court held that a plaintiff cannot establish causation simply by alleging and subsequently establishing that the price of the security on the date of purchase was inflated because of a misstatement made by the issuer.[67] Since the complaint alleged only that the asthma-medication delivery device misrepresentations resulted in the plaintiffs paying artificially inflated prices for Dura securities and that they suffered damages, the Court concluded that the complaint was legally insufficient and remanded the case.[68]

IV. ISSUES REMAINING OPEN

The Court's holding in *Dura* is extremely narrow. It settles only one issue: a plaintiff who merely alleges and subsequently establishes that a positive, material misstatement in violation of Rule 10b-5 inflated the price she paid for a security has not done enough to establish causation in a fraud-on-the-market action for damages. The pleadings must provide in addition some indication of the loss and the causal connection the plaintiff has in mind.[69] And proof at trial must provide evidence that the inflated purchase price proximately caused an economic loss.[70] The Court, however, did not specify what kinds of allegations and proofs would be sufficient to meet these standards. Specifically, there are two large, open questions. One concerns what constitutes a loss – specifically whether a plaintiff would ever be allowed to establish that a misstatement caused a loss in a situation in which the price at the time suit is brought (or, if earlier, the time of sale) is higher than the purchase price. Stated in more general terms, the first large, open question is whether a plaintiff's loss (and hence damages) is limited to his actual loss – that is, the difference between purchase price and the price at time of sale. The second large, open question concerns what, beyond the allegation that the misstatement inflated the purchase price, would constitute a sufficient "indication of the loss and the causal connection" for purposes of pleading and what, for purposes of proof at trial, would constitute the kind of evidence sufficient to establish that there had been an inflation in price that proximately caused an economic

---

[66] *See, e.g.,* Semerenko v. Cendant Corp., 223 F.3d 165, 185 (3d Cir. 2000); Robbins v. Koger Props., Inc., 116 F.3d 1441, 1148 (11th Cir. 1997).

[67] Dura Pharms., Inc. v. Broudo, 544 U.S. 336, 338 (2005).

[68] *Id.* at 346–48.   [69] *Id.* at 346–47.

[70] *Id.* at 345–46.

loss. In particular, is it necessary for the plaintiff to plead and prove a price drop immediately following the public announcement of the truth? Or can the pleadings or proof at trial consist of some other kind of indication that the purchase price had been inflated by the misstatement and that the market had later realized the true situation dissipating this inflation?

A. *Sale Price Above Purchase Price*

Consider the situation in which the price at time of sale (or, if earlier, at time the suit is brought) is higher than the price at time of purchase but not as high as it would have been had not a misstatement-caused inflation in price dissipated in the interim. In other words, other news in the interim that was relevant to the issuer's future but unrelated to the subject matter of the misstatement was, on balance, sufficiently positive that it pushed the price up more than it had been pushed down by the dissipation of the inflation.

In one sense of the word, the plaintiff has suffered no loss. She sold, or at time of suit would have been able to sell, the share for more than she paid for it. In such a situation, application of the loss-causation rule developed in the context of a traditional reliance-based action would bar recovery. This rule required that the purchased security had declined in value from what was paid (or was sold at a loss) and that the decline or loss was in some way reasonably related to the falsity of the statement that induced the purchase.[71] This also appears to be the position urged on the Court by the defendants in *Dura*, even though *Dura* was a fraud-on-the-market suit, not a traditional reliance-based suit.[72]

In another sense of the word, however, the plaintiff has suffered a loss. Assuming that she does not sell before full market realization of the true situation, the defendant's misstatement has made her worse off in an amount equal to its inflation of the purchase price. But for the misstatement, she would have paid exactly that much less for the share; yet her return over her period of ownership (however long, and from whatever mix of dividends, distributions, and sales proceeds that she receives) would have been just as

---

[71] *See, e.g.,* Emergent Capital Inv. Mgmt. v. Stonepath Group, Inc., 343 F.3d 189, 197 (2d Cir. 2003). The loss-causation rule in traditional reliance-based actions and a rationale for its *ex post* perspective for assessing whether a loss has occurred is discussed *supra* section II.

[72] The question that the defendants successfully sought to have the Court certify was whether a plaintiff in a fraud-on-the-market suit must demonstrate loss causation by pleading and proving a causal connection between the misstatement and a subsequent decline in price. Petition for Writ of Certiorari, *Dura*, 544 U.S. 336 (No. 03–932), 2003 WL 23146437. *See also,* John C. Coffee, *Loss Causation After "Dura": Something for Everybody,* N.Y. L. J., May 20, 2005, at 5.

great.[73] Interestingly, the U.S. government, while arguing in its amicus briefs in *Dura* that the Ninth Circuit ruling in *Dura* should be reversed, took the position that the plaintiff in the situation being considered here has suffered a loss.[74]

The Court explicitly reserved decision on this matter. It did so by first noting that when a share purchaser who claims that the purchase price has been inflated by a misrepresentation later sells at a price below the purchase price, the lower price may be the result of factors unrelated to the misrepresentation, not the dissipation of an inflated price. The Court then went on to observe that unrelated factors can also push the sale price above the purchase price, stating: "The same is true in respect of a claim that a share's higher price is lower than it would otherwise have been – a claim we do not consider here."[75]

B. Sufficient Pleadings and Proofs at Trial That the Misstatement Caused a Loss

What constitutes sufficient pleadings and proofs at trial that the defendant's misstatement inflated the purchase price in a way that resulted in a loss to the plaintiff? To see the matters left open by the Supreme Court in this regard and the variety of considerations relevant to the task of future courts in shaping definitive rules with regard to these open matters, it is helpful to consider four different situations. In each, a plaintiff-purchaser in a fraud-on-the-market action claims that she was injured by a defendant-issuer's misstatement. At some point after the purchase, there is an unambiguous public announcement by the issuer that the original statement was false. For simplicity, assume that

---

[73] This statement is somewhat of an oversimplification, as it assumes that the misstatement does not enable management to operate the firm in a different way. It is quite possible that the misstatement allows managers more slack, and so they run the firm less profitably, or that the misstatement permits managers to obtain more compensation. Both are actions that would reduce future returns to the plaintiff. Or the misstatement could allow the firm to obtain financing on more favorable terms, thus possibly increasing the value of the firm. Each of these possibilities, however, raises issues of corporate and securities law that differ from the cause of action under study here.

[74] In its briefs, the government makes statements such as "the inflation attributable to the untruth . . . could also be removed through an increase in price that is smaller than it otherwise would have been . . ." Brief for the United States as Amicus Curiae Supporting Petitioners at 7, *Dura*, 544 U.S. 336 (No. 03–932), 2004 WL 2069564; and "a price decline may not be a necessary condition for loss causation, however, because the inflation attributable to the fraud could be reduced or eliminated even if there were a net increase in price." Brief for the United States as Amicus Curiae at 13, *Dura*, 544 U.S. 336 (No. 03–932), 2004 WL 1205204.

[75] *Dura*, 544 U.S. at 343.

suit is brought immediately after the announcement (as soon as the market has had a chance to reflect any reaction to the announcement of the truth).[76] Two other assumptions will be made in this initial discussion of the four situations; these assumptions will be dropped in subsequent discussion. One initial assumption is that the plaintiff purchases her shares immediately after the misstatement (as soon as the market has had a chance to reflect any reaction to the original misstatement). The other is that in each of the four situations, the purchase price is greater than the share price at the time the suit is brought (and, if the plaintiff sold before the suit was brought, the price at time of sale as well).

Ultimately, when the discussion of the remaining open issues is complete, the implications of four potentially critical variables will have been considered: (1) Was there a significant price drop after the unambiguous public announcement of the falsity of the misstatement or not? (2) Did the plaintiff continue to hold her shares until after this public announcement of the truth or did she sell earlier? (3) Did the plaintiff purchase the shares immediately after the misstatement was made or later? and (4) Was the sale price lower or higher than the purchase price? The implications of the fact that most fraud-on-the-market actions are class actions will also be considered.

1. The First Situation: Price Drops Immediately after the Public Announcement of the Truth While Plaintiff Still Holds Shares

In the first situation, the plaintiff still holds the shares at the time suit is brought. She alleges and proves at trial that immediately after the announcement of the falsity of the misrepresentation, the price dropped significantly.

There is little doubt that this plaintiff satisfies the Court's requirements under *Dura* concerning causation. The drop in price after the announcement strongly indicates that the misstatement, when made, inflated price. It would simultaneously indicate, consistent with the efficient market hypothesis, that after the announcement, the market realized the true situation, thereby dissipating the inflation in price. The misstatement caused the plaintiff to pay more than she would have otherwise and, because she held her shares until the inflation had dissipated, he or she did not recoup her injury through a sale at a similarly inflated price. Thus she suffered a loss as a result of the

---

[76] This assumption is made for expositional convenience to avoid needing to describe separately the state of affairs in which the plaintiff sells after the public announcement but before the suit is brought from the state of affairs in which the plaintiff still holds the shares at the time suit is brought. Any differences in the results between these two states of affairs is not important for points I make in this discussion.

misstatement.[77] Given these considerations, the plaintiff's allegation of the price drop immediately after the announcement of the falsity of the misstatement would certainly satisfy the Court's requirement that the plaintiff allege "some indication of the loss and causal connection." Proof of this price drop at trial would be a strong indication both that the misrepresentation inflated the purchase price and that the inflation later dissipated before the plaintiff sold, thereby proximately causing a loss.[78]

What, though, about cases in which, unlike this first situation, there is no share-price drop immediately following the announcement? Is there any other kind of evidence that satisfies the Court's loss-causation requirements and, if so, under what circumstances? Some of the circuit court opinions cited by the defendants in *Dura* appear to suggest that nothing else would do.[79] But there are respectable arguments for allowing submission of a broader range of evidence on the matter, as is elaborated just below in the discussion of the second and third situations, and the Supreme Court has left this question open.

[77] I assume throughout this chapter that the impact on the underlying fundamental value of the issuer's shares of the facts asserted by the misstatement, if these facts were true, would remain constant. *See infra* section VI.E for further discussion of this assumption.

[78] Modern corporate finance teaches us that calculations of price drops or increases of this sort should, when possible, be done on an adjusted basis using the market model to take into account the influence of other factors that are simultaneously moving share prices in the market generally. RONALD J. GILSON & BERNARD S. BLACK, THE LAW AND FINANCE OF CORPORATE ACQUISITIONS 194–95 (2d ed. 1995). While courts and securities litigants increasingly recognize that price drops and increases should be calculated in this fashion, the practice is far from universal. All of the inferences in this chapter that I suggest can be derived from the fact that price drops or increases are stronger when they are calculated on a market-adjusted basis. Where the plaintiff submits only an unadjusted price change as evidence supporting his claim that the misstatement inflated his purchase price, it is appropriate for the defendant to be able to introduce market-adjusted data. If the a defendant's data convincingly show that there has been no price change on a market-adjusted basis, the inferences suggested here that can be drawn from an adjusted price change would be unwarranted. Where the plaintiff does submit to a market-adjusted price change as evidence supporting his claim that the misstatement inflated his purchase price, it is also appropriate that the defendant be allowed to introduce any evidence that some other firm-specific event occurred simultaneously that can explain the price movement. The inferences in this chapter that I suggest can be derived from price drops or increases assume that the defendant presents no persuasive evidence of this kind. If in fact the defendant does introduce evidence that some other firm-specific event unrelated to the misstatement or its correction explains the price change, then again the inferences suggested here would be unwarranted.

[79] Semerenko v. Cendant Corp., 223 F.3d 165, 185 (3d Cir. 2000); Robbins v. Koger Props., Inc., 116 F.3d 1441, 1148 (11th Cir. 1997). Each of these cases calls for pleading and proof that there was a causal connection between the misstatement and a subsequent decline in price. It is not clear whether these courts maintain that to establish the causal connection, the decline in price needs to be subsequent to the public announcement of the truth or only subsequent to the original misstatement.

2. The Second Situation: Price Does Not Drop Immediately after the Public Announcement of the Truth While Plaintiff Still Holds Shares

In this second situation, unlike the first, there is no significant price drop immediately after the announcement of the falsity of the misstatement. Since we assume that suit is brought immediately after the announcement and that the price after the announcement is lower than at the time of purchase, there has been a price drop at some point, just earlier than the announcement. Like in the first situation, the plaintiff still holds the shares at the time suit is brought.

In this second situation, the plaintiff should again easily be able to allege and prove that the market realized the true situation. This is because the issuer made an unambiguous public announcement that the earlier misstatement was false. The efficient market hypothesis tells us, therefore, that to the extent, if any, that the misstatement inflated the purchase price, the price after the public announcement was no longer inflated by the misstatement. Thus, to the extent that the misstatement caused the plaintiff to pay more than she otherwise would have, she did not recoup her injury through a sale at a similarly inflated price. As a consequence, if the misstatement did inflate the purchase price, it caused the plaintiff to suffer a loss.

Did the misstatement in fact inflate the purchase price, however? The fact that there was no negative price reaction after the unambiguous announcement is unhelpful to the plaintiff's claim, but it does not rule out the possibility that the misstatement inflated the purchase price. This is because the misstatement might initially have inflated the share price, but the market may have realized the true situation prior to the public announcement of the truth. Complete market realization of the true situation in this context means that the price is no longer any higher than it would have been if the misstatement had never been made. Prior to an unambiguous public announcement, the operation of one or more phenomena may lead to a complete market realization of the truth. One way is a series of earlier, smaller disclosures by the issuer or others that gradually led market participants whose actions set price to conclude that the misstatement was false. Another is that the price was pushed back to the level it would have been but for the misstatement as a result of trading by insiders or others based on nonpublic information or rumors concerning the true state of affairs. Another would be a growing quiet awareness on the part of certain highly sophisticated market participants – arbitrageurs and sell-side analysts – that previously publicly available facts, which for a time had gone unnoticed or seemed unimportant, were in fact inconsistent with the misstatements. Yet another possibility is that, without the issuer recanting its earlier misstatement, the higher earnings or sales in the future that one would have predicted based on the misstatement simply did not materialize or the poor financial condition of the issuer, which the misstatement masked, subsequently became obvious.

In *Dura*, the Supreme Court's requirements concerning how a plaintiff establishes that a misstatement caused a loss are phrased in terms of what more, beyond inflation in the purchase price, needs to be pled and proved. The Court's decision to phrase its requirements in these terms was presumably due to the way that the Ninth Circuit opinion in *Dura* phrased its holding. Unfortunately, phrasing the loss-causation requirements in these terms is likely to lead to new confusion. In the very common situation in which the plaintiff still holds the shares after the public announcement of the falsity of the misstatement, the something more is the public announcement. As just discussed, where the plaintiff already has clearly established that the misstatement inflated the purchase price, the public announcement is surely enough additional evidence to establish that the plaintiff suffered a loss. Indeed, the only coherent story that the Court tells to explain how an inflated purchase price might not lead to a loss is where the investor resells at the still-inflated price.[80] The efficient market hypothesis rules out any continuing inflation in price once there has been an unambiguous public announcement of the falsity of the misstatement.

There is thus an irony in the Supreme Court's phrasing of its loss-causation requirements in terms of what more needs to be established beyond the inflation in purchase price. For a plaintiff who still holds shares at the time of the public announcement, if anything is going to be difficult to establish, it is that the purchase price was inflated, not the something more. I suspect that in cases such as this second situation, in which there is no significant share-price drop immediately following the public announcement, the issue of whether the misstatement inflated the purchase price is in fact the issue troubling the Court as well. The Court is probably concerned that, in many of these cases, there was in fact no inflation in the first place and hence no possibility that misstatement caused a loss. The misstatement, although arguably facially material, did not inflate the purchase price and unrelated factors caused the share-price drop observed prior to the public announcement.[81]

In some cases resembling this second situation, the misstatement did inflate the purchase price and hence certainly did cause the plaintiff a loss; in others it did not inflate the purchase price and hence could not possibly have caused a loss. The existence of both of these possibilities gives rise to a question that will have to be addressed by future courts: when there is no significant

---

[80] *See infra* section V.B.   [81] *See infra* section V.B.

price drop after the public announcement of the falsity of the misstatement, what alternative kinds of evidence, if any, will the plaintiff be allowed to introduce in order to establish that the misstatement inflated the purchase price?

The strongest alternative evidence would be a showing that the misstatement itself, when initially made, was immediately followed by a significant price increase. This kind of evidence should be at least as acceptable as evidence of a significant price drop at the time of the public announcement of the falsity of the misstatement because it is at least as good a market confirmation of the importance of the misstatement. The problem, however, is that of all of the misstatements that do inflate the purchase prices of the issuers' shares, probably most are made to avoid disappointing expectations rather than to increase expectations, which means they are not followed by an immediate significant price increase.

Thus, it is important whether other, less definitive kinds of evidence of purchase price inflation are also acceptable to prove loss causation. If less definitive evidence is allowed, it would need to relate to a combination of showings. First, the plaintiff would need to establish that the misstatement was self-evidently important in the sense that, if it were considered reliable, it would significantly affect investors' expectations concerning the issuer's future returns. The importance of the statement in this sense is something that could be established, for example, by testimony of analysts or industry experts. Such testimony would tend to be more persuasive if it was empirically supported by studies showing the effect of similar announcements on the share prices of other firms. Second, the plaintiff would need to establish that the misstatement was in fact believed by the participants in the market whose actions set prices. One indication of the extent to which it was believed by this set of participants would be the reactions of analysts or the financial media at the time the misstatement was made. Finally, the plaintiff would have to explain how a claim that the misstatement inflated the purchase price could be consistent with the absence of a price decline immediately after the later public announcement of its falsity. Such an explanation would presumably require the testimony of financial economists or securities market professionals able to point to grounds for believing that, by one or more of the other routes discussed above, the market was realizing the true situation prior to the public announcement. The more persuasive the first two showings (the self-evident importance of the misstatement and its acceptance as true by the market), the less complete this third showing (the explanation of how the market realized the true situation prior to the public announcement) needs to be for the overall case to be convincing.

Nothing in the Supreme Court's holding in *Dura* rules out the use of these other, less definitive kinds of evidence. Since market realization of the true situation by routes other than a public announcement is not uncommon, allowing submission of these other kinds of evidence will permit actions to succeed in the many cases where the purchase price genuinely was inflated but there was no negative price reaction immediately after the announcement. On the other hand, because these other kinds of evidence are less reliable than either a price drop immediately after the announcement or a price increase immediately after the misstatement, allowing them will also permit more actions to succeed where in fact the misstatement did not inflate the purchase price.

Of all of the kinds of cases in which a plaintiff might claim market realization of the true situation by other routes prior to an unambiguous public announcement of the falsity of the misstatement, the easiest to show are those involving allegations that the price dropped after either (1) the higher earnings or sales in the future that one would have predicted based on the misstatement did not materialize, or (2) the poor financial condition of the issuer, which the misstatement masked, subsequently became obvious. Indeed, how to deal with these kinds of allegations has been a central question in many of the lower-court fraud-on-the-market causation cases decided since the Supreme Court's decision in *Dura*.

In some of these cases, courts refuse to accept such allegations as satisfying the loss-causation requirement under circumstances suggesting that they might as a general matter always insist on an allegation of price drop after the misrepresentation itself has been unambiguously identified and corrected.[82]

---

[82] For example, in an unpublished opinion, the Sixth Circuit affirmed a district-court dismissal with prejudice of a complaint alleging that during the first half of 2001, Kmart improperly reported, as a reduction in current expenses, rebates that it hoped to receive before the end of the year. D.E.&J. Ltd. P'ship. v. Conway, 133 Fed. App'x 994, 996–97 (6th Cir. 2005). The complaint alleged a sharp drop in share price in later 2001 after Kmart reported flat sales in September and declining sales in November and December; a further 60 percent price drop followed Kmart's announcement of filing for bankruptcy on January 22, 2002. The complaint alleged as well that starting on January 25, 2002, there had been various announcements suggesting accounting improprieties, capped by a restatement of 2001 earnings on May 15, 2002, which included a reversal of the treatment of the hoped-for rebates. *Id.* at 996–97, 999–1001. There was no allegation of a drop in price after the May 15, 2002, restatement. *Id.* at 1001. The court found that "D.E.&J.'s causation theory looks remarkably like Broudo's allegations in his complaint [in *Dura*]." *Id.* at 1000. In support of this finding, the court stated, "D.E.&J. never alleged that Kmart's bankruptcy announcement disclosed any prior misrepresentation to the market," and "D.E.&J. has done nothing more than note that a stock price dropped after a bankruptcy, never alleging the market's acknowledgment of prior misrepresentations that caused that drop." *Id.* These statements come close to saying that price drops following disclosures that reveal the true situation are not sufficient to establish loss causation because

If this interpretation is correct, the implicit rule seems harsh, since often the announcement of the falsity of the misstatement is the last act in a drama in which the true troubled situation had become apparent well before.

Admittedly, the disappointment concerning earnings that leads to a price drop may only be at most in part due to an earlier misstatement. Similarly, the revelation of poor financial condition leading to a price drop may only at most have been partly hidden by an earlier misstatement. Thus, in each case, the price drop that follows these events does not show with the same clarity that the misstatement in fact inflated price in the first place as would a price drop that follows an unambiguous public announcement of the falsity of the misstatement. This is a particularly difficult problem where an issuer's share price has dropped substantially, and it is obvious that at least some significant portion of decline in the market's valuation is due to factors unrelated to the misstatement.

On the other hand, sometimes the relationship between an original misstatement and at least a portion of the subsequent disappointment or revelation is fairly clear, for example, when premature earnings recognition in violation of generally accepted accounting principles (GAAP) is followed within a few quarters by an earnings disappointment of a similar magnitude. A dollar more in the earlier period obtained through premature recognition is bound to mean a dollar less in some subsequent period. If the market did not understand at the time of the earlier period earnings announcement that the earnings for that period had been enhanced in this way, falsely optimistic expectations about subsequent period earnings were bound to develop and ultimately bound to be disappointed. In apparent recognition of the existence of such circumstances

they do not specifically identify the misstatement itself and announce its falsity. *See also In re Tellium, Inc. Sec. Litig.*, No. 02-cv-5878, 2005 U.S. Dist. LEXIS 19467 (D.N.J. June 30, 2005); *In re Bus. Objects S.A. Sec. Litig.*, No. C 04-2401 MJJ, 2005 U.S. Dist. LEXIS 20215 (N.D. Cal. July 27, 2005).

Taking a perhaps more middle ground, the court in *Porter v. Conseco, Inc.*, No. 1:02-cv-01332-DFH-TAB, 2005 Dist. LEXIS 15466 (S.D. Ind. July 14, 2005), granted without prejudice a defendant's loss-causation-based motion to dismiss a complaint alleging major accounting irregularities and a drop in price after the company made an announcement revealing that it was performing poorly but not disclosing the existence of the irregularities. The court said that "this is not a case where plaintiffs can point to a sharp drop in the company's stock price following the announcement of the allegedly concealed truth. The stock had long since hit bottom before these alleged misrepresentations." *Id.* at 12. The court noted that plaintiffs claimed in argument that the truth was beginning to "leak out" and thus was contributing to the slide in share prices. The court responded that "whether the [*Dura* Court's] use of the phrase 'leak out' shows that plaintiff's suggestion would be sufficient under *Dura Pharmaceuticals* is not clear. It is clear, however, that this theory is certainly not what plaintiffs have alleged in the operative complaint." *Id.*

and the resulting harshness of an absolute bar, other courts have denied loss-causation-based defendant motions to dismiss or for summary judgment where the plaintiffs have alleged that the price dropped when the higher earnings or sales in the future that one would have predicted based on the misstatement did not materialize, or when the poor financial condition of the issuer, which the misstatement masked, subsequently became obvious.[83]

3. The Third Situation: Price Does Not Drop Immediately after Public Announcement of the Truth and Plaintiff Has Sold Shares Earlier

In this third situation, like in the second, there is a price drop prior to the announcement of the falsity of the misstatement, but there is no significant price drop immediately after the announcement. Unlike in the second situation, however, the plaintiff sells before the announcement. In this third situation, to prove that the misstatement caused a loss, the plaintiff must show both that the misstatement inflated the purchase price and that his sale occurred after at least partial market realization of the true situation. To establish that the misstatement inflated price, the plaintiff would need to make the same showings, as would the plaintiff in the second situation, with regard to the self-evident importance of the misstatement and its acceptance by the market as true. The third showing relating to how the market realized the true situation prior to the public announcement of the misstatement's falsity takes on new importance, however. This is because the plaintiff will not only need to explain defensively why the lack of market reaction to the announcement

---

[83] *See, e.g., In re* Daou Sys., Inc. Sec. Litig., 411 F.3d 1006 (9th Cir. 2005) (reversing a district court's grant of a defendant's loss-causation-based motion to dismiss a complaint alleging accounting violations involving premature recognition of income and a stock-price drop after a later announcement that disclosed disappointing earnings but not the fact that the disappointing earnings were the result of prematurely recognized income in earlier periods); *In re* Immune Response Sec. Litig., 375 F. Supp. 2d 983 (S.D. Cal. 2005) (denying a defendant's loss-causation-based motion to dismiss a complaint alleging (1) misstatements that predicted likely Food and Drug Administration approval of an anti-HIV drug and that asserted certain favorable test results and (2) alleging a price drop after publication of an academic paper contested by the issuer that cast doubt on the test results and a further price drop after a financial coventurer pulled out); *In re* Loewen Group, Inc. Sec. Litig., No. 98–6740, 2005 U.S. Dist. LEXIS 23841 (E.D. Pa. Oct. 18, 2005) (denying a defendant's loss-causation-based motion for summary judgment with regard to a suit in which plaintiffs provided evidence that the issuer overstated income by failing, when booking zero-interest installment sales, to discount to present value the future installments and that share prices dropped after the company's announcement of $80 million in charges for "reserves and other adjustments" that did not reveal that a portion of the charge was to account for the previously disregarded imputed interest, but where the plaintiff produced no evidence that the share price dropped after a later disclosure of the accounting irregularity itself).

of the falsity of the misstatement does not undermine the plaintiff's other evidence showing the misstatement's importance and acceptance as true but also must affirmatively show that the partial or full market realization of the true situation occurred prior to sale of the shares.

This difference is significant. At least where share price continued to fall after the plaintiff's sale, any weakness in the plaintiff's showing that the decline prior to his sale was due to market realization of the true situation cannot, unlike in the second situation, be compensated for by the strength of his showings relating to the misstatement's self-evident importance and acceptance as true. The plaintiff needs to establish that market realization of the true situation occurred prior to his sale in order to show that he did not recoup his injury through resale at an inflated price. The lack of a significant price drop after the announcement of the falsity of the misstatement – despite a strong showing of the self-evident importance of the misstatement and its market acceptance as true – may be just as easily explained as the result of a market realization of the true situation after the plaintiff's sale as before. Again, while nothing in the Supreme Court's *Dura* opinion rules out the acceptability of the kinds of evidence that the plaintiff in this third situation would need to introduce, a presentation of the same evidence by the plaintiff in the third situation would be less reliable in showing the misstatement really caused the plaintiff economic disadvantage than if the same evidence were introduced by the plaintiff in the second situation. This lower level of reliability provides a rationale for a bright-line rule prohibiting a finding of loss causation in cases resembling this third situation but not prohibiting such a finding in cases resembling the second situation. The existence of a rationale does not necessarily mean, however, that such a bright-line rule should be adopted. Again, there is the familiar trade-off involved in adopting such a rule. On the one hand, it prevents the introduction of evidence that is less reliable, and thus it will block actions that otherwise would have succeeded where in fact the misstatement did not cause the plaintiff economic disadvantage. On the other hand, it will also block actions that otherwise would have succeeded where in fact the misstatement did cause the plaintiff economic disadvantage.

4. The Fourth Situation: Price Drops Immediately after the Public Announcement of the Truth but the Plaintiff Sells Earlier
In this situation, like in the first, there is a price drop immediately after the public announcement of the falsity of the misstatement. Unlike in the first situation, but like the third, the plaintiff sells before the announcement. The plaintiff in this situation cannot claim a loss based on the portion of inflation in his purchase price indicated by the price drop at the time of the

public announcement. This is because he sold before market realization of this portion of the inflation. Thus, the price he received still reflected some inflation, thereby allowing him to recoup of that portion of his injury. To prove that the misstatement caused any loss, the plaintiff must both show that the misstatement inflated his purchase price by more than was indicated by the price drop after the public announcement and that his sale was after the market realization of the facts relating to this additional inflation.

This plaintiff's proof problems are therefore essentially identical to the plaintiff in the third situation. He cannot use the price drop after the public announcement to establish that his purchase price was inflated in a way that caused him a loss. He needs to show the existence of some additional inflation that is not indicated by a postannouncement price drop and he needs to show that market realization of the true situation with regard to this additional inflation occurred prior to his sale. As a consequence, future courts face the same range of possible rules concerning what evidence to admit with regard to this fourth situation as they do with regard to the third. Whatever set of rules the courts choose to deal with one situation should be applied to the other as well.

5. Changing the Four Situations to Reflect a Later Purchase

The four situations assume that the plaintiff purchases his or her shares immediately after the misstatement (as soon as the market has had a chance to reflect any reaction). What if the plaintiff purchases after that point but before the public announcement of the truth? A later purchase may alter the analysis because, to the extent, if any, that the market realized the truth by the time of the purchase, the inflation in the purchase price would be commensurately dissipated, along with the potential loss.

The fact that the purchase was made later should not alter any conclusions with regard to the first situation, in which the price drops after the public announcement of the falsity of the misstatement and the plaintiff is still holding her shares. Assuming that the plaintiff is not claiming an inflation in purchase price greater than what is indicated by the price drop after the public announcement, the market clearly had no realization of the true situation until the announcement and therefore not until after the plaintiff's purchase.[84] Her purchase price would have involved the full amount of the inflation caused

---

[84] Such a plaintiff, of course, might claim there was additional inflation that was not reflected in the price drop after the announcement because the market partially realized the true situation prior to the announcement. This portion of the plaintiff's claim is the same as the claim made by the plaintiff in the second purchase-time-changed situation, discussed just below in the text, and should be treated accordingly by the courts.

by the misstatement. Thus, the analysis made of the first situation as originally portrayed is equally applicable here and the plaintiff should easily be able to meet the Court's requirements in *Dura* concerning pleading and proving loss causation.

In the second purchase-time-changed situation, in which there is no price drop after the public announcement of the truth and the plaintiff is still holding the shares, the plaintiff needs to prove that the misstatement inflated price by a showing that the misstatement was self-evidently important and was accepted by the market as true. He also needs to reconcile the claim of price inflation with the absence of a price drop after announcement through an explanation of how the market realized the true situation prior to the public announcement. It was observed earlier, in the discussion of the second situation as originally portrayed, that the more persuasive the showings of the self-evident importance of the misstatement and its acceptance as true by the market, the less complete the explanation of how the market realized the true situation prior to the public announcement needs to be for the overall case to be convincing. Where the situation is changed so that the plaintiff makes his purchase later, however, this explanation of how the market realized the true situation takes on independent importance. This is because the plaintiff, to establish that he suffered a loss, needs to show that the market has not already fully realized the situation at the time of purchase. This change in the second situation, with the plaintiff purchasing later, consequently converts it to one that resembles the original portrayal of the third situation, in which the plaintiff buys right after the misstatement but sells before the public announcement.[85]

Because of this resemblance, the analysis made in the original portrayal of the third situation is equally applicable to this changed version of the second situation. As a consequence, future courts face the same range of possible rules concerning what evidence to admit with regard to this changed version of the second situation, with the plaintiff purchasing later, as they do with regard to the third situation as originally portrayed. Again, whatever set of rules they choose to apply to one should be applied to the other as well.

---

[85] In the second situation, as originally portrayed, I suggested that an alternative way for the plaintiff to demonstrate that her purchase price had been inflated was to introduce evidence that there was a price increase immediately after the misstatement was made. If the plaintiff could successfully show such a price increase, this would be sufficiently convincing evidence of the misstatement inflating her purchase price that she would not need to provide an explanation of how the market realized the true situation prior to the public announcement. With the second situation changed to reflect the plaintiff purchasing later, however, the plaintiff would need to provide such an explanation, in order to show that market realization had not occurred before her purchase.

The same can be said of changing the third and fourth situations to reflect a later purchase by the plaintiff. Whether the plaintiff purchases immediately after the misstatement (as the situations were originally portrayed) or later, the plaintiff's challenges are the same. She must demonstrate the existence of price inflation without the aid of a price drop after the announcement, and her explanation of how the market realized the true situation takes on importance independent of that demonstration.

6. Class Actions Typically Involve a Mix of These Situations

Most fraud-on-the-market actions are class actions. The typical class is composed of all persons who purchased an issuer's shares from the time of the misstatement until the time of the public announcement of its falsity. Thus, the class will contain plaintiffs in each of the situations described above as originally portrayed and as changed to reflect a later purchase time. These realities are something that will inevitably need to be considered by future courts as they fashion rules to deal with these situations. These class actions fall into two categories: instances in which the public announcement is followed by a significant price drop and instances in which it is not.

The analysis of class actions in which there is a price drop immediately following the public announcement of the truth is very straightforward. Assuming that there is no claim of inflation in purchase price beyond what is indicated by the price drop after the public announcement, the market clearly had no realization of the true situation until the announcement and therefore not until after the purchases by all of the members of the class.[86] For any member of the class still holding the shares at the time the suit is brought, whenever they were purchased, meeting the Court's requirements in *Dura* concerning pleading and proving loss causation should be easy. For the rest of the members of the class, meeting these requirements should be impossible because they sold prior to the announcement and thus recouped all of the claimed inflation.

The analysis of class actions in which the public announcement of the truth is not followed by an immediate significant price decline raises more issues. It is important to stress, however, that for the class as a whole, the proof problems are simpler than in many of the individual claims considered in the situations

---

[86] Similar to the discussion of individual claims in section IV.A.5 *supra*, there might be a claim that there was additional inflation that was not reflected in the price drop after the announcement because the market partially realized the true situation prior to the announcement. This portion of the claim is the same as the claim in a class action where the public announcement is not followed by an immediate significant price drop and should be treated accordingly by the courts.

above. This is because for every share purchased at least once between the time of the misstatement and the time of the public announcement, one or more members of the class suffers losses that in the aggregate equal the amount, if any, by which the share's price was inflated at the time of its initial purchase. If the share were purchased only once during the class period, then the single purchaser suffers the full loss. If the initial purchaser sells it prior to the end of the class period and the price at the time of her sale is still inflated to one extent or another, she will recoup part or all of her injury. But the second buyer of this share, if he holds until the suit is brought, sustains whatever portion of the loss was not sustained by the first buyer. If there are three or more purchases of the share during the class period, the same process is at work. Whatever portion of the loss is not sustained by the earlier purchasers is sustained by the later ones. Fundamentally, for the class as a whole, the situation is akin to the second situation (in which the plaintiff still holds her shares at the time of suit), but the situation is changed, as discussed above, to reflect that some of the shares purchased during the class period were initially purchased at a point in time later than immediately after the misstatement.

Probably, however, some members of the class would have purchased immediately after the misstatement, and others close enough to the date of the misstatement that if there was any inflation caused by the misstatement, its dissipation was unlikely to have already occurred. As far as the class as a whole is concerned, the shares initially purchased by these class members, even if sold by them prior to the announcement, are more akin to the second situation as initially portrayed, in which the individual plaintiff purchases immediately after the misstatement is made and still holds her shares at the time the suit is brought. With regard to these shares, one or more members of the class will, in aggregate, suffer losses equal to the full amount by which the price was initially inflated by the misstatement. Thus, the methods of proving that the class as a whole suffered at least some losses are the same as for the individual claimant in the originally portrayed second situation. One method of proof is to show that there was a price increase immediately following the misstatement. If there was no such increase, the other way of showing that the class as a whole sustained at least some losses is to establish that the misstatement inflated the price by a showing that the misstatement was self-evidently important and was accepted by the market as true, reconciling the claim of price inflation with the absence of a price drop after announcement through an explanation of how the market realized the true situation prior to the public announcement. Like the second situation as originally portrayed, to prove that the class as a whole suffered at least some damages, the explanation of how the market realized the true situation takes on no independent significance: the more persuasive the showing of the self-evident importance of the misstatement and its acceptance as true by the market, the less complete the explanation of how the market realized the true situation prior to the public announcement needs to be for the overall case to be convincing. As long as it is established that the misstatement inflated the price for each of the shares initially purchased immediately or soon after the misstatement was made, it follows that one or more members of the class suffered a loss that in aggregate equals the full amount by which the misstatement initially inflated the share price.

C. Combining the Open Questions

I have discussed the two large questions left open by the Court's opinion in *Dura* separately from each other in order to make clear what is at stake with each. Under some circumstances, there is a possible interaction between the two, however. Consider each of the four situations described above as initially portrayed, except this time with the modification that the purchase price is less than, not greater than, the share price at the time the suit is brought (and, if the plaintiff sold before the suit was brought, than the price at the time of sale as well).

1. Revisiting the First Situation

In the first situation, in which the announcement of the falsity of the misstatement is immediately followed by a significant stock-price drop and the plaintiff still holds the shares at the time suit is brought, this changed assumption that the price at the time of suit is higher than the purchase price turns out to be unimportant. This is because the significant price drop after the announcement is a very strong indication that the misstatement did inflate the purchase price. The fact that the price after the announcement is still higher than the purchase price does very little to undermine this conclusion since the drop after the announcement strongly suggests that the increase before the announcement was due to unrelated factors. Since the plaintiff clearly held the shares until after market realization of the true situation, the misstatement, which inflated her purchase price, unquestionably makes her economically worse off. The case is essentially as strong for providing compensation to the plaintiff in this price-trend-modified version of the first situation as it is in the first situation as originally portrayed. Unless the ultimate rule turns out to be that under no circumstances can there be compensation without an *ex post* loss, which in my view would be unfortunate,[87] the plaintiff in this

---

[87] *See supra* section IV.A.

price-trend-modified version of the first situation, with the price at the time of suit greater than purchase price, should still meet the Supreme Court's pleading and proof requirements under *Dura* concerning causation.

2. Revisiting the Second and Third Situations

In the second and third situations, however, where there is not a significant price drop after the falsity of the misstatement is announced, the fact that the price at time the suit was brought (or, in the third situation, at the time of sale) was higher than the price at time of purchase weakens the plaintiff's claim that the misstatement inflated the price.[88] In these situations, if the misstatement had in fact inflated the price, the dissipation of the inflation would have needed to occur between the time of purchase and the time of the announcement of the falsity of the misstatement (or, in the case of the third situation, the time of sale) and this dissipation would have exerted downward pressure on price. As for the other influences on price during this period, unrelated to the misstatement, there is just as great a probability that they, too, on a net basis, would have exerted a downward force on price as an upward one. This means that if there was any inflation to be dissipated, the combination of the dissipation of the inflation and the other unrelated influences on price were more likely to be negative than positive.[89] Thus, standing alone as a single piece of evidence, the fact that the price at the time of suit or earlier sale is higher than at the time of purchase suggests that it is more likely than not that there never existed any misstatement-caused inflation in the first place. Moreover, the greater the increase in price, the more likely this piece of evidence suggests that there was no inflation from the misstatement.

The fact that the price went up does not, of course, rule out the possibility that there was inflation in price due to the misstatement: as discussed earlier, the other unrelated influences on price might well on a net basis have been positive and enough so to more than counterbalance the downward force exerted on price from dissipation of an inflation due to the misstatement. The increase in price is simply, on a probabilistic basis, a negative piece of evidence to be weighed against whatever positive pieces of evidence the plaintiff might present in her efforts to show the self-evident importance of the misstatement and its acceptance as true by the market and to explain how the market realized

---

[88] The exception to this statement is when the price rose immediately after the misstatement was made.

[89] To be more precise, this statement would need to be modified to recognize that such unrelated factors push price up or down from a path that reflects the fact that, over the long, run share prices on average tend to grow. For relatively short periods of time, such as one or two quarters, however, this growth factor is likely to be small relative to the other factors at work.

the true situation prior to the public announcement of its falsity. Thus, one approach future courts might take is simply to consider all of these positive pieces of evidence offered by the plaintiff and, if they are persuasive enough to overcome the negative inference flowing from the fact that the price went up, find that the plaintiff established that the misstatement inflated price.

Alternatively, future courts might construct one of a number of possible bright-line rules triggered by the price at time of suit or earlier sale being higher than the purchase price. The most extreme rule for cases that otherwise resemble the second or third situations as originally portrayed would be an absolute bar on payment of damages. There exists a rationale for such a bright-line rule even if the law develops in a way that permits compensation despite the lack of an *ex post* loss in cases in which there is either a significant price drop immediately after the announcement of the truth (i.e., cases resembling the first situation) or in which there is a significant price rise immediately after the misstatement. If a case has neither of these characteristics, the plaintiff's argument that the misstatement inflated the price would, if allowed, have to rest on her showing of the self-evident importance of the misstatement and its acceptance as true by the market and her explanation of how the market realized the true situation prior to the public announcement of its falsity. The justification for a bright-line rule banning any such case would be that the plaintiff's argument is inherently weakened by the fact that the price at the time suit is brought is higher than the purchase price.

A less draconian bright-line rule would be an absolute bar on payment of damages only where the increase in price between time of purchase and time suit was brought (or earlier sale) was substantial relative to past fluctuations in price. Another approach would be to bar compensation unless the plaintiff can meet the burden of establishing the existence of unrelated factors that could be expected to increase price by more than he claims the misstatement inflated price.

With all of these bright-line rules, the usual trade-off is involved: the more restrictive the rule in terms of what evidence can be introduced, the more cases that will be blocked in which the misstatement in fact does cause the plaintiff economic disadvantage and the more cases that will be blocked in which it in fact does not.[90]

---

[90] My colleague Professor John Coffee favors a bar of some sort to recovery where the price at the time suit is brought (or, if earlier, at time of sale) is higher than the purchase price. Coffee, *supra* note 72, at 5. It is unclear, however, whether he favors a blanket bar to all such actions. He may simply favor a bright-line rule barring recovery unless there is strong, definitive evidence that the purchase price was inflated in the first place. In other words, he might allow recovery in the first situation, involving a price decrease after the announcement of the truth, or where

3. Revisiting the Fourth Situation

Again, assume the price at the time of sale is greater than the purchase price. Consider, with this price-trend modification in assumptions, the fourth situation, in which the share price drops significantly immediately after the announcement of the truth but where the plaintiff has sold her shares before that point. As noted in the earlier discussion of this fourth situation as originally portrayed, the plaintiff cannot claim a loss based on the portion of inflation in his purchase price indicated by the price drop at the time of the public announcement.[91] To prove that the misstatement caused him any loss, the plaintiff must show both that the misstatement inflated his purchase price by more than was indicated by the price drop after the public announcement and that his sale was after market realization of the facts relating to this additional inflation. The modifying fact that the price at time of sale is greater than the purchase price has the same significance as it does in modifying the second and third situations. Thus, this plaintiff's proof problems are essentially identical to the proof problems of the plaintiff under the price-trend-changed assumption in the second and third situations discussed just above, and the analysis set out just above is equally applicable to this modified version of the fourth situation. If courts use some kind of bright-line rule in these price-trend-modified second and third situations, they should use the same bright-line rule here.

V. THE COURT'S REASONING IN *DURA*

The Supreme Court describes the Ninth Circuit holding concerning what a securities fraud plaintiff needs to establish to prove "that the defendant's

there is a price rise immediately after the original misstatement, but otherwise bar recovery where the price at time of suit (or earlier sale) is higher than the purchase price.

Coffee's reasoning really only supports this latter, narrower bar. His stated concern is with what the absence of an *ex post* loss says about the likelihood that the price was inflated in the first place, not an insistence that an investor must suffer an *ex post* loss to have been made economically worse off by a misstatement. Coffee writes, "Economically, there is little conceptual difference between a price decline because of the discovery of a prior misstatement and a price that does not change because positive and negative news have offset each other." *Id.* at 8. He poses the following hypothetical, however. The share price increases by $5 from time of purchase to time of suit. A plaintiff claims that a misstatement inflated the price by $10 and that the market realization of the truth has dissipated this inflation while macroeconomic news has boosted the price by $15. Thus, the $5 price increase is consistent with the plaintiff's claim that the misstatement made him $10 worse off. But it is also consistent with the misstatement having caused no inflation in price and macroeconomic news boosting price by only $5, in which case the misstatement had no effect on the plaintiff's welfare. The hypothetical, Coffee says, illustrates the danger of "'phantom losses' that have no corroboration in actual market movements." *Id.*

[91] *See supra* section IV.B.4.

fraud caused an economic loss" as simply "that 'the price' of the security '*on the date of purchase* was inflated because of the misrepresentation.'"[92] The Court rejects this holding, stating, "In our view, the Ninth Circuit is wrong,"[93] and concluding, "normally . . . in fraud-on-the-market cases . . . an inflated purchase price will not itself constitute or proximately cause the relevant economic loss."[94] The Court gave a number of reasons for reaching this conclusion. These reasons, when scrutinized, appear to be rather confused and unfortunately do not provide much helpful guidance concerning how future courts should decide the open issues delineated above.

A. An Inflated Price Results in No Loss at Time of Purchase

The Supreme Court states that "as a matter of pure logic, at the moment the transaction takes place, the plaintiff has suffered no loss; the inflated purchase payment is offset by ownership of a share that *at that instant* possesses equivalent value."[95] The Court is thus apparently equating the value of a share at any moment in time to its market price at that time even when that price has been distorted by a misstatement. This rather slippery use of the term *value* is apparently based on the idea that the plaintiff could at the moment of a security's purchase turn around and resell it at the same price as he bought it. Using *value* in this way is contrary to one of the fundamental concepts in modern corporate finance – the value of a share means the expected dividends and other distributions, discounted to present value, that the holder or holders of the share, whoever that may be over time, will receive during the life of the issuing firm.[96] It also ignores that the primary purpose of the securities laws, including their antifraud provisions, is to promote economic efficiency and fairness by trying to minimize the gap between price and value as it is understood in this corporate finance sense. The market, with its capacity to digest information possessed by many different participants relevant to predicting what the issuer's future dividends and other distributions will be, is a very powerful appraiser of value but not when price is distorted by a material misstatement. More accurate share prices (i.e., prices that are closer to their fundamental values) enhance the efficient functioning of our economy by being better signals of where scarce capital should flow and by aiding in the mechanisms that provide appropriate discipline and incentives to management. Fairness is also related to minimizing the differences between price

---

[92] Dura Pharms., Inc. v. Broudo, 544 U.S. 336, 338 (2005) (citation omitted).
[93] *Id.*   [94] *Id.* at 342.
[95] *Id.*   [96] BREALEY ET AL., *supra* note 9, at 61–65.

and fundamental value. The Court's equating of value with price obscures the fact that while the plaintiff might be able instantly to turn around and sell for the same inflated price that he paid, eventually the truth will come out and eliminate the inflation. Thus, someone will be left holding the bag, having paid the premium but not able to resell at the premium.

The Supreme Court's use of the term *value* is odd for a second reason as well. Fraud-on-the-market suits are also available to sellers who sell at a price that has been depressed due to a negative misstatement. It seems unlikely that the Court would say the depressed price that the plaintiff received in such a case equaled the value of the share she gave up because she could have instantly turned around and repurchased the share for the same deflated price. Presumably, the Court would recognize that the plaintiff suffered a loss at the time of sale unless she in fact repurchased her shares at that same deflated price before the market realized the true situation. This hypothetical concerning a plaintiff-seller and a negative misstatement is completely symmetrical to one involving a plaintiff-purchaser and a positive misstatement, and there is no apparent rationale for treating them differently.

The Supreme Court's suggestion that a share's value equals its price is also at odds with established securities law when it comes to the calculation of damages. The standard measure of damages in Rule 10b-5 actions, including the Court's own jurisprudence on the matter, is the out-of-pocket measure (i.e., the extra amount that the plaintiff pays at the time of purchase because of the misstatement, assuming no resale at a price that is still inflated by the misstatement to one extent or another).[97] This could hardly be an appropriate measure of damages if value equals price at the time of purchase.

B. No Inevitable Link between an Inflated Share Price and Later Economic Loss

Having dismissed the idea that a loss could occur at the time of purchase, the Supreme Court argues that there also might not be a loss later, saying, "the logical link between the inflated share price and any later economic loss is not invariably strong."[98] In support of this second argument, the Court starts with the observation that "if, say, the purchaser sells the shares quickly before

---

[97] *See* Randall v. Loftsgaarden, 478 U.S. 647, 662 (1986); Estate Counseling Serv., Inc. v. Merrill Lynch, Pierce, Fenner & Smith, Inc., 303 F.2d 527, 532 (10th Cir. 1962); LOSS & SELIGMAN, *supra* note 34, at 4409–13.

[98] Dura Pharms., Inc. v. Broudo, 544 U.S. 336, 342 (2005).

the relevant truth begins to leak out, the misrepresentation will not have led to any loss."[99] It is certainly true, as already discussed, that it would be a mistake to grant damages to such a purchaser. The reason for not granting damages, however, is not that the purchaser did not incur an injury at the time of purchase as a result of defendant's wrongful misstatement; he did suffer an injury by having to pay more than he otherwise would have but for the misstatement. The reason for not granting damages is that the purchaser has received a benefit arising from the same wrong in an amount equal to the injury he suffered earlier. Indeed, a bar on the payment of damages to the extent that the plaintiff recoups his injury by sale at a still-inflated price is exactly the Ninth Circuit rule on damages, one set out by Judge Sneed in his concurring opinion in *Green v. Occidental Petroleum Corp.*,[100] which is a standard textbook case on the matter. Thus, any implication in the Court's opinion that the Ninth Circuit holding in *Dura* would have led to such a purchaser receiving damages is unfounded.

The Supreme Court then goes on to deal with the situation in which the purchaser does not sell until after truth has come out:

> If the purchaser sells later after the truth makes its way into the market place, an initially inflated purchase price *might* mean a later loss. But that is far from inevitably so. When the purchaser subsequently resells such shares, even at a lower price, that lower price may reflect . . . other events.[101]

Here the Court is simply wrong. If the truth makes its way into the market, the initially inflated price will inevitably result in a loss. Whether it is the original purchaser of the share or some later purchaser, some investor will be unambiguously economically disadvantaged because the misstatement inflated his purchase price. The investor who purchased the stock when its price was inflated and who is still holding it when the truth comes out will have paid more for the share than he would have but for the misstatement and will not be able to recoup this injury by selling at a similarly inflated price. This is because the efficient market hypothesis, the foundation on which the fraud-on-the-market theory is built, assures us that once the truth comes out, the price will no longer be inflated.

The rationale that the Court provides for its incorrect conclusion involves some odd form of backward reasoning. The issue the Court was purporting to

---

[99] *Id.*
[100] Green v. Occidental Petroleum Corp., 541 F.2d 1335, 1341–46 (9th Cir. 1976) (*per curium*).
[101] *Dura*, 544 U.S. at 342–43.

address was not whether every misstatement that at some point later is followed by a price drop inevitably means that the misstatement has caused a loss. That is obviously not true. The misstatement might not have inflated price in the first place, and the drop would therefore have to be the consequence of some unrelated factor, not the dissipation of inflation. The issue the Court was purporting to address was whether there is inevitably a loss where price was inflated by a misstatement and the truth later came out. The fact that not every price drop is evidence that price has been inflated by a misstatement is irrelevant because the proposition the Court was exploring assumed the price was inflated. While the statement clearly fails to support logically the Court's conclusion that price inflation due to a misstatement followed by the truth coming out does not inevitably lead to a loss, it probably does reflect the Court's appropriate concern with the reliability of evidence used to establish that a price was inflated in the first place.

C. The Ninth Circuit Holding Lacks Precedent

The Supreme Court also criticizes the Ninth Circuit holding as "lack[ing] support in precedent."[102] When past cases are examined carefully, however, there is not very much precedent relevant to what needs to be shown to establish causation in a fraud-on-the-market case. This lack of precedent going either way is hardly surprising given how new the cause of action is. The precedent that does exist is in fact fairly evenly split.

The Supreme Court starts by referring to what needs to be shown to establish causation in common law deceit actions.[103] The cases and commentary that it refers to, however, relate to traditional reliance-based actions, since the fraud-on-the-market theory is not a common law doctrine. As discussed in sections I and II, the causal link between the defendant's wrongful act and the plaintiff's injury is entirely different in a traditional reliance-based action than in a fraud-on-the-market action. Therefore, while, as Joel Seligman says, the decision in *Dura* is notable for its close reliance on common law concepts,[104] the common law cases on causation provide very little meaningful guidance to the question before the Court. The Court's review of circuit-court federal securities law Rule 10b-5 opinions suffers to some extent from a similar problem. Two of the four cases cited, *Emergent Capital Investment Management, LLC v. Stonepath*

---

[102] *Id.* at 343. [103] *Id.* at 343–44.

[104] Louis Loss, Joel Seligman, & Troy Paredes, Securities Regulation 1096 (Supp. 2007).

Group, Inc.[105] and *Bastian v. Petren Resources Corp.*,[106] are traditional reliance-based actions, not fraud-on-the-market actions.

When it comes to actual fraud-on-the-market cases, the Court cites only one case, *Robbins v. Koger Properties, Inc.*,[107] which holds that a showing that the price at the time of purchase was inflated by the misstatement is insufficient to constitute loss causation.[108] And while the Court refers to the "uniqueness" of the Ninth Circuit's perspective on this question,[109] it fails to note that the Eighth Circuit had adopted the same rule as the Ninth.[110]

VI. RESOLVING THE OPEN ISSUES

This chapter has identified two large questions left open by the Court's decision in *Dura*. The first is whether a plaintiff would ever be allowed to establish that a misstatement caused a loss in a situation in which the price at the time suit is brought (or, if earlier, the time of sale) is higher than the purchase price. The second concerns what, beyond the allegation that the misstatement inflated the purchase price, would constitute a sufficient "indication of the loss and the causal connection" for purposes of pleading and what, for purposes of proof at trial, would constitute the kind of evidence sufficient to establish that there had been an inflation in price that proximately caused an economic loss. I will address each of these issues specifically and then consider some larger questions relevant to their resolution.

[105] Emergent Capital Inv. Mgmt., LLC v. Stonepath Group, Inc., 343 F.3d 189 (2d Cir. 2003).
[106] Bastian v. Petren Research Corp., 892 F.2d 680 (7th Cir. 1990).
[107] Robbins v. Koger Props., Inc., 116 F.3d 1441 (11th Cir. 1997). *Robbins*, which is not a very persuasively argued case, is discussed in more detail *supra* section II.C.3. The court in addition cites *Semerenko v. Cendant Corp.*, 223 F.3d 165 (3d Cir. 2000), which is also a fraud-on-the-market case. In *Semerenko*, the Third Circuit in dicta appears also to reject the inflation theory of loss causation, stating "that an investor must also establish that the alleged misrepresentation proximately caused the decline in the security's value to satisfy the element of loss causation." *Id.* at 185. The *Semerenko* court's concern is that where "the value of the security does not actually decline as a result of an alleged misrepresentation . . . the cost of the alleged misrepresentation is still incorporated into the value of the security and may be recovered at any time simply by reselling the security at the inflated price." *Id.* The court made this statement to suggest that earlier Third Circuit opinions that appeared to adopt the price-inflation theory of loss causation might be wrong. What the Third Circuit rule is at this point was not tested by this case, however, since the court found that the complaint alleged that the stock involved "was 'buoyed' by the defendants['] alleged misrepresentations, and that it dropped in response to disclosure of the alleged misrepresentations. . . ." *Id.* at 186. The appellate court would have vacated the district court's grant of defendants' motion to dismiss under either approach.
[108] *Dura*, 544 U.S. at 343–44.   [109] *Id.* at 345.
[110] Knapp v. Ernst & Whinney, 90 F.3d 1431, 1438 (9th Cir. 1996); Gebhart v. ConAgra Foods, Inc., 335 F.3d 824, 831 (8th Cir. 2003).

A. *Price at Time of Suit Higher than Purchase Price: Limiting Recovery to Actual Losses*

There should not be a blanket rule barring damages in fraud-on-the-market suits in which the price at the time suit is brought (or, if earlier, the time of sale) is higher than the purchase price or, more generally, a rule limiting recoveries to actual *ex post* losses. Such a rule would be a relic carried over without reason from traditional reliance-based actions, in which, unlike fraud-on-the-market actions, there is some rationale for a focus on *ex post* losses.[111]

1. Case in Which Misstatement Clearly Inflated Plaintiff's Purchase Price

In a case in which the price at the time of suit is higher than the purchase price, but in which it is clear that the misstatement inflated the plaintiff's purchase price and that she has not recouped her injury through a sale prior to complete market realization of the true situation, the defendant's misstatement has unquestionably made the plaintiff worse off in an amount equal to the misstatement's inflation of purchase price. But for the misstatement, the plaintiff would have paid exactly that much less for the share and received in return the same share with the same value. A rule prohibiting compensation in such a case would result in a lack of balance in outcomes depending on whether, after the purchase, other news affecting the fortunes of the issuer, unrelated to the misstatement, is positive or negative.[112] Investors would have

---

[111] *See supra* section I.B.

[112] A requirement of limiting recovery to actual losses, as an application of the traditional loss-causation requirement to fraud-on-the-market cases would do, poses problems even when the sale price is less than the purchase price if the difference is not as much as the misstatement-inflated price. The following examples illustrate the point. In the first example, XYZ corporation violates Rule 10b-5 by falsely announcing on June 1 a large increase in the sales of its food division. This inflates XYZ's share price by $10, resulting in its shares trading at $60 instead of $50. Later the same day, A buys a share in the secondary market at the $60 price. Two things happen thereafter during the month of June: the Bolivian government confiscates XYZ's mineral properties in Bolivia (part of a business unrelated to food) and the market realizes the truth about the food division's sales. As a result, by July 1, the price has gone down from $60 to $30 (i.e., the confiscation subtracts $20 from the price and the realization of the truth about the food sales subtracts another $10, for a total decline of $30). On July 1, suit is brought. A has not sold. Under the approach advocated here, A's loss due to the misstatement is $10 because the misstatement caused him to pay $10 more than he otherwise would have. He would receive no compensation for the additional $20 because what happens to the share price after the purchase is irrelevant to his injury. Application of the traditional loss-causation theory would also result in the same $10 loss from the misstatement, but the reasoning would be very different: A suffers a loss because of the $30 price drop but only $10 is considered caused by the misstatement because the other $20 in decline is not a reasonably foreseeable consequence of the misstatement.

to suffer the full downside risk associated with unrelated bad news. They would not be able, however, to enjoy fully the upside risks associated with unrelated good news, because any such gains would cancel out, where present, their otherwise valid cause of action for damages from a misstatement that inflated their purchase price. This lack of balance in outcomes is not only arbitrary, it is inefficient. It distorts incentives for investors who seek to profit through hard work by anticipating, ahead of the market, both good and bad news. Such activities are socially useful because they help improve the accuracy of share prices. More accurate prices help allocate scarce capital to the most promising investment projects and assist in the mechanisms that discipline management and provide incentives.

2. Case in Which It Is Not Clearly Established That the Misstatement Inflated the Plaintiff's Purchase Price

Now consider the situation where the plaintiff has not clearly established one or more of the essential elements causally linking the misstatement to a loss, that is, that the misstatement inflated the issuer's share price in the first place, that some or all of the inflation still remained when the plaintiff made her purchase, and that the inflation still present at the time of purchase had dissipated in part or in whole by the time of sale. In such a situation, the fact that the price at the time suit is brought (or, if earlier, the time of sale)

In the second example, all the facts are the same except that in June, XYZ, instead of being a target of a Bolivian confiscation, discovers oil in Indonesia. By July 1, the price has gone down to only $55 (i.e., the oil discovery adds $5 to the price and the market realization of the truth about the food sales subtracts $10, for a net loss of $5). Under the approach recommended here, A again has incurred a $10 loss because the misstatement caused him to pay $10 more than he otherwise would have for shares. Application of the traditional loss-causation requirement, in contrast, would result in the recognition of $5 in loss because that is all that the price has gone down.

As noted in the text, requiring the same loss causation showing in fraud-on-the-market cases as in traditional reliance-based cases results in a lack of balance in outcomes depending on whether, after the purchase, other news affecting the fortunes of the issuer is positive or negative. Investors must suffer the full downside risk associated with bad news. If Bolivia confiscates XYZ's mineral properties, as in the first example above, A suffers the full $20 loss associated with the confiscation, since his right of recovery is still limited to $10, the amount by which market realization of the truth concerning the food division sales depressed the price. Under this approach, investors cannot, however, fully enjoy the upside risks associated with good news, because any such gains will be eroded by market realization of the truth. If XYZ instead discovers oil in Indonesia, as in the second example above, A's damages would be $5, since that is all that the price declined. A receives none of the $5 that the good news is worth. He would be able to sell the security for $55 and receive $5 in damages for a total of $60, exactly what he paid. In contrast, under the approach recommended here, A would enjoy the full $5 value of the good news. He could sell the security for $55 and receive $10 in damages, for a total of $65, $5 more than he paid.

is higher than the purchase price has some probative value. At a minimum, it is negative evidence that should be weighed against whatever affirmative evidence the plaintiff introduces with regard to these elements. Moreover, as discussed in section IV, there is a rationale for bright-line rules triggered by this fact that would bar damages under some circumstances. In deciding how compelling the rationale is for adopting any such bright-line rule, however, the lower courts should bear in mind that the arbitrariness and inefficiencies that would result from a blanket rule that never allows recovery when the price at time of suit (or earlier sale) is greater than the purchase price would still to some extent be present as well with more narrowly tailored bright-line rules applicable in only certain situations. Such rules are bound to cut out some cases where in fact the misstatement did inflate the price.

B. Sufficient Pleadings and Proofs at Trial That the Misstatement Caused a Loss

A threshold question is whether it is necessary for the plaintiff to plead and prove a price drop immediately following the public announcement of the truth. The discussion in section IV suggests that such a requirement, while it has a rationale, would be too strict and that the plaintiff should be able to introduce at least some other kinds of evidence showing that the purchase price had been inflated by the misstatement and that the market had later realized the true situation, thereby dissipating this inflation. To start, an immediate significant increase in share price following a misstatement is good evidence that the misstatement inflated price as a significant price drop following a public announcement of the falsity of the misstatement. Even if there is no price drop following the public announcement, a plaintiff who purchased immediately after such a misstatement was made and was still holding after the unambiguous public announcement of the falsity of the misstatement is very likely to have suffered a loss. The share price increase after the misstatement was made is a very strong indication that it inflated the plaintiff's purchase price. The public announcement of the truth while she is still holding the shares assures that the inflation has fully dissipated and that she cannot recoup her injury by a resale at the inflated price.

Limiting recovery to cases in which there is either a price drop after the public announcement or an increase in price at the time the misstatement is made has an attractive simplicity. Nevertheless, there are good arguments for allowing a plaintiff to submit less definitive kinds of evidence at least under some circumstances. Market realization of the true situation by another route in advance of an unambiguous public announcement of the falsity of a misstatement is not uncommon, and so many price inflating misstatements would not be actionable if less definitive evidence were prohibited.[113] Moreover, a blanket rule against submission of such less definitive kinds of evidence would encourage an issuer that made a misstatement to let the truth out slowly over time in bits and pieces so that no single announcement has a market-adjusted price drop associated with it sufficiently large to be statistically significant. I have discussed in section IV plausibly available kinds of evidence that could be quite persuasive as to importance of the misstatement, its acceptance as true by the market, and how the market realized the true situation prior to the public announcement. I also suggested that in the typical class action, at least a portion of the shares were purchased at time of misstatement or close enough to it that no dissipation of any inflation is likely to have occurred. As far as damages owed to the class as a whole is concerned, these shares are like the shares of persons in the second situation as originally portrayed and discussed in section IV, who purchased immediately after the misstatement and still held the shares at the time suit was brought (which is after the inflation, if any, was fully dissipated). Thus, if the lawyers for the class can make a persuasive argument that there was an initial inflation of price, then clearly, in the aggregate, members of the class suffered at least some losses as the result of the misstatement, regardless of the time and rate of dissipation of the inflation between the making of the misstatement and the public announcement.

If less definitive kinds of evidence are allowed, the pleading standards need to be carefully thought through. The Supreme Court stated that ordinary pleading rules are not meant to impose a great burden on a plaintiff but that "it should not prove burdensome . . . to provide a defendant with some indication of loss and the causal connection that the plaintiff has in mind."[114] Perhaps a bit more ominously for plaintiffs, it also said it would "assume, at least for argument's sake, that neither the Rules [of Civil Procedure] nor the securities statutes impose any special further requirement" beyond the Federal Rules of Civil Procedure Rule 8(a)(2) requirement of "a short and plain statement of

---

[113] As previously noted *supra* note 74, the U.S. solicitor general and the SEC urged the Supreme Court to reverse the Ninth Circuit ruling in *Dura*. In their brief arguing for a grant of certiorari, they drew a distinction, as ultimately does the Court and as is done here, between an investor who purchases a share whose price has been inflated by a misstatement and sells while the price is still inflated and an investor who does not sell "until the market price reflects the true facts that had been concealed by the fraud." In terms of how the market comes to reflect these facts, the brief interestingly says: "This will most commonly occur when the truth is revealed in whole or in part through corrective disclosure. That, however, is not the only way the fraud may be revealed. Events may also effectively disclose the truth." Brief for the United States as Amicus Curiae, *supra* note 74, at 11.

[114] Dura Pharms., Inc., v. Broudo, 544 U.S. 336, 347 (2005).

the claim showing that the pleader is entitled to relief."[115] Ultimately, though, whether this standard is met depends on the contours of what needs to be proved at trial. The pleading with respect to the self-evident importance of the misstatement under the assumption that it is reliable should be satisfied if it is facially material. In essence, the Court already accepted this idea when it blessed the fraud-on-the-market theory in *Basic*. Evidence concerning the market acceptance of the misstatement as true should be available to plaintiffs without discovery, and so requiring specific allegations with respect to this matter would not necessarily be very burdensome. Evidence supporting an explanation of how the market realized the true situation prior to the unambiguous public announcement may be more difficult to obtain. Moreover, as we have seen, for some plaintiffs – ones who purchased right after the misstatement was made and were still holding their shares when suit is brought – and for class-action lawyers showing that at least some damages are owed to the class, a persuasive showing of the importance of the misstatement and its acceptance as true by the market can substitute for a complete explanation of how the market realized the true situation. Thus, at least in these kinds of cases, a requirement of specific allegations with regard to this explanation seems unwarranted.

C. The Relevance of the Private Securities Litigation Reform Act

The Private Securities Litigation Reform Act (PSLRA) added section 21D(b)(4) to the Securities Exchange Act of 1934 (Exchange Act). This provision is titled "Loss Causation" and provides that plaintiffs in private actions "shall have the burden of proving that the act or omission of the defendant... caused the loss for which the plaintiff seeks to recover damages."[116] The government argued before the Supreme Court in *Dura* that this provision codifies the need for plaintiffs in fraud-on-the-market cases to establish traditional loss causation with the requirement of a discrete drop in price after an unambiguous announcement of the falsity of the misstatement and a limit on recovery equal to the difference between the purchase price and the sale price.[117] The weakness of this argument is that it begs the question of what is the loss with respect to which causation must be shown. The approach advocated in this chapter is that for fraud-on-the-market cases, the loss with respect to which the plaintiff must show causation is the inflation in the price the plaintiff paid minus the amount, if any, by which share price at time of suit (or, if earlier, sale) is still inflated.

---

[115] *Id.* at 346.   [116] 15 U.S.C. § 78u-4(b)(4) (2000).
[117] *See, e.g.*, Brief for the United States as Amicus Curiae, *supra* note 74, at 10–13.

The language of section 21D(b)(4) is fully consistent with the concept that the loss that the plaintiff must show was caused by the defendant's misstatement and that the misstatement resulted in her paying too much for the security.[118] Indeed, in section 21D(b)(4), the "loss" that is referred to is "the loss for which the plaintiff seeks to recover damages," and, as noted earlier, the out-of-pocket measure of damages is the measure conventionally applied by courts in Rule 10b-5 actions. Price inflation is the type of loss that most closely corresponds with this measure of damages. Moreover, the PSLRA's legislative history supports the conclusion that a showing of price inflation satisfies the requirements of section 21D(b)(4). The Conference Report, in explaining that the purpose of section 21D(b)(4) is to require the plaintiff to plead and prove that the misstatement "actually caused the loss incurred by plaintiff," goes on to state, "For example, the plaintiff would have to prove that the price at which the plaintiff bought the stock was artificially inflated as a result of the misstatement."[119] It is also significant that there existed appellate decisions

---

[118] The government seeks to deny that this is a reasonable reading of the provision by stating "a loss is a decline in value, and in a fraud-on-the-market case, that necessarily occurs at a point in time *after* the purchase." Brief for the United States as Amicus Curiae Supporting Petitioners, *supra* note 74, at 7–8. This narrow interpretation of the word *loss* seems contradicted by the government elsewhere in this same brief and in its own earlier brief in support of the defendant's certiorari petition. In these briefs, the government makes statements such as "the inflation attributable to the untruth . . . could also be removed through an increase in price that is smaller than it otherwise would have been . . ." *id.* at 7; and a "decline in price may not be a necessary condition for loss causation, however, because the inflation attributable to the fraud could be reduced or eliminated even if there were a net increase in price." Brief for the United States as Amicus Curiae, *supra* note 74, at 13. An additional problem with this narrow reading of *loss* arises in the case of a fraud-on-the-market suit by a plaintiff who sold shares of an issuer for less than he otherwise would have received because of a negative misstatement on the part of the defendant and never repurchases the shares. According to the logic of the narrow definition, even though the plaintiff never repurchases, he does not suffer a loss until after market realization of the truth. Such a conclusion defies common sense.

[119] H.R. Rep. No. 104-369, at 41 (1995) (Conf. Rep.), *reprinted in* 1995 U.S.C.C.A.N. 740. In terms of congressional intent concerning the meaning of the word *loss* in § 21D(b)(4), the government argues that, notwithstanding this example, Congress must have intended to require a showing of a loss after purchase because the PSLRA also added to section 12 of the Securities Act of 1933 (Securities Act) a provision that it referred to as relating to "loss causation." The addition to section 12 enables defendants to reduce liability to the extent that he can show that the amount otherwise recoverable represents amounts "other than the depreciation in value of the . . . security" resulting from the misstatement. The government states, "[T]here is no reason to believe that Congress had two different standards of loss causation in mind when it enacted the PSLRA." Brief for the United States as Amicus Curiae Supporting Petitioners, *supra* note 74, at 8. The problem with the government's argument is that the *prima facie* measure of damages in a section 12 claim is recissionary: the difference between the price paid and the price at the time of suit. Thus, any loss-causation limitation on section 12 damages would inevitably have to be phrased in terms of a reduction in damages so measured. In contrast, the ordinary measure of damages in a Rule 10b-5 action is the out-of-pocket measure, and hence

prior to the passage of the PSLRA holding that a showing of price inflation is sufficient to demonstrate loss causation.[120]

D. Should Fraud-on-the-Market Suits Be Discouraged by a Restrictive Rule of Causation?

Some academic commentators have indicated a preference for fairly restrictive rules relating to causation. My colleague Professor John Coffee, based on his doubts about the overall desirability of fraud-on-the-market suits in the first instance, argues for requiring a discrete drop in price after an unambiguous announcement of the falsity of the misstatement and limiting recovery to the difference between the purchase price and the sale price, both akin to traditional loss causation.[121] He argues that these more restrictive rules would limit the number of fraud-on-the-market actions. This is desirable because limiting the number of actions means limiting the amount of associated transaction costs.[122] These costs are primarily the fees that both sides pay to the legal profession, costs that are ultimately borne by shareholders. Coffee points out, correctly, that in the secondary-market-trading cases, where fraud-on-the-market causes of action arise, the losses by the plaintiff-purchaser, who pays too much, are counterbalanced by the gains of the seller, who is paid too much.[123] The seller is usually also an outside investor, unrelated to the suit, who is equally in the dark. From a societal point of view, therefore, because issuers pay most of the damages, which ultimately come from the pockets of issuer shareholders, fraud-on-the-market suits primarily redistribute wealth among innocent investors. Accordingly, Professor Coffee feels that the compensatory justification for such suits is weak,[124] a conclusion with which I tend to agree.

Fraud-on-the-market actions can have an efficiency justification as well, however, and this justification may be much stronger than the compensatory justification. As Professor Coffee acknowledges, such actions deter corporate misstatements.[125] A lower level of corporate misstatements increases share-price accuracy. Greater share-price accuracy makes the economy more efficient through improvements in how new projects in the real economy are

---

there is no need to phrase a limitation on these damages in terms of a depreciation in the value of the security.

[120] *See, e.g., In re* Control Data Corp. Sec. Litig., 993 F.2d 616, 619–20 (8th Cir. 1991) ("To the extent that the defendant's misrepresentations artificially altered the price of the stock and defrauded the market, causation is presumed.").

[121] John C. Coffee Jr., *Causation by Presumption? Why the Supreme Court Should Reject Phantom Losses and Reverse* Broudo, 60 Bus. Law. 533, 537 (2005).

[122] *Id.* at 542   [123] *Id.* at 534.

[124] *Id.* at 542–43.   [125] *Id.* at 543.

selected for implementation and, by increasing the effectiveness of a number of devices that limit the extent to which managers of public corporations place their own interests above those of their shareholders, through improvements in how existing projects are run.[126] An expectation of a lower level of corporate misstatements also lowers investor precaution costs, the resources secondary market traders and their advisers expend trying to detect misstatements so as to avoid losing transactions.

The question of the role of private civil damages litigation in deterring issuer misstatements in situations in which neither the issuer nor its insiders engage in significant trading is a complicated one. It involves a variety of rules beyond causation requirements, including, among others, rules determining how difficult it is to sue various potential defendants (e.g., issuers, directors and officers, control shareholders, accountants), the amounts that such defendants would be expected to pay out in damages, and the fees to plaintiffs' class action lawyers. Mandatory periodic disclosure rules and rules concerning related issuer, officer, and gatekeeper liability are relevant as well. In addition to deterring misstatements, the design of this whole complex of rules needs to be concerned with the incentives of issuers to make truthful statements in situations in which there is no duty to disclose and with the incentives of different kinds of investors to gather, analyze, and act on information.[127] It is desirable to have a set of rules that, working together, encourage suits in which the efficiency benefits exceed the costs and that discourage suits in which the opposite is the case. Personally, I believe that the prevailing set of

---

[126] *See* Merritt B. Fox, *Retaining Mandatory Securities Disclosure: Why Issuer Choice Is Not Investor Empowerment*, 85 VA. L. REV. 1335, 1358–69 (1999). Professor Robert Thompson expresses some reservations concerning the use of securities fraud suits to perform these functions, writing that "state law of fiduciary duty and the deference inherent in the business judgment rule provide both a check on possible management abuse of their authority and considerable room for management to make decisions free of second-guessing by courts." Robert B. Thompson, *Federal Corporate Law: Torts and Fiduciary Duty*, 31 J. CORP. L. 877, 889 (2006) (citations omitted). Because of the way fraud-on-the-market suits deter managerial abuse, however, it is not clear that they really deprive management of the room they need to make decisions or give courts the ability to second-guess management's substantive decisions. Fraud-on-the-market suits deter managerial behavior only indirectly by encouraging honesty in disclosure. Abuse that cannot be hidden is abuse that will probably not be undertaken. It is not a court's view of what constitutes abuse that managers fear, however; it is the market's and the public's views. While it is true, as Thompson points out, that a management that chooses to abuse is likely to make an actionable misstatement to hide it, the court simply has to judge whether a material misstatement has been made, not whether or not the underlying behavior constitutes abuse.

[127] *See* Zohar Goshen & Gideon Parchomovsky, *The Essential Role of Securities Regulation* (Colum. Law and Econ. Working Paper No. 259, 2004), *available at* http://ssrn.com/abstract= 600709 (discussing civil liability rules with regard to incentives of investors).

rules is not perfect. They encourage some kinds of suits in which the costs exceed the deterrence value and discourage some other kinds of suits in which their deterrence value would exceed their costs. Imposition of a traditional loss-causation rule in fraud-on-the-market suits does not appear to be a rational way of remedying this problem, however. It will arbitrarily cut out plaintiffs in cases in which positive news unrelated to the misstatement has counterbalanced the effect on price from the market realization of the misstatement. There is no reason to think that the deterrence value of these cases is any less or their costs any greater than those of cases in which traditional loss causation can be demonstrated. It will also cut out all cases in which there is no drop in price after the unambiguous announcement of the falsity of the misstatement. This seems arbitrary with respect to cases where there is other clear evidence of price inflation. Again, compared to cases in which traditional loss causation can be demonstrated, the deterrence value should be no less and, as explored here, the costs should not be dramatically greater.

E. The Assumption of Constant Impact

I assume throughout this chapter that the facts asserted by the misstatement would, if they had been true, have had a constant impact on the underlying fundamental value of an issuer's shares. For many kinds of misrepresentations, this assumption is a reasonably close approximation of reality. To illustrate, consider issuer A, with 5 million shares outstanding, that falsely stated that it had an extra $60 million in cash in its treasury. If the issuer had really had this $60 million in cash in the treasury at the time of the original misstatement, the fundamental value of each share would have been increased by $12. The same would be true if the issuer had really had this $60 million in the treasury at the time of the announcement of the truth.

For other kinds of misstatements, this assumption of constant impact is not a reasonable approximation of reality. To illustrate this second kind of misstatement, consider issuer B, also with 5 million shares outstanding, which falsely stated that it had an extra 1 million barrels of oil in storage. If the issuer had really had those 1 million barrels of oil at the time the misrepresentation was made and the price of oil was $60, the fundamental value of each share would again have been increased by $12. Suppose, though, that between the time of the misstatement and the time when the truth was announced, the price of oil decreased to $50 per barrel. By the time of the announcement of the truth, then, if the issuer had really had those 1 million barrels of oil in storage, the fundamental value of each share would have been increased by only $10. Thus, the impact of the facts asserted by the misstatement on the underlying fundamental value of an issuer's shares, which remained constant in the first example, dropped by $2 in the second example.

I employ the constant-impact assumption because, despite its deviation from reality with regard to this second type of misstatement, it simplifies the discussion of the most important issues related to loss causation without a serious loss of generality. For some kinds of cases, the lack of reality in the assumption has no impact at all on the analysis. Consider again the misstatements by issuer A and issuer B in the context of cases resembling the first or second situations discussed in section III, in which an investor buys immediately after the misstatement and holds the shares until after the public announcement of the truth. An investor who buys a share of A pays $12 more per share than he would have but for A's misstatement, and the same is true of an investor who buys a share of B.[128] As a consequence, the misstatement caused each of the investors a $12 loss. This is because each paid $12 too much and did not recoup any of that loss by selling at a price that was to any extent still inflated by the misstatement.

Where an investor purchases later than immediately after the misstatement or sells before the market fully realizes the true situation, the assumption of constant impact may be more problematic, but it still has a rationale. This is because the efficient market hypothesis guarantees that the impact of the facts asserted by the misstatement on the underlying fundamental value of an issuer's shares at the time of the misstatement is an unbiased estimate of this impact at any point in the future as well. In other words, the value that the market would assign to each share of B at the time of the misstatement reflects both the chance that the price of oil in the future might go up and the chance that it might go down. As a consequence, it would not be unreasonable to have a rule that there is no loss in the case of an investor in our example who purchased a share of B immediately after the oil misstatement, when, if fully believed, it inflated the price by $12, and who sold shortly before the announcement of the truth, when, if the misstatement was still fully believed, it inflated the price by only $10. The value the market assigned to this nonexistent oil at the time of the investor's purchase reflected the possibilities both that the price of oil might go up, which at time of sale would have resulted in a share price inflation of more than $12, and that it might go down. Thus, it can be argued, while the misstatement is a but-for cause of the $2 shortfall, it is not a proximate cause. This is because, at the time the investor purchased the share, the misstatement – if the investor were to sell before market realization

---

[128] In each, for purposes of expositional convenience, I assume that the market fully believes the misstatement at the time it is made. This assumption is not necessary for the point to hold.

of the truth – was as likely to have resulted in a gain from an increase in the amount the misstatement inflated price as to have resulted in a loss from a decrease in the amount the misstatement inflated price. Under this argument, it is the decrease in the price of oil, not the issuer's misstatement, that is the legal cause of the $2 shortfall.

Dura does not decide whether an economic disadvantage at time of sale arising out of a fall in the underlying value of a falsely claimed asset, such as this $2 shortfall, should be considered a loss caused by the misstatement. Cases may arise, of course, that require resolution of this question, but beyond my observation that a reasonable argument could be made that such a shortfall should not be considered a loss, I do not pursue the issue further here. The constant-impact assumption helps us keep our focus on what I believe are the two most important questions for loss causation – Did the misstatement inflate price in the first place? and Has the inflation dissipated by time of sale? – questions that are involved in every fraud-on-the-market case.

VII. CONCLUSION

This chapter has evaluated the issues remaining open after the Supreme Court's decision in *Dura*. Analytically, in an action for damages based on the fraud-on-the-market theory, for a positive misstatement to cause an investor to suffer a loss, (1) the misstatement must inflate the market price of a security, (2) the investor must purchase the security at the inflated price, and (3) the investor must not resell the security sufficiently quickly that the price at the time of sale is still equally inflated. *Dura's* narrow holding is that a plaintiff cannot establish causation merely by pleading and proving that the misstatement inflated price. Future courts have thus been left the task of designing a comprehensive set of rules concerning what the plaintiff must plead and prove, and the acceptable forms of evidence, concerning each of these three critical elements. I have tried to suggest a number of considerations that can help them do that in a way that minimizes the conflict between the two important social aims of deterring corporate misstatements and limiting the transaction costs associated with civil litigation.

One important matter on which the Court expresses no opinion is whether loss causation can ever be established when the price at the time suit is brought (or, if earlier, at the time of sale) is higher than the purchase price. This chapter concludes that a blanket rule against actions in which the price has increased would be inappropriate because there are situations in which the price has increased but each of the three critical elements can still be reasonably easily and definitively established. When one or more of these elements cannot be reasonably easily and definitively established, however, a price increase is a negative piece of evidence concerning whether the misstatement inflated the price, and a bright-line rule barring actions when price has increased might be appropriate at least under some specified circumstances.

The other important matter on which the Supreme Court expresses no opinion is whether the plaintiff must plead and prove a price drop immediately following the unambiguous public announcement of the falsity of the misstatement. Again, this chapter concludes that a blanket rule requiring such a showing is inappropriate. Other ways of demonstrating that the misstatement inflated the price are sufficiently reliable that they should be allowed under at least some circumstances. The absence of a price drop after the announcement, however, makes it less clear when the inflation dissipated, which is relevant to whether the plaintiff both bought at a time when the price was still inflated (if it ever was inflated) and sold at a time when it was no longer inflated. Some plaintiffs can show the other two elements reasonably easily and definitively, for example, plaintiffs who purchase the security immediately after the misstatement is made and still hold it at the time of the public announcement of its falsity. For plaintiffs whose purchase and sale timings do not fit this profile, it may be appropriate to bar actions where there is no postannouncement price drop. This problem is less critical for class actions because at least minimum losses to the class as a whole can be established without concern as to when the inflation dissipated.

9 From Boardroom to Courtroom to Newsroom

The Media and the Corporate Governance Scandals

Kathleen F. Brickey

The first trial is always in the court of public opinion.
– Donald Watkins, legal adviser to HealthSouth's CEO Richard Scrushy

Enron and its progeny spawned an unprecedented amount of press coverage. To their credit, the media comprehensively covered allegations of widespread accounting fraud as serious and important news. Major newspapers deserve special credit for the breadth and depth of their coverage.

While it was a safe assumption that the sagas of Enron and – to a lesser extent – media icon Martha Stewart would receive sustained media attention, the sheer magnitude of the corporate governance scandals fueled extraordinary coverage of massive frauds at WorldCom, Tyco, HealthSouth, and Adelphia, to name but a few. Before Enron collapsed into bankruptcy and became mired in a complex Web of investigations, few would have predicted that the editors of the *Wall Street Journal* would devote significant resources – including prominent front-page space – to criminal investigations and prosecutions on a long-term basis. But, to the *Journal's* credit, it did.

Apart from the value that intensive coverage of virtually every aspect of the corporate meltdown provided the papers' general readership, the press also helped inform public debate about how such massive frauds could have occurred over a prolonged period of time without detection. For elected officials, business executives, legal and accounting professionals, academicians, and corporate governance activists, the burning question was, What went wrong and how can we fix it? The remarkable thing is that, thanks to media saturation, almost everyone knew something about it.

Kathleen F. Brickey is James Carr Professor of Criminal Jurisprudence, School of Law, Washington University in St. Louis. Special thanks to Dania Becker and Sharon Palmer for their exceptional research and editorial assistance. This chapter is adapted from an article that appeared in the *Journal of Corporation Law* at 33 J. CORP. L. 625 (2008).

Yet despite all the spilled ink, the Enron fiasco came close to being one of the "biggest failures in financial journalism."[1] One of the most perplexing questions is why the financial press was asleep at the switch when Enron collapsed. Why was the news so late? How could the seventh-largest company in the country melt down in a mere twenty-four days with so little forewarning? How could the *Houston Chronicle* – whose headquarters were only a stone's throw from Enron's – come so close to missing the biggest business story of the year?[2]

To be sure, there were clues to be found. In a March 2001 *Fortune* article, "Is Enron Overpriced?"[3] Bethany McClean raised what, in retrospect, should have been a provocative question: How does Enron make money? At the time, her query might have seemed mildly out of sync. Enron was, after all, a major corporation that *Fortune* had ranked as the most innovative company in the country[4] and one of the "100 Best Companies to Work For."[5]

But McClean's research unearthed some ominous warning signs about Enron's financial soundness. In the first nine months of 2000, for example, Enron's debt rose by nearly $4 billion, and almost all of its earnings in the previous two years had come from sales of assets that Enron inexplicably booked as recurring revenue. Yet despite the obvious implications of her article, neither Wall Street nor the financial press rose to the challenge.

Enron's fortunes took a turn for the worse when CEO Jeff Skilling abruptly resigned in August 2001 for unspecified personal reasons, after just six months on the job. Skilling's sudden departure raised red flags for the *Wall Street Journal* reporters John Emshwiller and Rebecca Smith. Why, they asked, would Skilling – who described himself as "brilliant,"[6] said he had never failed at anything,[7] and had recently been featured on the cover of *Worth*[8] magazine as one of the top CEOs in the country – suddenly walk away at the pinnacle of his career? And why would he abandon a $20 million severance

---

[1] Kelly Heyboer, *The One That Got Away*, AM. JOURNALISM REV., Mar. 2002, at 12.

[2] *Id.*

[3] Bethany McLean, *Is Enron Overpriced?*, FORTUNE, Mar. 5, 2001, at 122 [hereinafter McLean, *Enron Overpriced?*].

[4] Bethany McClean & Peter Elkind, *The Guiltiest Guys in the Room*, FORTUNE, June 12, 2006, at 26.

[5] Heyboer, *supra* note 1. In 2001, the year Enron imploded, it was ranked twenty-second on the list. Kenneth L. Lay, *Guilty, Until Proven Innocent*, Speech at the Houston Forum (Dec. 13, 2005) (on file with author) [hereinafter Lay Speech].

[6] Bethany McLean, *Enron's Power Crisis*, FORTUNE, Sept. 17, 2001, at 48 [hereinafter McLean, *Power Crisis*].

[7] *Id.*   [8] *The 50 Best CEOs*, WORTH, May, 2001.

package and become obligated to repay a $2 million loan that Enron would have forgiven had he stayed on just another four months?[9]

In the meantime, analysts reported what they described as "aggressive" insider selling of stock by Enron executives, who collectively sold 1.75 million shares in 2001 while the price of the stock was going down.[10]

Then came the bombshell. In October, as Emshwiller and Smith continued to dig deeper to find out why Skilling had suddenly left, Enron announced a $618 million third-quarter loss and a $1.2 billion reduction of shareholder equity. Twenty-four days later, Enron descended into the hell of the largest corporate bankruptcy in U.S. history, intense regulatory scrutiny, and criminal investigation. The nation's seventh-largest corporation, it seems, was a financial house of cards. Where were all the financial journalists?

Enron's October earnings report spawned an unprecedented amount of press coverage. The *Wall Street Journal* and the *New York Times* alone featured more than 250 Enron stories in the ten weeks between the earnings announcement and the end of the year.

During the following four years, Enron and other financial fraud scandals remained major fixtures in the national press. Indeed, in May 2006 – the month in which the verdict in the Skilling-Lay trial was announced – the Enron scandal was the third-most-reported story in both the *Journal* and the *Times*. Only terrorism and illegal immigration received more coverage.

Thus, despite a sluggish start at the gate, the media ultimately provided comprehensive and sustained coverage of a seemingly endless stream of scandals and their aftermath. Ironically, journalists' failure to pursue the Enron story early in the game ultimately underscored how important its later comprehensive coverage was to understanding the breadth and depth of the corporate governance scandals. Yet despite much praiseworthy reporting, press coverage of five high-profile criminal trials arising out of corporate governance scandals raised troubling questions about media judgment and restraint.

In section I of this chapter – "Juries, the Media, and the Courts" – jury deliberations in the trial of Tyco's CEO Dennis Kozlowski and the jury selection process in the Martha Stewart trial provide the focal point. During the Kozlowski trial, several newspapers, including the *Wall Street Journal*, broke with journalistic tradition by publishing personal details about a juror who reportedly flashed an OK sign to the defense table during jury deliberations. The ensuing publicity over the courtroom incident ultimately led to a mistrial by media. In the Martha Stewart trial, intense media interest in

---

[9] McLean, *Power Crisis, supra* note 6, at 48.   [10] *Id.*

covering all aspects of the proceeding led some journalists to violate a judicial order against contacts with jurors until their service was over. Concern about overly aggressive media coverage prompted the judge to modify the jury selection process, which in turn produced – at least in part – a trial without media.

Section I – teases out the legal and practical implications of these two scenarios and suggests that journalistic mishaps like the one in the Tyco trial could well have the effect of encouraging risk-averse jurists like the judge in the Stewart trial to adopt more restrictive rules governing media coverage of high-profile trials.

Section II – "The Media as Public Relations Machine" – explores the growing phenomenon of high-profile defendants' use of well-orchestrated and increasingly costly multimedia campaigns to "set the record straight." The prosecutions of Arthur Andersen for shredding Enron documents and of Enron CEO Ken Lay for defrauding Enron investors provide the backdrop for exploring this phenomenon. They illustrate how high-profile defendants can (and increasingly do) use public relations campaigns to demonize prosecutors, witnesses, and the press to exonerate themselves. The case of HealthSouth's CEO Richard Scrushy builds on that theme but adds another troublesome dimension – the use of race and religion to manipulate the outcome of a trial. Section II uses these three prosecutions to explore the potential corrosive effect such public relations strategies can have on the criminal justice system.

The concluding section – "Praise or Blame?" – posits a series of questions raised by the analyses in sections I and II that reveal growing points of tension between the media and the courts. While there may be no definitive answers to any or all of the queries posed, the chapter concludes by suggesting that, if continued unchecked, aggressive media tactics in high-profile trials are likely to invite greater judicial scrutiny of media coverage and of the roles that defendants and defense lawyers play in manipulating the press to sway public opinion. Simply put, thoughtful journalists and lawyers – perhaps even publicists – who value the media's continued ability to fulfill its watchdog role would be well advised to consider the wisdom of exercising self-restraint.

Three appendices at the end of the chapter provide a "media-centric" postscript on coverage of the corporate governance scandals. Appendix A discusses traditional print source coverage and the Enron "media frenzy" that Ken Lay and Jeff Skilling blamed for Enron's collapse. Appendix B examines recent innovations, including the creation of a special media room in Houston's federal courthouse, that are transforming coverage of major trials by the mainstream media. And last, Appendix C considers two issues that take on increased significance in the age of electronic journalism – source credibility and the permanency (or lack thereof) of information that has historical value.

I. JURIES, THE MEDIA, AND THE COURTS

Recent high-profile trials have increasingly thrust jurors into the limelight. To be sure, interviews with jurors at the end of a trial can shed light on the dynamics of jury deliberations and the idiosyncrasies of individual jury members. Chappel Hartridge, an outspoken juror who commented extensively on the Martha Stewart trial, is a prime example.

Hartridge spoke at length in widely covered interviews soon after the guilty verdicts were announced. Some thought his opinions on the symbolic meaning of the verdicts suggested that he misunderstood his role as a juror and used the verdict to vent his anger about stock fraud and corporate greed – notwithstanding that the core charges in the case were about lying and obstruction of justice.[11] To others, his public comments about Martha Stewart herself suggested that class bias that may have compromised her right to a fair trial.[12]

But while widespread coverage of Hartridge's public comments is illustrative of intense and legitimate media interest in the inner workings of high-profile trials, overly aggressive media tactics during the course of the trial can skew the balance between the public's right to know and the parties' interest in receiving a fair trial. It is to this balance that we now turn.

A. Mistrial by Media

One of the most stunning clashes between competing media and judicial interests occurred near the end of contentious jury deliberations in the six-month criminal fraud trial of Tyco's CEO Dennis Kozlowski. It began when Ruth Jordan – then known only as Tyco Juror No. 4 – reportedly flashed the defense table an OK sign.[13]

In its coverage of this courtroom scene, the *Wall Street Journal* broke with journalistic convention and published Jordan's name, even though the trial was

---

[11] Hartridge thought the verdict might be "a victory for the little guy who loses money in the markets because of these types of transactions." Mem. of Law in Supp. of Martha Stewart's Mot. for New Trial Pursuant to Fed. R. Crim. P. 33, at 14, United States v. Stewart, No. S1–03-Cr-717 (MGC) (S.D.N.Y. Mar. 31, 2004) (on file with author).

[12] *Id.* at 14–15.

[13] David Carr & Adam Liptak, *In Tyco Trial, an Apparent Gesture Has Many Meanings: Publicity to Prompt Mistrial Motion*, N.Y. TIMES, Mar. 28, 2004, at C1; Mark Maremont & Kara Scannell, *Tyco Jury Resumes Deliberating: Defense Fails in Mistrial Bid Based on Media Coverage of Jury, but Incident Could Fuel Appeal*, WALL ST. J., Mar. 30, 2004, at C1.

still under way.[14] Jordan immediately became the subject of public ridicule. Not to be outdone, the *New York Post* published a front-page caricature of Jordan complete with a prominent OK hand signal and the caption "Ms. Trial." Accompanying articles called her a "'Holdout' Granny," a "braggart," and a "batty blueblood."[15] The next day, the *New York Times* published a picture of the *Post's* front-page sketch and ran an article on the decision other papers had made to disclose Jordan's identity.[16] The *Times* story did not, however, identify her by name.

These articles sparked a spirited debate about the propriety of the decision by some papers to publish her name. But they also unleashed a barrage of publicity that identified her as a seventy-nine-year-old retiree with a law degree who was somewhat standoffish and, perhaps, a wee bit stingy (no Christmas bonuses for the door guard at her apartment building).

This and other unwelcome public attention put Jordan in the spotlight while she was still participating in jury deliberations. The publicity spawned several anonymous communications, including a threatening letter, that "severely distressed" and "terrified" her.[17] And while she initially told the judge she could continue deliberating, the fallout from the media frenzy ultimately led the judge to declare a mistrial.[18]

Apologizing to a jury that had already deliberated for twelve days, the presiding judge said it was "a shame" that the system "could not protect the process sufficiently" to permit them to reach a verdict.[19] Although he did not elaborate further, Judge Obus alluded to "efforts to pressure the jury from the outside" in announcing his decision to end the trial.[20]

Was it appropriate for the *Journal* and the *Post* to break with tradition and risk the possibility of causing a mistrial? To ask this question is not to deny the

---

[14] The *Journal* first identified Jordan in an article in its online version and later included her name in a print story. Perhaps because Kozlowski was a native of Newark, New Jersey, the *Newark Star-Ledger* also published her name.

[15] Carr & Liptak, *supra* note 13; Matthew Rose, *Behind the Tyco Mistrial: Judge Faults Media's Moves*, WALL ST. J., Apr. 5, 2004, at B1.

[16] Carr & Liptak, *supra* note 13.

[17] Andrew Ross Sorkin, *Judge Ends Trial When Tyco Juror Reports Threat: Verdict Was Seen as Near: Prosecutors Plan to Retry 2 Executives Accused of Stealing Millions*, N.Y. TIMES, Apr. 3, 2004, at A1 [hereinafter Sorkin, *Judge Ends Trial*]. After the mistrial was declared, threats against Jordan were posted on Yahoo!'s message boards along with her name and address. David Carr, *Some Critics Say Naming a Juror Went Too Far*, N.Y. TIMES, Apr. 3, 2004, at B1 [hereinafter Carr, *Naming Went Too Far*].

[18] Mark Maremont, *Tyco Juror Maintains Her Stance*, WALL ST. J., Apr. 8, 2004, at B2; Mark Maremont & Kara Scannell, *Tyco Juror Denied to Rest of the Panel That She Gave "OK,"* WALL ST. J., Apr. 7, 2004, at C1; Andrew Ross Sorkin, *No O.K. Sign and No Guilty Vote by Juror No. 4*, N.Y. TIMES, Apr. 7, 2004, at A1 [hereinafter Sorkin, *No O.K. Sign*].

[19] Sorkin, *Judge Ends Trial, supra* note 17.   [20] *Id.*

newsworthiness of the story. Just as the public had an interest in knowing what influenced Chappel Hartridge's vote to convict in the Martha Stewart trial, the public had a legitimate interest in knowing what courtroom observers saw in the Tyco trial. If Jordan flashed an OK sign in open court, the gesture might have signaled that she had made up her mind and that a mistrial was imminent. Indeed, a jury note sent to the judge the previous week complained that the atmosphere in the jury room had become "poisonous" and the deliberative process was "irreparably compromised."[21] So it is possible, but by no means certain, that the deliberations would have come to a halt in any event.

But the relevant question is whether we really know the meaning of Jordan's hand gesture. When he declared the mistrial, Judge Obus described it as "equivocal."[22] And after the mistrial was declared, Jordan denied that she had ever signaled OK.[23]

But why, you might ask, wasn't this reported before the end of the trial when the original stories ran? The answer is, quite simply, that during the media frenzy that led to the mistrial, reporters could not get her side of the story because court rules prohibited press contact with sitting jurors during the trial. And, of course, Jordan reportedly gave the controversial signal while the jury was still deliberating.

In consequence, the furor leading up to the mistrial was based only on what reporters thought they saw Ruth Jordan do in open court. They could not "check the facts" because they could not ask Jordan – the most relevant source of information – about what, if anything, she intended to convey. Nor could they ask her fellow jurors how they interpreted the incident. Thus, the reports leading to the declaration of a mistrial were based on only one side of the story – what some court observers thought appeared to be an OK signal. But the meaning and significance of the gesture – if there was a gesture – remained the subject of a considerable dispute.[24]

So assuming *arguendo* the story was worth covering – but also acknowledging that the reporting was, of necessity, one-sided – what did the personal details about Ruth Jordan add to the newsworthiness or importance of the report? Was it necessary to provide her name, picture, and background in order to convey what reporters saw (or thought they saw) in open court? Did the importance of this information to the press outweigh the risk that she would be subjected to intense public pressure to change her mind?

---

[21] Rose, *supra* note 15.   [22] Carr, *Naming Went Too Far, supra* note 17.

[23] Carr & Liptak, *supra* note 13; Mark Maremont & Kara Scannell, *Tyco Juror Denied to Rest of the Panel That She Gave "OK,"* WALL ST. J., Apr. 7, 2004, at C1; Sorkin, *No O.K. Sign, supra* note 18.

[24] Carr & Liptak, *supra* note 13.

The journalists should have more carefully weighed the consequences of precipitating a mistrial near the end of jury deliberations. The judge's decision to end the trial without a verdict was precipitated by forces operating outside the courtroom and jury room.[25] Ruth Jordan would not have received the threatening letter if her name had not been publicly disclosed, and it is not entirely clear that the jury was deadlocked.

Indeed, some jurors expressed surprise and disappointment when the mistrial was declared, saying they had resumed their deliberations in earnest and were close to reaching a verdict. In the words of one juror, "We were on the verge this morning of coming up with our verdicts.... It was going to be the day."[26] Others who spoke about the jury's progress said they would probably have acquitted the defendants on some counts, convicted them on others (including "[a] lot of the most extreme" grand larceny charges), and perhaps have deadlocked on the rest.[27]

Instead, the trial ended prematurely in response to a chain of events precipitated by the press. This result is particularly unfortunate in light of the enormous amount of resources invested in the six-month trial and the cost of trying the case again. Not surprisingly, the prosecutor immediately announced that he would seek a retrial. And yes, at the end of the second trial – which lasted "just" four months – the jury found the defendants guilty as charged on twenty-two of twenty-three counts.[28]

But apart from the time and expense of a retrial, what are the potential implications of the media's abrupt departure from journalistic norms?

B. Trial without Media

To put the previous question in perspective, consider how the clash between competing media and judicial interests could play out differently, as it had earlier in the Martha Stewart trial. Stewart was accused of deceiving regulatory authorities to conceal the reason she sold all of her ImClone stock on December 27, 2001. Although Stewart claimed that the timing of the sale was driven by an earlier agreement with her broker to sell when the price fell below $60 per share, the government charged that she sold the stock after receiving

---

[25] As one attorney quipped to reporters after the mistrial, the media "are now the defense lawyer's secret weapon.... I have a trial coming up in October and I want you there." Carr, *Naming Went Too Far, supra* note 17.

[26] Sorkin, *Judge Ends Trial, supra* note 17.   [27] *Id.*

[28] Andrew Ross Sorkin, *Ex-Chief and Aide Guilty of Looting Millions at Tyco: 2nd Trial for Kozlowski: Lawyers Plan Appeal – Conviction Is Latest in Corporate Scandals*, N.Y. Times, June 18, 2005, at A1.

a tip that her longtime friend and founder of ImClone was selling his stock that day. Coincidentally (or not), the tip came the day before the Food and Drug Administration formally notified ImClone that its application to market a new cancer drug would be denied. And, of course, the agency's denial of the application triggered a precipitous decline in the price of ImClone's stock.

From the outset, the investigation into Stewart's fortuitously timed sale attracted enormous media attention that predictably intensified as her trial date approached. The unusual level of publicity understandably fed concerns about impaneling unbiased jurors, and this prompted Judge Cedarbaum to follow a two-phase jury selection process.[29]

First, several hundred prospective jurors were called to the courthouse to fill out a lengthy background questionnaire. After reviewing the completed questionnaires, lawyers on both sides then made challenges for cause. And when the challenges were resolved, the remaining members of the jury pool were questioned outside the presence of other prospective jurors in Judge Cedarbaum's robing room – a procedure that both the prosecution and defense agreed would promote juror candor.

Before jury selection began, the government – on behalf of all parties to the case – expressed concern that media representatives would try to interview prospective jurors, and the prosecutor asked the court to remind the press that contact with prospective jurors was forbidden.[30] Judge Cedarbaum responded by issuing an order banning press contacts with any potential or selected jurors or their families until their jury service was complete.[31] The order explained that this step was needed to preserve the integrity of the jury selection process and to protect the parties' right to a fair trial.

Before prospective jurors filled out the background questionnaires, Judge Cedarbaum had admonished them not to publicly disclose the contents. But by the next day, someone had violated the confidentiality order by posting paraphrased parts of the questionnaire on the Internet.[32]

Although there was no evidence that non-Internet media played any role in the posting, the government asked Judge Cedarbaum to exclude the press from voir dire questioning and to prohibit the publication or disclosure of

[29] Slip Opinion, United States v. Stewart, No. 03-Cr-717 (MGC), slip op. at 1–2 (S.D.N.Y. May 5, 2004) (on file with author).

[30] ABC, Inc. v. Stewart, 360 F.3d 90, 94 (2d Cir. 2004).

[31] Order, United States v. Stewart, No. 03-CR-717 (MGC) (S.D.N.Y. Jan. 2, 2004) (on file with author). Orders barring communications between members of the press and jurors and their families are typical in both criminal and civil trials.

[32] ABC, 360 F.3d at 94. The paraphrased portions were posted on the celebrity gossip Web site Gawker (http://www.gawker.com), and the person who posted them claimed to be a member of the jury pool.

who was in the jury pool.[33] The government's letter request, which had not been publicly disclosed, arrived on Judge Cedarbaum's desk the same day she received a letter from reporters asking whether the oral questioning of prospective jurors would occur in open court. The reporters' letter asked her to allow pool reporters to cover voir dire if she intended to exclude the media.[34]

Without affording media representatives notice or an opportunity to be heard, Judge Cedarbaum issued a two-page order barring the press from the proceedings.[35] Citing rampant media speculation about the identities of prospective jurors that made it highly likely that their names and answers to voir dire questions would be published, the order also provided that "no member of the press may sketch or photograph or divulge the name of any prospective or selected juror."[36]

But what harm could come from disclosing jurors' identities? Judge Cedarbaum found that publication of personal information – or even the possibility that it might be disclosed – created a "substantial risk" that prospective jurors would be reluctant to provide "full and frank answers" to questions during voir dire.[37] And if prospective jurors were reluctant to provide candid responses about what they had read or heard and whether they had preconceived opinions about the case, that would impede prosecution and defense efforts to effectively screen out potential bias.

To accommodate First Amendment interests, however, Judge Cedarbaum's order did permit publication of a transcript of each day's proceedings, but with the identities of prospective jurors and any "deeply personal information" redacted.[38]

The decision to exclude the public and the press from observing voir dire was highly unusual. Potential jurors are ordinarily questioned in open court,

---

[33] *Id.* Neither defendant objected.

[34] *Id.* at 94–95. This request was not unprecedented. Pool reporters were permitted to cover voir dire proceedings in the trials of Imelda Marcos and Sheik Omar Abdel Rahman. *Id.*

[35] Order, United States v. Stewart, No. 03-CR-717, 2004 U.S. Dist. LEXIS 426 (S.D.N.Y. Jan. 15, 2004). The order was based roughly on the following findings of fact:

> (1) The Stewart case had attracted unusually widespread media attention;
> (2) The press had indulged in rampant speculation about the identities of prospective jurors;
> (3) Paraphrased parts of the juror questionnaire had been published on the Internet in violation of Judge Cedarbaum's directive that its contents not be disclosed (the order defined the term *press* to include Internet media);
> (4) There was a "substantial likelihood that some members of the press [would] disclose the names of prospective or selected jurors with their responses to voir dire questions," Jan. 15, 2004 Order, *supra*, at *1; and
> (5) There was no less restrictive way to promote juror candor.

[36] 1 *Id.* at *3.   [37] *Id.* at *1.
[38] *Id.* at *3.

and the Supreme Court has repeatedly recognized a constitutional right of public access to criminal trials,[39] including the voir dire phase.[40]

Not surprisingly, the order was implemented over strong First Amendment objections from the press. A coalition of news organizations moved to vacate or modify the order to eliminate its three most objectionable parts: (1) closing the voir dire proceedings; (2) requiring jury anonymity; and (3) prohibiting the publication of juror's names, regardless of how reporters had discovered them.[41] Denying the coalition's motion, Judge Cedarbaum reiterated her concerns about intense media interest in the case and added yet another to the mix: the press had aggressively tried to approach jurors who came to the courthouse to fill out the questionnaires despite her order prohibiting press contacts and communications with prospective or selected jurors.[42]

The coalition appealed the closing of voir dire proceedings to the Second Circuit, which held that it was inappropriate to exclude the public and the press.[43] Although the court acknowledged that the right of access to criminal trials sometimes must yield to "higher values"[44] (e.g., the defendant's right to a fair trial and the jurors' privacy interests), the strong presumption favoring open access is difficult to overcome. The court unanimously ruled that, before ordering closure of a trial or voir dire, the trial judge must make specific findings that demonstrate (1) a "substantial probability" that the publicity would prejudice the defendant's right to a fair trial and that prejudice would be avoided by closure and (2) that there were no other reasonable ways to protect the defendant's right to a fair trial.[45]

The court found that extensive media interest is an inadequate ground for closing a criminal proceeding and that Judge Cedarbaum's other findings of fact fell short of the mark. Judge Cedarbaum's order did not cite any improper media conduct or violation of a court order.[46] Moreover, while her order cited the potential chilling effect that media presence might have on prospective jurors during voir dire, the court found it highly unlikely that they would be willing to reveal bias against Stewart while she was seated in the room but would be more reluctant to do so when reporters were added to the mix.[47] Nor did the order identify any particularly controversial subject Judge Cedarbaum

---

[39] Globe Newspaper Co. v. Sup. Ct., 457 U.S. 596, 605–06 (1982); Richmond Newspapers, Inc. v. Virginia, 448 U.S. 555, 580 (1980).

[40] Press-Enterprise Co. v. Superior Court, 464 U.S. 501, 504–10 (1984) [hereinafter *Press-Enterprise I*].

[41] ABC, Inc. v. Stewart, 360 F.3d 90, 95–96 (2d Cir. 2004).

[42] *Id.* at 96.   [43] *Id.* at 93.

[44] *Press-Enterprise I*, 464 U.S. at 510.

[45] Press-Enterprise Co. v. Superior Court, 478 U.S. 1, 14 (1986).

[46] *ABC*, 360 F.3d at 101. *But see supra* text accompanying note 42.

[47] *Id.*

thought would be explored during voir dire.[48] Thus, the court held that the order excluding the press from voir dire questioning impermissibly infringed the First Amendment right of public access to the proceedings.

Notwithstanding that the court reaffirmed the media's right to observe the voir dire phase of the trial, the coalition's victory was largely Pyrrhic. By the time the court's decision was announced, the jury had been seated and the trial was well under way. Other restrictions on the press remained firmly in place, moreover. Although the coalition had unsuccessfully challenged Judge Cederbaum's rules on juror anonymity and press contact with jurors, it did not pursue those issues on appeal. Thus, the court's ruling left unscathed both the ban on publishing the jurors' names or likenesses and the prohibition against press contacts with jurors or their families until the jurors' service was complete.

C. Implications for the Future

Press speculation about the likely composition of Martha Stewart's jury and the controversial outing of Ruth Jordan in the Tyco case raise some provocative questions about coverage of high-profile criminal trials. Are these highly publicized incidents likely to precipitate more (and more frequent) judicially imposed restrictions on how journalists ply their trade?[49]

Notably, journalists who covered the Tyco and Stewart trials were on significantly different legal footing. The *Wall Street Journal* and *New York Post* were well within their legal rights. Since no law was broken, their decision to publish Jordan's name was a discretionary, if questionable, judgment call.

In contrast, if media representatives who covered the Martha Stewart trial had published Chappel Hartridge's name before the end of the trial, their violation of Judge Cedarbaum's order would subject them to possible citation for contempt and jail time, a step that judges are increasingly – and in journalists' views, alarmingly – willing to take.[50]

[48] *Id.* at 101–02.
[49] Restrictions on press coverage of voir dire and on disclosure of jurors' identities were also imposed in the trials of HealthSouth CEO Richard Scrushy and star investment banker Frank Quattrone. Simon Romero & Kyle Whitmire, *Former Chief of HealthSouth Acquitted in $2.7 Billion Fraud: Case Fails to Sway Jury in Scrushy's Hometown*, N.Y. TIMES, June 29, 2005, at A1; Simon Romero & Kyle Whitmire, *Scrushy on Trial: Class, Race and the Pursuit of Justice in Alabama*, N.Y. TIMES, May 31, 2005, at C1; Kara Scannell & Randall Smith, *Ban on Publishing Jurors' Names Is Upheld*, WALL ST. J., Apr. 15, 2004, at C1; Kara Scannell & Randall Smith, *Quattrone Judge Bars Divulging Juror Names*, WALL ST. J., Apr. 14, 2004, at C1.
[50] *New York Times* reporter Judith Miller spent eighty-five days in jail after being held in contempt for violating a court order to reveal a confidential source who leaked Central Intelligence Agency operative Valerie Plame's identity. Mark Silva, *CIA Inquiry Shifts Focus to VP's Aid: N.Y. Times Reporter Breaks Her Silence*, CHICAGO TRIB., Oct. 1, 2005, at C7. According to the

Thus, through the simple expedient of issuing a judicial order prohibiting the press from divulging jurors' identities, the Tyco judge would have had far more leverage over media treatment of Juror No. 4. And while journalists defended the decision to publish Jordan's name, legal commentators suggested that risk-averse judges will neither accept nor rely on journalistic norms to police media self-restraint. In addition to fueling more (and more creative) judicial curbs on coverage of high-profile trials, journalists might also encounter other (perhaps equally unwelcome) changes in the ways trials are conducted, including preemptive restrictions such as increased use of sequestered or anonymous juries.[51]

Simply put, media editors and producers would be well advised to consider whether departures from established journalistic norms are tantamount to an open invitation for courts to exert a greater degree of control over press coverage of high-profile trials.[52]

II. THE MEDIA AS PUBLIC RELATIONS MACHINE

The post-Enron proliferation of high-profile prosecutions has brought with it vigorous public relations campaigns by defendants and their lawyers. This phenomenon has undoubtedly been fueled by media interest in the prosecutions, which translates into greater media access for the participants. In addition to the standard fare of speeches, interviews, and press releases, Web sites have added a new dimension to the mix and have become the medium du jour for "setting the record straight."[53] E-mails, letter-writing campaigns, and even newspaper ads have also proved to be instrumental in orchestrating the public relations wars.[54]

Reporter's Committee for Freedom of the Press, at least fifteen journalists have been jailed for refusing to disclose confidential sources since 1984. John M. Ryan, *Jail Time for Journalists*, CHICAGO TRIB., July 24, 2005, at C1.

[51] Carr, *Naming Went Too Far*, *supra* note 17. [52] *See* Carr & Liptak, *supra* note 13.

[53] Shortly after they were indicted, Martha Stewart and HealthSouth CEO Richard Scrushy launched Web sites through which they and their lawyers aggressively defended themselves. Arthur Andersen's public Web site also played a major role in the firm's fight to avoid indictment and conviction. Kathleen F. Brickey, *Andersen's Fall from Grace*, 81 WASH. U. L.Q. 917, 943–44 & n.139 (2003). High-profile defendants can gain a marketing advantage through the use of sponsored-link providers in Internet search engines. Payment of a price per hit helps ensure that the defendant's Web site will be displayed at or near the top of the list of hits a search generates. A Washington-based litigation media consultant estimated that it cost Ken Lay several thousand dollars for each quarter of a year that his Web site was listed as a top-sponsored link. Mary Flood, *Lay Is Paying to Tell His Side of the Story: He's Giving Major Search Engines Pennies a Hit to Make Sure His Web Site Gets Top Billing*, HOUSTON CHRON., Jan. 10, 2002, at A1.

[54] Arthur Andersen used its vast e-mail system to communicate with its employees to generate letter-writing campaigns, Brickey, *supra* note 53, at 942–44, and Milberg Weiss used its e-mail

The accounting firm Arthur Andersen was the first in the post-Enron con-
stellation of high-profile defendants to launch an all-out offensive to clear the
firm's name, spending $1.5 million over four months to burnish its reputation.[55]
Not to be outdone, Martha Stewart spent at least $1 million on jury experts and
public relations consultants who convened focus groups (at an estimated cost
of more than $10,000 per group), polled New York residents by phone (also
said to be expensive), created a Web site that attracted millions of hits and
generated nearly one hundred thousand sympathetic e-mail messages (cost
unknown),[56] arranged carefully orchestrated interviews with Larry King and
Barbara Walters shortly before the trial began,[57] and hired consultants to help
select a jury they hoped would be sympathetic to successful businesswomen
(estimated cost of up to $500,000).[58]

Although in some instances these public relations efforts have been wildly
successful, others have at times embarrassingly backfired and focused attention
where it was most unwanted. Nonetheless, wisely or not, public relations ploys
of every stripe have become an integral part of the defense strategy in celebrity
trials. So how could the media possibly resist?

A. The Demon Card

Arthur Andersen waged a highly aggressive public relations campaign to avoid
criminal prosecution for obstruction of justice in connection with its shredding
of tons of Enron-related documents. From the outset, Andersen's multipronged
public relations efforts were highly effective.

On one front, Andersen sought to humanize the story by spotlighting the
thousands of employees who stood to lose their jobs if the firm were criminally
charged.[59] Andersen even enlisted the legendary former UCLA basketball

system to advantage by sending messages that directed recipients to its Web site. Amanda
Bronstad, *A Web-Savy Firm*, NAT'L L.J., May 29, 2006, at 10.

[55] Constance L. Hays & Leslie Eaton, *Martha Stewart, Near Trial, Arranges Her Image*, N.Y.
TIMES, Jan. 20, 2004, at A1.

[56] *But see supra* note 53 and accompanying text.

[57] Her lawyers had approved the Walters and King interviews but were surprised by an earlier
interview, published in the *New Yorker*, that Stewart decided to do on her own.

[58] Hays & Eaton, *supra* note 55.

[59] Andersen's heavy investment in Internet and telecommunications technology made grassroots
organizing a relatively simple task. Chicago executives in Andersen's internal technology
services operation could dial seven digits on their phone and reach any Andersen employee
worldwide. "Imagine having an 85,000-person discussion group," he said. John Schwartz,
Arthur Andersen Employees Circle the Wagons, N.Y. TIMES, Mar. 22, 2002, at C1. The company's
Internet connections enabled it to send mass e-mail communications to employees telling them
how to contact congressional representatives and the media. The employees, in turn, were able
to send their own mass e-mail messages to politicians and reporters.

coach John Wooden to help draft a letter calling on President Bush to intervene on Andersen's behalf.[60]

In contrast with its effort to put a human face on the firm, a second prong of Andersen's strategy was to demonize the prosecutors. From the outset, Andersen claimed that criminal prosecution of the firm would be unjust and "an extraordinary abuse of prosecutorial discretion."[61] Using every possible opportunity to elaborate on this theme, Andersen legal documents called the government's decision to prosecute the firm "extraordinary," "an unprecedented exercise of prosecutorial discretion," and "a gross abuse of governmental power."[62] Andersen even claimed that the prosecution was politically motivated.[63]

Andersen's Web site was also instrumental in its effort to discredit the government's case. It prominently posted documents that its lawyers prepared, claiming myriad "factual and legal errors" in the indictment and calling the obstruction of justice charge "false and wholly unsupported by the facts."[64] A series of press releases posted on the Web site repeatedly reinforced those themes.[65] And then there were full-page ads published in the *Wall Street Journal* – including Coach Wooden's letter to the president.[66]

Not surprisingly, legal arguments embedded in Andersen's campaign to discredit the case found their way into mainstream media coverage.

Articles liberally quoted everything from Andersen's Web site postings to documents its lawyers prepared.[67] Language found in Web site postings and

---

[60] Flynn McRoberts, *Repeat Offender Gets Stiff Justice*, CHICAGO TRIB., Sept. 4, 2002, at A1.

[61] Press Release, Statement by Arthur Andersen, LLP (on file with author) (Mar. 14, 2002) [hereinafter Andersen March 14 Press Release].

[62] Letter from Richard J. Favretto of Mayer, Brown, Rowe & Maw, to Michael Chertoff, Assistant Attorney General at 1 (Mar. 13, 2002) (on file with author) [hereinafter Favretto Letter].

[63] Such claims are easy to make but hard to accept given that the firm's political action committee put Andersen among the top-five corporate contributors to the Bush campaign, BARBARA LEY TOFFLER, FINAL ACCOUNTING – AMBITION, GREED, AND THE FALL OF ARTHUR ANDERSEN 251 (2003), to say nothing of the improbability that a Bush administration Justice Department would be out to get an auditor for a big energy company. And lest we forget, Andersen itself overtly sought political relief.

[64] *Updated Analysis on the Justice Indictment of Andersen: The Government's Factual and Legal Errors* at 1 (Mar. 15, 2002) [hereinafter *Andersen Analysis*] (on file with author).

[65] *See, e.g.*, Andersen March 14 Press Release, *supra* note 61.

[66] Advertisement, *Arthur Andersen, LLP, Injustice for All*, WALL ST. J., Mar. 27, 2002, at A10–11; Advertisement, *Arthur Andersen, LLP, Why We're Fighting Back*, WALL ST. J., Mar. 20, 2002, at A5.

[67] *See, e.g.*, Adrien Michaels & Peter Spiegel, *Request for a Speedy Trial May Be Slow in Coming Court Case*, FIN. TIMES, Mar. 20, 2002, at 40 (quoting *Andersen Analysis*, *supra* note 64); Jackie Spinner and Susan Schmidt, *Andersen Wants Quick Trial on Obstruction Charge; Accounting Giant Faces Rising Number of Defections by Clients*, WASH. POST, Mar. 16, 2002, at E01 (same); Zachary Coile, *U.S. Issues Blistering Andersen Indictment; Action Threatens Survival of Enron*

press releases appeared in documents filed with the court. Sound bites in interviews with the press echoed the defense team's legal claims. And so it went down the line. And when all was said and done, Andersen's legal and public relations strategies had become so closely intertwined that it was hard to tell one from the other.[68] All this with a generous boost from the press.

As one might expect, the government cried foul. Prosecutors complained that Andersen's campaign was designed to "flood the public record" with slanted and inaccurate claims.[69] Government lawyers were concerned that the repetition of Andersen's misleading and manipulative statements in the press could influence the recollection and testimony of witnesses called to testify at Andersen's trial.[70] Indeed, prosecutors even suggested that some of Andersen's highly unusual tactics bordered on witness coaching.

Although these concerns did not translate into concrete judicial rulings, they raised fundamental questions about the potential impact Andersen's public relations campaign could have on the case. Not only was Andersen's strategy to bring public pressure to bear on the decision whether to prosecute; its effort to try the case in the court of public opinion also had significant potential to taint the jury pool.

The case against Andersen moved along with "giga-light speed."[71] Not so with Enron's CEO Ken Lay, whose prosecution proceeded at a far more stately pace. Bearing that in mind, Ken Lay's tale begins with a showcase event held on the eve of his trial.

On December 13, 2005 – nearly a year and a half after his indictment for conspiracy and fraud – Lay gave a speech before five hundred or so Houston

Accounting Firm, San Francisco Chron., Mar. 15, 2002, at A1 (same); Kurt Eichenwald, *Grand Jury Being Misused as Investigator, Andersen Says*, N.Y. Times, Mar. 26, 2002, at C1 (quoting Andersen's motion to quash); Jerry Hirsch, Edmund Sanders, & Jeff Leeds, *Auditor Balks at Guilty Plea in Enron Case: Andersen Says Its Destruction of Papers Does Not Warrant a Plea Bargain That Could Be Firm's Death Sentence*, L.A. Times, Mar. 14, 2002, Bus. Sec., at 1 (quoting Favretto Letter, *supra* note 62); Susan Schmidt, *Andersen Refuses to Plead Guilty: Firm Could Be Indicted Today*, Wash. Post, Mar. 14, 2002, at A01 (same).

[68] Brickey, *supra* note 53, at 944–45.
[69] Government's Mem. of Law in Opp. to Def. Andersen's Mot. to Quash Subpoenas and Limit Grand Jury Proceedings, at 4–8 (Mar. 28, 2002) (on file with author).
[70] *Id.* at 2.
[71] Kurt Eichenwald, *Andersen Wins an Early Trial as Date Is Set for May 6*, N.Y. Times, Mar. 21, 2002, at C1. Andersen was convicted after lengthy jury deliberations, but the Supreme Court overturned the conviction because of an erroneous jury instruction. Arthur Andersen LLP v. United States, 544 U.S. 696 (2005).

business and academic leaders. Enron was the subject of his talk, of course, and the speech received widespread national media attention.[72]

But what made this event so noteworthy? Every Houstonian in the audience already knew the story of Enron's collapse, and his speech drew what the *Houston Chronicle* described as "polite applause."[73] National media interest in his speech would be understandable if this had been the first time Lay had spoken out since his indictment, but he had long since turned to the media to get his version of the truth publicly told.

Thus, for example, immediately after appearing in court to plead not guilty the year before, Lay and his lawyers went directly to a crowded hotel ballroom where he held an hour-long televised press conference. Pursuing a bold, if risky, strategy, he described the events leading up to Enron's collapse, explained his then-controversial sales of Enron stock, and fielded more than a dozen questions from reporters.[74] His press conference launched a media blitz that included an appearance on CNN's *Larry King Live*[75] and an interview of his lead lawyer on CBS's *MarketWatch*.

So back to the Houston speech on the eve of the trial. Ken Lay spoke at length about what a good company Enron was and the constructive role he had played in building it. He also proclaimed his love of the company and his sadness at the loss of jobs and Enron's good name. But there is little new

---

[72] *See, e.g.,* John Emshwiller, *Lay to Testify at His Enron* Trial, WALL ST. J., Dec. 14, 2005, at B3; Kristen Hays, *Enron Founder Lay Asks Ex-Employees for Help*, ST. LOUIS POST-DISPATCH, Dec. 14, 2005, at B7; Carrie Johnson, *Enron Judge Refuses to Issue Gag Order*, WASH. POST, Dec. 17, 2005, at D2 [hereinafter Johnson, *Judge Refuses Gag Order*]; Carrie Johnson, *Enron Prosecutors Seek Gag Order After Speech*, WASH. POST, Dec. 16, 2005, at D2 [hereinafter Johnson, *Prosecutors Seek Gag Order*]; Joseph Nocera, *Living in the Enron Dream World*, N.Y. TIMES, Dec. 28, 2005, at B1; Simon Romero, *Enron's Chief Offers His Case*, N.Y. TIMES, Dec. 14, 2005, at C1; *U.S. Asks for Gag Order After Lay's Speech*, WALL ST. J., Dec. 16, 2005, at C4.

[73] Mary Flood, *Setting the Stage: Vocal Lay Foreshadows Defense in Speech: Ex-Enron Chief Says His Trust in Fastow was "Fatally Misplaced,"* HOUSTON CHRON., Dec. 14, 2005, at A1 [hereinafter Flood, *Setting the Stage*].

[74] Transcript, Ken Lay Press Conference at Doubletree Hotel, Houston, Tex. (July 8, 2004) (on file with author) [hereinafter Press Conference Transcript]; John R. Emshwiller, Rebecca Smith, Kara Scannell, & Deborah Soloman, *Lay Strikes Back as Indictment Cites Narrow Role in Enron Fraud*, WALL ST. J., July 9, 2004, at A1; Mary Flood, Tom Fowler, & Michael Hedges, *Lay: It Wasn't Criminal: The Charges: Lay Hit with 11 Counts, Including Wire and Bank Fraud, and Making False Statements: His Reaction: Ex-Enron Chairman Calls Collapse "a Tragedy" But Does Not Equate It to a Crime*, HOUSTON CHRON., July 9, 2004, at A1; Kristen Hays, *Ken Lay Proclaims Innocence in Fraud Case: Indictment Accuses Former Enron Exec of Conspiracy in Collapse*, ST. LOUIS POST-DISPATCH, July 9, 2004, at C1; Kara Scannell & Rebecca Smith, *Former Enron CEO Makes His Case on Television*, WALL ST. J., July 9, 2004, at B1.

[75] Transcript, CNN's *Larry King Live*, Interview With Ken Lay (July 12, 2004) (on file with author) [hereinafter Interview Transcript].

here to provide grist for the mill, except what one reporter described as its
"[a]ggressively self-pitying" content and tone.[76]

Apart from feeling persecuted by the government, Lay was pointedly angry at
the Enron Task Force. He charged that aggressive prosecutors had unleashed
a "wave of terror" in their relentless pursuit of criminal cases, leaving no
stone unturned to look for crimes where none existed. He also criticized the
prosecutors for prolonging the Enron investigation well beyond the projected
time line for completing it.[77] But this, too, was old news. Lay had publicly
blasted the prosecution on this point a year before.

But his December pretrial speech personalized the attack by raising a question about the lead prosecutor, Andrew Weissmann, who had left his post
with the Enron Task Force in July. Calling Weissmann's departure "sudden
and unexpected," Lay asked whether it was a "coincidence" that he left the
prosecution team "only days" after defense lawyers had filed a motion alleging prosecutorial misconduct in handling the case.[78] Lay's speech did not
directly accuse Weissmann of misconduct, but the pointed reference to him
was clearly a smear by innuendo. The alleged "coincidence" that Weissmann
left the Enron Task Force just as the defense team was crying foul was later
repeated in an article in the *Legal Times* soon after the Skilling-Lay trial got
under way.[79]

Yet as the *Houston Chronicle* inconveniently observed the day after the
speech, Weissmann's departure had been planned – and was expected by his
fellow prosecutors – months in advance.[80] And less than two weeks before
Lay gave his speech, Judge Sim Lake ruled that the defense had produced no
evidence of prosecutorial misconduct.[81] The reference to Weissmann in Lay's

---

[76] Nocera, *supra* note 72.   [77] Lay Speech, *supra* note 5.

[78] *Id.*

[79] The *Legal Times* reported that "Andrew Weissmann resigned from the Task Force in July 2005 –
which happened to be when defense lawyers in the Lay and Skilling case said they were going
to file a motion alleging prosecutorial misconduct." Miriam Rozen, *Enron Team Looks to
Bolster Its Record*, LEGAL TIMES, Feb. 6, 2006, at 12.

[80] Flood, *Setting the Stage*, *supra* note 73. *See also* Interview with Andrew Weissmann, Former
Director, Enron Task Force, New York, N.Y., 14 CORP. CRIME REP. 9, 14–15 (Feb. 27, 2006).
Weissmann decided to leave once it became clear that the months-long trial would last well
into 2006, John R. Emshwiller, *Head of Enron Task Force to Resign: Departure Comes as Group
Still Faces Its Biggest Test: The Trial of Lay, Skilling*, WALL ST. J., Jul. 19, 2005, at C3, and
he timed his departure to coincide with the end of the Enron broadband services trial. Flood,
Setting the Stage, *supra* note 73.

[81] Mary Flood, *Judge Turns Back Defense: He Sees No Evidence of Misconduct by Prosecution*,
HOUSTON CHRON., Dec. 2, 2005, at Bus. 1. Judge Lake said the public had a right to know
whether there had been prosecutorial misconduct, but that if there had been no wrongdoing
the allegations should be "publicly dispelled." *Id.*

speech was, of course, intended to blunt the effect of Judge Lake's ruling and plant the seeds of distrust among potential Houston jurors.

Another notable aspect of the speech was its timing – scarcely a month before the trial was expected to begin. And, perhaps, equally important, it previewed the key points of Lay's defense: (1) that the prosecution was trying to criminalize legitimate business activity that officers of publicly held corporations engage in every day; (2) that the scope of the wrongdoing was limited, that it was orchestrated by a handful of bad apples without the knowledge of the top executives or the board, and that CFO Andy Fastow (whom Lay called "despicable and criminal") played the role of culprit in chief;[82] (3) that aggressive prosecutorial tactics had driven innocent Enron employees to plead guilty and become cooperating witnesses because they were running out of money to defend themselves; (4) that Enron was a successful company that went into bankruptcy not because it was insolvent but because of liquidity problems; (5) that Enron's collapse into bankruptcy was triggered by the bursting of the stock market bubble and by media coverage of possible wrongdoing by Fastow, which prompted a loss of investor confidence; and, last but not least, (6) that Lay would testify at his trial.

Perhaps the reason why the speech drew only "polite" applause was best captured in a *Houston Chronicle* reporter's quip. Lay seemed to be talking not to the businesspeople and academics in the audience but to the jury that would ultimately sit in judgment[83] and to former Enron employees whom he urged to come forward and "join in this fight."[84] Simply put, Lay needed two things: a sympathetic jury and the cooperation of potential defense witnesses who had made it clear that they would invoke their Fifth Amendment privilege and refuse to testify.

These sentiments echoed much of what he said on *Larry King Live* the week after his indictment was announced. But the Larry King interview was punctuated with references to the "media frenzy"[85] accompanying Enron's

[82] Fastow, who had pled guilty and was cooperating with the government, was scheduled to be a key witness for the prosecution at Lay's trial.

[83] Flood, *Setting the Stage, supra* note 73. His attempts to impugn the credibility of Andy Fastow and other cooperating witnesses who would testify at trial and to call into question the motives of the Enron Task Force in bringing the prosecution prompted the government to seek a gag order prohibiting out of court statements before the trial. Johnson, *Prosecutors Seek Gag Order.* Calling Lay's speech "a drop in the bucket" relative to other media coverage of the scandal, the judge denied the motion. Johnson, *Judge Refuses Gag Order, supra* note 72.

[84] Lay Speech, *supra* note 5.

[85] Lay also used the term *media frenzy* at the press conference he held on the day of his arraignment. Press Conference Transcript, *supra* note 74. When asked why the public did not believe he was out of the loop at Enron, he said that media publicity had "lock[ed] in a lot of views" about Enron's culture and that "we've seen some of that even popularized in TV movies." *Id.*

collapse, which became one of the most stunning claims he made in his testimony at trial: the *Wall Street Journal* did it.

The *Journal's* "complicity" in Enron's demise began in mid-October 2001, when the paper ran a series of articles that raised serious doubt about "the bona fides of Andy Fastow"[86] and his off-book partnership called LJM. The first article was published the day after Enron announced its third-quarter net loss and huge write-down in shareholder equity. Despite clear market concerns reflected in Moody's decision to put Enron securities on a credit watch for a possible downgrade, and notwithstanding that the *New York Times* and the *Financial Times* were giving major coverage to the Enron story and that *Fortune* magazine had published an early article that questioned how Enron made money,[87] Lay accused the *Wall Street Journal* of conducting a witch hunt that "kicked off a shockwave among investors" and caused a market panic that led to Enron's collapse.[88]

Although he never identified any inaccuracies in the stories, Lay testified at trial that he thought the early articles "mischaracterized the true health and the true condition of Enron and overemphasized – primarily overemphasized the LJM matter and Andy Fastow and things that we . . . thought had become history."[89] Thus, in the end, Ken Lay turned on the media he had earlier turned to as a way to "start telling my story" and "get more of the truth" publicly told.[90]

Lay's codefendant Jeff Skilling also spoke out about Enron's fall, motivated (he said) by the need to get the truth about Enron publicly told. Like Lay, Skilling gave media interviews (including an interview on *Larry King Live*) and blamed the *Wall Street Journal* for Enron's downfall. But unlike Lay, who invoked his Fifth Amendment right to remain silent,[91] Skilling gave sworn testimony before the SEC and testified under oath at congressional hearings, where he sparred with members of the House Energy and Commerce Committee in full view of cameras and the press.[92]

---

[86] Transcript, Opening Statement of Mike Ramsey, Counsel for Ken Lay, at 537 (Jan. 31, 2006), United States v. Skilling, No. CRH-04–25 (S.D. Tex. 2006) (on file with author) [hereinafter Trial Transcript].

[87] McLean, *Enron Overpriced?, supra* note 3, at 122.

[88] Trial Transcript, *supra* note 86 (questioning of defendant Ken Lay by defense attorney George Secrest) (Apr. 24, 2006).

[89] *Id.* (questioning of defendant Ken Lay by prosecutor John Hueston) (Apr. 27, 2006).

[90] Interview Transcript, *supra* note 75.

[91] Richard A. Oppel Jr. & Joseph Kahn, *Enron's Ex-Chief Harshly Criticized by Senate Panel: Both Parties Join in Fray; Lay Appeals to Congress Not to Rush to Judgment, and Then Takes the Fifth,* N.Y. TIMES, Feb. 13, 2002, at A1.

[92] Skilling told the Committee he believed Enron failed because of a lack of confidence in the company triggered partly by media reports that set off alarm bells for investors and creditors. Tom Hamburger & Greg Hitt, *House Panel Challenges Skilling over Role at Enron: Executive*

At trial, Skilling told the jury that Enron's death spiral had been helped along by a witch hunt that originated with Congress, regulators, and the press. More specifically, he pointed to the *Fortune* magazine article that first cast doubt on Enron's credibility and the *Wall Street Journal* article that was published the day after Enron announced substantial third-quarter losses in October 2001.

Like Lay, Skilling testified that the *Journal* article had managed to transform "good" news (a $618 million third-quarter loss and a $1.2 billion write-down in shareholder equity) into "bad" (implying wrongdoing by Andy Fastow in his dealings with LJM). But Skilling went so far as to say the *Fortune* and *Journal* articles were so one sided that he believed both had been "planted by short sellers."[93]

So Jeff Skilling – who had recently been touted as one of the country's brightest business leaders[94] and had granted interviews with the likes of Larry King to get the Enron story told – now blamed the media for conducting a witch hunt that unfairly maligned the company and its top management.

Yet scarcely three weeks after his conviction, Skilling said in an interview that his willingness to speak up before the trial – particularly his discussions with the SEC – had been a mistake that helped the prosecution.[95] And the forum he chose for this interview? The *Wall Street Journal*, of course.[96] Oh, the irony of it all.

B. *The Race and Religion Card*

Religion has, for better or worse, been part of the legal scene in the post-Enron era. Religion became part of Ken Lay's public persona at least as early as his July 2004 interview on *Larry King Live*, in which he discussed his own upbringing as the son of a Baptist minister and his belief that faith would sustain him throughout his legal ordeal.[97] He also liberally injected religious references into his first day of testimony at the criminal-fraud trial,[98] insisting

Denies Knowledge About Partnership Details and Fastow Takes Fifth, WALL ST. J., Feb. 8, 2002; Lorraine Woellert, *The-Reporter-Did-It-Defense: Ken Lay Claims the Press Sped Enron's Fall by Scaring Investors; Does He Have a Case?*, BUS. WK., May 8, 2006, at 34.

[93] Trial Transcript, *supra* note 86 (testimony of Jeff Skilling) (Apr. 10, 2006). The articles were published about six months apart.

[94] Wendy Zellner, *Derring-Do in the Corner Office*, BUS. WK., Feb. 21, 2001, at 80.

[95] John Emshwiller, *In New Interview, Skilling Says He Hurt Case by Speaking Up: Former Enron President Says He Can Survive Jail; Depressing Days in Bed*, WALL ST. J., June 17, 2006, at A1.

[96] *Id.*   [97] Interview Transcript, *supra* note 75.

[98] Alexei Barrionuevo & Simon Romero, *Ken Lay Opens Up to the Jury: A Folksy Defense in Enron Trial*, N.Y. TIMES, Apr. 25, 2006, at C1 (noting Lay's "ready references to his faith in God"); *Excerpts from Testimony by Enron Founder Ken Lay*, WALL ST. J. ONLINE, May 2, 2006 (observing that on his first day on the stand, "Lay worked in references to his faith at every opportunity") (on file with author).

that he would not have engaged in criminal conduct because it would be contrary to his "moral compass and religious faith."[99]

To the casual observer, there seemed to be nothing cynical about Lay's emergence as a man of faith. Although his frequent public references to his religious beliefs on the nation's airwaves and on the stand may have been in part an effort to burnish his image as the congenial, decent man who was for years a pillar of the Houston community, they nonetheless seemed sincere. Nothing suggested that his was a last-minute conversion.

Not so with HealthSouth's CEO Richard Scrushy, who began to practice his religion in a very public way when the time was ripe. Before his fraud indictment and throughout the lengthy criminal trial,[100] Scrushy made every effort to develop a public persona that would resonate with a jury from Birmingham, Alabama.

The initial challenge for the white multimillionaire to connect with the jury pool began with demographics. Nearly 75 percent of Birmingham's population is African American.[101] Scrushy thus anticipated – correctly – a strong minority presence on the jury. Eleven of the eighteen veniremen were African American, and of the twelve jurors who completed the deliberations, half were black.[102]

Scrushy began with his legal team, which was an evolving work of art.[103] His chief legal adviser was Donald Watkins, a wealthy African American businessman and entrepreneur who could readily connect with a predominantly black jury.[104]

---

[99] Greg Farrell, Lay: No "Simple Answer" on Failure: "American Dream" Became "Nightmare," USA TODAY, Apr. 25, 2006, at B1.

[100] Scrushy was allegedly the mastermind behind a $2.7 billion fraud at HealthSouth.

[101] U.S. Census Bureau, http://quickfacts.census.gov/gfd/states/01/010700.html (last visited Aug. 16, 2007). African Americans also constitute about 40 percent of the population in Jefferson County, where Birmingham is located.

[102] Nine of the sixteen jurors and alternates were African American. Dan Morse, For Former HealthSouth Chief, An Appeal to Higher Authority: As Fraud Trial Nears an End, Scrushy Preaches in Church, Interviews Ministers on TV; Not Aimed at Jurors, He Says, WALL ST. J., May 13, 2005, at A1.

[103] Scrushy went through at least four teams of lawyers before the case went to trial. See Carrick Mollenkamp, Behind the Scrushy Defense: Shifting Teams, Feuding Lawyers; HealthSouth Founder Taps a Birmingham Attorney in Unorthodox Strategy; Celebrating in the Wine Cellar, WALL ST. J., Feb. 2, 2005, at A1 [hereinafter Mollenkamp, Behind the Scrushy Defense].

[104] Although his lead trial counsel was Jim Parkman, Scrushy tapped Watkins as his chief legal adviser. Watkins had not practiced law for more than five years, but he masterminded the sometimes-unorthodox defense strategy Scrushy's team of advisers pursued. In exchange for his agreement to interrupt his efforts to buy a Major League Baseball team, Watkins required a $5 million retainer. Greg Farrell, Scrushy's Lawyer Says Lay Strategy Was Wrong: "You Never, Ever Put the CEO on the Witness Stand," USA TODAY, May 30, 2006, at B3 [hereinafter Farrell, Scrushy's Lawyer]; Mollenkamp, Behind the Scrushy Defense, supra note 103.

Watkins's first priority was to reshape Scrushy's public image from that of a wealthy and imperious businessman into that of a fundamentalist Christian who came from humble origins and identified deeply with issues of race, class, and the civil rights struggle. In his words, "The first trial is always in the court of public opinion, and it comes down to community support and good will."[105]

Scrushy molded his private life to mirror his legal and public relations strategy. First, he left the predominantly white Vestavia Hills evangelical church he had been attending to join the Guiding Light Church – a predominantly black congregation with about four thousand members.[106] His switch to Guiding Light coincided with a $350,000 gift he made to the church, a precursor to donations totaling more than $1 million he gave to Guiding Light Ministries in 2003.[107]

Then he began preaching at other fundamentalist churches – often black or predominantly black congregations. During the year of the fraud trial, he and his wife preached at more than forty Birmingham churches[108] "to share [their] testimonies of the trials and persecution" they had experienced at the government's hands.[109] That same year, Scrushy's foundation gave more than $800,000 to churches whose pastors and congregants regularly attended his trial.[110] And just a month before the trial began, he became an ordained, nondenominational Christian minister.[111]

---

[105] Farrell, *Scrushy's Lawyer, supra* note 104. Watkins's view was that only when the client had his public relations strategy in place could he turn his attention to a trial strategy.

[106] Morse, *supra* note 102. Denying that the switch had anything to do with his legal problems, he explained that he "felt called to attend" Guiding Light after watching its pastor on television while he was exercising. Simon Romero, *Will the Real Richard Scrushy Please Step Forward: Race, Religion and the HealthSouth Founder's Trial*, N.Y. Times, Feb. 17, 2005, at C1 [hereinafter Romero, *Please Step Forward*]. Or, in the alternative, he abandoned Vestavia Hills because he felt "judged" by his fellow congregants. Thomas S. Mulligan, *Jurors Struggle in Scrushy Fraud Case: The Judge Tells Them to Keep Trying; The Former Executive Has Mounted a Vigorous Public Defense*, L.A. Times, June 4, 2005, at A1.

[107] Greg Farrell, *Former HealthSouth CEO Scrushy Turns Televangelist*, USA Today, Oct. 26, 2004, at 1B [hereinafter Farrell, *Scrushy Turns Televangelist*]; Peggy Gargis & Karen Jacobs, *Scrushy Acquittal Gets Alabama Hallelujahs, Boos*, Reuters, June 29, 2005, *available at* http://www.tiscali.co.uk/news/newswire.php/news/reuters/2005/06/29/business/ scrushyacquittalgets alabamahallelujahboos.html?page=2.

[108] Michael Tomberlin, *Scrushy Charity Gave to Churches: Foundation Sent $700,000 to Groups Supporting Him*, Birmingham News, Dec. 25, 2005, at 1D [hereinafter Tomberlin, *Charity Gave to Churches*].

[109] Michael Tomberlin, *Scrushy Widens Ministry: Web Site Details Roles as Pastor, Televangelist*, Birmingham News, Mar. 10, 2006, at B1.

[110] *Id.*; Tomberlin, *Charity Gave to Churches, supra* note 108.

[111] Morse, *supra* note 102; *Scrushy Starts Ministry as Trial Nears: Kingdom Builders Will Offer Services Including Mortgages, Insurance and Healthcare, He Says*, L.A. Times, Apr. 17, 2006, at C2 [hereinafter *Scrushy Starts Ministry*].

But Scrushy's media strategy had also transformed the CEO and minister into a broadcast personality as well. Before he was formally charged, he appeared in a *60 Minutes* interview with Mike Wallace, having waited "for the right opportunity . . . to tell his story."[112] And while he was under indictment, Scrushy and his wife, Leslie, launched a thirty-minute television show that aired five days a week.[113] The morning talk show, called *Viewpoint*, provided a forum for discussing news stories "truthfully and accurately, free from the bias of mainstream media."[114] The program often featured black ministers from the Birmingham community as guests.[115]

And just who bankrolled this operation? The time slot was purchased by Word of Truth Productions, an affiliate of the Guiding Light Church.[116] The program's only sponsor was Alamerica Bank, which was run by Donald Watkins, Scrushy's top legal adviser.[117]

But that's only the beginning. While the Birmingham trial was in progress, a second program, *The Scrushy Trial with Nikki Preede*, aired daily on another local channel. As its title suggests, *The Scrushy Trial* was devoted exclusively to favorable reporting on – what else – the Scrushy trial. And, in what a cynic might call an extreme example of synergy: (1) Scrushy's son-in-law had spent $2 million to buy a controlling interest in the same station not long before the trial began;[118] (2) the producer of *The Scrushy Trial* was a former member

---

[112] 60 Minutes Interviews Richard Scrushy, http://www.richardmsrcushy.com/newsdetail. aspx?News_ID= 2News_ID=2 (posted Oct. 13, 2003) (last visited on Nov. 7, 2003) (quoting Scrushy's legal adviser Donald Watkins). A week later, in an interview on the Birmingham talk show *The Breakfast Club*, Watkins defended Scrushy's refusal to testify at the congressional hearing and discussed his tenure at HealthSouth. *Available at* http://www.richardmscrushy. com/newsdetail.aspx?News_ID-6 (last visited on Nov. 7, 2003).

[113] Although Scrushy said he would not discuss the evidence in the case, he said he would "deal with the facts behind some of the personal attacks that have been made against me." *Scrushys Will Host Talk Show on WTTO, available at* http://www.al.com, Feb. 28, 2004 (archived on Mar. 3, 2004, by the author). The early morning show conveniently aired each day before the trial resumed. Morse, *supra* note 102.

[114] *Viewpoint* with Richard and Leslie Scrushy, posted on http://www.morningviewpoint.com (archived on Mar. 3, 2004, by the author).

[115] By Scrushy's own lights, his program featured guest appearances of at least two hundred ministers in the span of a year. Morse, *supra* note 102.

[116] Tom Bassing, *Scrushy and Wife Take to the Airways*, BIRMINGHAM BUS. J., Mar. 2, 2004, *available at* http://birmingham.bizjournals.com/birmingham/stories/2004/03/01/daily10.html. The *Viewpoint* time slot followed a show featuring taped Guiding Light Church worship services.

[117] Michael Tomberlin, *Scrushys' TV Show at the Bottom of Ratings*, http://www.al.com, Mar. 3, 2004 (archived on Mar. 3, 2004, by the author). *See supra* notes 104–05 and accompanying text.

[118] When Scrushy later established his own congregation, it met in his son-in-law's television studio. Michael Tomberlin, *Scrushy "Radioactive" After Trial: Business, Ministry Look Dim, Experts Say*, BIRMINGHAM NEWS, June 30, 2006, at 6A [hereinafter Tomberlin, *Scrushy "Radioactive"*]; *Scrushy Starts Ministry, supra* note 111. The *Viewpoint* set also served as the

of Scrushy's country music band; (3) the program's legal commentator, who appeared on the show about three times a week, had previously been on Scrushy's legal team; and (4) after he bought the station, Scrushy's son-in-law aired *Viewpoint* twice a day in the time slot next to *The Scrushy Trial* show.[119] An attempt to sway the jury?[120] *Res ipsa loquitor.*

Scrushy's Web site and television show were highly critical of the mainstream media, but his antipathy toward the press culminated in yet another bold attention-grabbing move three weeks before his trial began: he sued the *Birmingham News* for libel.[121] The complaint contained twelve counts of libel, a single count of "tortuous [sic] interference with a contract,"[122] and one count of intentional infliction of emotional distress.[123]

His press release announcing the lawsuit decried the "drumbeat of libel by the *Birmingham News*."[124] But judging from the complaint's thin litany of libels, one could easily conclude that the lawsuit was more a publicity stunt than a serious legal claim.[125] For example, one "libel" published by the *News*

background for a Scrushy news conference at which he proclaimed his innocence the day before he was arraigned in Montgomery on bribery charges. Simon Romero, *A High-Profile Trial, a TV Show and a Son-in-Law in Charge*, N.Y. TIMES, Nov. 7, 2005, at C4 [hereinafter Romero, *A High-Profile Trial*].

[119] Chad Terhune & Evelina Shmukler, *"Scrushy Trial" on Local TV Is Family Affair*, WALL ST. J., Feb. 15, 2005, at B1; Michael Tomberlin, *TV Station Covering Trial Has Ties to Scrushy*, BIRMINGHAM NEWS, Feb. 9, 2005, at 1D. The show's host, Nikki Preede, had once done a brief public relations stint for a law firm that represented Scrushy. Terhune & Shmukler, *supra*.

Consistent with the prosecutor's complaint that Scrushy's defense team had seized every opportunity to "stand on the corner to be interviewed" on *The Scrushy Trial* show, Scrushy advisers gave reporters covering the trial plastic spatulas emblazoned with a quote from the opening statement for the defense: "No matter how thin you make it, there's two sides to every pancake." *Id.* And as one commentator wondered, "What's next? Will Scrushy have a blimp over the courthouse, too?" *Id.*

[120] Scrushy, of course, denied that he had any connection with the program. But after the prosecutor voiced concerns about it, the judge instructed the jury not to watch it or any other program related to Scrushy or HealthSouth. *Id.* Scrushy also regularly held "press conferences" during the trial. Gargis & Jacobs, *supra* note 107.

[121] Complaint, Scrushy v. Birmingham News, No. CV 2005 002496 (Jefferson County, Ala. Cir. Ct., Mar. 20, 2004) (on file with author) [hereinafter Complaint].

Scrushy had earlier planned to start his own statewide newspaper to compete with the *Birmingham News*. Michael Tomberlin, *Talk Show Debuts*, BIRMINGHAM NEWS, Mar. 2, 2004.

[122] Complaint, *supra* note 121, at 19, 20. See also Press Release, Richard Scrushy Files Suit Against *The Birmingham News*, Dec. 20, 2004 (on file with author) [hereinafter Scrushy Press Release].

[123] Complaint, *supra* note 121, at 20–21.　　　[124] Scrushy Press Release, *supra* note 122.

[125] Among the most ludicrous examples of the "drumbeat of libel" are two cartoons – one depicting a prison, surrounded by barbed wire, bearing the name "Richard M. Scrushy Correctional Facility," and another showing Scrushy "on Santa's bad list." Scrushy Press Release, *supra* note 122. After his criminal trials were complete, the lawsuit was dismissed with prejudice on the filing of a joint motion by both parties. Michael Tomberlin, *Scrushy, News File to Dismiss Lawsuit: Spokesman Says Other Legal Issues Pressing*, BIRMINGHAM NEWS, Mar. 21, 2006, at

was that Scrushy "chose not to answer questions from Congress, even refusing to proclaim his innocence in the financial scandal engulfing the company he created."[126]

But as the *New York Times* and the *Wall Street Journal* (accurately) reported, Scrushy did invoke his Fifth Amendment privilege at a hearing before the House Energy and Commerce Committee on October 16, 2004, just weeks before he was indicted.[127] And yes, timing is everything. Scrushy refused to testify before the Committee only a few days after his self-serving moment in the sun had aired on *60 Minutes*.[128]

But Scrushy's media machine was anything but one-dimensional. A few weeks before he was indicted, he launched a personal Web site[129] "to fulfill[] two immediate needs" – to tell his side of the story and to correct inaccuracies about his case.[130] He described the Web site as

> a medium to help set the record straight and level the playing field. No longer will the public have to be content with a single, one-sided presentation of the facts filtered through and reflecting the personal prejudices of various news reporters. Those stories will be challenged and corrected.[131]

The Web site also served as a forum for Scrushy's lawyers to respond from "an objective viewpoint" to questions about his strategies. The initial posting nicely sums up Scrushy's need to speak through unfiltered media: "[W]e cannot continuously issue press announcements for local distribution . . . or continuously 'negotiate' comments for publication by local and national media. This case has received national and international attention, and the Web site gives us an international medium through which to communicate."[132]

1D; Dismissal, Scrushy v. Birmingham News, No. CV 2005 002496 (Jefferson County, Ala. Cir. Ct., Mar. 27, 2006) (on file with author).

[126] Scrushy Press Release, *supra* note 122.

[127] Milt Freudenheim, *Former Chief of HealthSouth Refuses to Respond at Hearing: Scrushy Asserts Fifth Amendment*, N.Y. TIMES, Oct. 17, 2003, at C7; Carrick Mollenkamp, *HealthSouth's Ex-Chief Invokes Right to Silence: Scrushy Refuses to Answer Questions from Lawmakers but Criticizes Investigators*, WALL ST. J., Oct. 17, 2003, at A7 [hereinafter Mollenkamp, *Ex-Chief Invokes Right to Silence*].

[128] Freudenheim, *supra* note 127; Mollenkamp, *Ex-Chief Invokes Right to Silence*, *supra* note 127. After Scrushy refused to testify, the committee played an eight-minute excerpt of the broadcast interview and wondered aloud why he would be unwilling to say the same thing to the Committee. *Id.*

[129] *Available at* http://www.richardmscrushy.com.

[130] *Id.*

[131] *Richard Scrushy Launches Web site*, *available at* http://www.richardmscrushy.com/newsdetail. aspx? News_ID=8 (quoting Tom Sjoblom, then attorney for Scrushy) (archived by author Nov. 7, 2003).

[132] *Id.*

The transformation of Scrushy's public persona through preaching, broadcasting, and the Internet not only raised his visibility in the local black community; it had a spillover effect in the courtroom. One tangible sign of this was a group of loyal followers – most of them black, many of them ministers – who became known as the "amen corner" in the courtroom. From as few as six to as many as two dozen strong, they often attended the criminal trial, filling the seats on Scrushy's side of the courtroom. Many brought Bibles with them, some wore vestments, and most gave approving nods when they thought the defense scored points against the government.[133] They even prayed with Scrushy in the courtroom in the jury's presence during breaks in the trial[134] and incurred the wrath of courthouse security workers when they tried to distribute pro-Scrushy leaflets as jury deliberations began.[135]

All told, Scrushy's media and public relations strategy succeeded in transforming the trial into a narrative about class and race rather than a forum for resolving accusations of a $2.7 billion accounting fraud.[136] This turn of events confounded many observers because Scrushy was, after all, a white multimillionaire, and all of the witnesses against him were white. His strategy was nonetheless highly effective. After lengthy deliberations that appeared to be headed for a deadlocked jury, the verdict was not guilty on all counts.[137]

---

[133] John Archibald, *Weird Stuff at Work at Scrushy Trial*, BIRMINGHAM NEWS, June 12, 2005, at 15A; Romero, *Please Step Forward*, *supra* note 106. *See also* Gargis & Jacobs, *supra* note 107 (quoting the pastor of a black congregation, who said that "[t]here were pastors and prayer warriors who were here in court daily supporting him. . . . We said all along that the prosecution didn't prove its case against him."); Ann Woolner, *Blacks Fill Scrushy's Amen Corner*, BIRMINGHAM NEWS, Feb. 6, 2005, at 1B.

[134] Simon Romero & Kyle Whitmire, *Writer Says Scrushy Paid Her to Write Favorable Articles*, N.Y. TIMES, Jan. 20, 2006, at C3 [hereinafter Romero & Whitmire, *Writer Says Scrushy Paid Her*].

[135] Jay Reeves, *Race Plays Subtle Role in Scrushy Trial*, May 22, 2005, http://www.cbsnews.com/stories/2005/05/22/ap/business/mainD8A8CMoGo.shtml (last visited Oct. 11, 2006). Continued media ploys during the trial and deliberations would not necessarily be lost on the jurors. The jury was never sequestered. Archibald, *supra* note 133.

[136] Reeves, *supra* note 135; Mulligan, *supra* note 106.

[137] Jerry Mitchell, *Scrushy's Home Victory Shows Venue Matters*, CLARION-LEDGER (Jackson, Miss.), July 14, 2005, at A6.

He was acquitted despite substantial evidence linking him to the fraud, partly because the jury doubted the credibility of a lengthy parade of cooperating witnesses who testified against him. Reed Abelson & Jonathan Glater, *A Style That Connected with Hometown Jurors*, N.Y. TIMES, June 29, 2005, at C1; Dan Morse et al., *HealthSouth's Scrushy Is Acquitted: Outcome Shows Challenges for Sarbanes-Oxley Act: SEC Suit Still Ahead; No Job Offer from Company*, WALL ST. J., June 29, 2005, at A1 [hereinafter *Scrushy Is Acquitted*]; Kyle Whitmire, *Jurors Doubted Scrushy's Colleagues*, N.Y. TIMES, July 2, 2005, at C5 [hereinafter Whitmire, *Jurors Doubted Scrushy's Colleagues*].

Scrushy also seems to have benefitted from the so-called *CSI* effect, a phenomenon attributed in part to the television show *CSI*, which is about crime scene investigation. Linda Deutsch,

The cause for celebration was, as it turned out, relatively short-lived. Within six months of his acquittal, Scrushy once again found himself embroiled in controversy, this time on two separate fronts. One related to a newly disclosed component of his public relations campaign during the trial. Two people from Birmingham, both of whom were associated with the Believers Temple Church, claimed that Scrushy had paid them to drum up support in the black community during the trial.

The first allegations were made by Audrey Lewis, who worked as a freelance writer and an administrator at the church. Lewis charged that she had been paid to write favorable articles about Scrushy for publication in the *Birmingham Times*, the city's oldest black-owned newspaper.[138] She said Scrushy had suggested topics for her stories and had reviewed at least two of the four articles before they were published;[139] that she had been paid $10,000 through a

"CSI" and "Law & Order" Lead Jurors to Great Expectations, ST. LOUIS POST-DISPATCH, Jan. 30, 2006, at D1. CSI investigators' heavy reliance on high-tech forensic evidence in run-of-the-mill cases – where such evidence is exceedingly rare – is thought to foster unrealistic expectations among jurors sitting in actual trials. Some Scrushy jurors faulted the prosecution for failing to produce fingerprint evidence linking Scrushy directly to the fraud. Abelson & Glater, *supra* note 137; Morse et al., *Scrushy Is Acquitted, supra*; Simon Romero & Kyle Whitmire, *Former Chief of HealthSouth Acquitted in $2.7 Billion Fraud: Case Fails to Sway Jury in Scrushy's Hometown*, N.Y. TIMES, June 29, 2005, at A1; Chad Terhune & Dan Morse, *Why Scrushy Won His Trial and Ebbers Lost*, WALL ST. J., June 30, 2005, at C1; Kyle Whitmire, *Determined to Find Guilt, but Expecting Acquittal*, N.Y. TIMES, June 29, 2005 at C5; Whitmire, *Jurors Doubted Scrushy's Colleagues, supra*.

[138] The *Birmingham Times*, which was published weekly, had a circulation of about sixteen thousand. Payments by corporations and the government to promote what passes for independent commentary have also recently come to light. *See, e.g.*, Abby Goodnough, *U.S. Paid 10 Journalists for Anti-Castro Reports: Some Are Fired for Radio and TV Deals*, N.Y. TIMES, Sept. 9, 2006, at A9 (reporting that the Bush administration's Office of Cuba Broadcasting had paid newspaper and broadcast journalists to provide commentary critical of Castro; one journalist reportedly received $175,000 between 2001 and 2006); Thom Shanker, *No Breach Seen in Work in Iraq on Propaganda*, N.Y. TIMES, Mar. 22, 2006, at A1 (reporting finding that the U.S. military had paid a public relations firm to plant favorable articles in Iraqi news sources); Philip Shenon, *G.M. Entangled in Pay-for-Publicity Dispute*, N.Y. TIMES, Apr. 28, 2006, at A19 (reporting that a public relations firm apologized after admitting it may have offered money to independent commentators to garner public support for General Motors' buyout plan; that Republican lobbyist Jack Abramoff paid at least two writers to publish articles supporting his clients' interests; and that the Bush administration had paid writers and commentators to promote the No Child Left Behind initiative); Ian Urbina & David D. Kirkpatrick, *For Ex-Aide to Bush, an Arrest Is a Puzzling Turn*, N.Y. TIMES, Mar. 14, 2006, at A1 (observing that conservative columnist and talk-show host Armstrong Williams generated controversy by accepting $240,000 from the Bush administration to promote the administration's education initiatives).

[139] Romero & Whitmire, *Writer Says Scrushy Paid Her, supra* note 134; Michael Tomberlin & Russell Hubbard, *Minister: Scrushy Paid to Build Black Support; Ex-CEO Says "Shyster" Stalked, Tried to Con Him*, BIRMINGHAM NEWS, Jan. 20, 2006, at A1.

public relations firm controlled by the founder of the *Birmingham Times*;[140] and that she had also received a $2,500 personal check from Charles Russell – a Scrushy spokesman and prominent crisis communications consultant – toward the end of the trial.[141]

Lewis, who was part of a group that regularly attended the trial and prayed with Scrushy in the courtroom, said, "I did everything possible to advocate for his cause."[142] Titles of her articles ranged from *Scrushy's Binding Ties to the African-American Community* to *Another Great Day for the Defense* and *Everything but the Kitchen Sink*.[143] In her first story, she wrote that Scrushy's worst offense had been "giving support to a race of people that have been oppressed for hundreds of years" and that the government had "absolutely no solid evidence linking him to a crime."[144] The day the case went to the jury, a front-page piece she wrote read, "[P]astors and community leaders have rallied around Scrushy showing him the support of the Christian and African American community."[145]

Scrushy, of course, denied he had paid her to write flattering articles. Although he did not deny that he had reviewed several of the stories before publication, he claimed that Lewis had only e-mailed the unedited articles so he could check for factual inaccuracies.[146] Despite the tug of war over whose story was closer to the truth, one thing is undeniably clear: Lewis did receive thousands of dollars from the Scrushy camp.

During the trial, Scrushy signed a $20,000 retainer agreement with a local public relations firm to perform marketing and public relations functions. The same day, Lewis received a $5,000 check from the public relations firm, and she received another $6,000 not long after that. It seems highly improbable that more than half of the $20,000 retainer would have quickly wound up in her hands, but it did. And it is more than passingly strange that the public relations firm that wrote the checks was owned by the founder of the *Birmingham Times* – the paper that published her highly favorable stories.[147]

---

[140] The newspaper's publisher said he was unaware of any financial ties between Lewis and Scrushy. Romero & Whitmire, *Writer Says Scrushy Paid Her*, *supra* note 134.

[141] She decided to go public with the story because "Scrushy promised me a lot more than what I got." *Id.*

[142] *Id.*

[143] Jerry Underwood, *New Scrushy Battle Might Get Smelly*, BIRMINGHAM NEWS, Jan. 22, 2006, at D1.

[144] Evan Perez & Corey Dade, *Scrushy Denies Trying to Buy Support: HealthSouth Ex-CEO Paid PR Firm, Writer and Pastor During His Criminal Trial*, WALL ST. J., Jan. 20, 2006, at A12.

[145] Romero & Whitmire, *Writer Says Scrushy Paid Her*, *supra* note 134.

[146] Perez & Dade, *supra* note 144.

[147] Oh, and by the way, the founder's son just happened to be the paper's publisher.

At the same time these allegations were revealed, Herman Henderson –
the pastor of the Believers Temple Church – also claimed he had been paid
by Scrushy to garner support in the black community. He said Scrushy had
agreed to pay him $5,000 a month for two years to perform public relations work
during and after the trial. In exchange for the payments, Henderson agreed
to enlist support for Scrushy among black ministers, arrange opportunities for
Scrushy to preach in black churches, and transport black supporters to the
courthouse during the trial.[148]

Scrushy denied he had ever hired Henderson to do anything for him and
called the pastor a "shyster" and a "con"[149] – an assessment that some of
Henderson's fellow pastors uncharitably shared.[150] But regardless of whether
the allegations were true, they gained traction in the press and cast Scrushy in
a far less favorable light.

Then there was the matter of a federal bribery indictment. The second
indictment charged that Scrushy had funneled two payments of $250,000 each
to the Alabama governor in exchange for a seat on the state's hospital board,
which oversees decisions on construction of new health-care facilities in the
state.[151] Although the bribery indictment was handed up in Montgomery rather
than in Birmingham, in some respects, the ensuing scenario aptly illustrated
the adage that the past is prologue.

Just weeks before Scrushy was arraigned on the bribery charges, his son-in-
law bought a Montgomery-area television station,[152] and shortly before the trial
began, the Montgomery station began airing *Viewpoint* – Scrushy's religious
talk show – five times a week. The addition of the Montgomery station to the
son-in-law's television venture increased the potential audience for Scrushy's
Viewpoint show to roughly a million viewers.[153]

And adding a new wrinkle to his now-familiar theme, not long before his
Montgomery bribery trial began, Scrushy launched a new ministry, Kingdom
Builders International, whose grand design was to build churches and provide
food and clothing for needy African children. The Web site for the ministry,
which was launched about five weeks before the start of the trial, explained

[148] *Id.* Other black ministers who supported Scrushy disputed Henderson's account.
[149] *See* Tomberlin & Hubbard, *supra* note 139.
[150] *Id.* Scrushy told reporters, "You need to know that I'm about ready to sue him for extortion."
Id.
[151] *Briefing*, Toronto Star, Feb. 15, 2006, at E5. The governor and two of his top aides were also
charged.
[152] The $235,000 package deal included two low-powered stations in the Montgomery area.
Michael Tomberlin, *Scrushy Kin Buying Into Capital TV Market*, Birmingham News,
Nov. 1, 2005, at D1.
[153] Romero, *A High-Profile Trial*, *supra* note 118.

several secondary yet complementary missions.[154] Kingdom Builders held its inaugural founders' meeting at a Birmingham hotel just five days before jury selection in the bribery trial began.[155] Also not long before the trial, the Scrushys were "ordained" as pastors and ministers of Grace and Purpose Church, which Scrushy had founded and whose congregation met at the Birmingham television station his son-in-law owned.[156]

Scrushy's increasingly religious public persona led skeptics to suggest the new ministry was either a "savvy public relations move" or an effort "to build an empire,"[157] and they questioned whether he had "found" religion or "used" it.[158]

But some things never change. As in Birmingham, Scrushy's legal team was a work in progress. The week before trial, Scrushy hired black civil rights lawyer Fred Gray to join his defense team. To the dismay of the lead prosecutor (who also was black), Gray's opening argument likened Scrushy to Gray's famous former clients – civil rights activists Rosa Parks and Martin Luther King Jr.[159]

Thus, as he had in the Birmingham fraud trial, Scrushy sought to curry favor in Montgomery by playing the race and religion card before a jury whose racial composition was substantially the same as the Birmingham jury. But Montgomery isn't Birmingham, and Scrushy's strategy failed. At the end of the day, the jury found him guilty as charged.

III. PRAISE OR BLAME?

The public has been well served by sustained coverage of the complex legal and regulatory ground out of which the corporate governance scandals arose. To its credit, the press has, in the main, acquitted itself well. But media coverage of the ensuing investigations and trials has also raised a host of provocative questions about judgment, professionalism, and restraint.

---

[154] Michael Tomberlin, *Scrushy Widens Ministry: Web Site Details Roles as Pastor, Televangalist,* BIRMINGHAM NEWS, Mar. 10, 2006 [hereinafter Tomberlin, *Scrushy Widens Ministry*]. *See also* http://www.richardmscrushy.com [hereinafter Scrushy Web site].

[155] *Scrushy Starts Ministry*; Observer, *Finding His Religion,* FIN. TIMES, May 3, 2006, at 12. *See also* Scrushy Web site, *supra* note 154.

[156] Tomberlin, *Scrushy Widens Ministry, supra* note 154.

[157] Tomberlin, *Scrushy "Radioactive," supra* note 111.

[158] Gargis & Jacobs, *supra* note 107.

[159] Valerie Bauerlein, *Opening Arguments Made in Scrushy Bribery Trial,* WALL ST. J., May 2, 2006, at C3; Rick Brooks, *Scrushy, in Federal Bribery Trial, Revives Tack from Fraud Acquittal,* WALL ST. J., MAY 1, 2006, at C3; KYLE WHITMIRE, *Trial Begins for Former Alabama Governor,* N.Y. TIMES, May 2, 2006, at A16. The prosecutor complained that the reason Gray had been added to the defense team was so he could play the race card by drawing these analogies.

How can courts best accommodate the First Amendment interests of the press while protecting the parties' interest in a fair and impartial jury when media icons like Martha Stewart are on trial? Was it appropriate for the *Wall Street Journal* and the *New York Post* to break with journalistic tradition and risk the possibility of causing a mistrial in the Tyco case? Unrestrained journalistic zeal can, after all, skew news-gathering and reporting functions and invite increased judicial restrictions on the press.

Then there are more generalized questions of somewhat broader import. How prevalent is manipulation of the press by media-savvy defendants? Should we be concerned about well-orchestrated campaigns to publicly impugn the motives and integrity of prosecutors and attack the credibility of witnesses before trial? Or about enlisting the media to play on the passions of the community from which the jury will be drawn?

On the one hand, media manipulation can undermine the legitimacy of the courts and the press. On the other hand, "[i]t's not illegal to buy popularity."[160] But relentless media manipulation raises serious questions about journalistic credibility and independence and about the potential for extrajudicial forces to inappropriately influence the outcome of a trial.

These are notable points of tension between the media and the courts, whose respective roles in preserving the public's right to know and ensuring a fair trial sometimes seem at odds. And, as can readily be seen, it is not always easy to discern the proper balance between competing goals of the media and the courts. But if the press is to effectively perform its watchdog role, it should be mindful of the occasional need to watch itself.

APPENDIX A: TRADITIONAL PRINT SOURCE COVERAGE

Traditional print source coverage of the Enron scandal began with Bethany McLean's March, 2001 article in *Fortune* magazine, "*Is Enron Overpriced?*"[161] While the article raised substantial questions about how Enron made money, there were few answers to be found. The article nonetheless laid the foundation for further investigation by others into the complex accounting schemes that ultimately brought Enron down. Enron officials challenged McLean's premise that Enron's apparent profitability might well be a matter of smoke and blue mirrors. When her article was published, 13 of 18 analysts rated Enron a buy at $75 a share. At the same time, Enron officials were trying to convince

---

[160] Evan Perez & Corey Dade, *Scrushy Denies Trying to Buy Support: HealthSouth Ex-CEO Paid PR Firm, Writer and Pastor During His Criminal Trial*, WALL ST. J., Jan. 20, 2006, at A12.

[161] Bethany McLean, *Is Enron Overpriced?*, FORTUNE, Mar. 5, 2001, at 122. References to traditional print source coverage are to newspapers, magazines, and books.

Wall Street that the stock should have been valued at $126. In a September 2001 article, "Enron's Power Crisis," McLean foresaw a bleaker picture as she reported on Enron's deteriorating relationship with Wall Street, which had worsened with Skilling's departure as CEO in August.[162]

Enron was certainly not the only corporate fraud story in 2001. At about the same time that Enron was a top item of media interest, other major, publicly held corporations were caught in more pedestrian forms of corporate wrongdoing.[163] While many of these scandals attracted prolonged public scrutiny and resulted in the imposition of significant fines, the media attention was generally short-lived and sporadic compared with the marquee attention that Enron received.

The release of Enron's earnings report on October 16, 2001, revealing a $618 million third-quarter loss was a watershed event. Between the report's release and the end of the year, the *Wall Street Journal* featured ninety-eight Enron stories, most of which were investigative reports by John Emschwiller and Rebecca Smith. Although Enron CEOs Ken Lay and Jeff Skilling would later blame Enron's downfall on the negative effects of the *Journal's* coverage, the *New York Times'* coverage was even more extensive. Between Enron's October earnings report and the end of the year, the *Times* ran 155 Enron stories. Thus, exhaustive coverage by the *Times* and other major papers – as well as extensive reporting in major business magazines – belie the claim that Enron's downfall was largely attributable to a witch hunt conducted by the *Wall Street Journal*.

The Enron story remained a major fixture in national newspapers from January 2002 through May 2006, when the trial of Skilling and Lay ended with guilty verdicts. During this sustained period, the *Journal* featured 386 stories, while Enron captured a spot on the front page of the main section 49 times and on the front page of the "Money and Investing" section another 135 times. And during the pre-verdict coverage in May 2006, Enron was the second-most-reported story in both the *Journal* and the *Times*, lagging only behind illegal immigration. Remarkably, Enron was the subject of more features in

---

[162] Bethany McLean, *Enron's Power Crisis*, FORTUNE, Sep. 17, 2001, at 48.

[163] In the first eighteen following McLean's first Enron story, for example, Citigroup settled fraud allegations involving its subsidiary, TAP Pharmaceutical was fined $875M for a Medicare/Medicaid kickback scheme, Xerox was fined $10M by the SEC for faulty accounting, Carnival was fined $18M for falsifying records of oil discharges at sea, Schering-Plough was fined by the FDA $500M for violating current good manufacturing practices regulations, Tenet Healthcare was fined $55.8M for defrauding Medicare/Medicaid, Coca-Cola was sued for human-rights abuses at a foreign bottling subsidiary, and Bristol-Myers Squibb was sued for making false claims to the FDA. Bill Wasik, *Dismal Beat: The March of Personal-Finance Journalism*, HARPER'S MAGAZINE, Mar. 1, 2003, at 81.

both papers than were stories about oil prices, the new head of the CIA, and the Abramoff lobbying scandal.

Notwithstanding its sluggish start on the Enron beat, the *Houston Chronicle* ultimately emerged as the preeminent source of Enron coverage. In all, from March 2001, when the first questions about Enron were asked, until May, 2006, when the guilty verdicts were announced, the *Chronicle* ran almost two thousand separate Enron stories. Yet while reporters from other news outlets began to question Enron's business in early Fall 2001, the *Chronicle* did not begin heavily covering the story until after the startling third quarter earnings report in October 2001.[164]

While the major newspapers and magazines were busy uncovering the story behind Skilling's sudden departure as CEO, the managing editor of the *Chronicle* sent just one beat reporter to interview him. And when Skilling declined to offer any explanation beyond "personal reasons" for stepping down, the *Chronicle* failed to dig deeper to find one until after the third-quarter earnings report was released two months later.

After the disastrous earnings report became public, the story could no longer be ignored, and the *Chronicle's* coverage increased dramatically. Between the release of the earnings report and the end of the year, the *Chronicle* ran 143 stories about the energy giant's ensuing downfall, and most of the business staff and many general assignment reporters in Houston, New York, and Washington, D.C., were assigned to the story. The paper also set up a dedicated Enron Web page that became a rich resource that provided archived news articles, court documents, transcripts, and other topical material.

Enron was selected as one of the top three stories of 2001 by *Fortune* magazine (finishing behind 9/11 and the economic recession), and reporting on Enron was prominently featured in the first edition of *Best Business Crime Writing of the Year* in 2002 and *The Best Business Stories of the Year* in 2003.

The Enron story also spawned an abundance of books written about various aspects of the scandal. The most notable titles were written by the journalists who covered the story from its inception. They include *Conspiracy of Fools* by Kurt Eichenwald of the *New York Times*, *24 Days* by Rebecca Smith and John R. Emschwiller of the *Wall Street Journal*, and *Enron: The Smartest Guys in the Room* by *Fortune's* Bethany McLean and Peter Elkind. The *Smartest Guys in the Room* won the Strategy and Business Best Book Title for 2003, the award for Choice Outstanding Academic Title, and was made into a documentary that earned widespread critical acclaim.

---

[164] Between March and October 2001, the *Chronicle* ran fifty-one stories about Enron, mostly about the general business of the company.

APPENDIX B: THE CHANGING FACE OF MEDIA COVERAGE

In addition to comprehensive trial coverage in traditional print sources, Internet coverage of the trial of Enron's Jeff Skilling and Ken Lay was also extraordinary. Even though TV cameras and recording devices were not allowed in the courtroom, the public gained "remarkable insight into the daily proceedings" of the trial largely because of extensive Internet coverage.[165]

The most innovative aspect of Enron trial coverage was largely made possible by Judge Sim Lake's creation of a special media room. In response to intense media interest in the trial (and, perhaps, to correspondingly more limited courtroom space), Judge Lake created a specially equipped room where journalists could watch the trial and ply their trade. The media room, which had space for roughly one hundred journalists, provided them "a closed-circuit feed of the witness stand and a wireless internet connection to the outside world."[166] While notebook computers were allowed inside the room, recording devices and phones were not.

The prohibition against phones and recording devices required journalists in the media room to rely on the Internet as a medium for real-time communication of information about the trial. The extent of their reliance on the wireless Internet connection was evident early in the trial when the WiFi network became overloaded, forcing technicians to install a new router.

Creation of a media room from which journalists could simultaneously observe the trial and report on it via the Internet thrust online journalism to the forefront of trial coverage by the mainstream media. The *Houston Chronicle* Web site provided the most comprehensive media coverage of the Enron trial, although the *Wall Street Journal* and *New York Times* Web sites were not far behind. All three Web sites had special sections devoted to the Enron scandal with new, trial-related articles appearing almost daily. On the *Wall Street Journal Online*, articles relating to the current day's proceedings were frequently updated as notable courtroom developments occurred.

The *Houston Chronicle's* Web site had three blogs that were updated several times a day during the trial. The first, the Trial Watch blog, gave a blow-by-blow account of the court proceedings; the second, the Legal Commentary blog, provided analysis by legal scholars and attorneys; and the third, Loren Steffy's Business blog, offered opinion on the trial.

---

[165] Mike Tolson, *The Enron Verdict: Coverage Entering New Phase for Media*, HOUSTON CHRON., May 30, 2006, at Bus. 1.
[166] *Id.*

The *Houston Chronicle* was by no means the only major paper to use blogs. Although the *New York Times* did not run a blog, both Peter Lattman of the *Wall Street Journal* and Frank Aherns of the *Washington Post* blogged the trial. Noting the public's reliance on media blogs as a means of gathering instantaneous information about the Enron trial, Mr. Aherns said that hits on the *Washington Post's* Web site increased significantly when he decided to blog directly from the media room in Houston instead of relying on periodic reports from the *Post's* courtroom reporter.[167]

The three papers' Web sites also provided extensive background information about Enron from its founding to its collapse and about the ensuing investigations and trials.[168] These background resources provided significant supplements to current news articles, placed contemporaneous events in context, and provided a better understanding of the underlying issues in the trial. The Web sites also provided links to audio sound bites and video footage of important interviews, analysis, and commentary about the trial.

Another remarkable aspect of Internet coverage of the Enron trial was that it made court documents, exhibits, and trial transcripts widely available. Defense exhibits were accessible through Ken Lay's personal Web site, and the Justice Department took the unusual step of posting the prosecution's exhibits on its own Web site.[169] But the Justice Department and personal Web sites are just the tip of the iceberg. As part of its reporting of the Enron scandal, the *Houston Chronicle* Web site also featured an extensive number of court documents, transcripts, and exhibits.[170] While the *Wall Street Journal* and *New York Times* provided similar, but more limited, offerings, both provided links to FindLaw.com, which also had a wide array of Enron documents in a special Enron section of its Web site.

Internet coverage of the Enron trial far exceeded both traditional print source and television coverage. Thus, for example, CBS and ABC did not even

---

[167] One indication of the extent to which blogging has changed the speed with which information (and much misinformation) spreads is found in how quickly news of – and a wild assortment of theories about – Ken Lay's death was disseminated. During June, the terms "Ken Lay" and "Kenneth Lay" appeared an average of 46 times a day on blog postings, and in the first twelve hours after he was pronounced dead on July 5, 2006, his name appeared in 871 postings. Del Jones, *Bloggers Weigh in Fast with Theories on Lay's Death*, U.S.A. TODAY, Jul. 6, 2006, at 2B.

[168] The background information included profiles of the defendants, key witnesses, and prosecution and defense lawyers, along with a time line of major events.

[169] With the creation of the Justice Department's Corporate Fraud Task Force in response to the Enron scandal, however, indictments, informations, deferred prosecution agreements, and similar materials became available online for approximately ninety corporate fraud prosecutions on the Task Force Web site.

[170] The *Houston Chronicle* had links to the jury instructions, prosecution and defense exhibits, and a redacted indictment, among other trial documents.

interrupt national programming to report the jury's guilty verdict on Skilling and Lay, and NBC interrupted programming for only a little over three minutes to report their convictions. In contrast, daily traffic on the *Houston Chronicle's* Web site was up twenty percent on the day of the verdict, "spiking immediately after the verdict" was announced.[171] "The spike prompted the [Web site] to move temporarily to a text-only home page[,]" and "[a]t midday the Enron story by itself account[ed] for as much as a fourth of the site's traffic."[172]

The combination of articles, background information, documents, exhibits, transcripts, and blogs available via the Internet provided a wealth of information about the Enron trial. The Internet allowed interested members of the public to learn the details about the rise and fall of Enron and to follow the trial of Skilling and Lay on a real-time basis. Public access to sources ranging from primary documents to the views of the many journalists, legal scholars, and lawyers who supplied input provided an extraordinary wealth of information to those who followed the trial.

APPENDIX C: POSTSCRIPT ON PERMANENCY

Apart from the Internet's many advantages, reliance on Internet coverage has its own distinct disadvantages. Perhaps the most problematic issue is the lack of permanency of much of the information that appears on the Internet. Although permanency issues may not affect those who merely seek instant news coverage of a story, the lack of historical value can be problematic for journalists, authors, and academics.

The *New York Times, Wall Street Journal,* and *Houston Chronicle* all have online archives for articles that have appeared both online and in print.[173] But permanency issues arise with respect to Web site only articles, blog postings, and the special online sections that emerged during the Enron trial. The *Houston Chronicle's* policy is to let Web site-only articles expire without being archived and to make the in-depth Enron special coverage Web pages accessible for an indeterminate period of time.[174] The *Wall Street Journal's* special Enron coverage will remain available "for as long as [editors decide] there is

[171] Fritz Lanham & Mike McDaniel, *The Enron Verdict: For the Media, a Chapter Closes,* HOU. CHRON., May 26, 2006, at A6.

[172] *Id.*

[173] The *New York Times* online archives date back to 1852, the *Houston Chronicle* to 1985, and the *Wall Street Journal* to 1996.

[174] E-mail from Mike Read, Web Operation Editor at the Houston Chronicle (June 26, 2006, 11:05:13 CST) (on file with author).

news to write about."[175] Thus, much of the Enron coverage that has potential historical value and that pushed the Internet to the forefront of mainstream media coverage will be lost unless individual researchers have archived the material themselves.

Permanency issues also occur with Findlaw, another Internet source of legal news. With the passage of time, links may no longer be functional or lead the reader to unrelated alternate pages[176] or no longer contain meaningful information.[177]

Similar permanency problems arise with personal Web sites, which are increasingly being used by defendants in corporate governance scandals to conduct aggressive public relations campaigns and to counter what they perceive as biased or incomplete mainstream media coverage. Yet while both Martha Stewart and Arthur Andersen effectively used personal Web sites to promote their cause, neither Web site exists today. Lost with their Web sites was a wealth of valuable information about their respective prosecutions, legal strategies, and public relations campaigns.

Martha Stewart's Web site provides an instructive example. On two occasions when she posted letters to Web site visitors, the postings were taken down almost immediately and then re-posted after ill-advised statements[178] or language from earlier drafts[179] had been removed. While the revised letters

---

[175] E-mail from *Wall Street Journal Online* Customer Support (June 26, 2006, 15:51:41 CST) (on file with author).

[176] Thus, for example, Findlaw's Enron section provides a link for a book called "Anatomy of Greed" by Brian Cruver, a former Enron employee. BRIAN CURVER, ANATOMY OF GREED: THE UNSHREDDED TRUTH FROM AN ENRON INSIDER (Carroll & Graf Publishers 2002). But clicking on the link now takes the reader to www.anatomyofgreed.com, a site where one can apply for a cash advance.

[177] For example, the link to Arthur Andersen's homepage, www.arthurandersen.com, leads to the Chicago-based company's current homepage, which has no navigational ability or information beyond an address and phone number. The Web site Andersen originally launched was removed after the firm's trial and conviction.

[178] Immediately following her conviction on March 5, 2005, Stewart posted an open letter on her Web site. Language from the original letter stating "I have done nothing wrong" was quickly changed to read "I am obviously distressed by the jury's verdict." John Lehmann, *Martha's Head: Jury Convicts Her on 4 Counts; May Spend 10–18 Mos. in Pen; Business Empire Crumbling*, N.Y. POST, Mar. 6, 2004, at 2.

[179] On July 15, 2004, a draft of Martha Stewart's pre-sentencing letter to Judge Cedarbaum was accidentally posted shortly after her sentence was handed down. The draft was quickly removed and replaced with the final letter that was sent to Judge Cederbaum. Constance L. Hays, *Stewart's Letter to the Judge Shows Up Online, in Two Versions*, N.Y. TIMES, Jul. 19, 2004, at C5. The removed draft contained "a long apologia" for Sam Waksal's sale of ImClone stock the day before the FDA denied approval to market the company's most promising new drug. The draft also offered an explanation for Stewart's parallel sale of her own ImClone stock (which was the genesis of the criminal charges against her), pointedly referred to a juror that

remained on the Web site, the originals that had been briefly but imprudently posted were permanently gone.[180]

Finally, increased reliance on the Internet leads to greater credibility concerns. Unlike official newspaper Web sites, much of the information on the Internet is unreliable. For example, during Martha Stewart's trial, a number of satirical sites with similar Web addresses popped up. Additionally, following Ken Lay's death, Internet conspiracy theories were rampant.[181] While those who followed the scandals closely would have been unlikely to confuse official Web sites with unofficial ones, it could have been more difficult for the casual observer to evaluate the credibility of unofficial information. Suffice it to say that these sources thus require a heightened level of individual scrutiny.

On balance, the permanency and credibility issues raised by Internet coverage are a small price to pay for the increased news coverage provided by the Internet. Traditional news print articles are still available and are now more readily accessible through the vast electronic archives provided by newspaper Web sites. Without the Internet, much of this information would not be available to the general public.[182] That the information may not be permanent or may require a greater level of scrutiny to assure its credibility are relatively small prices to pay for the advantages of increased and instantaneous Internet coverage.

her lawyers had accused of lying on the jury screening questionnaire, and a statement that her future was "unfortunately" in the hands of the judge to whom the letter was addressed. All of these references were excised from the letter that was actually sent.

[180] Although the impermanency of these Web postings can be problematic from the perspective of those who want to do historical research on the case, from Martha Stewart's perspective the ability to quickly change the ill-advised open letter she posted after her conviction allowed her to avoid another potential legal complication. Thus, the ability to change or remove Web postings at will facilitates spontaneous communication, in contrast with the more controlled and calculated responses appearing in newspapers and on television.

[181] Tom Zeller Jr., *A Sense of Something Rotten in Aspen*, N.Y. TIMES, Jul. 10, 2006. Various Web sites and blogs reported that Ken Lay had not in fact died and provided numerous explanations – some quite preposterous – about his death and whereabouts.

[182] Scholars, lawyers, and journalists, on the other hand, may have access though other Internet sources such as LexisNexis and Westlaw, or though microfiche or microform archives available at major libraries and newspapers.

PART FOUR

DELAWARE VERSUS CONGRESS

*On the Federalization of
Corporate Governance*

10 How Delaware Law Can Support Better Corporate Governance

James D. Cox

Corporate governance, or more particularly, improving corporate governance, has been an important national topic for decades – indeed from the first appearance of the public corporation. Within this discourse, we frequently find that the public and academics alike have short memories. We too frequently focus on the present more than on the sweep of history. So it is with the present corporate governance discussions. We tend to begin with the collapse of Enron in late 2001 and focus on the most recent tinkering with governance, such as the New York Stock Exchange's (NYSE) and Nasdaq's listing requirements and the novel, albeit discrete, federal incursion into the domain of corporate governance with the passage of the Sarbanes-Oxley Act. But corporate governance has a much longer history, and it is instructive to identify the forces that support the evolution of governance practices. For example, forty years ago, we were debating whether there should be a critical mass of independent directors on public company boards; critical mass was thought to be a distinct minority of two or three, and audit committees were just barely being discussed as a governance tool. Within a decade, each of these practices became common not because of listing requirements but because of the development of best practices. The efficiencies inherent with independent voices on the board and assigning recurring tasks – compensation, interaction with the auditors, and nominating new board members – to specialized committees led to the modern board structure. The task of the board was seen as monitoring, and much of its work was carried out through committees. The financial reporting failures epitomized by Enron can be seen as redefining critical mass. Two or three good men or women out of nine is no longer good enough to get the job done. Hence, the listing requirements changed to reflect this call for even more independent oversight.

James D. Cox is Brainerd Currie Professor of Law, Duke University.

Can courts play a role in nudging emerging practices in the direction of becoming best practices? We can ponder what role the courts play in the evolution of best practices. To be sure, courts have been innovative (or at least responsive to innovative lawyers who appear before them) in melding old law with a new governance paradigm. The best illustration of this is the advent of the special litigation committee.[1] Here we find courts deftly grafting the monitoring role of independent directors to the historical relic of the demand requirement in derivative suit litigation. The resulting product is a mechanism by which the corporate body can be resuscitated to opine in a demand excused case whether the corporation's interests are advanced by the derivative suit's continuance. Similarly, a specially impaneled committee of independent directors can be used to clothe a self-dealing merger with the characteristics of arm's-length negotiations.[2] The Delaware judiciary was a leader in stamping its early approval on each of these innovative uses of emerging best practices.

The enactment of the Sarbanes-Oxley Act has sparked a new perspective on the role of the United States' foremost corporate legal standard setter, the Delaware courts. This perspective has a smattering of conspiracy theory, whereby the Delaware bench, bar, and legislature (and no doubt the governor, too) maneuver the law to preserve the rents that this small state garners by its being the haven of U.S. corporations (and limited liability partnerships for that matter). The term *conspiracy* may be too harsh, but Machiavellian gamesmanship may not be too far from how we characterize what some see as the politics of the Delaware courts. We are all now familiar with the thesis: Delaware, needing the substantial contributions that corporate franchise fees provide its treasury, believes that its primary threat is federalization of corporate law. Thus, the Delaware courts and legislature pursue a common strategy that is designed to erode any momentum that may be gathering for such a relocation of authority over corporate law. To paraphrase a classic remark, every so often, the Delaware courts must sacrifice a corporate executive so that freedom may reign for the managerial multitude. This thesis explains why we are treated episodically to the Delaware Court of Chancery's baton coming down on the skull of an officer or director. But in most instances, when conduct is questioned, the executives receive a reassuring pat on the back, not a crunching blow to their plans.

---

[1] *See* James D. Cox, *Searching for the Corporation's Voice in Derivative Suit Litigation: A Critique of Zapata and the ALI Project*, 1982 DUKE L.J. 959 (reviewing the doctrinal developments shaping the contemporary use of investigative committees).

[2] *See, e.g.*, Kahn v. Lynch Commc'n Sys., Inc., 669 A.2d 79, 84 (Del. 1995).

This chapter's thesis is consistent with the preceding explanation of what motivates Delaware jurisprudence. However, my focus is on the methodology that would allow the Delaware courts to reach conclusions with a healthy respect for the political situation in which they find themselves. My thesis is straightforward. The principles enshrined in the Delaware courts' holdings too frequently fail to embody substantive guidance, at least not in ways that can reinforce good corporate practice. Simply stated, for most of Delaware fiduciary duty law, "there is no there there," as the saying goes. Because of the vacuousness of Delaware fiduciary duty law, there is no substantive reinforcement of the various structural directives that arise from listing requirements, Sarbanes-Oxley, or even the development of best practices. This, in the eyes of this author, is a sadly missed opportunity to use the expressive power of the Delaware courts to move managers toward best practices.

I. THE DUTY-OF-CARE MUDDLE

Delaware has rendered its judgment in the closely watched (notorious?) Disney-executive compensation case.[3] My purpose here is not to evaluate the correctness of the result in that case, which dismissed the plaintiff's charges of misconduct on the part of Disney's CEO and the Disney board in the employment of Michael Ovitz and, more particularly, his ensuing compensation contract and costly termination. *Disney* does, however, provide a rich illustration of what is wrong with Delaware jurisprudence.

Disney, like so many other corporate law cases, begins with the talisman of the business judgment rule.[4] As is frequently the case, the analysis begins with a nod to the socially desirable objective that law should encourage managerial risk taking, and this objective is joined with the equally well-respected consciousness that business decision making is not within the unique competence of the judiciary. Certainly, hiring and firing a senior executive fits neatly into risky and important decisions that are best laid with the board and its management team, not with the Delaware judiciary. Hence, not only does the business judgment rule carry a fairly high presumption of no second-guessing of the substance of a decision, but also this is manifested in the deference implicit in the chancellor's factual holdings. *Disney* shows that this presumption goes also to the process by which the decision was made, a point examined more fully later in this chapter.

---

[3] *In re* Walt Disney Co. Derivative Litig., 906 A.2d 27 (Del. 2006), *aff'g* 907 A.2d 693 (Del. Ch. 2005).

[4] *Disney*, 906 A.2d at 52.

Disney and many other important Delaware cases begin their formulation of the role and importance of the business judgment rule by invoking *Aronson v. Lewis*.[5] This is a very curious precedent for divining the content of the business judgment rule. To be sure, the Delaware Supreme Court took the opportunity in *Aronson* to set forth the importance of the business judgment rule. What makes its own decision and the reliance of subsequent courts on that decision so curious is the failure of *Aronson* to understand that the matter before it was light-years away from the type of matter that legitimately invokes the commercial considerations that support the business judgment rule.

The issue before the court in *Aronson* was whether the derivative-suit plaintiff was excused before commencing her derivative suit from making a demand on the board of directors to bring the suit. Using the issues posed by whether to excuse a demand on the board of directors in *Aronson* to announce the objectives of the business judgment rule's deference to managers is a bit like purchasing oranges with which to make an apple pie. There is good reason to conclude that the directors' response to a demand should not carry the same presumptive weight that courts accord directors' judgments in traditional business matters. The considerations that justify the overwhelming deference that courts accord directors' decisions in normal commercial transactions do not justify the same deference when a committee of the directors recommends dismissal of a derivative suit or when evaluating the board's rejection of a demand that has been made. For example, if a court is asked to review the directors' decision to acquire Blackacre for a price that is alleged to be too high, the court must weigh that prayer with a healthy respect that, if it does set aside the board's judgment respecting the price, the deciding directors are likely liable for any consequential damages for their decision. Furthermore, if courts fail to insulate directors from such second-guessing, this will discourage many from agreeing to be (outside) directors and also will discourage risk taking by boards of directors. There are, therefore, several justifications for judicial deference to business decisions by boards of directors. But a decision as to whether a derivative suit should go forward is not a business decision. If the court permits a derivative suit to proceed in the face of a recommendation of the company's directors that the suit is not in the company's best interest, there is no personal liability on the part of the deciding directors that ensues as a consequence of the court substituting its judgment for that of the board. Simply stated, there is no causal relationship between courts upsetting the directors' rejection of a demand and the responsibility of the deciding directors. Thus, there is no need in situations such as *Aronson* for the reviewing court to temper its review

[5] Aronson v. Lewis, 473 A.2d 805, 812 (Del. 1984).

out of concern for either managerial risk taking or the ability of corporations to recruit well-qualified candidates to their boards. Also consider that the deference called for by the business judgment rule is based on the sound belief that, as between a court and captains of industry, the latter are more natural repositories for understanding matters of finance, production, marketing, and the like. This, indeed, is the true wisdom of the business judgment rule. On the other hand, managerial experience and expertise in assessing the merits of a suit would appear no better, and quite likely a good deal less, than the experience and expertise of the derivative suit court. Thus, courts can justifiably be less deferential in the demand-on-director area, such as *Aronson*, than they are when called upon to review director judgments in other contexts.[6] That such sharp distinctions were not understood by either *Aronson* or *Disney* is cause to wonder whether Delaware is blind or just unqualifiedly promanagement.

The above distinction is what underlies the universal demand approach that was first embraced by the American Law Institute (ALI) and later incorporated into the Model Business Corporation Act (Model Act), and has now become the law in a distinct minority of the states. Why has Delaware not so rationalized its treatment of the demand requirement? Perhaps the easy answer here is that Delaware sees itself as a leader and not a follower. Equally plausible is that the *Aronson* standard for deciding demand futility, being couched in terms of whether the facts pose a "reasonable doubt" of a lack of independence on the part of the deciding directors or whether the challenged transaction is the product of a "valid exercise of business judgment,"[7] are so inherently vacuous as to permit Delaware's politics to guide results in the individual case. But in failing to adopt the universal demand requirement, Delaware has also failed to embrace the notion that oversight is the central function of the board. That is, by preserving the excuse-of-demand approach, Delaware focuses on whether a majority of the board is implicated in the underlying wrongdoing; the court does not focus, as the ALI and Model Act require, on the appropriate oversight by independent directors when confronted with notice of a corporate cause of action. This difference is not subtle but of fundamental importance in identifying the functions of outside directors. That is, in Delaware, the first line of responsibility is the court, whereas under the universal demand approach it is with the corporation's independent directors.

---

[6] *See In re* PSE & G S'holder Litig., 801 A.2d 295 (N.J. 2002) (while adopting *Aronson's* two-pronged approach, the court goes to some length to stress that the approach in practice will entail less deference than arises in a standard business judgment inquiry).

[7] *Aronson*, 473 A.2d at 814.

The backwaters of Delaware jurisprudence in *Disney* become even murkier. Consider the following from the Delaware Court of Chancery:

> [I]f the directors have exercised their business judgment, the protections of the business judgment rule will not apply if the directors have made an "unintelligent or unadvised judgment." Furthermore, in instances where directors have not exercised business judgment, that is, in the event of director inaction, the protections of the business judgment rule do not apply. Under those circumstances, the appropriate standard for determining liability is widely believed to be gross negligence. . . . [8]

Perhaps it is unduly technical to question why, if there is a conclusion that a decision is "unintelligent" or "unadvised," there needs to be a separate inquiry into the presence of gross negligence. A simple answer is that the unintelligent decision needs to be sufficiently extreme, just as does the inaction, to invoke liability. This explanation sharpens the point raised later – namely whether the conduct that is to be assessed against the gross negligence standard is the decision itself or the process by which the decision was reached. And, if it is the latter, is the assessment guided by announced criteria intended to strengthen governance in corporations or by shallow considerations such as whether the deciding directors were the CEO's relatives? As we will see, in Delaware the answer to each of these is no.

Disney cites extensively to *In re Caremark International Derivative Litigation*,[9] in which former Chancellor Allen reasons that the business judgment rule is "process" oriented, so that the focus is on the good faith of the deciding directors and the rationality of the process they follow.[10]

The focus is not on the wisdom of the resulting decision. Chancellor Allen further reasons that, "where a director in fact exercises a good[-]faith effort to be informed and [a good-faith effort] to exercise appropriate judgment, he or she should be deemed to satisfy fully the duty of attention."[11] Here we see the issues in full. A process-focused business judgment rule should meld nicely with corporate governance considerations. After all, governance is all about process – who decides and, more important, what process is more likely to ensure a rich vetting of the corporate interests implicated by a transaction. Indeed, in a perfect world, we would expect a symbiotic relationship between judicial holdings and the development of best practices. Courts should announce, or

---

[8] *In re* Walt Disney Co. Derivative Litig., 907 A.2d 693, 748 (Del. Ch. 2005) (citing for "unintelligent or unadvised judgment" *Mitchell v. Highland-Western Glass*, 167 A. 831, 833 (Del. Ch. 1933), and *Smith v. Van Gorkom*, 488 A.2d 858, 872 (Del. 1985)).
[9] *In re* Caremark Int'l Derivative Litig., 698 A.2d 959 (Del. Ch. 1996).
[10] *Id.* at 967.   [11] *Caremark*, 698 A.2d at 968.

at least celebrate, the steps expected to be taken for an appropriate judgment to be reached. That is, courts can use the facts before them to announce steps that they believe necessary for there to be a rational exercise of judgment.

Consider in this respect *Smith v. Van Gorkom*,[12] in which the Delaware Supreme Court shocked the corporate world by holding that the Transunion directors acted with gross negligence in accepting the offer to sell the firm for nearly a 50 percent premium. Among the facts relevant to this discussion are that the offering price was based on calculations of whether Transunion was an appropriate candidate for a leveraged buyout assuming a private equity investment of $200 million and a five-year horizon; that Van Gorkom, the CEO, presented the $55-per-share price to the buyer without consulting with either his senior management or the board of directors; that the board approved the sale at a meeting without advance knowledge of the substance of the meeting; that a copy of the term sheet was not circulated at the board meeting when the sale was approved; and that the board did not have the benefit of a fairness opinion prepared by an investment banking firm or, for that matter, by anyone else.

Van Gorkom was an excellent opportunity for the court to announce a few minimal practices it would expect CEOs and boards to follow. While the above facts are set forth in the court's opinion, the opinion weaves none of them into its holding. For example, perhaps the most glaring weaknesses were the absence of an investment banker's fairness opinion or Van Gorkom's failure to incorporate his management team into formulating possible approaches to the firm's problem of high cash flow, no taxes, and valuable accumulated tax credits. Instead of examining what precisely he should have done, *Van Gorkom* fuzzes the point by offering that retaining investment bankers is not essential (although casual observation before and certainly after *Van Gorkom* clearly suggests otherwise). Moreover, its holding provides no emphasis on Van Gorkom's failure to bring his team into the process or on just what process would have better represented the interests of the Transunion shareholders. Thus, among the questions we might ask after *Van Gorkom* is, Just what should be the impact of the prevalent practice of employing investment bankers? Similarly, what weight should be given to Van Gorkom's failure to seek the counsel of not just his senior officers but also the board?

Twenty years later, the same problem arose in *Disney*, where the facts clearly involved another freewheeling executive: what did the Delaware court think of this behavior, and what normative suggestions does it offer? Whereas *Van Gorkom* is amazingly quiet on what it believed would have been better

---

[12] Smith v. Van Gorkom, 488 A.2d 858 (Del. 1985).

practices to follow, *Disney*, much to the credit of Chancellor Chandler, does chastise the freewheeling behavior of CEO Michael Eisner and the board's lax oversight of him:

> Eisner's actions in connection with Ovitz's hiring should not serve as a model for fellow executives and fiduciaries to follow. His lapses were many. He failed to keep the board as informed as he should have. He stretched the outer boundaries of his authority as CEO by acting without specific board direction or involvement.... To my mind, these actions fall far short of what shareholders expect and demand from those entrusted with a fiduciary position.[13]

But note the disconnect the court creates between the absent best practices and its holding as to whether the conduct falls outside the protection of the business judgment rule. The court dismisses the action against all the parties, including Eisner, reasoning in part that "standards used to measure the conduct of fiduciaries under Delaware law are not the same standards used in determining good corporate governance."[14] Are we to conclude that well-received notions of governance standards assume no significance in deciding whether directors have acted rationally? Or are we to conclude that the breach here was not so severe a departure from the norms of other CEOs in similar circumstances as to rise to a gross departure? And, if it is the latter, just why isn't Eisner's departure so extreme as to be actionable? The vacuousness of both *Van Gorkom* and *Disney* allows the court free rein in any subsequent cases. This is fertile soil for those who harbor notions of conspiracy. And for us nonconspirators, we can only cry shame: Both cases would have been a wonderful opportunity to invoke the expressive value of the law. Each would have been a great opportunity to place an important stamp on just why it is that corporate practices followed by others are good practices for all.

To its credit, the Delaware Supreme Court in *Disney* provides some emphasis of just what practices the Disney board could, as a matter of good corporate governance, have followed:

> In a "best [practice]" scenario, all committee members would have received, before or at the committee's first meeting... [to consider the Ovitz contract] a spreadsheet or similar document prepared by (or with the assistance of) a compensation expert.... Making different, alternative assumptions, the spreadsheet would disclose the amounts that Ovitz could receive under the OEA [the employment contract] in each circumstance that might foreseeably arise. One variable in the matrix of possibilities would be the cost to Disney

[13] *In re* Walt Disney Co. Derivative Litig., 907 A.2d 693, 762–63 (Del. Ch. 2005).
[14] *Id.* at 772.

of a non-fault termination for each of the five years of the initial term of the OEA. The contents of the spreadsheet would be explained to the committee members, either by the expert who prepared it or by a fellow committee member similarly knowledgeable about the subject. The spreadsheet, which ultimately would become an exhibit to the minutes of the compensation committee meeting, would form the basis of the committee's deliberations and decision.

Had that scenario been followed, there would be no dispute (and no basis for litigation) over what information was furnished to the committee members or when it was furnished. Regrettably, the committee's informational and decisionmaking process used here was not so tidy.[15]

Against this template, Justice Jacobs then proceeds to assess the steps that the Disney compensation committee did employ, as well as those of the full board, concluding that their conduct was reasonable, albeit falling short of the more optimal best-practices standard. In doing so, he elevates the importance of best practices as well as provides important guidance as to what they mean. Similarly, his consideration of the various steps that the Disney directors did take in retaining and terminating Ovitz further steel the place for thoughtful procedures and deliberations in the advice that corporate lawyers will give their clients in the future. What we can hope is that the approach taken by the Delaware Supreme Court in *Disney* elevates best practices to a presumptive standard so that those who fall short bear the burden of persuasion that their conduct was nonetheless reasonable or, at least, did not change the result from what would have occurred had best practices been followed.

II. THE GOOD-FAITH MUDDLE

Corporate lawyers and academics cast their gaze toward the chimney above the Delaware Supreme Court. Will white or black smoke be emitted? The former signals the anointment of a holy trinity for fiduciary obligations: duties of care, loyalty, and good faith; the latter means something quite different. But what?

The notion that there is a freestanding obligation of good faith can at least be traced to Chancellor Allen's *Caremark* opinion.[16] This decision clearly will rank as one of the most significant decisions in Allen's remarkable tenure as Delaware chancellor. The opinion is all the more remarkable by the fact that most of its qualities are dicta. The opinion arose in his approval of a

---

[15] *In re* Walt Disney Co. Derivative Litig., 906 A.2d 27, 56 (Del. 2006).
[16] *In re* Caremark Int'l Derivative Litig., 698 A.2d 959 (Del. Ch. 1996).

derivative suit settlement in which small tribute was awarded to the attorneys in compensation for the mild corporate therapeutics agreed to in the settlement. In a now-famous statement, Chancellor Allen defined in *Caremark* the absence of good faith as "sustained or systematic" inattention.[17] As stated more recently by the Delaware Court of Chancery in *Disney*:

> [I]ntentional dereliction of duty, a conscious disregard for one's responsibilities, is an appropriate (although not the only) standard for determining whether fiduciaries have acted in good faith. Deliberate indifference and inaction in the face of a duty to act is, in my mind, conduct that is clearly disloyal to the corporation. It is the epitome of faithless conduct.[18]

This statement of the duty of good faith was affirmed by the Supreme Court.[19] There is good cause to question whether *Disney's* formulation of good faith is at odds with that in *Caremark*. In *Caremark*, Allen emphasizes the failure of a firm to install law-compliance programs where the circumstances clearly would have called for such monitoring. The tone is one of conscious disregard rather than the more purposeful, deliberate tone in *Disney*. Moreover, the chancery court in *Disney* appears to cabin good faith to instances where the directors have a separate duty to act, such as in mergers.[20] Why should the monitoring role be so constrained? But more important, is a court acting responsibly by even making such a suggestion? More significant, from a governance perspective, *Caremark* makes clear that company directors have a duty to install reasonably designed compliance systems. The expressive power of *Caremark*, regardless of the trivial issue before the court, is beyond doubt. After *Caremark*, multiple cottage industries flourished – those probing in executive and legal education programs the change introduced by *Caremark* and the ongoing consulting for compliance programs. Each was accelerated by *Caremark*. It is a dramatic illustration of the important thesis of this chapter: Delaware should not miss opportunities to endorse best practices through the expressive power of its opinions.

To be sure, the emerging good-faith requirement, at least as it applies to abdication of directorial oversight, is borne of the necessity of the immunity shield that Delaware and most other states authorize corporations to provide

[17] *Id.* at 971.
[18] *In re* Walt Disney Co. Derivative Litig., 907 A.2d 693, 755 (Del. Ch. 2005) (emphasis in original).
[19] *In re* Walt Disney Co. Derivative Litig., 906 A.2d 27, 62 (Del. 2006). It should also be noted that the Delaware Supreme Court does not view "good faith" as a separate duty but as falling within the continuum of obligations that span the duties of care and loyalty. *See* Stone *ex rel.* Amsouth Bancorporation v. Ritter, 911 A.2d 362 (Del. 2006).
[20] *In re* Walt Disney Co. Derivative Litig., 907 A.2d 693, 754–55 (Del. 2006).

their directors.[21] Under the Delaware formulation of the immunity statute, directors *qua* directors are not liable for damages for breaches of care but are responsible for other types of breaches. Thus, characterizing the misconduct as a breach of the fiduciary duty of good faith and defining that duty as other than being solely care based preserves a cause of action against slumbering, slothful, neglectful directors. So understood, we should compare *Disney* and *Caremark* with abdication cases generally to isolate opinion qualities that relate to improving corporate governance through the expressive power of the court.

Hoye v. Meek[22] held liable the nonresident chair and president of Guaranty Trust Company, a bank that failed quickly and spectacularly due to securities speculation by Guaranty's officers. Meek spent most of his time in Vermont rather than in Ponca City, Oklahoma, where the bank was located. The daily operations of the bank were overseen by Meek's son, Maxwell, who spoke on the phone regularly with his father. This worked for seven years, but Maxwell, believing that interest rates would fall, began highly leveraged purchases of Government National Mortgage Association (GNMA) certificates. The leverage purchases violated Guaranty's internal policies. But worse yet, interest rates rose, causing the GNMA certificates to lose their value so that, in two years of initiating the leveraged GNMA purchases, the bank was insolvent.

Hoye clearly identifies that "the breach of duty resulted from both his delegation of authority to Maxwell without adequate supervision and his failure to avert Guaranty's continued exposure to increasing indebtedness."[23] The obligations of Meek and other directors could not be more clearly expressed.

Similarly, *In re Abbott Laboratories Derivative Shareholder Litigation*[24] arose from the substantial losses suffered by Abbott Laboratories as a consequence of a $100 million fine (the largest ever imposed by the Food and Drug Administration [FDA]) and the required destruction of certain of its inventories, which together prompted a charge to earnings of $168 million. The facts revealed that over a six-year period, there were thirteen separate inspections of two Abbott facilities, with some inspections lasting two months. As a result, numerous warnings (so-called 483 letters and other letters) were issued by the FDA to Abbott regarding product contamination. Each warning letter contained the standard FDA notice that failure to correct could result in a variety of sanctions. The senior officers were aware of the warning letters, as was the audit committee. Abbott's SEC filings, signed by its directors, also referred to

---

[21] *See, e.g.,* DEL. CODE ANN. tit. 8, § 102(b)(7) (2006) (immunizing directors from liability for damages except for certain actions, including those undertaken other than in good faith).

[22] Hoye v. Meek, 795 F.2d 893 (10th Cir. 1986).

[23] *Id.* at 896.

[24] *In re* Abbott Labs. Derivative S'holder Litig., 325 F.3d 795 (7th Cir. 2003).

the ongoing inspection problems with the FDA. In holding that a reasonable doubt for excusing a demand on the board had been alleged by the facts, the court concluded:

> [W]e find that six years of noncompliance, inspections, 483s, Warning Letters, and notice in the press, all of which then resulted in the largest civil fine ever imposed by the FDA and the destruction and suspension of products which accounted for approximately $250 million in corporate assets, indicate that the directors' decision to not act was not made in good faith and was contrary to the best interests of the company.[25]

Sleeping in the face of such warnings is clearly proscribed in *Abbot*, and the message is equally clear to public directors that they need to take seriously not just warnings but also the risks the firm regularly confronts. Note also that there is no haven in *Abbot* for the directors due to their not being under some independent duty to be watchful. Their duty to be watchful exists in all circumstances, not just, as *Disney* holds, when board action is commanded by corporate statute.

III. THE BIG MUDDLE – USURPATION OF CORPORATE OPPORTUNITY

No area of Delaware corporate law is more indeterminate than that of the usurpation of a corporate opportunity.[26] The vagaries of Delaware's – and for that matter, most other states' – treatment of fiduciaries appropriating corporate opportunities for themselves is best understood by comparing the cleaner and more rationalized approach recommended by the American Law Institute (ALI). The ALI's *Principles of Corporate Governance* eliminate much of the uncertainty in dealing with this question because it treats the matter as a governance matter and not a legal dispute.[27] It does this by first clearly defining what is a corporate opportunity, discretely varying the definition so that more is included for senior officers than for outside directors. Second, the provision treats opportunities as a breach unless their acquisition by the fiduciary was first reviewed by the company, either through its board of directors or through its stockholders. It is the latter step that directs the focus on governance, not

[25] *Id.* at 809.
[26] *See generally* JAMES D. COX & THOMAS LEE HAZEN, COX AND HAZEN ON CORPORATIONS § 11.08 (2d ed. 2003).
[27] ALI PRINCIPLES OF CORPORATE GOVERNANCE: RESTATEMENT AND RECOMMENDATIONS § 5.05 (1992).

litigation, and, by doing so, reinforces the monitoring role of the board of directors.

In contrast, Delaware embraces a litigator's dream of ambiguity via a multi-factor approach that defies certainty. In doing so, it expressly disavows a blanket requirement of presenting the opportunity to the board. Instead, Delaware pursues a mixed line-of-business and interest-and-expectancy standard that, as a practical matter, is a factor analysis whereby a variety of considerations are weighed, with only one being the prior rejection of the opportunity by the board.[28] In doing so, it is joined by most other state courts; only a few have taken the more predictable corporate governance approach proposed by the ALI.

The differences here are not questions of whether wrong results are reached by rejecting the cleaner ALI approach. It may be that the results in individual cases would not be different had the manager presented the opportunity to the corporation before seizing it; the very factors weighed by the courts in those cases may also cause the firm's board to reject the opportunity. Even if this were the case – and we will never know what would have occurred – two points appear clear. First, examining opportunities through the internal procedures of the corporation is much more expeditious and less costly than after-the-fact litigation in individual cases. Second, adopting the ALI approach has powerful expressive effects regarding the centrality of potential conflicts of interest being worked through the corporation's internal procedures. Lodging this question with corporate boards stimulates them to develop internal procedures for resolving such questions and related matters. This places the board where it needs to be: monitoring the activities of senior management.

IV. THE ULTIMATE MUDDLE – DEFENDING CONTROL

Three decades ago, Professor William Cary published his now-classic article calling for federally imposed minimum corporate standards.[29] The article rekindled a debate about whether there should be federal corporate law. It is safe to say that presently we do have federal law, at least as it applies to judgment defensive maneuvers – it is the law of Delaware. One cannot find an approach at odds with the formula set forth by the Delaware Supreme Court in *Unocal v. Mesa Petroleum Co.*[30] Under the first step of *Unocal's* formulation, the incumbent board has the burden of proving that it acted in good faith and

---

[28] *See, e.g.,* Broz v. Cellular Info. Sys., Inc., 673 A.2d 148, 155 (Del. 1996).

[29] William L. Cary, *Federalism and Corporate Law: Reflections upon Delaware,* 83 YALE L.J. 663 (1974).

[30] Unocal Corp. v. Mesa Petroleum Co., 493 A. 2d 946 (Del. 1985).

with reasonable basis to believe the suitor posed a threat to the company or its shareholders. As originally formulated, the second step called upon the reviewing court to assure that the defensive maneuver bore a reasonable relationship to the identified threat. Overall, the Delaware courts continue to characterize its *Unocal* analysis as entailing "intermediate scrutiny"* of a board's defensive maneuver. Within months of deciding *Unocal*, the Delaware Supreme Court, in *Moran v. Household International, Inc.*,[31] weakened its promise by upholding a board's unilateral alteration of governance mechanisms through the poison pill that was adopted when there was no immediate threat of a takeover. The ultimate qualification of *Unocal* occurs within its second step, so that instead of a delicate balancing of the impact of a particular defensive maneuver against the threats posed by a change of control, the inquiry is whether the defense was coercive, preclusive, or beyond a range or reasonableness.[32] Hence, what is intermediate about the courts' scrutiny under *Unocal* is the allocation of the burden of proof to the board to show its lawyers and investment bankers provided a sufficient record of their deliberations in opposing the bid. Evidence of *Unocal*'s evisceration is the near-universal success those adopting defensive maneuvers enjoy when their actions are challenged.[33]

The most dramatic illustration within the takeover arena of an opportunity to marry good governance to substantive law is in the case of the poison pill. Before the poison pill, a suitor could directly approach the target firm's stockholders with its bid. This mechanism is resorted to when the target board refuses to enter into a merger or sale of its assets; under either approach, corporate mechanics permit the transaction only with the support of the target board. Hence, the received governance model is that the target board can be bypassed so that shareholders themselves can decide whether to accept the bidder's offer to tender their shares. The genius of the poison pill is that it alters this scenario by forcing the bidder to persuade the target board that it must redeem the pill. Absent redemption, pursuit of the takeover will give rise to draconian effects on the target and its suitor.

---

* *See* Ronald Gilson & Ranier Kraakman, Delaware's Intermediate Standard for Defensive Tactics: Is There Substance to Proportionality?, 44 Bus. Law. 247 (1989).

[31] Moran v. Household Int'l, Inc., 500 A.2d 1346 (Del. 1985).

[32] *See, e.g.,* Unitrin, Inc. v. Am. Gen. Corp., 651 A. 2d 1361, 1388 (Del. 1995); Paramount Commc'ns, Inc. v. Time, Inc., 571 A. 2d 1140 (Del. 1989).

[33] *See* Robert B. Thompson & D. Gordon Smith, *Toward a New Theory of the Shareholder Role: "Sacred Space" in Corporate Takeovers*, 80 Tex. L. Rev. 261 (2002) (reviewing thirty-four chancery court and eight supreme court decisions and finding that only chancery court decisions pre-*Paramount* upset defensive maneuvers and no supreme court decision has upset a defensive maneuver under *Unocal*). To be sure, the change of control decisions under *Revlon* carry somewhat greater success for the plaintiffs, but this, too, is marginal.

Given the business judgment rule's heavy overlay regarding the need to encourage risk taking, as well as its deference to the vision of a firm's managers and directors, board and management decisions made in the heat of a contest for control quite naturally call for a deferential attitude on the part of the reviewing court. However, this deference is not justified by concerns of risk or unique vision when there is not then an immediate threat to control. Failing to note this distinction has caused the Delaware courts, as well as their sister courts, to devoutly apply *Unocal*. This blind obeisance prevents them from nudging governance practices in a better direction. That is, instead of *Moran* examining the poison pill through the lens of *Unocal*'s two-pronged test, why did the court not view the maneuver as the agent inserting itself between the principal and the third party? This was the perspective that caused Chancellor Allen in *Blasius Industries, Inc. v. Atlas Corp.*[34] to condition any unilateral board action that interfered with the ongoing exercise of a stockholder's franchise upon proof there is a compelling justification for such unilateral action. Instead of the sterile and now-empty *Unocal* vessel in which all takeover defenses are collected, a more norm-oriented judiciary should single out those that directly alter the firm's governance. On this area, much along the reasoning of *Blasius*, matters of good faith and encouraging risk taking are not germane to resolving the impropriety of an agent changing the owner's rights as an owner. Far better in such circumstances is to heavily qualify the pill. In *Moran*, where there was no outstanding bid, conditioning the court's holding on there being a stockholder meeting within sixty or ninety days to ratify the pill would have greatly respected the governance rights of the firm's owners.

More broadly, courts considering defensive maneuvers should begin their analysis not with the business judgment rule but with a statement of what good governance practices call for under the circumstances. The business judgment rule should be seen as an instrument to carry out this vision and not a shade that blocks vision. It may well be that courts could view certain defensive maneuvers, such as poison pills and golden parachutes, as acceptable on the condition that they are subject to periodic ratification by the stockholders. This approach is not legislating standards but rather defining the meaning of existing concerns of good faith and reasonableness.

V. CONCLUSION

The most powerful protection against wrongdoing or simple misdirection of corporate assets is good corporate governance. What is good corporate

---

[34] Blasius Indus., Inc. v. Atlas Corp., 564 A.2d 651 (Del. Ch. 1988).

governance is not a static or finite concept. Most of what we associate with corporate governance emerges from best practices that are accepted into the marketplace. It is now time for the courts to weave this process into their decision making. Simply put, courts need to view their mission more broadly than just deciding disputes. Otherwise, they leave too much clutter in their wake. Most important, courts deciding corporate matters need to see themselves in the norms business. Firm and crisp announcements of contemporary expectations regarding how companies conduct their affairs need to become more common in the court's holdings. And when there is a departure from such norms, as in *Disney*, the court must carefully weigh just why that breach is not so consequential as to decide the case. Also, attention to governance should cause courts to be less blinded by the standard arguments regarding the need to encourage risk taking and the expertise of the board. These factors may well apply to the question of what strategic alliances the firm should pursue; they hold no sway on whether a poison pill once adopted should have an infinite existence. Thus, the conditioning of holdings on a future ratification of the stockholders is a truly intermediate position courts can take and one that would squarely place the courts where they need to be – embracing governance in their holdings.

11 Federalism versus Federalization

Preserving the Division of Responsibility in Corporation Law

E. Norman Veasey, Shawn Pompian, and
Christine Di Guglielmo

An efficient division of responsibility and the specialization that necessarily accompanies it lie at the heart of any successful business enterprise.[1] The same principle applies with equal force to the institutions charged with regulating those enterprises or adjudicating their conduct. Since the enactment of the Securities Exchange Act of 1934 (1934 Act), the prevailing division of responsibility in the United States has broadly followed a federal model: the federal government has limited itself (with important exceptions) to disclosure issues in regulating the flow of information from public corporations to the securities markets, and the states have established the legal framework governing a firm's internal affairs. There is also a third, ambiguous area that some describe as the regulation of voting procedure. That is a term that has some surface legitimacy, but there is a concern that it may sometimes be used as a bootstrap argument for increased federalization.

---

[1] "Those ten persons, therefore, could make among them upwards of forty-eight thousand pins in a day. Each person . . . might be considered as making four thousand eight hundred pins in a day. But if they had all wrought separately and independently, and without any of them having been educated to this peculiar business, they certainly could not each of them have made twenty, perhaps not one pin in a day. . . . " ADAM SMITH, AN INQUIRY INTO THE NATURE AND CAUSES OF THE WEALTH OF NATIONS pt. I.I.3. (1776). "Specialization is for insects." ROBERT HEINLEIN, TIME ENOUGH FOR LOVE (1973).

E. Norman Veasey is Senior Partner of the firm of Weil, Gotshal & Manges, LLP, and retired Chief Justice of Delaware. Shawn Pompian graduated from the University of Virginia School of Law in 2000 and served as a judicial clerk to Chief Justice Veasey from 2000 to 2001. He is currently Attorney Adviser in the Office of the Legal Adviser at the U.S. Department of State. Christine Di Guglielmo graduated from the University of Pennsylvania Law School in 2003 and served as a judicial clerk to Chief Justice Veasey from 2003 to 2004. She is currently Associate at the firm of Weil, Gotshal & Manges, LLP. The authors also wish to acknowledge the invaluable assistance of Rob Eaton, a 2005 summer associate at Weil, Gotshal & Manges, LLP. The views expressed in this chapter are solely those of the authors. This chapter originally appeared in 2 THE PRACTITIONER'S GUIDE TO THE SARBANES-OXLEY ACT at V-5-1 (John J. Huber et al. eds., 2006).

The division of authority between federal disclosure regulation and state primacy over internal affairs naturally led to the evolution of specialized institutions to govern different facets of business. The federal government, particularly the Securities and Exchange Commission, developed an elaborate regulatory apparatus devoted to monitoring and controlling the disclosure of information to the markets.[2] For their part, state lawmakers defined the rights and obligations of a firm's owners and managers, as well as governing state disclosure issues. Delaware, in particular, embraced the federalism model and adopted a wide range of innovations – most notably, the establishment of a neutral body of experts to review and recommend changes to its corporation law and the cultivation of a cadre of judges and lawyers with special expertise in business law.

Despite occasional federal incursions into the states' traditional domain, this division of responsibilities survived more or less intact for nearly seventy years. In 2001, however, a wave of highly publicized scandals broke at prominent public corporations such as Enron, WorldCom, and Tyco. The scandals, which followed closely on the heels of the now-infamous bursting of the technology bubble, precipitated the passage of the Sarbanes-Oxley Act of 2002 (Sarbanes-Oxley),[3] a loose package of federal legislation ostensibly intended to rein in corporate executives run amok and restore investor confidence.

Unlike most of the federal initiatives that preceded it, Sarbanes-Oxley established some mandatory rules governing the internal affairs of publicly listed corporations. Not only were these rules arguably unrelated to the corporate scandals they were supposed to address, but they also represented a perceptible shift in the established federal-state division of authority. And, perhaps more ominously, Sarbanes-Oxley seemed to presage further federal incursions of corporate governance and lawyer regulation – either directly through the SEC or indirectly through listing requirements promulgated by the stock exchanges. Sarbanes-Oxley and the SEC rules that have flowed from it thus squarely present the question whether substantive regulation of corporate governance is best undertaken at the state or national level (or some combination thereof).

[2] The SEC often attempts to achieve substantive regulatory goals through the mechanism of disclosure. For some examples in the Sarbanes-Oxley context, see *infra* section II; see also Robert B. Thompson & Hillary A. Sale, *Securities Fraud as Corporate Governance: Reflections upon Federalism*, 56 VAND. L. REV. 859, 860 (2003) (arguing that "federal securities law and enforcement via securities fraud class actions today has become the most visible presence in regulating corporate governance").

[3] Sarbanes-Oxley Act of 2002, Pub. L. No. 107–204, 116 Stat. 745 (codified as amended in scattered sections of 15 U.S.C.).

The guiding principle of the corporate governance regime in Delaware and most other states is that each corporation should be free to choose – within broad limits – the governance mechanisms appropriate for its situation. Although there is wide latitude for private ordering, corporations that choose poorly are punished in the first instance by the markets, which discount the share price of companies with an inappropriate internal governance structure. The rationale behind the enabling approach taken by the states is straightforward: corporations (particularly major public corporations) represent a highly diverse group of entities. It would be virtually impossible to devise a set of governance rules that fits even a majority of firms.

Superficially at least, the incentive for some to pursue federal regulation of corporate governance is also quite simple: because malfeasance, misfeasance, or nonfeasance by corporate managers – particularly if widespread – can have a substantial effect on the national capital markets, it is argued that those managers should be subject to a uniform set of governance rules established at the national level. Without uniform national rules, the argument goes, management will cause their companies to incorporate in states with the weakest regulation of management activities.

This argument loses much of its force on closer scrutiny. One is reminded of an intense debate about thirty years ago on the subject of whether there should be federal chartering or federal minimum standards for directors' duties. This debate was sparked by the late Professor William L. Cary, of Columbia Law School, who contended the following in several writings[4] in the mid-1970s:

> [I]n my opinion the time has come for us to consider a Federal Minimum Standards Act. There has been a deterioration of corporate standards, and I think it is safe to say that Delaware has been the sponsor and the victim of this unhappy denouement. As has been stated already in this room, there has been a race for the bottom.[5]

There was some academic agreement with this thesis at the time, and there was some strong disagreement. The late S. Samuel Arsht, then arguably the dean of the Delaware Corporate Bar, stated:

> I submit that Professor Cary's analysis of the Delaware experience is biased, unscholarly and wholly unfair. If these articles had to measure up to the

---

[4] William L. Cary, *Federalism and Corporate Law: Reflections upon Delaware*, 83 YALE L.J. 663 (1974); William L. Cary, *A Proposed Federal Corporate Minimum Standards Act*, 29 BUS. LAW. 1101 (1974).

[5] William L. Cary, *Summary of Article on Federalism and Corporate Law*, 31 BUS. LAW. 1105 (1976).

required standards of an SEC disclosure document, they would be found woefully deficient. . . .

On the merits, Professor Cary has failed to make out a case of any need for a federal minimum standards act. To the extent that he has sought to bootstrap his proposal by pointing the finger of scorn at Delaware his arguments do not do him credit.[6]

Also, in a well-reasoned article with a persuasive economic analysis, Ralph Winter, now a senior federal circuit judge of the U.S. Court of Appeals for the Second Circuit, wrote a paper in 1977 engaging this debate and concluding "that state corporate legal systems do protect shareholders and that state regulation is generally preferable to federal regulation."[7] Judge Winter's analysis also concludes:

An expanded federal role in corporate governance would almost surely be counterproductive. At the federal level, there is no mechanism by which optimal legal rules governing the shareholder-corporation relation can be determined. . . .

Once federal legislation is enacted, it will be very difficult to correct, no matter how wrong it may be. Not only will bureaucrats view the legislation as a cornerstone of the Republic and perhaps seek to expand its jurisdiction and their own, but even the most demonstrably foolish rule will lead to calls for more rather than less regulation. . . . At present, the case for federal intervention (except for takeover statutes) lacks both a theoretical and empirical basis. Worse, it finds its sole political sustenance in a movement that has little sympathy for shareholders as investors or for the survival of the private sector in general.[8]

Despite the intensity of this debate in the 1970s, federal intrusion into state corporation law and litigation came in fits and starts, but no broad-based preemption came about until the Sarbanes-Oxley era.

[6] S. Samuel Arsht, Reply to Professor Cary, 31 Bus. Law. 1113, 1123 (1976). Professor Cary's "summary" and Arsht's "reply" were part of a symposium held June 13–14, 1975, at the Airlie House in Virginia. The February 1976 special issue of volume 31 of Business Lawyer was devoted to the entire proceedings of that symposium, titled "An In-Depth Analysis of the Federal and State Roles in Regulating Corporate Management."

[7] Ralph K. Winter Jr., State Law, Shareholder Protection, and the Theory of the Corporation, 6 J. Legal Stud. 251 (1977). This article originally formed chapter 2 of a book prepared by Judge Winter titled Government and the Corporation, published by the American Enterprise Institute for Policy Research. The foregoing quotation appears at page 5 of his American Enterprise Institute chapter.

[8] Ralph K. Winter, Government and the Corporation 44–46 (1978); see also Ralph K. Winter, Contractual Freedom in Corporate Law: The "Race for the Top" Revisited: A Comment on Eisenberg, 89 Colum. L. Rev. 1526 (1989); Ralph K. Winter, Protecting the Ordinary Investor, 63 Wash. L. Rev. 881 (1988).

In contrast to the states' approach, the nascent federal governance regime established by Sarbanes-Oxley contemplates at most three categories of corporations: (1) private corporations that are not directly subject to federal requirements, (2) public corporations that must satisfy the minimum standards of Sarbanes-Oxley, and (3) listed public corporations that must satisfy both the Sarbanes-Oxley requirements and additional rules established by the stock exchanges.

Not surprisingly, these categories have proved to be a poor fit for many of the firms to which the regime applies. Preoccupied by the spectacular failures of Enron, WorldCom, and others, Congress clearly fixed its attention on the practices of the largest listed public companies while disregarding the significant and costly impact of its legislation on the legions of smaller public corporations. As a result, the smaller public companies face substantial costs for implementing governance practices mandated by Sarbanes-Oxley that were designed for much larger enterprises. These compliance costs can be expected to lead many medium and small public companies to delist or to go private, or to defer or forgo going public.

This chapter concludes that the unintended consequences of the federal regime are the direct result of Congress legislating outside its area of expertise and its proper role, thus changing the regulatory division of responsibility. Unlike Delaware, which has extensive institutional experience with corporate governance issues, Congress, the SEC, and the federal courts are ill prepared for a significant foray into substantive corporate governance rules. Moreover, the habit of Congress in addressing financial market regulation only in moments of real or perceived crisis is not well suited to the proper role of governmental authority in establishing transparent, administrable, and flexible rules that will apply to a diverse population of firms. Equally important, given its wide-ranging interests and short attention span, Congress is not well suited to monitor the effects of its legislation or to enact prompt reforms to address deficiencies in the operation and consequences of the legislation it has inflicted on business enterprises.

In short, Congress and the SEC should leave the states to regulate the internal affairs of businesses and return to their own area of expertise: ensuring that public companies present uniform, and uniformly vetted, information to the capital markets.[9] In the graphic metaphor depicted by Vice Chancellor

---

[9] This is not to suggest that federal preeminence in the regulation of securities is unassailable. Professor Roberta Romano, for example, has presented a compelling argument that the states should have a greater role in this area as well. *See* Roberta Romano, *Empowering Investors: A Market Approach to Securities Regulation*, 107 YALE L.J. 2359, 2361 (1998) (advocating

Leo Strine, the federal government has a proper and useful "lane" in which to travel but should be reluctant to "veer out of its lane."[10]

This chapter is organized into four sections. Section I presents a brief overview of the traditional federal-state division of responsibility in business regulation. Section II discusses the components of Sarbanes-Oxley and provides an assessment of their impact on the traditional federal-state balance. Section III addresses corporate governance regulations promulgated by the SEC and national stock exchanges in the wake of Sarbanes-Oxley. Section IV explains why the states, particularly Delaware, are better suited than the federal government to handle substantive corporate governance issues.

I. OVERVIEW OF THE INTERNAL AFFAIRS DOCTRINE AND THE FEDERAL-STATE BALANCE

Any analysis of whether recent corporate governance initiatives at the federal level upset the delicate balance between federal and state regulation of corporations must begin with a review of the history of business regulation in this country and the basic principles that underlie our system of federalism.

During the late colonial and early federal periods, each corporation existed only as a product of state chartering and was subject to careful legislative monitoring to ensure that corporations served a public interest.[11] By the turn of the twentieth century, however, the number and variety of corporations had increased substantially, the regulatory significance of state charters had declined dramatically, and companies were increasingly privatized.[12] State courts thus gradually developed a common law of corporate governance based on principles of fiduciary duty.[13] After the birth of this state common law of corporate regulation, concerns about trust abuses began to attract regulation of some corporations at a national level.[14]

"a market-oriented approach of competitive federalism that would expand, not reduce, the role of the states in securities regulation").

[10] *See* Leo E. Strine Jr., *The Delaware Way: How We Do Corporate Law and New Challenges for Free Market Economies* 23 (Wash. Legal Found.: Critical Legal Issues, Working Paper Series No. 133, 2005) (urging the federal government not to "veer out of its traditional lane" on matters of corporate governance).

[11] Myron T. Steele, Distinguished Jurist Lecture at the University of Pennsylvania, *in* Practising Law Institute, What All Business Lawyers and Litigators Must Know About Delaware Law Developments 431, 437–38 (Mar. 3, 2005).

[12] *Id.* at 438–39.

[13] *See id.* at 439 ("In the world of modern capitalism, the 'public' side of the corporation evolved into the dispersed interests of ownership. As a result, some mechanism was required to isolate the corporation's welfare from that of its promoters. Recognizing the primacy of corporate fiduciary duties provided the solution.").

[14] *Id.*

From the early twentieth century forward, federal business regulation grew in fits and starts but stood in a cautious balance with state corporate law. Then, in 1933, Congress enacted the Securities Act. That act was followed in 1934 by the Securities Exchange Act, which created the SEC.[15] Professor Joel Seligman has described the SEC's regulation of proxies under section 14(a) of the 1934 Act as the first regulation of corporate governance by the federal securities laws.[16] From 1934 through 2002, however, the SEC focused primarily on disclosure regulation as a means to ensure proper functioning of the securities markets[17] and to facilitate the effectiveness of the stockholders' franchise.[18] With the focus on disclosure, the SEC largely refrained from regulating the aspects of corporate governance that have traditionally been the province of state law – that is, the principles that work to balance power among stockholders, directors, officers, and other corporate constituents.[19]

This division of responsibility for lawmaking and regulation, including concerning corporations, between the state and national governments is the foundation of our system of federalism. It ascribes certain matters to state control, certain matters to the national government, and certain matters to concurrent state and federal regulation. Under this system of federalism, the national government has only the limited powers that are enumerated in the Constitution; all other matters are left to regulation under the state's police

---

[15] 15 U.S.C. § 78d (2005).

[16] Joel Seligman, *The SEC at 70: A Modest Revolution in Corporate Governance*, 80 NOTRE DAME L. REV. 1159, 1162 (2005).

[17] There is significant debate over whether the SEC's authority relates primarily to disclosure regulation. See, e.g., the discussion of the stockholder access proposal in section III.A. *Cf.* Mark J. Roe, *Delaware's Competition*, 117 HARV. L. REV. 588, 615–16 (2003) ("Although the formal division of authority is said to be that the SEC forces disclosure and regulates stock trading while the states handle the internal affairs of shareholder-director relations, savvy lawyers, judges, and analysts know better. Much substantive law can be – and is – made by the SEC in the name of disclosure. *Ex ante*, to force disclosure that 'this company is run by thieves' usually keeps the thieves out."); *id.* (arguing that the federal government determines the content of state corporation law, through the threat of federal preemption should states adopt corporate laws of which the federal government does not approve). *But cf.* Roberta Romano, *Is Regulatory Competition a Problem or Irrelevant for Corporate Governance?*, 21 OXFORD REV. ECON. POL'Y 212 (2005) (critiquing Roe's thesis and arguing that the federal government's regulation of disclosure does not dictate the substance of corporation law).

[18] This latter mission is one shared by Delaware courts, which have been strongly protective of stockholders' franchise rights. *See* Blasius Indus. Inc. v. Atlas Corp., 564 A.2d 651, 663 (Del. Ch. 1988); Loudon v. Archer-Daniels, 700 A.2d 135 (Del. 1997); MM Cos. v. Liquid Audio, Inc., 813 A.2d 1118 (Del. 2003).

[19] *Cf.* Seligman, *supra* note 16, at 1169 ("[C]orporate governance was generally considered to be a matter of state law outside the scope of what the SEC should address. . . . [O]ver time there had evolved an implicit understanding that absent countervailing circumstances requiring federal preemption, areas such as corporate governance would remain exclusively or largely matters of state law.").

powers.[20] With respect to matters that the national government has the power to regulate, it may choose to regulate concurrently with the states, to leave the regulation entirely to the states, or to exercise sole authority in the area. When Congress does enact legislation on a subject that falls within its enumerated powers, the doctrine of federal preemption guides the determination of whether Congress has chosen to share authority with the states or to exercise sole authority on the subject by preemption of state regulation.

When Congress legislates in a field that traditionally has been occupied by the states, one must consider whether that legislation preempts state authority in that field.[21] That analysis begins "with the assumption that the historic police powers of the States were not to be superseded" by federal legislation unless "that was the clear and manifest purpose of Congress."[22] The "perplexing question" of whether Congress has completely preempted state regulation or, through its choice of regulatory measures, has left the power of the states intact except where state and federal laws conflict may be answered by reference to the evidence of Congress's intent as gleaned through review of the regulatory scheme itself:

> The scheme of federal regulation may be so pervasive as to make reasonable the inference that Congress left no room for the States to supplement it. Or the Act of Congress may touch a field in which the federal interest is so dominant that the federal system will be assumed to preclude enforcement

---

[20] *See* U.S. Const. amend. X ("The powers not delegated to the United States by the Constitution, nor prohibited by it to the States, are reserved to the States respectively, or to the people."); Gonzales v. Raich, 545 U.S. 1, 51 (2005) (O'Connor, J., dissenting) ("Congress cannot use its authority under the [Commerce] Clause to contravene the principle of state sovereignty embodied in the Tenth Amendment. Likewise, that authority must be used in a manner consistent with the notion of enumerated powers – a structural principle that is as much part of the Constitution as the Tenth Amendment's explicit textual command."); Gibbons v. Ogden, 22 U.S. 1, 190–95 (1824) (stating that the federal government's powers consist only of those enumerated in the Constitution, and that the Constitution's grant of federal power over commerce "among the several States" does not grant power over commerce that is internal to a single state); *id.* at 195 ("The genius and character of the whole government seem to be, that its action is to be applied to all the external concerns of the nation, and to those internal concerns which affect the States generally; but not to those which are completely within a particular State, which do not affect other States, and with which it is not necessary to interfere, for the purpose of executing some of the general powers of the government.").

[21] Rice v. Santa Fe Elevator Corp., 331 U.S. 218, 230 (1947); *cf. also Gonzales*, 545 U.S. at 41 (O'Connor, J., dissenting) ("We enforce the 'outer limits' of Congress' Commerce Clause authority not for their own sake, but to protect historic spheres of state sovereignty from excessive federal encroachment and thereby to maintain the distribution of power fundamental to our federalist system of government. One of federalism's chief virtues, of course, is that it promotes innovation by allowing for the possibility that 'a single courageous State may, if its citizens choose, serve as a laboratory; and try novel social and economic experiments without risk to the rest of the country.'") (citations omitted).

[22] *Rice*, 331 U.S. at 230.

of state laws on the same subject. Likewise, the object sought to be obtained by the federal law and the character of obligations imposed by it may reveal the same purpose. Or the state policy may produce a result inconsistent with the objective of the federal statute.[23]

States have traditionally and actively regulated the internal affairs of corporations.[24] Thus, federal law will preempt such state regulation only if Congress shows a clear and manifest purpose to do so. This principle has been reflected in a number of court decisions explicating the internal affairs doctrine. The internal affairs doctrine – derived from a series of federal court decisions considering the validity of various federal business regulations – essentially embodies preemption analysis in the corporate law context and serves as a choice-of-law principle. The doctrine covers two principal areas. First, the internal affairs doctrine provides that state, not federal, law will generally govern the internal affairs of corporations. It also provides that the state law that will control those internal affairs is that of the state in which the company is incorporated.[25]

In *VantagePoint Venture Partners 1996 v. Examen Inc.*, the Delaware Supreme Court applied the choice-of-law aspect of the internal affairs doctrine to decide whether a corporation's preferred stockholders had a right to a class vote on a merger. The corporation, Examen, claimed that the preferred stockholders did not have such a right under Delaware law and the preferred stock's certificate of designations. VantagePoint, a preferred stockholder, claimed that the preferred stockholders were entitled to a class vote because Examen was a "quasi-California corporation" under section 2115 of the California Corporations Code and therefore subject to California Corporations Code section 1201(a), which entitled the preferred stockholders to a class vote. The court held that the issue of whether the preferred stockholders were entitled to a class vote "clearly involve[d] the relationship among a corporation and its shareholders."[26] Therefore, the court held, "Delaware's well-established choice of law rules and the federal constitution mandated that

---

[23] *Id.* at 230–31.

[24] *See, e.g.*, CTS Corp. v. Dynamics Corp. of Am., 481 U.S. 69, 89 (1987) ("No principle of corporation law and practice is more firmly established than a State's authority to regulate domestic corporations. . . ."); Lyman P.Q. Johnson & Mark A. Sides, *Corporate Governance and the Sarbanes-Oxley Act: The Sarbanes-Oxley Act and Fiduciary Duties*, 30 Wm. Mitchell L. Rev. 1149, 1192 (2004) ("States, not the federal government, traditionally have regulated corporate governance.").

[25] *See* VantagePoint Venture Partners 1996 v. Examen, Inc., 871 A.2d 1108, 1112 (Del. 2005) ("The internal affairs doctrine is a long-standing choice of law principle which recognizes that only one state should have the authority to regulate a corporation's internal affairs – the state of incorporation.").

[26] *Id.* at 1116.

Examen's internal affairs, and in particular, VantagePoint's voting rights, be adjudicated exclusively in accordance with the law of its state of incorporation, in this case, the law of Delaware."[27]

In the federalism area, the internal affairs doctrine has been developed in a series of frequently cited federal court decisions. In *Santa Fe Industries, Inc. v. Green*,[28] the U.S. Supreme Court considered the coverage of section 10(b) of the Securities Exchange Act of 1934[29] and SEC Rule 10b-5[30] in the context of a going-private, short-form merger. The Court refused "to federalize the substantial portion of the law of corporations that deals with transactions in securities, particularly where established state policies of corporate regulation would be overridden," without a clear expression of congressional intent to enter that regulatory domain.[31] Following their receipt of notice of a short-form merger, minority stockholders of Kirby Lumber Corporation sued in federal court, claiming that the merger grossly undervalued the minority stock. The minority stockholders alleged that the merger violated federal law because the merger was not based on any justifiable business purpose and the minority did not receive prior notice of the merger. In addition, they alleged that the undervaluation itself constituted actionable fraud under Rule 10b-5.

The U.S. District Court for the Southern District of New York dismissed the action for failure to state a claim on which relief may be granted. The Court of Appeals for the Second Circuit reversed. That court agreed that the undervaluation itself did not support a claim under federal law. But the court held that the plaintiffs did state a claim for relief based on their allegation that the majority breached its fiduciary duty to the minority by effecting a short-form merger without any justifiable business purpose and without prior notice to the minority.[32] The court held that neither misrepresentation nor

---

[27] *Id.*   [28] 430 U.S. 462 (1977).
[29] 15 U.S.C. § 78j (2006).
[30] Rule 10b-5 provides:

It shall be unlawful for any person, directly or indirectly, by the use of any means or instrumentality of interstate commerce, or of the mails or of any facility of any national securities exchange,

(a) To employ any device, scheme, or artifice to defraud,
(b) To make any untrue statement of a material fact or to omit to state a material fact necessary in order to make the statements made, in the light of the circumstances under which they were made, not misleading, or
(c) To engage in any act, practice, or course of business which operates or would operate as a fraud or deceit upon any person, in connection with the purchase or sale of any security.

17 C.F.R. § 240.10b-5.
[31] *Santa Fe Indus.*, 430 U.S. at 479.   [32] *Id.* at 469–70.

nondisclosure was a necessary element of a Rule 10b-5 violation and that the rule covered "breaches of fiduciary duty by a majority against minority shareholders without any charge of misrepresentation or lack of disclosure."[33]

The Supreme Court rejected the interpretation of Rule 10b-5 by the court of appeals to the extent that it relied on the use of the word *fraud* in the rule to encompass all breaches of fiduciary duty in connection with a securities transaction.[34] The Court noted that the scope of Rule lob-5 was limited to the scope of power granted by Congress to the SEC under section 10(b). The Court interpreted section 10(b) as covering only conduct involving manipulation or deception.[35] Because the Court determined that the transaction as alleged in the complaint did not involve deception or manipulation, it held that the transaction did not violate section 10(b) or Rule 10b-5.[36]

The Court focused primarily on the language of the statute in concluding that Rule 10b-5 did not permit a cause of action for breach of fiduciary duty as alleged in the complaint. But, importantly, it also observed that "[a] second factor in determining whether Congress intended to create a federal cause of action in these circumstances is whether the cause of action [is] one traditionally relegated to state law."[37] The Court noted that Delaware law provided the minority stockholders with a cause of action that would enable them to recover the fair value of their shares and that leaving the minority stockholders to pursue that remedy would be entirely appropriate.[38] The Court expressed concern that interpreting Rule lob-5 as covering the conduct alleged in the complaint would "bring within the Rule a wide variety of corporate conduct traditionally left to state regulation. . . . [T]his extension of the federal securities laws would overlap and quite possibly interfere with state corporate law."[39] The Court thus "adhere[d] to the position that 'Congress by § 10(b) did not seek to regulate transactions which constitute no more than internal corporate mismanagement.'"[40]

That conclusion of the court represents the crux of the internal affairs doctrine: the internal affairs of corporations will be left to state oversight unless Congress explicitly indicates its intent to exercise control in that area. The Court of Appeals for the D.C. Circuit further developed the internal affairs doctrine in *Business Roundtable v. SEC*.[41] In that case, the Court held that SEC

---

[33] *Id.* at 470 (quoting the opinion of the court of appeals) (internal quotation marks omitted).
[34] *Id.* at 472.   [35] *Id.* at 473.
[36] *Id.* at 474.
[37] *Id.* at 478 (second alteration in original) (internal quotation marks omitted).
[38] *Id.*   [39] *Id.* at 478–79.
[40] *Id.* (quoting Superintendent of Ins. v. Bankers Life & Cas. Co., 404 U.S. 6, 12 (1971)).
[41] 905 F.2d 406 (D.C. Cir. 1990).

Rule 19c-4, which barred self-regulating organizations (SROs) from "listing stock of a corporation that takes any corporate action 'with the effect of nullifying, restricting or disparately reducing the per share voting rights of [existing common stockholders],'"[42] exceeded the SEC's authority under section 19 of the Securities Exchange Act of 1934 because the rule "directly control[led] the substantive allocation of powers among classes of shareholders."[43] As in *Santa Fe*, the Court disavowed federal involvement in regulating the internal relationships among corporate constituents absent a finding of an express congressional intent to do so.

In considering the SEC's authority to enact Rule 19c-4, the *Business Roundtable* court acknowledged two aspects of the SEC's authority over the SROs under section 19. First, it recognized that, under section 19(b), the SEC had the power to approve changes to the SROs' rules. Second, the court noted the SEC's power to impose amendments to the SROs' rules for any of several reasons, including "in furtherance of the purposes of [the Exchange Act]."[44] The issue therefore centered on what "purposes" of the Exchange Act might be furthered by Rule 19c-4. The SEC argued, among other things, that section 14 of the Exchange Act (pertaining to the SEC's authority to regulate the proxy process) demonstrated a purpose to ensure fair stockholder suffrage.[45] The court decided that the legislative purpose on which the SEC's authority rests can only be "defined by reference to the *means* Congress selected[; otherwise] it can be framed at *any* level of generality – to improve the operation of capital markets, for instance."[46] The court determined that section 14 showed that Congress's primary concern was disclosure to stockholders through control of the proxy process.

The court held that Rule 19c-4

> directly interferes with the substance of what the shareholders may enact. It prohibits certain reallocations of voting power and certain capital structures, even if approved by a shareholder vote subject to full disclosure and the most exacting procedural rules. In 1934 Congress acted on the premise that shareholder voting could work, so long as investors secured enough information and, perhaps, the benefit of other procedural protections. It did not seek to regulate the stockholders' choices. With its step beyond control of voting procedure and into the distribution of voting power, the Commission would assume an authority that the Exchange Act's proponents disclaimed any intent to grant.[47]

---

[42] *Id.* at 407 (alteration in original).   [43] *Id.*
[44] *Id.* at 408–09 (quoting § 19(c), 15 U.S.C. § 78s(c)) (alteration in original, emphasis omitted).
[45] *Id.* at 410.   [46] *Id.*
[47] *Id.* at 411.

The court observed that state law governs the distribution of powers among corporate constituents, and Rule 19c-4 stepped beyond disclosure and into that area of state regulation.[48] It opined that the Exchange Act draws an "intelligible conceptual line excluding the Commission from corporate governance."[49] That line falls between substantive regulation of stockholders' choices and procedural regulation of the voting process through regulation of disclosure. Under *Business Roundtable*, then, the SEC has authority over certain procedural aspects of stockholder voting – in particular, the disclosures that must be made in connection with the solicitation of proxies – but may not control the substance of corporate governance, such as the distribution of power among corporate constituents.

In *Kamen v. Kemper Financial Services, Inc.*,[50] the U.S. Supreme Court again emphasized that distinction between substance and procedure. In *Kemper*, a plaintiff brought a derivative suit to enforce section 20(a) of the Investment Company Act (ICA),[51] which prohibits materially misleading proxy statements. In derivative suits, the claim belongs to the corporation, and the stockholder asserting the claim must make demand on the board of directors or show that demand is excused. The plaintiff alleged that demand was excused because it was futile, but the district court dismissed the suit on the ground that plaintiff had not pleaded sufficient facts excusing demand to satisfy Federal Rule of Civil Procedure 23.1. The court of appeals affirmed, adopting as a federal common law rule the American Law Institute's "universal demand rule," which abolishes the demand futility exception to the demand requirement.[52]

The Supreme Court reversed, holding that "the function of the demand doctrine in delimiting the respective powers of the individual shareholder and of the directors to control corporate litigation clearly is a matter of 'substance,' not 'procedure.'"[53] The Court explained that the application of the demand requirement in a suit under the ICA would be governed by federal law.[54] Where the federal law did not involve a "distinct need for nationwide legal standards" or a directly applicable statutory scheme, however, the Court held that federal courts should look to state law to fill any gaps in the federal law, particularly where the gaps bear on the allocation of power among corporate constituents.[55] The Court decided that, by determining who has the power to

---

[48] *Id.* at 411–13.
[49] *Id.* at 413; *see also* CTS Corp. v. Dynamics Corp., 481 U.S. 69, 86 (1987).
[50] 500 U.S. 90 (1991).   [51] 15 U.S.C. § 80a-20(a) (2006).
[52] *Kemper*, 500 U.S. at 94.   [53] *Id.* at 96–97.
[54] *Id.* at 97.

control corporate litigation, the demand requirement related to the allocation of power within a corporation.[56] Because it also concluded that the demand requirement was not inconsistent with the policies underlying the ICA, the Court held that federal courts adjudicating cases under the ICA must apply the demand futility exception as provided by state law.[57] *Kemper* thus emphasized the primacy of state law in defining the relationships among corporate constituents.

The Court of Appeals for the D.C. Circuit recently distinguished *Business Roundtable* when faced with a case challenging the SEC's authority under the ICA to adopt a rule bearing on corporate governance. In *Chamber of Commerce v. SEC*,[58] the court upheld an SEC rule that required that an investment company have a board with at least 75 percent independent directors and an independent chair for the company to engage in transactions otherwise prohibited by the ICA. The Chamber of Commerce argued that the rule exceeded the SEC's power because the ICA did not grant the SEC authority to regulate corporate governance. The court disagreed, finding that the SEC did not exceed its authority by adopting the rule. The court found that the purposes of the ICA included "tempering the conflicts of interest" inherent in investment company structure and that Congress had selected regulation of the governance structure of investment companies as a means to achieve that purpose.[59] The court left undisturbed the internal affairs and preemption principles articulated in *Business Roundtable*, but found that the express provisions of the ICA authorized the SEC's rule. *Chamber of Commerce* thus reinforces the importance of evaluating preemption questions and issues relating to agency authority only by reference to the means and ends contemplated in the precise statutory context in which they arise.

II. SHIFTING THE BALANCE: THE SARBANES-OXLEY ACT OF 2002

Placed in historical context, Sarbanes-Oxley marks a perceptible change in the division of responsibility between the federal government and the states. More to the point, it represents a substantial federal incursion into the regulation of corporate governance that was traditionally left to the states under the internal affairs doctrine. To determine the extent of this incursion, this section undertakes a review of each component of Sarbanes-Oxley and how those components fit within the traditional federal-state balance.

---

[55] *Id.* at 98–99.
[57] *Id.* at 108–09.
[59] *Id.* at 139.

[56] *Id.* at 101.
[58] 412 F.3d 133 (D.C. Cir. 2005).

A. *Sarbanes-Oxley Provisions within the Traditional Federal Competence*

While Sarbanes-Oxley strays significantly beyond the boundaries of the internal affairs doctrine, many of its provisions stay well within (or involve a minimal expansion of) preexisting federal law.

1. Audit Regulation and Oversight

The centerpiece of the Sarbanes-Oxley Act is the regulation of accounting practices in connection with the audit of public companies. Indeed, of all Sarbanes-Oxley's reforms, the establishment of standardized accounting regulation (and the attendant provisions) may very well have the most lasting and far-reaching effect on the operation of the securities markets. More important for present purposes, the regulation of public company audits is closely related to the disclosure standards that are at the heart of the federal regulatory regime. Accordingly, in our view, this component of Sarbanes-Oxley is consistent with the traditional focus of federal regulation.

At the center of the audit reforms was the creation of the Public Company Accounting Oversight Board (PCAOB).[60] Sarbanes-Oxley charges the PCAOB with establishing a registration and oversight scheme for all accounting firms that prepare audit reports for public companies.[61] Thus, the PCAOB essentially has exclusive statutory power to establish (in consultation with advisory groups and other experts) uniform "quality control" and ethical standards for the preparation of public company audits, subject to the approval of the SEC.[62] The PCAOB also has authority to monitor the performance of registered accounting firms through inspections and to enforce compliance with the audit standards it adopts.[63]

---

[60] The PCAOB is not a federal government agency but a private, nonprofit corporation with authority to oversee and regulate audit practices pursuant to Sarbanes-Oxley. *See* Sarbanes-Oxley § 101(a)-(b).

[61] *See* Sarbanes-Oxley § 101(c). Registration with the PCAOB is required for any accounting firm that wishes to participate in the preparation or issuance of an audit report for an issuer subject to the U.S. securities laws. *See id.* § 102(a). The registration application requires disclosure of the applicant's annual fees received for audit and nonaudit services; its general financial information; the persons associated with the firm; and any civil, criminal, or administrative disciplinary actions taken against the applicant. *See id.* § 102(b)(2); *see also* PCAOB Rules 2100 through 2106 (July 16, 2003), *available at* http://www.pcaobus.org/Rules/Rules_of_the_Board/Section_2.pdf (governing the registration of public accounting firms).

[62] *See* PCAOB Release No. 2003–06 (Apr. 18, 2003); Sarbanes-Oxley § 107 (establishing SEC oversight responsibility over PCAOB).

[63] *See* Sarbanes-Oxley §§ 101(c)(3)-(4), 104, 105 (establishing PCAOB authority to conduct inspections of and to initiate investigations and disciplinary proceedings against public accounting firms).

Congress did not leave the formulation of audit regulations entirely up to the PCAOB, however. Instead, Sarbanes-Oxley directs the PCAOB to adopt a set of mandatory standards. For example, in accordance with the directions set out in Sarbanes-Oxley, PCAOB regulations require accounting firms to maintain for at least seven years sufficient documentation to support the conclusions in each audit[64] and to obtain independent reviews of each audit report by a second audit partner or another qualified independent reviewer.[65] Also in accordance with the Sarbanes-Oxley directives, PCAOB regulations require a separate audit of the issuer's internal controls over financial reporting detailing any material flaws or weaknesses in the internal controls (along with an explanation of how the auditor tested the controls).[66] Following the directives in Sarbanes-Oxley, the PCAOB regulations essentially contemplate an elaborate multiphase process to evaluate both the issuer's internal controls over financial reporting and management's assessment of those controls.[67]

In addition to the rules specifically mandated by Sarbanes-Oxley, Congress instructed the PCAOB to establish regulations in a number of areas without directly specifying the content of the regulations, including regulations governing the acceptance and continuation of audit engagements and the supervision of audits.[68] Until the PCAOB develops final rules in these areas, public accounting firms are required to comply with the standards set out in the Statement of Auditing Standards, Statements on Quality Control Standards, and Code of Professional Conduct, established by the American Institute of Certified Public Accountants.[69]

---

[64] *See* Sarbanes-Oxley § 103(a)(2)(A)(i); *see also* PCAOB Auditing Standard No. 3 – Audit Documentation (June 4, 2004), *available at* http://www.pcaobus.org/Rules/Rules_of_the_Board/Auditing_Standard_3.pdf (implementing document preparation and retention requirements).

[65] *See* Sarbanes-Oxley § 103(a)(2)(A)(ii); *see also* PCAOB Interim Quality Control Standards, *available at* http://www.pcaobus.org/ Standards/Interim_Standards/Quality_Control_Standards/index.aspx (establishing standards for concurring partner opinions based on Am. Inst. of CPAs SEC Practice Section §§ 1000.08(f), 1000.39).

[66] *See* Sarbanes-Oxley § 103(a)(2)(A)(iii); *id.* § 404(b); *see also* PCAOB Auditing Standard No. 2 – An Audit of Internal Control over Financial Reporting Performed in Conjunction with an Audit of Financial Statements § 14 (Mar. 9, 2004), *available at* http://www.pcaobus.org/Standards/Standards_and_Related_Rules/Auditing_Standard_No. 2.aspx (establishing requirements for audit of internal controls). The results of the internal controls audit are to be included in the issuer's annual report.

[67] Daniel L. Goelzer & Phoebe W. Brown, *The Work of the Public Company Accounting Oversight Board, in* 1 THE PRACTITIONER'S GUIDE TO THE SARBANES-OXLEY ACT, at IV-1-1 (2004).

[68] *See* Sarbanes-Oxley § 103(a)(2)(B).

[69] *See* PCAOB Interim Rules 3200T, 3400T, 3700T, *available at* http://www.pcaobus.org/Standards/Interim_Standards/index.aspx; *see also* PCAOB Release No. 2003–005, at 9–14, *available at* http://www.pcaobus.org/rules/docket_004/2003–04-18_release_2003_005.pdf (setting out rule-making priorities and agenda).

While the PCAOB is explicitly charged with regulating the conduct of public company audits, Sarbanes-Oxley left the SEC to select an appropriate body to establish the substantive accounting rules to be applied in audits.[70] Not surprisingly, the SEC reaffirmed the Financial Accounting Standards Board (FASB), which has long set the *de facto* accounting standards for public companies, as the body designated to establish "generally accepted" accounting principles for public company audits.[71]

The introduction of uniform regulations for audit practices and the establishment of the PCAOB to police those practices generally fall well within the traditional federal regulation of financial disclosure. Indeed, from its inception, the SEC has had the authority to establish the form and content of financial statements for public companies, as well as the methods by which those statements are prepared.[72]

Alas, even in this field, Sarbanes-Oxley did not always respect the federal-state balance. Although Congress wisely left most substantive audit and accounting rules to be devised by the PCAOB and FASB, it apparently could not resist mandating at least some specific audit standards for public firms. Some of these mandates, such as the audit documentation requirements, do not intrude on public companies' internal affairs. In contrast, by requiring all public companies to perform regular audits of their internal controls, Congress has (at least indirectly) sought to regulate the companies' corporate governance and has imposed substantial compliance costs on small public firms for which extensive internal controls audits do not make economic sense.[73] As a general rule, decisions on the scope of a public company audit should be left to the sound discretion of the issuer's audit committee (under state law) and its auditor rather than to one-size-fits-all federal regulation.

---

[70] *See* Sarbanes-Oxley § 108(b).

[71] *See* SEC Release No. 47,743 (Apr. 25, 2003) (reaffirming the status of the FASB as a standard setter for accounting rules).

[72] *See, e.g.,* Securities Act of 1933 § 7, 15 U.S.C. § 77g (prescribing the information required in a registration statement); Securities Act of 1933 § 19, 15 U.S.C. § 77s(a) (authorizing the SEC to make rules regarding "the items or details to be shown in the balance sheet and earning statement, and the methods to be followed in the preparation of accounts" related to registration statements); Securities Act of 1933 § 28, 15 U.S.C. §§ 77aa(25), (26) (describing the balance-sheet and earnings-statement requirements for registration statements); Securities Exchange Act of 1934 § 3(b), 15 U.S.C. § 78c(b) (SEC rule-making authority to define accounting terms); Securities Exchange Act of 1934 § 12(b), 15 U.S.C. § 78l(b) (registration application requirements for listed securities); Securities Exchange Act of 1934 § 13(b), 15 U.S.C. § 78m(b) (SEC rulemaking authority for "the items or details to be shown in the balance sheet and earning statement, and the methods to be followed in the preparation of [periodic] reports").

[73] There is every reason to expect that issuers will produce an audit of internal controls over financial reporting where the value of the additional information to investors exceeds the cost of producing the audit. This decision is best left to the individual issuer, however, because the cost-benefit calculation is necessarily firm specific.

For the most part, however, the audit practice regulations and standards under Sarbanes-Oxley entrench a welcome uniformity not only to the accounting principles applied in public company financial statements but also to the methods by which those financial statements are vetted by independent auditors.[74] Such uniformity is valuable because it facilitates the comparison of different firms' financial statements, and it tends to increase investor confidence in the results disclosed by the firms.[75]

2. Executive Certification of Financial Statements

To avoid the unseemly spectacle of high-ranking corporate officers disavowing responsibility for filings with the SEC, Sarbanes-Oxley requires the chief executive officer and the chief financial officer of each public company to certify that the company's quarterly and annual reports do not contain any material misstatements and "fairly present in all material respects the financial condition" of the company.[76] The signing officers must also certify that the company has implemented appropriate internal controls, that management has evaluated those controls as of the end of the period covered by the report being filed, and that the company's auditor has been notified of any material weaknesses in the controls.[77]

This certification provision effectively imposes a duty on the signing officers to develop internal controls and disclosure controls and procedures sufficient to ensure that they have the information necessary to verify the content of the firm's periodic reports – regardless of whether such controls and procedures

---

[74] The European Union is also moving toward greater uniformity in the preparation of the financial statements of companies listed in its member states. Beginning on January 1, 2005, all financial statements prepared for listed firms were required to conform to International Financial Reporting Standards. *See So Far, So Good,* ECONOMIST, June 18, 2005, at 73.

[75] Auditors play a central role in the financial markets precisely because they act as "reputational intermediaries" who vouch for the material accuracy of the data disclosed by management. *See* John C. Coffee Jr., *Understanding Enron: "It's About the Gatekeepers, Stupid,"* 57 BUS. LAW. 1403 (2002) (describing the role of reputational intermediaries in verifying and certifying corporations' statements about themselves). Uniform audit practices may enhance this function by increasing transparency of the audit process and by establishing benchmarks for use by analysts and investors. Of course, in a functioning market, one would expect public accounting firms to follow best audit practices even in the absence of such regulations; if they did not, investors would discount the value of the shares of issuers that hired them. Nevertheless, uniform audit rules are probably necessary to the extent that comparisons of the technical aspects and details of audits and audit procedures are beyond the ken of even trained market analysts.

[76] *See* Sarbanes-Oxley § 302(a)(1)-(3).

[77] *See* Sarbanes-Oxley § 302(a)(4)-(5); 17 C.F.R. § 240.13a-15 ("Each such issuer's management must evaluate . . . the effectiveness of the issuer's disclosure controls and procedures, as of the end of each fiscal quarter. . . . "); 17 C.F.R § 240.15d-15 (same).

would be mandated as a matter of state law. As a practical matter, however, the certification is little more than a device to ensure that high-ranking executives are ultimately responsible for any material misstatements in the company's filings. This does not represent a substantial departure from prior federal law.[78] Moreover, state law undoubtedly requires management to exercise reasonable control over the activities of the corporation, including the implementation of an appropriate system for reporting information up the chain of command.[79]

In short, while the Sarbanes-Oxley certification provision indirectly imposes a minimum federal governance standard on corporations, it does not significantly intrude on existing state law – at least so long as Congress does not later mandate the implementation of specific internal controls.

3. Prohibition on Insider Trades during Pension-Fund Blackout Period

As Enron's shares fell precipitously during its implosion, a number of Enron executives limited their exposure to further losses by unloading their shares in the company. Unfortunately, Enron employees who held company shares in their pension plans were unable to follow suit because the implosion occurred in the middle of a trading blackout period while the Enron pension plan changed administrators. To prevent similar inequitable outcomes in the future, Sarbanes-Oxley prohibits officers or directors from trading any shares in the company acquired in connection with their service as an officer or director during pension blackout periods.[80] As this provision does not have a direct impact on corporate governance and is related to federal regulation of both insider trading and pension plans, the pension blackout provision does not represent an expansion of federal power into fields previously reserved to the states.

---

[78] *See* Roberta Romano, *The Sarbanes-Oxley Act and the Making of Quack Corporate Governance*, 114 YALE L. J. 1521, 1541 & n.56 (2005) ("CEOs and CFOs had always been required to sign the annual report and were liable for knowingly filing fraudulent reports as well as for inadequate internal controls.").

[79] *See, e.g.*, Graham v. Allis-Chalmers, 188 A.2d 125, 130 (Del. 1963) ("[D]irectors of a corporation in managing the corporate affairs are bound to use that amount of care which ordinarily careful and prudent men would use in similar circumstances. Their duties are those of control, and whether or not by neglect they have made themselves liable for failure to exercise proper control depends on the circumstances and facts of the particular case."); *In re* Caremark Int'l, Inc. Derivative Litig., 698 A.2d 959, 970 (Del. Ch. 1996) (recognizing that the board of directors has a duty to implement an adequate reporting system in the corporation but leaving "the level of detail that is appropriate for such an information system" to the "business judgment" of the board).

[80] *See* Sarbanes-Oxley § 306(a)(1); *see also* 17 C.F.R. pts. 240, 245, 249 (implementing blackout prohibition through SEC rules).

4. Enhanced Criminal Penalties

Among the most publicized provisions of Sarbanes-Oxley were those related to the criminal penalties for certain violations of the federal securities laws. In addition to establishing new criminal offenses related to document retention[81] and expanding the federal obstruction statute,[82] Sarbanes-Oxley expanded the federal mail-fraud statute to impose substantial sanctions on executives who certify public filings that they know to be inaccurate, misleading, or otherwise in violation of the requirements of Sarbanes-Oxley.[83] Sarbanes-Oxley also substantially increased the maximum fines and jail sentences that may be imposed in securities fraud prosecutions,[84] and it directed the U.S. Sentencing Commission to review the Federal Sentencing Guidelines for obstruction of justice and related securities offenses with a view to increasing the relevant penal ties.[85] These provisions of Sarbanes-Oxley simply enhance the existing federal system of criminal penalties associated with securities fraud and therefore fall well within the traditional federal competence.[86]

---

[81] Section 802 of Sarbanes-Oxley, codified at 18 U.S.C. § 1519, makes it a criminal offense to alter or destroy corporate records with the purpose of impeding a federal investigation. Another portion of section 802, codified at 18 U.S.C. § 1520, makes it a criminal offense for public accounting firms to engage in knowing violations of the audit paper retention requirements.

[82] Section 1102 of Sarbanes-Oxley, codified at 18 U.S.C. § 1512, expands the federal obstruction statute to include tampering with a document for the purpose of impeding an investigation. Section 1107, codified at 18 U.S.C. § 1513, expands the federal obstruction statute to prohibit knowing interference with a person's employment because the person cooperated with a federal investigation. To protect whistle-blowers, Sarbanes-Oxley also prohibits retaliation against the employee of a public company for cooperation with a federal investigation, and it authorizes an aggrieved whistle-blower to initiate a civil action for reinstatement and/or compensatory damages. See Sarbanes-Oxley § 806.

[83] See Sarbanes-Oxley § 906. Sarbanes-Oxley also clarified that the federal wire fraud statute applies to securities fraud and to conspiracies and attempts to commit a securities fraud. See id. § 807 (wire fraud); id. § 902 (attempt and conspiracy).

[84] See Sarbanes-Oxley § 903(a) (wire fraud); id. § 903(b) (wire fraud); id. § 904 (ERISA); id. § 1106 (securities fraud). Sarbanes-Oxley expands other remedies against violators of the securities laws. For example, it makes debts from securities fines not dischargeable in bankruptcy, increases the statute of limitations for securities fraud, authorizes the SEC to temporarily freeze assets in connection with securities investigations, and authorizes the SEC to prohibit individuals from serving as officers or directors of public companies. See Sarbanes-Oxley § 803 (bankruptcy amendment); id. § 804 (statute of limitations); id. § 1103 (temporary freeze); id. § 1105 (authorization to censure individuals).

[85] See Sarbanes-Oxley § 805 (obstruction sentencing guidelines); id. § 905 (wire-fraud sentencing guidelines); id. § 1104 (securities-fraud sentencing guidelines).

[86] The same can be said of the provision making it a crime for officers or other agents to "tak[e] any action to fraudulently influence, coerce, manipulate, or mislead any independent public or certified accountant... for the purpose of rendering [the company's] financial statements materially misleading." Id. § 303(a). This provision falls squarely within the federal sphere, as it protects the integrity of the audit process and the resulting financial statements filed with the SEC.

5. Additional Disclosure Requirements

In keeping with the traditional federal emphasis on disclosure regulations, Sarbanes-Oxley expands the existing reporting obligations of public companies. In particular, it requires firms to disclose the following in their periodic reports:

- Any "material correcting adjustments" to financial statements identified by the company's auditor;[87]
- All "material off-balance sheet transactions, arrangements, obligations (including contingent obligations), and other relationships of the issuer with unconsolidated entities;"[88]
- *Pro forma* figures that are reconciled with the issuer's results under generally accepted accounting principles;[89]
- Management's assessment of the company's internal controls, audited in accordance with the rules established by the PCAOB;[90]
- The company's code of ethics for senior financial officers (or the reason the company has not adopted such a code);[91] and
- The members of the company's audit committee who are "financial experts" (or the reason there are no financial experts on the committee).[92]

To improve monitoring of public company disclosures, Congress also directed the SEC to review the periodic reports of public companies "on a regular and systematic basis," paying particular attention to companies that (1) have issued material restatements of results, (2) have experienced unusual share-price volatility, (3) have the largest market capitalization, (4) have an unusually high market price to earnings ratio, or (5) have a significant effect on "any material sector of the economy."[93]

Although the disclosure components of Sarbanes-Oxley seem most obviously within the traditional responsibility of the federal government, several of these provisions arguably amount to oblique corporate governance directives. For example, requiring each public company to disclose any financial experts on its audit committee is a not-so-subtle signal that the SEC (and investors) should look unfavorably on companies that do not have such experts.[94] Nevertheless, a disclosure-oriented approach to federal regulation

[87] Sarbanes-Oxley § 401(a).
[88] *See id.* § 401(a).
[89] *See id.* § 401(b).
[90] *See id.* § 404.
[91] *See id.* § 406(a).
[92] *See id.* § 407.
[93] *See id.* § 408(a). Sarbanes-Oxley also requires issuers to disclose "on a rapid and current basis" any material changes in their operations or financial condition. *Id.* § 409.
[94] As explained *supra*, requiring management to conduct an internal controls audit represents a similar form of indirect corporate governance mandate. *See* Jesse A. Finkelstein & Mark J.

in this area is clearly preferable to substantive mandates; for example, the SEC presumably will not view a company with suspicion if the company can present a satisfactory explanation of why it does not have a financial expert on its audit committee. Of course, these disclosure requirements may be an indication of future expansions of federal regulation in this area. In their present form, however, the Sarbanes-Oxley disclosure provisions generally represent an unremarkable extension of existing federal disclosure regulations.

6. Summary

As the foregoing analysis makes clear, a sizable portion of Sarbanes-Oxley fits comfortably within existing federal law governing securities fraud and disclosures by public companies. Any regulatory expansion raises the possibility of conflict with state law,[95] however, and Congress should be cognizant of the interaction between any federal law or regulation and state law.

B. Sarbanes-Oxley Provisions within the Traditional State Competence

The more worrying aspects of Sarbanes-Oxley are those that represent an expansion of federal authority into areas of corporate governance traditionally regulated by the states. This section discusses a number of components that present just such a concern.

1. Regulation of Nonaudit Services

The revelation of vast accounting irregularities (and, in some cases, outright fraud) at companies such as Enron and WorldCom raised questions about the efficacy of their independent auditors. In particular, observers questioned

Gentile, *Relationship to State Law, in* 1 THE PRACTITIONER'S GUIDE TO THE SARBANES-OXLEY ACT, at V-4-22 (2004) (discussing various "therapeutic" disclosure requirements promulgated by the SEC as a means to influence corporate behavior); *see also id.* at V-4-30 (arguing that required disclosures of a code of ethics for the chief financial officer indirectly conflicts with state policy to leave such issues to the discretion of the corporation).

[95] Conflict may exist even in areas that have been subject to federal regulation for quite some time, as shown by a recent decision of the Delaware Court of Chancery. *See* Newcastle Partners, L.P. v. Vesta Ins. Group, Inc., 887 A.2d 975 (Del. Ch. 2005) (mem. op.) (requiring that a company proceed with a court-ordered annual meeting, despite the company's argument that proceeding with the meeting would cause the company to violate SEC proxy rules because it was not prepared to issue an annual report and proxy statement or information statement); *cf. id.* at 981–82 ("[T]he [federal and state] provisions do not actually conflict. Rather, they both serve the same purpose of helping to safeguard the shareholders' foundational voting rights. . . . Any suggestion that there is an irreconcilable conflict between the [court's order for the company to hold the annual meeting] and SEC statutes and regulations would both misconstrue the scheme of federal proxy regulation and weaken a basic premise of American corporate law that is a defining characteristic of our federal system.").

whether an auditor could provide a truly independent review and evaluation of a company's financial statements if the auditor also earned substantial fees from the company for other, nonaudit services – fees that the auditor stood to lose if the audit turned up problems with the company's books. To address this perceived conflict, Sarbanes-Oxley forbids accounting firms from providing certain nonaudit services to the public companies they audit.[96]

By dictating what services a company may and may not purchase from a public accounting firm – a decision that would otherwise be governed by state law – this provision marks a clear departure from the traditional disclosure-oriented approach of federal securities laws. Congress, in effect, has made a substantive business decision on behalf of every public company in the United States. But these implementing rules leave much to the audit committee to determine (except for enumerated prohibited items). In the absence of any empirical evidence that the provision of nonaudit services may compromise the work of an independent auditor,[97] however, there is no reason to believe that state law fiduciary duty principles were insufficient to address any potential conflicts that may arise from a company's purchase of multiple services from its auditor.[98]

2. Audit Committee Composition

In apportioning responsibility for the various accounting scandals, Congress clearly believed that failures in board oversight were at least partly to blame. To address these perceived failures, Sarbanes-Oxley requires that all of the

---

[96] *See* Sarbanes-Oxley § 201(a). Prohibited nonaudit services include, among other things, bookkeeping, information technology, appraisals, outsourcing of human resources or other management functions, investment banking, and legal advice. *See id.* Auditing firms may perform other services, such as tax preparation, that are not explicitly prohibited "only if the activity is approved in advance by the audit committee of the issuer." *See id.* §§ 201–02. It is unclear why Congress viewed these other services as less of a threat to the auditor's independence than the prohibited services, except perhaps that they are less likely to result in substantial fees or perhaps have been traditionally provided by auditing firms.

[97] *See* Romano, *supra* note 78, at 1533–37 (describing studies addressing whether the provision of nonaudit services compromises the quality of audits). Given that the studies have not found any impairment to audits performed by accounting firms that performed multiple services for the issuer, there is also no basis to argue that corporate management uses purchases of nonaudit services to influence the results of audits.

[98] Section 203 of Sarbanes-Oxley, which requires accounting firms to rotate the lead audit partner for each public company every five years, suffers from the same infirmity. Here again, Congress has mandated a business decision that would ordinarily be taken by the company's board of directors or audit committee subject to state law fiduciary duties – namely whether it makes sense to change the lead partner on the audit. Ominously, Congress also directed the comptroller general to study the effects of requiring public companies to rotate entire accounting firms. *See* Sarbanes-Oxley § 207.

members of a listed company's audit committee be independent directors (as defined in the Act).[99] The theory behind this rule is that independent directors will cast a more critical eye on the company's financial statements, thus providing a more effective check on management abuses.[100]

Commentators, including the Delaware courts, have long advocated majority-independent audit committees for public companies as a corporate best practice.[101] But there is an important distinction between aspirational guidelines and mandatory rules: the best practice for some (or even most) public companies is not necessarily the best practice for all such companies.[102] Congress has thus negated the more flexible case-by-case approach of state law by declaring that all public companies must have fully independent audit committees regardless of the circumstances. So long as insider directors are not subject to some particular conflict of interest, it is not clear that they should automatically be prohibited from serving on the audit committee.[103] Indeed, there may be good reasons to have insider members of the audit committee, particularly given that insiders often have an in-depth understanding of the firm's accounts that may be lacking among independent directors.

In accordance with the above analysis, federal regulation in this area should be limited to the disclosure of audit committee members and should not extend to substantive regulation of audit committee composition. This approach would allow investors to make judgments about the likely quality of board oversight of a company's financial statements while leaving the company sufficient flexibility to select the best available members for their audit committee.

3. Executive Bonuses

Among the measures designed to increase the accountability of top executives, Sarbanes-Oxley requires the CEO and CFO of public companies to forfeit any

---

[99] See Sarbanes-Oxley § 201 (directing the SEC to promulgate rules requiring the exchanges to adopt listing standards on audit committee composition); Finkelstein & Gentile, *supra* note 94, at V-4-13, V-4-14 (discussing SEC rules and stock-exchange listing standards for audit committees).

[100] See Romano, *supra* note 78, at 1530–31.

[101] See, e.g., Ralph K. Winter Jr., *State Law, Shareholder Protection, and the Theory of Competition*, 6 J. LEGAL STUD. 251, 287 (1977). Similarly, beginning in 1999, the exchanges required listed companies to have at least three independent directors on their audit committees. See Finkelstein & Gentile, *supra* note 94, at V-4-12.

[102] As stated by the Delaware Supreme Court in its 2000 decision in the *Disney* case, "Aspirational ideals of good corporate governance practices . . . can usually help directors avoid liability. But they are not required by the corporation law and do not define standards of liability." Brehm v. Eisner, 746 A.2d 244, 256 (Del. 2000).

[103] An insider-dominated audit committee theoretically presents a potential conflict, as insiders might engage in lax oversight of the company's accounts as a means to increase their compensation. But there is a lack of empirical evidence supporting a correlation between complete audit committee independence and audit quality. See Romano, *supra* note 78, at 1532–33.

incentive compensation and any profits from trading in the company's shares that they receive during the twelve-month period after the company discloses a material noncompliance with reporting rules "as a result of misconduct."[104] The idea is that executives should not profit personally from the accounting misstatements made on their watch. Ultimately, however, decisions about the appropriate compensation for executives (or the forfeiture of that compensation) should be left up to the board of directors.

A mandatory federal rule requiring forfeiture essentially strips the board of its power under state law to fix executive compensation and to determine whether executives should be made to return any compensation to the company as a result of any potential misconduct. While the forfeiture rule may not come into play in many cases,[105] there is a well-founded concern that this provision represents a first step toward more generalized federal regulation of executive compensation.[106] Indeed, as discussed in H.R. 4291 below, a bill has already been introduced in the U.S. House of Representatives that would require a separate shareholder vote to approve certain executive compensation plans.

4. Executive Loans

Embedded in the "Enhanced Financial Disclosures" section of Sarbanes-Oxley is arguably the clearest federal incursion into areas traditionally governed by state law: a new general prohibition on corporate loans to officers and directors.[107] This provision is presumably a response to well-publicized abuses of executive loan programs in which executives covered various personal expenses with funds from company loans. State law generally permits loans by a corporation to its officers "whenever, in the judgment of the directors, such loan . . . may reasonably be expected to benefit the corporation."[108]

Yet there is no evidence that state laws on fiduciary duty were inadequate to address these abuses. To the contrary, state fiduciary law is expressly designed

---

[104] *See* Sarbanes-Oxley § 304.

[105] Because it is unclear what constitutes "misconduct" under section 304, the potential scope of the forfeiture obligation is ambiguous. *See* Finkelstein & Gentile, *supra* note 94, at V-4-28.

[106] *See* Roberta S. Karmel, *Realizing the Dream of William O. Douglas – The Securities and Exchange Commission Takes Charge of Corporate Governance*, 30 DEL. J. CORP. L. 79, 106 (2005) (suggesting that the executive compensation provisions in Sarbanes-Oxley could support an attempt by the SEC to regulate the makeup of corporate compensation committees). For their part, the New York Stock Exchange and Nasdaq rules require compensation issues at listed companies to be decided by independent directors. *See* Finkelstein & Gentile, *supra* note 94, at V-4-16 (discussing exchange rules governing compensation and arguing that regulation of compensation "create[s] new substantive obligations where none previously existed under state law").

[107] *See* Sarbanes-Oxley § 402. The only exception to this rule is for companies that provide loans or credit to the public on the same terms in the ordinary course of their business. *See id.*

[108] DEL. CODE ANN. tit. 8, § 143.

to deal with situations in which executives misappropriate corporate funds or otherwise attempt to loot the corporate treasury. Moreover, a blanket ban on loans to all executives is the worst kind of one-size-fits-all rule and has the effect of prohibiting a large swathe of legitimate transactions that benefit both the companies and investors. For example, the ban on loans seems to cover unremarkable practices, such as loans to facilitate the exercise of executive stock options, which tend to align executives' interests with those of stockholders, or loans to support executive relocation at the company's request.[109]

Here again, rather than banning the potentially beneficial provision of executive loans, federal regulation in this area could simply have required public companies to disclose in greater detail the amount and terms of any loans to executives. This approach would allow analysts and investors to review the nature of loans provided to executives and to reach a judgment whether the loans are beneficial to the company or reflect a failure of proper board oversight. Tellingly, only one witness who testified before Congress during the Sarbanes-Oxley hearings advocated a ban on loans to executives; most advocated simple disclosure of the amount and terms of executive loans in SEC filings.[110] By establishing a blanket prohibition on potentially beneficial conduct that is subject to effective regulation under state law, Congress took over a field traditionally reserved to the states – and it did so in a manner likely to be detrimental to the investors it meant to protect.[111]

5. Rules of Lawyer Conduct

With a view to encouraging knowledgeable insiders to identify improper activity by management, Sarbanes-Oxley directs the SEC to adopt rules of professional responsibility that require any lawyer who practices before the SEC

---

[109] Finkelstein & Gentile, *supra* note 94, at V-4-23–25 (observing that Sarbanes-Oxley could be read to prohibit loans to facilitate the exercise of options, cash advances, advances of defense costs in stockholder litigation, and the use of a company credit card); Romano, *supra* note 78, at 1538 (discussing the use of corporate loans to facilitate the exercise of options); *see also id.* at 1539 (citing studies indicating that "most loans' purpose is one of incentive alignment").

[110] *See* Romano, *supra* note 78, at 1538. Indeed, the use of executive loans "had not been a component of recent policy discussions" and had not "generat[ed] scholarly controversy." *Id.*

[111] The prohibition on executive loans is also likely to have other unintended side effects and to lead to anomalous results. Professor Romano notes that regulating compensation is virtually impossible and may ultimately be detrimental to the company; when the government bans a particular practice, parties will simply find an alternative (often less desirable and more expensive) means to procure a similar result. *See* Romano, *supra* note 78, at 1539. Jesse Finkelstein and Mark Gentile further observe that, although corporations may not make loans to their own executives or directors, they may make loans to executives and directors of their subsidiaries. *See* Finkelstein & Gentile, *supra* note 94, at V-4-24.

to report material violations of the securities laws "up the ladder" within the company until the attorney receives an appropriate response.[112] Under the SEC rule implementing this provision, the lawyer is also permitted to notify the SEC of a material violation without the issuer's consent if the disclosure is necessary (1) to prevent a violation that is likely to cause substantial harm, (2) to prevent perjury, or (3) to rectify a past violation that was furthered by the attorney's services.[113] The SEC has a further provision "on hold" that would require a mandatory "noisy withdrawal" of the lawyer under certain conditions.[114] The SEC would be well advised to keep this provision on hold or to drop it altogether. Indeed, state ethics rules already permit some disclosure of client information to prevent or rectify fraud or to permit a noisy withdrawal and sometimes mandate that action.[115]

The promulgated SEC rules are expressly contemplated by Sarbanes-Oxley but remain firmly in traditional federal territory only to the extent that they prescribe rules of professional conduct for lawyers practicing before the SEC. The problem is that the rules are very broad and are not necessarily limited to lawyers who practice directly before the SEC; they may also cover the armies of lawyers who participate indirectly in securities filings or investigations.[116] Because federal standards prevail in the event of a conflict with state lawyer-conduct standards,[117] state law rules circumscribing the reporting of misconduct to promote confidentiality of client communications may be preempted for a substantial number of lawyers.

---

[112] *See* Sarbanes Oxley § 307; *see also* 17 C.F.R. § 205.3(b). Under the SEC rule implementing this provision, an attorney must report a "material violation" of the securities laws to the appropriate authority within the issuer where a "prudent and competent" attorney would "conclude that it is 'reasonably likely' that a material violation has occurred, is ongoing, or is about to occur." 17 C.F.R. § 205.2(e); *see also* Implementation of Standards of Professional Conduct for Attorneys, Exchange Act Release No. 47,276 (Jan. 29, 2003).

[113] *See* 17 C.F.R. § 205.3(d)(2); *see also* Finkelstein & Gentile, *supra* note 94, at V-4-18–19 (discussing the potential breadth of the SEC rules of professional conduct for attorneys).

[114] Proposed 17 C.F.R. § 205.3(d)(l)(A) (requiring an outside attorney to withdraw from the representation if the attorney does not receive an appropriate response and requiring the attorney to notify the issuer that the withdrawal was based on "professional considerations"); Proposed 17 C.F.R. § 205.3(e) (requiring the issuer to notify the SEC of the withdrawal and the related circumstances); *see also* Implementation of Standards of Professional Conduct for Attorneys, Exchange Act Release No. 47282 (Jan. 29, 2003).

[115] *See* ABA Model Rules of Professional Conduct Rules 1.2(d), 1.6, 1.16, 4.1.

[116] Specifically, the rules cover attorneys (1) who represent clients in any formal SEC "proceeding" (as that term is defined in 17 C.F.R. § 201.101(9)), (2) who make filings with the SEC, or (3) who represent clients in SEC investigations. *See* 17 C.F.R. § 201.102(b) (representation in a proceeding); 17 C.F.R. § 201.102(d)(2) (representation in a filing); 17 C.F.R. § 203.3 (making Rule 102(e) applicable to investigations).

[117] *See* Sarbanes-Oxley § 205.

This potentially vast preemption of state law is not justified by any failure of state regulation of lawyers. More important, federal intervention in this area threatens to undermine the delicate balance established under state law between the interests of the public and the interests of the corporate client.

III. ANALYSIS OF REGULATIONS FOLLOWING SARBANES-OXLEY

A number of post–Sarbanes-Oxley regulatory developments in the federal arena raise significant federalism questions. The SEC's proposed stockholder access rule raises questions concerning the SEC's authority to regulate corporate internal affairs as well as the wisdom of federalizing such regulation. Changes to the listing requirements of the SROs raise similar questions. A bill recently introduced in Congress by U.S. Representative Barney Frank raises the question of whether regulation of executive compensation should be federalized. This chapter addresses these developments in turn.

A. *The SEC's Stockholder Access Proposal*

In 2003, the SEC proposed Rule 14a-11, which under certain circumstances would permit stockholders to access a company's proxy statement for the purpose of nominating candidates for the board of directors.[118] Under this proposed stockholder access rule, stockholders or groups of stockholders owning more than 5 percent of the company's stock for at least two years would be able to include nominees to the board on the company's proxy materials if one of two triggering events occurred:[119] (1) if stockholders approved a stockholder proposal submitted by a stockholder group owning at least 1 percent of the company's stock to opt into the stockholder access system or (2) if 35 percent of the stockholders withheld their votes from a management nominee to the board.[120] At the annual meeting in the year following the occurrence of either triggering event, the company would be required to include in its proxy materials a candidate nominated by a stockholder or group holding the required amount of stock.[121]

---

[118] Security Holder Director Nominations, Exchange Act Release No. 48,626 (proposed Oct. 14, 2003). This is at least the third time that the SEC has considered providing for direct stockholder access to the company's proxy for the purpose of nominating directors. *See* Seligman, *supra* note 16, at 1162, 1163–65.

[119] Roel C. Campos, *The SEC's Shareholder Access Proposal: It Still Has a Pulse*, Remarks at the Yale Law School Center for the Study of Corporate Law (Jan. 10, 2005), *in* PRACTISING LAW INSTITUTE, WHAT ALL BUSINESS LAWYERS AND LITIGATORS MUST KNOW ABOUT DELAWARE LAW DEVELOPMENTS 1147, 1149 (2005).

[120] *Id.* at 1149.   [121] *Id.*

Proposed Rule 14a-11 proved highly controversial, drawing more than four-teen thousand comments.[122] Many of the comments received by the SEC centered on the structure of the triggering events,[123] whether the effects of Sarbanes-Oxley and related reforms should be evaluated before enacting a stockholder access rule,[124] and the SEC's authority to enact the rule.[125] The proposal has now faltered and is perhaps dead.[126] Nevertheless, it merits con-sidering whether the rule would be a valid product of SEC authority and advisable as a matter of federalism.

There is significant disagreement, even among the commissioners them-selves, over whether the SEC has the authority to enact Rule 14a-11.[127] The SEC claims as the source of its authority section 14(a) of the Exchange Act, through the enactment of which, the SEC asserts, Congress intended to ensure fair corporate suffrage for stockholders.[128] Critics of the proposed rule contend

[122] *Id.; see also* John C. Coffee Jr., *Federalism and the SEC's Proxy Proposal*, N.Y.L.J. 5 (Mar. 18, 2004), *available at* http://www.sec.gov/rules/proposed/s71903/s71903-816.pdf (describing the stockholder access proposal as "the most controversial and important proposal to emanate from the SEC in over a decade").

[123] *See, e.g.*, Letter from ABA, Section of Business Law, to SEC (Nov. 3, 2003), *available at* http://www.sec.gov/rules/proposed/s71903/abal110303.htm; Letter from ABA, Sec-tion of Business Law, to SEC (Jan. 7, 2004), *available at* http://www.sec.gov/rules/proposed/s7l903/aba10704.htm (acknowledging that stockholder access should be permitted only where a triggering event signals strong stockholder dissatisfaction with the company's nomination process but questioning the ability of the proposed triggering events to reflect such dissatisfaction).

[124] *See, e.g.*, Letter from ABA, Section of Business Law, to SEC (Jan. 7, 2004), *available at* http://www.sec.gov/rules/proposed/s71903/aba010704.htm ("This subject can be revisited in the future after evaluating whether these recently enacted reforms and other changes in company practices have resolved the concerns that the direct access proposals seek to address.").

[125] *Compare* Letter from ABA, Section of Business Law, to SEC (Jan. 7, 2004), *available at* http://www.sec.gov/rules/proposed/s7l903/abao10704.htm (arguing that the stockholder access rule would create "a substantive right of access for shareholders that would impinge on corpo-rate law – including valid provisions of a corporation's organizational documents – [and thus] would raise serious issues regarding the Commission's authority"), *with* Coffee, *supra* note 122 (observing that "[t]he legality of proposal Rule 14a-11 depends upon where courts draw the line between the realm of corporate governance, regulated primarily by state corporate law, and the realm of securities regulation, where the SEC is the primary regulator," and arguing that proposed Rule 14a-11 is a "procedural" rule that falls within the SEC's authority).

[126] *See* E. Norman Veasey & Christine T. Di Guglielmo, *What Happened in Delaware Corporate Law and Governance from l992–2004? A Retrospective on Some Key Developments*, 153 U. PA. L. REV. 1399, 1505 n.473 (2005) (noting that the stockholder access proposal "now appears to be dead").

[127] *See* Karmel, *supra* note 106, at 126–27 (stating that "[a]t least one sitting SEC Commissioner, [Paul S. Atkins,] has expressed serious doubt about the SEC's authority to promulgate a rule mandating shareholder access to management's proxy."); Campos, *supra* note 119, at 1160.

[128] Security Holder Director Nominations, Exchange Act Release No. 48,626 (proposed Oct. 14, 2003), at text accompanying notes 46–48.

that director nominations are a matter of corporate internal affairs controlled by state law, citing *Santa Fe Industries* and *Business Roundtable*.[129] Proponents of the rule argue that, under state law, stockholders are entitled to nominate directors but that the proxy rules create obstacles to the exercise of that right that the proposed rule seeks to remove in a balanced way.[130] The SEC expressly disclaims any attempt to create a stockholder right to nominate directors. Instead, it insists that the proposed rule would merely regulate the manner by which that right is exercised through regulation of the company proxy, only where state law permits stockholder nominations.[131]

Professor John Coffee has asserted that section 14(a) grants the SEC sufficient authority to adopt the stockholder access rule. He argues that section 14(a) is not limited to disclosure but, by requiring that anyone who solicits proxies must comply with the SEC's regulations, the section authorizes the SEC to ensure a right of fair corporate suffrage.[132] Professor Coffee understands the SEC's power as extending to the regulation of voting procedure and believes that the stockholder access proposal fits within that domain.[133] He cites a "long list of respected commentators" as understanding the SEC's power with respect to the proxy rules as based on a policy goal of placing an absent stockholder in an equivalent position with a stockholder who attends the annual meeting.[134] Because a stockholder in attendance at an annual meeting may nominate a director from the floor, such commentators suggest, a stockholder participating in the meeting by proxy should also be permitted to nominate a director via proxy.

---

[129] *See* Letter from ABA, Section of Business Law, to SEC (Jan. 7, 2004), *available at* http://www. sec.gov/rules/proposed/s71903/aba010704.htm ("The director election process is a fundamental element of corporate governance provided for and controlled by state law. It includes the right of shareholders to elect directors and govern the director nomination process, and reflects a balance of rights and responsibilities between shareholders and directors that is important to our system of corporate economic enterprise."). *See also supra* this chapter for discussion of *Santa Fe Industries* and *Business Roundtable* and the internal affairs doctrine.

[130] Campos, *supra* note 119, at 1160.

[131] Security Holder Director Nominations, Exchange Act Release No. 48,626 (proposed Oct. 14, 2003), at text following note 58 ("Nothing in the proposed procedure establishes a right of security holders to nominate candidates for election to a company's board of directors; rather the proposed procedure involves disclosure and other requirements concerning proxy materials that are conditioned on the existence of such a right under state law and the occurrence of specified events.").

[132] John C. Coffee Jr., *Remarks at Roundtable Discussion Regarding Proposed Rules Relating to Security Holder Director Nominations* (Mar. 10, 2004) (transcript available at http://www.sec. gov/spotlight/dir-nominations/transcript03102004.txt).

[133] *Id.*

[134] Coffee, *supra* note 122, at note 13 and accompanying text.

The Task Force on Shareholder Proposals of the Committee on Federal Regulation of Securities of the American Bar Association's Section of Business Law (the Committee), co-chaired by Todd Lang and Charles Nathan, submitted comments regarding proposed Rule 14a-11, arguing that the rule would exceed the SEC's authority because it would constitute a federal grant of a right to stockholders that does not exist under state law. The Committee contends that the rule is a substantive, not a procedural, rule of the commission, and therefore falls outside the scope of the SEC's authority.[135] The Committee summarized its position as follows:

> The Commission's authority to regulate director nominations is confined to disclosure and voting procedures related to proxy solicitations. State corporate law otherwise governs the director nomination process and does not provide shareholders a right of access to the company's proxy materials, although such a right may be established and the director nomination process may be regulated under organizational documents and by board action. Preemption of state corporate law in this fundamental area of corporate governance cannot be implied from the Commission's general powers; it can only result from direct Congressional action. Accordingly, the creation by the Commission of a substantive right of access for shareholders that would impinge on corporate law – including valid provisions of a corporation's organizational documents – would raise serious issues regarding the Commission's authority. This would include access requirements that conflict with the exercise of board or nominating committee responsibilities with respect to the nominating process or the use of company proxy materials, whether undertaken to implement listing standards or to achieve other legitimate corporate purposes. Rule 14a-8 is not precedent for creation of such an access right because matters relating to the election of directors are excluded from the Rule's scope, reflecting the design and use of Rule 14a-8 for other purposes. Therefore, the limited access to company proxy statements provided by Rule 14a-8 is not determinative of the Commission's authority to adopt an access rule involving the director selection process. The Commission's exercise of authority in this area must separately be supported by considerations involving disclosure or voting procedures.[136]

Critics and proponents alike of the stockholder access proposal agree that the SEC's authority in this area is limited. That is, assuming the SEC has authority to regulate voting procedure, it may not venture into the area of substantive regulation of corporate governance without an express grant of

---

[135] Letter from ABA, Section of Business Law, to SEC (Jan. 7, 2004), *available at* http://www.sec .gov/rules/proposed/s71903/aba010704.htm.
[136] *Id.*

authority by Congress to do so. Thus, the definition of *procedure* becomes important. The disagreement revolves around whether the stockholder access proposal constitutes a substantive regulation or a limited procedural one.

The better view of the issue, in our judgment, is that the proposed stockholder access rule would go beyond the SEC's authority over disclosure and voting procedure and move into the substantive regulation of the balance of power among corporate constituents. Under traditional state law principles, directors are responsible for nominating directors and for controlling the company's proxy materials. The stockholder access proposal would expand stockholder power in both of these areas. Rule 14a-11 would not simply place an absent stockholder in the same position as one who actually attended the meeting and could nominate a director from the floor. A stockholder who attended the meeting would still be required to obtain sufficient votes for her candidate to be elected – an unlikely result for a floor nomination because the proxies would already have been submitted. Rule 14a-11 would give the nominator the benefits of soliciting votes and access to the corporation's pockets to do so, a benefit stockholders have never had before. In contrast, the stockholder access rule would permit the stockholder to make the nomination and solicit votes in support of her candidate in advance of the meeting and at the company's expense.

The timing of the stockholder access proposal suggests another interesting view of the SEC's authority with respect to the proposal. The SEC's authority under the Securities Act and the Securities Exchange Act has traditionally been understood as extending to regulation of disclosure and voting procedure. It could be argued that by legislating concerning so many aspects of corporate governance, Sarbanes-Oxley has eroded the distinction between substantive internal affairs and disclosure. If so, the statute may implicitly grant authority to the SEC beyond the disclosure and limited procedural areas. That argument is without force, however, for two reasons. First, the internal affairs doctrine holds that, unless Congress demonstrates an express intent to regulate corporate internal affairs, regulation will be left to the states. Thus, an implicit eroding of a traditional distinction will not be sufficient to grant the SEC authority in a new, substantive area of law. Second, as discussed above, Sarbanes-Oxley's corporate governance provisions largely function through the mechanism of disclosure. Thus, the traditional means-end distinction is actually sustained – or even reinforced – by Sarbanes-Oxley. That is, the SEC's authority over securities issuers is exercised by requiring disclosure of corporate governance structures, not by mandating the structures themselves.

Regardless of whether the stockholder access proposal is ultimately adopted by the SEC and challenged in court, it highlights important federalism questions. If it is adopted and challenged, it will present another opportunity for the courts to refine the boundary between state and federal regulation of corporate governance. And even if it is not adopted, the proposal stands as evidence of a move toward federalization of corporate governance and the willingness of federal actors to venture further into a quintessentially state area of regulation.

The foregoing discussion, of course, addresses only the SEC's authority to adopt Rule 14a-11. It does not consider whether adoption of the rule would be advisable as a policy matter. In this regard – and as will be discussed in more detail below – the development of corporate law is best left to the states. Jurisprudentially, state law in this area is typically more flexible and balanced than federal law.[137] In our view, state legislatures and courts (especially expert business courts like the Delaware Court of Chancery) are better positioned to respond more appropriately to perceived needs for change or in a contextual fact setting than are Congress or the many federal judges in nearly one hundred federal district courts. Finally, Rule 14a-11 could create a perverse incentive for states to opt out of allowing stockholder nominations entirely, creating a race to the bottom among state corporate laws in the context of stockholder suffrage. Without such an incentive for states to enact a blanket prohibition on nominations by stockholders, state law retains the benefits of its enabling approach and allows states to leave open the possibility of stockholder nominations where they suit the circumstances of a particular company.

The weakness of the basis for federal (i.e., SEC) activity in the law governing the voting by stockholders for the election of directors and the complexity of that issue on the merits, apart from federalism concerns, have caused a shift in focus from federal to state law. Now the analysis on voting for directors has shifted to an examination of state default rules. The Committee on Corporate Laws of the Section of Business Law of the American Bar Association is studying whether to recommend changes in the Model Business Corporation Act (in effect in some form in a majority of states) where the default provision (section 7.28(a)) provides that directors shall be elected by a plurality (not a majority) of the votes cast, even in an uncontested election, unless the articles of incorporation provide otherwise. Delaware, where the law is not based on the Model Act, has a similar but slightly different default formulation and permits opting out of the statutory default in the certificate of incorporation or in the bylaws.

The Corporate Laws Committee has set forth in a discussion paper the issues and some options in this complex area and, in response to its invitation,

---

[137] *See* Veasey & Di Guglielmo, *supra* note 126, at 1413 & n.39.

has reviewed many comments.[138] Meanwhile, there is much activity among investor groups and some private ordering by corporations in adopting guidelines obliging directors who receive a majority of withhold votes to resign. At this time, the issue remains in flux, although the focus is definitely on state law, not SEC regulation.[139]

B. Recent Amendments to the SROs' Listing Rules on Corporate Governance

Following Sarbanes-Oxley, in late 2003, the SEC approved amendments to the listing standards of the principal SROs, including the New York Stock Exchange (NYSE).[140] The amendments regulate a variety of corporate governance issues. The federalism implications are similar to those raised by SEC rule making like the stockholder access proposal but are perhaps both narrower and broader in the listing standard context. They are narrower because the listing standards do not constitute direct federal regulation of corporate governance. They are broader because the SROs are not necessarily subject to the same constitutional limits on authority as are the federal government and its agencies. In addition, because the SEC exerts considerable influence over the listing standards adopted by the SROs, those standards do constitute indirect federal regulation of corporate governance.

---

[138] Committee on Corporate Laws, *Discussion Paper on Voting by Shareholders for the Election of Directors* (2005), *available at* http://www.abanet.org/buslaw/committees/CL270000pub/directorvoting/20050621000000.pdf.

[139] The Corporate Laws Committee noted in its release of September 26, 2005, that it had received "many helpful observations and comments in the 36" letters commenting on its Discussion Paper. The Committee noted that it "is continuing its objective and intensive work on this subject." Significantly, the Committee noted the following:

> One positive development is the growing trend of voluntary adoption by certain corporations of corporate governance guidelines that address the failure of nominees to satisfy a minimum vote requirement. One such guideline is that exemplified by the action of the board of directors of Pfizer, Inc. (as well as similar action and variations thereon by other companies), to the general effect that a nominee for director must tender his or her resignation to the board of directors for action by the board in the event that the nominee "receives a greater number of votes 'withheld' from his or her election than votes 'for' such election." The Committee is looking at whether there are suitable ways in the Model Act to reinforce this kind of voluntary initiative. The Committee is continuing as well to study other director voting issues, including those identified in the Discussion Paper.

[140] Many other SROs similarly amended their listing standards around the same time. Unless noted otherwise, this discussion will focus on the NYSE listing standards as an example of the federalism issues presented by corporate governance provisions of the SRO rules.

At the outset, it is important to note that the SEC must approve the SROs' listing standards before they may take effect.[141] The listing standards therefore should not be viewed as purely private, contractual, nonfederal requirements but as part of the federal regulatory landscape.[142] In addition, beyond the SEC's authority to approve (or reject) listing standards presented to it by the SROs, the SEC engages in a process of "regulation by raised eyebrow,"[143] through which it encourages SROs to adopt as listing requirements corporate governance standards that the SEC does not have the political wherewithal – or perhaps even authority – to enact directly as SEC rules.

The 2003 amendments to the NYSE's listing standards require that companies satisfy a number of corporate governance mandates in order to be listed on that stock exchange. First, listed companies must have a board comprising a majority of independent directors, and the listing standards now define *independence* for this purpose and mandate that the board identify the independent directors and disclose the basis for that determination.[144] Second, the new standards require that listed companies' nonmanagement directors regularly meet in executive sessions without management present.[145] Third, the amendments require that each company have a nominating or corporate governance committee and a compensation committee comprised entirely of independent directors, and prescribe certain processes that those committees must follow and duties for them to perform.[146] Fourth, the listing standards

---

[141] *See* 15 U.S.C. § 78s(b) (requiring that the SROs submit proposed rule changes to the SEC for review, public comment, and SEC approval before they become effective).

[142] *Cf.* Donald E. Schwartz, *Federalism and Corporate Governance*, 45 OHIO ST. L.J. 545, 574 (1984) ("The Company Manual of both the New York and American Stock Exchanges is an important source of de facto law for affected companies in major respects.").

[143] Bus. Roundtable v. SEC, 905 F.2d 406, 410 n.5 (D.C. Cir. 1990) (quoting Schwartz, *supra* note 142, at 571). Donald Schwartz has described the SEC's influence over the SROs as follows:

> The creation of audit committees was central to the SEC objective to influence the control system. Rather than adopt a controversial requirement, the Commission exerted its influence on the New York Stock Exchange to have it adopt such a rule for companies listed on the Exchange. This may be seen as regulation by raised eyebrow. The SEC has the power to compel stock exchanges to adopt rule changes under section 19(c) of the 1934 Act. Whether the SEC had the power to require the exchanges to adopt rules regarding corporate governance is an open question, but in any event, the Commission, through a speech by its then chairman, Roderick Hills, suggested that this was a good idea for the Exchange, and the New York Stock Exchange responded by adopting such a rule. As a result, all New York Stock Exchange listed companies now have audit committees that are essentially independent.

Schwartz, *supra* note 142, at 571 (citations omitted).

[144] NYSE, LISTED COMPANY MANUAL §§ 303A.01-02 (2004), *available at* http://nysemanual.nyse.com/LCM/Sections.

[145] *Id.* § 303A.03.   [146] *Id.* §§ 303A.04-05.

now state that each listed company must have an audit committee that satisfies the requirements under the SEC's Rule 10A-3,[147] as well as specifying
a number of other requirements and processes for the audit committee and
its members.[148] Fifth, under the amendments, listed companies must give
stockholders the opportunity to vote on most equity compensation plans.[149]
Sixth, the amendments mandate that listed companies adopt and disclose
their own corporate governance guidelines that address, at minimum, a specific list of corporate governance issues.[150] Seventh, the amendments similarly
require that companies adopt and disclose a code of business conduct and
ethics.[151]

Because these listing rules constitute indirect federal regulation of internal
corporate affairs, they raise the same policy questions concerning imposing
corporate governance rules at a national level that are raised by Sarbanes-
Oxley. Without the overlay of the SEC's influence over the SROs' listing
standards, the SROs might resemble states in the sense that they constitute
separate regulating bodies that may benefit investors by engaging in regulatory
competition in order to attract companies to list on their exchange. The SEC's
role in "encouraging" the SROs to adopt corporate governance rules as listing
standards, however, undermines any such analogy between the states and the
SROs. Instead, the SROs can be seen as functioning as cogs in the federal
regulatory machine. As a result, the standards of the different SROs are likely
to converge toward a federal agenda, limiting any competition among them
for listings. In addition, any potential efficiency in adopting rule changes
is muted by the time required for public comment and SEC review and
approval. Finally, by prescribing specific corporate governance rules, the new
SRO listing standards resemble "the statutory- and rule-based prescriptive
methodology" generally employed in federal business regulation, instead of
the common-law principles and enabling statutes that define state regulation
of corporations.[152] The convergence of corporate governance listing standards
among the different SROs highlights the problems created by the prescriptive
approach. The SROs' other listing requirements and the characteristics of the
firms that list on them are quite different, suggesting that the SROs would

---

[147] *Id.* § 303A.06.   [148] *Id.* § 303A.07.
[149] *Id.* § 303A.08.   [150] *Id.* § 303A.09.
[151] *Id.* § 303A.10.
[152] Steele, *supra* note 11, at 437; *see also* William B. Chandler III & Leo E. Strine Jr., *The New Federalism of the American Corporate Governance System: Preliminary Reflections of Two Residents of One Small State*, 152 U. Pa. L. Rev. 953, 960 (2003) (noting "the overall discord between the prescriptive quality of the 2002 Reforms – particularly the proposed Exchange Rules – and the enabling approach to corporate regulation taken by the Delaware General Corporation Law").

probably be better than the SEC at crafting listing standards that would be best suited to the particular needs and interests of the corporations that list with them.

C. H.R. 4291 – Federalizing Regulation of Executive Compensation

On November 10, 2005, Barney Frank of Massachusetts introduced a bill in the House of Representatives that would expand federal regulation of executive compensation. H.R. 4291 proposes amendments to the Securities Exchange Act, purportedly for the purpose of requiring "additional disclosure to shareholders of executive compensation."[153] The language of the bill reveals, however, that its passage would expand federal involvement in executive compensation far beyond regulation of disclosure.

The bill does begin by requiring certain disclosures regarding executive compensation. It provides that issuers must include in their annual reports and in management's proxy solicitation materials "a comprehensive statement of such issuer's compensation plan" for certain senior executives. That disclosure regarding the compensation plan must include information about the following:

> (i) any type of compensation (whether present, deferred, or contingent) paid or to be paid to such [executives], including
>> (I) an estimate of the present value of any accrued pension of such officers;
>> (II) the estimated market value of any other benefits received by such officers; and
>> (III) any agreements or understandings concerning any type of compensation;
> (ii) the short- and long-term performance measures that the issuer uses for determining the compensation of such principal executive officers and whether such measures were met by such officers during the preceding year; and
> (iii) the policy of the issuer adopted pursuant to the rules promulgated under paragraph (3).[154]

Such disclosure requirements could fall within the traditional federal realm of regulation of corporate disclosures. But the bill then adds a requirement that the proxy solicitation materials that include the required disclosure regarding executive compensation "shall require a separate shareholder vote to approve

---

[153] H.R. 4291, 109th Congress (1st Sess. 2005).   [154] *Id.* § 2(a).

such compensation plan."[155] That requirement interferes with the states' traditional role in regulating the distribution of power among corporate constituents and, thus, the internal affairs doctrine.[156]

Because H.R. 4291, if enacted, would represent a direct congressional action regulating corporate governance, it would not implicate the issues concerning federal regulatory authority discussed in section I (so long as it falls within Congress's broad power under the Commerce Clause, which it most likely does). But it would implicate all the policy reasons for maintaining the appropriate division of responsibility for regulation of corporate governance between the state and federal governments that are discussed in the next section of this chapter.

It is highly unlikely that this bill will pass, at least in this form. The SEC staff is, however, working on further rule-making initiatives relating to enhanced disclosure requirements on various aspects of executive compensation.[157] Careful implementation of best practices concerning executive compensation – and corresponding adoption of compensation plans that appropriately reflect the needs and strategies of the corporations the executives lead – is the best prophylaxis against further federal intrusion into executive compensation decisions.[158] If, despite adherence to such practices, government intervention proves necessary, regulation of executive compensation is best left to the states.

V. PRESERVING THE TRADITIONAL FEDERAL-STATE BALANCE

Our analysis to this point has focused on the effects of Sarbanes-Oxley and other reforms of corporation regulation on the division of labor between the federal and state governments. It has established that Sarbanes-Oxley and related

---

[155] The bill proposes similar disclosure of and separate stockholder vote to approve "any agreements or understandings that [a person soliciting votes in connection with an acquisition, merger, consolidation, or proposed sale or other disposition of substantially all the assets of an issuer] has with [certain senior executives] of such issuer (or of the acquiring issuer) concerning any type of compensation (whether present, deferred, or contingent) that are based on or otherwise relate" to the transaction at issue. *Id.*

[156] *See* Bus. Roundtable v. SEC, 905 F.2d 406, 411 (D.C. Cir. 1990) (stating that, in enacting the Securities Exchange Act, "Congress acted on the premise that shareholder voting could work, so long as investors secured enough information and, perhaps, the benefit of other procedural protections. It did not seek to regulate the stockholders' choices").

[157] Alan L. Beller, *Remarks Before the Conference of the NASPP, The Corporate Counsel and the Corporate Executive* (Oct. 20, 2004), *available at* http://ww.sec.gov/news/speech/spch102004alb.htm.

[158] *See* William B. Chandler III, *When Boards Make (or Allow) Bad Decisions – Anatomy of a Board Liability Case*, Address at the NACD Annual Corporate Governance Conference (Oct. 25, 2005) ("[T]he entire matter of executive compensation . . . will either be regulated by you, *the fiduciaries, or by the politicians.*").

reforms do in fact represent a marked shift toward greater federal regulation of internal corporate affairs, but it has not evaluated in detail whether this shift is good, bad, or indifferent. As explained in this section, the expansion of federal regulatory authority beyond those areas directly related to the operation of the securities markets is both detrimental to investors and an inefficient allocation of responsibility among regulators.

A. *Investor Benefits of State Regulation*

The central question for any scheme of business regulation is whether it provides a net benefit to investors, the ultimate beneficiaries of any such regulatory scheme.[159] The exclusive state regulation of corporate governance yields benefits to investors that they would not receive under a federal regime. The theory behind this proposition is well established: states compete with one another to attract corporate charters (and the attendant incorporation revenues) and, in the process, produce regulations with an optimal balance between management and stockholder interests.[160] Corporate managers will seek to incorporate in states with optimal corporate regulation because their interests are aligned with those of stockholders – that is, they want to maximize the value of the firm's shares. Managers who incorporate in states with lax regulation will find that investors discount the firm's share price (thereby raising its cost of capital) to account for the increased probability of management abuses. Under this view, Delaware became the preeminent state of incorporation because it has a superior regulatory regime and provides superior ancillary services – such as a judiciary with special expertise in business law and a well-developed body of case law in the field.[161]

---

[159] Of course, a complete recitation of the long-standing and well-documented debate over the desirability of state regulation in this area is beyond the scope of this chapter. Nevertheless, this section highlights a number of points raised in the debate that are instructive in evaluating the impact of Sarbanes-Oxley.

[160] *See* Winter, *supra* note 101, at 289.

[161] Over the years, commentators have identified a number of positive factors that likely contribute to Delaware's central role in corporation law. For example, because Delaware depends on incorporation revenues rather than ordinary tax revenues from companies headquartered in Delaware, there is no need for state lawmakers to formulate laws to suit the interests of a few big statewide employers. *See* ROBERTA ROMANO, THE GENIUS OF AMERICAN CORPORATE LAW 38–39 (1993). Similarly, incorporation revenues – which make up a sizable proportion of Delaware's budget – function as a bond that would be forfeited if Delaware were not responsive to the needs of corporations and their investors. *See id.* To preserve this income stream, Delaware lawmakers have taken a number of precautions to ensure that the state's corporation law reflects the most advanced thinking in the area while remaining stable and predictable. Thus, the Delaware corporation law is subject to regular review by experts, but any changes must be approved by a two-thirds majority of both houses of the legislature.

In contrast, some scholars argue that competition among states in corporation law actually yields regulation that entrenches corporate management (at investors' expense) because state lawmakers seek to please corporate managers who control the decision where to incorporate.[162] A more nuanced version of this race-to-the-bottom theory holds that state competition results in value-enhancing regulation of corporations for some issues but favors managers over investors on other issues, such as hostile takeovers.[163] Other scholars take a different approach, arguing that states do not, in fact, engage in regulatory competition at all; instead, each state simply seeks to protect incumbent managers of its local businesses.[164] Under any of these lines of reasoning, they argue,

See id. at 41–42. Demonstrating their commitment to remain at the forefront of legal and business developments in the field, members of the Delaware judiciary and bar are also prominent participants in the academic analysis of corporate regulation.

[162] See, e.g., William L. Cary, Federalism and Corporate Law: Reflections from Delaware, supra note 4, at 668–86; see also Lucian Bebchuk et al., Does the Evidence Favor State Competition in Corporate Law?, 90 CALIF. L. REV. 1775, 1780 (2002) ("Because managers have substantial influence over where companies are incorporated, a state that wishes to maximize the number of corporations chartered in it will have to take into account the interests of managers."). As numerous scholars have noted, this argument presupposes that investors will not discount the shares of companies incorporated in management-friendly states. See, e.g., Winter, supra note 101; FRANK H. EASTERBROOK & DANIEL R. FISCHEL, THE ECONOMIC STRUCTURE OF CORPORATE LAW 213–15 (1991) ("As a matter of theory, the 'race for the bottom' cannot exist.").

[163] See, e.g., Lucian Arye Bebchuk & Allen Ferrell, Federalism and Corporate Law: The Race to Protect Managers from Takeovers, 99 COLUM. L. REV. 1168 (1999) (arguing that the state-competition theory does not explain why many states have adopted restrictive antitakeover laws that serve only to protect management at the expense of shareholders); Bebchuk et al., supra note 162, at 1779 (arguing that "state competition induces states to provide rules that managers, but not necessarily shareholders, favor with respect to corporate law issues that significantly affect managers' private benefits of control, such as rules governing takeovers").

[164] See Marcel Kahan & Ehud Kamar, The Myth of State Competition in Corporate Law, 55 STAN. L. REV. 679 (2002–2003) (arguing that states do not actually compete in corporation law because most states do not collect significant revenues from incorporation). Similarly, scholars have argued that any competition for corporate charters takes place between the corporation's home state and Delaware because those are the legal regimes with which corporate advisers are most familiar. See Bebchuk et al., supra note 162, at 1784 ("[C]ompetition is highly imperfect in that Delaware faces scant competition in the market for out-of-state incorporations; firms largely incorporate either in Delaware or in the state of their headquarters."); Robert Daines, The Incorporation Choices of IPO Firms, 77 N.Y.U. L. REV. 1559, 1562 (2002) ("Firm choices are thus oddly 'bimodal' – they operate as if there is no national market but a single choice: their home jurisdiction or Delaware. The nationwide search for attractive legal rules that Cary feared and Winter cheered does not appear." (citation omitted)). Daines suggests that one reason for the "bimodal" operation of incorporation choices is that lawyers strongly influence incorporation choice, and lawyers generally are familiar with the corporation law of their home state and Delaware, which serves as a "common law language" of corporation law. This then creates a "network effect," which further increases the prominence of Delaware law. See Daines, supra at 1580–82, 1587–88 ("For instance, as the number of firms incorporated in a state increases, the amount of litigation increases, which may clarify the law, provide valuable

Delaware dominates state corporation law not because it has produced optimal regulations but because it is most likely to protect management. Thus, it is argued that federal intervention (or the threat of intervention) represents the only viable means to restrain the management-friendly excesses of Delaware law.[165] Indeed, several scholars have suggested that the federal government itself should be viewed as the principal competitor in corporation law alongside Delaware.[166]

Not satisfied to leave the debate over the merits of state competition at the level of theory, scholars have constructed a series of event studies in an attempt to assess how investors value the state of a firm's incorporation. These studies essentially track the movements of a firm's share price immediately after it announces its intention to reincorporate in Delaware. If the share price goes up (after controlling for other factors), one can infer that investors take a positive view of the overall package of Delaware corporation law.[167]

Of the reincorporation event studies completed to date, all have found positive abnormal returns associated with a decision to reincorporate in Delaware and half have found statistically significant positive abnormal returns.[168]

training to judges, and increase the availability of cheap legal advice. In addition, the more firms that incorporate in a given state, the more likely the legislature may be to update the state's corporate code.").

[165] *See, e.g.*, Lucian Arye Bebchuk, *Federalism and the Corporation: The Desirable Limits on State Competition in Corporate Law*, 105 HARV. L. REV. 1435 (1991) (arguing that federal intervention in corporate governance is justified where necessary to prevent redistributions of wealth from stockholders to management or to address effects of regulation on third parties other than stockholders and management); William L. Cary, *Federalism and Corporate Law: Reflections upon Delaware*, 83 YALE L.J. 663, 702–03 (1974) (advocating a federal statute prescribing, among other things, fiduciary duties of officers and directors, a "fairness" standard for transactions with directors, and mandatory stockholder approval of various corporate transactions).

[166] *See, e.g.*, Mark J. Roe, *Delaware's Politics*, 118 HARV. L. REV. 2491 (2005) (arguing that the threat of federal intervention establishes limits on Delaware's ability to act); Roe, *supra* note 17 (arguing that state competition is less important in corporation law than the threat of federal intervention); Lucian Bebchuk & Allen Ferrell, *A New Approach to Takeover Law and Regulatory Competition*, 87 VA. L. REV. 101, 105 (2001) (proposing a nonmandatory federal corporate governance regime that firms can choose instead of the state options); Renee M. Jones, *Rethinking Corporate Federalism in the Era of Corporate Reform*, 29 IOWA J. CORP. L. 625 (2004) (arguing that Sarbanes-Oxley influenced the Delaware judiciary and that "vertical competition" – that is, the threat of federal intervention – is more effective than "horizontal" state competition).

[167] *See* Sanjai Bhagat & Roberta Romano, *Event Studies and the Law: Part II: Empirical Studies of Corporate Law*, 4 AM. L. & ECON. REV. 380, 381–83 (2002) (describing event-study methodology).

[168] *See id.* at 383–84 (2002) ("All [eight] of the studies find positive abnormal returns, with four finding a significant positive stock return at the time of the announcement of the domicile change. . . ."); *see also* Romano, *supra* note 161, at 18 ("[W]hile several studies have found significant positive stock price effects on firms' reincorporation to Delaware, no study has

Similar event studies indicate that investors may even evaluate specific statutory changes by state legislatures – particularly those concerning takeovers.[169]
Taking a different approach, a study by Robert Daines found that firms incorporated in Delaware were worth an average of up to 2 percent more than firms
incorporated in other states.[170]

These studies provide powerful evidence[171] that investors place a positive
value on incorporation in Delaware and that Delaware's dominant position
in corporation law is likely the result of its success in competing against other
states for corporate charters. In other words, the studies support the contention
that investors benefit from competition among states in corporation law – not
only because state competition yields better regulation than would the federal
government on its own but also because it allows states to experiment with
their regulations while being subject to market discipline.[172]

B. The Division of Responsibility

The case for leaving the regulation of internal corporate affairs to the states
does not rest solely on theories of state competition, however. To the contrary,
state regulation in this area is desirable because it is part of a sensible division of responsibility that plays to the strengths of the different regulators.[173]

---

found a negative stock price effect as Cary would predict."). Moreover, there is evidence that
the positive, abnormal returns are indeed attributable to the decision to reincorporate rather
than some other factor, such as the simultaneous disclosure of a new business plan. *See* Bhagat
& Romano, *supra* note 167, at 385 (citing study finding no statistical difference in returns based
on the reason for reincorporating). *But see id.* at 388 (discussing study finding a difference in
returns based on the reason for reincorporating).

[169] *See* Bhagat & Romano, *supra* note 167, at 389–90 (discussing event studies of changes in
Delaware law).

[170] *See* Robert Daines, *Does Delaware Law Improve Firm Value?*, 62 J. Fin. Econ. 525, 532 (2001).
The study also found that firms incorporated in Delaware were significantly more likely to
receive takeover offers and were more likely to be sold than firms incorporated in other states.
Id. at 541. *But see* Bebchuk et al., *supra* note 162, at 1785–86 (citing studies completed after
1999 finding no correlation between firm value and Delaware incorporation).

[171] *But cf.* Bebchuk et al., *supra* note 162, at 1791–97 (arguing that the event studies finding positive,
abnormal returns on reincorporation in Delaware do not provide any meaningful evidence of
beneficial state competition). *But see* Bhagat & Romano, *supra* note 167, at 384 (arguing that
the flaws identified by Bebchuk, Cohen, and Ferrell are not significant and do not affect the
implications of the event studies).

[172] *Cf.* Gonzales v. Raich, 545 U.S. 1, 41 (2005) (O'Connor, J., dissenting) (describing as "[o]ne of
federalism's chief virtues . . . the role of States as laboratories" that may "'try novel social and
economic experiments without risk to the rest of the country'" (quoting New State Ice Co. v.
Liebmann, 285 U.S. 262, 311 (1932) (Brandeis, J., dissenting))).

[173] In addition, the drawbacks that sometimes accompany state regulation are not present in
this context. Unlike the devolution of insurance regulation to the states, for example, state

While federal regulators have both the expertise and the administrative capacity to regulate nationwide securities markets, the states – and, in particular, Delaware – are better placed than the federal government to regulate the internal affairs of corporations.

As an initial matter, the federal government is not well suited to the nuanced regulation of the fiduciary duties that lie at the heart of corporation law.[174] Fiduciary duty law is by its nature fact intensive. Fiduciary relationships arise in the context of complex and constantly evolving long-term arrangements and therefore do not lend themselves easily to bright-line rules or detailed regulations.[175]

Sarbanes-Oxley, however, does not account for the complexities of the corporate environment. Rather than setting broad standards and allowing public companies some leeway in determining how best to comply with those standards, Sarbanes-Oxley "prescribe[s] the precise means by which directors and officers are to pursue certain ends."[176] Delaware fiduciary law, by contrast, promotes good governance practices while "recogniz[ing] that what generally works for most boards may not be the best method for some others."[177] Delaware's approach, which relies on the courts to define what is required of officers and directors on a case-by-case basis, ensures that firms can select the appropriate governance regime for their situation. This flexibility, so vital to maintaining a sensible, effective regulatory regime for corporate governance, is too often absent from Sarbanes-Oxley.

Failing to address the diversity of firms that are subject to a regulatory regime is not merely a theoretical problem; it has important practical consequences. By resorting to inflexible rules applicable to all public companies regardless of the circumstances, Sarbanes-Oxley indiscriminately imposes substantial compliance costs on those companies. Small firms, in particular, bear a heavy

regulation of corporate governance does not require companies to comply with multiple regulatory regimes; a corporation's internal affairs are governed only by the law of the state of its incorporation.

[174] Some scholars have argued that Delaware courts leave case law indeterminate to make it more difficult for other states to emulate. *See* Ehud Kamar, *A Regulatory Competition Theory of Indeterminacy in Corporate Law*, 98 COLUM. L. REV. 1908 (1998). Although Delaware's flexible "enabling" approach to corporate governance inevitably requires a case-by-case analysis of fiduciary duties in marginal cases, Delaware case law produces relatively clear guidance in the vast majority of cases. *See* Leo E. Strine Jr., *Delaware's Corporate-Law System: Is Corporate America Buying an Exquisite Jewel or Diamond in the Rough? A Response to Kahan & Kamar's Price Discrimination in the Market for Corporate Law*, 86 CORNELL L. REV. 1257, 1259 (2001).

[175] *See* Daines, *supra* note 164, at 1582–83 ("Fiduciary duty rules are difficult to reduce to simple statutory rules (given the nature of opportunism and the difficulty of predicting and legislating to prevent future conflicts) and are instead regulated by a body of precedent.").

[176] Chandler & Strine, *supra* note 152, at 979.   [177] *Id.*

burden under Sarbanes-Oxley. As Professor Roberta Romano has observed, recent surveys suggest that Sarbanes-Oxley more than doubled the fixed costs of being a public company and that the costs of complying with the Sarbanes-Oxley internal audit requirements among smaller public companies "are an order of magnitude greater than larger companies' [costs]."[178] More generally, the tendency of Congress to impose mandatory requirements applicable to large numbers of diverse businesses inevitably leads to unintended compliance costs and rules that may be both under- and overinclusive.

In addition, while courts in states such as Delaware, New York, and California have developed extensive case law addressing myriad fact patterns, federal regulators have no such repository of specialized institutional knowledge. Delaware, in particular, has amassed a wealth of case law and has accumulated substantial expertise in the regulation of corporate fiduciaries. It may be that the federal courts (if given sufficient time) could eventually assemble a repository of case law of comparable size, but busy federal district judges are unlikely to seek out the sort of specialized knowledge of corporate affairs that characterizes the Delaware Supreme Court and Court of Chancery.[179]

Finally, it is worth noting as a general matter that the process of federal legislation is particularly ill equipped to deal with corporate governance issues. As Roberta Romano has explained in detail, Congress typically legislates on financial issues only in times of economic crisis, which results in hastily formulated laws that are seldom revisited.[180] In contrast, Delaware's legislature and its courts have built an excellent record of responding promptly to both legal and business developments as they arise.[181] To facilitate this process, Delaware has established a process by which its corporation law is reviewed by an expert panel charged with recommending revisions where appropriate.

VI. CONCLUSION

Federalism concerns in the context of corporation law raise myriad philosophical and practical questions. There may be broad constitutional limits on the

---

[178] Romano, *supra* note 78, at 1520–21; *see also* David Wighton, *The Boardroom Burden: Calls for Reform Are Replaced by Concern That Corporate Shake-Up Has Gone Too Far,* FIN. TIMES, June 1, 2004, at 9 (reporting that International Paper spent $10 million on compliance with section 404 of Sarbanes-Oxley in 2004 and that "General Electric has spent $30[million] and 250,000 hours of employee time putting similar 404 measures in place").

[179] *See* Veasey & Di Guglielmo, *supra* note 126, at 1505.

[180] Romano, *supra* note 78, at 1592–94.

[181] *See* Roberta Romano, *The States as a Laboratory: Legal Innovation and State Competition for Corporate Charters,* 23 YALE J. ON REG. 209, 225–26 (2006) (comparing the median time for Delaware statutory amendment in response to a Delaware Supreme Court decision (two years) with the time for congressional response to a U.S. Supreme Court decision (twelve years)).

power of Congress to legislate in areas of traditional state regulation, but it is fair to assume for present purposes that Congress has preemptive powers it has not yet used in the corporate area. This chapter has questioned whether Congress has already gone too far in the Sarbanes-Oxley Act by regulating internal corporate affairs that are traditionally the domain of the states. Given the improbability of a congressional volte-face on this issue, however, it is probably a moot point. In contrast, the desirability of further federal regulation of corporations remains an open issue – and one that will come to the fore if another major scandal should produce a public outcry similar to that generated by Enron, WorldCom, and the like. There is already a heated debate whether the SEC has the power to, or should, enlarge its rule-making efforts by taking action on shareholder voting for directors.

This chapter has argued that further federalization of corporation law would be problematic both because it would be unlikely to benefit investors and because the federal government is ill equipped to handle regulatory responsibility for internal corporate affairs. Although state and private ordering initiatives to improve corporate governance are a work in progress, they are a powerful example of the benefits of leaving the regulation of internal corporate affairs to dynamic bodies with the greatest interest and expertise in the field. In short, given the complexity of the interaction between federal and state regulation of corporations, unthinking expansion of federal power is plainly not the answer. This is not the time for sloganeering or knee-jerk reactions. This is the time for careful analysis.

PART FIVE

COMPARATIVE CORPORATE GOVERNANCE

12 Regulatory Differences in Bank and Capital Market Regulation

Hideki Kanda

I. INTRODUCTION

It is well known that financial systems around the world can be roughly distinguished as either bank-based systems or capital-market-based systems. Whether and to what extent this distinction is meaningful is controversial.[1] The answer depends upon what we consider. From a regulatory perspective, two prototypical forms of regulation correspond to the counterparts of this distinction, and thus we observe regulatory differences between the bank system and the capital market system.[2]

In this chapter, I place particular emphasis on the costs of regulation and the enforcement thereof. I argue that these costs are important determinants when any given jurisdiction chooses a financial system. From this perspective, this chapter has two purposes. First, I briefly describe prototypical forms of regulation in the bank system and the capital market system. I also briefly discuss the change in the regulatory focus over time in both bank and capital market regulation. This change has resulted from environmental change in the banking and capital markets. Second, I examine the descriptive and prescriptive question of which system is, and should be, adopted in any given country once the costs of regulation and enforcement are seriously considered. The

---

[1] See, e.g., Rafael La Porta et al., *Investor Protection and Corporate Governance*, 58 J. Fin. Econ. 3 (2000) (arguing that outside investor protection rather than bank- or capital-market-based systems is important).

[2] Franklin Allen & Douglas Gale, Comparing Financial Systems (2000); Franklin Allen & Douglas Gale, *Comparing Financial Systems: A Survey* (Wharton Sch. FIC, Working Paper No. 01-15, 2001).

Hideki Kanda is Professor of Law, University of Tokyo. An early version of this chapter was written for policy makers in Asian jurisdictions and presented at the Asian Development Bank Institute/ Wharton seminar "Regulatory Differences between the Banking Sector and the Securities Market," on July 26–27, 2001. It was published in 2 U. Tokyo J.L. & Pol. 29 (2005).

cost of writing proper regulation and the cost of enforcing such regulation are sometimes overlooked, but if these costs are taken into account seriously, we can better understand (as a descriptive matter) why the bank-based system is adopted in some jurisdictions and the capital market-based system is adopted in other jurisdictions. This chapter presents a blunt hypothesis that the bank system is better where the economy is small, while the capital market system is better where the economy is large.

Section II offers a brief general discussion on the costs of regulation and enforcement. Section III explores regulatory differences between the bank system and the capital market system, and the problems associated with these systems. The long-term credit bank system is also briefly addressed as an intermediate system. Section IV asks the question of which system is and should be better. Section V presents my preliminary conclusion.

II. COSTS OF REGULATION AND ENFORCEMENT

If some form of regulation in the financial sector is justified, no regulatory system functions well unless accompanied by proper regulation and enforcement thereof. What is proper is thus the primary concern for policy makers. The starting premise should be to acknowledge the simple fact that the costs of regulation and the costs of enforcement are not zero. In other words, the value of regulation must be determined by both its benefits and its costs. Through consideration of these benefits and costs, how to design and maintain effective regulation and an enforcement system thereof is the key issue for any jurisdiction.

Imagine a world with only one simple rule: do not do bad things. This rule may be appealing; what it says is quite right, and it covers all possible situations. However, when a problem arises, who makes the decision, and based on what specific criteria? Applying this abstract rule (appropriately) to each specific situation or problem would be an extremely difficult task. Thus, in this world, the cost of enforcing the rule would be prohibitively high, and so the rule would not work at all in practice.

The reason every jurisdiction has complex rules is simple: the enforcement of rules is costly. In other words, to reduce the cost of enforcement, there must be specific rules. The problem is that if one attempts to write too many specific rules, writing such rules is costly because it is not easy to write specific rules so as to cover all possible situations or problems that may arise. In short, the optimal level of specificity in writing rules is difficult to determine, even from the enforcement perspective alone. In reality, a variety of factors other than enforcement affect rule making in any jurisdiction, and so rule making is more complex and contingent. Although one can list major factors that should be considered in rule making in the financial sector, specific regulatory rules inevitably vary from jurisdiction to jurisdiction. Each jurisdiction should adopt specific regulatory rules that fit the jurisdiction best by carefully examining the enforcement environment and other factors in that jurisdiction.

III. REGULATORY DIFFERENCES IN THE BANK SYSTEM AND THE CAPITAL MARKET SYSTEM

A. *The Bank System*

Under the bank system, a bank funds itself by taking deposits from those who have money and uses the money for lending to those who need capital. This simple bank system is very popular in most Asian jurisdictions and elsewhere still today.

Why we need regulation in this straightforward scheme is not simple. Generally, there are two realities that justify bank regulation. One is that it is impractical for dispersed depositors to monitor the bank effectively in an organized fashion because of the collective action problem. Thus, regulators monitor banks on behalf of dispersed depositors.[3] Second, banks often participate in (and sometimes operate) payment systems that inevitably accompany systemic risk, thus producing a negative externality. Failure of one payment transaction may lead to a disaster, so participants call for some form of regulation to deal with this systemic risk.[4]

There are many well-known problems with this bank system, and this chapter is not the place to explore the entire picture. I list three problems here. First, banks have incentives to continue lending until they fail. In most jurisdictions, some form of deposit insurance protects depositors in case of a possible bank failure, and to protect the payment system and the jurisdiction's economy, the central bank and/or the government usually extends help through various rescue measures if a bank, particularly a large bank, fails. Generally speaking, this typical moral hazard problem is not easy to solve.

Second, banks face not only credit risk related to borrowers but, especially today, market risk and other risks as well. Banks today tend to have financial assets, such as bonds, that are subject to market risk, and even loans are often securitized and thus produce market risk. Other risks include operational risks such as that of sudden and unexpected computer breakdown. In short, banks face many risks.

---

[3] *See* Mathias Dewatripont & Jean Tirole, The Prudential Regulation of Banks (1995).
[4] *See generally* Charles Goodhart, Financial Regulation: Why, How and Where Now? (1998).

Third, while banks bear these risks, depositors usually bear only the credit
risk of the bank with which they deal. Often deposit insurance protects depositors (up to a certain amount), which results in almost no risk for depositors.
This means that risks are not diversified or spread out among many investors
but are instead taken somewhat concentrically by the bank. This form of risk
taking leaves banks vulnerable, especially today when risks exist more widely
and are spread across country borders. Banks, as intermediaries, are centralized
risk takers.

Bank regulation is basically designed to respond to these problems. First, the
most important part of today's bank regulation ensures proper risk management
by banks. Excessive lending, sometimes coupled with a sudden downturn in
the economy (known as bursting of asset bubbles in Japan and elsewhere), has
led to bad-loan problems in many jurisdictions in Asia and elsewhere. Regulators today require banks to make proper and strict assessments of each loan
in the bank's asset portfolio. Regulators also undertake strict on-site examina-
tions of banks on a regular basis. Regulators take "prompt corrective actions"
when a bank's capital decreases below a certain level. These strong and active
interventions by regulators are understood to be necessary in the bank system
today. While enhancing the transparency of banks is considered important,
market discipline is often not practicable, even though academics often argue
that it should be.

From a policy maker's perspective, the bank system may seem relatively easy
to regulate because there is a clear focal point for the regulator to examine:
the bank. Unless banks fail, it is considered that there is no problem. However,
experience shows that maintaining perpetual bank solvency is not an easy task
and that the costs of regulation are thus very high. Banks frequently fail in
most countries. If regulation fails and banks fail, the result is often disastrous,
as experienced by Japan and other jurisdictions in the 1990s.

Historically speaking, the paradigm of bank regulation has changed over
time.[5] While the purpose of bank regulation remains the same – that is, ensuring soundness of banks – specific measures of bank regulation have changed.
Former regulation prohibited competition among banks and required banks
to maintain sound asset portfolios. Environmental changes in recent decades,
however, brought about a change in this old-fashioned regulatory strategy.
Today, competition among banks is considered desirable, and thus interest
rate regulation, branch regulation, and other forms of anticompetition regulation have been removed in most industrialized countries. The philosophy
of regulation of banks' asset portfolios has also changed. It formally prohibited certain high-risk investments per se, while today regulation focuses on

[5] *See generally* Robert C. Clark, *The Soundness of Financial Intermediaries*, 86 YALE L.J. 1 (1976).

maintaining the proper level of capital, not on particular investments in the bank's asset portfolio.

Over the past decades, technological change and deregulation have increased the risks that banks face. Banks today face not only credit risk of borrowers but market risk as well. Additionally, banks engage not only in traditional banking business activities but in new business activities as well, and banking institutions often shape financial conglomerates that engage in various kinds of financial business activities. Moreover, economies of scope and economies of scale tend to produce large banking institutions. These modern institutions are often said to be "too big to fail" and their business activities are too complex for regulators to understand and monitor properly. The asymmetry of information between banks and regulators is so great today that regulators are poorly equipped for direct intervention in bank activities. Consequently, regulatory measures have changed from direct regulation to indirect regulation. In other words, traditional regulation directly controlled risks by, for example, prohibiting risky investments. In contrast, modern regulation looks only at capital, and capital regulation also relies on internal control and accounting systems by banks themselves.

The regulatory treatment of bank failure is also understood to be important. There are several different possible causes for bank failure, including bad management, fraud, and external economic conditions. However, the failed bank's assets disappear quickly and speedy regulatory intervention is called for.

The outcomes of bank failures may differ depending upon legal, regulatory, and political environments. Deposit insurance schemes play an important role, not simply as providing insurance in the traditional sense but also as suppliers of financial assistance and as purchasers of bad assets (where permitted). The purpose of postinsolvency intervention by bank regulators (or special treatment for failed banks) is understood to avoid confusions and to protect the payment system. It is not to rescue the individual banks in question.

The above overview of bank regulation shows where the costs of bank regulation primarily lie. First, there is the cost of providing proper deposit insurance. Second, regulation tries to prevent bank failure by requiring soundness of banks. Third, bank failure results in an enormous cost, as postinsolvency treatments often carry very high costs.

B. *The Capital Market System*

1. Basic Regulation
Under the capital market system, borrowers obtain funds not through banks or similar intermediaries but directly from capital markets. Investors in the

capital market, unlike depositors, take investment risks – that is, the risk of the borrower's failure. While intermediaries exist between borrowers and investors in the form of brokers and dealers, they do not take investment risks in the same way that banks do. Consequently, the regulatory focus is different from that of the bank system.

While capital markets are both well-developed and well-functioning markets as compared to product and other markets, they operate in highly regulated environments. Highly organized securities markets on stock exchanges also operate in highly regulated environments. The reason there is more rather than less regulation in capital markets than in other markets stems from the historical aim of securities regulation: the protection of public investors against manipulative and deceptive activities by securities brokers. Thus, securities regulation in most jurisdictions emerged with, and is centered upon, the idea of retail investor protection.

In general, the capital market system is understood to be better than the bank system in the following sense: various risks, including borrowers' credit risk and market risk, are spread out and taken by dispersed investors rather than by intermediaries. This also means that borrowers can fund larger amounts of money from the capital market than from the bank. The cost of capital is therefore usually less in capital market financing than bank financing, if all other things are equal. However, there are problems with the capital market system as well, and there are costs of regulation and enforcement.

First, in the capital market system, there are numerous opportunities for fraudulent activities, including manipulation, insider trading, and so on. Intermediaries who pass investment and other risks on to investors also have incentives to defraud public investors.

Second, capital markets are relatively difficult to regulate because, unlike in the bank system, there is no single focal point on which regulators can focus. Regulators must regulate the market entirely, and due to the nature of the capital market, regulatory failure would lead to disaster.

How to regulate capital markets is not an easy question. Indeed, the benefits of capital market regulation have not been well established in empirical literature by academics.[6] However, experience in the United States, where we find the most advanced capital markets, suggests the need for three strong sets of regulation in order for capital markets to function properly: (1) strong investor protection; (2) a strong watchdog or enforcement agency, like the U.S. Securities and Exchange Commission; and (3) strong regulation of intermediary

[6] *See, e.g.*, Roberta Romano, *Empowering Investors: A Market Approach to Securities Regulation*, 107 YALE L.J. 2359 (1998).

institutions. From a policy maker's perspective, preparing and maintaining such regulations is quite costly.

First, strong investor protection is usually ensured by two well-known regulatory schemes: mandatory disclosure and antifraud regulation. Additionally, further regulation is usually called for to deal with the collective action problems faced by public bondholders in relation to debt securities. For instance, the U.S. Trust Indenture Act of 1939 provides certain safeguards to protect public bondholders.

Second, the complexity of enforcement of capital market regulation should not be underestimated. For disclosure regulation to work, proper accounting rules and proper auditing requirements must be provided. A good auditor system (or certified public accountant system) must be developed. Also, both for disclosure and antifraud rules, there must be a strong watchdog or enforcement agency, such as the SEC. Finally, private enforcement is probably important, given the complexity of capital market regulation. Defrauded investors must be given a chance to resort to legal remedies. Additionally, for such private enforcement to work, a well-functioning judicial system, with reliable courts and private lawyers, must be established.

Third, as discussed subsequently, today the capital market system does not imply a lack of intermediaries. Intermediaries such as investment funds and pension funds are popularly observed in today's capital markets throughout the world. Thus, proper regulation of these intermediaries is necessary. Usually these institutions act in the capacity of a fiduciary, and so a strong fiduciary duty, such as regulation of conflict-of-interest transactions, must be imposed on them. Again, enforcement must be effective here.

In the following, I examine only the costs of disclosure regulation and its enforcement. However, a similar analysis would also apply to antifraud regulation.

The value of disclosure has been well recognized, and the relationship between the amount of information available in the marketplace and the efficiency of the stock market has been well analyzed. Why the law must require firms to disclose certain information, however, is not entirely clear. Nevertheless, most industrialized economies today have a legal system of mandatory disclosure. In fact, civil law countries have a register system of merchants that provides specific information regarding the amount of stated capital, the names of officers and directors, and other pertinent information about business entities. In many jurisdictions, securities law provides a detailed and complex disclosure system for large public companies.

The value of disclosure depends on the value of information being disclosed. In general, information being disclosed consists of two kinds: accounting and nonaccounting information. For accounting information to be useful, it must be based on proper accounting treatment. What is proper accounting, however, is not entirely clear and is much debated today. The global trend is that the importance of market-value accounting is increasingly recognized. Today, the efforts to harmonize the accounting standards are under serious discussion.[7] Additionally, proper auditing requirements are the key for accounting information to be reliable. Needless to say, there must also be a well-functioning and reliable system of auditing professionals.

Mandatory disclosure, however, has both benefits and costs. Its value depends on other elements of corporate governance. Among various determinants of corporate governance, or how companies are run, it is well known that two are most important: the method of finance and the ownership structure. First, for the method of finance, jurisdictions can be classified as either bank-centered systems or capital-market-centered systems. Because capital markets function better when more information is available in the marketplace, disclosure is more important and more valuable in the capital-market-centered system. In other words, in any given country's policy, increased emphasis on the disclosure system means increased emphasis on the capital-market-based system.

Second, where ownership is concentrated, investors are able to collect necessary information about the firm by themselves rather than through the mandatory disclosure system. Where ownership is spread out, dispersed investors face a collective action problem and may benefit more from laws that mandate disclosure. This suggests that, where investors are more dispersed, the mandatory disclosure system is more valuable and more effective.

Other legal infrastructures are equally important for capital markets to function well and properly. One typical example is the rule regarding corporate takeovers. It is well known that corporate takeovers discipline inefficient management, but restrictive legal rules on corporate takeovers often emerge for political reasons. Where corporate takeovers become difficult due to regulatory restrictions, the value of capital markets is reduced from a corporate governance perspective.

---

[7] In 2002, the U.S. Financial Accounting Standards Board and the International Accounting Standards Board (IASB) acknowledged their commitment to the convergence of their respective accounting standards. FASB, Norwalk Agreement, *available at* http://www.fasb.org/news/memorandum.pdf (last visited Nov. 6, 2007).

Similarly, in 2007, the Accounting Standards Board of Japan and IASB indicated their commitment to convergence between Japanese GAAP and International Financial Reporting Standards. IASB, Tokyo Agreement, *available at* http://www.iasb.org/NR/rdonlyres/287C0E76-E95C-47FD-BC13-9C167757CDE7/0/PRonTokyoAgreement.pdf (last visited Nov. 6, 2007).

Disclosure mandated by law also has inevitable weaknesses. For instance, the most typical mandatory disclosure system is to require public companies to make periodic public disclosures. Disclosure is made quarterly in most jurisdictions, including the United States and Japan. The scope of information being disclosed is carefully delineated by law, and the key information being disclosed consists of accounting and financial data. Such periodic disclosure, however, has at least two flaws. First, there is a time lag between the date when disclosure documents, typically the firm's financial statements, are prepared and when they are actually disclosed. In Japan, the legal rule is that the financial statements must be prepared and become public within three months of the cutoff date. For instance, an annual report must be prepared and become public within three months after the closing of the company's fiscal year. Thus, there is generally a three-month lag. Second, there is no obligation for the company to update the information supplied in the financial statements even if material events occur after the statements are prepared and become public. There is an exception that certain important events must be disclosed in a special report (the 8-K report in the United States), but this exception is not comprehensive.

To rectify these two flaws, a supplemental scheme has been developed. Stock exchanges and other self-regulatory organizations usually require what is known as timely disclosure, by which the company is required to disclose pertinent information more often, and sometimes in more detail, than is required by law. For instance, the Tokyo Stock Exchange requires listed companies to file summary financial statements within two months after the closing of the fiscal year and to file a special report for any event that would materially affect investor decision making as soon as such event occurs.

The other problem is that any regulatory rule must be enforced, and enforcement is often costly. Disclosure and accounting rules, particularly those for hard information such as data in a firm's financial statements, can be viewed as enforceable at low cost. For example, if a publicly held company keeps supplying false numbers in its financial statements, it is most likely to be uncovered and penalized in the marketplace. Thus, contrary to insider-trading rules, for instance, rules on disclosure and accounting are often self-enforcing. This implies that it is the value of the substantive rule that matters, not so much the cost or level of enforcement. In such situations, there is reason to expect that various jurisdictions' disclosure and accounting rules will converge in a more efficient direction.

The Enron debacle in the United States reminded us of the cost of enforcing disclosure regulation. Today, maintaining a reliable system of auditors and other gatekeepers is understood to be costly, and it is the price for using well-functioning capital markets.

2. Broker-Dealer Regulation

Regulation of broker-dealers has traditionally been part of antifraud regulation, and it prohibits brokers from defrauding customers, manipulating the market, and so on. Thus, the conduct rule – an extensive list of fraudulent conduct that is prohibited of broker-dealers – is the central part of such regulation. However, the same institution may serve as broker and dealer at the same time, and when the activities as dealer go wrong, the possibility of the broker's insolvency increases. Thus, the rule requiring brokers to segregate customers' assets from their own has become another important part of such regulation. However, even if these two rules are well written, they must be effectively enforced. In other words, if a broker violates a conduct rule or segregation rule and consequently becomes insolvent, its customers usually do not receive satisfactory remedies. Various forms of a safety net have been developed for such circumstances in most countries, such as the establishment of funds to provide defrauded customers with compensation up to a certain amount. The scope covered by such investor compensation schemes varies from jurisdiction to jurisdiction. For instance, in the United States and Japan, such schemes cover only segregation matters, but in the United Kingdom, they cover all kinds of broker misconduct.

Over the decades, the nature of the risk faced by broker-dealers has also changed. It used to be market risk, but today, as a result of the increase in off-exchange transactions, typically swaps and other over-the-counter derivatives transactions, broker-dealers face credit risk as well. Thus, today regulators usually require financial soundness of broker-dealers. As in bank regulation, regulators usually look at capital. Broker-dealer regulation is similar to bank regulation in this respect.

3. Regulation of Institutions

Developments in capital markets in the past decades produced the growth of institutional investors and new investment vehicles, typically mutual funds and pension funds, that can "fend for themselves," which led to the need for adjustment on the part of the traditional regulatory structure. The initial response to this institutionalization was to allow exemptions from the disclosure requirements in primary markets. Private placement exemptions were thus recognized in most jurisdictions. The next stage was to push exemptions a step further into the secondary markets and allow these sophisticated investors and investment vehicles to trade in less-regulated or unregulated markets.

Rule 144A in the United States was an ambitious step in this direction. Here, exemptions present a policy issue: whether we can live simultaneously with two markets, one for retail investors and the other for institutional investors. No satisfactory answer has yet been presented on this issue.

Investor institutionalization and the flowering of the asset management business had an impact on the structure of both capital markets and industrial organization.[8] Although the stock markets established at stock exchanges were formally the only places for stock tradings, investor institutionalization, coupled with advanced computer technologies, brought about many changes in stock trading. Stock exchanges have faced direct competition with various (off-exchange) electronic trading systems, and the structure of stock markets has become more complex. This has raised a difficult regulatory issue of whether and how to regulate these electronic trading systems.

The ownership structure of public firms was also affected. The traditional model of the separation of ownership and control, by which shares of public firms are anonymously held by many dispersed public investors, did not reflect the real world in most jurisdictions. Instead, the shares of public firms became commonly held by a relatively small number of institutional investors and retail investors.

Consequently, dual governance problems came to public attention. First, we now observe increased discussion about when and how institutional investors exercise their shareholder rights in the firms whose shares they own and about whether increased activism by institutional stockholders is a good thing for a national economy. Second, governance within these institutions themselves became an important issue. The key question is how the management of these institutions should be accountable to their public beneficiaries, and whether some form of regulation should be installed to secure their accountability. This regulation has a primary focus on governance, centering upon applying fiduciary principles with a view to preventing conflicts of interest and protecting public beneficiaries. Additionally, the regulation of retail marketing of the units of the pool became an important issue.

The real development in this area, however, was not as straightforward as one might expect. The United States enacted federal investment company regulation as early as 1940. The regulation has worked well, but in the United States, pooled investment funds are subject to fragmented regulation. Until 1999, the Glass-Steagall Act prohibited commercial banks from sponsoring

---

[8] *See generally* Joel Seligman, The Transformation of Wall Street: A History of the Securities and Exchange Commission and Modern Corporate Finance (2003). *See also* Robert C. Clark, *The Four Stages of Capitalism*, 94 Harv. L. Rev. 561 (1981).

mutual funds, and a separate area of pooling and management by commercial banks, known as common and collective trusts, had developed. Additionally, commodity pools are regulated by a separate statute and by a separate regulator. Similar developments have occurred in relation to real estate investment trusts. In Japan, in 2000, the Investment Trusts and Companies Act opened a door to establishing a pooled investment fund that invests in a wide range of financial assets, including real property. However, commodity funds are regulated by a separate statute and by a separate regulator. In contrast, in 1986, the United Kingdom introduced a comprehensive regulatory framework in this area in its Financial Services Act, which became the Financial Services and Markets Act in 2000. A variety of pooling and management schemes are categorized as "collective investment schemes" and are subject to uniform regulation under the Financial Services and Markets Act.

It is difficult to evaluate which country's regulation is most desirable. Fragmented regulation in the United States and Japan has produced continuous disputes among participants regarding jurisdictional and related issues. It may also have hindered the development of new schemes and thereby increased costs in each national economy. Fragmented industries, however, may compete with one another under different sets of regulation, and this may be better than a world in which all industries are subject to uniform functional regulation.

4. Summary

As described above, under the capital market system, three sets of regulation are understood to be necessary for capital markets to function properly: (1) strong investor protection (disclosure, antifraud regulation, and broker-dealer regulation), (2) a strong watchdog or enforcement agency, and (3) strong regulation of institutional investors. Preparing, maintaining, and enforcing these sets of regulation are costly.

C. *The Long-Term Credit Bank System*

Japan and some other economies have developed an intermediate system between the simple bank system and the simple capital market system – the long-term credit bank system. Under this system, a long-term credit bank, on behalf of borrowers, goes to capital markets and funds there by issuing bank notes or bank debentures. The bank, in turn, uses the proceeds for long-term lending.

At first glance, this system appears to combine the advantages of the bank system and the capital market system. Investors usually do not take risks other than the risk of the long-term credit bank's failure, and regulators have a focal point for regulating. Additionally, money can be obtained from a wide investor base for the long term.

Under this system, the soundness of long-term credit banks is the key, and therefore if one long-term credit bank fails, it would lead to a greater disaster than when one ordinary bank fails under the simple bank system. This suggests that even stronger regulation is necessary for long-term credit banks than under the simple bank system. However, the long-term credit bank system may be worth trying in some jurisdictions where developing capital markets with proper regulation is time consuming and costly. Once again, the overall advantage of adopting this system depends on many factors that exist in particular jurisdictions, and one cannot say in general terms that this system is better or worse than other systems of finance.[9]

IV. WHICH SYSTEM?

While it is difficult to assess exactly the costs of regulation and enforcement in the bank system and the capital market system, it seems that capital market regulation is more costly than bank regulation. As discussed above, capital market regulation must reach a wider range of matters, and particularly for disclosure and antifraud regulation, the effectiveness of regulation very much depends on other legal infrastructure, such as the existence of effective gate-keepers, a strong enforcement agency, and a well-functioning and reliable judicial system.

Thus, although many reservations may have to be made, as a prescriptive matter, in countries whose economies are small, the bank system is probably better. The relative costs of regulation and its enforcement between the two systems may matter more in such countries. In contrast, as the size of an economy becomes larger, the benefit of the capital market system – that is, providing capital at cheaper cost – may offset or outweigh the costs of regulation and its enforcement. If so, in a country whose economy is relatively large, the capital market system is better.

Note that, in reality, there is almost no country where only one of these systems exits. In all industrialized countries, the bank system and the capital market system coexist. In those countries, banks primarily provide borrowers with liquidity, and capital markets provide them with capital. Thus, in the real

---

[9] In Japan, two of the three long-term credit banks failed in 1998. The remaining bank and the successor banks of the failed two banks chose to become ordinary banks. As a result, long-term credit banks do not exist today.

world, the costs and benefits of the two systems must be considered in aggregate rather than separately for each of the systems. This makes prescription more complex and more ambiguous.

Additionally, the globalization of financial markets may have an impact on even small economies. Borrowers in small countries may go out and fund in capital markets outside their own countries more cheaply if effective capital market regulation is in place in the economies where they fund. In other words, a country may be able to borrow regulation from outside, although I will not further address the costs associated with such borrowing in this chapter.

V. CONCLUSION

One system does not fit all economies. Each jurisdiction must make a policy decision in choosing a system that fits its situation best. Whether one financial system is better than others depends on many factors, including those not discussed in detail in this chapter, such as corporate governance. This chapter has emphasized the importance of regulation and its enforcement. Regulatory differences must be properly recognized in choosing a financial system, and the costs of regulation and enforcement are the key when any jurisdiction makes its choice. Finally, it should be noted that there are additional costs when a jurisdiction moves from one system to another. For instance, insofar as long-term debt finance is concerned, Japan has been moving from the bank system to the capital market system and abolishing the long-term credit bank system. The costs associated with this move are substantial, and for that reason, the move has been taking more time than expected.

13 European Corporate Governance after Five Years with Sarbanes-Oxley

Rainer Kulms

I. REGULATORY CHALLENGES FOR THE EUROPEANS

A. *The EU Commission's Action Plan*

The May 2003 European Union (EU) Action Plan *Modernising Company Law and Enhancing Corporate Governance in the European Union*[1] came in the wake of the Sarbanes-Oxley Act.[2] The European Commission (the Commission) acknowledged that, "[i]n many areas, the EU shares the same broad objectives and principles of the Sarbanes-Oxley Act and in some areas robust, equivalent regulatory approaches already exist in the EU." In October 2004, the European Commissioner for the Internal Market, Taxation and Customs proposed to "converge" U.S. and European thinking in order to narrow the gap between a rules-based, law-enforcement-oriented approach and a comply-or-explain policy based on general principles.[3]

Financial scandals send out different regulatory messages depending on whether they occur in an outsider economy with dispersed ownership or a

---

[1] *Modernising Company Law and Enhancing Corporate Governance in the European Union – A Plan to Move Forward*, COM (2003) 284 final (May 21, 2003).

[2] The Sarbanes-Oxley Act of 2002, Pub. L. No. 107–204, 116 Stat. 745 (2002).

[3] Frits Bolkestein, European Comm'r for the Internal Mkt., Taxation & Customs, Corporate Governance in the European Union, Speech Before The Hague (Oct. 18, 2004) ("[T]he approaches on both sides of the Atlantic are quite different. The European approach is essentially based on a principle and 'comply or explain' basis. The U.S. approach is rule-based and relies more on law enforcement. What is important on both sides of the Atlantic, we aim for the same basic goals. Wherever possible, we should aim to converge our thinking, before laws are made. If we do not do this, friction will arise; and we will be faced with downstream regulatory repair....").

Rainer Kulms is Senior Research Fellow, Max Planck Institute for Comparative and Private International Law and Lecturer at Law, University of Hamburg, Germany.

bank-centered economy with block holdings.[4] Against this background, the
Action Plan is a multipurpose response to internal and nondomestic policy challenges.[5] On an international level, it pledges to improve European
competitiveness as corporate scandals have changed the world of company
law.[6] From an intra–European Community perspective, the Action Plan tacitly acknowledges that supplying efficient and competitive rules for European
business has not always been a priority on the regulatory agenda.[7] By offering a
combination of mandatory and nonbinding policy measures the EU Commission focuses on improving corporate efficiency and shareholder and third-party
rights. Corporate governance problems are to be remedied by harmonizing disclosure, board structure, director liability, and capital requirements. Company
mobility and cross-border restructuring are to be facilitated.[8] A European Corporate Governance Forum is charged with the coordination and convergence
of national corporate governance codes.[9] The Commission's policy statement

---

[4] John C. Coffee Jr., A *Theory of Corporate Scandals: Why the U.S. and Europe Differ*, in
AFTER ENRON – IMPROVING CORPORATE LAW AND MODERNISING SECURITIES REGULATION IN
EUROPE AND THE U.S. 215 (John Armour & Joseph A. McCahery eds., 2006); *see also* Jennifer
Hill, *Corporate Scandals Across the Globe: Regulating the Role of the Director*, in REFORMING
COMPANY AND TAKEOVER LAW IN EUROPE 225 (Guido Ferrarini et al. eds., 2004) (comparing
Australian corporate scandals with their U.S. and U.K. counterparts).

[5] *Cf.* Frits Bolkenstien, European Comm'r for the Internal Mkt., Taxation, & Customs, The EU
Action Plan for Corporate Governance, Speech in Berlin, Germany (June 24, 2004).

[6] *See, e.g.*, William Bratton, *Enron and the Dark Side of Shareholder Value*, 76 TUL. L. REV. 1275,
1299–1331 (2002); Andrea Melis, *Corporate Governance Failures: To What Extent Is Parmalat a
Particularly Italian Case?*, 13 CORP. GOVERNANCE 478 (2005); *German Business – Dark Days
for Volkswagen*, ECONOMIST, July 16, 2005, at 55; Guido Ferrarini & Paolo Giudici, *Financial
Scandals and the Role of Private Enforcement: The Parmalat Case* 5 (European Corporate
Governance Inst., Law Working Paper N. 40/2005, 2005). The breakdown of the Dutch com-
pany Royal Ahold NV is atypical for corporate financial scandals in continental Europe. Royal
Ahold had dispersed shareholders, but its management structures were ill equipped for a com-
pany, double listed at the New York Stock Exchange, and acting in a globalized environment.
Moreover, there was considerable gatekeeper failure. For a comprehensive study, see Abe de
Jong et al., *Royal Ahold: A Failure of Corporate Governance* (European Corporate Governance
Inst., Finance Working Paper No. 67/2005, 2005).

[7] *Report of the High Level Group of Company Law Experts on a Modern Regulatory Framework for
Company Law in Europe* (Nov. 4, 2002), *available at* http://www.europa.eu.int/comm/internal_
market/en/company/company /modern/consult/report_en.pdf. On the work of the High Level
Expert Group, cf. Jaap Winter, *EU Company Law at the Cross-Roads*, in REFORMING COMPANY
AND TAKEOVER LAW, *supra* note 4, at 3.

[8] Winter, *supra* note 7, at 12. For a survey, cf. Klaus Hopt, *European Company Law: Where Does
the Action Plan of the Commission Lead?*, in CORPORATE GOVERNANCE IN CONTEXT 119 (Klaus
J. Hopt et al. eds., 2005).

[9] *See* Bolkestein, *supra* note 3 ("The objective of gathering a small group of very knowledgeable
people [i.e., the European Corporate Governance Forum] is to help the convergence of
national efforts, encourage best practice, and advise the Commission. It will, however, not
provide advice or expertise on legislative initiatives.").

adds a dose of realism. In light of numerous national corporate governance codes,[10] centralized regulatory action will be taken only where the growing integration of the capital markets calls for a unified approach.[11] The European Union law principles of subsidiarity and proportionality will be observed.[12] The Commission does not explain, however, whether this is a statement in favor of regulatory competition, so that centralized regulation would have to address only negative externalities arising from national lawmaking.[13] Moreover, there is potential tension between the various policy goals proclaimed by the Commission. Favoring harmonization over regulatory competition might enable the European Union to offer a countermodel toward standards set by other international players.[14] A unified policy assumes that externalities may arise under decentralization, neglecting the competitive potential of rule making by local authorities. The public consultation assessing the Commission's policies under the Action Plan indicates a preference for more enabling legislation, allowing for greater diversity among the various national legal orders.[15]

[10] *Cf.* the study commissioned by the European Commission, Weil, Gotshal & Manges LLP, *Comparative Study of Corporate Governance Codes Relevant to the European Union and Its Member State*, On Behalf of the European Commission, Internal Market Directorate General (in Consultation with the European Association of Securities Dealers and the European Corporate Governance Network) 74 (Jan. 2002), *available at* http://ec.europa.eu/internal_market/company/docs/corpgov/corp-gov-codes-rpt-part1_en.pdf.

[11] *Modernising Company Law, supra* note 1, at 11.

[12] *Modernising Company Law, supra* note 1, at 12; *cf.* Charles McCreevy, European Comm'r for Internal Mkt. & Servs., The European Corporate Governance Action Plan: Setting Priorities, Speech in Luxembourg (June 28, 2005); Gerard Hertig & Joseph A. McCahery, *An Agenda for Reform: Company and Takeover Law in Europe, in* REFORMING COMPANY AND TAKEOVER Law, *supra* note 4, at 21, 30.

[13] Rather obliquely, the Commission makes a convergence argument. *See* Charles McCreevy, European Comm'r for Internal Mkt. & Servs., Future of the Company Law Action Plan, Speech in Copenhagen (Nov. 17, 2005) ("Corporate governance practices vary among Member States because of their different economic, social and legal traditions. Nevertheless, there is a clear market-driven trend towards convergence in Europe.... [M]arket participants, including investors, have every interest in taking the view that such convergence is vital for integration of our capital markets – and even for economic growth.... [T]he Commission has recognized that... soft law instruments such as recommendations, rather than prescriptive detailed legislation, are most appropriate. In so doing, the Commission [is] conscious of the need not to overburden companies with too much regulation."). *Cf.* Amir N. Licht, *Regulatory Arbitrage for Real: International Securities Markets in a World of Interacting Securities Markets*, 38 VA. J. INT'L L. 563, 588 (1998); Roger Van den Bergh, *The Subsidiarity Principle in European Community Law: Some Insights from Law and Economics*, 1 MAASTRICHT J. EUR. & COMP. L. 337, 343 (1994); Winter, *supra* note 4, at 13.

[14] *Cf.* Jan Von Hein, *Competitive Company Law: Comparisons with the USA, in* MODERN COMPANY LAW FOR A EUROPEAN ECONOMY 25, 31 (Ulf Bernitz ed., 2006).

[15] Directorate Gen. for Internal Mkt. & Servs., *Consultation and Hearing on Future Priorities for the Action Plan on Modernising Company Law and Enhancing Corporate Governance in the European Union – Summary Report* (2006), *available at* http://ec.europa.eu/internal_

The Commission has embarked on a single market review scrutinizing the
regulatory burden of the European Company Law Directives.[16]

B. *Europe's Capital Market Systems*

The member states of the European Union have embraced two different
capital market systems, thereby defying the teachings of Berle and Means.[17]
In analyzing bank-centered and market-centered financial systems, La Porta,
Lopez-de-Silanes, and Vishny have emphasized the crucial importance of
corporate law protection for investors; they elaborate on their former analysis of legal systems and argue for strong securities laws for the benefit of
investors' rights.[18] But this does not adequately reflect the regulatory challenges the European Commission and the member states are faced with.
The European Union of 2007 includes countries that readily subscribe to
the market-centered ideal of a capital market, new member states that are
emerging from the transformation process,[19] and those that Professor Roe

market/company/docs/consultation/final_report_en.pdf. On the economics of harmonization,
see EILIS FERRAN, BUILDING AN EU SECURITIES MARKET 122 (2004) (evaluating the regulatory
process for European securities law-making); Luca Enriques & Matteo Gatti, *The Uneasy Case
for Topdown Corporate Law Harmonization in the European Union*, 27 U. PA. J. INT'L ECON. L.
939 (2006); Emanuela Carbonara & Francesco Parisi, *The Economics of Legal Harmonization*
(George Mason Univ. Law and Econ. Res. Paper Series 05–40, 2005), *available at* http://ssrn.
com/paper=870519; Luca Enriques, *EC Company Law Directives and Regulations: How Trivial
Are They?* (European Corporate Governance Inst. Law Working Paper No. 39/2005, 2005)
(citing efficiency reasons).
[16] Charles McCreevy, European Comm'r for Internal Mkt. & Servs., Hearing on Future Priorities
for the Action Plan on Company Law and Corporate Governance, Closing Remarks in Brussels
(May 3, 2006); Charles McCreevy, European Comm'r for Internal Mkt. & Servs., Company
Law and Corporate Governance Today, Speech in Berlin, Germany (June 28, 2007).
[17] ADOLF A. BERLE & GARDINER C. MEANS, THE MODERN CORPORATION AND PRIVATE PROP-
ERTY (1932); *cf.* John C. Coffee Jr., *The Rise of Dispersed Ownership: The Roles of Law and the
State in the Separation of Ownership and Control*, *in* CAPITAL MARKETS AND COMPANY LAW
664 (Klaus Hopt & Eddy Wymeersch eds., 2003).
[18] Rafael La Porta et al., *What Works in Securities Laws?* (NBER Working Paper No. W9882, July
2003), *available at* http://www.nber.org/papers/w9882; on the effects of corporate law protection
on valuation, cf. Rafael La Porta et al., *Investor Protection and Corporate Valuation*, 57 J. FIN.
1147 (2002).
[19] *Cf.* Maciej Dzierżanowski & Piotr Tamowicz, *Setting Standards of Polish Corporate Governance: A Polish Experience with Drafting Codes*, 4 EUR. BUS. ORG. L. REV. 273 (2003); Andras
Kisfaludi, *The Harmonisation of Hungarian Company Law*, 5 EUR. BUS. ORG. L. REV. 705
(2004); Katharina Pistor, *Patterns of Legal Change: Shareholder and Creditor Rights in Transition Economies* (European Bank for Reconstruction and Dev., Working Paper No. 49/2000,
2000).

would classify as "social democracies."[20] For historical reasons, these "socially democratic" countries are also bank-centered economies.[21] There is evidence that the block holdings in the stakeholder economies are disintegrating, due to the increase in cross-border acquisitions and pressure from institutional investors.[22] Moreover, in the aftermath of Basel II, the insider type of a capital market may well be unable to generate sufficient funds for venture capital companies and to respond to a changing climate in international investment behavior.[23] Thus, even in the traditional insider capital market systems bank-centered models of corporate governance and more market-oriented patterns of behavior do coexist. National legislators appear to be faced with the unenviable task of accommodating the concerns of market-oriented investors without offending openly the interests of the path-dependent constituencies.[24] From the perspective of the European Commission, this implies a double transition challenge. The new member states of the European Union are reluctant to jeopardize their emancipation from state-controlled economies toward an outsider market model. And the more seasoned member states on the

---

[20] MARK J. ROE, POLITICAL DETERMINANTS OF CORPORATE GOVERNANCE 112 (2003) (on concentrated ownership as facilitating social democracies).

[21] Coffee, *supra* note 17, at 705; *cf.* Enrico C. Perotti & Ernst-Ludwig von Thadden, *The Political Economy of Corporate Control and Labor Rents*, 114 J. POL. ECON. 145 (2006).

[22] Theodor Baums & Kenneth Scott, *Taking Shareholder Protection Seriously? Corporate Governance in the United States and Germany*, 53 AM. J. COMP. L. 31, 58 (2005); Coffee, *supra* note 17, at 676; Jeffrey Gordon, *The International Relations Wedge in the Corporate Convergence Debate*, *in* CONVERGENCE AND PERSISTENCE IN CORPORATE GOVERNANCE 161, 176 (Jeffrey Gordon & Mark Roe eds., 2004); Hertig & McCahery, *supra* note 12, at 24; Harald Baum, *Change of Governance in Historic Perspective: The German Experience* (European Corporate Governance Inst., Law Working Paper No. 39/2005, 2005).

[23] *Cf.* BANK FOR INTERNATIONAL SETTLEMENTS – BASEL COMMITTEE PUBLICATIONS NO. 107 (June 2004); BASEL II: INTERNATIONAL CONVERGENCE OF CAPITAL MEASUREMENT AND REVISED FRAMEWORK, *available at* http://www.bis.org/publ/bcbs107.htm; Roland Kirstein, *The New Basel Accord, Internal Ratings, and the Incentives of Banks*, 21 INT'L REV. L. & ECON. 393, 402 (2001).

[24] Klaus J. Hopt, *Common Principles of Corporate Governance in Europe?*, *in* CORPORATE GOVERNANCE REGIMES – CONVERGENCE AND DIVERSITY 176, 183 (Joseph McCahery et al. eds., 2002) (addressing path-dependent differences in corporate governance between the United Kingdom and Germany); *cf.* DOUGLASS C. NORTH, INSTITUTIONS, INSTITUTIONAL CHANGE AND ECONOMIC PERFORMANCE 99 (1990) (on the path-dependent character of incremental change); Ronald J. Mann & Curtis J. Milhaupt, *Path Dependence and Comparative Corporate Governance*, 74 WASH. U. L.Q. 317 (1996) (on the contribution of path dependence to corporate law scholarship); see also the analysis of Lucian Arye Bebchuk & Mark J. Roe, *A Theory of Path Dependence in Corporate Ownership and Governance*, 52 STAN. L. REV. 127 (1999) (on the persistence of path dependence in the face of globalization).

European continent have to open up their economies and legal systems to "outsiders."[25]

3. Outline
This chapter will analyze the implications of the European Commission's Action Plan in light of U.S. experiences with the Sarbanes-Oxley Act. Both U.S. federal legislators and the European Commission defend centralized rule making by arguing that corporate scandals have undermined public confidence in the capital markets. In this context, the Commission has been criticized for taking a merely reactive approach toward the Sarbanes-Oxley Act instead of protecting the strength of the diversity of national corporate law systems within the European Union.[26] This amounts to a rather broad-brush criticism that the European Commission is deliberately playing the globalization argument to impose harmonized corporate governance standards on national legal systems. A closer look suggests that a constitutional argument is involved, focusing on the advantages and externalities of decentralized rule making in the European Union.

European policy making relies on three regulatory mechanisms: deregulation as a private market solution, national regulatory devices as an instrument of home country control, and the harmonization of EU regulation.[27] In a nutshell, the current debate on corporate governance is primarily about the merits of centralized rulemaking where member state law is thought to yield unsatisfactory results.[28] It would seem, though, that, in the age of globalization, European regulatory issues go well beyond the inquiry of whether the market for corporate law is so conditioned as to allow for regulatory competition among the member states.[29] In continental Europe, corporate law

[25] Cf. John C. Coffee Jr., *The Future as History: The Prospects for Global Convergence in Corporate Governance and Its Implications*, 93 Nw. U. L. Rev. 641 (1999) (on transition processes toward dispersed ownership); Katharina Pistor, *Enhancing Corporate Governance in the New Member States – Does EU Law Help?*, in Law and Governance in an Enlarged European Union 339, 352 (George Bermann & Katharina Pistor eds., 2004) (fears that accession countries may have adopted a "comply but don't enforce strategy" with respect to certain EU regulatory action on corporate law matters).
[26] Karel Lannoo & Arman Khachaturyan, *Reform of Corporate Governance in the EU*, 5 Eur. Bus. Org. L. Rev. 37 (2004).
[27] Wolfgang Kerber, *Interjurisdictional Competition Within the European Union*, 23 Fordham Int'l. L.J. 217, 243 (2000).
[28] This includes an argument that regulatory competition is ill equipped to overcome local rent-seeking. Cf. Van den Bergh, *supra* note 13, at 346.
[29] See analyses by Tobias H. Tröger, *Choice of Jurisdiction in European Corporate Law – Perspectives of European Corporate Governance*, 6 Eur. Bus. Org. L. Rev. 3 (2005); Luca Enriques,

standards are a public good, traditionally supplied by national legislators.[30] Globalization defies conventional wisdom that deficiencies of a public good can be overcome by regulatory intervention. Rather, competitive efficiency dictates that a public good should be privatized, thereby subjecting its provision to the workings of the market mechanism.[31] For the European Commission and the member states, corporate law is a test case for the merits of regulatory action or private contracting on a market for the most efficient rules.

This article addresses corporate governance aspects of the Sarbanes-Oxley Act. But it is not intended to develop a comprehensive analysis of congressional attitudes toward capital markets. Rather, the evaluation of the Act should add insights to the regulatory debate on centralized and decentralized rule making in federal rule-making systems. The Commission's Action Plan on Corporate Governance in Europe was preceded by the detailed Financial Services Action Plan designed to create a level playing field for issuers and investors. This is a corollary to the U.S. debate on whether federal securities regulation should also include capital-market-related aspects of corporate governance. The implementation of the Commission's Action Plan will be assessed, evaluating regulatory options in light of globalization, private ordering, and the jurisprudence of the European Court of Justice (ECJ) on company mobility. The ECJ's jurisprudence is understood as a mechanism for containing negative externalities of national company laws. In assessing its regulatory strategy, the European Commission should concentrate on rule making that forces disclosure of information.

EC Company Law Directives and Regulations: How Trivial Are They? (European Corporate Governance Law Working Paper No. 39/2005, 2005) (citing efficiency reasons and arguing that regulatory competition between the member states of the European Union is severely restricted so that a race to the bottom is highly unlikely). For a more optimistic stance on regulatory competition, see John Armour, *Who Should Make Corporate Law? EC Legislation versus Regulatory Competition, in* AFTER ENRON, *supra* note 4, at 497.

[30] In this context, corporate statutes and their liability rules are prone to suffer from a tragedy of the commons situation: Regulatory protectionism motivates national officials to yield intrajurisdictional efficiency at the expense of interjurisdictional efficiency. *Cf.* Michael I. Krauss, *Product Liability and Game Theory: One More Trip to the Choice-of-Law Well,* 2002 BYU L. REV. 759, 782 (2002) (relying on the prisoner's-dilemma approach); William Powers, *Some Pitfalls of Federal Tort Law Reform Legislation,* 38 ARIZ. L. REV. 38, 909, 910 (1996).

[31] *Cf.* Gillian K. Hadfield & Eric L. Talley, *On Public versus Private Provision of Corporate Law,* 22 J.L. ECON. & ORG. 414, 417 (2006); Christoph Engel, *Wettbewerb als sozial erwünschtes Dilemma* (Preprints of the Max Planck Inst. for Res. on Collective Groups, 2006/12, 2006), *available at* http://ssrn.com/abstract=902813.

II. CORPORATE GOVERNANCE UNDER THE
SARBANES-OXLEY ACT

A. *A Level Playing Field for Domestic and Foreign Issuers*[32]

1. Basic Concepts

The Sarbanes-Oxley Act of 2002 has its friends and foes.[33] As it redesigns the role of law in corporate governance, it changes the balance between federal and state laws.[34] The mandatory provisions of the Act are intended to address what has been regarded as a major deficiency of the contractual approach to corporate governance.[35] In this, an attempt is made to restore investor confidence and to reduce the probability of a market crash.[36] The Act is critical of capital market standards developed by self-regulatory organizations. The notion of auditor peer review is denounced, and the Public Company Accounting Oversight Board (PCAOB) is established to oversee the audit of public companies subject to the federal securities laws.[37] Operating as a nonprofit organization, the PCAOB is empowered to adopt or modify auditing and related quality control standards and prohibit categories of consulting services, if necessary for investor protection. Much to the chagrin of the European Commission,

---

[32] William H. Donaldson, Chairman, SEC, U.S. Capital Markets in the Post-Sarbanes-Oxley World: Why Our Markets Should Matter to Foreign Issuers, Speech in London (Jan. 25, 2005), *available at* http://www.sec.gov/new/speech/spch012505whd.htm.

[33] For an evaluation of the Sarbanes-Oxley Act after five years of enactment, see Donald C. Langevoort, *The Social Construction of Sarbanes-Oxley*, 105 MICH. L. REV. 1817 (2007) (after a careful assessment, Langevoort makes a "best guess that SOX's impact on doing business will be a subtle 'accountability creep'" rather than a dramatic post-SOX epiphany, as part of a long-running narrative about the boundaries and norms of corporate governance in a world that both celebrates and worries about private economic power").

[34] Conversely, a one-size-fits-all approach to listing standards for director independence has the effect of federalizing state corporate laws. *See* Stephen M. Bainbridge, *A Critique of the NYSE's Director Independence Listing Standards*, 30 SEC. REG. L. J. 370 (2002).

[35] Larry E. Ribstein, *Market vs. Regulatory Responses to Corporate Fraud: A Critique of the Sarbanes-Oxley Act of 2002*, 28 J. CORP. L. 1 (2002).

[36] *Cf.* Donald Langevoort, *Managing the "Expectations Gap" in Investor Protection: The SEC and the Post-Enron Reform Agenda*, 48 VILL. L. REV. 1139 (2003); Frank Partnoy, *Why Markets Crash and What Law Can Do About It*, 61 U. PITT. L. REV. 741 (2000).

[37] JOEL SELIGMAN, THE TRANSFORMATION OF WALL STREET: A HISTORY OF THE SECURITIES AND EXCHANGE COMMISSION AND MODERN CORPORATE FINANCE 738–41 (3d ed. 2003); Neil H. Aronson, *Preventing Future Enrons: Implementing the Sarbanes-Oxley Act of 2002*, 8 STAN. J.L. BUS. & FIN. 127, 133 (2002); Joel Seligman, *No One Can Serve Two Masters: Corporate and Securities Law After Enron*, 80 WASH. U. L.Q. 449, 473–99 (2002) [hereinafter Seligman, *No One Can Serve Two Masters*]; *cf.* Joel Seligman, *Cautious Evolution or Perennial Irresolution: Stock Market Self-Regulation During the First Seventy Years of the Securities and Exchange Commission*, 59 BUS. LAW. 1347, 1370–77 (2004) (discussing private regulation of the stock market).

foreign auditors will have to register with the PCAOB if they want to do business in the United States.[38]

Under title III of the Sarbanes-Oxley Act, audit committees are entrusted with playing a vital role in guaranteeing market transparency.[39] They have to establish confidential procedures to allow whistle-blowing on accounting and auditing matters.[40] Audit committee members are to be recruited exclusively from the independent directors of the company. The audit committee nominates the accounting firm. It is the audit committee the accountants will have to report to.[41] By emphasizing the role of the audit committee, federal legislators have opted for an improved scheme of accountability in which independent directors play a decisive role in overseeing corporate executives.[42] This has caused considerable uneasiness among issuers from national corporate law systems with two-tier boards where independent directors on the managing board are unknown.[43] It is also a problem for German supervisory boards subject to the mandatory rules of the Codetermination Act.[44] The Securities and Exchange Commission has strived to accommodate the concerns of foreign issuers by striking a balance between the legislative intent of Congress and non-U.S. corporate life.[45] For practical matters, the result has been a

[38] The Sarbanes-Oxley Act of 2002 § 106, 15 U.S.C. § 7216 (2006).

[39] Seligman, *No One Can Serve Two Masters, supra* note 37, at 498; Aronson, *supra* note 37, at 137.

[40] The Sarbanes-Oxley Act of 2002 § 301, 15 U.S.C. § 78j-1 (2006). But see the critical assessment by Jonathan Macey, *Getting the Word Out About Fraud: A Theoretical Analysis of Whistleblowing and Insider Trading*, 105 MICH. L. REV. 1899 (2007) (warning that the high costs of investigating a whistle-blower's complaint may outweigh the benefit of the whistle-blower provisions of the Sarbanes-Oxley Act).

[41] The Sarbanes-Oxley Act of 2002 §§ 202, 204, 15 U.S.C. § 78j-1 (2006). Moreover, Nasdaq Corporate Governance Standards now require all related party transactions to be approved by the company's audit committee or a comparable independent body of the board. *NASD and NYSE Rulemaking: Relating to Corporate Governance*, Exchange Act Release No. 48,745, 81 SEC Docket (CCH) 1586 (Nov. 4, 2003).

[42] Seligman, *No One Can Serve Two Masters, supra* note 37, at 499.

[43] John C. Coffee Jr., *Racing Towards the Top? The Impact of Cross-Listings and Stock Market*, 102 COLUM. L. REV. 1757, 1825 (2002); Roberta S. Karmel, *The Securities and Exchange Commission Goes Abroad to Regulate Corporate Governance*, 33 STETSON L. REV. 849, 875 (2004); Larry E. Ribstein, *International Implications of Sarbanes-Oxley: Raising the Rent on US Law*, 3 J. CORP. L. STUD. 299, 306 (2003).

[44] On German codetermination rules, see Katharina Pistor, *Codetermination: A Sociopolitical Model with Governance Externalities, in* EMPLOYEES AND CORPORATE GOVERNANCE 163 (Margaret M. Blair & Mark J. Roe eds., 1999); Horst Siebert, *Corporatist versus Market Approaches to Governance, in* CORPORATE GOVERNANCE IN CONTEXT, *supra* note 8, at 281, 298.

[45] Standards Relating to Listed Company Audit Committees, Exchange Act Release No. 47,654, 79 SEC Docket (CCH) 2876 (Apr. 9, 2003); Roel C. Campos, Comm'r Sec. & Exch. Comm'n, Embracing International Business in the Post-Enron Era, Speech in Brussels (June 11, 2003), *available at* http://www.sec/gov/new/speech/spcho601103rcc.htm; Donaldson, *supra* note 32.

functional convergence toward the corporate standards introduced by U.S. legislation.[46]

To ensure truthful reporting, the Sarbanes-Oxley Act requires the chief executive officer and the chief financial officer to certify periodic reports.[47] The sanction is personal liability; executives will forfeit their bonuses if their company has to make a restatement due to misconduct amounting to material noncompliance with statutory requirements. The SEC is empowered to issue rules requiring domestic and foreign issuers to include in their annual report a statement on internal control mechanisms.[48] A comply-or-explain approach is pursued as listed companies are bound to a code of ethics.[49] The Sarbanes-Oxley Act proceeds to further lay down federal standards by barring corporate officers and directors from selling securities during a blackout period if such securities were received in connection with employment at their company. Federal rules prohibit loans to directors and officers.[50]

2. Regulatory Outlook

The Sarbanes-Oxley Act is a bipartisan piece of legislation that was drafted with great speed and less-than-astute reflection on the extent to which state corporate law rules are capable of handling financial scandals of Enron-like dimensions.[51] Even supporters of a far-reaching federal securities regime do

---

[46] Ribstein, *supra* note 43, at 318.

[47] The SEC applies this certification requirement to foreign issuers as well. *See* Certification of Disclosure in Companies' Quarterly and Annual Reports, Exchange Act Release No. 46,427, 78 SEC Docket (CCH) 875 (Aug. 28 2002); Karmel, *supra* note 43, at 861.

[48] The Sarbanes-Oxley Act of 2002 § 404, 15 U.S.C. § 7262 (2006). *See* Alan L. Bellier, Dir. of the Div. of Corporation Fin., SEC, Investors, the Stock Market, and Sarbanes-Oxley's New Section 404 Requirements, Speech in New York (Jan. 12, 2005), *available at* http://www.sec. gov/news/speech/spch011205alb.htm. Foreign issuers have been granted an extension for first-time compliance with section 404 by the SEC. Management's Report on Internal Control over Financial Reporting and Certification of Disclosure in Exchange Act Periodic Reports of Non-Accelerated Filers and Foreign Private Issuers, Exchange Act Release No. 51,293, 84 SEC Docket (CCH) 3226 (Mar. 2, 2005). For an overall cost-benefit analysis of section 404, see Joseph A. Grundfest & Steven E. Bochner, *Fixing 404*, 105 Mich. L. Rev. 1643 (2007).

[49] The code of ethics applies to foreign issuers as well. Karmel, *supra* note 43, at 869. In commenting on the code of ethics, the European Commission internal market director-general, Alexander Schaub, feared that imposing such a requirement on the CEO and senior financial officers would tend to obscure the collective responsibility of the board as envisaged by the European corporate governance schemes. Alexander Schaub, European Comm'n Internal Mkt. Dir. Gen., Commentary on S7-40-02 (Nov. 29, 2002).

[50] *Cf.* Lawrence A. Cunningham, *The Sarbanes-Oxley Yawn: Heavy Rhetoric, Light Reform (and It Might Just Work)*, 35 Conn. L. Rev. 915, 959 (2003).

[51] *Cf.* Gary M. Brown, *Changing Models in Corporate Governance – Implications of the Sarbanes-Oxley Act, in* Corporate Governance in Context, *supra* note 8, at 143; Joseph A. Grundfest, *Punctuated Equilibria in the Evolution of United States Securities Regulation*, 8 Stan. J. L.

not pretend that the mere enactment of corporate governance rules will restore investor confidence. For them, the Act will have to be supplemented by an activist SEC enforcement program,[52] greater private litigation, more spirited board members, and the workings of market forces.[53] It is precisely the power of these market forces that has led critics to believe that the regulatory thrust of this legislation is doubtful. Critics claim that corporate governance should be returned to the states whose regulatory competition will bring about the most efficient approach to governing corporate financial scandals.[54] Markets, imperfect as they are, should be allowed to respond with greater speed and precision to corporate governance failure.[55] Professor Cunningham feels that the congressional effort to shape new rules adds little to what is not already established law.[56] Management discussion and analysis disclosures under the securities acts are to be made with greater frequency, including information on long-term contractual obligations and debt.[57] It would seem, however, that these duties to disclose do not amount to a full "risk discussion and analysis."[58] The Sarbanes-Oxley Act expands the role of independent directors on the audit committee, only to rely on state law to develop corporate fiduciary duties and to accommodate the code of ethics.[59]

If, on the other hand, federal legislation improves transparency on the marketplace then it is difficult to maintain that the U.S. Congress should not

Bus. & Fin. 1 (2002); Roberta Romano, *The Sarbanes-Oxley Act and the Making of Quack Corporate Governance*, 114 Yale L.J. 1521 (2005); Seligman, *No One Can Serve Two Masters, supra* note 37, at 516.

[52] *See* Roberta S. Karmel, *Realizing the Dream of William O. Douglas – The Securities and Exchange Commission Takes Charge of Corporate Governance*, 30 Del. J. Corp. L. 79 (2005). In this context, the enforcement biases of the SEC and its staff will have to be evaluated. *Cf.* Stephen J. Choi & A.C. Pritchard, *Behavioral Economics and the SEC*, 56 Stan. L. Rev 1 (2003) (assessing the circumstances under which a regulator should rely on "a hybrid between government oversight and market-based regulators, including self-regulatory organizations").

[53] Seligman, *No One Can Serve Two Masters, supra* note 37, at 516; Bengt R. Holmström & Steven N. Kaplan, *The State of U.S.: Corporate Governance: What's Right and What's Wrong?* 27 (European Corporate Governance Inst., Finance Working Paper No. 23/2003, 2003).

[54] Romano, *supra* note 51, at 1599; *cf.* Roberta Romano, *Is Regulatory Competition a Problem or Irrelevant for Corporate Governance?* (Yale Law School Research Paper No. 307, 2005), *available at* http://ssrn.com/abstract=693484.

[55] Ribstein, *supra* note 35, at 48.   [56] Cunningham, *supra* note 50, at 986.

[57] Jeffrey N. Gordon, *Governance Failures of the Enron Board and the New Information Order of the Sarbanes-Oxley*, 35 Conn. L. Rev. 1125, 1139 (2003).

[58] Langevoort, *supra* note 36, at 1156; *cf.* Joshua Ronen, *Post-Enron Reform: Financial Statement Insurance and GAAP Re-visited*, 8 Stan. J.L. Bus. & Fin. 39, 65 (2002) (suggesting an amendment to the current conceptual framework of GAAP to allow for more precise statements on management projections).

[59] Aronson, *supra* note 37, at 138; Lyman P.Q. Johnson & Mark A. Sides, *The Sarbanes-Oxley Act and Fiduciary Duties*, 30 Wm. Mitchell L. Rev. 1149, 1209 (2004).

regulate corporate governance-related issues.[60] This is an argument against decentralized rule making, tacitly assuming that the Sarbanes-Oxley Act has brought forth efficient enforcement mechanisms.[61] In this context, congressional efforts to curb class-action litigation may be counterproductive to a vigorous enforcement of improved corporate governance standards.[62] Conversely, the holding of the U.S. Supreme Court in *Central Bank of Denver*[63] severely restricts shareholders' ability to sue auditors for aiding and abetting in a management scheme to defraud shareholders and potential investors.[64] The Sarbanes-Oxley Act is silent on gatekeeper liability.[65] But it has stirred a debate on the viability of U.S. accounting standards. It has been suggested that a more principles-based approach would enable an auditor to police with greater consistency the governance failures that have surfaced during the Enron scandal.[66] From a European perspective, the debate on a rules-based approach is of great interest, as it foreshadows transatlantic consensus building toward the mutual recognition of accounting standards. There is one aspect of the debate that deserves particular attention from European and member state lawmakers. Bebchuk and Hamdani emphasize that states tend to enforce corporate law rules through private litigation, whereas federal authorities combine public and private enforcement mechanisms.[67] If one accepts the concept of "regulation through litigation,"[68] an increase in shareholder litigation is likely,

---

[60] Langevoort, *supra* note 36, at 1152. But see the model of choice-enhancing (nonmandatory) federal intervention in takeover law and incorporation rules proposed by Lucian Arye Bebchuk & Allen Ferrell, *A New Approach to Takeover Law and Regulatory Competition*, 87 Va. L. Rev. 111 (2001); Lucian Arye Bebchuk & Assaf Hamdani, *Vigorous Race or Leisurely Walk: Reconsidering the Competition over Corporate Charters*, 112 Yale L.J. 553 (2002).

[61] *See* Lucian Arye Bebchuk & Assaf Hamdani, *Federal Corporate Law: Lessons from History*, 106 Colum. L. Rev. 1793 (2006) (arguing for a more proactive approach by federal lawmakers toward corporate law).

[62] John C. Coffee Jr., *Gatekeeper Failure and Reform: The Challenge of Fashioning Relevant Reforms*, 84 B.U. L. Rev. 301 (2004) (favoring reform without abandoning the securities class action); *see also* John C. Coffee Jr., *Reforming the Securities Class Action: An Essay on Deterrence and Its Implementation*, 106 Colum. L. Rev. 1534 (2006).

[63] Cent. Bank of Denver, N.A. v. First Interstate Bank of Denver, N.A., 511 U.S. 164 (1994); on the scope of *Central Bank*, see SEC v. Fehn, 97 F. 3d 1276 (9th Cir. 1996).

[64] The debate continues in the post-Enron era. *See* SEC v. Lucent Techs., Inc., 363 F. Supp. 2d 708, 723–25 (D.N.J. 2005) (discussing the various approaches taken by federal courts).

[65] See the criticism in Coffee, *Gatekeeper Failure*, *supra* note 62, at 347, and his evaluation of the regulatory policy options after the Sarbanes-Oxley Act, John C. Coffee Jr., Gatekeepers: The Professions and Corporate Governance (2006).

[66] See the analysis by William W. Bratton, *Rules, Principles, and the Accounting Crisis*, 5 Eur. Bus. Org. L. Rev. 7 (2004).

[67] Bebchuk & Hamdani, *supra* note 61, at 1821.

[68] *See* Regulation Through Litigation (W. Kip Viscusi ed., 2002), *available at* http://www. aei-brookings.org/publications/abstract.php?pid=253. For a European perspective, see Guido

aiming at a clarification of what a decisive accounting principle is.[69] Alternatively, clearer rules on auditor liability might counterbalance an influx of shareholder litigation.[70]

B. International Accounting Aspects

Section 108(d) of the Sarbanes-Oxley Act charges the SEC with the preparation of a study on whether the U.S. financial reporting system should adopt a principles-based accounting system. In the aftermath of Enron, the financial community had assumed that a rules-oriented approach had contributed to a culture of noncompliance, as there was no guidance to novel transactions.[71] Wall Street intermediaries associated principles-based accounting with the International Financial Reporting Standards (IFRS), hoping for more rents from listing foreign business.[72] The 2003 SEC study "Adoption by the United States Financial Reporting System of a Principles-Based Accounting System"[73] contains a carefully balanced analysis of U.S. generally accepted accounting principles (GAAP) and international accounting standards (IAS). The study notes that current U.S. GAAP is based on a conceptual framework that combines detailed rules with general principles for further guidance.[74] The SEC's study moves for an objectives-based approach that does not exclusively rely on the true and fair view method. In fact, it combines principles

---

Ferrarini & Paolo Giudici, *Financial Scandals and the Role of Private Enforcement: The Parmalat Case, in* ARMOUR & MCCAHERY, AFTER ENRON, *supra* note 4, at 158, 193.

[69] Coffee, *Gatekeeper Failure, supra* note 62, at 344.

[70] *Id.* at 350; *see also* Stephen Choi, *Market Lessons for Gatekeepers*, 92 NW. U. L. REV. 916 (1998) (advocating that the issuer and the gatekeeper contract over the share of the gatekeeper's liability with respect to the issuer's investors); Frank Partnoy, *Barbarians at the Gatekeepers? A Proposal for a Modified Strict Liability Regime*, 79 WASH. U. L.Q. 491 (2001). *But see* Reinier H. Kraakman, *The Anatomy of Third-Party Enforcement Strategy*, 2 J.L. ECON. & ORG. 53 (1986) (warning against a strict gatekeeper liability regime).

[71] Bratton, *supra* note 66, at 10.

[72] *Id.* at 7. *Contra* William J. Carney, *Jurisdictional Choice in Securities Regulation*, 41 VA. J. INT'L L. 717, 723 (2001) (maintaining that U.S. exchanges will pressure the SEC into accepting "some form of international disclosure standards as substitute for American standards"); *accord* Frederick Tung, *From Monopolists to Markets? A Political Economy of Issuer Choice in International Securities Regulation*, 2002 WIS. L. REV. 1363 (2002).

[73] SEC, OFFICE OF THE CHIEF ACCOUNTANT & OFFICE OF ECONOMIC ANALYSIS, A STUDY PURSUANT TO SECTION 108(D) OF THE SARBANES-OXLEY ACT OF 2002 ON THE ADOPTION BY THE UNITED STATES FINANCIAL REPORTING SYSTEM OF A PRINCIPLES-BASED ACCOUNTING SYSTEM (July 2003), *available at* http://www.sec.gov/news/studies/principlesbasedstand.htm.

[74] *Cf.* Scott Taub, Deputy Chief Accountant, SEC, Remarks Before the 2003 Thirty-First AICPA National Conference on Current SEC Developments (Dec. 11, 2003), *available at* http://www.sec.gov/news/speech/spch121103sat.htm.

with rules-oriented implementation guidance.[75] The study emphasizes the crucial importance of enforcement procedures that include oversight over the auditors and litigation. An objectives-based approach should not provoke an increase in litigation if auditors establish adequate documentation procedures.

Since 2003, the SEC has increasingly evaluated both the domestic and international impacts of its regulatory policy on financial reporting. In a domestic context, statements by SEC officials focus on the viability of a principles-based approach.[76] On an international level, the SEC has moved from granting exemptions to Europeans[77] to a more comprehensive approach, emphasizing aspects of converging accounting standards.[78] Adopting objectives-based rules should not conflict with IAS and should foster global accounting standardization. This is part of the SEC's policy to increase comparability for investors by facilitating global capital formation and creating greater competition among stock exchanges.[79] The SEC currently accepts foreign statements based on IAS. European issuers will have to file reconciliation with U.S. GAAP only if they have invoked an exemption from IAS, which is possible under the

[75] James L. Kroeker, Deputy Chief Accountant, SEC, Remarks Before the 2007 Conference on Principles-Based Accounting and the Challenges of Implementation, New York (Apr. 4, 2007), *available at* http://www.sec.gov/news/speech/2007/spcho40407jlk.htm.

[76] *See* Cynthia A. Glassman, Comm'r, SEC, Complexity in Financial Reporting and Disclosure Regulation, Remarks Before the 25th Annual USC Leventhal School of Accounting SEC and Financial Reporting Institute Conference, Pasadena, Calif. (June 8, 2006), *available at* http://www.sec.gov/news/speech/2006/spech/060806cag.htm; Kroeker, *supra* note 75; John M. White, Dir. of Div. of Corporation Fin., SEC, Principles Matter, Speech at Practicing Law Institute Conference, New York (Sept. 6, 2006), *available at* http://ftp.sec.gov/news/speech/2006/spcho9090909jww.htm. This includes specific regulatory relief and simplification for smaller companies.

[77] *Cf.* Kristina Sadlak, *The European Commission's Action Plan to Modernize European Company Law: How Far Should the SEC Go in Exempting European Issuers from Complying with the Sarbanes-Oxley Act?*, 3 BYU INT'L L. & MGMT. REV. 1 (2006).

[78] *See* Conrad Hewitt, Chief Accountant, SEC, Remarks at IASC Foundation: IFRS Conference, Zurich, Switzerland (May 23, 2007), *available at* http://www.sec.gov/news/speech/2007/spcho52307cwh-2.htm.

[79] *See* Roel C. Campos, Comm'r, SEC, The Global Market Place and a Regulatory Overview, Speech in Amsterdam, Netherlands (Sept. 17, 2004), *available at* http://www.sec.gov/news/spcho91704rcc.htm; Robert K. Herdman, Chief Accountant, SEC, Moving Toward the Globalization of Accounting Standards, Speech in Cologne, Germany (Apr. 18, 2002), *available at* http://www.sec.gov./news/speech/spch554.htm; Susan Koski-Grafer, Senior Assoc. Chief Accountant, SEC, Understanding the Financial Infrastructure for Globalization, Speech in Tampa, Fla. (Feb. 4, 2005), *available at* http://www.sec.gov./news/speech/spcho20202skg.htm; Donald T. Nicolaisen, Chief Accountant, SEC, A Securities Regulator Looks at Convergence, Statement (Apr. 2005), *available at* http://www.sec.gov/news/speech/spcho40605dtn.htm.

relevant European Union regulation.[80] At the time of this writing, the SEC was soliciting public comment on eliminating the reconciliation requirement if foreign private issuers file an English-language version of their financial statement that complies with IFRS.[81]

Although the SEC recognition of IFRS-based statements would considerably reduce the cost of entering the U.S. market (for companies with multiple listings),[82] marked policy differences between the U.S. and the European Union persist. The SEC staff has expressed confidence in an independent accounting-standards setter with simple majority voting.[83] A green paper by the European Commission criticizes the activities of the IASB and states that they should be subject to greater scrutiny to also reflect the interests of stakeholders.[84] This appears to suggest that the Commission would wish to

---

[80] First-Time Application of International Financial Reporting Standards, Exchange Act Release No. 51,535, 85 SEC Docket (CCH) 406 (Apr. 12, 2005).

[81] Press Releases 2007–105, SEC Announces Roundtable Discussion Regarding Mutual Recognition (May 24, 2007), *available at* http://www.sec.gov/news/press/2007/2007–105.htm; Press Release 2007–128, SEC Soliciting Public Comment on Eliminating Reconciliation Requirement for IFRS Financial Statements (July 3, 2007), *available at* http://www.sec. gov/news/press/2007/2007–105.htm. The European Commission and the SEC have been promoting convergence between GAAP and IFRS to eliminate the reconciliation requirement. *See* Annette L. Nazareth, Comm'r, SEC, Remarks Before the Institute for International Bankers Annual Conference, Washington, D.C. (Mar. 13, 2006), *available at* http://www.sec. gov/news/speechspch031306aln_iib.htm.

[82] *Cf.* Craig Andrew Doidge, *U.S. Cross-Listings and the Private Benefits of Control*, 72 J. FIN. ECON. 519, 524 (2004); DEUTSCHES AKTIENINSTITUT, DUAL LISTING – EINE ÖKONOMISCHE ANALYSE DER AUSLANDSNOTIERUNGEN DEUTSCHER UNTERNEHMEN (2005); DEUTSCHES AKTIENINSTITUT, DELISTING UND DEREGISTRIERUNG DEUTSCHER EMITTENTEN IN DEN USA – STATUS QUO, ÄNDERUNGSVORSCHLÄGE UND ERGEBNISSE EINER BEFRAGUNG US-NOTIERTER UNTERNEHMEN (2004) (studies analyzing dual listing decisions of German companies and delisting decisions of German companies listed in the United States, based on questionnaires); *see also* Roel C. Campos, Comm'r., SEC, Regulatory Role of Exchanges and International Implications of Demutalization, Speech in Armonk, N.Y. (Mar. 10, 2006), *available at* http://www.sec.gov./news//speech/spch031006rcc.htm. For a critical assessment of the costs of the Sarbanes-Oxley Act for cross-listed firms, see Kate Litvak, *Sarbanes-Oxley and the Cross-Listing Premium*, 105 MICH. L. REV. 1857 (2007).

[83] Donald T. Nicholaisen, Chief Accountant, SEC, Remarks Before the Public Hearing on the IASC Constitution Review, Baruch College, N.Y. (June 3, 2004), *available at* http://www.sec. gov/news/speech/spch060304dtn.htm.

[84] *Commission Green Paper on Financial Services Policy (2005–2010)* (May 2005), *available at* http://ec.europa.eu/internal_market/finances/docs/actionplan/index/green_en.pdf ("The debate about the future governance, funding and political accountability of global standard-setting bodies, such as the International Accounting Standards Board, are of growing political importance. The Commission considers that public oversight of these structures must be strengthened, to ensure appropriate reflection of stakeholders, satisfactory transparency, due process and sustainable financing."). *See also* Charles McCreevy, European Comm'r for Internal Mkt. & Servs., Governance and Accountability in Financial Services, Speech in Brussels, Belgium (Feb. 1, 2005); Matthias Schmidt, *On the Legitimacy of Accounting Standard Setting*

include stakeholders in a centralized regulatory policy.[85] It also underlines the need for a coherent regulatory policy approach towards nongovernmental standards setting and private lawmaking in corporate governance.

III. EUROPEAN CORPORATE GOVERNANCE IN THE AGE OF SARBANES-OXLEY

A. *Transatlantic Messages and Regulatory Choices*

In scrutinizing the costs and benefits of the Sarbanes-Oxley Act, commentators proceed on a common assumption: a strong, liquid securities market is predicated on an informational model of transparency that enables investors to make an informed judgment on a buy-or-sell decision. Ideally, the close interface between securities regulation and corporate governance will reduce agency and information costs, thereby shielding shareholders and the capital market from executive wrongdoing.

Historically, it has been the mission of the Commission to implement the right of establishment as embodied in article 44 (2)(g) (ex article 54) of the EC Treaty. In acting on the advice of the High Level Expert Group on Company Law,[86] the Commission favors a combination of policies. The Action Plan calls for regulatory action on investor-oriented information and company-mobility related issues to achieve deep securities markets. Such a unified approach would support the hypothesis that securities regulation follows major crises in capital markets.[87] But there is very little agreement within the European Union that an efficiency-minded Commission should embark on imposing corporate governance standards on member states. Post-Enron, member states have taken action to address corporate governance problems,[88] thereby begging

---

by *Privately Organised Institutions in Germany and Europe*, 54 SCHMALENBACH BUS. REV. 171 (2002).

[85] Cf. the legislative policy statement in the consultation document prepared by the European Commission Directorate-General for Internal Market and Services, *Consultation on Future Priorities for the Action Plan on Modernising Company Law and Enhancing Corporate Governance in the European Union* (2005), *available at* http://europa.eu.int/comm/internal_market/en/company/news/index/htm ("[T]he application of better regulation strategy and principles in the field of company law and corporate governance will involve . . . the organization of systematic consultation on all future initiatives. . . . ").

[86] *See supra* note 7.

[87] Stuart Banner, *What Causes New Securities Regulation? 300 Years of Evidence*, 75 WASH. U. L.Q. 849 (1997); Coffee, *supra* note 17, at 669.

[88] On post-Enron corporate governance reform initiatives in the member states of the European Union, see Luca Enriques, *Bad Apples, Bad Oranges: A Comment from Old Europe on Post-Enron Corporate Governance Reforms*, 38 WAKE FOREST L. REV. 911 (2003).

the question of whether regulatory competition will result in better investor protection laws.[89] This is not just an issue of member states defending their own turf. In implementing the short-term measures of its Action Plan, the European Commission has assumed that centralized action is superior to member states' policies on corporate governance and securities regulation.[90] The recent policy announcements on simplifying community legislation in the area of company law and reducing the regulatory burden suggest that the Commission has begun to recognize the changing regulatory sentiment, thereby relinquishing the traditional rhetoric of harmonizing national laws to overcome internal trade barriers.[91]

B. European Securities Regulation

The first attempt to develop a regime of European securities regulation dates back to 1977, when the Commission issued a recommendation for a code of conduct for securities transactions. Two years later, harmonization policies introduced the Listing Particulars Directive, which was followed by further issuer-disclosure measures.[92] The European Commission sought to foster a single capital market by focusing on mutual recognition of national securities laws without establishing meaningful common disclosure standards.[93] The home member state was to control the EU-wide activities of its issuer, but European minimum standards had little effect. The member states largely retained

[89] *Cf.* Stephen Choi, *Law, Finance, and Path Dependence: Developing Strong Securities Markets*, 80 TEX. L. REV. 1657 (2002); Wolfgang Kerber, *Interjurisdictional Competition Within the European Union*, 23 FORDHAM INT'L L. J. 217, 230 (2000); Roger Van den Bergh, *Economic Criteria for Applying the Subsidiarity Principle in the European Community: The Case of Competition Policy*, 16 INT'L REV. L. & ECON. 363, 366 (1996); Van den Bergh, *supra* note 13, at 343.

[90] *See* the criticism by Frank H. Easterbrook, *Federalism and European Business Law*, 14 INT'L REV. L. & ECON. 125 (1994) (discussing regulatory choices in the European Community). For a *tour d'horizon* through the European Union's choices, see Eddy Wymeersch, *About Techniques of Regulating Companies in the European Union*, in REFORMING COMPANY AND TAKEOVER LAW, *supra* note 4, at 145.

[91] Heike Schweitzer & Christoph Kumpan, *Changes of Governance in Europe, Japan, and the US, Discussion Report*, in CORPORATE GOVERNANCE IN CONTEXT, *supra* note 8, at 695; *Commission Communication on a Simplified Business Environment for Companies in the Areas of Company Law, Accounting and Auditing* (July 10, 2007), available at http://ec.europa.eu/internal_market/company/docs/simplification/com2007-394-en.pdf; McCreevy, *supra* note 13 (recommending a "light touch" approach in corporate governance matters).

[92] Niamh Moloney, *New Frontiers in EC Capital Markets Law: From Market Construction to Market Regulation*, 40 COMMON MKT. L. REV. 809, 810 (2003).

[93] Emilios Avgouleas, *The Harmonisation of Rules of Conduct in EU Financial Markets: Economic Analysis of Subsidiarity and Investor Protection*, 6 EUR. L.J. 72, 77 (2000); *see generally* Niamh Moloney, EC SECURITIES REGULATION 69 (2002); Moloney, *supra* note 92, at 810.

regulatory supremacy in securities regulation matters. Compared to other financial centers, the European capital market suffered from fragmentation.[94] In developing liquid markets, continental Europe lagged behind the United Kingdom. Member states with less exposure to international capital markets tended to ignore the global implications of domestic securities regulation.[95] The classic divide between bank-centered and market-centered corporate governance mechanisms had left its mark on company-related information as continental Europe paid very little attention to the interface between the securities regulation and corporate governance standards.[96] Thus, it was feared that continued market fragmentation with an embryonic European securities regulation would severely curtail the benefits of the single European currency.

In 1999, the Commission published the Financial Services Action Plan (FSAP)[97] in support of deep securities markets with adequate investor protection. The FSAP proposes a coherent approach to integrated securities wholesale markets by taking regulatory action on the mutual recognition of prospectuses, unlisted start-up companies, disclosure, and corporate governance. It is the express wish of the European Commission to eliminate investment restrictions in order to create a "level playing field for similar financial products."[98] The 2001 report of the Committee of Wise Men on the Regulation of European Securities Markets under the chairmanship of Alexandre Lamfalussy (Lamfalussy Report)[99] pushes for an efficient regulatory system and common rules of interpretation.[100] The Lamfalussy Report suggests midterm regulatory action on a single prospectus for issuers, the modernization of listing requirements, home-country control of primary markets and the definition of an investor, the adoption of the international accounting standards, and the single passport for recognized stock markets.[101] The Lamfalussy Report is also aware of the cumbersome decision-making procedures at Brussels and makes a plea for a fast-track mechanism for adopting European securities legislation.[102]

---

[94] SELECT COMMITTEE ON EUROPEAN UNION, REPORT, 2003, H.L. 45–14.
[95] SELECT COMMITTEE ON EUROPEAN UNION, REPORT, 2003, H.L. 45–105.
[96] *Cf.* Werner F. Ebke, *The Impact of Transparency Regulation on Company Law,* in CAPITAL MARKETS AND COMPANY LAW, *supra* note 17, at 178.
[97] COMMUNICATION OF THE EUROPEAN COMMISSION, FINANCIAL SERVICES: BUILDING A FRAMEWORK FOR ACTION no. 17 (1999); *cf.* FERRAN, *supra* note 15, at 43 (on the regulatory thrust of the FSAP).
[98] BUILDING A FRAMEWORK FOR ACTION, *supra* note 97, at no. 18.
[99] FINAL REPORT OF THE COMMITTEE OF WISE MEN ON THE REGULATION OF EUROPEAN SECURITIES MARKETS (Feb. 15, 2001), *available at* http://ec.europa.eu/internal_market/securities/docs/lamfalussy/wisemen/final-report-wise-men_en.pdf.
[100] *Id.* at 10.   [101] *Id.* at 13.
[102] *Id.* at 22; FERRAN, *supra* note 15, at 75; Gerard Hertig & Ruben Lee, *Four Predictions About the Future of EU Securities Regulation,* 3 J. CORP. L. STUD. 359, 370 (2003) (warning that the

The member states have reacted to the signals from the marketplace and the need for greater investor protection. There is a trend in the member states to establish integrated financial market regulators.[103] Corporate governance codes are operative.[104] Due to these national developments, member states implement and enforce European Union securities legislation with varying enthusiasm. From a constitutional point of view, it is asked whether there are alternatives superior to centralized European legislation and whether the envisaged regulatory action is mindful of the policy implications for global financial markets.[105] Nonetheless, the Lamfalussy Report has unleashed (centralized European) regulatory activity to such an extent that, in 2004, the European commissioner for internal market and services diagnosed certain "regulatory fatigue" among the members of the financial services industry.[106] Even the most faithful implementation of the Lamfalussy Report is unlikely to lead to a single European market in finance. The absence of common rules on clearance and settlement and of minimum standards for taxation is a barrier to a truly single European market.[107] The green paper on financial services policy identifies corporate governance principles, company law reform, accounting, and statutory auditing as policy areas complementary to securities regulation.[108] In the following, a brief survey is given introducing European Union capital market directives with implications for corporate governance. Takeover law is not addressed, as the relevant directive has not brought about a substantial harmonization of member states' laws.[109]

---

envisaged fast-track procedure will fail in the day-to-day politics of the European Union and that a European SEC (ESEC) with soft enforcement powers will be established).

[103] Andreas Grünbichler & Patrick Darlap, *Integration of EU Financial Markets Supervision: Harmonisation or Unification, Austrian Financial Market Authority*, 12 J. Fin. Reg. & Compliance 36 (2004). Professor Grünbichler is the executive director of the Austrian Financial Markets Authority.

[104] *Cf. Weil, Gotshal & Manges LLP, supra* note 10.

[105] United Kingdom, Joint Report by HM Treasury, the Bank of England, and the Financial Services Authority, *After the EU Financial Services Action Plan: A New Strategic Approach* 3 (May 2004). This also includes a consistent regulatory approach when adopting new directives. *See* European Central Bank, Governing Council, *Review of the Application of the Lamfalussy Framework to EU Securities Markets Legislation* (Working Paper, Feb. 17, 2005), *available at* http://www.ecb.int/pub/pdf/other/lamfalussy-reviewen.pdf.

[106] Charles McCreevy, European Comm'r for Internal Mkt. & Servs., Assessment of the Integration of the Single Market for Financial Services by the Commission, Speech in Paris, France (Dec. 6, 2004), *available at* http://europa.eu/rpaid/presRelesasesAction.do?reference=SPEECH/04/515&language=EN&guiLanguage=en.

[107] Select Committee on European Union, Report, 2003, H.L. 45–19.

[108] *Green Paper, supra* note 84.

[109] This is largely because of the opt-out provisions under the Directive, which make a common regime on antitakeover defenses highly unlikely; see article 12 of the Council Directive (EC) No. 2004/25 on Takeover Bids, O.J. (L 142) 12 of Apr. 30, 2004. Commission Report on the

1. Initial Public Offerings – The Prospectus Directive

The European Union Prospectus Directive seeks to provide for a prospectus that can be used as a "single" passport throughout Europe after having been cleared by one competent member state authority.[110] It is the express hope of the drafters of the Directive that this passport will create a large, liquid, and integrated capital market, thus enabling firms to raise capital on a community wide basis. The requirements under the Directive are to be understood as minimum standards that do not prevent member states or any other competent authority (including an exchange) from imposing other requirements, notably regarding corporate governance. The Directive distinguishes between debt securities offered pursuant to an offering program and all other offerings that are classified as equity securities. The prospectus shall contain information concerning the issuer and the securities to be offered. A summary is to be given in nontechnical language, which shall convey the essential characteristics and risks associated with the issuer, any guarantor, and of the rights attaching to the securities. There is no duty to update information regularly. The prospectus is valid for twelve months, and issuers are under a duty to provide new information after such a period has lapsed. The Directive is less clear on the responsibility of executive directors making false statements in the prospectus than U.S. securities regulations. Various degrees of liability may develop, as article 6 of the Directive contains only a very broad statement on civil liability rules.[111] Responsibility may attach either to the issuer as a whole

---

Implementation of the Directive on Takeover Bids, Staff Working Document (Feb. 21, 2007), *available at* http://ec.europa.eu/internal_market/company/docs/takeoverbids/2007-02-report_en.pdf (the many options and exemptions afforded under the Directive may actually create new barriers among the member states); *cf.* Matteo Gatti, *Optionality Arrangements and Reciprocity in the European Takeover Directive*, 5 EUR. BUS. ORG. L. REV. 553 (2005).

[110] European Parliament and Council Directive (EC) No. 2003/71 on the Prospectus to be Published When Securities Are to Be Offered to the Public or Admitted to Trading and amending Directive (EC) 2001/34, O.J. (L 345) 64 of Dec. 31, 2003); for a detailed analysis, see FERRAN, *supra* note 15.

[111] Article 6 on Responsibility attaching to the prospectus:

> 1. Member States shall ensure that responsibility for the information given in a prospectus attaches at least to the issuer or its administrative, management or supervisory bodies, the offeror, the person asking for the admission to trading on a regulated market or the guarantor, as the case may be. The persons responsible shall be clearly identified in the prospectus by their names and functions or, in the case of legal persons, their names and registered offices, as well as declarations by them that, to the best of their knowledge, the information contained in the prospectus is in accordance with the facts and that the prospectus makes no omission likely to affect its import.
>
> 2. Member States shall ensure that their laws, regulation and administrative provisions on civil liability apply to those persons responsible for the information given in a prospectus. However, Member States shall ensure that no civil liability shall attach to any person solely

or to its administrative, management, or supervisory bodies; the offeror; the trader seeking admission to a regulated market; or the guarantor. Civil liability for a false summary of information shall only lie if it contributes to a statement falsifying the entire prospectus.

2. Disclosure – Transparency on Secondary Markets

Investor protection and the efficiency of the primary markets are to be supplemented by the European Union directive on the harmonization of transparency requirements about issuers whose securities have already been admitted to trading on a secondary market.[112] The member state of the issuer's choice shall determine the legal regime on disclosure for the issue of nonequity securities. Otherwise, the issuer's member state of incorporation shall be controlling.[113] Market transparency dictates that security issuers provide for a regular flow of information by annual reports, a condensed half-yearly report, and interim management statements regarding material events that may affect the financial situation of the issuer and its subsidiaries.[114] The annual and interim reports shall be drawn up in accordance with IAS in order to provide a true and fair view of the issuer's assets, liabilities, financial position, and profit or loss.[115] Shareholders acquiring or disposing of major holdings shall notify the issuer, who, in turn, has to make public without delay any change in the rights of holders of such shares.[116] In view of Europe's marked difference between bank-oriented and market-based corporate governance systems, disclosure with secondary market relevance adds a twist to the debate on ownership and control. Transparency is intended to operate as a tool for controlling issuers from an insider's and outsider's perspective.[117] With respect

on the basis of the summary, including any translation thereof, unless it is misleading, inaccurate or inconsistent when read together with the other parts of the prospectus.

However, Member States shall ensure that no civil liability shall attach to any person solely on the basis of the summary, including any translation thereof, unless it is misleading, inaccurate or inconsistent when read together with the other parts of the prospectus.

[112] European Parliament and Council Directive (EC) 2004/109 on the Harmonization of Transparency Requirements in Relation to Information About Issuers Whose Securities Are Admitted to Trading on a Regulated Market and Amending Directive (EC) 2002/34 O.J. (L 390) 38 of Dec. 31, 2004; on the member states' attitude toward the Transparency Directive, see FERRAN, *supra* note 15.

[113] Art. 2(1)(i) of the Directive. For issuers from third countries, the legal regime of the primary market is controlling. Such issuers shall file their annual reports in the member state where registered for their initial offering under the Prospectus Directive.

[114] *Cf.* Preamble 2 of the Directive and arts. 4, 5, 6.

[115] Preamble 9 of the Directive and art. 4.   [116] Arts. 9, 16 of the Directive.

[117] *Cf.* Ebke, *supra* note 96, at 173; Klaus J. Hopt, *Modern Company and Capital Market Problems: Improving European Corporate Governance After Enron*, 3 J. CORP. L. STUD. 221, 241 (2003);

to responsibility and liability, the Directive confers discretion on the member states, which may decide against a system of personal sanctions.[118]

3. International Accounting Standards for Listed Companies

Companies listed within the European Union have applied international accounting standards since January 1, 2005.[119] As IAS ushers in a more investor-oriented account on the state of the company, the board of directors is subject to greater scrutiny by capital markets. This introduces an informational model to Europe that is to facilitate investor decision making, thus putting less emphasis on risk-containment strategies for creditors.[120]

Technically, many European companies, unlisted as they are, may defy a call for more market information, preferably adhering to their traditional accounting standards.[121] But it is unclear to what extent nonlisted companies will have to succumb to market pressures to use IAS as well, thereby assuring a greater degree of comparability.[122] A recent draft by the International Accounting Standards Board (IASB) argues for specific accounting standards for

Jens Wüstemann, *Disclosure Regimes and Corporate Governance*, 159 J. INSTITUTIONAL & THEORETICAL ECON. 717, 719 (2003) (comparing disclosure in outsider and insider-control systems).

[118] Article 7 of the Directive on Responsibility and Liability stipulates:

> Member States shall ensure that responsibility for the information to be drawn up and made public in accordance with Articles 4, 5, 6 and 16 lies at least with the issuer or its administrative, management or supervisory bodies and shall ensure that their laws, regulations and administrative provisions on liability apply to the issuers, the bodies referred to in this Article or the persons responsible within the issuers.

[119] See article 2 of the Regulation (EC) No. 1606/2002 of the European Parliament and of the Council on the Application of International Accounting Standards, O. J. (L 243) 1 of Sept. 11, 2002 ("'[I]nternational accounting standards' shall mean International Accounting Standards (IAS), International Financial Reporting Standards (IFRS) and related interpretations ... issued or adopted by the International Accounting Standards Board"). To attain the status of European Community Law, standards promulgated by the IASB have to be adopted by the Commission, see arts. 3, 6 (2) of Regulation (EC) 1606/2002.

[120] For the European Commission, the regulation is instrumental in bringing common accounting standards to an integrated European capital market and preparing corporate Europe for the challenges of globalization. Charles McCreevy, European Comm'r for Internal Mkt. & Servs., IFRS – No Pain, No Gain?, Speech at the Official Opening of the FEE's (Fédération des Experts Comptables Européens) new offices, Brussels, Belgium (Oct. 18, 2005), *available at* http://europa.eu.int/rapid/pressReleasesAction.do?reference=SPEECH/05/621&forma.

[121] Karel Van Hulle, *Financial Disclosure and Accounting, in* CAPITAL MARKETS AND COMPANY LAW, *supra* note 17, at 171; *cf.* Ian Dewing & Peter Russell, *Accounting, Auditing and Corporate Governance of European Listed Countries: EU Policy Developments Before and After Enron*, 42 J. COMMON MKT. STUD. 289 (2004) (on the difficulties in moving towards international accounting standards).

[122] See Britta Carstensen & Peter Leibfried, *Auswirkungen von IAS/IFRS auf mittelständische GmbH und GmbH & Co. KG*, 2004 GMBH-RUNDSCHAU 864 (2004) (analyzing the costs and benefit for nonlisted midsize companies voluntarily undertaking to observe IAS); Jonathan

"small and medium-sized entities," as users' needs and cost-benefit considerations are different from those of large listed corporations.[123] In making its plea, the IASB recognizes that small- and medium-sized entities have to address capital market concerns, as when they publish their financial statements for the benefit of external users. Such external users may include, *inter alia*, banks, credit-rating agencies, prospective business partners, and nonmanaging shareholders.[124]

Traditional European company law for public limited companies (i.e., listed companies) is still based on the concept of a statutory minimum capital as a device for shareholder and creditor protection.[125] When the European Commission prepared the Regulation on the International Accounting Standards, it found no major conflict with the Community rules on accounting.[126] There is, however, a potential for open conflict between investor information as envisaged by IAS and creditor protection by capital maintenance rules.[127] Without attacking openly the minimum capital rules of the Second Company Law Directive, the ECJ has questioned the signaling effect of national rules on legal capital for creditor protection purposes.[128] The High Level Expert Group supports a differentiated approach toward legal capital, which is to be supplemented by corresponding liability rules.[129] Although member states are softening their stance on minimum capital for private companies, their position on public listed companies is less flexible. The Directive (EC) 2006/68 pledges to simplify the mandatory rules on capital formation, maintenance,

Rickford, ed., *Reforming Capital – Report of the Interdisciplinary Group on Capital Maintenance*, 15 EUR. BUS. L. REV. 919 (2004) (evaluating the convergence effects after introducing IAS in the European Union).

[123] International Accounting Standards Board, *Basis for Conclusions on Exposure Draft: IFRS for Small and Medium-Sized Entities* (Feb. 2007).

[124] *Id.*; cf. the empirical study in BUNDESVERBAND DER DEUTSCHEN INDUSTRIE (CONFEDERATION OF GERMAN INDUSTRY & ERNST & YOUNG, RECHNUNGSLEGUNG IM UMBRUCH 40 (2005) (evaluating the largely positive attitude of German nonlisted midsize companies toward such accounting standards).

[125] Wolfgang Schön, *The Future of Legal Capital*, 5 EUR. BUS. ORG. L. REV. 429, 438 (2004).

[126] Van Hulle, *supra* note 121, at 159.

[127] Wolfgang Schön, *Wer schützt den Kapitalschutz?*, 166 ZEITSCHRIFT FÜR DAS GESAMTE HANDELSRECHT 1 (2002).

[128] This is, however, a criticism that was made in the context of private, nonlisted companies. *See* Kamer van Koophandel en Fabrieken v. Inspire Art Ltd., ECJ C-167/01 (Sept. 30, 2003), *available at* http://curia.eu.int/en/content/juris/index_form.htm; on legal capital as a signaling device, cf. John Armour, *Legal Capital: An Outdated Concept?*, 7 EUR. BUS. ORG. L. REV. 5, 25 (2006); John Armour, *Share Capital and Creditor Protection: Efficient Rules for a Modern Company Law*, 63 MOD. L. REV. 355, 359 (2000); Peter O. Mülbert & Max Birke, *Legal Capital – Is There a Case Against the European Legal Capital Rules?*, 3 EUR. BUS. ORG. L. REV. 695, 727 (2002).

[129] *Cf.* Thomas Bachner, *Wrongful Trading – A New European Model for Creditor Protection?*, 5 EUR. BUS. ORG. L. REV. 293 (2004).

and alteration, but it does not change the established balance between share-holders and creditors.[130]

4. Statutory Audit

In developing a coherent strategy on the statutory audit, the European Commission attempts to combine several prongs of capital market policy. Regulating the single market for auditing services is to safeguard harmonized financial disclosure and the establishment of a pan-European capital market. However, the role of the auditor will be strengthened to improve corporate governance and investor confidence in market efficiency.[131] In a first move, the Commission's 2002 Recommendation on Statutory Auditors' Independence laid down core principles on professional standards, auditor responsibility, conflicts of interest, and internal safeguard mechanisms for auditing firms.[132] The impact of the Enron and the Parmalat scandals and the Sarbanes-Oxley Act finally convinced the Commission openly to acknowledge the interface between market transparency, professional auditing, and corporate governance.[133] In May 2006, the European Parliament and the Council adopted a new directive on the statutory audit "to rebuild trust in the audit function."[134] The Directive prefers regulatory action over market control by relying on board-of-directors-centered governance and public oversight.[135] Efficient public oversight at the

---

[130] European Parliament and Council Directive (EC) No. 2006/68 of Sept. 6, 2006, amending Council Directive (EEC) No. 77/91 as regards the formation of public limited liability companies and the maintenance and alteration of their capital, O. J. (L 264) 32 of Sept. 6, 2006.

[131] Anita I. Anand & Niamh Moloney, *Reform of the Audit Process and the Role of Shareholder Voice: Transatlantic Perspectives*, 5 EUR. BUS. ORG. L. REV. 232, 283 (2004).

[132] European Commission Recommendation (EC) No. 2002/590, Statutory Auditors' Independence in the EU: A Set of Fundamental Principles, O.J. (L 191) 22 of July 19, 2002.

[133] *See* European Commission Communication to the Council and the European Parliament, *Reinforcing the Statutory Audit in the EU*, COM (2003) 286 final (May 21, 2003) (the Communication refers expressly to the Sarbanes-Oxley Act), *available at* http://eur-lex.europa. eu/LexUriServ/site/en/com/2003/com2003_0286en01.pdf.

[134] European Parliament and Council Directive (EC) No. 2006/43 of May 17, 2006, on Statutory Audits of Annual Accounts, amending Council Directive (EEC) No. 78/660 and Council Directive (EEC) No. 83/349/EEC and repealing Council Directive (EEC) No. 84/253, O.J. (L 157) 87 of June 9, 2006, *available at* http://eur-lex.europa.eu/LexUriServ/site/en/oj/2006/l_ 157/l_15720060609en00870107.pdf; see the preparatory documents introduced by the European Commission, Proposal for a Directive of the European Parliament and of the Council on Statutory Audit of Annual Accounts and Consolidated Accounts and Amending Council Directive (EEC) No. 78/660 and Council Directive (EEC) No. 83/349, Mar. 16, 2004; Memorandum, European Commission Proposal for a Directive on Statutory Audit: Some Frequently Asked Questions, Mar. 16, 2004.

[135] *See* art. 41; Benito Arruñada, *Audit Failure and the Crisis of Auditing*, 5 EUR. BUS. ORG. L. REV. 635 (2004).

member state level requires that auditors be registered, subject to investigations by nonaudit professionals.[136] Independence from the audited company
dictates that the auditor is not involved in its management decisions and does
not have any financial, business, employment, or other relationship.[137] The
Directive stops short of outlawing auditor consultancy work for the audited
company.[138] But auditors have to establish that such work will not compromise
their independence. In what is a considerable departure from market mechanisms, member states will have to lay down rules on audit fees, outlawing
contingency fees, and cross-subsidization between income from auditing and
nonauditing services.[139] The Directive provides for auditor rotation,[140] and in
reaction to the Parmalat scandal, the auditor of a conglomerate group shall
also be responsible for the audit report on the consolidated accounts.[141]

C. Implementing the Action Plan on Corporate Governance

1. Audit Committees

The Directive on the statutory audit emphasizes the importance of an external audit for capital market transparency. In order to buttress the link between
internal governance mechanisms and meaningful auditing procedures, article
41 of the Directive provides for the establishment of an audit committee.[142] It
has to be composed of the nonexecutive members of the administrative body,
members of the supervisory body of the audited entity, or members appointed
at the shareholders' meeting.[143] At least one member of the audit committee has to be independent with competence in accounting or auditing.[144]

---

[136] Council Directive (EC) No. 2006/43 arts. 15 et seq., 31.
[137] *Id.* at art. 23(1).   [138] *Cf.* Arruñada, *supra* note 135, at 639.
[139] Council Directive (EC) No. 2006/43 art. 25.   [140] *Id.* at art. 43.
[141] *Id.* at art. 27(a).
[142] On the interface between corporate governance, external audits, and capital market transparency, cf. Peter Nobel, *Audit Within the Framework of Corporate Governance, in* CAPITAL
MARKETS AND COMPANY LAW, *supra* note 17, at 207.
[143] Art. 41(1) of the Council Directive (EEC) No. 2006/43:

> Each public-interest company shall have an audit committee. The Member State shall
> determine whether audit committees are to be composed of non-executive members of
> the administrative body and/or members of the supervisory body of the audited entity
> and/or members appointed by the general meeting of shareholders of the audited entity.
> At least one member of the audit committee shall be independent and shall have
> competence in accounting and/or auditing.

[144] The European rules auditing committees are inspired by the Sarbanes-Oxley Act. The U.S.
requirements on auditor oversight have also operated as a powerful incentive for some
member states to model their national oversight mechanisms after the Sarbanes-Oxley Act.
FERRAN, *supra* note 15, at 228. In administering the Sarbanes-Oxley Act, the SEC accepts

The audit committee shall monitor the financial reporting process, the effectiveness of the company's internal and risk-management systems, and the statutory audit. Procedures for reviewing internal whistle-blowing procedures, however, are relegated to the nonbinding Recommendation on Independent Directors.[145] The (statutory) auditor shall be nominated by the audit committee for appointment by the general meeting of the shareholders.[146] The auditor or the auditing firm shall report to the auditing committee.[147] From the point of view of harmonizing corporate governance, the future of pan-European audit committees is somewhat clouded. After intensive debate in the Law Committee of the European Parliament, a compromise was reached, allowing member states to derogate from the provisions on the statutory audit if listed companies have a similar body with comparable functions.[148]

2. Amending the Accounting Directives and Collective Board Responsibility

Accounting rules serve capital market transparency. They are a proxy for disclosure.[149] Thus, the June 2006 Directive of the European Commission aims at increased liability of board members with respect to financial statements.[150] The Directive imposes collective responsibility on the members of the administrative, management, or supervisory bodies for drawing up the annual or consolidated accounts, the annual or consolidated annual report, and the corporate governance statement. The annual report shall also contain information on special purpose entities and on transactions between the company and related persons where such a transaction is material and has not been concluded under normal commercial conditions. The corporate

---

that the nonexecutive members of the audit committee of nondomestic issuers may include labor representatives. Alan L. Beller, Dir. Div. of Corporation Fin., SEC, Regulation in a Global Environment, Speech in Berlin, Germany (Apr. 20, 2004), *available at* http://www.sec. gov/news/speeh/spchalbo42004.htm.

[145] *See infra* section III.3.c.

[146] Council Directive (EEC) No. 2006/43, arts. 37, 41(4).

[147] *Id.* at art. 41(5).

[148] *See Report* (Confederation of German Industry: Bundesverband der Deutschen Industrie, NvWR), July 2005, at 138.

[149] *Cf.* Jens Wüstemann, Institutionenökonomik und internationale Rechnungslegungsordnungen 1, 16 (2002).

[150] European Parliament and Council Directive (EC) No. 2006/46 of June 14, 2006, amending Council Directive (EEC) No. 78/660 on the Annual Accounts of Certain Types of Companies, Council Directive (EEC) No. 83/349 on Consolidated Accounts, Council Directive (EEC) No. 86/635 on the Annual Accounts and Consolidated Accounts of Banks and Other Financial Institutions and Council Directive (EEC) 91/674 on the Annual Accounts and Consolidated Accounts of Insurance Undertakings, *available at* http://eur-lex. europa.eu/smartapi/cgi/sga_doc?smartapi!celexplus!prod!DocNumber&lg=en&type_doc= Directive&an_doc=1991&nu_doc=674.

governance statement is to disclose information regarding the company's adherence to a national corporate governance code, the applicable control and risk-management systems, and a description of shareholders' rights. The Directive favors a comply-or-explain approach toward company application of a national corporate governance code.[151] Contrary to U.S. practice under the Sarbanes-Oxley Act, EU law refrains from requiring boards to certify the effectiveness of internal control mechanisms.[152] Member states are, however, authorized to introduce a more rigid regime on corporate governance and transparency.[153] The Directive does not change current liability rules. After the European Commission had published a draft of the Directive,[154] member states indicated that they did not wish to modify established concepts of personal liability, thereby reflecting the U.S. debate on the scope of liability for false statements under section 10(b) of the Securities Exchange Act of 1934.[155] The responsibility of the member of the administrative, management, or supervisory bodies will be conditioned on the individual member's scope of professional duties in the day-to-day business of the company.[156]

The Directive recognizes the regulatory burden for smaller- and medium-size enterprises. It raises the compliance thresholds so that member states may authorize a greater number of companies to prepare abridged accounts and notes to the accounts.[157]

---

[151] Cf. *Statement of the European Corporate Governance Forum on the Comply-or-Explain Principle*, Brussels (Feb. 22, 2006), *available at* http://ec.europa.eu/internal_market/company/ecgforum/index.en.htm.

[152] The European Corporate Governance Forum, *Statement on Risk Management and Internal Control* (June 2006) (denying the need for introducing a legal obligation for boards to certify the effectiveness of internal controls at the EU level, referring somewhat generally to a trade-off between the benefits of additional statutory requirements and the regulatory burden and costs for companies).

[153] In 2006, the German government suggested that the officers of a corporation certify that the annual accounts give a true view of the financial situation, properly describing the decisive chances and risks. Cf. Cordula Heldt & Sascha Ziemann, *Sarbanes-Oxley in Deutschland? Zur geplanten Einführung eines strafbewehrten "Bilanzeides" nach dem Regierungsentwurf eines Transparenzrichtlinie-Umsetzungsgesetzes*, 17 Neue Zeitschrift für Gesellschaftsrecht 652 (2006).

[154] Press Release, European Comm'n, Accounts: Commission Proposes Collective Board Responsibility and More Disclosure on Transactions, Off-Balance Sheet Vehicles and Corporate Governance (Oct. 28, 2004), *available at* http://europa.eu/rapid/pressReleasesAction.do?reference=IP/04/1318&language=en&guiLanguage=en.

[155] See In re Enron Corp. Sec., Derivative and ERISA Litig., 235 F. Supp. 2d 549 (S.D. Tex. 2002); SEC v. Lucent Techs., 363 F. Supp. 2d 708, 723 (D.N.J. 2005).

[156] See Report (Confederation of German Industry: Bundesverband der Deutschen Industrie, NvWR), Apr. 2005, at 67.

[157] DG Internal Market, *Report on Impacts of Raised Thresholds Defining SMEs – Impact Assessment on Raising the Thresholds in the 4th Company Law Directive* (EEC) No. 78/660 *Defining Small- and Medium-Sized Companies* (Dec. 2005), *available at* http://ec.europa.eu/internal_market/accounting/docs/studies/sme_thresholds_en.pdf.

3. Independent Directors

In February 2005, the Commission issued a nonbinding recommendation, inviting member states to take regulatory action on listed companies by introducing nonexecutive or supervisory directors on a mandatory or comply-or-explain basis.[158] Less strict than Nasdaq standards,[159] the Recommendation refrains from specifying the ratio between independent directors and other members of the board.[160] The Commission strikes a balance between one-tier and two-tier corporate governance systems, as independent directors may either be added to the board of directors or to the supervisory board. Boards should be so organized that a sufficient number of independent nonexecutive or supervisory directors play an effective role in key areas where the potential for conflict of interest is particularly high. Nomination, remuneration, and audit committees should be established to make recommendations to the board. At least a majority of the members of the audit committee should be independent. The Recommendation attempts to bridge the gap between bank-centered and capital-market-centered systems. For companies with dispersed ownership, the involvement of independent board committees is to ensure manager accountability to weak shareholders. Independent committees of companies with large block holdings are thought to protect the interests of the minority shareholders. Compared to section 301 of the Sarbanes-Oxley Act, the Recommendation contains a rather mild admonishment to review procedures on whistle-blowing, implying that the status quo in member state law will not be affected.[161] Implementing whistle-blowing rules will bring a cultural change to some European countries. So far, U.S. companies with European subsidiaries have encountered legal difficulties in attempting to comply with the Sarbanes-Oxley Act. In France, anonymous whistle-blowing

[158] European Commission Recommendation (EC) No. 2005/162 on the Role of Non-Executive or Supervisory Directors of Listed Companies on the Committees of the (Supervisory) Board, O.J. (L 52) 51 of Feb. 25, 2005, *available at* http://eur-lex.europa.eu/LexUriServ/site/en/oj/2005/l_052/l_05220050225en00510063.pdf.

[159] Revised Rules 4200 (a)(15) & 4350 (c)(1) of the Nasdaq Compliance Standards mandate that a majority of the board be independent. SEC, NASD and NYSE Rulemaking: Relating to Corporate Governance, Exchange Act Release No. 48,745, 81 SEC Docket (CCH) 1586 (Nov. 4, 2003), *available at* http://www.sec.gov/rules/sro/34-48745.htm.

[160] This is because of differences in member state laws on the composition of the board that distinguish companies with widely held shares from others (leaving aside the specific problem of how to accommodate German laws regarding codetermination on supervisory boards).

[161] Section 4.3.8 of annex I to the Recommendation (EC) No. 2005/162 stipulates:

> The audit committee should review the process whereby the company complies with *existing provisions* [emphasis added] regarding the possibility for employees to report alleged significant irregularities in the company, by way of complaints or through anonymous submissions, normally to an independent director, and should ensure that

hotlines are in conflict with data protection laws, as they would give rise to an internal climate of defamation.[162] In Germany, the approval of the Works Council has to be sought.[163]

4. Disclosure of Directors' Remuneration

The Commission recommendation on the remuneration regime for directors of listed companies[164] supplements the policy on audit committees. The Recommendation emphasizes the interface between internal corporate control mechanisms and transparency for the benefit of investors.[165] The Recommendation envisages that member states take regulatory action to require a listed company to disclose its remuneration policy in an annual report. Such remuneration may be included in the annual report, attached to the report, or made independently. The statement should also explain the company's approach to termination periods and payments in the directors' contracts. The Recommendation suggests that the total remuneration and other benefits granted to individual directors over the relevant fiscal year be disclosed in the annual report. Member states are urged to empower shareholders to control the company's remuneration when the annual general meeting is held.[166] This includes a shareholder vote on share-based remuneration schemes.

5. Shareholders' Rights

Buying shares confers the full scope of rights on the purchaser. Thus, bargaining on shareholders' rights appears to be quintessentially a matter of private

arrangements are in place for the proportionate and independent investigation of such matters and for appropriate follow-up action.

Cf. the comparative study on whistleblowing rules, Matthias Schmidt, *"Whistle-blowing" Regulation and Accounting Standards Enforcement in Germany and Europe – An Economic Perspective*, 21 INT'L REV. L. & ECON. 143 (2005).

[162] Commission Nationale de l'Informatique et des libertés, Délibération No. 2005-111 (CEAC/Exide Technologies) & Délibération No. 2005-110 (McDonald's France/McDonald's Corporation U.S.) (May 26, 2005).

[163] Arbeitsgericht [Labor Court Wuppertal] June 15, 2005, 5 BV 20/05, 2005 ZEITSCHRIFT FÜR WIRTSCHAFTSRECHT 1334 (2005); cf. Simon, Case Note, 2005 DER BETRIEB 1800.

[164] European Commission Recommendation (EC) No. 2004/913 Fostering an Appropriate Regime for the Remuneration of Directors of Listed Companies, O.J. (L 385) 55 of Dec. 29, 2004, *available at* http://europa.eu.int/eur-lex/lex/en/repert/1710.htm.

[165] Press Release, European Comm'n, Directors' Pay – Commission Sets Out Guidance on Disclosure and Shareholder Control (Oct. 6, 2004), *available at* http://ec.europa.eu/internal_market/company/directors-remun/index_en.htm.

[166] Germany has introduced a statutory regime of disclosure that allows an opt-out of transparency on individual director remuneration if the general meeting of shareholders consents. Holger Fleischer, *Das Vorstandsvergütungs-Offenlegungsgesetz*, 2005 DER BETRIEB 1611 (2005).

ordering that does not require regulatory intervention. Nonetheless, nondomestic shareholders may experience difficulties in exercising their right to vote in a cross-border context. On June 12, 2007, the Council of Ministers adopted a directive on the exercise of certain rights of shareholders in listed companies.[167] The Directive lays down basic rules on advance information on shareholders' general meetings, electronic participation in these meetings, and *in absentia* voting, and it abolishes all forms of share blocking.[168] Issuers do not have a right to opt out of the envisaged legislation even if the shareholders' meeting so decides. The Commission has refrained from introducing mandatory rules related to the exercise of voting rights, such as stock lending, depository receipts, and language requirements, acknowledging that some leeway for private ordering might be preferable.[169]

The Report of the High Level Group of Experts notes that proportionality between ultimate economic risk and control normally requires control rights reflecting the amount of share capital owned.[170] In corporate practice control enhancing mechanisms abound.[171] The consultation on the Commission's Action Plan revealed that plans for regulatory measures will receive a mixed welcome. Issuers emphasize the freedom of contract and reject the need for intervention at the EU level. On the other hand, representatives from the investing community (shareholders' associations and institutional investors) support regulatory action in order to curtail the role of dominant shareholders.[172] Currently, the Commission carries out an impact assessment

---

[167] Provisional Text of the Directive of the European Parliament and of the Council, European Union – The European Parliament & Council of Ministers (June 1, 2007), *available at* http://www.consilium.europa.eu/uedocs/cms_data/docs/2004/7/9/1994.pdf; Press Release, European Comm'n, Corporate Governance: Directive on Shareholders' Rights Formally Adopted (June 12, 2007), *available at* http://ec.europa.eu/internal_market/company/shareholders/indexa_en.htm.

[168] *See* art. 4 et seq. of the Directive.

[169] Recital 4 of the introductory remarks to the Directive describes the regulatory purposes as an attempt to lay down certain "minimum standards . . . with a view to protecting investors and promoting the smooth and effective exercise of shareholder rights attaching to voting shares." *See* Consultation Document by the European Comm'n, Internal Mkt. & Servs. DG, Fostering an Appropriate Regime for Shareholders' Rights, MARKT/13.05.2005 (Apr. 30, 2007), *available at* http://ec.europa.eu/internal_market/company/docs/shareholders/consulation2_en.pdf.

[170] *See Report of the High Level Group, supra* note 7.

[171] *Commission Study on Proportionality Between Ownership and Control in EU Listed Companies* (June 2007) (referring to multiple voting rights shares, nonvoting shares (without preference), nonvoting preference shares, pyramid structures, depository certificates, voting rights ceilings, golden shares, cross-shareholdings, and shareholder agreements), *available at* http://ec.europa.eu/internal_market/company/docs/shareholders/study/final_report_en.pdf.

[172] *See* Directorate General, *supra* note 15, at 8.

to determine the need and potential scope of a regulatory instrument at the EU level.[173]

IV. WHITHER EUROPEAN CORPORATE GOVERNANCE?

A. *Private Ordering and Externalities – The European Court of Justice on Company Mobility*

Officials in the United States have occasionally noted a transatlantic convergence between U.S. and European regulatory concepts.[174] There are similarities between the short-term priorities of the EU Action Plan and the standards set by the Sarbanes-Oxley Act and its federalizing strategy. Comparative corporate governance reveals that convergence toward international standards creates unstable punctuated equilibriums, occurring intermittently on selected

---

[173] Press Releases, European Comm'n, Commission Publishes External Study on Proportionality Between Capital and Control in EU Listed Companies (June 4, 2007), *available at* http://europa.eu/rapid/preeReleasesAction.do?reference=IP/07/751&format=HTML&aged=0&language=EN.

[174] Conrad Hewitt, Chief Accountant, SEC, Remarks at Baruch College, New York (May 3, 2007), *available at* http://www.sec.gov./news/speech/2007/spcho50307cwh.htm; Ethiopis Tafara, Dir., Office of Int'l Affairs, SEC, Remarks Before Transatlantic Financial Market Symposium Panel, "The Road to Regulatory Convergence: Where Are We and Where Are We Going?" Luxembourg (Apr. 27, 2005), *available at* http://www.sec.gov/news/speech 042705et.htm; Scott A. Traub, Deputy Chief Accountant, SEC, International Convergence and Public Oversight of Accounting and Auditing Standards, Speech in Amman, Jordan (May 20, 2004), *available at* http://www.sec.gov.news /speech/spcho52004sat.htm; *cf.* Maria Cardilli, *Regulation Without Borders: The Impact of Sarbanes-Oxley on European Companies*, 27 Fordham Int'l L.J. 785 (2004); Ronald J. Gilson, *Globalizing Corporate Governance: Convergence of Form or Function*, 49 Am. J. Comp. L. 329 (2001). A dialogue has been established to come to terms with the extraterritorial implications of the Sarbanes-Oxley Act and European securities regulation. *See The U.S.-EU Regulatory Dialogue and Its Future, Hearing Before the Committee on Financial Services – U.S. House of Representatives*, 108th Cong. 100 (May 13, 2004); Hans-Jürgen Hellwig, *The Transatlantic Financial Markets Regulatory Dialogue*, in Corporate Governance in Context, *supra* note 8, at 363. The April 2007 "Framework for Advancing Transatlantic Economic Integration Between the United States of America and the European Union" calls, *inter alia*, for a continued informal financial markets dialogue on the implementation of the Basel II rules and for the mutual recognition of U.S. GAAP and IFRS. Press Release on the U.S.-EU Summit, annex 6, White House, Framework for Advancing Transatlantic Economic Integration Between the United States of America and the European Union (Apr. 30, 2007), *available at* http://www.whitehouse.gov./news/releases/2007/04/print/20070430-4.html; *see also* Kern Alexander et al., *Transatlantic Financial Regulatory Dialogue*, 7 Eur. Bus. Org. L. Rev. 647 (2006) (on the transatlantic regulatory dialogue); Press Release 2007–105, SEC, SEC Announces Roundtable Discussion Regarding Mutual Recognition (May 24, 2007), *available at* http://www.sec.gov./news/press/2007/2007–105.htm.

issues.[175] Nowadays, even insider systems experience change, and national lawmakers implement regulatory standards typical of capital markets with dispersed ownership.[176] Analyzing capital markets from a globalization perspective does not explain, however, why centralized European action should be taken instead of relying on the forces of the marketplace.[177] Apparently, centralized rule making dominates decentralization where the externalities of national legal systems cannot be properly internalized.[178] The ECJ's jurisprudence on company mobility illustrates that private ordering is a viable alternative to centralized rule making.[179] By examining national company laws on their compatibility with the (European) internal market, the ECJ redefines the trade-off between decentralized rule making and the negative externalities of national legislative efforts.[180]

1. Regulatory Entry and Exit under the Freedom of Establishment

The ECJ favors a deregulatory approach by implementing the freedom of establishment under the EC Treaty.[181] A series of judgments guarantees free

---

[175] William Bratton & Joseph McCahery, *Comparative Corporate Governance and Barriers to Global Cross Reference*, in CORPORATE GOVERNANCE, *supra* note 24, at 23, 24, 37; *cf.* Jonathan Rickford, *Corporate Governance Systems – How Much Convergence?*, in CORPORATE GOVERNANCE IN THE US AND EUROPE – WHERE ARE WE NOW? 25 (Geoffrey Owen et al. eds., 2006).

[176] In this context, Professors Bratton and McCahery diagnose a trade-off between ownership concentration, monitoring, and management initiative and private rent seeking, which may affect national convergence processes. Bratton & McCahery, *supra* note 175, at 29.

[177] *Cf.* Nicolas Jabko, *The Political Foundations of the European Regulatory State*, in THE POLITICS OF REGULATION 2002 (Jacint Jordana & David Levi-Faur eds., 2004) (questioning the link between European integration and globalization).

[178] Jean-Jacques Laffont & Wilfried Zantman, *Information Acquisition, Political Game and the Delegation of Authority*, 18 EUR. J. POL. ECON. 407, 417 (2002).

[179] *See* Jean-Jacques Laffont & Jerome Pouyet, *The Subsidiary Bias in Regulation*, 88 J. PUB. ECON. 255, 266 (2003) (on how the negative side effects of local government can be checked by (regulatory) competition among the various jurisdictions and by centralized rule making).

[180] *Cf.* Luca Enriques & Martin Gelter, *Regulatory Competition in European Company Law and Creditor Protection*, 7 EUR. BUS. ORG. L. REV. 417 (2006).

[181] The freedom of establishment for corporate organizations is guaranteed by articles 43 and 48 of the EC Treaty.

    EC Treaty art. 43:

> Within the framework of the provisions set out below, restrictions on the freedom of establishment of nationals of Member States in the territory of another Member State shall be prohibited. Such prohibition shall also apply to restrictions on the setting-up of agencies, branches or subsidiaries by nationals of any other Member State established in the territory of any Member State.

> Freedom of establishment shall include the right to take up and pursue activities as self-employed persons and to set up and manage undertakings, in particular companies or firms within the meaning of the second paragraph of 48, under the conditions laid

entry to the host state, thus facilitating corporate relocation decisions.[182] Non-domestic European companies are entitled to access to justice in the host state irrespective of whether they have been incorporated under the laws of another member state. Creditor protection is a valid regulatory policy purpose. But a foreign European company may commence business activities without depositing funds to satisfy potential creditor claims. Conversely, it is illegal to apply specific liability rules to a director of a nondomestic company no longer operative in its country of incorporation. Absent fraud, it is legitimate to circumvent restrictive laws of one member state and resort to the more liberal company law regime of another.[183] Private companies are entitled to demonstrate mobility by consummating a cross-border merger.[184]

The ECJ's rulings on regulatory exit are less far reaching. In the *Daily Mail* case, a British statute was upheld that conditioned a corporate-relocation decision upon the payment of a *de facto* exit tax.[185] Since then, no tax-related

> down for its own nationals by the law of the country where such establishment is effected, subject to the provisions of the chapter relating to capital.
>
> EC Treaty art. 48:
>
> > Companies or firms formed in accordance with the law of a Member State having their registered office, central administration or principal place of business within the Community shall, for the purposes of this chapter, be treated in the same way as natural persons who are nationals of Member States.
> > "Companies or firms" means companies or firms constituted under civil or commercial law, including cooperative societies, and other legal persons governed by public or private law, save for those which are non-profit making
>
> Consolidated Version of the Treaty Establishing the European Community, Dec. 24, 2002, O.J. (C 325) 33.

[182] ECJ judgments, Case No. C-221/97, Centros Ltd. v. Erhvervs- og Selskabstyrelsen, 1999 E.C.R. I-1459 (1999); Case No. C-208/00, Überseering B.V. v. Nordic Construction Co. Baumanagement GmbH (NCC), 2002 E.C.R. I-9919 (2002); Case No. C-167/01, Kamer van Koophandel en Fabrieken v. Inspire Art Ltd. (2003); Case No. C-411/03, SEVIC Systems AG, 2005 ECR I-10805 (2005).

[183] See ¶ 95 et seq. of the ECJ's judgment Case No. C-167/01, Kamer van Koophandel en Fabrieken v. Inspire Art Ltd. (2003) ("[T]he reasons for which a company chooses to be formed in a particular Member State are, save in the case of fraud, irrelevant with regard to application of the rules on freedom of establishment.... [T]he fact that the company was formed in a particular Member State for the sole purpose of enjoying the benefit of a more favourable legislation does not constitute abuse even if that company conducts its activities entirely or mainly in that second State....").

[184] See ECJ Judgment in the SEVIC case, *supra* note 182; Behrens, Case note, CMLR 43, 1669 (2006); *see also* the Directive of the European Parliament and of the Council on Cross-Border Mergers of Limited Liability Companies, O.J. (L 310) of Dec. 13, 2005.

[185] ECJ judgment, Case No. 81/87, The Queen v. H.M. Treasury and Comm'rs of Inland Revenue, *ex parte* Daily Mail & General Trust plc., 1988 E.C.R. 5483 (1988). A Hungarian court has requested a preliminary ruling that may give the ECJ a chance to reassess its holding in the *Daily Mail* case and to specify the conditions for regulatory exit from member states: Reference

relocation cases have come to the ECJ.[186] It is, therefore, uncertain whether
the ECJ may mellow its stance on tax aspects of company mobility.[187]

2. The ECJ's Major Beneficiaries: Private Companies

It is no coincidence that private companies have become the motor for company mobility and regulatory competition in corporate Europe. National regulatory policies for private companies and partnerships are less restrictive,[188]
hence the relative ease for European judges to intervene and foster company
mobility. The ECJ's agnosticism toward pseudoforeign companies has paved
the way for free regulatory choice and private ordering. The English Private
Limited Company stands to become the major beneficiary of this state of
European Community law. Investors opt for this type of business organization, continue to have it registered in the United Kingdom and coordinate
their activities from the head office on the European continent.[189] There is no
taxable income in the United Kingdom, and shareholders reap the benefits
of English company law, which they consider to be of greater appeal than its

for a Preliminary Ruling from the Szegedi Ítéótábla (Court of Appeal of Szeged) Case No.
C-210/06P, Cartesio Oktató és Szolgáltató Bt., O.J. (C 165) 17 of July 15, 2006.

[186] The X and Y and de Lasteyrie du Saillant cases involve tax liabilities of individuals who held
shares of European multinational companies. See ECJ judgments, Case No. C-436/00, X and
Y v. Riksskatteverk (2002); Case No. C-9/02, Hughes de Lasteyrie du Saillant v. Ministère
de l'Économie, des Finances et de l'Industrie (2004). See also Case No. C-292/04, Meilicke,
Weyde & Stöffler v. Finanzamt Bonn-Innenstadt (2007).

[187] For a detailed analysis, see Gero Burwitz, Tax Consequences of the Migration of Companies: A
Practitioner's Perspective, 7 EUR. BUS. ORG. L. REV 589, 596 (2006).

[188] In the debate on company mobility in the EU, the factual settings of the cases before the
ECJ are often overlooked. See the Centros, Überseering, and Inspire-Art rulings, supra note
182 (dealing with close corporations or private companies). See also Joseph McCahery, Har-
monization in European Company Law: The Political Economy of Economic Integration, in
EUROPEAN INTEGRATION AND THE LAW – FOUR CONTRIBUTIONS ON THE INTERPLAY BETWEEN
EUROPEAN INTEGRATION AND NATIONAL LAW TO CELEBRATE THE 25TH ANNIVERSARY OF THE
MAASTRICHT UNIVERSITY'S FACULTY OF LAW 155 (D. Curtain et al. eds., 2006). Cf. JOSEPH
A. MCCAHERY & ERIK P.M. VERMEULEN, TOPICS IN CORPORATE FINANCE: UNDERSTANDING
(UN)INCORPORATED BUSINESS FORMS 9 (2005) (assessing the legal regime for closely held
firms); Larry E. Ribstein, Why Corporations?, BERKELEY BUS. L.J. 1 183, 191 (2004) (analyzing
the choice between corporation and partnership from a U.S. perspective).

[189] It is estimated that some thirty thousand private limited companies have moved headquarters to
Germany; Andre O. Westhoff, Die Verbreitung der limited mit Sitz in Deutschland, 97 GMBH-
RUNDSCHAU 525, 528 (2006); Harry Rajak, The English Limited Company as an Alternative
Legal Form for German Enterprise, 2005 EWS 539 (2005); Marco Becht et al., Corporate
Mobility Comes to Europe: The Evidence (Working Paper, Université Libre de Bruxelles &
Saïd Business School, Oxford University, 2005).

continental European counterparts.[190] Some member states have taken up the competitive challenge, modernizing their laws on private companies.[191]

In favoring private companies over listed corporations, the ECJ's holdings on company mobility might be thought to be incoherent.[192] But this reflects the balance of power among the member states, the European Commission, and the European judges. The corporate law policies of the member states have tended to establish a noncooperative equilibrium, foreclosing regulatory choice and interjurisdictional competition to corporations.[193] Although the ECJ has the means to mold Community law, it has attempted to use its discretionary power in a spirit of cooperation to avoid alienation with the major regulatory players in the European Union.[194] Member states are still reluctant to bestow free regulatory choice on listed corporations. Rules on stakeholder protection place considerable barriers on the road to exit from one corporate law jurisdiction.[195] Nonetheless, the importance of private companies for listed corporations should not be underestimated. Listed corporations have begun to rely on (more liberal) private company law vehicles to escape the constraints of their domestic corporate law rules. In creating foreign private (holding) companies, mergerlike devices are put into effect.[196] There are also signs that

---

[190] The same practice is observed with respect to private limited companies established in offshore centers such as the British Virgin Islands or the Cayman Islands. The provisions of the EC Treaty on the freedom of establishment are equally applicable to these companies.

[191] *See* Harm-Jan De Kluiver, *Private Ordering and Buy-Out Remedies Within Private Company Law: Towards a New Balance Between Fairness and Welfare?*, 8 EUR. BUS. ORG. L. REV. 103 (2007) (on the Private Company Law Reform in the Netherlands); Ulrich Seibert, *Close Corporations – Reforming Private Company Law: European and International Perspectives*, 8 EUR. BUS. ORG. L. REV. 83 (2007) (on German reform projects).

[192] *Cf.* Horatia Muir Watt, *Experiences from Europe: Legal Diversity and the Internal Market*, 39 TEX. INT'L L.J. 429, 450 (2004).

[193] *Cf.* Christian Kirchner et al., *Regulatory Competition in EU Corporate Law After Inspire Art: Unbundling the Delaware Product*, 2 ECFR 2, 159, 176 (2005) (pointing to the switching costs an established company would face in migrating from one national legal order to another); Joseph A. McCahery & Erik P.M. Vermeulen, *Does the European Company Prevent the "Delaware-effect"?* (Tilburg University, TILEC Discussion Paper DP 2005–10, 2005) (arguing that "there are few political incentives for lawmakers to pass legislation that might serve to disrupt the EU's non-competitive equilibrium in company law").

[194] Robert Cooter & Josef Drexel, *The Logic of Power in the Emerging European Constitution: Game Theory and the Division of Powers*, 14 INT'L REV. L. & ECON. 307, 324 (1994).

[195] In Germany, for example, local interest groups heavily defend the country's codetermination laws. For an analysis, see Katharina Pistor, *Codetermination: A Sociopolitical Model with Governance Externalities, in* EMPLOYEES AND CORPORATE GOVERNANCE 163 (Margaret M. Blair & Mark J. Roe eds., 1999).

[196] Foreign holding companies are exempt from German laws on codetermination. BAG [Federal Labor Supreme Court] Feb. 14, 2007 (7 ABR 26/06); OLG [Court of Appeal Düsseldorf] Oct. 30, 2006 (26 W 14/06 AktE).

competition from private company law[197] and globalization will push national legislators toward reform: legislative activities of the European Union are designed to extend corporate mobility to listed corporations.[198]

3. Regulatory Policy Implications

The ECJ's rulings on company mobility make an attempt to attack the negative externalities of national corporate law systems by emphasizing private choice and the freedom of establishment. But private ordering is not unlimited. It has to internalize spillovers arising from regulatory differences between national legal orders.[199] Member states are authorized to derogate from the freedom of establishment for "grounds of imperative national interest."[200] However, this caveat should not be overestimated. It rather acknowledges the evolution of company law. As corporate law systems have ceased to be all-encompassing regulatory devices, there is a need for allocating the spheres of influence of various national laws.[201] Traditional legal terminology classifies this regulatory problem as an issue of whether mandatory law takes precedence over private choice.[202] From a transnational point of view, this requires a policy decision on the extent to which the host state may control the internal affairs

---

[197] *Cf.* Vino Timmerman, *Welfare, Fairness and the Role of Courts in a Simple and Flexible Private Company Law*, EUR. BUS. ORG. L. REV. 326 (2007).

[198] *See* European Parliament and Council Directive (EC) No. 2005/56 on Cross-Border Mergers of Limited Liability Companies, O.J. L (310) 1 of Nov. 25, 2005 and the European Commission Proposal for a Fourteenth European Parliament and Council Directive on the Transfer of the Registered Office of a Company from One Member State to Another with a Change of Applicable Law (XV/D2/6002/97-EN REV.2).

[199] The ECJ's approach may lead to conflicts between national systems of creditor protection under company and insolvency laws. *Cf.* Horst Eidenmüller, *Free Choice in International Corporate Law: European and German Corporate Law in European Competition Between Corporate Law Systems*, in ECONOMIC ANALYSIS OF PRIVATE INTERNATIONAL LAW 187, 199 (Jürgen Basedow & Toshiyuki Kono eds., 2006) (arguing against harmonizing creditor protection standards by centralized EU legislative action, favoring compulsory insurance for the benefit of tort creditors); Gerard Hertig & Hideki Kanda, *Creditor Protection*, in THE ANATOMY OF CORPORATE LAW: A COMPARATIVE AND FUNCTIONAL APPROACH 70, 78 (Reinier Kraakman et al. eds., 2004) (noting a considerable degree of international convergence in the rights of corporate creditors); Andrew Keay, *Directors' Duties to Creditors: Contractarian Concerns Relating to Efficiency and Over-Protection of Creditors*, 66 MOD. L. REV. 665, 687 (2003); Roger Van den Bergh, *Regulatory Competition or Harmonization of Laws? Guidelines for the European Regulator*, in THE ECONOMICS OF HARMONIZING EUROPEAN LAW 27, 32 (Alain Marciano & Jean-Michel Josselin eds., 2002). In this context, the case for regulatory competition in creditor protection is investigated by Enriques & Gelter, *supra* note 180, at 417.

[200] *See* the ECJ's jurisprudence, *supra* note 182.   [201] *Cf.* Muir Watt, *supra* note 192, at 452.

[202] *Id.* at 443; Fabio Morosini, *Globalization and Law: Beyond Traditional Methodology of Comparative Legal Studies and an Example from Private International Law*, 13 CARDOZO J. INT'L & COMP. L. 541, 559 (2005).

of a foreign company.[203] Ultimately, this begs the question of whether private international law rules are capable of recalibrating conflicting regulatory concepts in corporate law.[204] It is against this background that the European Commission will have to decide when to take centralized regulatory action for private companies.[205]

Marked differences between private companies and listed corporations tend to obscure a surprising regulatory policy overlap. Lawmakers may be driven by path dependence in corporate law systems and concerns about national sovereignty and personal rent seeking. But globalization forces them to face competitive processes and private ordering under foreign legal orders as they ponder centralized regulatory action. In this context, the European Union will have to decide to what extent it is prepared to accept external private ordering or standards setting from nongovernmental or nondomestic institutions.

B. Information-Forcing Rules

Regulatory competition does not automatically guarantee better rules and optimal corporate charters. It may be deficient or too slow to counterbalance the effects of national policies.[206] The U.S. debate on regulatory competition illustrates that, absent strong markets, high corporate law standards are not self-evident. Such competition will be beneficial only if it is "exit-less" and will result in a "race to the top." [207] A closer scrutiny of the current regulatory climate in the European Union suggests that regulatory competition among the member states has its problems.[208] Tax is an important issue[209] and so

---

[203] Cf. Andrea J. Gildea, Überseering: A European Company Passport, 30 BROOK. J. INT'L L. 257, 260 (2004).

[204] Cf. Paul F. McGreal, The Flawed Economics of the Dormant Commerce Clause, 39 WM. & MARY L. REV. 1191, 1275 (1998); Horatia Muir Watt, European Integration, Legal Diversity and the Conflict of Laws, 9 EDINBURGH L. REV. 6, 16 (2004–2005).

[205] Proposals for a European Statute on Private Companies have been greeted with little enthusiasm. See Charles McCreevy, European Comm'r for Internal Mkt. & Servs., Addressing the European Parliament Committee on Legal Affairs (Nov. 21, 2006); McCreevy, supra note 16.

[206] Cf. Damien Gerardin & Joseph A. McCahery, Regulatory Co-opetition: Transcending the Regulatory Competition Debate, in THE POLITICS OF REGULATION, supra note 177, at 90.

[207] John C. Coffee Jr., Law and Regulatory Competition: Can They Co-Exist?, 80 TEX. L. REV. 1729, 1735 (2002).

[208] Jens Christian Dammann, Freedom of Choice in European Corporate Law, 29 YALE J. INT'L L. 477, 492 (2004); Tröger, supra note 29, at 14.

[209] The ECJ judgment in the Marks & Spencer case has only removed very specific tax law obstacles to company mobility in Europe. See ECJ, Case No. C-446/03, Marks & Spencer, plc v. David Halsey (Her Majesty's Inspector of Taxes) (2005) (ruling on tax deductibility of losses in multicountry corporate groups), available at http://curia.eu.int/en/content/juris/index_form .htm.

are the obstacles to enforcing investor rights.[210] National governments have a strong incentive to offer high standards in securities regulation and corporate law to nondomestic investors.[211]

In evaluating the future of its Action Plan, the European Commission will have to consider the complexities of regulatory processes at the member state level and the cost of introducing centralized rules.[212] The U.S. securities regulation teaches that lack of information is a threat to transparency and active liquid markets.[213] The European Commission should, therefore, concentrate on information-forcing rules to maintain a high standard of market transparency.[214] Centralized regulatory action requires a cost-benefit analysis and a scrutiny of rent-seeking behavior and of the spillover effects of national corporate laws.[215] It is a matter of political controversy whether the Commission should become active only in cases of market failure during competitive regulatory processes.[216] It would nonetheless seem that European Commission action is apposite where the negative externalities of national legal systems have

---

[210] Cf. the analysis by Eidenmüller, *supra* note 199 (citing factual obstacles); Kirchner et al., *supra* note 193 (emphasizing the switching costs an established company would face in migrating from one national legal order to another).

[211] Enriques, *supra* note 15. *But see* McCahery & Vermeulen, *supra* note 193 (arguing that "there are few political incentives for lawmakers to pass legislation that might serve to disrupt the EU's non-competitive equilibrium in company law").

[212] For an assessment of the future of the Action Plan, see Theodor Baums, *European Company Law Beyond the 2003 Action Plan*, 8 EUR. BUS. ORG. L. REV. 143 (2007).

[213] SEC v. Infinity Group Co., 212 F.3d 180, 191 (3d Cir. 2000) ("[T]he securities laws were intended to provide investors with accurate information and to protect the investing public from the sale of worthless securities through misrepresentations.") (citing H.R. Rep. No. 85, 73d Cong., 1st Sess., at 1–5 (1933); *cf.* STEPHEN BREYER, REGULATION AND ITS REFORM 26 (1982); Stefan Grundmann, *Regulatory Competition in European Company Law: Some Different Genius?*, in CAPITAL MARKETS IN THE AGE OF THE EURO – CROSS-BORDER TRANSACTIONS, LISTED COMPANIES AND REGULATION 561, 573 (Guido Ferrarini et al. eds., 2002); Stefan Grundmann, *The Structure of European Company Law: From Crisis to Boom*, 5 EUR. BUS. ORG. L. REV. 601, 617 (2004).

[214] In this, a distinction has to be made between corporate finance, company formation, and restructuring. Grundmann, *Some Different Genius?*, *supra* note 213, at 578; *accord* Hertig & McCahery, *supra* note 12, at 24. *See also* ECJ, Criminal Proceedings Against Berlusconi, Adelchi, Dell'Utri et al., joint cases C-387/03, C-391/02 and C-403/02 (2005) (emphasizing the importance of disclosure of annual financial statements); Niamh Moloney, *Confidence and Competence: The Conundrum of EC Capital Market Law*, 4 J. CORP. L. STUD. 1, 22 (2004).

[215] *Cf.* BREYER, *supra* note 213, at 23; Oliver Budzinski, *Towards an International Governance of Transborder Mergers? – Competition Networks and Institutions Between Centralism and Dualism*, 36 N.Y.U. J. INT'L L & POL. 1, 47 (2003); Stefan Grundmann & Wolfgang Kerber, *European System of Contract Laws: A Map for Combining the Advantages of Centralised and Decentralised Rulemaking*, in AN ACADEMIC GREENPAPER ON EUROPEAN CONTRACT LAW 295, 300 (Stephen Grundmann & Jules Stuyck eds., 2002).

[216] *Cf.* Gerardin & McCahery, *supra* note 206, at 99; Katharina Pistor & Chenggang Xu, *Incomplete Law*, 35 N.Y.U. J. INT'L L. & POL. 931, 962 (2003).

to be offset in order to clear the way for company and investor mobility.[217] In the following, the Commission's action plans will be briefly reassessed to ascertain whether centralized regulatory action is necessary.[218]

C. Cases for Centralized European Regulatory Action

1. Action Plans – Enabling to Establish More Transparency?

The Prospectus and the Transparency Directives are designed to force disclosure. They are intended to create a level playing field within the European Union to enable issuers freely to offer securities and to empower investors to make buy-and-sell decisions on the basis of a minimum content of comparable information. With respect to general securities regulation and supervision, member states converged on the single regulator model.[219] But elsewhere, there is diversity. The directives do not prevent issuers from voluntarily subscribing to higher standards of disclosure in order to make a first-class offering of securities. Information-forcing rules cannot bridge the gap between outsider and insider systems on the financial markets. The European definition of securities falls considerably behind the almost all-encompassing coverage of the U.S. securities acts. It is the responsibility of each member state to develop civil liability rules. In this, rules on liability for making false statements have to be improved, especially in countries that are slowly moving from an insider system to an open-market approach.[220] The latest experience with member states legislating on (criminal) liability for false financial statements suggests that European Union regulatory action is necessary to maintain minimum standards.[221] From the point of view of improving transparency of capital

---

[217] *Cf.* Easterbrook, *supra* note 90, at 128; Gerardin & McCahery, *supra* note 206, at 92; Roger Van den Bergh, *Towards an Institutional Legal Framework for Regulatory Competition in Europe,* 53 KYKLOS 435, 458 (2000); Klaus Hopt, *Company Law in the European Union: Harmonization and/or Subsidiarity?,* 1 INT'L & COMP. CORP. L.J. 41, 52 (1999); Stephen Woolcock, *Competition Among Rules in the European Market, in* INTERNATIONAL REGULATORY COMPETITION AND COORDINATION 289, 300 (William W. Bratton et al. eds., 1996).

[218] Martin Gelter & Mathias Siems, *Judicial Federalism in the ECJ Berlusconi Case: A Political Choice Analysis,* 46 HARV. INT'L L. J. 487, 504 (2005) (assuming that industry pressure has led the European Commission to act on the interface between corporate governance and securities regulation).

[219] FERRAN, *supra* note 15, at 225. Elsewhere, member states' sensitivities have to be taken into account. *Id.* at 227.

[220] See recommendations in Klaus J. Hopt & Hans-Christoph Voight, *Empfehlungen,* PROSPEKT- UND KAPITALMARKTINFORMATIONSHAFTUNG 1 (Klaus J. Hopt & Hans-Christoph Voigt eds., 2005).

[221] See factual analysis in the opinion of the Advocate-General *Kokott,* of Oct.14, 2004, in the ECJ joint Cases No C-387/02, C-391/02 and C-403/02, Criminal Proceedings Against Berlusconi et al.

markets, it is regrettable that the Prospectus and Transparency Directives remain silent on whistle-blowing.[222]

The Directive providing for collective board responsibility and the Recommendation on Director Remuneration support the information-forcing function of European legislation. It is also possible to reconcile the Draft Directive on the statutory audit with the transparency requirement. But it remains doubtful whether the proposed legislation will substantially improve the quality of the audit. Obviously, the position of the statutory auditor in corporate governance systems with prevailing block holdings creates loyalties different from companies with dispersed ownership. This situation might be overcome by mandating that statutory auditors be nominated by minority shareholders. It is less clear, however, whether this is a matter to be regulated by the European Union. Arguably, implementing a directive on statutory audits imposes an obligation on the member states to introduce corresponding liability rules and to protect the specific interests of minority shareholders in insider corporate governance systems.[223] This verdict would also apply to the audit committee and the Commission Recommendation on Independent Directors. Audit committees are an important mechanism to safeguard transparent decision-making procedures in the corporate setting that the Sarbanes-Oxley Act envisages. In corporate governance systems with block holdings, it is vital to ensure that minority shareholders have the right to nominate an independent director who protects their interests. It is unlikely that such an institution will be brought about by private ordering.[224]

2. Cross-Border Mergers

Under the laws of most member states, mergers are possible only between two resident national companies.[225] The ECJ judgment of December 13, 2005,

---

[222] Accepting whistleblowing would, in fact, be an acknowledgment of failing external corporate governance mechanisms. It is unclear, though, what whistle-blowing can actually achieve, as it comes at a time when basic institutions of corporate governance are malfunctioning. Macey, *supra* note 40, at 1917.

[223] *Cf.* Gelter & Siems, *supra* note 218, at 504.

[224] In this context, it should not be overlooked that even under the Sarbanes-Oxley Act there are limits to director independence. *Cf.* Lucian Arye Bebchuk & Jesse Fried, PAY WITHOUT PERFORMANCE 28, 202 (2004). This problem is likely to be magnified where an independent director is nominated by the minority shareholders.

[225] But see the Austrian-German cross-border merger case decided by Oberster Gerichtshof [OGH] [Supreme Court] Mar. 20, 2003, Zeitschrift für Unternehmensrecht 1086 (Austria); Georg Wenglorz, *Die grenzüberschreitende "Heraus"-Verschmelzung einer deutschen Kapitalgesellschaft: Und es geht doch!*, 58 BETRIEBSBERATER 1061(2004).

has determined that this position is in conflict with Community law: inter-European mergers are to be allowed.[226] But for practical (e.g., tax) reasons, important barriers to cross-border mergers will remain.[227] It is obvious that private ordering will not bring about an efficient solution, as information-forcing procedures are severely restricted by member state laws. In October 2005, the EU Directive on cross-border mergers became effective.[228] It has to be implemented by the member states by the end of 2007. Under the Directive, the assets of the merging companies are transferred to the new company. The merging companies do not have to go into liquidation. Conversely, a merger by acquisition of the merging company can be executed without liquidating the target company.[229] During the merger proceedings, the respective national laws will be observed, but a "reconciliation" between conflicting national company law concepts will take place. This does not, however, apply to national law rules on creditor protection, which continue to apply to the premerger creditors of the merging companies. The Directive provides for conflict-of-law rules on codetermination.[230]

3. The Statute for the European Company (Societas Europaea)

The Council Regulation on the Statute for a European Company sets out to provide for enabling rules for private ordering where public limited liability companies engage in transnational activities within the Community or plan for a cross-border joint venture merger without having to dissolve the company in one jurisdiction and reincorporate in another.[231] Public and private limited liability companies of different member states may establish a Societas

[226] ECJ, Case No. C-411/03, SEVIC Sys. Aktiengesellschaft v. Amtsgericht Neuwied (2005), *available at* http://curia.eu.int/en/content/juris/index_form.htm.

[227] *Cf.* Stefan Leible & Jochen Hoffmann, *Grenzüberschreitende Verschmelzungen im Binnenmarkt nach "Sevic,"* 52 RECHT DER INTERNATIONALEN WIRTSCHAFT 161 (2006).

[228] *See* Directive, *supra* note 198.

[229] Art. 14 of the Council Directive (EC) No. 2005/56 on cross-border mergers.

[230] *See* Press Release, European Comm'n, Commission Welcomes Council Agreement on Making Cross-Border Mergers Easier (Nov. 25, 2004) (IP/04/1405), *available at* http://europa.eu/rapid/searchAction.do; Charles McCreevy, European Comm'r for Internal Mkt. & Servs., Statement on the Adoption of the European Parliament Opinion on the Cross-Border Mergers Directive (May 10, 2005), *available at* http://ec.europa.eu/internal_market/company/mergers/index_en.htm; *Report* (The Confederation of German Industry, Bundesverband der Deutschen Industrie, NvWR), Mar. 2005, at 44.

[231] Council Regulation (EC) No. 2157/2001 on the Statute for a European Company (SE), O. J. (L 294) 1 of Nov. 10, 2001; Carla Tavares Da Costa & Alexandra de Meester Bilreiro, THE EUROPEAN COMPANY STATUTE 37 (2003). For country reports on member states implementing the regulation, see THE EUROPEAN COMPANY – ALL OVER EUROPE (Krzysztof Oplustil & Christoph Teichmann eds., 2004).

Europaea (SE) as a holding company[232] or as a subsidiary.[233] Beginning in
article 37, the Council Regulation authorizes existing public limited liability
companies to opt for a conversion into a SE.[234] By the end of June 2007,
seventy-four SEs had been established in the European Union, and an additional group of fifteen was still in the planning phase. Virtually all financial
and real estate SEs have very few employees. There is a considerable number
of "shelf companies" without any noticeable business activities.[235]

The Regulation does not purport to create a federal company law for the
Community. The law of the member states where the SE has its registered
office is largely controlling. The dichotomy between one-tier and two-tier corporate governance systems remains intact.[236] Thus, there may be a German
type of SE as well as a U.K. equivalent with diverging rules on capital maintenance and emission of securities. With some justification, the Regulation
on the European Company has been criticized for achieving too little when
it comes to setting down common principles for European governance.[237]
Moreover, legal uncertainty from a conflict-of-laws perspective persists. But
this tends to underrate the potential of the Regulation for jurisdictional competition. The European Company will help to overcome national law barriers
to mobility. National companies may adopt the form of a European Company
and migrate in due course to an investor-friendly country.[238] The Regulation
is likely to overcome the obstacles that English law has created towards the
reincorporation of companies.[239] This, in turn, should contribute to regulatory

---

[232] Arts. 2(2), 32 et seq. of the Council Regulation on the Statute for a European Company.

[233] Arts. 2(3), 35 of the Council Regulation on the Statute for a European Company.

[234] Recently, the German chemical company BASF moved for conversion into a SE, arguing,
inter alia, that after conversion, the supervisory board would be smaller, thereby providing for
a more efficient corporate governance structure with less labor representatives under German
codetermination laws. *See* Revised Satzung BASF (Statutes of the BASF Corporation) of Mar.
16, 2007, *available at* http://www.corporate.basf.com; Magazin Mitbestimmung 06/2007,
available at http://www.boeckler.de.

[235] Statistical data on the European company (Societas Europaea) can be obtained at http://www.
seeurope-network.org and http://www.worker-participation.eu/about_wp, research networks
organized under the auspices of the European Trade Union Institute for Research, Education,
and Health and Safety.

[236] Peter Böckli, *Konvergenz: Annäherung des monistischen und des dualistischen Führungs- und
Aufsichtssystems, in* Handbuch Corporate Governance 201, 204 (Peter Hommelhoff et al.
eds., 2003).

[237] *See* Luca Enriques, *Silence Is Golden: The European Company as a Catalyst for Company
Law Arbitrage*, 4 J. Corp. L. Stud. 77 (2004) (analyzing the relevant legal literature).

[238] *Id.* at 80.

[239] *Id.* at 82; *cf.* Brian R. Cheffins, Company Law – Theory, Structure and Operation 427
(1997) (on the position of English Law toward a market for incorporation in the European
Union).

arbitrage and to regulatory competition within the European Community.[240] The combination of both the Statute for a European Company and the jurisprudence of the ECJ on company mobility should operate as an incentive for member states to compete for more efficient national company and securities laws.

D. Decentralized Enforcement in Member States

This chapter has argued for an information-forcing approach to corporate governance in the European Union to create transparent markets. If rules on transparency and liability are to be meaningful, powerful enforcement is vital.[241] Even after the 1995 Private Securities Litigation Reform Act in the United States, private litigation still adds to SEC enforcement polices. Pretrial discovery in the United States combined with U.S. rules of costs contribute to disclosure of information, which lends credibility to securities litigation and established principles of corporate governance. European lawyers are still unfamiliar with the idea of acting like a "private attorney-general"[242] who polices private behavior and contributes to rule making by litigation.[243] But it is precisely this threat of litigation that would greatly help open up insider types of capital markets, as management would have to justify activities before a more general public.[244] In fact, a two-step process is warranted. Shareholder litigation has to become a meaningful tool for shareholders who do not or cannot sell their shares at an acceptable price. This will require greater open-mindedness toward class-action-like procedures and rules on discovery, which reflect the specific challenges of litigating capital market and corporate governance issues in court. It is unrealistic to make a plea for European civil

---

[240] Enriques, *supra* note 237, at 83.

[241] This includes speedy administration of justice. *See* DANIELA MARCHESI, LITIGANTI, AVVOCATIE MAGISTRATI 20 (2003) (analyzing speed and cost of judicial proceedings in the member states of the European Union).

[242] The European Commission now endorses private enforcement as a complement to public enforcement of antitrust law, noting that collective actions (i.e., litigation) consolidate a large number of smaller claims. *Commission Green Paper on Damages Action for Breach of EC Antitrust Rules* (Dec. 19, 2005) COM (2005) 672 final; European Commission Staff Working on the Green Paper SEC (2005) 1732, *available at* http://ec.europa. ed/comm/competition/antitrust/actionsdamages/documents.html.

[243] *Cf.* Rafaele Lener, *L'introduzione della class action nell'ordinamento italiano del mercato finanziario*, 32.2 GIURISPRUDENZA COMMERCIALE 269/I (2005); *Les 'class actions' devant le juge français: Rêve ou Cauchemar*, 394 PETITES AFFICHES/LA LOI/LE QUOTIDIEN JURIDIQUE No. 115 (2005).

[244] *Cf.* Baums & Scott, *supra* note 22, at 71 (on enforcement problems under German law).

procedure converging on U.S. rules for class actions.[245] But specific provision
has to be made for empowering those dispersed shareholders who would otherwise shy away from litigating their rights. The United Kingdom has recently
introduced group litigation orders.[246] Germany enacted rules mildly reminiscent of class-action procedures on collectively litigating issues of evidence.[247]
It is to be hoped that investor pressure will push member states toward establishing powerful enforcement mechanisms,[248] which will be handled by competent judges.[249]

IV. CONCLUSION

Major financial scandals on both sides of the Atlantic have provided the
European Union and its member states with an opportunity to reevaluate their
regulatory approaches toward corporate governance and securities regulation.
The Commission's Action Plan proposes corporate governance measures that
converge on standards introduced under the Sarbanes-Oxley Act.[250] As the
Commission assesses its long-term strategy under the Action Plan, a policy shift
toward less mandatory and more enabling EU legislation is discussed.[251] This
may reflect a regulatory climate different from that of the United States at the

---

[245] See the analysis by J. Sordet, *Vers des Securities Class Actions à la Française*, 392 PETITES
AFFICHES/LA LOI/LE QUOTIDIEN JURIDIQUE No. 244, 4, 5 (2003) (on the current rules of
French civil procedure for collective action), and the cautious plea by L. Magnier, *Les Class
Actions d'Investisseurs en Produits Financiers*, 394 PETITES AFFICHES/LA LOI/LE QUOTIDIEN
JURIDIQUE No. 115, 33 (2005) (on a class-action type of remedy in securities litigation in France).

[246] U.K. DEPT. FOR CONSTITUTIONAL AFFAIRS, CIVIL PROCEDURE RULES PART 19.10 (Group
Litigation), *available at* http://www.dca.gov.uk/civil/procrules_fin/contents/parts/part19.htm#
ruleIDAC025E.

[247] BGBl. I No. 50 of Aug.19, 2005, at 2437; *cf.* Heiko Plassmeier, *Brauchen wir ein Kapitalanleger-
Musterverfahren? – Eine Inventur des KapMuG*, 8 NEUE ZEITSCHRIFT FÜR GESELLSCHAFT-
SRECHT 609 (2005). On the legislative history, see Fabian Reuschle, *Möglichkeiten und Grenzen
kollektiver Rechtsverfolgung*, 2004 WERTPAPIER-MITTEILUNGEN 966, 972 (2004).

[248] *Cf.* Gerard Hertig, *Convergence of Substantive Law and Convergence of Enforcement: A Comparison*, in CONVERGENCE AND PERSISTENCE, *supra* note 22, at 328, 333; Hopt, *supra* note 217,
at 58.

[249] *Cf.* Luca Enriques, *Do Corporate Law Judges Matter? Some Evidence from Milan*, 3 EUR. BUS.
ORG. L. REV. 765 (2002).

[250] See Mathias Siems, DIE KONVERGENZ DER RECHTSSYSTEME IM RECHT DER AKTIONÄRE 428
(2005) (analyzing the conditions for convergence of shareholder rights in the age of globalization and Europeanization).

[251] On the law-making processes in multilayer regulatory systems, cf. Jody Freeman, *The Private
Role in Public Governance*, 75 N.Y.U. L. REV. 543, 550, 664 (2000); Wolfgang Kerber & Klaus
Heine, *Zur Gestaltung von Mehr-Ebenen-Rechtssystemen aus ökonomischer Sicht*, in VEREIN-
HEITLICHUNG UND DIVERSITÄT DES ZIVILRECHTS IN TRANSNATIONALEN WIRTSCHAFTSRÄUMEN
(Claus Ott & Hans-Bernd Schäfer eds., 2002) (analyzing decentralized rule making under
default rules and federal systems); see also the European Commission's cautious approach

time Congress debated the Sarbanes-Oxley Act. The European Commission is faced with market-centered economies, insider systems, and capital markets in which the impact of globalization is felt. Throughout the member states, the degree of private law enforcement is remarkably weak. National rules on civil procedure constitute an important barrier to shareholder activism, and rules on whistle-blowing and liability differ considerably.

Traditionally, European company law and problems of corporate governance have been classified as policy issues over whether or not to harmonize member states' laws. Ironically, the ECJ's jurisprudence on company mobility both alleviates and aggravates the strain on national corporate law systems. The ECJ has opened up new opportunities for regulatory competition, private ordering, and arbitrage among the legal orders of the member states. This will not undo all the obstacles to the freedom of establishment in cross-border investment. Private companies are the major beneficiaries of the ECJ's holdings. Existing and new enterprises respond differently to regulatory competition.[252]

But regulatory competition will force the member states to internalize the negative effects of their national laws and to facilitate private ordering and attract foreign investors.[253] In this context, national legislators increasingly favor liberalization and voluntary standards, both on a domestic and on a European Union level.[254] There is a trade-off between the microeconomic aspects of corporate contracting and its macroeconomic side effects.[255] There is also a trade-off between the informational advantages of regional government

toward coregulation, *in Commission White Paper on European Governance,* COM (2001) 428 final (July 25, 2001).

[252] Zsuzsanna Fluck & Colin Mayer, *Race to the Top or Bottom? Corporate Governance, Freedom of Reincorporation and Competition in Law* (European Corporate Governance Working Paper No. 90/2005, 2005).

[253] In the long run, this should also contain rent-seeking behavior and regulatory capture in the member states. On regulatory capture as an important element of the economic theory of regulation, see Jonathan R. Macey, *Corporate Law and Corporate Governance – A Contractual Perspective,* 18 J. CORP. L. 185, 205 (1993).

[254] *Cf.* Gerardin & McCahery, *supra* note 206 (arguing for a new model of intra- and extragovernmental cooperation, which they term *regulatory co-opetition*); Steen Thomsen, *The Hidden Meaning of Codes: Corporate Governance and Investor Rent-Seeking,* 7 EUR. BUS. ORG. L. REV. 845 (2006). This policy approach is also endorsed by the European Corporate Governance Forum, *Statement on the Comply-or-Explain Principle* of Feb. 22, 2006, *available at* http://www.europa.eu.int/comm/internal_market/company/docs/ecgforum/ecgf-comply-explain_en.pdf.

[255] *Cf.* Paul B. Stephan, *Regulatory Competition and Cooperation: The Search for Virtue, in* TRANSATLANTIC REGULATORY COOPERATION – LEGAL PROBLEMS AND POLITICAL PROSPECTS 169, 190 (George A. Bermann et al. eds., 2000); Henri Tjiong, *Breaking the Spell of Regulatory Competition. Reframing the Problem of Regulatory Exit* (Preprints aus der Max-Planck-Projektgruppe Recht der Gemeinschaftsgüter, 2000/13), *available at* http://papers.ssrn.com/paper.taf?abstract_id=267744.

and the externalization effects of national legal systems.[256] The European Commission should, therefore, concentrate on information-forcing regulatory action that removes obstacles to cross-border activities within the EU and private ordering.[257]

Regulatory competition among the member states does not necessarily guarantee that the national legal orders will converge on the international standards of corporate governance to which the Commission's Action Plan subscribes.[258] This suggests a need for centralized regulatory action, assuming that the Commission's position in the international competition among regulators will be strengthened. It is perhaps a matter of conjecture whether the Commission's assessment of the implications of globalization is apposite. But in the long run, a combination of both – globalization and competitive efficiency – may eventually force the European Union and the classic nation-states to accept more private ordering and out-of-state lawmaking by transnational, non-European, or nongovernmental institutions.

[256] Laffont & Zantman, *supra* note 178, at 417.
[257] This includes a policy debate on standards for creditor and investor protection and on whether freedom for choosing an insolvency regime should be granted. Eidenmüller, *supra* note 199; Horst Eidenmüller, *Efficient Creditor Protection in European Company Law*, 7 Eur. Bus. Org. L. Rev 1 (2006).
[258] Von Hein, *supra* note 14, at 32.

Epilogue

Three Secular Trends of Corporate Law

Joel Seligman

I feel a little bit like I'm Huck Finn at my own funeral. I've never heard so many kind words, and it's been deeply moving. I've had to pinch myself occasionally to remember I'm still alive. I do want to note, for the record, that while I'm becoming a university president, I'm still going to play a role in securities law. This has been my life as a scholar since I began many years ago, and I'm looking forward particularly to working with Troy Paredes on the fourth edition of the *Securities Regulation* treatise, what will now be the Loss, Seligman, and Paredes treatise.

The greatest joy of my academic life has been my friends. To see the number of colleagues in this room is especially moving. Harvey Goldschmid, for example, whom I met my first day on the job in August of 1974 at a conference that Elliot Weiss helped organize, provides a sense of continuity for my entire career.

Since the purpose of this conference is to reflect on the new corporate law, let me offer a few thoughts on where we are going by addressing three secular trends, which in the decades to come will have a good deal to do with the development of corporate governance standards.

The first general trend of corporate governance has been the growing irrelevance of state corporate law. This trend dates back decades. It is a study in abdication. It is a study of common law techniques that were the great achievement of nineteenth-century jurisprudence, that do not work well for the application of standards to the largest corporations today. Delaware, at most, is an occasional and episodic residual claimant in articulating the standards by which corporations are now governed. It is striking when you think

---

Joel Seligman is President, University of Rochester, and former dean and Ethan A. H. Shepley University Professor at Washington University School of Law. What follows are edited remarks delivered at a conference held in his honor, where the chapters of this book were initially presented.

about the major scandals of the past few years, how thoroughly irrelevant state corporate law was to the deterrence or remedy of so much that occurred beginning with Enron.

Why was that so? There are traditional critiques of state corporate law focusing on limitations with jurisdiction and venue, or on the fact that it doesn't have an enforcement agency. But there is a more fundamental point, and that is the very limitation of the common law itself. The common law is judge-made law. It operates in a fact-specific way. The common law is reactive to cases brought before it. The common law is largely incapable of developing detailed standards. What we have seen in the response of the law-creating community in recent decades, and on the part of boards of directors, is an almost urgent need to know what is the right thing to do. The common law can occasionally tell you what you should not do. It is generally inadequate for prescription.

Throughout the twentieth century, we saw the virtual total abdication of the common law from the regulation of insider trading, even before the Securities and Exchange Commission came into existence, largely because of its commitment to the doctrine of privity or the difficulty of enforcing common law standards interstate. Even much more important, by the early 1930s the duty of care had often become largely irrelevant, and the duty of loyalty has become increasingly irrelevant. The effective legal standards with which corporations comply today have been transformed from difficult-to-enforce duties in state courts into precise and detailed statutes and rules that are enforced through federal disclosure or fraud standards.

Disclosure standards today are the essence of what we mean by the "duty of loyalty" and the "duty of care." When you look at the leading corporations in this country and compare the number of instances in which one has been successfully sued in a state law duty-of-care or duty-of-loyalty suit with the number of instances in which they have been held liable under the federal securities laws, in all their permutations, the federal securities laws dwarf the state law standards.

Let me take this point further. The abdication of state law standards has accelerated in the very recent past precisely because of the mandatory disclosure system. This achievement in the past few years has been fundamental, particularly with regard to auditing and accounting. Accounting is an area that Louis Brandeis urged is the very essence of governance. By that, he referred to how boards of directors in fact manage corporations. Internal accounting controls matter. Public reports matter. This is an area in which state law has been generally absent. To be sure, there have been occasional cases. But when you focus on the audit breakdowns that we saw in the recent past, the state law is essentially nowhere to be seen.

We are seeing right now a new abdication, of less consequence, but clearly obvious in its implications, in the area of executive compensation. The waste doctrine is not dead, but it is largely so. It is a doctrine that has been very difficult to enforce in the state of Delaware for decades because of the mechanisms by which one could dismiss a derivative action before trial. But after Chancellor Chandler's *Disney* decision,[1] you are essentially seeing a process by which an area where state law has proved to be ineffectual will inevitably be succeeded by progressively more detailed federal standards.

Does this mean that state corporate law will become entirely irrelevant? No – it still has a role. But, with respect to the largest business corporations, it is a shrinking one. As we look into the future, this sense of abdication in state response will continue, because the very nature of state corporate law jurisprudence is ill equipped to deal with the complexity and technicality of the management of the giant corporation today.

To be precise, there are three underlying reasons why state law is ill equipped to address governance in large corporations.

First, it is too fact specific. For example, in the version of the recent *Disney* chancery court case that I mentioned, 103 of 174 pages (59 percent) addressed material facts. The pivotal lead issue of waste was addressed in three pages. The essence of the common law is to resolve the case before the court rather than develop standards applicable to future behavior.

Second, it can be erratic. Common law often appears to be less settled than statutory law. There are many illustrations of this. But again, to rely on the *Disney* case, it comes as a shock to see this decision emerge as a principal vehicle for the development of a new or significantly amplified duty of good faith, which Chancellor Chandler informs us subsumes both the duty of care and the duty of loyalty.[2]

---

[1] *In re* Walt Disney Co. Derivative Litig., 907 A.2d 693 (Del. Ch. 2005).
[2] *Id.* at 755 (citations omitted):

> To act in good faith, a director must act at all times with honesty of purpose and in the best interests and welfare of the corporation. The presumption of the business judgment rule creates a presumption that a director acted in good faith. In order to overcome that presumption, a plaintiff must prove an act of bad faith by a preponderance of the evidence. To create a definitive and categorical definition of the universe of acts that would constitute bad faith would be difficult, if not impossible. And it would misconceive how, in my judgment, the concept of good faith operates in our common law of corporations. Fundamentally, the duties traditionally analyzed as belonging to corporate fiduciaries, loyalty and care, are but constituent elements of the overarching

Third, it is too standardless: the more important point is that state corporate law lacks the standards of both federal securities laws and self-regulatory organizations in the most fundamental areas of corporate governance, which include the duties of the board, its audit committee, and its internal and outside auditors. The purpose of common law is essentially compensatory and requires thoughtful judgment about a detailed case record. But from the point of view of deterrence and predictability, it is a weak reed on which to rely. How, to take the *Disney* case again, should compensation be determined? Obviously, only after a reasonable investigation and in good faith. But what does that ultimately tell you about magnitudes, comparators, or process? Both federal law and the self-regulatory organization standards have gone considerably further to provide operational standards on which major corporations can rely.

Let me turn to a second secular trend, and, from my point of view, a more complex one. This is the role of federal securities laws. If the probability is that state law will atrophy in its application to large corporations over time, I would suggest the probability for federal securities laws in the decades to come will continue to be a pendular or erratic process. By that, I mean periods of significant standard-creating activity, as we've seen in the aftermath of Enron and the Sarbanes-Oxley Act, alternating with periods of underbudgeting and understaffing, as we saw in the late 1990s and may be entering again. The SEC's role will fluctuate for a number of reasons.

Federal securities laws are highly reactive to the very deficiencies of state law. The SEC is the basic enforcement agency for corporate law. Federal securities law resolves problems with respect to jurisdiction and venue. Federal law provides the detailed standards. Here is where you have the enforcement mechanisms. At the same time, the SEC is subject to the risk of overbureaucratization, which occurs because of the ever-growing complexity of new SEC initiatives.

Let me offer an illustration. I was struck less by the Sarbanes-Oxley Act's section 404, which has become a buzzword for the expense of compliance with internal controls, than I was by the Public Company Accounting Oversight Board's (PCAOB) Auditing Standard No. 2, which was its key enforcement mechanism. Section 404 is a very short provision in a very long statute. There

concepts of allegiance, devotion and faithfulness that must guide the conduct of every fiduciary. The good faith required of a corporate fiduciary includes not simply the duties of care and loyalty, in the narrow sense that I have discussed them above, but all actions required by a true faithfulness and devotion to the interests of the corporation and its shareholders.

was little testimony with respect to section 404. It was one of a panoply of concepts. Auditing Standard No. 2 was a standard that showed some, but not sufficient, attention to the consequences of applying the new standards to small and medium companies as well as large ones. It is a standard that the SEC approved during a period in which it was swamped with rule-making responsibilities under the Sarbanes-Oxley Act.

There was consideration given to what the likely consequence of adopting section 404 would be and the enforcement of it through both SEC rules and PCAOB standards. But the predictions turned out to dramatically understate the costs of compliance.

It is typical, for example, whether you look at the new National Market System (NMS) standards or the securities offering proposals, that the SEC adopts complex rules. They are long. They are detailed. They are precise and they risk backlash in a way that is somewhat different than the SEC experienced before. When money is on the line, the SEC always risks backlash. When you rework systems through the NMS or through section 404, it may be wise. It may be defensible. But it is likely to be a process by which, when you have an agency adopting as many detailed rules as the SEC does, the periodic backlash will contribute to erratic pendulum swings in terms of congressional and White House support.

I believe that the pendulum process itself is not wise for sound public policy. It has led to alternating periods in which fraud has become a more serious problem and in which Congress has provided significant support that too often is followed by periods of insufficient support from Congress or the White House. The SEC, as important and dominant as it is in corporate governance today, is an agency whose stability is not as sure as it is sometimes believed to be. I've become concerned, as I've studied recent rule adoptions, that when you have an agency vulnerable to criticism that it has been insensitive to the cost or compliance burdens involved in new standards, this further aggravates the SEC's pendular support.

In the future, both state-proposed law and the SEC may be transformed by a third secular trend, which in the long run may prove to be the most significant – the internationalization of standards. For more than twenty years, the SEC has haltingly moved toward a multijurisdictional system of disclosure standards.[3] There has been progress developing common accounting standards through the International Accounting Standards Board and the International

---

[3] *See, e.g.*, 2 LOUIS LOSS, JOEL SELIGMAN, & TROY PAREDES, SECURITIES REGULATION 796–98 (4th ed. 2007) (reciprocal and common prospectus approach); *id.* at 798–803 (Canadian multijurisdictional approach).

Organization of Securities Commissions (IOSCO).[4] In recent years, cross-border securities transactions have dramatically increased.[5]

At the same time, cross-border fraud has increased. In recent years, the SEC has frequently and successfully litigated fraud cases against defendants who inappropriately relied on Regulation S when there has been a *prima facie* violation of the Securities Act and the securities involved are "part of a plan to evade the registration provisions of the Securities Act."[6]

Nonetheless, a new regime of securities regulation may emerge with a blue-ribbon tier of issues, at least in the United States, the European Union, and in Japan, subject to new international standards initially for reporting and accounting standards. This may also result in international corporate governance standards.

Inevitably, there will be pressure as international standards become more prominent to reduce compliance burdens in the United States both at the state and at the federal levels. At the state level, this may lead to a new type of federal corporate governance statute, intended not to increase regulatory burdens, but to simplify comprehension of the United States' system by corporations with headquarters abroad. At the federal level, this will mean inevitable compromises in the application of federal securities standards.

---

[4] *See, e.g.*, International Disclosure Standards, Exchange Act Release No. 7745, 70 SEC Docket (CCH) 1474 (Sept. 28, 1999) (adopting IOSCO standards to be part of federal securities laws); James D. Cox, *Regulatory Duopoly in U.S. Securities Markets*, 99 COLUM. L. REV. 1200 (1999); Symposium, *International Accounting Standards in the Wake of Enron*, 28 N.C. J. INT'L. L. & COM. REG. 725 (2003).

[5] *E.g.*, in 2002, foreign purchases of U.S. securities equaled $549 billion. 2003 SECURITIES INDUSTRY FACT BOOK 74. As of December 31, 2004, there were 1,240 private issuers registered and reporting with the SEC. Of these, 497 were from Canada, 107 from the United Kingdom, 86 from Israel, 40 from Brazil, 39 from Mexico, 34 from the Netherlands, 33 from France, and 31 from Japan. No other country had more than thirty companies. In the United States, 439 companies were on the NYSE, 60 on the Amex, 246 on the Nasdaq NMS, 45 on the Small Caps, and 450 in the OTC. SEC, Foreign Companies Registered and Reporting with the U.S. SEC (Dec. 31, 2004).

[6] *See, e.g.*, Geiger v. SEC, 363 F.3d 481, 488 (D.C. Cir. 2004) (transaction amounted to a design to evade registration when there was "[resort] to fraud"); SEC v. Autocorp Equities, Inc., 292 F. Supp. 2d 1310, 1327–28 (D. Utah 2003); In re Charles F. Kirby, 2000 SEC LEXIS 2681 (SEC Dec. 7, 2000) ("Regulation S is not available with respect to any transaction or series of transactions that, although in technical compliance with these rules, is part of a plan or scheme to evade the registration provisions of the [Securities Act]."); SEC v. Corp. Relations Group, Inc., No. 6:99-cv-1222-Orl.-28KRS, 2003 U.S. Dist. LEXIS 24925 (M.D. Fla. Mar. 28, 2003) ("The evidence shows no confusion or misapprehension on the part of the defendants, but rather a calculated albeit failed attempt to evade a regulation that they well understood."); SEC v. Softpoint, 958 F. Supp. 846, 860 (S.D.N.Y. 1997) (Regulation S shelters only *bona fide* overseas transactions); SEC v. Schiffer, 1998 Fed. Sec. L. Rep. (CCH) ¶ 90,247 (S.D.N.Y. June 10, 1998) (Regulation S is not available for "bogus" transactions).

Whether international standards will largely supplant state and federal disclosure or accounting standards for large corporations in the United States is a riveting question in the early twenty-first century. It is already clear that challenges with respect to standard setting may prove to be easier than challenges with respect to enforcement. Will there be an international SEC? If so, will it be modeled after the U.S. version, whose purpose is to be an investor's advocate, or after the United Kingdom's Financial Services Authority, which is widely viewed as more focused on promoting the United Kingdom's securities markets than the investor? Will an international SEC simply address securities or also banks, insurance companies, and hedge funds? Who will be the judiciary?

When I accepted a position to begin my career in academic administration in the fall of 1994, I did so with the belief that virtually everything likely to occur in federal securities law had been accomplished for the foreseeable future. After I accepted a position to become a law school dean, control of Congress changed, the Private Securities Litigation Reform Act of 1995 was enacted, and the pace of change accelerated. So my closing remark is a humble one. One can identify trends; one can never be certain about the pace of change. Nonetheless, as Newton sagely observed: "Fortune favors the prepared mind."

Index

ABA. *See* American Bar Association
Abbott Laboratories decision, 345, 346
Abramoff, J., 320n138, 346
advisory board model, 52, 66, 92n159. *See also*
    monitoring board
AFSCME. *See* American Federation of State,
    County and Municipal Workers
AICPA. *See* American Institute of Certified
    Public Accountants
ALI. *See* American Law Institute
American Bar Association (ABA)
    Conference Board and, 42, 44
    Corporate Laws Committee, 383
    Director's Guidebook and, 35–44
    liability and, 94
    Model Act and, 50, 383
    monitoring model and, 22, 35–44, 46, 66n16
    Principles and, 16, 39, 50
    SEC and, 381, 383
    structural model and, 36
    See also specific topics
American Federation of State, Country and
    Municipal Workers (AFSCME), 200
American Institute of Certified Public
    Accountants (AICPA), 71, 367
American Law Institute (ALI), 46, 47–53, 339,
    346
    CORPRO and, 47–50
    Eisenberg and, 19n7, 34, 47. *See also*
    Eisenberg, M.
    Model Act and, 46n120, 339
    monitoring model and, 19n7, 22, 34, 46–54,
    66n16. *See also* monitoring board
    outside directors and, 51, 52n137
    Principles and, 22, 34, 39, 46, 50, 346–347
    social responsibility and, 45, 51

universal demand rule, 363
    See also specific topics
American Society of Corporate Secretaries
    (ASCS), 35
Angelides, P., 231
Aronson decision, 338, 339
Arrow, K., 223
Arsht, S. S., 353–354
Arthur Andersen case, 305–306, 330
ASCS. *See* American Society of Corporate
    Secretaries
audit committee
    accounting and, 5, 63, 76, 78
    Action Plan and, 437
    alternative mechanisms and, 78
    common law and, 462
    conservatism and, 81–88, 94
    COSO and, 71
    earnings management and, 5, 74, 82–83
    expertise and, 63, 74, 75, 78, 82. *See*
    expertise
    fair value and, 85, 89
    financial reporting and, 71, 74, 75, 168–171
    function of, 82
    incentives and, 83n118, 88, 89
    independence and, 51, 62, 64, 70, 74, 374,
    462. *See also* independent directors
    insiders and, 374
    internal controls and, 70–71
    managerial abuse and, 88–89
    NYSE and, 70, 71
    SOX and, 72, 81, 90, 374, 421, 452. *See also*
    Sarbanes-Oxley Act
    SEC and, 70–73, 385n143. *See also*
    Securities and Exchange Commission
    See also specific topics

467

Printed in the United States
By Bookmasters